The Letters and Diaries
of
John Henry Newman

The Letters and Diaries
of
John Henry Newman

Edited at the Birmingham Oratory
with notes and an introduction
by

Charles Stephen Dessain

of the same Oratory

and

Thomas Gornall, S.J.

Volume XXXI
The Last Years
January 1885 to August 1890

With a Supplement of Addenda to Volumes XI – XXX

CLARENDON PRESS · OXFORD

1977

Oxford University Press, Walton Street, Oxford OX2 6DP

OXFORD LONDON GLASGOW NEW YORK
TORONTO MELBOURNE WELLINGTON CAPE TOWN
IBADAN NAIROBI DAR ES SALAAM LUSAKA ADDIS ABABA
KUALA LUMPUR SINGAPORE JAKARTA HONG KONG TOKYO
DELHI BOMBAY CALCUTTA MADRAS KARACHI

© The Birmingham Oratory 1977

Newman, John Henry
    The letters and diaries of John Henry Newman.
    Vol. 31. The last years, January 1885 to
    August 1890; with a supplement of addenda to
    volumes XI – XXX.
    Index.
    ISBN 0–19–920083–1
    1. Dessain, Charles Stephen 2. Gornall, Thomas
    262'.135'0924   BX4705.N5
    Newman, John Henry
    Roman Catholic Church – Clergy – Correspondence,
    reminiscences, etc.

Printed in Great Britain by
Cox & Wyman Ltd,
London, Fakenham and Reading

Preface

WITHOUT the gradual building up at the Birmingham Oratory of a very full collection of Cardinal Newman's correspondence (an account of which will be found in the Introduction to Volume XI), the present work could not have been undertaken. Its aim is to provide an exhaustive edition of Newman's letters; with explanatory notes, which are often summaries of or quotations from the other side of the correspondence. Some of these letters *to* Newman, when they appear to have particular importance, or to be necessary for following a controversy, are inserted in the text. Every one of the letters written *by* Newman is included there, in chronological sequence. Should there eventually be any of his letters, whose existence is known to the editor, but of which he has failed to obtain a copy, this will be noted in its place. On the other hand, no attempt has been made to include a list of letters written by Newman and now lost, nor the brief précis he occasionally made of his reply, on the back of a correspondent's letter, although these are utilised for the annotation.

In order that the text of each letter may be as accurate as possible, the original autograph, when it still exists, or at least a photographic copy of it, has been used by the editor as his source. (The very few cases in which he has been content with an authenticated copy will be noted as they occur.) Always the text of the autograph is reproduced, or, when the autograph has disappeared, that of the copy that appears most reliable. When only Newman's draft exists, that is printed. The source used in each case is to be found in the list of letters by correspondents.

Such alterations as are made in transcribing the letters aim, without sacrifice of accuracy, at enabling them to be read with ease. Newman writes simply and has none of those idiosyncrasies which sometimes need to be reproduced for the sake of the evidence of one kind or another which they provide.

The following are the only alterations made in transcription:

ADDRESS AND DATE are always printed on the same line, and at the head of the letter, even when Newman puts them at the end. When he omits or gives an incomplete date, the omission is supplied in square brackets, and justified in a note unless the reason for it is obvious. The addresses, to which letters were sent, are included in the list of letters by correspondents. The information derived from postmarks is matter for annotation.

THE CONCLUSION of the letter is made to run on, irrespective of Newman's separate lines, and all postscripts are placed at the end.

NEWMAN'S CORRECTIONS AND ADDITIONS are inserted in their intended place. His interlinear explanations are printed in the text in angle brackets ⟨ ⟩, after the word or phrase they explain. His erasures are given in footnotes when they appear to be of sufficient interest to warrant it. Square brackets are reserved for editorial additions. All Newman's brackets are printed as rounded ones (the kind most usual with him).

NEWMAN'S PARAGRAPHS AND PUNCTUATION are preserved, except that single quotation marks are printed throughout, and double ones for quotations within them. (Newman generally used the latter in both cases.) Further, a parenthesis or quotation that he began with the proper mark but failed to complete, or completed but did not begin, is supplied. All other punctuation marks supplied by the editor are enclosed in square brackets. Newman's dashes, which frequently do duty either for a full stop, a semicolon or a comma (especially when he is tired or writing hurriedly), are represented by a '—' with a space before and after. His spelling and use of capitals are left unchanged, but 'raised' letters are lowered in every case.

NEWMAN'S ABBREVIATIONS are retained in the case of proper names, and in the address and conclusion of each letter, since these are sometimes useful indications of his attitude at the time. In all other cases, abbreviations are printed out in full, where Newman employs them.

When he uses the initials of proper names, the full name is normally inserted in square brackets after the initials, at the first occurrence in each letter, and more often if it seems advisable in order to avoid confusion. No addition of the full name is made in the case of Newman's correspondent, whether his initials occur at the beginning of the letter or in the course of it.

When Newman uses only a Christian name, the surname is sometimes added in square brackets for the reader's convenience. The Christian names of members of the Oratory, since they are of frequent occurrence, are listed in the index of proper names and the reader is referred to surnames.

When transcription is made from a PRINTED SOURCE, typographical alterations clearly due to editor or printer are disregarded.

Sometimes Newman made HOLOGRAPH copies of his letters or of portions of them, when they were returned to him long after they had been written. In order that the reader may be able to see how much he copied and what changes he introduced, the copied passages are placed in quarter brackets ⌐ ¬, and all additions of any importance included in the text in double square brackets, or, where this is impracticable, in the annotation.

Newman's letters are printed in CHRONOLOGICAL ORDER, with the name of his correspondent at the head (except that those of each day are arranged alphabetically), and, when more than one is written to the same person on the same day, numbered, I, II. In the headings the name of the correspondent is given in its most convenient form, sometimes with Christian names in full, sometimes only with initials.

THE LIST OF LETTERS BY CORRESPONDENTS, at the end of each volume, shows whether the source used was an autograph, draft, printed source or copy, and in the last case, whether a holograph made by Newman later; and gives the present location of the source, as well as of any additional holograph copies or drafts. When a letter, or a considerable portion of it, has been printed in a standard work, references are given; but mistakes or omissions in these previous publications are noticed, if at all, in the annotation.

THE LETTERS WRITTEN TO NEWMAN, when inserted in the text, are printed in type smaller than that used for Newman's own letters, and headed by the name of the correspondent. These letters are not arranged in chronological order, but are placed either just before or just after the letter of Newman to which they are related. A list of them is given at the end of each volume in which they occur. These and the quotations from letters in the annotation are always, unless otherwise stated, printed from autographs at the Birmingham Oratory, and are transcribed in the same way as Newman's letters.

NEWMAN'S DIARIES COVER THE YEARS 1824 to 1879 (with a gap from July 1826 to March 1828). They are written in a series of mottled copy books, 12 × 18½ centimetres, printed for a year each, and entitled *The Private Diary : arranged, printed, and ruled, for receiving an account of every day's employ-ment . . .'* with the exception of the four periods July 1847–May 1850, January 1854–January 1861, January 1861–March 1871, March 1871–October 1879, each of which is contained in a somewhat thicker copy book.

These diaries are printed complete for each day in which Newman has made an entry, except that the lists of people to whom he has written or from whom he has received letters are omitted, as not being of sufficient general interest. The original diaries are, of course, available for consultation. At the end of each diary book are various notes, lists of addresses, of people to be prayed for, accounts, etc. These, also, are omitted, except for occasional dated notes of events, which are inserted in their proper place. Of the rest of the notes, some are theological and will be reserved for a volume of Newman's theological papers, and others will perhaps have room found for them in any fuller edition of *Autobiographical Writings*.

Newman compiled with his own hands, on quarto sheets sewn together, a book of *Chronological Notes*, drawn largely from the diaries. Any new matter in these *Notes* is printed in italics with the appropriate diary entry. (It should be noted that the diary entries themselves were sometimes written up con-siderably later than the events they record).

Each volume is preceded by a brief summary of the period of Newman's life that it covers. Summary, diaries and annotation give a roughly biographical form to the whole, and will, it is hoped, enable the ordinary reader to treat it as a continuous narrative.

THE BIOGRAPHIES OF PERSONS are collected in the index of proper names at the end of each volume, in order to simplify the annotation of the letters. Occasionally, when a person is mentioned only once or twice, and a note is required in any case, biographical details have been given in the notes, and a reference in the index. Volume XXI, being the first of a new period in Newman's life, contains an account of every person mentioned, with the exception of a few for whom a notice seemed unnecessary, and of still fewer who have not yet been identified. The indexes of Volume XXII and of subsequent volumes will contain notices of persons who appear in them for the first time, and references back, in the case of those who have been noticed in an earlier volume. (The editor will be grateful for information as to persons not identified.)

These notices have been compiled from such various sources — books of reference, letters at the Oratory, information supplied by the families or religious communities of the persons concerned, and by librarians and archivists — that the giving of authorities would be a very complicated and lengthy process. Like others faced with the same problem, the editor has decided usually to omit them. References are given, however, to *The Dictionary of National Biography*, or *The Dictionary of American Biography*, in all cases where there is an article there, and failing them, to Boase's *Modern English Biography* or Gillow's *Bibliographical Dictionary of the English Catholics*. When all the volumes of letters have been issued, a final index volume will be compiled for the whole work.

This Volume XXXI ends with Newman's death on 11 August 1890. A Supplement contains all the letters which have come to light too late for inclusion in their chronological place in Volumes XI to XXX, or of which a more accurate text has been found. These additional letters have new page-numbers marked with an asterisk, and a separate index.

Volumes I to X, covering Newman's Anglican period, will now appear. For the practical reasons which led to publishing first the letters of the Catholic period, see the Introduction to Volume XI.

Contents

Abbreviations in Volume XXXI

THE abbreviations used for Newman's works are those listed in Joseph Rickaby, S.J., *Index to the Works of John Henry Cardinal Newman*, London 1914, with a few additions.

References to works included by Newman in his uniform edition are always, unless otherwise stated, to that edition, which was begun in 1868 with *Parochial and Plain Sermons*, and concluded in 1881 with *Select Treatises of St Athanasius*. From 1886, until the stock was destroyed in the 1939–45 war, all the volumes were published by Longmans, Green and Co. They are distinguished from other, usually posthumous, publications by having their date of inclusion in the uniform edition in brackets after the title, in the list of abbreviations below. The unbracketed date is, in every case, the date of the edition (or impression) used for giving references. (Once volumes were included in the uniform edition the pagination usually remained unchanged, but there are exceptions and minor alterations.)

Add.	*Addresses to Cardinal Newman with his Replies etc. 1879–82*, ed. W. P. Neville, 1905.
Apo.	*Apologia pro Vita Sua* (1873) 1905.
Ari.	*The Arians of the Fourth Century* (1871) 1908.
Ath. I, II	*Select Treatises of St Athanasius*, two volumes (1881) 1920.
A.W.	*John Henry Newman: Autobiographical Writings*, ed. Henry Tristram 1956.
Call.	*Callista, a Tale of the Third Century* (1876) 1923.
Campaign	*My Campaign in Ireland, Part I* (printed for private circulation only), 1896.
D.A.	*Discussions and Arguments on Various Subjects* (1872) 1911.
Dev.	*An Essay on the Development of Christian Doctrine* (1878) 1908.
Diff. I, II	*Certain Difficulties felt by Anglicans in Catholic Teaching*, two volumes (1879, 1876) 1908.
Ess. I, II	*Essays Critical and Historical*, two volumes (1871) 1919.
G.A.	*An Essay in aid of a Grammar of Assent* (1870) 1913.
H.S., I, II, III	*Historical Sketches*, three volumes (1872) 1908, 1912, 1909.
Idea	*The Idea of a University defined and illustrated* (1873) 1902.
Jfc.	*Lectures on the Doctrine of Justification* (1874) 1908.
K.C.	*Correspondence of John Henry Newman with John Keble and Others, 1839–45*, ed. at the Birmingham Oratory, 1917.
L.G.	*Loss and Gain: the Story of a Convert* (1874) 1911.
M.D.	*Meditations and Devotions of the late Cardinal Newman*, 1893.
Mir.	*Two Essays on Biblical and on Ecclesiastical Miracles* (1870) 1907.
Mix.	*Discourses addressed to Mixed Congregations* (1871) 1909.
Moz I, II	*Letters and Correspondence of John Henry Newman*, ed. Anne Mozley, two volumes, 1891.

O.S.	*Sermons preached on Various Occasions* (1870) 1927.
P.S. I–VIII	*Parochial and Plain Sermons* (1868) 1907–10.
Prepos.	*Present Position of Catholics* (n.d. 1872) 1913.
S.D.	*Sermons bearing on Subjects of the Day* (1869) 1902.
S.E.	*Stray Essays on Controversial Points* (private) 1890.
S.N.	*Sermon Notes of John Henry Cardinal Newman, 1849–1878*, ed. Fathers of the Birmingham Oratory, 1913.
T.T.	*Tracts Theological and Ecclesiastical* (1874) 1908.
U.S.	*Fifteen Sermons preached before the University of Oxford* (1872) 1909.
V.M., I, II	*The Via Media* (1877) 1908, 1911.
V.V.	*Verses on Various Occasions* (1874) 1910.

*　　　*　　　*

Boase	Frederick Boase, *Modern English Biography*, six volumes, Truro 1892–1921.
Butler	Cuthbert Butler, *The Life and Times of Bishop Ullathorne*, two volumes, London 1926.
de Lisle	E. S. Purcell, *Life and Letters of Ambrose Phillipps de Lisle*, two volumes, London 1900.
D A B	*Dictionary of American Biography*, London, 1928–36.
D N B	*Dictionary of National Biography*, to 1900, London, reprinted in 1937–8 in twenty-two volumes, the last being a Supplement *D N B*, Suppl.
D N B, 1901–11	*Dictionary of National Biography*, 1901–11, three volumes in one.
DR	*Dublin Review.*
D T C	*Dictionnaire de Théologie Catholique*, Paris, 1903–50.
Gillow	Joseph Gillow, *Bibliographical Dictionary of the English Catholics*, five volumes, London 1885 and later.
Liddon's *Pusey* I–IV	H. P. Liddon, *Life of Edward Bouverie Pusey*, four volumes, London 1893–7.
Newman and Bloxam	R. D. Middleton, *Newman and Bloxam*, London 1947.
Purcell	E. S. Purcell, *The Life of Cardinal Manning*, two volumes, London 1895.
Trevor I	Meriol Trevor, *Newman the Pillar of the Cloud*, London 1962.
Trevor II	Meriol Trevor, *Newman Light in Winter*, London 1962.
Ward I, II	Wilfrid Ward, *The Life of John Henry Cardinal Newman*, two volumes, London 1912.

Introductory Note

DURING 1885 Newman became involved in his last public controversy. Throughout his lifelong defence of Revealed Religion he had always insisted on the reasonableness of the act of faith, but had refused to accept the narrow rationalist definition of reason. Reason, he maintained, could not be considered independently of the first principles and assumptions from which it proceeded, or of the moral character of the person making use of it. In the *Contemporary Review* for May 1885 there appeared an article by the Congregationalist A. M. Fairbairn, Principal of Airedale Theological College, Bradford, which accused Newman of philosophical scepticism and of withdrawing the proofs of religion from the realm of reason into that of conscience and imagination. Newman was gradually persuaded that the misunderstanding must be set right and was hard at work in July and August on his article, 'The Development of Religious Error', which appeared in the *Contemporary Review* for October. It was his last explanation of the relations between reason and faith, and the final clarification of his teaching. As a test case of the corrosive effect of rationalistic first principles he took the Christian teaching on eternal punishment. He insisted that he accepted the doctrine 'on the simple word of the Divine Informant', but went on to show 'the disintegrating consequences of letting it go'. Here was an example of a wrong first principle leading to the development of religious error, and the rejection of the revealed doctrine led to the undermining of belief in the Atonement and of the Incarnation itself.

Newman reprinted his article early in 1886 for private distribution, adding a lighter postscript on Fairbairn's description of his language about reason as 'almost impious'. Meanwhile Fairbairn had countered with another article, 'Reason and Religion', in the *Contemporary Review* for December 1885. Newman drew up a reply, chiefly with Catholics in view, lest they should misunderstand him and take scandal. He decided, however, after consulting Lord Blachford, that it was unbecoming to continue the controversy. He printed his reply and sent it to a few interested persons, including Fairbairn, who acknowledged it courteously. Newman reprinted it with his first article, privately, in the small volume *Stray Essays*, in 1890. Both are included in *The Theological Papers of John Henry Newman on Faith and Certainty*, Oxford 1976, where the reply has been published for the first time. The lighter postscript is reproduced below as Appendix 1.

Earlier in 1885, before these preoccupations, Newman was in frequent correspondence with Anne Mozley, who at the end of January accepted the task of editing a memoir and letters covering his Anglican period, *Letters and Correspondence of John Henry Newman during his Life in the English Church with a Brief Autobiography*, 'edited at Cardinal Newman's request'. He supplied most of the material, letters, early journals and the autobiography, but insisted that he must never see her work, which was to appear only after his death. He was to be treated as he and Keble had treated Richard Hurrell Froude when they published his *Remains*. Newman lent her books but said, 'I don't see you can learn from *me all* the books you want. This would be like packing the jury.' He commended Anne Mozley's formula, 'All to be as *true* and simple as I can make it'. She was allowed to consult Dean Church and Lord Blachford. To the latter Newman wrote on 14 September 1885: 'I thought that the three conditions of a friend, an Anglican and a contemporary, *if possible*, would give the prospect of a true account of what otherwise would be sure to be full of errors.' In the summer of 1887 Newman's letters were returned to him, but Anne Mozley made additions from other collections. When he died the work was ready and appeared early in 1891. She herself died on 27 June 1891 in her eighty-second year. Newman's trust was justified; *Letters and Correspondence*, in spite of its omissions, errors and silences, gave the substantially true account for which he had hoped. It was complemented by R. W. Church's history of the Oxford Movement, drafts of which he sent to Newman for criticism during the autumn and winter of 1885–6. Like Anne Mozley, Dean Church, who died on 10 December 1890, lived just long enough to complete his work. *The Oxford Movement* was published in 1891.

Newman also made provision for the continued publication of the uniform edition of his own works. In January 1885 he had occasion to write to C. J. Longman, and after a very amicable correspondence it was agreed that Longmans, Green and Co. should take over six of his volumes. The rest were added gradually as other publishers released them. Nor was Newman merely interested in his own works. On 21 September 1886 he wrote to Alfred Newdigate, promoter of the Art and Book Company for publishing Catholic books, 'I have long had an intense wish that English Catholics had what answers to a "Christian Knowledge Society".' To the same correspondent he wrote a week later, 'I think the papers and the programme of the Catholic Truth Society are excellent'. On the other hand, when, in 1887, it was proposed to present to Leo XIII for his sacerdotal jubilee all the books written by English Catholics during the previous half century, he was insistent that his should not be included. He stood by what he had written in 1879 to T. W. Allies, when a similar proposal was made: 'What many people think my best work is so flavoured with Protestantism that I could not send it to him (Leo XIII) without giving offence'. He refused to allow a presentation he thought presumptuous. He had no objection to a set of his works being presented to Queen Victoria by the Brothers of the London Oratory for her jubilee later in the same year. A message came back from Windsor Castle thanking for 'the beautiful present'.

To the end Newman remained mentally alert, and interested in all that was happening, but in the latter part of 1886 his physical powers grew weaker. He could no longer see to read by candle light, he was liable to falls, and he found great difficulty in writing, so that he had increasingly to resort to dictation. Of a letter he wrote to Charles Gore in November 1888, H. P. Liddon remarked, 'How the perfect and inimitable grace of courtesy which characterizes the Cardinal's writings survives – even the test of dictation.'

One of the last letters of any length which Newman wrote entirely with his own hand was that of 7 January 1887, in connection with the death of Principal Shairp. He spoke of his comfort 'in this day of religious indifference and unbelief' at the thought 'that a silent and secret process is going on in the hearts of many' bringing Christians together. It might lead to the spread of 'Divine Truth all over the world', or at least 'one can fancy such a return to primitive truth to be vouchsafed to particular countries which at present are divided and broken up into a hundred sects.' A few weeks later, on 24 February, he was writing of how 'those great and burning truths, which I learned when a boy from evangelical teaching, I have found impressed upon my heart with fresh and ever increasing force by the Holy Roman Church.' The lessons Newman learned during his last year at school were the turning point of his life. Even such a man of the world as Lord Rosebery, who came on 13 August 1890 to see Newman lying in state, sensed something of this: 'The Cardinal just like a saint's remains over a high altar, waxy, distant, emaciated, in a mitre, rich gloves whereon the ring (which I kissed) rich slippers. With the hat at the foot.

And this was the end of the young Calvinist, the Oxford don, the austere Vicar of St Mary's. It seemed as if a whole cycle of human thought and life were concentrated in that august repose. That was my overwhelming thought. Kindly light had led and guided Newman to this strange, brilliant, incomparable end.'[1]

---

[1] The Marquess of Crewe, *Lord Rosebery*, London 1931, II, pp. 356–7.

Summary of Events covered by this Volume

1885

27 January	Anne Mozley agrees to edit Newman's correspondence during his life in the Anglican Church.
7 March	Longmans Green and Co. take over the publication of six of Newman's works.
7 April	Newman is sent General Gordon's marked copy of *The Dream of Gerontius*.
26 August	Death of W. J. Copeland.
October	Newman's article 'On the Development of Religious Error' in answer to A. M. Fairbairn is published in the *Contemporary Review*.
2 December	Death of Miss M. R. Giberne.
December	Newman draws up notes in answer to a further attack in the *Contemporary Review* for December by A. M. Fairbairn.

1886

Early in March	Newman sends to A. M. Fairbairn a copy, privately printed, of his notes in answer to the latter's second article.
28–30 March	Newman stays with Dean Church at St Paul's, in order to attend the funeral of the dowager Duchess of Norfolk at the London Oratory.
September	After an illness Newman becomes physically weaker.
29 September	Newman allows three extracts from his works to be issued by the Catholic Truth Society, but permission is withheld by the publishers, Burns and Oates.

1887

January–July	Newman is still at work on new editions of his *Select Treatises of St Athanasius*.
10 August	Newman consults Dr Ogle in London.
17 August	Newman goes to London to consult the oculist Sir William Bowman.
18 August	Bishop Ullathorne, whose retirement is announced, visits Newman who asks for his blessing.

1888

1 January	Newman preaches at the Oratory at a celebration in honour of the sacerdotal jubilee of Leo XIII.
24 March	Emmeline Deane's portrait in oils of Newman is finished. (It now hangs in the National Portrait Gallery.)
4–5 June	Newman goes to London to sign his will, and visits F. S. Bowles at Harrow.
16 July	Newman, on the way to a short tour of North Wales, pays his last visit to the Dominican nuns at Stone.
28, 30 and 31 August	Newman attends the Birmingham Musical Festival.
October	Newman has a fall and receives the Anointing of the Sick.

1889

21 March	Death of Archbishop Ullathorne.
29 September	Newman writes to congratulate Cardinal Manning on his part in the settlement of the London dock strike.
About 14 November	Newman calls on George Cadbury at the Bourneville Works about the compulsory attendance of Catholic girl employees at his daily prayer meeting.
21 November	Death of Lord Blachford.
25 December	Newman says Mass for the last time.

1890

2 July	Newman receives an address from the Catholic Truth Society which is holding a conference in Birmingham, and makes a short speech in reply.
23 July	Newman gives out the prizes at the Oratory School and attends the Latin Play.
9 August	Newman's niece, Grace Langford, only child of his sister Harriett, visits Newman. He had not seen her since 1843, when she was three years old, after which time her mother, Mrs Thomas Mozley, had broken with him.
11 August	Newman dies of pneumonia in the evening.

The Letters and Diaries

of

John Henry Newman

Jany 1. 1885

Dear Mr Edwards

I am very glad to have your letter, and thank you for it. Gladly do I return your congratulations on the New Year. I am quite in the dark when it is that God will take me, for my worst trial of failing strength at present is nothing more serious than difficulty of writing and dimness of sight, but I have a clear consciousness of course that I cannot last long, nor indeed is any time long or short to one, who has lived so many years as I have.

I thank you for your beautiful New Year Card, and for the volume you give me. I suppose the latter is on the line of the 'Analogy' of a great English thinker, only more eloquent and practical.[1] I shall have much interest in reading it, when perhaps I shall find an explanation of some statements which at first sight are difficult, as, that holy men, when they get to heaven, do not help by their prayers the friends they have left behind them on earth. I thought Protestants allowed this, as not interfering with our Lord's Mediation.[2]

If you happen to write to Mr Fisher, pray wish him in my name a happy New Year. I hope he believes the assurance I gave him, at the time I protested against some words of his, that they would make no difference in my friendly feelings towards him — I often think of him.[3] I wonder what he thinks of Mr Bartlett's Article in the 'Contemporary' for January.[4]

Very truly Yours John H Card. Newman

TO LADY SIMEON

Jany 1. 1885

My dear Lady Simeon

A happy New Year to you and Queenie.[5] Thanks for your beautiful card. I would not limit myself to these few lines, were I able to write — but my

---

[1] Edwards wrote on 31 Dec. 1884: 'I send your Eminence a book which may perhaps interest you—The author an American was lately in this country and consulted me about publishing it. It has interested many thoughtful persons, and I think is likely to be useful.'

[2] Edwards replied on 23 Jan. that some Protestants allowed it, others did not, others did not know.

[3] See letters of 8 and 24 Feb. 1883 to Edwards, and 10 March to Fisher.

[4] R. E. Bartlett's article 'The Church of England and the Evangelical Party', the *Contemporary Review* (Jan. 1885), pp. 65–82, thought that the Evangelicals had declined and become more ecclesiastical. They shrank from the idea of a non-sacerdotal church and were no longer the bridge towards nonconformists which they had formerly been. Nor were they acting now as a moderating influence on the Broad Church. They should return to their ideal of godliness, rather than churchiness. Edwards replied on 23 Jan. that he had not yet heard Fisher's opinion on the article, 'though he, as well as us others, will be rather surprised to see Maurice and Kingsley claimed as "in the highest and purest sense, Evangelical."' Art. cit. p. 76.

[5] Lady Simeon's daughter, Catherine.

3

fingers are so stiff and weak that it is by an effort that I get through a few lines — else, I am quite well

Yours affectly J. H. Card. Newman.

TO HENRY JAMES COLERIDGE

Jany 2. 1885

My dear Fr Coleridge

I felt the great and kind thoughtfulness of your letter, for I was very anxious for news. It is indeed most strange, and, as you say, one trusts that, as the Providence is strange, so the design, which is involved in it, is strange and good also.[1]

I have a difficulty about your letters. I cannot leave them for others to see, yet I do not know how to destroy carefully written letters, which are to you perhaps formal memoranda without copy. Years ago, when I had sent a very confidential letter about a third person to a friend, after a while he wrote me word that he could neither keep it, nor destroy it — so he sent it me back. Shall I do the same with yours?

A happy new year to us all
Yours affectly J. H. Card. Newman

TO R. W. CHURCH

Jany 4. 1885

My dear Dean

Thank you for the trouble you have been at about Archdeacon Manning's call on me at Littlemore.[2] As the statement does not come from him, I do not think much of it.[3]

---

[1] This refers to the libel case in which Coleridge's nephew and niece, the children of Lord Coleridge, were involved. See letter of 23 Nov. 1884 to H. J. Coleridge.

[2] Dean Church wrote about the story broadcast by C. Kegan Paul that in Nov. 1843, after Manning had preached a 'no popery' and pro-puritan sermon in St Mary's, Oxford, Newman refused to see him when he called at Littlemore. See next note. Church wrote on 1 Jan., 'I have heard to-day from Kegan Paul. I find that I misunderstood him in giving Cardinal Manning as the Source and direct authority for the story. [See letter of 23 Dec. 1884 to Church] Paul seems to have heard it from more than one person.' One of these was J. A. Froude. Church added: 'But after Paul's article in the American "Century" [May 1883] was published, in which the story was told, Cardinal Manning "expressed his opinion of its (the Article's) accuracy without excepting this story; and before it was published he knew that I was going to write it (the Article), and gave me for the purpose of reproduction the portrait which appears in the front of the Number. I feel sure therefore," he goes on, "that if there had been any substantial error he would have let me know it. I have seen him many times since."

So that I ought to have said, *not* that he heard it from M.; but that M. did not contradict or correct it.

The reviewer in the Spectator (MacColl) [see Memorandum of 18 Nov. 1884] heard the story told by J.A.F. [Froude] some years ago: but the animus of the story was distinctly *not* against you.'

[3] Kegan Paul's article 'Cardinal Manning', the *Century Magazine* (May 1883) p. 129, explained that on the day the Gunpowder Plot was commemorated in the *Prayer Book*,

4

As to his *passing it by* in Mr Paul's Memoir of him, I will tell you why I think little of it. Curiously, the very same thing occurred in my own reading of his notice of *me*[1] I thanked him for it, for it was kindly written, and said no more — but a friend in this house said to me afterwards 'Do you see what you have done? you have let pass an unjustifiable, unfounded, offensive imputation on yourself and the Oratory. He violates private hospitality in disclosing and perverting what happened when he dined with the Fathers. He takes occasion to say that you showed your scorn of moral theology (casuistry) by keeping silence on one of the questions proposed at table for discussion.'[2]

Certainly this was a serious offence in him; it had nothing to do with my 'life' and was most untrue. He increased his fault by inserting a private letter of mine to some third person about the Inspiration of Scripture, a letter of which I have no cause to be ashamed, but which brought upon me from a D.D. almost a charge of heresy in the Tablet.[3]

If then in skimming through Mr Paul's article on myself (an operation almost as unpleasant to me when I am praised as well as when I am blamed), I did not observe what he said about our Fathers and their Superior, I can easily fancy Cardinal Manning sending back the statements of his visit to Littlemore without remark.

Yours affectly J. H. Card. Newman

P.S. Perhaps, hearing the Archdeacon was coming, I went out for a walk, and he could not believe I was not within. Of course Mr Paul must not know what I have told you: it is a thing done and over.[4]

5 Nov. 1843, 'Archdeacon Manning preached before the University of Oxford a violent tirade against Popery with a vehemence unusual in an English, and still more in an university pulpit. . . . Newman was then in retirement at Littlemore . . . Archdeacon Manning walked out to Littlemore to call upon him, but the report of the disastrous sermon had already preceded the preacher. The door was opened by one of those young men, the members of the quasi monastic community, who had to convey to the Archdeacon the unpleasant intimation that Dr Newman declined to see him. . . . So strangely do we change in these changing times, that it is hard to realize that the perplexed novice was Mr J. A. Froude.'

[1] This was Kegan Paul's article 'John Henry Cardinal Newman', the *Illustrated Century Magazine* (June 1882). See letter of 30 May 1882 to Kegan Paul.
[2] In art. cit., p. 285, that Newman chose to reply to the scriptural rather than the moral question proposed, was completely misinterpreted.
[3] See the letters of 14 June 1882 to Henry Bittleston and notes there.
[4] Church replied on 7 Jan., 'Of course I have not told Paul about your note. I have only said that as the story did not come from Cardinal Manning, you did not trouble yourself more about it.'
There is no trace of the story in any of Newman's letters at this period, and as he remarks in that of 23 Dec. 1884, he and Manning were corresponding in a confidential way at the time. Newman's diary for 6 Nov. 1843 simply has 'Manning called', and on 7 Nov. J. B. Mozley wrote to his sister that Manning, in spite of his sermon, 'went up to Littlemore and saw J.H.N. yesterday.' *Letters of J. B. Mozley*, edited by his Sister, London 1885 [1884], p. 149. cf. Memorandum of 18 Nov. 1884. The story continued to flourish after Newman's death. See *Purcell* I, p. 245 and G. D. Boyle, *Recollections*, London 1895, p. 238.

TO CHARLES SMYTH MORRIS [?][1]

Jan. 4. 1885

Dear Mr Morris

Of course your touching letter was a great pleasure and cause of rejoicing and thanksgiving to me, and now, if I have been slow to acknowledge it, do not impute this to indifference, for I have thought of you all along since it came to me, but because of my age I find it no easy task to form my letters more than a child does and that there are not a few persons to whom I have to write.

And now I am confident that He who has begun a good work in you will perfect it.[2] He never fails those who place themselves in His hands. I have lived a long life and can witness to His faithfulness. He is a true friend, and the more you can trust Him, the more you will gain from Him. May His abundant blessing be upon you now and ever. This is the fervent prayer for you of

Yours sincerely John H. Card Newman

TO MRS RICHARD WARD

Jany 4. 1885

Dear Louisa Ward

I should have thanked you long before this for sending me tidings which hardly surprised me,[3] had my power gone with my will — but, though I have by God's mercy few of the inconveniences of old age, I am very slow at correspondence, brain and fingers working only with an effort, and not successfully

I know how attached Emily Bowles was to her brother and how keenly she will feel his loss. This is the penalty most of us pay, if we are granted a long life.

Say all that is affectionate from me to Richard. I should rejoice to see you and him, should it so happen as you throw out, in fine weather. One of the great penances of delicate health at his age is that it throws a man out of work and the duties of life. Yet all circumstances have their compensations, and I doubt not that he has found or will find, his —

Yours affectly John H Card. Newman

---

[1] Charles Smyth Morris went up to New College, Oxford, in Oct. 1867, aged nineteen, and became a Catholic about 1883.

[2] *Philippians* I:6.

[3] Louisa Ward told Newman of the death of John, the eldest brother of Emily Bowles.

TO EMILY BOWLES

Jany 5. 1885

My dear Child

I have not written to you, because I knew of no words which were suitable to the rent of affection which was just now your trial. You have ever seemed to me a most united family, and I knew especially how you loved your brother John. I have done what lay in my power to do in saying Mass for your intention concerning him.

The sad tidings did not surprise me in consequence of what you said to me, but I was sorry to hear from Louisa Ward, that after all his departure was sudden.

Let me hear how you are, if you have any thing to tell me

Yours affectionately John H Card. Newman

TO W. S. LILLY

Jany 7. 1885

My dear Mr Lilly

My best New Year wishes for you and Mrs Lilly, if I have not sent them already.

The only criticism I see cause to make on your Dedication and Preface, is that they do not notice what is generally considered the true aspect of the heathen religions *as existing facts*,[1] suggested by St. Paul's words, 'Quod immolant Gentes, daemoniis immolant, et non Deo. Nolo vos socios fieri daemoniorum. Fugite ab idolorum cultura.'[2] 'Supersensible' may be devilish.

As a personal matter, I must quite negative having been indebted to Kant or Coleridge. I never read a word of Kant, I never read a word of Coleridge. I was not even in possession of a single work of Coleridge's. I could say the same of Hurrell Froude, and also of Pusey and Keble, as far as I have a right to speak of others.[3]

Very truly Yours, John H Card. Newman

P.S. Is it not usual at least once to say 'Your Lordship' in a letter to a Peer?[4]

[1] Newman is referring to the second edition of Lilly's *Ancient Religion and Modern Thought*, London 1885. The preface was the same as in the first edition of 1884, but the dedication, in the form of a long letter to Lord Ripon, was new. In it Lilly spoke of 'the supercilious contempt' of British officials towards the non-Christian religious systems of India. 'The creeds, the rituals, the institutions in which the highest conceptions, the deepest yearnings, the most sacred ties of millions of native fellow-subjects are embodied, surely deserve from us far other treatments than that,' p. ii. 'But woe to India and to England too, if the issue of that revolution is to sap all belief in supersensuous truth, and in the ethical obligations which find in supersensuous truth their only real sanction.' p. iii.

[2] I *Corinthians*, 10:20 and 14.

[3] This paragraph is inserted verbatim in letter of 17 Aug. 1884 to Lilly. See notes there.

[4] This phrase did not occur at all in Lilly's letter of dedication to Lord Ripon.

TO PHILIP SHERIDAN

Jany 7. 1885

Copy

Cardinal Newman hopes that Mr Philip Sheridan will pardon him if he asks a question in which Mr Sheridan has no concern.

Some years since a boy of the name of Philip Sheridan was placed at the Oratory School, Birmingham by his mother and after a time withdrawn. At the latter date the sum of £136 was due for pension and personal expenses to the Fathers of the Oratory, who not being then or since in possession of his mother's address have been unable to claim the sum of her. Is Mr Sheridan able to do them the great service of informing them how to direct to her?[1]

TO CHARLES JAMES LONGMAN

Jany 8. 1885

To Charles ⟨C. J.⟩ Longman Esqr
Dear Sir

I thank you for your letter and heartily return your friendly wishes for the New Year.[2]

I quite appreciate the value of your recommendation that I should order 1250 copies in my new Edition of my Apologia, but I doubt whether I can afford it. At my age, there is little chance of the outlay on it coming back in my life time. I wonder whether you could advise me as to selling the copyright of the book, according to an offer I have had, or as to accepting a royalty on it; but perhaps the question admits of no answer.

Very truly Yours J H N

TO LORD BRAYE

Jan. 9. 1885

My dear Lord Braye

Ever since the sacred season began, I have been wishing to send you and Lady Braye my best wishes and my blessing for the new year. Tardily indeed, but still heartily, I do so now. I am no politician — but it seems to me likely to prove an anxious year — though events commonly move slower, than they promise or threaten to do

Most truly Yours John H. Card. Newman

The Lord Braye

[1] Philip Sheridan was an Indian Mutiny veteran and for forty years Inspector-General of Mails in the Punjab, Postmaster-General of the Punjab, 1891–9, when he retired to Cork.
    Philip Sheridan the younger was at the Oratory School from 4 Nov. 1880 until the end of the summer term 1882.
[2] Longman wrote on 2 Jan. that Apo. was out of print and suggested a new edition of 1250 instead of the usual 750.

Jany 10? [1885]

(*copy*)

My dear Sir

Of course I should greatly prefer parting with the Apologia to your House instead of looking elsewhere; but I hardly thought you would care for a single volume.[1]

I am quite ready to treat with you on making over the sale of it to you on a royalty and should have very few conditions to make. One would be that I should have liberty to make literary corrections or alterations in the text, tho' at the end of 20 years I do not expect that I should use it. On the other hand I suppose you would have the right to publish it in any shape as regards size, paper, type etc. I believe I am correct in saying that Messrs Gilbert and Rivington have the stereotyped plates of it, which would become yours

Some difficulty might arise about the first and subsequent editions. I could not offer you the first — the difference between the two which is considerable is stated in the Advertisement prefixed to the volume Mr Kingsley's name is omitted in the second.

As to my other works which are not in your hands, I want advice about them sadly: but I hardly feel you would consider yourself able to give it — first because you may not be acquainted with them (I inclose a list of them) and secondly because they are in other hands[2]

J H N

TO T. W. ALLIES

Jan. 12. 1885

My dear Allies,

I have ever been so taken up by the duties immediately before me as to have no time for any other, and now what with the load of letters which oppress me, and my failing sight, and the weakness of my memory and my difficulty in writing, I cannot properly take in the interesting circular and private letter you sent me several months ago.

I feel with you that Catholics ought to contribute more for the healthy action of the Church, and yet when you look into the (state) of things in detail, we find that most of us are poor, and those who are rich do give largely.

Here I am reminded that I promised (did not I?) £10 a year to the School Fund.[3] I inclose a cheque, and wish you and yours a happy new year. I wish I was sufficiently bright in my head to write more.

Yours affecty John H. Card. Newman

[1] Longman replied on 9 Jan. to Newman's letter of the previous day that he would be sorry to let *Apo.* go to another publisher. He asked to make an offer either to buy the copyright or to sell on a royalty. Meanwhile he would print the usual edition of 750 copies.

[2] See letter of 15 Jan. to Longman.

[3] Allies was secretary of the Catholic Poor School Committee.

TO ALEXANDER DENNY

Jany 12. 1885

To Mr Denny (Pickering and Co)

I am sorry you do not aid me in entering the £40.0.0 in my account. Figures do not tell their own tale and in the course of my life I have been much perplexed to determine the mutual relation and the meaning of items as they occurred in an account. Even though as you say the printing went through your hands in other cases that does not explain this case in particular

You will do me a service then if you throw light upon this matter e.g. the date of it would be a gain

I do not know how I have deserved what seems to me an uncourteous mode of meeting a simple inquiry[1]

TO THEODORE FRIEDRICH ALTHAUS

Bm Jany 13. 1885

Dear Sir

I have received and read the Article on dear Mr Pattison, which you have been so good as to send me;[2] and though I had seen him in brief interviews only twice or thrice in the course of forty years, and only knew him as a junior in age and standing to myself, and never had such intimacy with him as yours has been, still your interesting and vivid notices of him fitted on to my own recollections of him with remarkable exactness, and not only revived, but in good measure interpreted them.

Much, alas, as, I fear, he differed from Catholics in religion, I must ever consider him a grave, cautious, conscientious thinker.

Since you have, as his gift, a copy of a volume of mine, which went from me to him, on its first publication, with many imperfections in it, I venture, in return for your article about him, to send you my second Edition, in which I removed some of them[3]

Yours faithfully John H. Card. Newman

[1] See letter of 17 Dec. 1884 to Pickering. On 13 Jan. Denny sent a calculation to account for the £40. See letter of 15 Jan. to him.

[2] Althaus, who went up to Lincoln College, Oxford, in 1877 and had been befriended by Mark Pattison, sent Newman a copy of *Temple Bar* (Jan. 1885), containing pp. 31–49 his article 'Recollections of Mark Pattison'.

[3] 'I next asked Pattison's advice as to reading Newman. "Well," he said, "of course the 'Apologia' has the great biographical interest to recommend it; but upon the whole I think the 'Discourses on University Education' would suit you best. I have the copy of the 'Discourses,' which Newman himself gave me: I should like you to have something of mine; if you can take the book I will give it you."' Art. cit., p. 47. See also letter of 21 Dec. 1856 to Pattison.

Althaus also remarked that in Pattison's study, 'On the mantelpiece, in a small frame, was a photograph of John Henry Newman.' Art. cit. p. 32.

TO W. H. KEATING

Jany 13. 1885

(Copy)

Dear Sir

I should long before this have thanked you for your obliging communication but for the pressure of correspondence which lay on me and required an immediate answer and the effort which writing causes. The refusal of the governing powers here to grant a Catholic people such as Ireland freedom of education is a great inconsistency and ought not to be tolerated any longer. I shall rejoice to receive the information which you promise me on a question which does not lie in the province of secular politics to be considered a[1]

TO ANNE MOZLEY

Jan 14. 1885

My dear Anne Mozley

The MS shall go to you at once. I have no *special* question to ask upon it — but, *supposing* it to be published as it stands, what would be the just criticisms on it?[2]

I have a great deal of Memorand [sic], letters from myself home, and from home to me — but not of a public nature — of which my correspondence with Harriett and Jemima reaches to 1845, the originals being with you. Also I have letters from abroad, of which James, for several reasons thought too highly [3]— the original rough copies of my Lyra Apostolica, and a large collection of my letters from friends and acquaintance — on the whole transcribed clearly.

I don't see that any portions of these can be introduced into the narrative, but my present notion is to append bits in the shape of Illustrations, viz No 1,

---

[1] The draft ends thus.

On 17 Dec. 1884 Keating sent a report of the proceedings at the Dublin University College historical society. He wrote: 'This University College, though deprived of the name of Catholic by a policy of which few can understand the meaning, is sole representative of the Catholic University begun a generation since, under such happy auspices. Your Eminence will perceive from this paper, that the blessing of the Holy See, and your own incomparable teaching, have *not* been without fruit: and that there is ground for abiding hope that the traditions of the erstwhile Catholic University will be worthily revived and produce results equal to the promise of their beginning. As your Eminence may have perceived, the future charge of this momentous question has been confided by the Irish Hierarchy to the hands of the Parliamentary Party of Ireland. The new demand for justice in this order has not yet been formulated . . .'

cf. letter of 23 April 1884 to Keating.

[2] This refers to Newman's Memoir of his life up to 1833, *A.W.* pp. 29–107. See also *Moz.* I between pp. 26 and 160. See letters of 20 Oct. and 24 Dec. 1884 to Anne Mozley, who wrote on 12 Jan. that, a Christmas family gathering having dispersed, she was now ready for the Memoir. For Anne Mozley's replies to this present letter see that of 16 Jan. to her. She was taking the first steps towards editing *Letters and Correspondence of John Henry Newman during his Life in the English Church.*

[3] See note to letter of 18 April 1878 to Anne Mozley.

No 2, No 3 etc etc thus No 1 Whether the Tractarian Movement owed any thing to Kant and Coleridge[1]
No 2 Lord Malmesbury's report of Mr Newman as College Tutor[2]
No — 3 Mr Newman in his relations with the Church Missionary Society[3]
No 4 Mr N's refusal to marry a parishioner who was unbaptized.[4]
No — Sir William Palmer's imputation [?] on Mr N. of a purpose, to be, while an English clergyman in communion with the Church of Rome etc.[5]
But I have no distinct preference for such an arrangement

Yours affectly J. H Card. Newman

TO ALEXANDER DENNY

January 15. 1885

Dear Mr Denny

If I understand your letter of the 13th it somewhat surprises me. Will [you] let me ask you a few questions

Of whom did you buy the paper, at the cost of £15.5.3. for the sixth edition of the second volume of my 'Historical Sketches'? Did I give you leave to buy it at all? Did you direct Messrs Gilbert and Rivington to print that 6th Edition at the cost of £22.17.0. Was this in consequence of directions from me?[6]

J H N

[1] See letters of 17 Aug. 1884 and 7 Jan. 1885 to W. S. Lilly; also that of 28 April 1885 to Anne Mozley. Anne Mozley replied on 16 Jan., 'Having been used to footnotes lately illustrative of the context [in her edition of Letters of the Rev. J. B. Mozley] my first idea was that they might be admitted here, but I see this must all come from your own hand. I am no judge in the question of Kant and Coleridge, and of course any thing you would think *suited* for a place in the narrative would interest the philosophical reader'.
[2] See letter of 8 Oct. 1884 to Lord Blachford and those of the month following. Anne Mozley replied on 16 Jan., 'My first thought was (before reading the MS.) that Lord Malmesbury *had* been answered by Lord Blachford — but on reading your feelings towards the Gentlemen Commoners [A.W. p. 89] — it puts him [Malmesbury] in a different and more aggressive position. Still if it would necessitate any lengthened explanation, I think you may spare yourself the trouble as in fact what the MS. says already is an answer to Lord M's story [,] is not compatible with it.
In looking over some old letters returned to me by Miss M. A. Dyson I found a testimony from my pen to your gift of *Silence* upon occasion commemorated by Lord B [Blachford]'.
[3] See V.M. II, pp. 1–7 and letter of 14 June 1883 to the editor of the Fortnightly Review. Also end of letter of 15 May 1885 to Anne Mozley.
[4] See Moz. II, pp. 55–63; Trevor I, pp. 169–71.
[5] See letter of 5 May 1883 to the editor of the Spectator. Anne Mozley replied on 16 Jan., 'Sir W. Palmer's imputation has in a sense been answered in the Apologia — though with no allusion to him — but anything you *wish* to say as an answer to a direct attack might come in well in this place. Still the reader of your works needs no such justification'.
[6] Denny replied on 16 Jan. that in his arrangements about H.S. II he had done what had been customary with Newman's volumes for the past six years, although sometimes these had been charged direct by the printers. Newman noted on the reply, 'N B Jany 17. I shall not answer this letter, since it would only lead to a dispute.'

Jany 15. 1885

Dear Sir

I am quite willing to accept the terms you propose for your having on a royalty the publication of my Apologia, and will subscribe the usual form of agreement when you send it to me.[1]

As to my other volumes, it strikes me, as you went so far last year as to accept Lord Coleridge's proposal of entering into correspondence with me on the subject of purchasing my copyrights, that it is possible you may be willing to take ⟨?⟩ other volumes besides the Apologia on a royalty also[2] E.g. The Idea of a University which you did originally publish in two separate volumes. A third volume on the same subject is published also by you now incorporated in the three volumes called 'Historical Sketches' which, I think, has gone through six editions. 'Discussions and Arguments' also seems one of the more popular volumes judging by the sale. Another is 'The Development of Doctrine' There are others, however, which from particular circumstances I might find myself in a difficulty in proposing to you.

I suppose there is no law standing in the way of my transference at my own will from one publisher to another works which the former publishes only on commission. Of course there is a rule of considerateness and courtesy.[3]

JHN

Jany 16. 1885

My dear Anne Mozley

I see I have completely puzzled you, and I am puzzled myself. One thing I ask of you not to send my MS back at once as you propose Think better of this by thinking longer. I am much gratified to have your praise, but I wanted from you something else, but I hardly know what I wanted, and time is going.[4]

[1] In reply to Newman's letter of 10 Jan. Longman replied on 13 Jan., that he would be glad to publish *Apo.* 'on the following terms.
(1) The stereoplates to be placed at our disposal free of charge,
(2) We to pay the entire cost of printing etc.
(3) We to pay a royalty of ¼ of the retail price of all copies sold . . .
(4) You would have the right to make small corrections . . . to make really extensive arrangements, the matter would no doubt be easily arranged between us.'

[2] See letters of 29 April and 17 May 1884 to Lord Coleridge, also those of May, June and 4 July 1884 to Longman, who now offered to give Newman 'any assistance in my power'.

[3] Longman replied on 19 Jan. that there was no law against changing a publisher unless the author had bound himself by contract not to do so. As to courtesy, there was nothing more than 'a natural feeling of consideration between parties'.

[4] Anne Mozley acknowledging Newman's Memoir, after she had read the first two chapters, on 15 Jan. wrote: 'I will only say now what indeed could not be otherwise that I have found it of absorbing interest What letters of boyhood were ever written before that show the mind as these do?
It seems to me to introduce a new form of biography'.
On 16 Jan. she wrote: 'I have just come to the end of the M S. So lost in it that I was

I am very well at present — but no one can reckon on his life at my age. Lord Blachford, as an independent witness confirmed me on my own idea that a Memoir of me up to 1845 should be written by an Anglican.[1] I doubt whether my Catholic Life can ever be written without causing much controversy, which ought not without strong reason to be allowed.

Then I thought how few there are now among Anglicans who know any thing about me, or would care to bother themselves with my collections of letters etc This led me in 1874 to write, as a specimen, the MS I have sent you, of what I should like This I sent to Jemima, but, tho' I dare say she felt, she showed, no interest in it, and I had it back.

As time has gone on, I have got more reconciled to the idea of its being not a mere specimen, but, as far as it goes, the memoir itself; but I should ask of the friend or well wisher into whose hands it came to exercise a judgment on every part of it, and omitting or inserting accordingly

And I speculated on his doing his work, (whether from my papers or from other informations in my life time,) and *that I should never see what he had done.*

If you look back on my letters already written to you, perhaps they will become clearer to you now.

Now, if you consent to keep MS a while, perhaps suggestions may occur, and may lead me to explain more fully my difficulties and wishes[2]

Yours affectly John H. Card. Newman

startled to come to the end so soon It seems to me wonderful for the absolute truth and fairness of the narrative so transparent is its flow.' To Newman's question of 14 Jan. 'What would be the just criticisms on it?' she replied 'that people will say it is *too short* they will wish for more.' See also postscript to letter of 19 Feb. to her. She concluded, 'the whole MS. shows a sweetness and tenderness most delightful to me as I read.'

[1] See letter of 20 Oct. 1884 to Anne Mozley.
[2] Anne Mozley wrote again on 17 Jan., 'By this time you will have received the MS . . . I heartily wish I had not been so precipitate . . . But I hope no harm is done and that you will let me have it back again. It is really a valuable document, so to call it. The truth is it never occurred to me that I might detain it any time. You mentioned Lord Blachford and he seemed to me to represent the ideal Protestant Editor.

If I have health for I too am old I think I might help in the way of illustration and additions to the context in my favourite form of footnotes. I look forward to the box of letters Jane [Mozley] has asked me to look over.' These were Newman's letters to his sister Jemima, also ones to Harriett in the eighteen twenties. Anne Mozley thought she 'might thus have suggestions to offer to who ever carried out your wishes'. She was encouraged by compliments she had received for her editing of *Letters of the Rev. J. B. Mozley.*

She went on to ask Newman not to leave his Memoir as a mere specimen but to continue it as he had intended. 'Would it not be well to do so? It may be an effort to resume a work left off in 1874 but your pen retains its cunning It should at any rate be explained what your original intentions were, and a sketch given of the following years more or less filled in — up at least to 1843. You once told me that you remember little of the time immediately before the act of 1845 but *something* said of that period would allow the insertion of some interesting letters, of which *I* have some which I think you would not be sorry to be given.

The Editorship of the work in prospect would have to be anonymous Who ever undertook the office might I should think reckon on the Dean's [Church] allowing himself to be consulted. You would rely on his taste feeling and judgment

It seems like a dream writing such a matter. Who ever is the survivor the work ought to be in hand as soon as there is the material from the hands of the author or the illustrator by contemporary letters etc.'

TO WILFRID OATES

Jany 17. 1885

(Copy)

Dear Mr Oates

You told me on Decr 13 that customers were waiting for Callista, and asked me about the Postscript (of the Advertisement) I sent it up at once asking for a revise.

This [is] Jany 17 and the Revise has not yet come

Also I asked for proof of the work itself[1]

J H N

TO MESSRS GILBERT AND RIVINGTON

Jany 19. 1885

(copy)

Cardinal Newman requests Messrs Gilbert and Rivington to place the stereotyped plates of the Apologia at the disposal of Messrs Longman and Co.

TO ALEXANDER DENNY

Jany 20. 1885

vid Denny's letter of Oct 30 1884 and mine of Nov 27 1884

Dear Mr Denny

In your letter of last Oct 30 you offered me a royalty on the sale of my works and on Nov 27 following not being satisfied with your terms I answered you that I 'must decline your proposal'

I have by this morning's post received a more advantageous offer for at present six of my works from a publishing firm and have definitively accepted it.[2]

I do not like to make any delay in informing you — but in a day or two I will write to you on the subject again

J H N

TO CHARLES JAMES LONGMAN

Jany 20. 1885

(copy)

My dear Sir

I agree to your terms for taking my six works on a royalty.[3] I am glad to receive your intimation about my other volumes, but I might seem abrupt to

---

[1] Oates promised to send half the proofs very soon, but see letter of 8 Feb. to him.
[2] See next letter.
[3] Longman replied on 19 Jan. to Newman's letter of the 15th. He offered to publish,

my present publishers, if I did not move now; as things stand, they knew last October that I was inquiring about royalties, and made me an offer, which I did not accept.

I will send you in a few days an account of stock, which is large

J H N[1]

TO ALEXANDER DENNY

[23 January 1885]

Dear Mr Denny

I am sorry to find that the copy of my letter of Decr [November] 27 which I kept does not run with what I sent to you. I suppose I thought that saying I had given up the idea of a royalty on my books, which till then I had entertained, implied, inclusively my declining your offer in particular.[2]

I had no thought of reviving the idea of a royalty, till an accident led to my having a better offer, and this from a very acceptable quarter

I transcribe the portion of my letter of Nov 27 as it stands in my copy

'I am sorry I have not answered your last letter before today, but I could not do so till this morning. I have now to say that I have given up the idea of letting my books on a royalty and therefore must decline your proposal.'

TO H. W. WRIGHT

Bm Jany 23. 1885

Dear Sir

I am glad to send you my leave to print the Hymn 'O God, the Lord' for the use of your Congregation[3]

Yours faithfully John H. Card. Newman

The Revd H W Wright

besides *Apo.*, the six stereotyped volumes mentioned in that letter, at a royalty of 25 per cent of the retail price. This would be paid in advance, even in the case of the stock Newman had in hand, provided it was not more than could be sold in two or three years.

Longman also offered to publish on a royalty any other of his works that Newman put in his hands.

See also letters of 3 Feb.

[1] On 20 Jan. the twin sisters Mrs Helen Paget and Mary Church visited Newman. Dean Church wrote on 21 Jan. to thank Newman for his 'kindness to those two audacious children of mine, who took on themselves to disturb you, and to whom their visit gave such extreme delight'.

[2] For Newman's draft see at 27 Nov. 1885. Denny wrote on 22 Jan. 'I have found your Eminence's letter of Nov. 27th, in which I do not find that you "declined our proposal". What your Eminence did write in that letter was, "I have given up the idea of a royalty for my books."'

[3] This was Newman's translation of the hymn for Sext, 'Rector potens, verax Deus', *V.V.*, p. 246, where it begins 'O God, who canst not change nor fail.' Originally in *Tract 75*, p. 68, he wrote 'O God, the Lord of place and time.'

Henry Wildey Wright, who took his B.A. at Magdalen College, Oxford, in 1832, was Vicar of St John's, Newcastle-on-Tyne, 1835–73, and then chaplain to the Institution for the Deaf and Dumb in the same city.

TO GEORGE T. EDWARDS

Jany 24. 1885

Dear Mr Edwards

Thank you for your beautiful hymn — if I were writing to Mr Fisher, and wished to be controversial, I should say 'I can't find in it Justification by Faith only', except in the sense in which we all hold it, Catholics as well as Protestants.[1]

I was sincerely concerned to hear from you the great affliction he has had lately.[2] We are all going sooner or later

Yours sincerely John H Newman

TO CHARLES JAMES LONGMAN

Jany 24. 1885

My dear Sir

The volumes of which I now send you the stock, are all stereotypes.

This leads me to mention the works which are not stereotypes. I do so because, since in one of your last letters you expressed a readiness to take on a royalty other of my volumes, you may prefer those which already have stereotype.

Should you take others, I should prefer, if it would suit you, not to make the engagement before the end of June.[3]

My remaining stereotype volumes are

1. Miracles
2 Volumes 1 and 2 Essays
3 Via 1 and 2
4. Difficulties of Anglicans Volume II — query about first volume?

Volumes not as yet stereotyped

1 Grammar of Assent
2 St Athanasius Vol 1 and 2
3 Theological Tracts
4 Position of Catholics
5 Verses including Dream of Gerontius
6 Loss and Gain a Tale
7 Callista a Tale

---

[1] See last note to letter of 1 Jan. to Edwards.
[2] Fisher's wife had died.
[3] Half a line follows, almost illegible.

Jany 25. 1885

My dear Stewart

Such cases as you mention have a special interest for me, as being examples of misfortune met or rather welcomed with resignation and with a brave spirit. Alas, we are already interested in a family of daughters parallel to those in whose behalf you write, the Miss Cannings. But I won't neglect your friends, if we can serve them

Yours affly J. H. Card. Newman

TO LORD BLACHFORD

The Oratory, Jan. 26th. 1885

My dear Blachford,

Thank you for the amusement your letter gave me. I will only specify the 'callida junctura.'[1] That the Trinity motto is Johnson's reference, I am sure so is Tom Warton his — but where does Johnson end and you begin? Is there a Pope common to you and Johnson? am I to keep Leo XIII, or to be made over to Leo X.?[2]

I suppose everyone is as anxious as I am about the Nile expedition — those who have relations on it far more so. Poor young de Lisle, a clever fellow, was a son of Ambrose Phillipps, and the third of a large family 3 of whom have died in the course of the year, and a comrade and great friend of one of the young Pollens, who, having to tow a boat up the rapids swimming, is invalided with fever. Other of our boys are there too.[3]

[1] Horace, *Ars Poetica*, 46–7.
[2] Lord Blachford wrote on 16 Jan.: 'I have been reading Boswell's Life of Johnson — actually for the first time. What do you say to the following
"Sir — your disquiet is a foolish affair. Why Sir if my wife bade me give you her love, she would never, to be sure, tell you to say nothing about it. No Sir. If the Pope, who I am informed is a man of sense intended to afford you a gratification, he would never have imposed a condition to destroy half its value. Mr Warton used to say at Trinity College "quod tacitum velis nemini dixeris" — and if the Pope had been ashamed of his affection for you, why Sir, he would have said nothing about it"
As somebody says "Them's my sentiments."' Lord Blachford was imitating Boswell's *Life of Samuel Johnson*. He wrote on 13 Jan. 1885: 'How very unkind of you to make me burn that letter — which is a *pièce historique* — to say nothing else of it. But I have done it. I am sincerely glad that you are getting your deserts — and it was very good of you to tell me of it.' This was evidently a laudatory message from Leo XIII. On 9 Jan. Dean Church wrote to Newman: 'It was very kind in you to let me know of the Pope's kind message to you. There is a fitness in it, which no one can overlook. But the fit things do not always happen; and this is of a piece with the Pope's insight and wisdom. You must let us rejoice with you. I wish I might tell Blachford. I am sure he would be glad.'
[3] This refers to the expedition sent out too late by Gladstone to rescue General Gordon. On this very day that Newman wrote Khartoum was stormed and General Gordon killed. Rudolph de Lisle, R.N., was sailing up the Nile with the Naval Brigade. He was killed at the battle of Abu Klea on 17 Jan. Francis Pollen, R.N., was originally a member of the same Brigade. De Lisle wrote home on 20 Dec., 'I wish indeed Pollen was with us, for he was always so bright and cheery till knocked down by that wretched fever . . .' H. N. Oxenham *Memoir of Lieutenant Rudolph de Lisle, R.N.*, London 1886, p. 214.

As to the expedition, has not Gladstone made imprudent promises, which it will be frightful to keep?

Yours affectionately, John H. Card: Newman.

P.S. It is to me a phenomenon of old age, that I cannot write without making mistakes.

TO MARGARET DE LISLE

[26 January 1885]

I am shocked to hear of your mother's and your new affliction. God alone can carry you and her through the trial. I can but give you my true sympathy; and I will say Mass for your dear brother.'[1]

TO JAMES BLAKE KAVANAGH

Jany 26 1885

Dear Dr Kavanagh

Thank you for your able and cogent argument.[2] I fear, however, that there are necessarily serious difficulties in making a practical application of it. It requires much thought and skill. I have been in the course of my life embarassed when young men would not accept views and reasonings which I felt myself to be indisputable, and we cannot forget this is an unbelieving age in a sense which could not be said 30 years back. The true, safe, and happy way is to believe what the Church teaches, but when we have to go down to deeper and elementary questions, then the teacher needs the grace of insight into hearts and natures ⟨intellects⟩ and the pupil ⟨student⟩ the grace of docility. You feel all this quite well, I know — but I am expressing what I feel myself

JHN

TO ANNE MOZLEY

Jany 26. 1885

Dear Anne Mozley

I have so much to say and find it so difficult to put it into order, and so little leisure, that I do not know how to write at all.

---

[1] See previous letter. Two of Rudolph de Lisle's brothers and also a brother-in-law died in 1883.

[2] On 12 Jan. Kavanagh sent a copy of his pamphlet *The Study of Mental Philosophy by Catholic Students in the Royal University of Ireland*, Dublin 1885. He was a member of its Senate and complained that certain other Catholic members wished 'to restrict the study of Mental Philosophy for Catholic Students to scholastic philosophy in its ancient forms'. He wished Catholic students to study modern manuals of scholastic philosophy, which, he felt, met the questions of the day. He thought that if Newman approved of 'an extended course of Mental Philosophy for Catholic Students' the matter would be settled.

Of course any one who puts on paper a Memoir of me, must do it in his own way, not in mine — what *I* have written would be a memorial of what I had thought would be best and so be valuable.[1]

I say this because you remark that readers will think what I have written too short — but the very reason I have written it has been to protest against such biographies as the present morbid taste of the public requires. If indeed there is more which it is reasonable and open to say, say it — but then it should be short; whereas a memoir commonly is *padded*, as I have observed in my Letter to Fr St John,[2] and that either with irrelevant matter or matter too private. Again, this padding is not only culpable in itself, but, breaks the thread of the narrative and is illogical and distracting, and leading to dipping into the pages instead of reading outright.

This leads me to notice another practice which has a serious effect upon the lucidity and continuity of a narrative, and that is the indulgence in foot notes. I am not speaking of yours in editing J B M's [Mozley] letters, but of the practice in itself. It turns my head to break off the text and to transport my eyes to the foot of the page. It does not matter in family and familiar *letters*, for they have no continuity, but it is intolerable in an argument or a narrative I suffered from it seriously in my 'Letter to a Magazine—[3]' On the Editor's allowing me to defend *in his pages* Pusey on Baptism I wrote certainly a very sharp letter — what was the Editor to do, considering his promise? he was equal to the occasion. He cleverly put not above a few lines of my answer in each page, filling up the space by his own long two columned representation of it. It effectually smothered me, and I had to retire from the contest. My own 'Athanasius' is another instance, but here the Notes suffered, not the text. In the new Edition they form a separate volume. In what I last wrote to you 'Number 1 Number 2 Number 3 etc etc'[4] answers to the Alphabetical Notes which form the second volume of the new Edition of Athanasius, notes *far too long* for foot notes.

I repeat it would be great gain to me to find you would undertake the task and perhaps you could not give me an answer till you have the letters and papers. I have said all I can say as things stand yet — what I have said will sufficiently explain my saying 'I am puzzled and perhaps shall puzzle you'[5]

Yours affectly J H Card. Newman

---

[1] See first note to letter of 16 Jan. to Anne Mozley.

[2] This was in the first paragraph of the note Newman wrote on 1 June 1874 'For Father Ambrose St John', as a preface to his *Autobiographical Memoir*. See *A.W.* p. 23.

[3] On this letter of Jan. 1837 to the *Christian Observer* see *Moz.* II, pp. 222–3. Newman republished it as *Tract 82*, 'Letter to a Magazine on the subject of Dr. Pusey's Tract on Baptism,' reprinted in *V.M.* II, pp. 143–94.

[4] See letter of 14 Jan. to Anne Mozley.

[5] Anne Mozley replied on 27 Jan., agreeing to undertake the task Newman proposed. 'I see it need not involve much personal responsibility . . . what I ask — *perhaps almost make a condition* — is if any difficulty arises when I feel my ignorance and incapacity too much for me I may consult Dean Church and through him Lord Blachford — or direct on occasion'.

TO CHARLES JAMES LONGMAN

Jany 27. 1885

Copy

Dear Sir

Thank you for the trouble you have taken as to the copies of 'Development etc' I have written to inquire.

As to my general statement, lest by some mistake I omitted to send you Messrs Gilbert and Rivington's autograph statement, I have begged them to send you another.

Messrs Pickering sent no autograph, merely confirmed *my* statement. In consequence, instead of sending you what I *now* send (paper B) I sent the paper A, which Pickering has attested.

I return your own paper as you wish.

Very truly Yours John H. Card Newman

P.S. As to 'Historical Sketches' vol 2 I think Edition 6 must have been printed before Edition 5 was sold off — each edition being of 500 copies, I suppose.[1]

TO CHARLES JAMES LONGMAN

January 31. 1885

To C J Longman Esqr

(copy)

Thank you for the great trouble you are taking about the stock of my volumes. For the moment I will confine myself to the question of the stock without going on to the question of royalties

I send you back your careful table, having made a copy of it,[2] also I think it best to send you some letters etc. which may throw light upon the matter, I have lettered them C D E F G H I J. I send all these to you in a separate parcel.

I can send you Pickering and Burns and Oates' annual statement in the 1881. 82. 83. Burns and O's up to 1884 if you like

I have written to Messrs Pickering and Messrs Burns and Oates as you wish me.[3]

---

[1] Wilfrid Ward visited Newman on 30 and 31 Jan. See the account in *Ward* II, pp. 490–7, and Maisie Ward, *The Wilfrid Wards and the Transition*, London 1934, pp. 109–14. Ward wished to consult Newman about lectures on unbelief he was to deliver at Ushaw College and about the biography he was preparing of his father.

[2] See next letter.

[3] On 30 Jan. Longman asked for further information as to stock and sales.

TO CHARLES JAMES LONGMAN (I)

The Oratory Birmingham Feb 3. 1885

(copy)

Dear Sir

I agree to the proposal you make me of the terms on which you will take on a royalty the sale of the six books I have offered.[1] May I not take for granted that you have satisfied yourself as to the stock of 'Development' in the hands of Messrs Gilbert and Rivington? I say this because in a paper which I sent you in their hand writing the stock is set down May 14. 1884 as 592, and in their return of the stock *at present* as 'none', whereas in your Table which you inclose in the letter just come, you put it down as at present 592, in accordance with their report last May.

This occurs to me to say in consequence of your words 'our estimate is for the stock on hand at the date of the *December account*'[2]

I will make a separate letter respecting the other works which it seems best to me to leave as they are at present till July 1st

I am etc J H N

TO CHARLES JAMES LONGMAN (II)

The Oratory, Birmingham Feby 3 1885

Dear Sir

Though certainly it would be a relief to me, if you took all my volumes, as you are taking the Apologia, and the six besides it — still I know so little about the usages of publishing that I prefer to make a proposal short of this, thus

My thought is to offer you those which are *stereotyped*, which I believe are these: — 1 volume Miracles 2 and 3 Essays — 4 and 5 Via Media — 6 and 7 Difficulties of Anglicans. These are all stereotyped except volume 1st. of 'Difficulties' with the stereotyping of which I should have to be charged. To these I should like to add as an 8th volume Grammar of Assent, which I should have to stereotype also.

If this was carried out, then, since the copyright of my volume on the Arians is in the hands of Messrs Pickering, I should go on to leave to them as publishers 'Athanasius' two volumes, and 'Theological Tracts' one volume, as being cognate in their contents to the Arians, altogether three volumes.

And I should leave with Messrs Burns and Oates what may be called 'School' and 'Public Library' volumes, viz 'Position of Catholics in England',

---

[1] See letter of 20 Jan. to Longman who wrote on 2 Feb. that he would pay £250 for the stock of these books and a royalty of a quarter on all future copies printed, the copyright to remain Newman's. Longman listed the stock, on inaccurate information. For a more exact list see last note to letter of 21 Feb. to him.

[2] Longman wrote on 5 Feb. that Gilbert and Rivington claimed to have 592 copies of *Dev.* whereas they only had 92, since delivered to Pickering. In consequence Longman deducted £29.12 from the sum due to Newman.

'Verses', 'Loss and Gain', and 'Callista', — altogether four volumes ⟨(The two volumes of Sermons accidentally omitted)⟩[1]

On a disposition of volumes such as this, perhaps there is no reason for my stipulating for the delay till July 1st.

I am &c J H N

P.S.   I must ask to delay my sending you the stock of these volumes till I hear what you think of this letter.[2]

TO GEORGE TEELING

Febr 3/85

My dear George

Thank you for your telegram. I made it known directly, sending it into the Church. I said Mass for dear Lord O'Hagan this morning.[3]

Yours affecly J. H. Card. Newman

TO EMILY BOWLES

Feb 5. 1885

My dear Child

It troubles me so to write, that I can't attempt a letter — but I write a line to ask whether your anxieties about Milton are less.[4] Your letter about your brother was very sad, but still very consoling

All kind thoughts of the Wards[5]

Yrs affly J H Card. Newman

TO MRS WILSON

Febr. 5. 1885

My dear Mrs Wilson,

Did I thank you for your kind remembrance of me at Christmas? If I did not, I do so now. I have so many letters to write and now it is difficult to form my A.b.c. letters.

God be with you – all his best blessings attend you

Most truly Yours John H. Card. Newman

[1] Newman added the bracketed words to the copy, which is in Neville's handwriting.
[2] See letter of 21 Feb. to Longman.
[3] Lord O'Hagan died in London on 1 Feb. 1885.
[4] Milton Hill was the home of the Bowles family at East Hendred, where Emily's eldest brother John had just died.
[5] The F. R. Wards and the Richard Wards.

Febr. 6. 1885

My dear Aubrey de Vere

I am a very bad person to ask for an opinion on a political question.[1] I was painfully struck with your concluding pages, but they went beyond politics — but the truth is that since 1832 I have no political views at all. I then thought what called itself the Reform Bill was a Revolution — indeed Lord John [Russell] so called it — and what you now truly call a Revolution is that same old act which was then by violence and blood-and-gutter Articles in the Times effected, though it has taken 50 years and more perhaps to carry it out.

You will say that patriots should make the best of things — but that is the duty of politicians. They have done so, and to have staved it off for 50 years, is no bad work, but *I* could as easily command a force in the Soudan, as give an opinion how to meet the Radical party. I think your Pamphlet a very good one, but I am ignorant of the elements of the question. I did not know what 'Proportional representation' meant, or 'single-member districts' till your Pamphlet told me; what I have felt all along most keenly since I went to Ireland is that, if a revolution was in progress in England, much more, alas, was it making its way in England [Ireland]

A gentleman of the name of Whitelaw of Ipswich has sent me a pamphlet titled 'Co-operative Voting secures Proportional Representation'[2]

Yours affectly John H Card. Newman

Sunday, Febry 8. 1885

Dear Mr Denny

I have agreed to give the sale of a certain number of my works to Messrs Longman on a royalty. How many is not yet decided — but the probability is that I should not offer to them Athanasius and Theological Tracts as being on cognate subjects with the Arians, of which you have the copyright. I shall let you have a list of them, most likely through Messrs Longman when the list is settled

If you have at hand a list of my stereotyped volumes I should be glad of a copy. Else it does not matter

J H N

---

[1] De Vere sent his *Ireland and Proportional Representation*, Dublin, 1885. He objected to the new Franchise Act, which with single member constituencies would throw nearly all the seats into the hands of the Nationalists. The friends of England in Ireland had been abandoned by the English political parties. At the end of his pamphlet de Vere maintained that in Ireland a social revolution was about to turn into a political one, while in England a political revolution had begun, which would eventually turn into a social one.

[2] George Whitelaw, *Co-operative Voting the only means to secure Proportional Representation*, London 1885.

Sunday Febry 8. 1885

Dear Mr Oates

You cannot be surprised at my looking for other publishers of my works, when as I am so sorry and vexed to have to say, it is so difficult to rely on your punctuality[1]

You told me last autumn when I agreed on your bringing out an edition of a 1000 copies of my 'Callista' that the publication of it would take place about the 31st of December last. We are now at the end of the first week of February, you have not got through the first sheet.

In consequence I am in correspondence with Messrs Longman with the intention of offering them the sale of some of my works on a royalty, and I must ask you to be so good as to tell me what stock you have in hand of my Grammar of Assent and of the first volume of the Difficulties of Anglicans, such stock most likely becoming Messrs Longmans from this date.

If for any reason you wish to cancel your agreement with me about the Edition of Callista, I am ready to entertain it — but, if you mean to carry it out, I think you should pay me the £50 for it *at once*.[2]

Feb 8. 1885

Copy

My dear Lady Simeon,

I can't help writing to you on a subject on which you have touched.

No one can go beyond me in my admiration of Gladstone in his private-public character, I mean as a man who in the midst of public affairs is true to religion and duty. But since 1874 many, I doubt not, as myself, have had grave and anxious thoughts about his future.

It used to be said of Lord John Russell that he never prospered politically after his change of policy and attack upon the Catholic Church and the Pope in 1851, and the needless and angry attack of Gladstone, apparently in return for the rejection by the Irish Bishops of his University Bill (which I wonder he could fancy their accepting) was a turning point in his career.[3] I have often asked myself whether he was to succeed after (to all appearances) so wanton an act. If Providence, not only judges us as individual persons, but interposes in the course of public affairs, I cannot certainly feel aught but awe and silent submission when I find a man, however exemplary personally, now smitten for using his great influence against the Spouse of Christ.

[1] See letters of 27 Nov. 1884 and 17 Jan. 1885 to Oates.
[2] This was the sum due on publication. It was paid on 28 March.
[3] See Volume XXVII, 'Introductory Note'.

Further, if my dates are correct, he wrote a letter after his ministry went out of office, saying he meant to give the few remaining years of life to preparing for eternity,[1] but in no long time we find him setting out on his Scotch (Midlothian) expedition, and ever since he has been in the hands of the enemies of all religion. Alas, Alas — that so it should be! and it makes me reflect how dreadful a fate perhaps dear Hope-Scott escaped, when he shrank from the public line to which his close friend and much loved companion so earnestly invited him, and died a Catholic. Did not the one follow the suggesttions of his guardian Angel, and the other was deaf to them, (tho' the occasion was different)?

With all my heart I trust and pray that the blow which has now fallen upon both him and us is all we shall have to suffer[2]

Yours affectly, John H. Card. Newman

(Enclosed)
Extract of a sermon preached before the University Decr 2. 1832.

... With these principles fresh in the memory ... what do all these symptoms show, but that the spirit of Saul still lives? that wilfulness, which is the antagonist principle to the zeal of David, the principle of cleaving and breaking down all divine ordinances, instead of building up. And with Saul's sin, Saul's portion awaits his followers — distraction, aberration; the hiding of God's countenance; imbecility, rashness, and changefulness in their councils; judicial blindness; fear of the multitude; alienation from good men and faithful friends, subserviance to their worst foes, the kings of Amalek and the wizards of Endor. So it was etc.

On the Sin of Saul.[3]

TO ANNE MOZLEY

Febr. 10. 1885

My dear Anne Mozley

First let me say that I wish you quite to understand that I am to have no part in any thing you write. I am neither to *see* nor to *suggest* knowingly any thing which you pen. This does not mean that neither you nor I am at liberty to introduce into your work *bodily* and with an *open profession* remarks or statements of mine, which you may wish to have, e.g. the whole of the memoir which I sent you to read, but you would not make yourself answerable for one word of it.

---

[1] This was Gladstone's letter of 13 Jan. 1875 to Lord Granville, published in all the newspapers, saying that 'retirement is dictated to me by my personal views as to the best method of spending the closing years of my life'. Philip Magnus, *Gladstone a Biography*, London 1954, p. 231.
[2] The blow was General Gordon's death, for which Gladstone was blamed.
[3] 'Wilfulness the Sin of Saul', *U.S.*, pp. 174–5.

And I should say that I sent that Memoir to you for quite a distinct reason — viz to set before you what *I* thought the *best* way of writing a memoir, viz. to be brief, not to pad, not to digress etc. etc, but not for me to *bind* you even to this. I consider you ought to pursue your own ideal of a Memoir, not mine, and that I should never see what would in fact be after my death. At the same time it is plain that I should not have taken the step of asking of you a great favour, if I did not believe that your ideal would not be very different from my own. And in particular, I should say I do not object to footnotes, if the possible evils, which I pointed out are kept in mind.

If you think it best to begin with the autograph Memoir I sent you, you can; and you can add to it, if you wish so that you *profess* to be adding. On this supposition your own independent work would commence in 1832, when I had just given up the Tutorship. At this time the influence of Hurrell Froude upon me was fully developed, and my University Sermon of December 2 1832, preached the day before I set out for Gibraltar is worth looking at, and then you are launched on your own work. The documents I should send you are my letters home and to my Sisters from 1815 to 1845, my Mother's to me from 1817 to 1836; perhaps some private memorandums from 1816 to 1828; my letters from abroad 1832–3 a number of notes on particular points, such as 'Number 1, Number 2, Number etc' spoken of in a recent letter,[1] none of them yet written; — my letters to Bowden, Keble etc Hurrell Froude for a long course of years — This is enough for the present.

You would find many letters of mine 1839–45 in Hope Scott's life. Vid. also Froude's Remains volume 1 and 2 ⟨?⟩

I am so very busy, that I must ask you to bear with some delay[2]

Yours affectly John H Card. Newman

TO CHARLES JAMES LONGMAN (I)

Febr 11. 1885

Dear Sir

There were several points which I had to clear up and bring together before writing, as you wished me, to Messrs Gilbert and Rivington and to Messrs Pickering and I was trying to save unnecessary correspondence. This is why I have delayed my answer to your letter of the 5th. And indeed I interpreted that letter to mean that you were intending to write to me.[3]

---

[1] Letter of 14 Jan. to Anne Mozley.
[2] Anne Mozley replied on 11 Feb. that she would throw herself into the material before writing anything herself, and that the letters must tell the story, 'my aim would be in my selection of letters etc to show a *character*.'

She went on to say 'Every letter of yours that I have seen — with thought or character in it — all tells the same way, is as it were a representative letter, as coming from the same mind and hand and *heart*. No one can help the book being interesting that has such letters in it'
[3] Longman wrote on 10 Feb. asking for further details as to the volumes he was to take over.

One reason was that I had given you as yet no voucher for the fact of my stereotypes.

Next I suspected I was wrong in saying the *second* volume of 'Difficulties' was stereotyped, and I think I was, for I have found a statement, (original I believe) of Messrs G. and R. [Gilbert and Rivington] in which certainly no mention is made of stereotypes of *either* volume. I inclose it.

Also I was not satisfied that they might not have to correct other statements about the general stock; however, as you make no difficulty about it in this morning's letter I shall put this aside.

I now send you with this letter the two letters. I send them to you, not to them, in accordance with your letter.[1]

I understand what you say about the deduction from the £250 on account of the stock of Development

This answers, I think, your letter of the 5th.

TO CHARLES JAMES LONGMAN (II)

Febr 12 ⟨11th?⟩ 1885

As to your letter of this morning, the volume of 'Difficulties' which I have thought was stereotyped was volume 2 not volume 1. ⟨I believe neither are stereotyped.⟩

The stereotyped 'Dream of Gerontius' is a reprint, selling for a shilling, in very small pages of one of the Poems of my 'Verses', a volume which is not stereotyped.

I inclose a third letter, viz to Messrs Burns and Oates, about the 'Grammar of Assent' and the 1st volume of 'Difficulties,' The second volume is in the hands of Messrs Pickering.[2]

TO CHARLES JAMES LONGMAN

Febr 13. 1885

Cardinal Newman begs to inform Messrs Longman that he has received the inclosed letter from Messrs [Burns] and Oates

---

[1] Newman kept copies of the two letters he enclosed: 'Cardinal Newman requests Messrs Gilbert and Rivington to deliver the stock of six volumes enumerated below to Messrs L. [Longman] and Co. on their application.' The list that followed contained eight volumes, *Idea, H.S.* I–III, *D.A., Dev.* and *Diff.* I and II.

'Cardinal Newman, in accordance with information he has already given to Messrs. Pickering, wishes them to deliver the stock of his six volumes enumerated below to Messrs. Longmans and Co. on their application, also to account to them instead of to him for all copies of these volumes sold after Decr. 17. last.' The list was the same except that *Diff.* I was omitted.

[2] 'Cardinal Newman, having placed his Grammar of Assent and 1st volume of "Difficulties" in the hands of Messrs Longman wishes Messrs Burns and Oates to be so good as to send Messrs Longman a report of the Stock of the above two volumes at present in Messrs Burns and Oates hands. Also he must ask them for an account of the sale of these two volumes during the past year.'

Messrs Burns and Oates have not yet replied to his request 'for an account of the sale of the two volumes during the past year.'[1]
Messrs Longman and Co

TO CHARLES JAMES LONGMAN

Febr 14. 1885

(in substance)
My dear Sir

I have just had brought to my mind that Mr Lilly some years ago had my leave to publish certain selections from my works which he called 'Characteristics.' At the time I did this, I took measures, as I believe sufficient to prevent this interfering with my copyright. However, you may consider it to interfere with the royalty.[2]

J H N

I will send Mr Lilly's volume

TO RICHARD MILLS

Febr 14. 1885

Dear Mr Mills

I am made very sad by the thought that we may be pressing rudely on the difficulties of the Trustees of Mr Wheble's property.

I write to you in confidence, asking your private opinion, whether there is any thing, which is possible to us, the doing which would be acceptable to them.

Would it be worth saying that the payment to us of the sums, which, in the course of this year will be incurred by them for the two boys might be delayed till next first of January?

I cannot disguise from you, speaking confidentially, that we are in want of money for carrying on the school; again few of our present Fathers have a knowledge of the school from its first years, or that interest in consequence in its old friends which long experience gives; still, I don't like to omit inquiring whether there is not something we can do from our respect and gratitude towards Mr Wheble's memory.[3]

J H N

---

[1] Newman made a note below this draft: 'N B Oates's return in his letter to me was
Difficulties volume I at present 342 sheets, 34 bound
Grammar of Assent ,,   ,,   286 ,,   73   ,, '
[2] See letter of 21 Feb. to Longman.
[3] Mills, who was the lawyer of the Wheble family replied gratefully on 17 Feb. Their money was in trust, but the situation had eased, and it was hoped to make the payment due to the Oratory School, for the two youngest sons of James Wheble, who died in 1884.

Febr 15. 1885

Dear Mr Oates

I am sorry to trouble you, but I really must beg you to answer the question contained in my letter to you, which came to you through Messrs Longmans, on the 12th or 13th inst. asking for an account of the sale during the past year of the Grammar of Assent and 1st volume of 'Difficulties.'[1]

J H N

TO HENRY EDWARD WILBERFORCE

Febr 18. 1885

My dear Harry

I rejoice to read your news about yourself, and congratulate you with all my heart on having persuaded a lady so good as you describe her to accept you, and I congratulate her on being sought for by so good a fellow as you.[2]

I send you both my blessing, and when you tell me the day of the wedding, I will, please God, say Mass for you and her

Yours very affectionately John H. Card. Newman

TO ANNE MOZLEY

Febr 19. 1885

My dear Anne Mozley

It is very difficult to write to you a logically consecutive letter because I have anxious business of various kinds on my mind, and my brain and my fingers are not what they were.

Lest I should forget to say let me say to you what no one knows but Fr Neville himself viz that *all* the MSS I send you are his property. They are all too in my writing. And if you tell me the name of the station nearest to Barrow (Cheleston?) [Chellaston] he will come over to you for an hour some morning which we agree upon and deliver them into your hands. There are *no* copies (unless indeed you can call the *originals* of those which Jane [Mozley] has, *copies*.) This makes me careful about transmission.[3]

---

[1] Oates replied on 16 Feb. with the required information.
[2] Wilberforce married Emily Mary, third daughter of R. S. Moody, on 29 April 1885.
[3] Anne Mozley wrote on 20 Feb. how very glad she was at the prospect of being able to talk to Neville.

At once, however, I shall send you back the Memoir with three *private* notes, which I wish you not to *keep* or to *use*, but to send back to me, (they are headed, A, B, C, and give you an idea of the *Notes* which I intend to append to my Memoir,) though they are not for publication but in order to give *you* what I call elbow room.[1]

I wish you to keep steadily in mind, and when you publish to make it known that I am cognisant of no part of your work. And I beg you to beware of panegyric, for this reason if no other, that it would provoke a re-action — Not that I am afraid of it, considering that even for your brother you have not indulged in too kind words.

Of course I do not object to your consulting your Sister Fanny, for whom I have much affection. Nor to Dean Church, but, I wish you could manage to account for what you were doing by saying that you had not taken the task out of your own head, that it came naturally to be your task, since you had so many letters of mine to or from my Mother and sisters, and that, tho' I knew what you contemplated, I had seen not a single word of what you were writing.

Of course I am not inflicting conditions on you — but wish your own judgment to consider what I have been saying.

I am rather perplexed what to send you — whether to begin with my school time or with 1816. Of course I cannot myself be the judge of myself, but, speaking with this reserve, I should say that it is difficult to realize or imagine the identity of the boy before and after August 1816, as the memoranda, still undestroyed, describe him. I can look back at the end of 70 years as if on another person, but even the period from 1816 to 1828 I shall not be able to send you without a great effort, though they are necessary to illustrate my Memoir, if you commence your volume with the Memoir.

And now I do not recollect of more to say.

Yours affectly John H Card. Newman

P S I am surprised you should think by shreds and tatters I meant to express contempt. Even a king's robe may be cut up into un[in]telligible bits. I have not looked out the passage — but I am sure I meant patches. Catholicism may be held in bits and pieces. But I will look [out] the place[2]

I suppose rooted is a mistake for routed.

---

[1] These were passages about the Oriel tutorship, which Newman cut out from his Memoir. They are in *A.W.* pp. 96–107.

[2] In her letter of 16 Jan. Anne Mozley had criticised Newman for speaking in his Memoir of 'routing out evangelical doctrines from' his Creed, and of 'certain shreds and tatters of evangelical doctrine hanging about his preaching.' *A.W.*, pp. 77 and 78, and *Moz.* I, pp. 120–1, where she misread 'rooted.'

My dear Wilfrid   Febr. 19. 1885

I am sorry I am able to do nothing more for le Serre, than send you the inclosed cheque

Yours affectionately John H Card. Newman

TO CHARLES JAMES LONGMAN

Dear Sir   Febr 21. 1885

As I now have not heard from you for a week, I am led to think that my letter informing you of Mr Lilly's 'Characteristics' has placed you in a difficulty. If so, be sure I am ready on my part if you wish it to cancel the copies of our agreement as regards the Apologia and other of my works, and to return to you the sum of £56.5, which you sent me lately.[1]

I only wish you to believe that there was nothing very strange in my not recollecting Mr Lilly's compilation till the time when I wrote to you about it. I have made no contract with either Mr Lilly or Messrs Paul and Co or Mr King who preceded them. I did not receive one shilling for the permission I gave Mr Lilly, and I am so used to grant permissions on a small scale for the use of my Volume of 'Verses' that such an act comes to me as a matter of course. My own motive in giving Mr Lilly the permission for the Characteristics was my belief that it would be a good advertisement of my volumes, and I am led, rightly or wrongly, to think that it has been so.

I will add that your reluctance in the first instance to part with the Apologia was a surprise to me, a very welcome surprise, and, as coming to me suddenly, required some little time more than I gave before I could collect my thoughts, and understand what such an act implied in its fulness.[2]

And, now, if you accept my offer to undo what we had so nearly brought to an end, I will though with sorrow close the correspondence by thanking you for the trouble you have taken for me, asking you to pardon my having caused it needlessly[3]

C. J. Longman Esqr   J H N

[1] This was the royalty on the new edition of *Apo.*
[2] See letter of 10 Jan. to Longman.
[3] Longman replied on 25 Feb., 'I must apologise for my silence which has I regret to find, given you a wrong conception, and I fear some worry. It was solely due to a complication as to the stock . . .' The existence of W. S. Lilly's *Characteristics* made no difference. Longman sent his (roughtly accurate) estimate of stock: *G.A.* 359, *Diff.* I, 376, *Diff.* II, 560, *Mir.* 230, *Ess.* I and II, 127, *V.M.* I, 344, *V.M.* II, 458. Only a small number of copies of each volume had been bound. For them all Longman would pay £300. There were no stereotypes of *G.A.* or *Diff.* I and II. These Newman would have to provide.
Longman finally said: 'I hope that this will satisfactorily conclude the negotiation. I have been anxious in conducting it to spare you labour and worry as far as I could, but I have been obliged to be somewhat troublesome.
May I finally express our very great satisfaction at the relations with yourself into which we are now entering.'

TO J. R. BLOXAM

Febr. 23. 1885

My dear Bloxam

Your kind remembrance for my birthday, as splendid as it is kind, has come safely, and I thank you for it[1]

Is not the state of things in the Soudan most distressing? It is a load to bear

Yours affly John H Card. Newman

TO BERNARD HENNIN

February 24th. 1885

My dear Bernard

You are one of those friends and well wishers, who have so kindly addressed to me letters of congratulation on my birthday, — letters which touched me much, and for your share in which I hereby offer you my sincere thanks.

Yours affectionately, John H. Card. Newman.

P.S.   I am obliged to send you a lithograph, since I write with difficulty.[2]

TO CHARLES JAMES LONGMAN

[25 February 1885]

My dear Sir

I am much obliged by your friendly letter, and am quite ready to sign the agreement for the eight volumes which you propose to send me, and to make over to you the stock of copies, about which you have taken so much trouble, for the sum of £300. I write by this post to the three firms who have the stock, directing them to send the copies to you.

I quite understand that I have to pay for the stereotyping of the three volumes, 'Grammar of Assent', and 'Difficulties felt by Anglicans' volumes 1 and two on this first new edition hereafter printed. I suppose you will deduct

---

[1] Bloxam sent Burke's *Peerage*, with a note inserted: 'With a thankful remembrance of the past, And with kindest wishes for the future, This volume is offered to the acceptance of His Eminence, Cardinal Newman, on the anniversary of his Birthday, By his ever grateful and affectionate servant and friend John Rouse Bloxam   Beeding Priory   February 21.   A.D. 1885.'

[2] The postscript was added in writing. On 24 Feb. Newman sent the same lithograph, without a postscript, to Sir William Henry Cope and John Hardman junior.

the cost of it in each case from the sum due to me for the royalty; but any mode you name will suit me.

Thank you for the words with which you conclude your letter. For my own part, let me say how much pleased and relieved I am to have been able to make this disposition of so much of what I have written[1]

J H N

TO J. R. BLOXAM

Febr 26. 1885

My dear Bloxam

Thank for me Mr Hessey for the gift of his new Publication   I have read quite enough of it to feel its impressiveness and value at this time, but I am too old to do justice to it[2]

Yours affectly John H Card. Newman

TO ANNE MOZLEY

Febr. 26. 1885

My dear Anne Mozley

I have many things to say, but I cannot recollect them all together.

First, there are a number of books you ought to have — I forget which — but e.g. You ought to have Hope Scott's Life — both because it may put ideas of arrangement etc etc into your mind whether you criticize the Editor or not — and because it contains many letters of mine. I will send it to you

Next, you ought to see my Via Media volume 2 which contains my Letter about the Church Missionary Society verbatim.[3] I can't recollect others just now.

I am in a difficulty what MSS to send you. You *have*, as having Jane's [Mozley] box, my letters to my Mother and Sisters, and I am proposing to send you my Letters from abroad.

But as to my letters in Jane's box from me to my Mother and Sisters, tell me the *first* and *last* date of each packet, and I shall be able to see how far my collection runs beyond yours.

One of my packets is 'from me to my Father, Mother, and Sisters', 1815 to 1827 — Have you got the originals of *these?*

---

[1] Longman replied on 26 Feb, promising, as soon as he had received the stock, to send the agreement. This he did on 7 March.

[2] R. F. Hessey, *Drifting into Unbelief. An Appeal to Thinking Men*, London 1885.

[3] See fifth note to letter of 14 Jan. to Anne Mozley.

Again, have you the packet 'to my two sisters, 1817 to 1828'? of course you have not.

Further — so widely has the world been thrown open since 50 years ago, that I may be very wrong in my *descriptions*, and *statement of facts* of all kind. Also my views of philosophies and of philosophers may be open to great criticisms in this learned time — (e.g. what I say of Berkeley) I feel then it may be a comfort to you to consult Dean Church on passages in my letters.

This letter must be taken into account before Fr Neville goes to you

Yours affectly John H Card. Newman

I send you by this post the Memoir with A, B, C. I shall register it.[1]

TO LOUISA ELIZABETH DEANE

Febr. 27. 1885

My dear Louisa,

I should have thanked you for your kind recollection of my birthday long before this, did I not find it so difficult to use my hand. Louisa [Deane] will, I know, let me thank her through you, and for a welcome and thoughtful pot of Mignonette.

Though I know no one in the Soudan, and scarcely any of their relatives, I am in real distress at the thought of what those relatives are suffering. Neither the Crimea nor the Indian Mutiny has come home to me, I don't know why, as this has. Perhaps it is because the misfortune is so wanton, and on that ground makes one so indignant. Five successful engagements, won at a cruel price, but all for nothing.

My kindest remembrances to Mr Deane.

Yours affly John H. Card. Newman

TO MARGARET DE LISLE

Febr. 27. 1885

Dear Miss de Lisle

I hope you can give me a favorable account of your Mother.

I have said three Masses for you and her, since I last wrote to you[2]

Most truly Yours John H Card. Newman

---

[1] Anne Mozley acknowledged Newman's packet on 27 Feb. and wrote: 'I have your letters to your mother and to Jemima . . . Your first letter to Jemima is Dec 1819 — and there does not seem to be any cessation of correspondence up to her death. Of your letters *to* your mother I think 1826 is the first date. You will remember an *old* letter dated 1816 sent *to* you at Ealing — Your mother writing in the crossing. There are none either to or from your father.

I have *not* the originals of the packet headed "to my father Mother and sisters 1815 to 1827" to ask for neither have I "to my *two* sisters"'

[2] See letter of 26 Jan. to Margaret de Lisle.

TO GERARD MANLEY HOPKINS

Febr. 27. 1885

My dear Fr Hopkins

Thank you for your very kind remembrance of my birthday I am so sorry to say my hand is too weak now to enable me to write — and I fear the weakness is permanent. I grieve to find you corroborat[e] from your own experience what other friends tell me about the state of Ireland   What are we coming to!

Yours affectly J H Card. Newman

TO JANE MOZLEY

Febr 27. 1885

My dear Jane

Thank you for your affectionate letter. I wish my hand was so strong and managable that I could write a letter with a more natural flow of words.

You seem to feel what is trying in your present useful employment. Every work has its good and its bad — and we have here quite enough experience of trouble in our own school here, to know how much those ladies sacrifice who devote themselves to the welfare and comfort of thoughtless boys. And the first year often or always is the worst.

Also you are necessarily a great comfort to Frank[1]

All this you know better than I can tell you — but sometimes it does some something to show sympathy when one can do nothing else — Therefore I have allowed myself to write these platitudes

Yours affly John H Card. Newman

TO ALFRED PLUMMER

Febr. 27. 1885

My dear Dr Plummer

I was much pleased to receive your birthday letter, and should have answered it sooner, did I not write now with much difficulty.

I was afraid that James Mozley's Letters would fail to excite interest, considering how many biographies have been published lately, but it seems to have been a success.[2] As to us undervaluing, as you think, Maurice and

---

[1] Francis Woodgate Mozley was a master at Bedford School and boarded some of the boys. His sister Jane kept house for him. See letter of 26 Feb. 1884 to her.

[2] Plummer wrote on 20 Feb., 'I have been reading with much interest and delight the Letters of Dr [J.B.] Mozley. What a contrast to the Reminiscences of his brother! [Thomas Mozley] It seems to me something like the difference between the earnestness of Tacitus and the Gossip of Suetonius. But one thing does surprise me in the Letters – the very low estimate expressed of the *ability* of Hampden and F. D. Maurice. That some of their views should be condemned is not more than one would expect; but that their intellectual power should be questioned so seriously was a new thing to me.'

Hampden you must recollect that the more active-minded men of the Movement were men who delighted in clearness of thought and statement, such as Hurrell Froude, Ward etc and they considered the two writers you have named most provokingly unintelligible. Yet my dear friend, Ambrose St John, professed to owe one of his first steps towards the Catholic Church to Maurice's book on Baptism;[1] and I think we all considered his Pamphlet in 1836 [1835], Subscription no Bondage a striking one.

As to Hampden, certainly, when in 1834 he came out with the Pamphlet which I have spoken of in my Apologia, no one could accuse him of ambiguity[2]

Most truly Yours John H Card. Newman

P.S.   I am very well, thank you, but very weak

TO FANNY MARGARET TAYLOR

Febr 28. 1885

Dear Sister in Christ

I had great admiration and respect for Lady Georgiana Fullerton — but I had very few opportunities of seeing her, and scarcely ever exchanged a letter with her.

I am sorry then I cannot help you in your excellent undertaking, except, as I do with all my heart, by sending you my blessing upon it[3]

Yours very truly John H Card. Newman

TO ANNE MOZLEY

March 3. 1885

My dear Anne Mozley

I fear my inconsecutiveness has perplexed you more than I had fancied, but recollect I told you I was perplexed and should perplex you, and you are quite right in cross-examining me.

As far as I recollect, I thought you would begin with my own memoir as it stands — when you spoke (as I understood you) of footnotes to it, such as you have put so well to James's letters, I considered that letters, being independent of each other and fragmentary, admit of footnotes without injury to them, but a logical, continuous Memoir does not, and I had such unpleasant experience of injury to *text* in the Christian Observer[4] and to *notes* in Athanasius, that I said that *long* Notes on my Memoir ought to be at the end, as in

[1] i.e. F. D. Maurice's *Second Letter to a Quaker* (1837) later published in *The Kingdom of Christ*, 3 vols., London 1838, vol. 1, pp. 65–160.
[2] *Observations on Religious Dissent* . . . See *Apo.* pp. 57–8.
[3] Lady Georgiana Fullerton died on 19 Jan. Her life was written by Mrs Craven. See letter of 12 Nov. 1885 to her.
[4] See third note to letter of 26 Jan. to Anne Mozley.

the Apologia, or in Athanasius edition 2. I referred (as an illustration) to a projected Number 1, Number 2 etc but *not as subjects* which *you* were to treat, but as instances which *I* had meant to write (and *still* mean) as an Appendix to my Memoir — and I sent you A. B. C as instances already written of such Notes, though not instances which were to be *published* by any one (certainly). I did not wish *you* to make Notes on this pattern, but I said that I certainly should dislike *foot* notes to my Memoir which hurt ⟨injured⟩ the swing of the narrative. Long Notes at the end was one way which I myself might take, you need not. If you confined your Notes on my Memoir to the foot, don't let them be long; that is all.

N B. Observe, I have all along been speaking on the question of *manner* or *structure* of your composition I do not interfere with matter or with opinion. And I am not speaking of *your* work itself, but of your handling my Memoir. I hope I am not puzzling by needless explanations.

As you seem to have seen Hope Scott's life, or some Review of it, I have no cause for sending it to you, I *had* two reasons for sending it — first because it contained letters of mine, and next because it has been praised as an instance of a good *editing*. I have often recommended Stanley's Life of Arnold as another instance, as the world has thought of a successful editing.[1] I did not thinking [sic] of wishing you to follow it, but I thought it might give you ideas.

There is one view of the proposed work which I hope is yours too — but it is too sacred for me to write about, tho' I could talk to you about it. No one but myself can know what acute pain Tom's book[2] gave me in the few pages I read of it — Not only its miserable *half* truths which he said of my dear Father, but the handling the subject at all — Who has so been treated as I ? So numerous are his mistakes, and so often cruel ones, that though I had the book in my hands scarcely five minutes, I have come across quite a crop of them, like Falstaff's 'blackberries.'[3]

Yours affly J H Card. Newman

P.S. I am very much afraid of perplexing and worrying you. When you ask how you are to know *what* are 'elbow room' matters, I should give, as an instance, personalities, as the A about Hawkins, mentioning his failing — yet you might find it *necessary* in your discretion in a particular case to make mention of faults as necessary for *fairness* or other reasons, *till* you had so decided, I think they should not be told to others, as I feared your circle of confidants would bring about

J H N

[1] Arthur Penrhyn Stanley, *The Life and Correspondence of Thomas Arnold, D.D.*, 2 volumes London 1844.
[2] T. Mozley, *Reminiscences chiefly of Oriel College and the Oxford Movement.* See letter of 9 June 1882 to T. Mozley. Anne Mozley replied on 5 March 1885: 'Tom has intellectual gifts but I believe they are counterbalanced by large deficiencies. I believe his want of sympathy is due to lack of imagination   I doubt if he can put himself into other people's frame of mind, or guess what they will feel.'
[3] Shakespeare, I *Henry IV*, II, iv, 265 'If reasons were as plenty as blackberries, I would give no man a reason upon compulsion.'

P.S.   I send you back the Alton letter you sent me — Addressed so much to me, except a separable bit, or even with that bit, it belongs to me. How did it get to my Mother or sisters? If you did not want it, I would ask for it.[1]

P.S.   (I repeat your words as perfectly agreeing with them 'Your own letters brought into use with every document you send me — All to be as *true* and simple as I can make it')[2]

TO SIR WILLIAM HENRY COPE

March 4. 1885.

My dear Sir William

I have had your kind letter in my mind ever since I received it, but I do everything so slowly now, especially the act of writing, that I have to beg my friends to excuse my want of punctuality, especially in correspondence. I write at the pace of a child making letters

I felt the compliment, a very great one, both of your collecting my published writings and your printing the list of them, and that you should think of sending them to some friends only increases the compliment.[3] I have thought that, as you have taken the trouble to record my beginnings, you would like also to have my endings — So I enclose a catalogue of my books as they stand at present — and I propose with your approval to have it printed in size and type to match yours — and to send you two or three copies

I hope you enjoy this mild season, though I am not quite sure that the coast which you are upon does not suffer from wind. It is my lot here to be in a house warm in winter as well as cool in summer — and, though March is a formidable month, at least I may say that hitherto I have got on without a cold

Most truly Yours John H. Card. Newman

Sir W. H. Cope. Bart

TO GEORGE WILLIAM COX

Mar 4. 1885

My dear Sir George

I thank you for your letter and reference to the late Bishop of Natal. I am sorry I am obliged to send you this shabby answer — but I have lost the use of

---

[1] Anne Mozley, who had sent this letter of 1816 on 2 March, returned it on 4 **March.**

[2] Newman quotes from Anne Mozley's letter of 2 March.

[3] *List of Works written and edited by his Eminence Cardinal Newman, in the library of Sir William H. Cope, Bart., at Bramshill,* not published. It contained works up to and including those of 1884.

See also letters of 25 May 1869, 26 Jan. 1879 and 17 Sept. 1880 to Cope.

my fingers and eyes and am forced to lithograph 'I regret to say I am too old to attempt to answer letters', instead of a more respectful reply[1]

Hoping you will excuse this in a man of my age

I am My dear Sir George Yours truly

John H Card Newman

TO JOHN WILLIAM OGLE

March 4 1885

My dear Dr Ogle

As I took up my pen to write these lines, I was told by Fr Neville that you had been corresponding about me with him. I have wished to write sooner, but do every thing, including the use of the pen, so slowly, that I am overset with arrears of work in every direction

Alas, the Tamer[2] failed with me. I think all my powers are failing tho' I have nothing positive the matter — but I doubt whether I should have strength to meet a sudden attack, whether it were an external accident or an illness.

What troubles me is that every morning brings its own work and more than I have time to get through so that the days go on, and I seem to have less and less chance of getting thro' current matters and beyond them into serious occupation[s] which have a claim on my thoughts

For the moment my greatest trouble is the feebleness of my fingers. My pace in writing is that of a child beginning the alphabet

And I am losing the power of spelling

Yours most truly J. H. Card. Newman

TO CHARLES RYDER

March 4. 1885

My dear Charles Ryder

I have been very much pleased and touched by the birthday letter addressed to me by yourself and the Collectors for the New Church.[3]

---

[1] Cox, who laid claim to a baronetcy, published *Life of John William Colenso*, two volumes, London 1888. Scholar of Trinity College, Oxford, in 1845, Cox adopted high church views and took orders. Towards the end of the fifties he became broad church and an ardent supporter of Bishop Colenso of Natal, who died in 1883. Cox's letter is not to be found, but in his book, I, pp. 449–52, he pointed out how Charles Kingsley 'hurled his lance' first at Colenso for not accepting all the wonderful events in the Bible as historical, and then at Newman for accepting, where the evidence was good, similar events in the history of the Church.

[2] This seems to refer to some remedy.

[3] Charles Ryder became the priest at Smethwick in 1882, and at once began collecting money for a new church, opened in 1893, to which Newman contributed. See letter of 20 March.

They must forgive me for my delay in acknowledging their kindness and the few words I use now in acknowledging it. But I do not write without effort, and with the slowness of a child – and, if I used ever so many words, I could not express as fully as I should like to do the gratification which their letter gave me.

I send you and them my blessing and am

Your and their sincere Friend John H Card. Newman

The Rev Charles Ed. Ryder

TO GEORGE T. EDWARDS

March 5. 1885

My dear Sir

Thank you for your remembrance of my birthday, and your kind letter. This house is so warm that I have not known that it was winter.

The lines which you inclosed are very beautiful. And I trust and believe that there are many Protestants besides the authoress, whose hearts respond to them.

Very truly Yours John H Card. Newman

TO SIR WILLIAM HENRY COPE

Bm March 9. 1885

My dear Sir William

I do not like longer to delay my thanks for your beautiful and curious volume, which came quite safe. It is in various respects a most interesting documentary work and our library here will be proud of having it.[1]

Most truly yours John H. Card Newman

TO WILLIAM HENRY ARCHER

March 10, 1885

My dear Sir W Archer

I thank you, though late, for your New Year's letter. I write with such difficulty now, that I have been obliged, by the necessity of letters to me which required an immediate answer, to postpone my acknowledgement of yours.

We have all been much gratified and encouraged, in the present anxious state of our foreign affairs, by the lively and practical interest taken in our

---

[1] This was Sir W. H. Cope's *Bramshill: its History and Architecture*, London n.d. Newman's copy is inscribed 'With the Authors kind regards.'

wellfare by our colonies. It is a fact which counterbalances many misgivings about our future[1]

I am very well, but still weak; but surprisingly well for my age

Most truly Yours John H Card. Newman

TO THOMAS LIVIUS

March 11. 1885

Dear Fr Livius

I thank you for your instructive and interesting Pamphlet. It is very kind in you to send it to me[2]

Yours very truly John H Card. Newman

TO THE ABBESS OF STANBROOK[3]

The Oratory March 12 1885

My dear Lady Abbess

I thank your kindness in sending me the Bishop of Newport's impressive and interesting Funeral Oration.[4]

I had not heard of Fr Shepherd's death, till it came to me. I grieve much for it, and condole with you on your great loss. I send you my blessing, and am Dear Lady Abbess

Your faithful servt J. H. Card. Newman

TO ANNE MOZLEY

March 13. 1885

My dear Anne Mozley

Fr Neville will be at your service next week, if it suits you, any day but Monday, you to fix the day.

He expects to be with you about noon or half past 11, and thanks you for

---

[1] Australia sent, amid scenes of great enthusiasm, a contingent of troops to support the British in the Sudan.

[2] Livius made a note on the autograph: 'The foregoing note was in answer to an Article of mine on the lawfulness of saying Holy Mass for a deceased Protestant, reprinted from the "Irish Ecclesiastical Record" [(March 1885), pp. 144–61] – which I had sent the Cardinal with my respectful compliments. Though I had sent it to several other distinguished Clerical Converts – Cardinal Newman was the only one to acknowledge it – J.L.' See also letter of 12 May to Livius.

[3] This was Gertrude d'Aurillac Dubois (1842–97), a French Huguenot who had become a Catholic. She came to Stanbrook to teach French, and in 1864 entered the convent. There she effected a great revival, being Abbess from 1872 until death.

[4] This was Bishop Hedley's *Funeral Oration of the Rev. Fr. J. L. Shepherd,* James Laurence Shepherd, from 1862 chaplain to the nuns at Stanbrook Abbey, who died on 30 Jan. 1885.

your offer to give him luncheon. As to the Waggonet this is very kind of you. If you can, it will be a real kindness, as he will have a heavy load with him

He will bring a list with him, and I think you should give a receipt and make it quite clear that the books are his property and must go back to him. There are no copies of some or most of them. The following will give you some idea of them

1. An abridged diary from 1804 to 1873[1]
2 private notes about me from 1804 to 1816[2]
3 letters ditto from 1816 to 1828
4 letters to and from home from 1815 to 1836 and 1845 (Five Books)
5 letters from abroad[3]
6 account of my illness in Sicily
7 Remains of Littlemore and St Clement's.
8 Letters to Miss M. R. Giberne
9 H W Wilberforce on my Sermons[4]
10 Two letters from me to the Christian Observer[5]
11 Five letters to the Record[6]
12 Suggestions about the Ch. Miss. Society in Via Media Number 1. Volume 2.[7]

Yours affectly J H Card Newman

TO ANNE MOZLEY

March 16. 1885

My dear Anne Mozley

Fr Neville wrote to you last night.

Two difficulties he will speak to you about. Of course Fanny's being in your confidence is no difficulty, but nephews and nieces is.[8] How can you keep out knowledge of some kind from Bonamy Price, the most liberal newsvendor in the literary world?[9] Your relations and friends, intimate and familiar as they are with you, will be sure to find out that there is a secret and a mystery.

---

[1] *Chronological Notes.*
[2] This was the two books, 'Early Journals' *A.W.*, pp. 149–213. See letter of 18 March to Anne Mozley.
[3] i.e. during the Mediterranean tour, 1832–3.
[4] 'F. Newman's Oxford Parochial Sermons', *D R* (April 1869), pp. 309–30.
[5] 'On the Study of Mathematics', the *Christian Observer* (May 1821), pp. 293 5; 'Hints to Religious Students at College' (Oct. 1822), pp. 623–6.
[6] 'On Church Reform', published in the *Record* in Oct. and Nov. 1833.
[7] See fifth note to letter of 4 Jan. to Anne Mozley.
[8] Anne Mozley wrote on 14 March that she was copying Newman's Memoir, and wished to keep it 'till I can read over my copy with my sister Fanny, to make sure of there being no errors.' On 2 March Anne Mozley had written that she was sure her nephews and nieces would rather the work 'was in the hands of one connected by family ties'.
[9] John Rickards Mozley was married to Edith daughter of Bonamy Price.

This requires an answer, and doubtless admits of one. The only matter which is a great difficulty is your sister Maria, not because she is *she*, but because she is *another*. When you enlarge the range of a secret, you break it. This is even more certain in the case of Dean Church, who would think it cruel to know such a secret about *me*, and not tell it to Blachford. You will say I ought to have thought of this before.

As far as the Dean is concerned, I think it may be met by reserving your consulting him, till you can show him all your difficulties of editing (if you shall have any) altogether on your *last* reading. By that time, I may be gone from this world. But what about Maria? how can you tell her something without telling her every thing without unkindness?

Do you think that, with honesty, you can say, if questioned that you were looking through 'family letters,' which you thought called for it, useful for the future? such are Harriett's and Jemima's, and even my Mother's, considering her as mother in law to your John and Tom.

The other difficulty is, What will you do with your book if I overlive its finishing? Neither I, nor Fr Neville must be allowed to come near it, for there must be no possible suspicion of our having any thing to do with it. This is a large subject.

Yrs affly J H Card. Newman

Send back A, B, C by Fr Neville

TO WILFRID WARD

March 16. 1885

My dear Wilfrid Ward

It pleases me very much to find you take so kindly the real affection I have for you — which has come to me as if naturally from the love I had for your Father. You can give me in return your prayers, which I need much.

I have little else to say to you — than this[1]

1. I don't know when I first knew your Father. He was one of a number whom I accidentally and gradually got intimate with. I got to know in this way many young men, some of whom ultimately went one way, some another. Lord Blachford, as much as any one made me intimate with him. I recollect Lord B. saying 'If Ward comes over he will go great lengths'

2. I am overburdened with letters of past times, and have been for *many* years burning or sorting them. It would be a great relief to come upon your Father's, and if I live, I shall, and will send them to you. I do every thing so slowly now, and get so soon tired.

3. I don't understand your last part. If you wish to refer to any thing I

[1] See note at end of letter of 27 Jan. 1885 to C. J. Longman. W. Ward wished to know the circumstances of Newman's first meeting with his father. He also asked whether Newman had letters of his father's.

wrote in the way of criticism, let me please have my letter back, and I will give you an answer. I think I said you had not made distinct enough that you were maintaining the reasonableness of 'The wish to believe', as in *two* ways an element in the search after, and the attainment of the Truth in ethical subjects[1]

Yours affectly John H. Card Newman

P.S. Your Father was never a High-churchman, never a Tractarian, never a Puseyite, never a Newmanite. What his line was is described in Apologia pp 163, etc

TO ANNE MOZLEY

March 18. 1885

My dear Anne Mozley

Fr William Neville returned highly pleased with your reception of him, and feeling that he had done me a service. For all this I warmly thank you.

But I think you hardly had read, perhaps not received, the letter you ought to have received yesterday morning which I sent you the day before viz. Monday the 16th. I say so because it was on a subject which (by Neville's silence about it in his report to me of his mission on his return last night) seems to have escaped you

I am appalled at your acquiescence as in a necessity, at the idea of a large circle knowing what you are undertaking in my behalf. I am not disputing it, but dismayed at it. It will soon lead to a paragraph in the Athenæum 'We understand the talented lady who has been successful in placing before the public the letters of Dr Mozley, is engaged in the same interesting work as regards the papers of Card. Newman.' This will be improved on by the 'Society' Papers.

But though I accept this as a necessity, if it is so, I cannot see that *my* letters to my Mother, my Sisters and others were ever the property of your Mother (Mrs Mozley) — nor do I think it good law, because my Executors and Heirs could hinder the holders of these letters publishing them, therefore *I* could be hindered by your nephews from publishing my own copies of my own.

But there is a more serious anxiety which comes upon me. If Fanny is to be consulted what to put in and what not, you will find yourself enlarging the number of those whom I contemplated as being allowed what I call 'elbow room.' Over and above that *discretion* which an Editor *must* have, I have considered that an Editor ought to have full command of, and above his facts, and, as the condition of his using them properly, must know more than

---

[1] See letters of 4 and 20 Dec. 1884 to W. Ward. There was not a second edition of his *The Wish to Believe*. See letter of 5 April 1886 to him.

legitimately belongs to him. Thus A which you have at my wish returned, was an instance of circumstantial extraordinary knowledge which would guide you in your use of letters etc which on the other hand, unlike A., did fall within the legitimate range of your subject matter[1]

But I could not consent to this 'elbow room' being shared by any one but yourself. And I am so sensitive on the point, that I must conclude this letter by earnestly asking you a special favour. It is to take Number 2[2] (consisting of *two* parts in roan covers and a larger cover including both) *and do it up and seal it, and keep it safe*, since I should like to see it once more *before* you use it.[3]

Yours affectly John H Card. Newman

(my hand is so weak I use an Amanuensis.)[4]

TO ANNE MOZLEY

March 20. 1885

My dear Anne Mozley

I am sorry to have given you the trouble of writing so long a letter[5]

I am still more sorry to have led you to enter into details in a way which is close upon a surrender of your own independence of judgment and action, which independence is one of the conditions of your undertaking as dear to me and as necessary as your right to consult Dean Church can be to you. Your work, I feel, would be worth nothing if it could be suspected of being under my supervision.

I think it best then to give you full elbow room to omit or to insert any part of what I have sent you, in (if you please) my very words, or again to show it to Dean Church; but I certainly should like to see Number 2 before I give you this full elbow room, as I am not sure that some things, as they stand in

---

[1] 'A' was the first of the passages concerning the Oriel tutorship, excised from the Memoir. See letter of 19 Feb. to Anne Mozley.

[2] See letter of 13 March to Anne Mozley, who wrote on 18 March: 'What I have been reading this morning in Number 2 prompts me to beg from you another form of assistance – the aid of your prayers that I may do the work as wisely faithfully and truly make it as good as it is within my limited powers to make it.'

[3] Anne Mozley also wrote on 18 March, her letter crossed Newman's, that it was impossible not to tell her sister Maria, who regarded it as a secret, what she was doing. Anne continued: 'Then as to Dean Church. I take rather a stronger ground of self defence. You will remember that I said I must make the liberty of consulting him a *condition* and of his conferring with Lord B [Blachford] You did not write for several days and my task weighed on my mind so I wrote — and he promised his counsel, and *asked* if he might tell Lord Blachford, which I agreed to. I have not heard since' See last note to letter of 26 Jan. to Anne Mozley.

[4] Only the conclusion and postscript are in Newman's hand.

[5] Anne Mozley wrote on 19 March that she had been obliged to take her sister Maria into her confidence, but that this confiding would be limited to four people, her other sister Fanny, Dean Church and Lord Blachford. She had spoken to Neville about having to tell her nephews and nieces, but it would be long before this need be done. 'I feel the necessity for secrecy and the wish for it as strongly as you can do'.

Anne Mozley then commented at length on the documents which Newman had sent, and the use to be made of them.

Number 2, may not be misunderstood. I wish them then sealed up till I have seen them.

I dare say I have not been consistent always in what I have said in the way of condition, but in so personal a matter I have been perplexed. Of course I feel it would be cruel, or rather impossible, to leave Maria out, but recollect you spoke only of Fanny.

Don't you pass through Birmingham to get to Bourn mouth — but London is perhaps the better intermediate. If you happened to do so, Fr Neville would be at the Station to take the Number 2 from you, if it is not too large for a lady's hand bag

Yours affly John H Card. Newman

TO CHARLES RYDER

March 20. 1885

My dear Charles

I want to pay the £30, which I promised towards your Church. To whom am I to address the cheque? to you or to Trustees?[1]

Yours affectly John H Card. Newman

TO WILFRID WARD

March 21 1885

Dear Wilfrid Ward

I return my letter of Decr 26/84.
You make what use you like of it[2]

Yrs affly J H Card. Newman

TO ANNE MOZLEY

March 22. 85

Dear Anne Mozley

I don't like to let the 'Number 2' go by the Post, even though it is registered.[3]

I am not sure I understand your letter, but, if you propose to break your journey at Birmingham I shall propose to you to let me secure you a room at the Plough and Harrow for the 30th or 31st. It is quite a place to recommend.

---

[1] See letter of 4 March to Ryder.
[2] See letter of 16 March to W. Ward.
[3] Anne Mozley wrote on 21 March, 'I do not know how to express my feelings on the trust you place in my judgment'.
She proposed to send Newman's Number 2 by registered post, since it would be ten days before she passed through Birmingham. When doing so, she would either have to break her journey there, or take a train which only stopped at Saltley, the other side of the town to Edgbaston.

My cousins, the Deanes, struck up quite a friendship with the Landlady last September. In this case, you would bring Number 2 with you.

If you *don't* break your journey at Birmingham, it will be easy to find some other plan, if you will let me know what you decide on as sooner as you can. E.g. Fr Neville could *easily* meet you at *Saltley*.

One caution I am led to give: — recollect what happened to poor Pusey When he left for Genoa, it is said that his housemaid burnt his precious MS notes on the Psalms to light the fire with. I suppose he did not lock them up and hide the key.

Yours affecty John H Card. Newman

TO CHARLES RYDER

Mar. 23. 85

My dear Charles

I enclose a cheque for my subscription to your Church

Yrs affectly John H Card Newman

TO BISHOP ULLATHORNE

March 23 1885

My dear Lord

I thank you for a sight of your Lordship's Report of the state of the Diocese, which I now return.

I do not wonder at the Cardinal Prefect being struck with a document so exhaustive and so interesting. It is a lasting Memorial of a great Episcopate[1]

Your Lordship's affecte Servt John H Card. Newman

TO ANNE MOZLEY

March 24. 1885

My dear Anne Mozley

I ought to have thought of the mental disturbance which a journey would give you, since I feel it so intensely myself.[2] So, as soon as I read your letter of last night, I felt I must take one of two courses, either ask you to keep Number 2 locked up with the rest, or to ask Fr Neville to run over to you at once and to receive Number 2 from you. Before I could ask him, he out of his head

---

[1] This was evidently the 'Relatio Status Diocesis Birmingamiensis 1884', sent to Cardinal Simeoni, Prefect of Propaganda, in the Archives, *S.R.C. 1883–4*, f 988 seq.

[2] Anne Mozley wrote on 23 March, 'You cannot feel more anxious for the safe delivery of the two books which together constitute Number *2* than I am or more alive to their value. It is a wonder to me as I read them to find myself allowed to do so.' She went on to speak of the risk of 'any bewilderment in travelling.' See letter of 30 March to her.

proposed it, but we both felt that his going to you must depend on your convenience

I know I distress [distrust] the post, irrationally, but a few facts are sufficient for the imagination, and, years indeed ago, a cheque was lost of £70 — and I hear complaints here lately of the receiving box being so full that a small hand could reach the last letters put into it. I had confidence in registration while it cost 4d — but twopence affects my imagination

So much I write before breakfast. I shall speak more decidedly when evening comes — for all is under your approval, whether you would let me place Number 2 in your charge, or whether you would allow Fr Neville to intrude upon you.

P M. 1 o'clock. Since I wrote the above, I find Fr Neville in bed with a bad cold. This settles two points – neither can he go to Barrow nor to Santley [Saltley] – i.e. he cannot be sure to go. Therefore I must ask you to *keep* Number 2, and to lock it up safely with the others in your closet

> Yours affectly John H Card Newman

Fr Neville hopes to write about your Train Paper tomorrow

TO JOHN WAUGH[1]

Birmingham, March 24. 1885.

Cardinal Newman wishes his fingers allowed him to write a longer letter than this. The statement is simply untrue that he ever for a moment has wished to return to the English Church. The Catholic Roman Church is the only oracle of Truth and Ark of Salvation, no other Communion has the promises, no other has the Grace of the Redeemer. St Paul did not tell Jews to remain Jews because they had [been] reared members of the Jewish Church; nor is it any reason why Protestant should remain Protestants because they were born Protestants.

May God enlighten you and guide you, and bring you into the full truth of the Gospel.

TO MRS WILLIAM BORLASE

March 30. 1885

Dear Mrs Borlase

Your sad letter could not take me by surprise.[2] Ever since the commencement of his illness he has day by day been in my mind When he is well enough

---

[1] Neville has written at the bottom of his copy of this extract:
'N.B. The owner of this cutting from a catalogue has written at the bottom of the printed extract thus:—
The original was sent to me in 1894, by John Waugh, C.E. my father's brother. N.W.'
[2] Mrs Borlase wrote about the illness of her uncle, W. J. Copeland, who died on 26 Aug. 1885.

to receive it, pray, give him the most affectionate message you can from me. He has been a true faithful friend to me and I feel great gratitude to him

I feel the kindness of your letter to us, and hope you will excuse my bad penmanship which is owing to my stiff fingers

Most truly Yours John H Card. Newman

TO ANNE MOZLEY

March 30, 1885

My dear Anne Mozley

I write you a hasty line to thank you for the trouble you are taking and to say that Fr Neville means on Wednesday to get to Saltley Station in such good time before 11.27, as to get a porter to help him to find you out in the Train. I hope it won't make you nervous[1]

Yrs affly J H Card. Newman

TO THE DUKE OF NORFOLK

April 6. 1885

My dear Duke

I wish all Easter blessings and graces on you and the Duchess and your little child.

This requires no answer, and I should not have written to tell you, what I trust you knew full well already without my telling, for you and yours are ever in my thoughts and I said Mass for the Duchess and your boy only this morning — but I have something to tell you which you will be glad to know.

We have made great reforms in our Domus arrangements under a new Father Minister, the younger Father Bellasis — and there is a proverb about new brooms. We have changed our servants and some of our tradesmen, with considerable success. The upshot is, that, having had our annual audit about a week ago, we find to our great satisfaction that the balance of our account is in our favour, not indeed a great sum, being six shillings, but every thing to us as being on the right side

So St Philip has been very good to us

Your Grace's affectionate Servt John H Card. Newman

The Duke of Norfolk E M

---

[1] Miss Mozley wrote on 26 March that she would hand over Newman's books, Number 2, on 1 April.

TO AN UNKNOWN CORRESPONDENT

April 6 1885

Dear Sir

As my hand is very weak, I hope you will excuse me if I leave your letter unanswered, except by the inclosed.[1]

I am, Dear Sir, Yours faithfully John H Newman

TO ANNE MOZLEY

April 7. 1885

Dear Anne Mozley

It is very good of you to write to me as soon as you got to your destination. You should have told me how you found Maria.

I return the paper, and letter – and hope I have pencilled my additions, not clearly I fear but, clearly enough.[2]

Yours affecly John H. Card. Newman

P.S.　All kind Easter greetings to you and Maria *Of course* Mr Wagner has applied to Dr F. G. Lee of Lambeth.

TO MARY MURPHY

April 7. 1885

Dear Mrs Murphy

Your letter and its contents took away my breath. I was deeply moved to find that a book of mine had been in General Gordon's hands, and that, the description of a soul preparing for death.[3]

---

[1] These four words and the date are added, and the word 'very' substituted for 'rather', in the lithograph.

[2] Anne Mozley wrote on 4 April after her arrival at Falmouth, enclosing an inquiry of Mr Wagner, concerning Newman's family.

[3] Mary Murphy wrote on 6 April from 10 Upper Mount Street, Dublin: 'Seeing that you are a large subscriber to the "Memorial Fund" for General Gordon, it strikes me, that you would be pleased to see the enclosed little book　It was given to my brother the late Mr Frank Power by General Gordon soon after his arrival in Khartoum. As you will see by the front page the pencil marking through the book is done by General Gordon himself　I need not say how highly I prize it, for many reasons so I will feel obliged if you will return it to me at your earliest convenience.' This was a copy of the small edition of *The Dream of Gerontius*. Power was *The Times* correspondent at Khartoum, which General Gordon reached on 18 Feb. 1884. On the same day he gave this marked copy to Power, who sent it to his sister. Gordon received the copy in Egypt and must have read it on his way to the Sudan. See end of letter of 19 May 1885 to Lord Blachford. His friend E. A. Maund wrote on 30 Jan. 1888 to Miss Gordon: 'It may interest you to know how it was that General Gordon had this little Roman Catholic poem with him in Khartoum.

The day he left, your brother related to me how his spiritual life was changed by what he experienced at his father's death-bed, as, gazing on his lifeless form, he thought: 'Is this what

I send it back to you, with my heartfelt thanks, by this post in a registered cover. It is additionally precious, as having Mr Power's writing in it[1]

Most truly Yours John H. Card. Newman[2]

TO R. J. CUERVO

Birmingham April 8. 1885

Sir

I fear from some mistake an answer was not sent to your obliging letter of some weeks since.

I beg now to acknowledge with many thanks the first livraison of M. Cuervo's Diccionario de la Lengua Castellana, begging of you the kind office of conveying my thanks to him.[3]

And I must ask you to excuse my bad handwriting, which must be considered the infirmity of old age.

I am, Sir Your faithful Servant

John H Card. Newman

TO WILFRID OATES

April 10. 1885

Dear Mr Oates

I can't say the look of your Volume, which I return pleases me. The marbled sides are dingy and wanting in neat workmanship.[4]

we all come to?" This led to a long discussion of death, when I remarked that some of his ideas reminded me of Dr. Newman's little Book, *The Dream of Gerontius*. Whereupon he said he should like to read it; and I promised to send it after him to Egypt. Your brother in a post-card, dated from Khartoum, 7 March, 1884, acknowledging the book says:

"My Dear Mr. Maund, — Your letter 25 January arrived today . . . , Thanks for the little book. . . .'" *General Gordon's Letters to his Sister*, London 1888, pp. 402–3.

[1] Gordon wrote in the fly leaf: 'Frank Power with kindest regards of C G Gordon 18 Feby 84.' Power wrote below this:
'Dearest M
I send you this little book which General Gordon has given me. The pencil marking thro' the book is his
Frank Power   Khartoum'.
On 10 Sept. 1884 Power steamed down the Nile to try to hasten the relieving force. His ship struck a rock and on 18 Sept. he was murdered.
See also William E. A. Axon, 'On General Gordon's Copy of Newman's "Dream of Gerontius",', the *Manchester Quarterly* (Jan. 1889), reprinted separately and also in *Longman's Magazine* (Oct. 1890), pp. 632–9.
[2] Neville made several transcriptions of Gordon's markings into copies of the Dream. The first was sent to Dean Church, who wrote to Newman on 10 April: 'You are indeed kind in letting me have a copy of the book with the pencil notes and marks. . . . All our party are alive to the interest of the book — one result was that they all went to get copies of the small edition . . .'
[3] Newman was sent the first 160 pages of R. J. Cuervo's *Diccionario de Construccion y Regimen de la Lengua Castellana*, Paris 1884.
[4] On 9 April Oates sent as a specimen a book that had been bound in half calf with paper sides. Newman had ordered two sets of his own works.

I certainly must have cloth sides, the backs being calf. And I understand you to say that the binding with these materials will cost 3/6 per volume, that is, six guineas for the 36 volumes.

I think it best, if I am right in this, to order at present only one, not two sets.

Also I wish the copy of Grammar of Assent to be one of those copies which run to 503 pages – the copy of Via Media volume 2 which runs to 433 pages, and of Theological Tracts which at p 299 has a note in small type

Very truly yours J. H. Card Newman

P.S. Perhaps I had better trouble you to send me a specimen of the calf and cloth you propose for the set.

TO R. W. CHURCH

April 12. 1885

My dear Dean

Thank you for your impressive Easter Sermon.[1]
It is 63 years today since I was elected at Oriel; the turning point of my life.

Yrs affly J. H. Card. Newman

TO AN UNKNOWN CORRESPONDENT

April 12. 1885

My dear Child

I mean, please God, to say a Mass every week for you for some time.

Yours affly John H Card. Newman

TO EDMUND STONOR

April 13. 1885

My dear Monsignor Stonor

I am sorry to be late in my offering, and thank you for your usual kindness in taking charge of it. Inclosed is a cheque for £20 Make my compliments to the good Preposto[2]

Yours most truly with best Easter greetings

J. H. Card. Newman

[1] 'The Resurrection from the Dead', preached on Easter Sunday 1885, and included in Church's *Cathedral and University Sermons*, London 1892, pp. 131–43.
[2] Provost of Newman's titular church, San Giorgio in Velabro.

April 16. [1885]

Cardinal Newman has to acknowledge the favour of the letter and article sent him by the Editor of the *Pall Mall Gazette*, and begs in reply to say that while he agrees with the Editor's statement of general principles, as contained in the article to which the Editor calls his attention, his knowledge of facts is commonly not such as to warrant his pronouncing a definitive judgment in its application to particular cases.[1]

TO THOMAS LIVIUS

April 21. 1885

Dear Father Livius

As you so kindly sent me your valuable Pamphlet on an interesting subject,[2] I think you will let me trouble you, at your leisure with the following question.

Can you refer me to any theological work, which treats of the 'justa causa' which is the condition of various exceptions to ecclesiastical rules? The absence of some explanations give rise to scruples or to license.

In illustration of what I mean, I will observe for instance

1. It is not without 'levis culpa' that the matins and lauds of the day are deferred till after Mass, *unless* there is a 'justa causa'.

But is it a justa causa, when a parochus in a large and populous cure, saying Mass at 7, finds, that from 8 to 11 a.m. are the only hours of the day which he can depend upon as vacant for saying office.[3]

2. Again — It is not without 'levis culpa' that a priest omits saying Mass *quotidie* unless he has 'justa causa'.

Now a priest of weak health was out on his holiday. He was not sure a holiday would do him good. It was a mere experiment. He said Mass at his place of recreation on Sundays and festivals — not on week days, because the Church was two miles off, and the walk and the Mass fatigued him. Was

---

[1] On 30 March the Russians defeated an Afghan force and the threat to India brought Great Britain and Russia to the verge of war, averted largely owing to the combined firmness and conciliation of Gladstone's government. The *Pall Mall Gazette* in a leading article on 15 April 'Why is the Pulpit silent?' complained that preachers, especially those of the Established Church were not warning against misjudging issues which involved war or peace. Copies of the article were sent to church dignitaries and their comments requested. Newman's letter appeared at the end of a further article in the *Pall Mall Gazette* on 18 April.
cf. letter of 23 April to Lord Blachford.
[2] See letter of 11 March to Livius.
[3] Livius replied on 25 April that he knew of no author who dealt with the general question ex professo, but after quoting at length about this particular case gave his opinion that it was lawful, one of the 'just causes' being 'periculum supervenientis occupationis'.

this a justa causa for his omission, or did he commit a venial sin, toties quoties?[1]

I beg to condole with the members of your body at the loss of so holy a man as Bishop Coffin.[2] And if Father Cyril Ryder is at home, I beg you to remember me kindly to him.

And pardon the bad penmanship of an old man

Most truly Yours John H. Card. Newman

TO LORD BLACHFORD

April 23. 1885

My dear Blachford

You will not be surprised at a confirmation of your letter for me in Re Malmesbury.

Our Father Ryder is told by his uncle 'Tom' that his brother-in-law, the late Sir George Grey, shortly before his death told him he was a witness or a party to the table-jerking of which poor James was the victim.[3]

What do you think of Foreign Affairs? My first years were passed in our then greatest war, and my last seem likely to see as great a one. Who will be 'our Pilot to weather the storm' that is upon us? Can Gladstone, even when all is known, come out with credit? Also G. when, about 1873, he said he was going to give his last years to personal duties, how wise and good he seemed! and how his good Angel must have sighed, when soon after he took the lead of the Radicals![4]

Are not the Afghans an [sic] indispensable to us in a war with Russia, and who can trust them? and what vulnerable point has Russia, while we have a hundred?

And that Gladstone, whose own boast was that he would not move without all Europe, should have turned all Europe against us![5] But what are your politics?

I write with great difficulty

Yours affectly John H Card. Newman

[1] Livius replied that there would be no sin, the priest's 'just causes' being his actual distance from the church and his weak health. See letter of 30 April.

[2] R. A. Coffin, who had become a Redemptorist and in 1882 Bishop of Southwark, died on 6 April. The words 'holy a man' have been almost obliterated by a large blot, but can be restored from Newman's draft.

[3] See letter of 8 Oct. 1884 to Lord Blachford and note there, also Piers Brendon, *Hurrell Froude and the Oxford Movement*, London 1974, p. 79. Lord Malmesbury had attributed to Newman incidents that concerned another Fellow of Oriel, William James.
Ignatius Ryder's aunt Anna Sophia married Sir George Grey of Falloden, the liberal statesman, who was at Oriel College from 1817 to 1821, when he took a first in Classics.

[4] See letter of 8 Feb. 1885 to Lady Simeon, and a fragment of an 1885 letter to R. W. Church, in *Ward* II, p. 513: 'What a dreadful thing this democracy is! How I wish Gladstone had retired into private life, as he seems to have contemplated some 10 years ago'.

[5] See letter of 16 April to the editor of the *Pall Mall Gazette*. Great Britain was at this time alienated not only from Russia and the Central Powers but also from France.

TO THOMAS EDWARD BRIDGETT

April 27. 1885

Dear Fr Bridgett

I thank you for your letter and Sermon.[1] They brought to my mind days long past. I thought it was at Easter 1836, not 1837, that your late Superior and Bishop came up to Oxford; but you must have better authority than my memory.[2] He was at that time a very attractive youth, from the expression, even more than the features, of his face. His expression was very sweet and modest, and these characteristics were combined with a playfulness and an evident sense of humour when he conversed, which, among the many dear friends I had at Oxford, was all his own.

On December 2. 1845, when (if I remember rightly) he was rather wavering, I took him down to Prior Park, where various converts had been, and there he was received on St Francis Xavier's day by Dr Brindle.[3]

I am touched by his liking for 'Loss and Gain.'[4] Some three years ago I heard of his interest in some of my volumes, so I sent him the revised edition of 'Athanasius' which had just been published.

It is difficult to condole with you — for a soul so ripe for heaven can do for us more when he is away than he could by his presence here

Yours faithful Servant John H. Card. Newman.

TO ANNE MOZLEY

April 28. 85

My dear Anne Mozley

Fr Neville is much obliged by your offer which will suit himself except the days. He must wait till you *next* go to Derby, unless that day will be far off, if you will notify him.[5]

[1] On 25 April Bridgett sent his *A Sermon preached at St Mary's, Clapham, at the Requiem Mass, celebrated on April 16th, 1885, the Octave Day of the Funeral of The Right Rev. Robert Aston Coffin, C.S S.R. Bishop of Southwark.*

[2] Bridgett, who was correct, said at the beginning of his sermon: 'The Bishop used always to speak of it as one of God's merciful providences to him, that when he went up to Oxford at the age of eighteen in the year 1837, he was admitted not merely to the acquaintance, but in spite of the disparity of their age, to the friendship of Mr Newman . . . It was from his books, his sermons and conversations, that the young Mr Coffin first learned to know something of Catholic doctrine and discipline . . . It was by Mr Newman's advice and under his guidance that he entered the ministry of the Anglican Church.' Bridgett went on to speak of the part Newman played in Coffin's becoming a Catholic, but did not mention that he had also become an Oratorian.

In his letter Bridgett wrote: 'The late bishop of Southwark talked to me so often of his old Oxford days, and we used to read together your Eminences works with such admiration and gratitude . . .'

[3] See diary for 2 and 3 Dec. 1845, and letter of 10 Dec. 1845 to Dalgairns.

[4] 'Two or three years after his conversion, Mr Newman wrote a tale . . . to which he gave the significant title "Loss and Gain." Father Coffin, to the end of his life, (or at least till his episcopate, for of that time I cannot speak) used to read that tale almost every year, and each time with greater thankfulness for the Gain, which made the loss seem always more insignificant.' Bridgett's *Sermon*, p. 7.

[5] See the postscript.

In that Note,[1] I meant to say it surprised me to find how many points I had hit upon *without* Coleridge (and Kant) which I thought had been my own — I did not mean with Lilly to say that I drank in from the atmosphere Kantism. (vid my University Sermons p 23)[2]

I expect Liddon will say something on the subject in Pusey's Life[3]

Yours affly John H Card Newman

P.S. I don't see you can learn from *me all* the books you want. This would be like my *packing* the Jury. You alone can *determine* what you *want*, tho' I alone can offer you what you don't know about

I feel Hutton's Article in the Contemporary, tho' highly coloured, and Principal Fairbairns in last February's Contemporary, are more exact than Lilly[4]

Fr Neville is writing to you. He means to take advantage of your offer, provided you go to Derby on *Thursday*.[5]

TO ANNE MOZLEY

April 29. 1885

My dear Anne M.

Excuse an abrupt letter.

Of course you may make a rule that you will limit your books and memorative documents to those which you can have all at once, from first to last — but you ought to be sure this will work well. E.g. there are my letters to Keble up to 1845 which you might have a wish to read, but which I should not like to part with for an unlimited time. There is the 'No. 2 in two parts' which I now send back to you by Fr Neville, which I should like to have before I die, say before a definite day.[6] Then there are my letters to Bowden and to H Wilberforce, and so on

---

[1] Anne Mozley wrote on 27 April that she had been reading W. S. Lilly's *Ancient Religion and Modern Thought*. 'He goes into Kant and Coleridge'. She then quoted from *Chronological Notes*, 'March. 27. 1835. "During this spring I for the *first time* read parts of Coleridge . . ."' *Moz.* II, p. 39.
The note to which Newman refers is that in letter of 14 Jan. 1885 to Anne Mozley. See third note there, and for the references to Lilly, letter of 17 Aug. 1884 to him.

[2] There a footnote says: 'The author was not acquainted, at the time this was written, with Mr Coleridge's Works, and a remarkable passage in his Biographia Literaria, in which several portions of this Sermon are anticipated . . .'

[3] Liddon's *Pusey*, I, p. 254.

[4] For R. H. Hutton's article 'Cardinal Newman', the *Contemporary Review* (May 1884), pp. 642–65, see letter of 6 May 1884 to him. Principal Fairbairn's 'Catholicism and Apologetics', the *Contemporary Review* (Feb. 1884), pp. 164–184, reprinted in *Catholicism: Roman and Anglican* London 1899, pp. 48–93, dealt with Newman's history in the concluding pages. He remarked on how English he remained: 'Cardinal Newman does not build on Thomas Aquinas or Bellarmine or Bossuet; they only supply the buttresses and pillars, the arches and gargoyles of his faith: his fundamental principles are those of Butler . . .' Fairbairn also spoke of the influence of Coleridge, who 'had made the speculative reason and the creative imagination become as sisters ministrant to faith'. pp. 177 and 179. In the reprint pp. 79 and 83.

[5] Neville handed over to Miss Mozley a parcel of books and papers on this day, 30 April.

[6] See end of letter of 18 March to Anne Mozley.

You may say, if you will and perhaps justly — 'I want to hinder this vast accumulation of documents — and therefore to send me all the correspondence you *could* send, is just to do what I don't want to do —' but I think you must make up *beforehand* what you aim at doing, prior to your deciding what books and documents you want. E.g. I am sending you by Fr N. letters bearing on the Hampden controversy — but you may tell him to take them back because you are not intending to touch on that controversy. Yet, it may be, though you don't so intend, you need a sight of these letters in order for them to act as giving you elbow room etc etc

My brain and my fingers conspire to blunt my power of explanation

Yrs affly J H Card Newman

TO THOMAS LIVIUS

April 30. 1885

Dear Father Livius

You have taken great trouble for me, and the best return I can make to you is to say that you have done me a very good service and that I am very grateful to you for it.[1]

As my fingers write so slowly and that slowness puts out my brain, I will not attempt to use many words, or much logic, but I will say that your general account of a justa causa, seems to me very good, that is, both simple and probable in itself and practically satisfying to the conscience. I think you refer to Scavini — my edition is not yours, but I think I have found your passage.[2]

Your answers to my questions are what I gave myself, but I had reasons for wishing a confirmation of my judgment, which I need not go into.

I wish I could in turn throw light upon your own question.[3] I am surprised that Eusebius's words are not enough for modern critics, Λῖνος πρῶτος μετὰ Πέτρον etc. Hist iii, 4.[4] Does he ever say that John was *Bishop* of Ephesus? — or, which is more to the purpose, that Paul was Bishop of Rome?

[1] See letter of 21 April to Livius and notes there.

[2] Livius replied on 25 April that he found no principle laid down by authors with regard to the 'justa causa', but formulated one as follows: 'Sicut ordinarie loquendo leges humanae, tum ecclesiasticae tum civiles — immo leges ipsae divinae purè positivae — sub gravi obligantes, cum gravi incommodo desinunt obligare — ; ita simili ratione, leges humanae, levis tantum obligationis, levi cum incommodo—seu aliis verbis ob causam proportionatè justam — obligare desinunt — Talis enim causa proportionate justa a transgressione legis excusare censetur — Conf. Scavini. De legibus M. Th. tom. i. n. 199.' Newman's edition of Petrus Scavini, *Theologia Moralis Universa*, was the second, Brussels 1847.

[3] Livius asked about the Roman episcopate of St Peter. His mother, who had been an intimate friend of F. W. Newman's first wife, tried to bring him back to a belief in the Christian truths. She was obliged to turn for help to a relative, Harold Browne, Bishop of Winchester, whose curate Livius had been for five years. The Bishop at the same time entered upon the controversy with Rome, maintaining that although St Peter as an apostle helped to found the church in Rome and was martyred there, it was clear from history that he was never *Bishop* of Rome.

[4] πρῶτος μετὰ Πέτρον τῆς 'Ρωμαίων ἐκκλησίας τὴν ἐπισκοπὴν ... κληρωθεὶς '[Linus] was Peter's first successor in the episcopate of the Church at Rome'.

As the office of Apostle eclipsed that of Bishop, is it wonderful that, while Eusebius distinctly says that *Peter* was succeeded in the Episcopate by Linus, he should *also* say 'After Peter *and Paul* comes Linus'. It is the same as saying 'after the Martyrdom of Peter and Paul came Linus,'[1] it is the notice of a date, as well as of a change of rulers.

In truth, however, for myself I have never rested the duty of being a Catholic on the Papal Supremacy — but ever (as I think,) upon the fact of the Catholic Church itself. This must be my apology for having so little to say in answer to your question — The existing Catholic Roman Church is the True Church, because it is the only representative and successor of the Apostolic Church, historically and in fact because it alone has the Four Notes; *because the only one* which has the bearing of a Prophet, the only organized, consistent outspoken etc

Most truly Yours J. H. Card. Newman

P.S.   I cannot accept Fr Addis's statements which I return.[2]

TO ANNE MOZLEY

May 3. 1885

Dear Anne Mozley

I have such abundant correspondence, that both Fr William and I, though we *quite* concur in the anticipation that you must at least look at the outside of it before you get to the end of your self denying work, both doubt whether you would not be losing time and trouble, by attempting a survey of it yet.

For instance have you settled whether to bind yourself to the Tractarian controversy, including such episodes as the Hampden? I should think you have settled *not*? Nor to the Number 90? No — you will not introduce either, except perhaps in their ethical aspect.

As to the Hampden, I am thinking that Liddon, in his Memoir of Pusey, will clear the ground for you tho' leaving you free to have your own judgments upon it in its details.

Again, Liddon may bring out Pusey's judgments of Number 90 — and I conceive you might do well, not to touch upon that matter. Keble saw Number 90 before publication — but not Pusey.

But here I am illustrating against my will, the very difficulty and danger I feel in seeing you just now. If you don't treat me as one dead, you cannot do your work. I withdraw all supposed unwillingness, on my part, which I have

---

[1] Eusebius, *Ecclesiastical History*, III, 2.
[2] Livius had consulted on St Peter's Roman episcopate William Addis, who maintained that the testimony for it was insufficient.
See letter of 7 May to Livius.

never felt or meant you to suppose, of your consulting Dean Church,[1] but I am much afraid of your spoiling your work, by letting it be fancied that I have had any thing to do with it.

Will it not be enough for me to say, 'Archdeacon Froude put into Keble's and my hands all Hurrell's Papers and Letters. I wish to be treated as we treated him. And, as our Memoir of him was after his death, so let the publication of mine be.'

Ever Yours affectly John H Card. Newman.

P.S. If you have reasons for coming now, which you feel to be sufficient to overcome my dissuasions, come by all means.[2]

TO JOHN HUNGERFORD POLLEN

May 6 1885

My dear Pollen

Your letter of this morning is most welcome, and I thank you for it. I thought it a very plucky thing your going all that way by yourself and I rejoice that you are back safe and sound.[3] Though no traveller myself, I can sympathise in what you tell me, I have gone through the Gibraltar galleries — and brought away from them at least one piece of knowledge, which, after all the change in the science of warfare, seems, (from the account of poor Colonel Stewart's bet [boat] on running over the rock on the Nile still to hold good,) that there are two ways of disabling a gun, spiking it, and knocking off the end of the trunnion.[4] Also I recollect a window in the galleries, from which you look down 800 feet sharp descent.

Well and I sympathise with you in the strange feeling of coming on deck of a morning and seeing before you Cadiz, Algiers, Palermo or Ithaca, like the

[1] See letters of 16 and 18 March to Anne Mozley.

[2] Anne Mozley replied on 4 May, 'I . . . *thoroughly* concur in your decision', and decided not to visit Newman.

[3] In Oct. 1884 Pollen went out to India where his son Walter was aide de camp to the Marquis of Ripon. Pollen returned with the Viceroy on his retirement at the end of the year, and they reached England in Jan. On 5 May he wrote to Newman: 'I have been to India as you know. I reached it over thousands of miles of sea and saw Gibraltar on the road . . . I went through the famous galleries, and worthily famous too. I thought also how magical it is to come upon a new place by *sea*! It seems to appear before you without any preliminary changes of soil or trees or languages. As for India, I started on a 1700 miles railway journey the evening I arrived in Bombay. . . . In the moonlight I saw cocoanut palms etc. — Yes. IT IS INDIA! Then by day I had huge apes on the side of the line, beautiful antelopes — resting in the long grass — green parrots flitting about — little striped squirrels innumerable nimbly running up and down over and under everything, brown faces white tunics and togas as of antique Romans, in short India. One of my first thoughts was what would your Eminence think of all this if you saw it? (You must know I had a certain Grammar of assent which I read and reread when disposed for serious reflection.)' After further descriptions Pollen ended, 'Well the book I took with me I also brought back Libri comitas fidelissima. I had the author always near me.'

[4] Colonel Stewart left Khartoum with Frank Power in Sept. 1884 with a view to hastening the force that was to relieve General Gordon. Their steamer struck a rock in the Nile, and Colonel Stewart spiked the steamer's gun before throwing it into the river. *The Times* 5 Feb. 1885), p. 5. He and his party tried to proceed by land but were killed.

rounds in a Magic Lantern though the middies and the crew take it as a matter of course.

One thing I confess lies outside my sympathy, though I confess it *touches* me much, and all the more, viz your having recourse to 'the Grammar of Assent' as a refuge from the palm trees and apes. My imagination will not take it in, except as a pendant to that great Ch Ch Greek scholar who to relieve himself of the excitement of the subjective [sic] mood, used to take up a volume of the Tracts of the Times. I think he told me so himself.[1]

Your sketchy account of India made me understand why the Russians should covet it.

I have heard nothing quite lately of your home anxieties, which are so great. I hope your wife bears them well.[2]

When you see Lord Ripon, please to tell him how I rejoice at his triumphant return.[3] I have not written my congratulations because I feel myself Passe and thereby privileged. Indeed I am really old now. I write slowly and with effort and pain, and have various small ailments which I am unable to throw off, and I am writing this as I lie upon a sofa.

Ever yours affectly John H Card. Newman

TO THOMAS LIVIUS

May 7. 1885

Dear Fr Livius

I am sorry to hear that accidental circumstances hinder your proceeding with the interesting subject you began. Any how the affirmative view must be a probable one.[4]

---

[1] William Linwood. See letters of 1 and 5 Oct. 1886 to Lord Blachford.

[2] Mrs Pollen went out to Egypt to nurse her son Francis. See third note to letter of 16 Jan. 1885 to Lord Blachford.

[3] In June Pollen sent Newman a copy of his privately printed *An Indian Farewell to the Marquis of Ripon*, describing the enthusiasm the Indians showed for him. It ended as follows:
'The Government of India had, for years passed, been bound by specific promises to admit native Indians to offices of trust and power in the civil service, and those promises had been discussed and renewed both in Parliament and in Council. Lord Ripon pushed them to their fulfilment. Then the very opposition and obloquy so unmerited, and in great measure "got up" by sections of the press, did but bring after it a counter current of popularity, as unreasonable opposition will. The Viceroy and the natives had a common cause, and were forced into it by the clamour of political opponents. To this we must add certain personal considerations. Simplicity of aim, an entire absence of irritation of temper under a trial, painful even when one is perfectly satisfied of its injustice; kindness of disposition, and modest but incessant devotion to the duties of his office.

Though no man in India made so little parade of his religion, he was known to be sincerely attached to it. If any Christianity can command the respect of Indians it is that form of it which recognizes counsels of perfection, and encourages renunciation of the world, and the cloistered life. Hindoos and Mahomedans, widely as their religions differ from that which he professes, are loyal to their own traditions, and are, above all, worshippers. The religious prejudices which threw an element of bitterness into the strife raised against Lord Ripon would help to turn attention on the part of native Indians to these considerations, and cast weight into the scale of opinion in his favour.'

[4] Livius wrote on the letter: 'The subject alluded to as interrupted — was the question of the validity of the Sacrament of Penance — as ministered through the Telephone — I had been

61

I hope you will not forget the subject of Mr Addis's letter. What is the reason he is not satisfied with the prima facie evidence of the case?[1]

Most truly Yours John H Card. Newman

TO THOMAS LIVIUS

May 12. 1885

Dear Fr Livius

I put your letter and its two inclosures into Fr Ryder's hands, as soon as I got them. He did not decide at once, and indeed, though he does not agree with Fr Flanagan's conclusion, nor with his grounds for it, neither does he follow you in your premisses *altogether*.[2] As he knows a good deal out of the beaten track of theological writers, and is often able to throw an unexpected light on disputed points, I shall be sorry if he does not take the subject up.

As to the see of Peter, I never meant to throw cold water on your purpose, which would be most inconsiderate in me and thoughtless, but to state my dissent from Mr Addis's opinion that it was purely a matter of *faith*.[3] You must excuse if I used any words inconsistent with this intention, and that, because my great difficulty in using my fingers acts upon my brain, confusing it, making me forget what I have to say and otherwise troubling me

One point indeed, most important I did leave out, and your last letter has reminded me of it — viz the positive *objections* to the fact of St Peter's Roman ἐπισκοπὴ,[4] as derived from Scripture — Certainly, these whether from St Paul's Epistles or from the Acts, should be decisively refuted — but I think that Catholic controversialists, without going the length of saying to Protestant opponents 'we accept the *doctrine* of the Roman Episcopate on simple faith in the infallible teaching of the Church,' are not driven in to the necessity of actually proving the *fact*.

The Bishop of W.[5] says 'I need not be a Catholic till you prove the Pope's Roman Episcopate.' We answer 'You need — because the Catholic Church is the only Ark of Salvation.' He rejoins 'How can you expect me to believe in a Church which teaches a mere figment?' We reply 'Of course we cannot, when

writing several articles about this time in the Irish Ecclesiastical Record.' (Oct., Dec. 1882, Feb., March, April 1883).

[1] See postscript to letter of 30 April to Livius, who wrote a second note on Newman's letter 'Circumstances put me in correspondence with Fr Addis an ex-Oratorian — who had the repute of being very learned, especially in the Fathers — on the subject of St Peter's Roman Episcopate. He expressed himself I thought very superficially, saying that this was unknown to the early Fathers — and that he should not believe it save on the word of the Church — not long after he apostatised from the Catholic Church and joined the Unitarians. J.L.'

[2] In the *Irish Ecclesiastical Record* (May 1885), pp. 334–8, J. S. Flanagan had raised objections against Livius's article defending the lawfulness of offering Mass privately for a deceased Protestant. See letter of 11 March to Livius. Ryder's reply was published in the *Irish Ecclesiastical Record* (Aug. 1885), pp. 541–6. See letter of 10 June to Livius.

[3] See letter of 7 May.

[4] 'episcopate'.

[5] 'Winchester (Harold Browne) with whom I had had some correspondence'. Note of Livius on the letter. See third note to letter of 30 April to Livius.

you have *proved* it a figment — but a fact is not disproved, because it is un-proved, much less if probable evidence can be adduced in its behalf. In this case the onus probandi that it is a fiction, against such authorities as Eusebius, (Caius,) Jerome and Cyprian, rests with you. These three cannot be said one to follow another, like a flock of sheep.' But I am getting now in to a further stage of the subject

Very truly Yours John H Card. Newman

TO EDWARD BELLASIS, JUNIOR

May 15. 1885

My dear Edward

I have only, this very minute, received your letter of February 4, addressed to Fr William, which contains a question to me.

I can only answer it, if I understand it, by saying how very pleasant it is to me to have such tokens of your love for me, as your whole action about my Terence, so munificent and so persevering, has been.[1] But, having done as much as you have, you have done enough. I have not that confidence in my own performance to think I can compete with a classical Jesuit —[2] and it was only because I was pressed, that I consented to let them be published.

I ought before now to have thanked you for your music — and I have been trying, not successfully as yet, to get Mr Alleguen to sing it with accompaniments from your brothers[3]

I am sorry to say I am losing the use of my fingers for writing — and this loss strangely acts on my brain and leads me to leave out words, spell wrongly etc. I[n] short I have lived 12 sevens.

Yours affly John H Card Newman.

TO THOMAS LIVIUS

May 15. 1885

Dear Fr Livius

I am sorry to say that Fr Ryder finds your subject to be too difficult to allow of his taking it up.[4] From what he says there is great complication in the opinions of divines. One question has occurred to me as arising out of it 'Is it allowable to say Mass for those souls who are in inferno?' Zacharia on Petavius

---

[1] Edward Bellasis had published *The New Terence at Edgbaston*: being notices of the performances in 1880 and 1881, third issue, London 1885.

[2] See op. cit., p. 10, note: 'In a notice of the "Pincerna," the "Spectator" tells us that the French Fr. J. Jouvency, S.J., who lived in the reign of Louis XIV, also revised Terence for Christian youth (i.e., *P. Terentii Comoediae expurgatae, cum interpretatione ac notis,* editio tertia, auctior . . . Rothomagi, 1703).'

[3] What follows has been cut out of the autograph and is supplied from a copy.

[4] See letter of 12 May to Livius.

I think says No, because it has never been done, but I *think* too that some Benedictines have done it[1]

Thank you for your letter

Very truly Yours John H Card Newman

I return the three letters, and your own

TO ANNE MOZLEY

May 15. 1885

My dear Anne Mozley

My stiff fingers are a sad impediment to my writing to you all I wish. Indeed I have various mementos that I am 12 times seven old.

I wrote a very confidential letter to the Dean the other day, forgetting he was out of England. I felt I might say much to him which to you I could not say without breaking my rule of not prompting you.[2] I am not sure you quite understand that rule.[3] It is not to force you to put into your Memoir of me just the parallel things which Keble and I put into our Memoir of Hurrell Froude, but to give you the same power over my MSS and the same right to insert or leave out at your own discretion (consulting the Dean, if you will) which Archdeacon Froude gave us in the case of Hurrell's MSS. As to the Dean, I wrote to him to give him the full leave of reading whatever you might send him for his opinion.

As to your letter which I am answering. I hope I shall not transgress my rule of not interfering with you (to reconcile you to which rule is my reason why I have told you of my letter to the Dean) if I suggest *subjects* as coming first in order after my own short Memoir of 1874. At all events such a suggestion may lead you to some clearer view of your work than you have at present. E.g.

 1. The process of thought by which I ceased to be evangelical; as found

---

[1] On this see Zacharia's note at the end of Petavius, 'De Angelis'. *De Theologicis Dogmatibus*, Venice 1757, III, pp. 98–9.

[2] Newman's letter is not to be found but Dean Church replied from Perugia on 16 May: 'Thank you very much for the confidence you repose in me. I cannot say how glad I am to hear of your purpose: glad that you should resolve to give us these authentic papers, and glad that you should have entrusted them to so faithful and capable an editor as Miss Mozley. I need not say that I am quite ready to accept the honour which you confer upon me, and I will do anything I can to be of use to her. She is a person to whom such a work is a religion. I know the pains which she took about James Mozley's letters. I will let her know as soon as we are in England.'

[3] See last paragraph in letter of 3 May to Anne Mozley, who wrote on 12 May: 'Sometime ago I *added* to a note I was writing to you that the only letters I had received from you were family letters ⟨except the M R G. [Giberne] ones⟩ – the best of *all* letters when the mind is given to them — but still I would remind you of the fact but I considered it was not for me to ask or suggest but for you to give such material as you wished and thought proper — so I tore up the note. Of course the "Extracts from Letters to friends" are just what I meant.

My feeling is always for private matters above public ones of which the interest is more passing Yet for the purpose of such a book — as the one in prospect *ought* to be — both classes may be called for. I can't sketch out a plan in prospect but perhaps I hope for myself that when the occasion comes I may know what to do.'

in the later detached current notes at the end of Number 2 part 1 and in the Private Journal of years 1825, 1826 etc

2 On the feelings under which I was ordained in 1824, not as feeling I was receiving a gift from the Apostolical Succession but because I was dedicating myself for ever, consecrating myself, to the Service of Almighty God.

3 My pamphlet in 1830 about the Ch. Miss. Society, which was not as my brother says, a 'bitter attack,' but a wish with Hawkins, R. Wilberforce and Hope Scott for its improvement[1]

4 The gradual and powerful influence of Hurrell Froude upon me.

I must stop, though I have only half answered your letter

Yours affly J H Newman[2]

TO CHARLES GORE

May 16. 1885

Dear Mr Gore

As you so kindly contrast books of mine, which you happen to have already in your Trinity library, with those which would come to it from me, I have the following difficulty, if I can rightly express it.[3]

It has been my practice, in sending to the press a new Edition of a volume to add to it, if I thought a necessity occurred, to add pages in defence of particular passages, as e.g. at the end of the Grammar of Assent. That is to say, the later edition is (as I should consider) a better book than the earlier. And I have left a memorandum that if any new edition is called for after my death, it should be printed according to the text of the last edition published in my life time. At the same time, my rule has been not to omit what I have already committed myself to, but to state my disapproval of it, or to explain, if necessary.

This being the case, I should not myself feel the difficulty of offering to the College any book which it has already, because the edition which I should offer, being the later, would be more complete; but how am I to hinder the editions I offer being inferior, that is, less complete than editions which are published next year?

I am making too much of this, I dare say; and ought to put it aside, for I

---

[1] See fifth note to letter of 14 Jan. 1885 to Anne Mozley.

[2] Anne Mozley replied on 20 May, thanking 'for *every* suggestion'.

[3] Gore wrote from Pusey House on 15 May: 'We should feel it a great honour and pleasure to have the gift of your Eminence's Books from yourself. I could not of course conceal from your Eminence that the College Library already contains a great number of them, but it would be of course a matter of the greatest interest to have them as a gift from yourself. In accordance with what I conceive to be your intention, I have not mentioned the matter to the President and Fellows, but only write to assure you that your Eminence's intended gift would be most acceptable to the College.

Venturing to ask for our work a share in your Prayers, I beg to remain Yours very respectfully   Charles Gore.'

Gore was a Fellow of Trinity College as well as Warden of Pusey House.

see no way out of it — yet I am glad to have mentioned it. If you cannot suggest any thing to the purpose, I shall proceed to write to the President.

I am losing my power of hand writing, which must be my excuse for this ill-looking letter. I do with all my heart wish success to the Pusey House, but not only negatively as a defence against infidelity, but positively as smoothing the way for the return to England of him who has the promises and the rights of the Christian Kingdom

Very truly Yours John H Card. Newman

TO JOHN PERCIVAL (I)

May 18. 1885

Cardinal Newman begs to thank the President and Bursars of Trinity College for their invitation of him to dinner on Trinity Monday June 1, and is sorry to be obliged, in consequence of his advanced age, to deny himself the pleasure of accepting it.

TO JOHN PERCIVAL (II)

May 18. 1885

My dear President

I have been asking myself how I could show that I was still mindful of the kindness done me by the College in giving me a place among its Fellows, now that I cannot longer present myself to them in person on the annual Gaudy; and the bold thought has come to me that, instead of myself, perhaps they would let me offer to them a set of the books I have published in the course of my life.

I know indeed how books grow on the shelves of a Library, and how precious in consequence is the space, and I shall be content if there is room only for some of mine; still, it seems a duty to offer all if I offer any, while, in order to give the Librarian a choice, I send you, with this letter, a complete list of them

I hope you will not think me unreasonable in thus writing to you

This May the 18th, on which I write is the Anniversary of the Monday on which in 1818 I was elected a member of your Foundation — May your yearly Festival ever be as happy a day to you all, as in 1818 it was to me.[1]

I am, My dear President Sincerely Yours

John H Card. Newman

P.S.   Excuse my handwriting: I am now scarcely able to form my letters.

[1] Percival replied on 21 May: 'We are indeed very grateful for your kind thought of the College and most gladly accept the offer of your books.
They will be placed in the Library on a shelf of their own as from the author and for the

TO LORD BLACHFORD

May 19. 1885

My dear Blachford

You have escaped a long letter by my difficulty of writing, and perhaps a short one will not unsuitably stand as a mode of thanking you for yours.

I wonder you don't go back further for our present leap in the dark — a leap which, coinciding with our foreign difficulties, is a most grave event.[1]

Why don't you go back to 1832? since which I personally have felt that I was not clever enough to have any politics. That so called Reform (tho' a Reform was necessary) was a party move in favour of Whiggism — and has not Reform been shamefully used, or shamelessly, by both parties as a party weapon since? Some years, I think, before Disraeli's and Gladstone's handling of it, I recollect an occasion when Lord John [Russell] shed tears in the House, when he found his Bill was not to pass,[2] he who had indirectly called the Act of 1832 scarcely less than a Revolution. Disraeli in 1865 ⟨?⟩ had this excuse, that he with many Tories thought that to lower the Franchise would be to increase the Aristocratic power, but what excuse has poor Gladstone for help-ing on the Radicals? How well it would be for him if he had carried out his resolution in 1874 ⟨?⟩ to give his last years to something giving more satis-faction than Radicalism, initiating his new career with a wanton attack upon the Catholic Church! We have been accustomed to say that Lord John never prospered after he attacked the Catholic Church.[3] How truly this is said I cannot tell; but it certainly has struck me that perhaps it can be said of Glad-stone. This is quite consistent with my acknowledgment of what is so admirable and high in Gladstone's character and conduct.

Well, I have done pretty well, considering what I said about short and long letters when I began. I will but say a word about Gordon.

What struck me so much in his use of 'The Dream etc' was that in St Paul's words he 'died daily' — he was always on his death bed, fulfilling the common advice that we should ever pass the day, as if it was to be our last[4]

Ever Yrs affectly John H Card. Newman

use of future generations of Fellows and Scholars; and, although we should not have ventured to ask for anything on so large a scale, as you have so kindly suggested that we may have the complete list, that is what we should desire.

I hope to have the pleasure of announcing your gift on Trinity Monday . . .' On that day, 1 June, Percival wrote again, after he had read out Newman's letter in Hall, and conveyed the thanks of all the members of the College.

[1] This refers to Gladstone's Franchise Act, passed at the end of 1884. See also letter of 8 Feb. 1885 to Lady Simeon.
[2] When withdrawing his Reform Bill on 11 April 1854.
[3] See letter of 11 Nov. 1850 to T. W. Allies.
[4] See letter of 7 April to Mary Murphy.

May 20th. 1885

My dear Child

I rejoice to see your handwriting, but, for me, my fingers have become so stiff that I write with effort and pain, and cannot write much.

I was amused at your friend's question. Is he infallible, that I am to take his word on trust and to answer his difficulty before he *proves* it? He speaks against the 'Infallible Church'; I had rather believe the infallible Church that St Catharine existed, than his fallible word that she never did. Of course he has a right to believe in his own infallibility, if he will — but he has no right to enforce it upon others, instead of proving its existence or else disproving St Catharine's.[1]

Do you recollect Mrs Glasses' direction in her cookery book, 'First catch your fish'[2] — The Church's infallibility is our fish, what is your friend's fish?

Yours affly John H Card. Newman

P.S.   You must not take this letter as a sharp one. Your friend should look into the Bollandists or Tillemont, if he wishes to have the judgment of Catholics. As to Butler, he only says that nothing is known about such a lady but what Eusebius says — How does this prove that she did not exist? Did Lycurgus not exist because nothing is know of him? Your friend is as bad as Kingsley.

May 21. 1885

My dear Anne Mozley

Your letter has just come. I have heard from Dean Church at Perugia.[3]

Now for the question of public events etc.[4] I cannot tell how much of my letters do *not* concern *me*, but I have a great collection of them.

First of mine to others — viz those which I gave you a list of when last I wrote — my letters to Miss Giberne (which have come back to me) to Church, to R F Wilson, to Bowden, to Keble etc.

Next two quarto books from 1828 to 1836 of public matters — two larger quartos from 1822 to 1836 of both public and personal matters

---

[1] On the question of whether St Catherine of Alexandria ever existed Miss Fitzgerald had referred to Alban Butler, *The Lives of the Fathers, Martyrs, and other Principal Saints, compiled from Original Muniments and other Authentic Records*, first published 1756–9. Butler said, 'Her acts are so much adulterated that little use can be made of them', and according to Assemani all we know of her is derived from Eusebius, 'though that historian mentions not her name.'

[2] According to *The Oxford Dictionary of Quotations* this is a misquotation from Hannah Glasse, *The Art of Cookery made plain and easy*, London 1747, who said 'Take your hare when it is cased.'

[3] See first note to letter of 15 May to Anne Mozley.

[4] See second note to letter of 15 May to Anne Mozley.

These great collections are either letters *from* me or *to* me; the name of the writer is given at the side of each letter with the unlucky omission of 'from'. When they are not *from* me they are *to* me.

There is another little confusion, arising from a change to chronological order from a chance transcription.

I cannot tell what use they will be to you, except certainly that they will bring before you the state of things. There is much gossip in them — they include my letters to Froude when he was in the West Indies — you could not do without the first Volume of Froude's Remains — a rare book now — but Fr Neville could lend it to you.

I must consider what I had better send you

Yours affectly J H Card. Newman

TO LORD BLACHFORD

May 23. 1885

My dear Blachford,

Thank you for your long and most welcome letter. I am pleased to think how very closely I follow what you said. That a Reform was needed in 1832, I thought I had quoted — but I thought of Lord John [Russell] and Lord Durham.[1]

I think that all praise is due to Gladstone for being so exemplary both personally and publicly as Prime Minister, and I am unspeakably shocked and indignant to be told, as you tell me, of his private character having been the butt of slander.

What has made me feel so bitterly which I do not know how to help, is the thought of the poor fellows in the Soudan.[2]

Yours affly John H. Card. Newman

PS. I congratulate you on having left at this season the 'fumum strepitumque'[3]

I am not quite easy about myself. I have small ailments which will not go, and I ask myself, Are they tokens of a break up, considering my age. 84 is twelve times seven; and seven is commonly considered a stage of life.

TO ANNE MOZLEY

May 27. 1885

Dear Anne Mozley

I am sending you a portmanteau, the contents of which (which I give overleaf) ought to give you trouble ⟨employment⟩ for a long time.

---

[1] These were leading radicals in the Government which carried the first Reform Bill.
[2] Gladstone was generally held responsible for the failure to save Khartoum.
[3] Horace, *Odes*, III, xxix, 12.

You ask you [me] about Froude's influence upon me. Accordingly Fr Neville has let me send you the first volume of his copy of the 'Remains', the reading of which has inexpressibly touched me now at the end of 50 years.

His letters to *me* are headed with a delta,δ and those which concern your question begin at p 245, (δ5). At the same time I should say the 'δ5' is unfair to me, as he misunderstood me. At the same time I have confessed in the Apologia that in 1826 and following years I had fallen into some lax opinions. ⟨Vid. pp 232, 233 in *the Remains*.⟩

I believe the *Greek* letters, prefixed to H. Froude's letters to Friends are repetitions, as far as possible, of the Greek letters appended to the Poems of the Lyra Apostolica

Lyra Ap.	Froude's letters to
α – Bowden	α his Father?
β – H. Froude	β William Froude?
γ – Keble	γ Keble
δ – Newman	δ – Newman
ε – R. Wilberforce	ε – R. Wilberforce
ζ – Isaac Williams.	ζ – Isaac Williams?

The additional letters I only partly make out

η – Rogers
θ – F. J. Christie
κ – Ogilvie?

Yrs affectly J H Card. Newman

MSS books sent to Miss Mozley at Barrow on Trent May 27. 1885
1. Bowden's Letters *from* me — six packets
2 My correspondence with (from and to) friends in four large quartos — from 1822 to 1828
3. Letters from me to Miss Giberne, to Church, to R. F. Wilson
4 Originals of the Lyra Apostolica
and besides
5 The first volume of Froude's Remains

TO RICHARD HIPPISLEY DOMENICHETTI

May 30. 1885

Dear Mr Domenichetti

I congratulate you on gaining what in my time at Oxford was the coveted prize of the year[1]

And I thank you very much for proposing to dedicate it to me. But the Provost surely is the person whose leave must be got, and I never heard of

---

[1] Domenichetti had just won the 1885 Newdigate Prize for English verse with a poem on 'The Thames'.

such a leave being given. I conceive the composition becomes the property of the University, from the time it is sent in.

This does not lessen the pleasant sense I have of the warmth of heart which has led you to your proposal

I write with much difficulty, so my letter must be short I give you my blessing

Yours very truly John H Card. Newman

TO MARGARET ELLEN JAMES

May 30. 1885

Cardinal [Newman] is sure that Miss James's letter did not reach him, or that he has answered it.[1]

The notion that he became a Catholic in order to get rid of doubts is utterly unfounded. He became a Catholic because our Lord set up a Church in the beginning as the Ark of salvation and the Oracle of Truth. And the *Roman* was it.

So he has said in all he has written. Look to his Apologia, his sermons to Mixed Congregations, the postscript to his Letter to the Duke of Norfolk, or to his Development of Christian Doctrine. He has never had a doubt since he became a Catholic. He became a Catholic because he was certain the Catholic was the true faith.

Miss James must excuse his bad writing but he writes with an effort and with difficulty.

TO J. R. BLOXAM

Rednal June 9. 1885

My dear Bloxam

The Sermon, which under a new name you inquire about, is one of my University Sermons, preached on Nov 4 1832 with the text 'The serpent deceived me and I ate.'[2]

Yrs affectly John H Card Newman.

[1] Neville copied out Miss James's letter accompanying a copy of this letter: 'Dear Fr Neville, The raison d'être of the letter was as follows — I was about to be received into the Catholic Church when my uncle Captain Jones-Parry wrote me a long letter on the subject in which he said "I believe Newman, the most pure and honest of all divines, turned simply because he was in a maze of perplexity and doubt, and the Church of Rome solved his doubts by saying "You shall not doubt."

That, on the face of it, would be rather a remarkable thing for the Church of Rome to do. However, as the Cardinal's great kindness was proverbial I thought I would ask him what his motive was . . .

Believe me, Yrs sincerely M. E. James'

[2] 'Human Responsibility, as Independent of Circumstances', *U.S.*, pp. 136–55. Bloxam had been asked for this information.

Rednall June 9. 85

My dear Wilfrid

I would gladly see your friend. The only difficulty is that at last the weather has let me come here, which the doctors have been urging me to do for the last six months. I wonder if it would be of use to him to say that I expect to be at the Oratory every Sunday.

I wish, however, he felt how easily he could get good advice in London. What could I do for him, which another priest could not? Don't suppose that I am unwilling to see him — but I don't see he ought to go out of his way to see me

Yours affecty John H Card. Newman

TO THOMAS LIVIUS

Rednall June 10. 1885

Dear Fr Livius

I am sorry to say that, in going to and fro between this place and Bm, I have mislaid your last letter. I hope I shall find it in a few days

Fr Ryder sent his paper to Fr Flanagan as to a friend — Fr Flanagan, thinking it unfair to suppress an argument which told against his own paper, sent it to the Record. This, I believe, is the state of things. Fr Ryder treats the subject *historically*[1]

Very truly Yours John H Card. Newman

TO H. H. HEAD[2]

June 13. 1885

Dear Sir

Your letter just received has been a great gratification to me. Excuse a short letter, written with the stiff fingers of an old man.

I had no expectation, when I wrote those two hymns, that they would be acceptable to others, as well as an outpouring of my own thoughts; but so it has turned out.

This being the case, I feel the same of much besides that I have written, that it has had its day, even if it ever attracted the notice of others; but, since

[1] See letters of 12 and 15 May to Livius.
[2] A note on the autograph says that this letter was addressed 'To H H Head Esq of India', and Head noted on it the date of Newman's death, signing 'HHH. Kendrapara. Orissa. Sep 7, 90.'

you ask me, I refer you then to the following volume, which I shall direct Messrs Burns and Oates, the publishers, to send to you, if conveyance is practicable. 'Verses on various occasions.'

God bless you and keep you

Very truly Yours John H Card. Newman

TO LADY WOLSELEY

Rednall June 19. 1885

Dear Lady Wolseley

I grieve to hear of your great loss, but the memory of your dear Father is a consolation to you which will be greater and greater, as time goes on.[1]

I will say Mass for him, please God, and, when I return to Birmingham will give your message to the Fathers there.

Excuse my bad writing; I am losing the use of my fingers.

Very truly Yours John H. Card Newman

TO THOMAS LIVIUS

June 21. 1885

Dear Fr Livius

Your MS has come quite safe

Fr Ryder thinks, at my suggestion, of sending you the proof of his article. I thought you might like to see it and this was the only way.

I wish I had eyes or head to profit by your MS

Most truly Yours John H Card. Newman[2]

TO H. P. LIDDON

Rednall June 26. 1885

Dear Canon Liddon

As the inclosed letter, written on the page of one of my letters to Keble, has turned up, I send it to you. Please burn it, if (as likely) you gain nothing from it

Very truly Yours John H Card. Newman

---

[1] Lady Wolseley's father was Daniel T. Murphy of San Francisco.

[2] Conclusion and signature are cut off but supplied in Livius's hand. He noted on the letter: 'Fr Ignatius Ryder's Article was on a subject about which I had written — The Lawfulness of saying Mass for a deceased Protestant — The Cardinal's signature was cut out — that I might supply an Australian Bishop with his autograph – he had begged hard for one'

TO THOMAS LIVIUS

Bm July 5. 1885

Dear Fr Livius

I am ashamed to have kept your Pamphlets so long without an answer. They are both of them interesting and instructive — and the one on the telephone on a subject new to me.[1] I send back the one in MS, and regret much that my knowledge of its subject is not such as to enable me to answer to your kindness in sending it by accompanying it with remarks upon it. I shall register it

Very truly Yours John H Card. Newman

TO W. H. KEATING

Bm July 13. 1885

Dear Mr Keating

I have been from home, or I should have answered you before now. I thank you for the welcome news you give me about the Catholic University and your kind language about myself. I am losing the power of using my hand in writing — so I must ask you to allow me to be brief I inclose the Autograph

Very truly Yours John H. Card. Newman

TO J. R. BLOXAM

July 15/85

My dear Bloxam

I am not likely to have any difficulty about my Tracts or my Letters – but of course I shall be glad to see them (in proof) before I decide.[2]

The[re] was a 'Nero del Nero' and others apparently not close relations of his. His pedigree etc is given in Bacci's life of him ii, 15. 2 and his connection with the *del* Nero's at iv, 8. 5[3]

Yours affectly J H Card Newman

[1] See letter of 7 May to Livius.

[2] Bloxam was proposing to print his correspondence in 1841 with Ambrose Lisle Phillipps, and to include notes and letters of Newman's relating to it. He wrote on 21 July, 'I venture to send you ten folios of my *copy* for the press of Mr Ambrose Phillipps' letters — they have all passed through Lockhart's hands'. Bloxam's plan for publication fell through, as had an earlier one. See *Newman and Bloxam*, p. 101.

[3] G. Bacci, *The Life of St Philip Neri*. A lady in Brighton was proposing to bring to see Bloxam a girl who was a descendant of a branch of St Philip Neri's family. This branch had lived for generations in Athens and claimed to have 'the jewelled crucifix of the Saint'. See letter of 4 Oct. to Bloxam.

July 22. 1885.

My dear Lady Simeon

I have been going to write to Queenie[1] to know how you were, so it rejoiced me to hear from you. I did not write, from the great difficulty I have now in using my fingers, which leads me not to write without something like necessity. And I am altogether more feeble, though Fr Neville thinks it right to deny it.

Thank you for your news. On the whole I think it good, though I feel what a lasting pain it must be to you, to be disappointed in the present results of Sir John's sacrifice.[2]

But if dear Ste ever becomes serious, as one cannot but hope he will be, the only religion which will have a hold on him is the Catholic, and he may be the means of influencing others.

I took it for granted that he was fairly off. How can youths be so foolish as not to let well alone.

Yesterday was our annual School Gaudy, so I will make it an excuse for a stupid letter.

Yours affly John H. Card. Newman

The Honble Lady Simeon

TO MRS F. J. WATT

July 22. 1885

My dear E. [Eleanor?]

I shall rejoice to see the boys. Only let me know *the day*.

Yours affly J H N

TO LORD BLACHFORD

July 27. 1885

My dear Blachford,

Thank you for your long letter. I was anxious to know whether we agreed together, and I think we do. Certainly Home Rule could only make matters worse, and end in Separation, but then, will not a continuance of things as they are be a chronic state worse than separation.

Perhaps, as men say, the land question is *the* difficulty — but my experience

---

[1] Lady Simeon's daughter Catherine.
[2] Sir John Simeon's eldest son had been married without permission in an Anglican church, see letter of 30 May 1872 to Lady Simeon, and now his brother Stephen was engaged to Louisa, elder daughter of Hugh Culling Eardley Childers, M.P., and was to be married in the same way on 10 Nov. 1885.

leads me another way. It may be said that John Bull acted on principle, but he tried to teach a people whose religion he ignored. Trinity College to this day is a standing offence. It gives the law to the intellectual, or at least the social life of Dublin. (N.B. My fingers will not let me write with due ease)

How differently have we treated Scotland! The old woman shied her stool at the Parson's head, and forthwith Presbyterianism was established.[1] Our (Irish) University asked for a charter, (not for money) in vain. Our Law students were not granted even the dispensation for 2 years out of 5 granted by Lincoln's Inn and the Temple to Oxford and Cambridge men. We kept up our University for 30 years, collecting for it, I am told, £5000 a year, but in vain. No: England was to be liberalistic, and therefore Ireland must be an exception to the rule.

Then as to Trade and Arts. One of our Professors told me, a competent authority, he could count up 20 trades which had disappeared from Dublin since the Union – and it was commonly said that the picture collections of noblemen had left the place from the same cause

And now, and only now, I come to the one remark which I had intended to make on your letter, but I have got into a wrong groove and have been unable to get out of it. I think what I have been saying accounts for what has often perplexed me, viz. the coolness with which Irish Nationalists hear the prophecy what great losses Separation will be, not to England merely, but to Ireland. They think that every change must be for the better, things cannot be worse than they are. We risk nothing, or very little. At all events if we gain Home Rule, we can *treat* with England — we shall offer terms with a high hand. We shall have an international court for the settlement of differences — the Westminster Parliament will cease any more to be 'omnipotent' — but I cannot go on writing, or you in labouring to decypher.

Yours affly J. H. Card. Newman.

TO MESSRS BURNS AND OATES

July 27. 1885

Cardinal Newman observes of Messrs Burns and Oates in answer to his [question], that he seems not to have put his question distinctly   His question was *when*, in what *month*, the stock of the two volumes went from their keeping to Messrs Longmans   He believes it was in February last, in which case the payment for the sale of those two volumes would be due to him not only up to Christmas 1884 but to Feb 1885. His question is whether he is right in thus stating, or should the payments respectively be more restricted He will be obliged by their returning the inclosed.[2]

---

[1] This was on 23 July 1637 in St Giles's Cathedral, Edinburgh, when the Prayer Book was first read. Episcopacy was abolished in the following year.

[2] Burns and Oates replied on 28 July that they had been mistaken in saying they had paid up to Christmas 1884. The correct date was 14 Feb. 1885.

July 28, 1885.

My dear Mr. Quinn,

I thank you for your notice of the annual meeting of your excellent and important society. I gladly send you, as asked, my blessing upon it, and will, please God, offer the Holy Sacrifice in its behalf.

Most truly yours John H. Card. Newman.

TO A DAUGHTER OF MRS F. J. WATT

July 30. 1885

My dear Child

I congratulate you on your prizes, and feel how pleasant it must be to you to be at home.

My love to all of you. Give the inclosed letter to Mama.

Yours affectly J. H. Card. Newman

TO J. F. X. O'CONOR, S.J.

July 31. 1885

My dear Rev. Father

On St Ignatius's day I can best hope you will receive my apology with kindness, for not being able to tell whether I have acknowledged to you the coming of your welcome gift or not. If not, I beg to do so now, asking you to ascribe it to an old man's deficient memory

Most truly Yours John H. Card. Newman

TO JOSEPH MONTEITH

Aug. 18. 1885

My dear Joseph

Thank you for your dear Father's book, and for your account of yourself and yours.[1] I was very glad to hear from you, and hope you will excuse this shabby answer, but I have lost the use of my fingers in writing

Yours affly John H Card. Newman

Pray thank your wife and Miss Fullerton for their kind remembrance of me

[1] Robert Monteith died in 1884.

TO MISS M. R. GIBERNE

Aug. 19. 1885

My dear Sister Pia

I have not forgotten your two sisters. It must be a great trial to you.[1] I have much difficulty in writing and now can write but a short letter. Also a matter is upon me quite requires a great deal of writing which does not allow of dictating. Give me some prayers for it.[2] I hope we have found some books of yours

My blessing on you
Yours affectly J H Card. Newman

TO ROBERT CHARLES JENKINS

August 25, 1885.

Dear Canon Jenkins,

I thank you for the beautiful lines you have sent me and your music, which is an additional kindness.

Did I acknowledge your last brochure?[3] If not, this comes not from my feeling (I grieve to say) that it was written with your usual fairness — but principally because I have lost my power of writing, and do not even make those 'Pothooks and hangers' without pain.

Excuse then this miserable letter.

Yours most truly J. H. Card. Newman.

TO MRS WILLIAM BORLASE

Aug 28. 1885

Dear Mrs Borlase

Your sad tidings could not take me by surprise.[4] I had been expecting it for months. I hope you are not knocked up with your anxieties and attentions.

---

[1] Two of Miss Giberne's sisters died, Caroline, aged 81, on 14 May, and Rebecca, aged 86, on 19 Aug. 1885.

[2] Newman was preparing his answer to A. M. Fairbairn. See letter of 9 Sept. to Percy William Bunting.

[3] Presumably Jenkins's *The Law and Practice of the Church of Rome in Cases of Heresy*, London 1885. Newman's copy is inscribed 'With affectionate respects from R.C.J.' He now sent H. Grotius, *Via ad Pacem Ecclesiasticam*, 1642, inscribing it to 'His Eminence Cardinal Newman from Robert C. Jenkins, Lyminge. August 27th 1885.'

[4] Mrs Borlase wrote on 26 Aug. to Neville to say that William Copeland had died that day.

Thank you for your letter. Excuse my bad writing. I seem to be losing the use of my fingers

Very truly Yours John H Card Newman

TO LORD BLACHFORD

Sepr 2. 1885

My dear Blachford,

I was very glad to hear from you. If my writing were not a difficulty to me, I should have challenged you. Dear Copeland's death I had been looking for daily for a long time. People all say I am looking well. I have nothing the matter but think I am weaker and weaker. My memory is bad.

I am startled at your having a criticism to make on my cousin's likeness — It was the most talking gay party I have had for many years. She and her sister were full of talk. I had never seen them before. By the time we had got sociable, in came Isy Froude (The Baroness) with the Baron whom I had never seen — he was a very nice fellow — and it may be I talked too much, and got tired. I was not aware of it.[1]

Every one was charmed with the picture and Harry Mozley took it to his Eton friends, and, whether from politeness or not, they spoke as much pleased. Can the autotype have hurt it?[2] This morning, curiously enough comes the inclosed from Ogle.[3]

See what a long letter I have written

Yours affly John H. Card. Newman

TO ANNE MOZLEY

Sept. 7. 1885

My dear Anne Mozley

Thank you for your sympathy. Dear Copeland was one of the faithfullest of friends, and a great loss. I write with such difficulty, that I write as little as I can — but I have managed to write out my letters to Keble. I think you would like to see them. I should propose to send you only the Anglican — they reach to May 1843, when I told him I was likely to be a Catholic I should not wonder if that date would be found to be the best that could be taken for the termination of your undertaking

Yours affectly John H. Card Newman

[1] This was Emmeline Deane's portrait. See second note to letter of 8 Sept. 1884 to Mrs Deane.

[2] 'A process of permanent photographic printing which reproduces photographs or works of art in monochrome.' *OED*. Those of Emmeline Deane's portrait were made by the Autotype Company, 74 New Oxford Street and cost one pound or one guinea.

[3] This was from John William Ogle, perhaps about Newman's health.

TO LORD BLACHFORD

September 8th. 1885.

My dear Blachford,

The Auto-type has come down here — Certainly I don't like it as much as I liked the Drawing itself – but my friends here, who had not seen it last year, are very much pleased.

I am ashamed of giving you trouble, but, unless (as is natural) you have burned Ogle's letter, please send it to me.

Yours affectionately, J. H. Card: Newman.

TO MISS M. R. GIBERNE

Septr 8. 1885

My dear Sister Pia,

I had your letters in my hands only the other day. I shall be sure to find them — and wish you to determine whether I should send them to you or to burn them. Recollect, I have made use of them in the Apologia.[1]

Mr Copeland, as you know is gone. My oldest living friends are, besides you, Rogers and T. Mozley — is it not so?

I have finished my article.[2] I don't think people will *like* it — but I am *satisfied* with it. My trouble with it has been very great. My memory goes before I have set down what I have in my mind, and I have been fagging six hours and more every day to find by next morning that it won't do — and I must do it over again   When I was once atop of the embankment all was right — but how should I get there

Ever Yours affectionately J H Card. Newman

TO PERCY WILLIAM BUNTING

Sept 9. 1885

Dear Sir

I ask to be allowed to insert in the Contemporary Review an answer to Principal Fairbairn's criticism of me in your number of last May.[3] The Article

---

[1] Miss Giberne had asked for Newman's letters to her to be returned to her. She wrote again on 10 Sept. 1885, 'it is my great and fervent wish for years to possess them once more before I die. Why, *they* with your published writings were the making of me'. She promised they would be returned to Newman after her death, if he wished.

[2] See next letter.

[3] A. M. Fairbairn's article was 'Catholicism and Modern Thought', the *Contemporary Review* (May 1885), pp. 652–74, reprinted in *Catholicism: Roman and Anglican*, third edition, London 1899, pp. 94–140. He accused Newman of philosophical scepticism and of withdrawing the proofs of religion from the region of reason into the realm of conscience and imagination.

will take from 8 to 10 of your pages. The copy is printing — I have done this for my own convenience; it will not interfere with your printer

I hope you will allow me to make two conditions 1. that I should not receive any payment for the Article and 2. that I retain the copy right of it.[1]

I am, Dear Sir, Yours faithfully

J H Card Newman

TO J. G. SNEAD-COX

Sent   Sept 9. 1885
Sir

I answer in the affirmative your question as to the authorship of the passage in the copy of the Tablet which you send me.

I suppose it is my contribution long ago to a volume of Testimonials on behalf of the Pope's Infallibility.[2]

J H N

TO LORD BLACHFORD

Sept. 14. 1885.

My dear Blachford

You know how very sensitive I am, more so because I am older — but let me say a word apropos of Miss Mozley's great kindness towards me. I wanted all my papers (down to *May 1843*, when I told Keble I was likely to be a Catholic) to be left on my death for the inspection of some contemporary of mine (they will be the property of Fr William Neville.) I mean, not only a contemporary, but an Anglican and a friend. I felt I could not escape the chance of the book making by strangers which pays so well, if I did not succeed in my own attempt. I thought that the three conditions of a friend, an

---

[1] On 10 Sept. John Rae replied on behalf of Bunting, editor of the *Contemporary Review*, 'Of course we assent to your conditions', and asked for Newman's article in time for the next number, where it appeared as 'The Development of Religious Error', the *Contemporary Review* (Oct. 1885), pp. 457–69, reprinted separately in 1886 by Burns and Oates, and (without its critical poscript) in *S.E.*, pp. 69–89, also in *The Theological Papers of John Henry Newman on Faith and Certainty*, Oxford 1976, pp. 140–9.

[2] Cox, who was editor of the *Tablet* wrote on 7 Sept. that in the issue for 5 Sept., p. 382, there was a quotation from Newman, taken from the Sydney *Freeman's Journal*.

Many correspondents had written to say that the greater part of the passage was in *Idea*. The passage consisted of extracts from the first edition of *Discourses on the Scope and Nature of University Education*, which Newman had sent to Valerian Cardella S.J., for an album of articles on St Peter. See letters of 29 March 1867 to Hope-Scott and 19 Sept. 1872 to Alfred Plummer.

In a first draft of his letter, instead of the second paragraph, Newman wrote: 'I suppose it is taken from a volume of Fr Cardella's containing testimonies in favour of the Pope's Infallibility to which I contributed from one of my Dublin Discourses. As he pressed that the extract should not appear in print elsewhere I complied with his wish which I could do without harm to the substance of my argument. There were other reasons for my concession of a literary nature relating to the composition of the whole book as I noticed in the advertisement of the 2nd Edition'. See *The Scope and Nature of University Education*, second edition, London 1859, p. vii, where Newman explained that he had 'removed from the text much temporary, collateral, or superfluous matter'.

Anglican and a contemporary, *if possible*, would give the prospect of a true account of what otherwise would be sure to be full of errors. Ah, if 'possible' – for there is another condition still. It would not be published till after my death. I could not let it be written with the chance, the opportunity of my seeing any part of it — yet every year takes away contemporaries.

Under these circumstances I read Miss M's volume of James Mozley's Letters —[1] and it struck me, I should be fortunate, if she would receive my papers with a view to using them in her own way. I wanted her to accept the full leave and discretion to use just what of them she would, making on my part two conditions, that it should not be published till after my death, and that I should not see any part of it, or hear about it in prospect.

Now I am come to my sensitiveness. I could not be in better hands than yours and Church's. I should be more than contented. You would not in all things agree with me — who would? but I should perfectly trust you both, as well as Miss M. I should be grateful. But let me be dead to it — don't speak about it to me — don't say whether it is 'interesting' or not. There is just this one thing I can't help having [hoping] and should be pleased to find — that my papers had come back to Wm Neville (tho' I am in no hurry for them) This would show the work was done, but I can't expect this will come to pass in my life time.[2]

Ever Yrs affly J. H. Card. Newman

TO ANNE MOZLEY

Sept 14. 1885

My dear Anne Mozley

I was shocked to hear of your accident.[3] The news came home to me the more sharply from the selfish reason that I am always slipping and tumbling myself, and, alas, without warning, or (as I think) imprudence on my part And I hear of so many parallel cases. We can only say that we are in God's Hands.

Thank Fanny [Mozley] for her letter, and beg her to let me know how you go on.

I had nearly finished my Letters up to May 1843, when I had to leave off to answer an Article against me in the Contemporary Review of last May, accusing me of scepticism. This will appear, I believe on next October 1. and after that date I mean to finish and send you the Letters.[4]

Yours affectly John H Card. Newman

---

[1] *Letters of the Rev. J. B. Mozley*, London 1885.
[2] On 5 Oct. Anne Mozley wrote to Newman: 'I have had letters lately from Lord Blachford and the Dean *very* satisfactory to me.'
[3] Anne Mozley fell down three steps, and broke her right wrist.
[4] See letter of 9 Sept. to Bunting. Anne Mozley wrote on 5 Oct. with her left hand, that she had read Newman's article in the *Contemporary Review* for Oct. 'with much interest and satisfaction. Your opponent deserves his set down, though that is scarcely the right word.'

TO LORD BLACHFORD

September 17th. 1885.

My very dear Blachford,

I don't like to be seeming to be striving for the last word — and I assure you I had nothing of any feeling you would wish away in noting the word 'interesting' — but the long and the short is that I am as if my skin was torn off (metaphorically) by the number of Memoirs written of me (written in kindness). Within this week. I hear that one of my Catholic life is coming out —[1] I do feel gratitude — and so I should to a surgeon who performed an operation upon me — But, besides this, in Miss Mozley's matter came the additional imagination lest I myself should have part in a work which I professed (however truly) so hugely to dislike; and 'interesting' was the first touch of my having a partnership in it. Forgive me if I have hurt you.

Yours affectionately, John H. Card: Newman.

P.S. I know well how anxious I was about the Oriel Election in 1833, but had quite forgotten it came into my letters.[2]

TO WILFRID MEYNELL

[20? September 1885]

Dear Mr Meynell

I am quite sure of your friendly purpose in putting together memorials of my Catholic life, but I am obliged, while thanking you for your telling me and for the feelings towards me you express, to say that it is my habitual ⟨long settled⟩ judgment that a memoir ought not to appear in the life time of its subject.[3] There is an additional awkwardness [?] in my own case — for I have been the subject of much controversy, and when there are two sides to a question, it may be equally difficult when it is brought before the public for parties interested in it to speak or to be silent upon it[4]

JHN

[1] See next letter.
[2] This refers to the Oriel Fellowship election, when Frederic Rogers (Lord Blachford), and Charles Marriott were elected. See Keble's letter of 11 April 1833 in *Moz*. I, p. 381, also p. 425 and *A.W.*, p. 134.
[3] Meynell wrote on 13 Sept. that he was about to publish 'a record of your Eminence's Catholic Life' in *Merry England* (Oct. 1885), under the pseudonym of 'John Oldcastle'. In fact it was described as 'Cardinal Newman Number', and was occupied entirely with him during the forty years after Oct. 1845, except for a dedication at the beginning to Cardinal Manning.
[4] Wilfrid Meynell replied on 21 Sept., 'Your Eminence's letter adds to the responsibility I have felt all along in the preparation of the Record. For, good or ill, it is out of my hands now and beyond recall; but I hope it is not arrogant in me [to] feel a certain hope that what has been done has been done in a manner not likely to incur your Eminence's displeasure, at least on the point indicated in your Eminence's letter'. Meynell added, 'When I undertook the task, I had no idea of its delicacy or difficulty. My own memory went back only to 1871; — and what I found antecedent to that, forced me to throw the Record into a rather unusual form, and to avoid the necessity for a consecutive biography'. See letter of 19 Oct. to J. G. Cox.

Septr 26. 1885

My dear Emmeline,

I have been rejoiced at your success, and thank you for your two Auto-types.[1] I am losing the use of my writing fingers, and must content myself with sending you only a few words.

All kind thought to your Father, Mother, Louisa, and all of you.

Yours affectionately John H. Card. Newman

TO AUBREY DE VERE

Sept 28. 1885

My dear Aubrey de Vere,

I am ashamed of my neglect. I inclose it. Our Protestant friends are somewhat dictatorial[2]

As I am writing, I am led to say that I hope I did not leave an impression on your mind that the pain I feel as to my Article is anything more than the chance of carrying some readers *from* the Church, in consequence of their abhorrence of the doctrine I maintained. I have no doubt it is the doctrine of the Church, and has claims on our faith.[3]

Yours affectly John H Card. Newman

TO J. R. BLOXAM

Oct. 4. 1885

My dear Bloxam

Thank you for your account of the Relic[4]

I feel honoured by the inclosed

Yrs affly J H Card Newman

[1] See letters of 2 and 8 Sept. 1885 to Lord Blachford.

[2] Aubrey de Vere replied on 29 Sept. 1885: 'Pray accept my thanks for sending me on the address to the Pope.' See letter of 9 Sept. 1885 to J. G. Cox.

[3] De Vere noted on the autograph 'Probably the Doctrine of "Eternal Punishment." A de V.' In his reply on 29 Sept. de Vere thanked for 'The Development of Religious Error' which Newman had given him, spoke of Fairbairn's 'most undiscerning eye,' and his un-founded charge, which ought never to have been made without ample quotations to substantiate it. However he had 'produced a result the opposite of that which he contemplated, through the clearer light which, both by your fresh statements, and by your quotations, you have now thrown on your opinions respecting the relations of Faith and Reason.'

De Vere then went on: 'I think that your remarks on the subject of "Eternal Punishment" also cannot fail to be of serious use. Thoughtful Protestants and Rationalists knew already that the Catholic Church held the doctrine in reality not semblance, and they cannot therefore be alienated from her by that belief, more than they are already alienated; while your statements will make them see that she holds it because it is part and parcel of the Christian Revelation, and must share the "reproach,' which authentic Christianity has always to meet.' See *S.E.* pp. 83–8, and *The Theological Papers of John Henry Newman on Faith and Certainty*, pp. 146–9.

[4] This was about the jewelled crucifix said to have belonged to St Philip Neri. See letter of 15 July to Bloxam. A. D. Wagner later brought it to Newman to look at, and it did not appear to be old.

Oct. 7. 1885

My dear Lord Braye

Thank you for your inquiries about me.

I am, thank God, quite well — but I am weaker, I think, than I was — certainly than when I last saw you.

With my best regards to Lady Braye

I am Most sincerely Yours John H Card. Newman

Justificata est Sapientia à filiis suis[1]

John H Card. Newman

Oct. 10. 1885

My dear Allies,

I write with such difficulty that I must content myself with sending your Wife and Daughter with yourself my best blessing, rejoicing to hear of Basil's [Allies] promotion, and welcoming in my judgment your daughter's new work as a very happy idea.[2]

Yours affectionately John H. Card. Newman

P.S. If any one has merit by becoming a Catholic you and Mrs A. have.[3]

P.S. My answer to Dr F. [Fairbairn] only takes the Popes for [granted?]. I thought that enough.[4]

Oct 10. 1885

Private

My dear Lord Archbishop

I have welcomed with the warmest interest the eloquent appeal of your University Board to the Catholics of the United States, which has come to me from America through the kindness of an anonymous friend.[5]

---

[1] *Matthew*, 11:19.

[2] Mary Allies was preparing *Leaves from St Augustine*, London 1886.

[3] Allies wrote on 9 Oct. 'But I am writing to you on an anniversary which has never been out of my thoughts since forty years ago you wrote to me on this day that you were to be received into the Church. [See letter of 9 Oct. 1845 to Allies.] "Merry England" is not the only one to remember that. I confess that your letter opened to me a prospect which was terrible — I must confess also that the forty years have been terrible to pass: and again, what might not be expected, that the *retrospect* of them is terrible.'

[4] See letter of 9 Sept. to Bunting. The copyist found a word illegible. Allies wrote on 27 Oct., 'No lady ever put so much into a P.S. as you do.'

[5] 'In the early fall of 1885 Bishop Spalding completed the text of a circular which was to

At a time when there is so much in this part of the world to depress and trouble us as to our religious prospects, the tidings which your Circular conveys of the actual commencement of so great an undertaking on the other side of the Ocean on the part of the Church will rejoice the hearts of all educated Catholics in these Islands.

With this thought before me, I cannot help feeling it to be out of place to notice what is merely personal to myself; still I may be allowed by your Grace and the other members of the Board briefly to express my deep sense of the singular honour they have done me by introducing into their appeal a quotation from what I wrote years ago upon the subject of Universities.

It leads me in simple gratitude, were I not already bound by faith and brotherly love, to pray for an abundant blessing from above on a design so necessary for the growth and stability of the Church in the vast regions which Divine Providence has opened upon her.[1]

I am My dear Lord Archbishop

Yours Grace's humble and affectionate servant,

John H. Card. Newman

His Grace The Archbp of Baltimore

TO ST GEORGE JACKSON MIVART

October 10. 1885.

My dear Mr Mivart,

I return you my best thanks for your friendly remembrance of me yesterday, a day of such solemn and joyful associations to myself.

Yours most truly John H. Card. Newman.

St George Mivart Esq.

TO ALEXANDER WOOD

[10 October 1885]

Dear Mr Wood

I thank you for your congratulations on my 40 years and your kind wishes for my future.[2]

be sent out to all interested parties in an effort to enlist support for the [Catholic] University [of America]. Gibbons gave his approval to the document, and later that autumn he received a letter from Cardinal Newman to whom a copy had been sent by an anonymous friend.' John Tracy Ellis, *The Life of James Cardinal Gibbons, Archbishop of Baltimore*, Milwaukee 1952, I, p. 396.

[1] On 24 Oct. Cardinal Gibbons thanked Newman for his letter, 'though you have reached the evening of life, you are still regarded by us all as a tower of strength.'
[2] Wood wrote on 9 Oct., writing 'Sept' by mistake, and congratulated Newman on the completion of forty years as a Catholic. He then drew Newman's attention to the articles 'Catholics at the English Universities' by R. F. Clarke, S.J. in the *Month*, (July, Aug., Sept. and Oct.)

I see so badly now, that I have not been able to read more than portions of the Month's Articles and what the writer says of Oxford as compared with the London University pleased me.[1] I am in no way able to form a judgment on the Articles as a whole; on the other hand whether a letter is to be written, none can decide with the authority of the President, and if it is to be written — but I do not think you could have a better judge about this than the President.

I read his letter with great interest, and enclose it with this

J H N

TO HENRY BEDFORD

Oct. 12th. 1885.

Dear Professor Bedford,

I was very sorry I missed you in the Summer, and thank you much for the Papers which have just come to me.

Very truly yours, John H. Card. Newman.

TO G. D. BOYLE

Oct. 17. 1885.

My dear Dean Boyle

I thank you for your letter and the inclosure. It was with much pain I saw the announcement of Principal Shairp's death.[2] I had felt a warm gratitude to him for the great kindness of various notices and criticisms he had published about me and was quite unprepared for the sad tidings. I shall ever think of him, as one who has done me great favours.

For your good Bishop's death of course I was quite prepared. I never was intimate with him, but I had known him close upon sixty years[3]

Very truly Yours John H. Card. Newman

The Very Rev. Dean Boyle

which spoke harshly of religion and morals at Oxford. Wood, a convert from Trinity College, Oxford, had been in correspondence with John Percival, the President. He sent Newman a letter of Percival's, and asked him 'to decide whether any notice should be taken of the articles, not on behalf of any plan for Catholics going to Oxford, but simply to vindicate Oxford itself against the attacks upon it.'

[1] In the last of his articles on 'Catholics at the English Universities', the *Month* (Oct. 1885), pp. 153–69, 'Examinations and Residence', Clarke compared the two ancient universities with London greatly to its disadvantage, 'it is a miserable substitute for the older Universities.' It had been generous towards Catholics, 'But the generosity was founded not on liberality, but on Liberalism; not on any love of Catholics, but on a general indifference to religion.' pp. 155–6.
[2] John Campbell Shairp died on 18 Sept. 1885.
[3] Boyle was Dean of Salisbury. George Moberly, Bishop of Salisbury from 1869, died on 6 July 1885. He became a Scholar of Balliol College, Oxford, in 1822, and was a Fellow, 1826–34.

TO J. G. SNEAD-COX

Oct. 17. 1885

(To the Editor of the Tablet)

We have been requested by Cardinal Newman to say that the Collection of his letters lately published in Merry England has been made without his knowledge or his sanction   He utterly disapproves of it.[1]

TO J. G. SNEAD-COX

Oct 20. 1885

To the Editor of the Tablet

Dear Sir

I feel your generosity in writing to me in behalf of Mr Meynell. But it is quite necessary for my own sake that I should insist on being cleared of any partnership in a publication of letters, some of which have an untold history, and none of which was intended to figure in a Collection

Since you have kindly interposed, I must ask you to gain from Mr Meynell some statement for the public eye, by which Americans as well as English purchasers may know that I was told nothing at all about the work till it was out of Mr Meynell's hands. Until I see this, I cannot withdraw my intention of publishing the notice I sent you, though certainly I will not ask you to let it appear in the Tablet.[2]

I am & J H N

[1] See letter of 20 Sept. to Meynell. Cox replied on 19 Oct. expressing willingness to publish Newman's note, but adding, 'At the same time . . . it is only with a deep reluctance that I make myself even the unwilling means of inflicting what I know will be a great pain and disappointment to Mr Meynell. Of all the men whom it has been my lot to know, there is no other who is animated with such consistently warm feelings of kindness and regard for your Eminence· And this public rebuke and "utter disapproval" can only be felt in proportion to the really unending loyalty and goodwill which he has always borne towards you . . . I shall still hope that it may be possible for the disclaimer to be made in some other way less certain to wound.'

Meynell, who on 8 Oct. had sent Newman a copy of Merry England for Oct., wrote again on 19 Oct. that he had published without asking permission 'lest I should seem to seek a sanction it would be difficult to refuse or to grant.' He also said that 'any thing which suggests that I have published private letters, or that I have professed to have your Eminence's sanction for what I did on my own responsibility, does me an injustice which is not so easily parried'.

[2] Cox replied on 21 Oct., 'I have written to Mr Meynell . . . and undertake that all possible publicity shall be given to the explanation you desire.

I am confident that Mr Meynell will willingly write a letter to the Tablet and any American paper yr Eminence may select . . .' See letter of 28 Oct. to Meynell.

TO WALTER L. DAVIS

Oct 20. 1885

Dear Sir

I thank you for your friendly letter.

You are right in supposing that the paragraph in the Globe has no other foundation that the passage in the Apologia[1]

I have had nothing to do with the Collection of my letters in the 'Merry England', which has much displeased me

Your faithful Servant John H. Card. Newman

TO JOHN WICKHAM LEGG

Oct. 20. 1885

Dear Sir

I wish I could aid you in your interesting undertaking, but it is close upon fifty years since I was led to inquire into the history of the Breviary, and my memory is not as strong as it used to be. I am sorry then to be obliged to leave your question unanswered.[2]

Your faithful Servant John H Card. Newman

TO EDWIN TREVELYAN

Oct 24. 1885

Dear Sir

The paragraph you refer to is from beginning to end a growth of the passage in my Apologia at pp 339–342, as you suppose[3]

Yours faithfully John H Card Newman

P S I have sent no 'letter' or 'message' to any one. I still hold by what I said in the Apologia

Edwin Trevelyan Esqr

---

[1] See letter of 24 Oct to Trevelyn.

[2] Legg published an edition of Cardinal Quiñones's Breviary, Cambridge 1888, and helped to found the Henry Bradshaw Society in 1890.

[3] The paragraph alluded to was an extract from the *Bath Chronicle* (22 Oct. 1885), 'At a Meeting last week of the Clerical Defence Institution at Bromsgrove, a letter was read from Cardinal Newman, saying that he regarded the English Church as the great bulwark in this country against Atheism and wishing all success to those defending her, in which he and his friends would join'.

The pages in *Apo.* are 'Note E. The Anglican Church'. See also letter of 21 March 1884 to Trevelyan.

TO C. F. AUDLEY[1]

Oct. 26. 1885.

Dear Sir,

I have had many inquiries such as yours. No. I have sent neither letter or message to any one. I doubt not the mistake has arisen from some one referring to my words in my Apologia pp 329 [339]–342, words which I hold by now. I agree with Cardinal Manning in his late declaration.[2] Excuse my bad writing.

Your faithful Servt John H. Card. Newman

TO ANNE MOZLEY

Oct 26th 1885

My dear Anne Mozley,

I am now getting anxious to know how you are. I have been afraid of writing to you, lest I should be troublesome.

Ask the sister who is with you at Barrow to send me two lines.[3]

Yours affectly John H. Card. Newman

TO MARGARET DE LISLE

Oct. 27. 1885

My dear Miss de Lisle

I read your letter with great satisfaction and thankfulness, God is indeed good to you. I doubt not you will have trials — but He who has given you so brave a heart, will not forsake you, but will bring you on triumphantly. Give me some notion of your movements in prospect, and, please God, I will say some Masses for you I say 'if He enables me'[4] because I am not so strong as I was. You must not forget me in your prayers. I say the same to Revd Mother[5]

Most truly Yours John H Card Newman

[1] A note with the copy says: 'Anonymous but with Mr Audley's two letters of Dec 16/64 Dec 26/64.'

[2] In a sermon preached in his Pro-Cathedral on 18 Oct. 1885 in defence of Christian schools Manning stated that 'it has been the Christian tradition of England from the sixth century down to the present day that has preserved the unity and the national character of England. Down to the year 1870 there was no education that was not Christian'. The *Weekly Register* (24 Oct. 1885), p. 519.

[3] Anne Mozley replied on 27 Oct. using her right hand, that she was going on well.

[4] I *Timothy*, 1:12.

[5] Margaret de Lisle was becoming a Franciscan nun at Mill Hill, under Mary Frances Basil.

October 28. 1885.

Dear Fr Rector

I have just received your very kind letter and thank you for it.[1] Considering my age, I do indeed need the prayers of all who are interested in me, and the prayers of the Passionist Fathers are especially grateful to me.

Sending you my Blessing

I am, Yours sincerely John H. Card. Newman

TO WILFRID MEYNELL

Oct 28. 1885

To Wilfrid Meynell Esq
My dear Sir

I thank you for the Notice relative to this month's Number of Merry England which you have inserted in the Weekly Register of last Saturday[2]

I cannot, however, be quite at peace with Mr John Oldcastle till he suppresses the very offensive caricature which disgraces his pages of my mother and her children[3]

J H N

TO LORD CHARLES THYNNE

Nov. 1. 1885.

My dear Lord Charles,

It is very kind in you to tell me of the singular mercy and love that our Lord is showing to you.[4] If you tell me on what day or days you desire a Mass for your intention, please tell me, it will please me so to say it.

Excuse my bad writing — I am losing the use of my fingers.

Most truly yours, John H. Card. Newman.

[1] Magee, a member of the Passionist Order, wrote from Broadway, Worcs., on 27 Oct. with what 'pleasure and instruction' he had read Newman's letters published in *Merry England*.

[2] The following note appeared in the *Weekly Register* (24 Oct. 1885), p. 526; 'John Oldcastle' was the pseudonym of Wilfrid Meynell, editor of the *Weekly Register*:

'Considering the great interest which must always attach to all that concerns Cardinal Newman, Mr John Oldcastle thinks he will not be held punctilious if he seeks permission to assume the sole responsibility for the arrangement of the October number of *Merry England*. In collecting together, as in a scrap book, some of Cardinal Newman's scattered public letters of the last forty years, for the main feature of what was intended to be an entirely spontaneous tribute to the interest of the occasion, Mr Oldcastle acted without his Eminence's knowledge or approval. And this statement Mr Oldcastle asks us to make, inasmuch as a less transitory interest has been aroused by the volume than was claimed for it, and a bound re-issue of it was first announced under a title which might possibly leave open the way to a misconception of the entirely unauthorized and incomplete character of the publication'.

[3] This was Miss Giberne's family sketch. See letter of 22 Sept. 1884 to Anne Mozley. Newman sent her a message on 26 May 1890, when she was engaged on *Moz.*, 'Please bring in if you can when speaking of family friends that the picture in "John Oldcastle's" book only represents him talking to his sister'.

[4] Lord Charles Thynne's wife had died in 1881, and he was now becoming a priest. He was ordained by Cardinal Manning in Rome in 1886.

TO G. D. BOYLE

Nov. 2. 1885

My dear Dean of Salisbury

It is very kind in you and Miss Weale to send me tidings of Sir William Palmer's death.[1] It took me by surprise, and brought to me the sad feeling, now so frequent, that another contemporary had passed away. I fear his life was not a happy one but I have heard very little about it.

Very truly Yours J. H. Card. Newman

TO J. SPENCER NORTHCOTE

Nov 2 1885

My dear Canon Northcote

I thank you for the pains you have taken so long to get me the little book. I will gladly send several of mine to Mr Caddie, who has been exceedingly civil[2]

Beveridge's book is a very impressive one with very little Protestantism in it. I had given to a Cousin who has long been dead

Very sincerely Yours John H Card. Newman

TO WILLIAM BARRY

The Oratory Nov 4. 1885

Dear Dr Barry

I thank you sincerely for your article about me in the Contemporary of this month. It is in form an answer to Dr Fairbairn, but from its impartiality and fairness it is really a defence of me.[3]

I require and desire no better defence, for it would be a great mistake in me, to suppose that any thing I have written, with whatever care, was not in some way or other open to criticism.

[1] William Palmer (of Worcester College), died towards the end of Oct. 1885. Boyle wrote on 1 Nov., 'Miss Weale, who has lived for many years in the parish of poor Sir W. Palmer, has asked me to forward the enclosed to you.

He expressed a desire that no obituary notice should be written about him, and seemed to wish to pass away unseen and forgotten.

It will awaken memories of old days. Dr Liddon has been here lately and we had a most interesting talk over the life of Dr Pusey which he is busy with now.'

[2] This was a copy of Beveridge's *Private Thoughts on Religion* containing on the fly-leaves an autograph letter of Newman to his cousin Harriett Fourdrinier. The holder of the book had only now kept his promise of returning it to its rightful owner, Mr Caddie. See letter of 25 Nov. 1881 to Northcote.

[3] 'Catholicism and Reason', the *Contemporary Review* (Nov. 1885), pp. 656–75. After explaining that no individual could be taken as in all things the spokesman of the Catholic Church, Barry defended Newman's teaching on reason and on conscience.

There is only one point to which I will call your attention. In an Oxford Sermon, preached in 1839, which Dr Fairbairn confuses with my 'Grammar of Assent' I have expressed a doubt whether the argument from *final causes* is, as facts stand, sufficient to prove the being of God[1] (vid. also 'the idea of a University' p 219) but that is not all one with denying that the *physical universe* was sufficient to prove it. On the contrary, I should maintain that the very fact of the world's existence implies an Almighty, intelligent, personal Creator. And again, the same great truth is proved from what I should call the argument from *design*, that is, from the wonderful order, harmony, unity, and beautifulness of the Universe as dwelt on in the Psalm 'Caeli enarrant'.[2]

I am, Dear Dr Barry Very truly Yours
John H Card Newman

P.S.   Since writing this, Fr Ryder has given me your message.

TO R. W. CHURCH

Nov. 4/85

My dear Dean

Your capital memoir of R.H.F. came right.

I will return as soon as I can — but I have been so busy. I have not had time to report to you its arrival.[3]

J.H.N

Dean Church

[Later in November 1885]

I think you have succeeded wonderfully in your account of R. H. Froude, and marvel how without knowing him you could be so correct.[4]

[Later in 1885]

'Charles Marriott' and 'Hampden' are first rate each in its own way. All are good and done as no one else could do them.[5]

---

[1] 'Faith and Reason, contrasted as habits of mind', *U.S.*, p. 194.

[2] *Psalm* 18:2. In the draft Newman inserted here: 'I should add that, tho' I have done my best to make my Anglican works theologically correct, I have not entirely succeeded.'

[3] Dean Church wrote on 26 Oct: 'You spoke in your last note to me about Hurrell Froude. Last year, I began to put together roughly some of what I could remember of the old days: and among these sketches was one of R H.F. — whom I never knew. But Blachford saw it, and added something of his own. Of course I do not want to trouble you with it — but I think I ought to ask you whether you would like to see it.'

Church had already written on 5 Oct., 'I tried about a year ago to put down what I could call to mind of the early days of the movement. I have not gone on with it, and I do not know that I shall do anything with what I have written. Blachford has seen it, and Anne Mozley; and I have let one or two other people see it. I think I ought to let you know that I have tried something of the kind and found it very difficult.' This was the beginning of Dean Church's *The Oxford Movement*, London 1891.

[4] Dean Church wrote on 16 Nov., 'I am most grateful to you for having read what I wrote, and for taking the trouble to send me notes about it. If ever anything comes of these

93

memoranda in the way of publication you may be sure that I will attend to what you have said. I do not trouble you with any more, because I do not want to take up your time. But you will quite understand that at any time they are at your service.'

Some of these notes were given to the Bodleian Library, and published by Dr R. W. Hunt, with the references to *The Oxford Movement* (1891 edition) in square brackets, in *Bodleian Library Record*, VIII, 1967–72, pp. 136–7:

'pp. 3, 4 [p. 34] 'patient winning considerateness' etc. ⟨Apolog. p. 23⟩. This was added by me to the text ⟨of the Apologia in proof⟩ at the suggestion of Rogers. I make a point of this because his account of Froude is less sunshiny than yours. I think it is always a matter of *conscience* with him ⟨Blachford⟩ (for which, I speak seriously, I reverence him) to be careful to state both sides of a thing or a man.

pp. 6–8 [pp. 36–8?] As to the Remains, Froude had said that the Reformers had set wrong a broken leg, and it must be broken again in order to set it rightly. The Remains and Number 90 were the re-breaking. It is a painful process; perhaps we are cross with the surgeon.

p. 9 [p. 41] I cannot help thinking that his great objection to Milton was his ⟨M's⟩ opinions, political and ecclesiastical.

p. 10 [p. 41] Pusey when writing against Rose was found fault with for speaking of '*Orthodoxism*' and was not acquitted by his critics when he said he meant *dry orthodoxy*. What would Burgon say to this explanation now?

p. 11 [p. 42] As to 'Froude's place in my heart', each Friend has his own place in a man's heart, and no one has another's place. When dear Froude was alive I had a far earlier friend John William Bowden, with whom I was so intimate, that, after his marriage he got into the habit as he told me, ⟨and I know⟩ of addressing his wife as 'Newman' and me as Elizabeth. My love of him, and my love of Froude were incommensurables.

p. 16 [48] You do not say, or perhaps think that I became a Catholic because I could not pronounce the ⟨Roman⟩ Church Antichrist — but I will recall some facts. Golightly went about repeating Baxter's saying 'If Rome is not Antichrist, she has bad luck to be so like it.' I answered 'Since Antichrist is (according to prophecy) to be like Christ, Christ must be necessarily like Antichrist': and I clenched my reply in the British Critic by showing that Baxter's party were as strong in maintaining that the church of England was Antichrist, as Baxter was in the case of the Roman Church. Moreover, though I cannot recollect every thing I have said about the alternative of Christ or Antichrist, so much I am quite sure of, that it was the alternative of the *Via Media* or not on which my conversion turned. I had begun to turn the whole Anglican position into a Via Media, and a Via Media after the pattern of Antiquity and then in July 1839 it flashed upon me that in Primiti[ve] History the Via M. was the seat of semi-ortho[do]xy as Monophytism was the middle point between Rome and Eutychianism. The alternative between Christ and Antichrist did not come into my great question. I will add my judgment that it is a fallacy by no means unfrequent with controversialists, to take for granted the arguments which such as I put out in a polemical work are his *own reasons* for conversion. All that he avouches is that he considers his arguments ⟨in controversy⟩ *good*. This of course does not apply to a work like my Apologia, which expressly professes to give my *personal* reasons; but I don't recollect ⟨that⟩ the *dilemma* of Christ and Antichrist ⟨is⟩ there.

p. 17 It is curious you should compare R.H.F. [Froude] to Pascal. Is not one of Pascal's characteristic features his melancholy? The literary men of Birmingham have fastened the likeness upon me, and, when they paid me the compliment some years ago of asking me to sit for an oil painting they agreed with the artist that he should represent me as *sad*. It was the combination of melancholy with a sense of humour and with wit, that they considered linked me to Pascal, and the artist told me that he had aimed at representing me as mourning for the loss of my friends — but how can Froude's high spirits and his go-a-head remind one of Pascal?

As to Blachford's remarks, they are as able, as interesting and as true as yours but they do not present to me so lovable a picture of R.H.F. as yours vid. what I have said supra ⟨on⟩ pp. 3, 4.

J.H.N.'

As to the portrait of Newman, see letter of 20 Jan. 1875 to an unknown correspondent.

[5] On 25 Nov. Dean Church wrote: 'I will send you some of the papers tomorrow. None of them profess to speak of you, though of course your name is everywhere. But I will send some of the early ones. I got down, in what I wrote, to Number 90. As you will see, they are rough, and doubtless full of mistakes; and I do not at all [know] what will become of them.'

Dear Sir   Nov. 5. 1885

I propose to publish my Article in the Contemporary of last October as a pamphlet next January. I shall give notice on the Title page that it comes from the Contemporary Review. I trust you will consider three months a sufficient interval from the date of its original appearance.[1]

Very truly Yours John H Newman

The Editor of the Contemporary Review

My dear Scratton   Nov 5. 1885

I can congratulate you at least on this, that the suspense and weariness of a lawsuit is over. And the law has so many chances.[2] Who after all has to pay? The cost may be more than what you get[3]

Yours very truly John H Card. Newman

Thos Scratton Esqr

[9 November 1885]

Cardinal N. wishes to express his sense of the kindness ⟨courtesy⟩ of the M of B [Mayor of Birmingham] in this fresh instance of an invitation from him to the Cardinal on a public occasion, and hopes the Mayor will not think him unmindful of it if he pleads his advanced age as his reason for declining it.[4]

My dear Allies,   Nov. 10. 1885.

It is not for want of pains that I have not found your letter.[5] My fear is that it has got into some packet of letters with which it has either nothing or little to do. Letters, which I feel to be personal, I burn, but yours was not really so.

---

[1] See second note to letter of 9 Sept. 1885 to Bunting.

[2] Scratton was engaged in a lawsuit against the Irish bishops and on 3 Nov. had been awarded £300 as compensation for his dismissal from the post of Secretary to the Catholic University, to which Newman had originally appointed him. See letter of 9 Oct. 1881 to Scratton. He wrote on 4 Nov. 1885, 'The conclusion is rather a painful wreck of my whole life, and I don't exactly see how I shall get on for the future.' Newman had suggested to him the dangers of litigation.

[3] Scratton replied on 6 Nov., 'Accept my grateful thanks for your kind congratulations on my being free — at least for a season — from the painful anxiety of a law-suit.' Most of the costs were to be paid by the Irish bishops. Scratton expected his own to be less than £100.

[4] The invitation must have been to the opening of the Art Gallery by the Prince of Wales on 29 Nov.

[5] This was a letter of 9 Sept. 1848 from Allies to Newman of which Allies had no copy. See letter of 29 Feb. 1880 to Allies, and his *A Life's Decision*, London 1880, p. 145.

One thing alone can be fancied — all my goods moved to St Wilfrid's, to Alcester Street, to Edgbaston since it was received, and the move has been from room to room, not from house to house, so that they never have been out of my room. Still there is the shipping and un-shipping three times. However, I have long been going through all my papers, and I will keep your letter in mind.

Yours affectly John H. Card. Newman

TO THOMAS MARTINEAU

Nov 10 [1885]

Dear Mr Mayor

I have just heard to my dismay that in my late answer to your kind invitation I have instead of 'fresh instance' written 'first instance'. I have a copy of it and thus I am able to hope and believe that it is only my bad writing which is the cause of so unlucky and so grave an accident.[1]

Your faithful Servt J H N

TO MRS AUGUSTUS CRAVEN

Nov. 17th [12], 1885.[2]

Dear Mrs. Craven,

Mr. Fullerton tells me that you have consented to write a Memoir of Lady Georgiana. I sincerely rejoice at such good news.

Since I have been a Catholic I have looked upon her with reverence and admiration for her saintly life. A character and mental history such as hers make her a fit representative of those ladies of rank and position in society who, during last half century, have thought it little to become Catholics by halves, and who have devoted their lives and all they were to their Lord's Service.

May I, without taking a liberty, express my feeling that the treatment of a life so full of interest seems naturally to belong to you?

I bid you God's speed in your undertaking, and I add my prayers to the many which are sure to accompany you in the course of it in proportion as it becomes known.[3]

Je suis, chère Madame Craven,

Votre fidèle seviteur John H. Card. Newman[4]

[1] The Mayor replied the same day that Newman's note had the words 'fresh instance'. He added, 'I can hardly regret that a mistaken impression as to what you had written arose in your mind, as it has given me the pleasure of receiving so graceful a correction of the supposed mistake'.

[2] This letter is dated 17 Nov. in the printed sources, but Mrs Craven's reply was written on 13 Nov.

[3] Mrs Craven's *Life of Lady Georgiana Fullerton* was published in Paris 1888, and edited by H. J. Coleridge, London 1888. See letter of 17 April 1888 to Mrs Craven.

[4] The conclusion exists only in French translation. Mrs Craven replied on 13 Nov. from Walmer Castle that she had been very ill and that Newman's letter gave her the encouragement she needed to continue with her task.

Nov 17 [12]. 1885[1]

My dear Mr Fullerton

I rejoice to find that Mrs Craven has undertaken the Memoir of Lady Georgiana. I inclose a note for her — and am sorry my fingers will not write more clearly   I wish you spoke more cheerfully of yourself

Very truly Yours John H Card. Newman

TO THE HON. MRS MAXWELL-SCOTT

Nov. 16. 1885

My dear Mamo

God speed you and your husband. I grieve that you must go, and am John Bull enough not to be sure of the 'Flowers' ascribed to foreign places. But with all my heart I pray that both of you may return full of satisfaction and thankfulness at the success of your expedition[2]

Yours affectly J. H. Card. Newman

TO H. P. LIDDON

Nov. 20. 1885

My dear Canon Liddon

I am sorry to say I recollect nothing of baptizing Mrs Pusey — but I have had so many changes of scene in my life that, excepting my own personal history and what bears upon it, my memory of events is very capricious and uncertain. Yet I can supply some circumstantial evidence in favour of what you surmise.[3]

1. I think Mrs Pusey is very likely to have felt scruples on the question of her baptism. In that last year of her life she had a profound awe of death.

2 Pusey would have certainly (I think) asked me to baptize her, if she was baptized, and the following extracts from my Private Journal show that I baptized *someone*, name not given, on the day you mention, and that just during that week dear Mrs P. was in Oxford.

Entries 1838.

'April 7.   Mrs Pusey returned from Town.
April 14.   Easter Eve. between 5 and 6 baptized —
April 17.   Pusey and family went to Clifton'

3. And now, the more I think of it, I think I certainly *did* baptize her.

Most truly Yours John H Card. Newman

[1] See first note to previous letter.

[2] Mrs Maxwell-Scott wrote on 15 Nov. to say that she and her husband were about to go for the winter to Florida, the 'Country of Flowers'.

[3] Liddon evidently asked about the conditional baptism which Newman gave Mrs Pusey on Holy Saturday, 14 April 1838. See Liddon's *Pusey*, II, pp. 89–91.

TO H. P. LIDDON

Nov. 23. 1885

My dear Canon Liddon

I thought of St Gregory, but I was previously sure that that gift was for the baptism of the little girl who died.[1] I even said 'I am sure he ⟨P.⟩ must have given me a book, if I baptized her ⟨Mrs P.⟩', yet I did not think of the coincidence of dates between St Gregory and my Private Journal. Is not my weak memory more than balanced by the circumstantial evidence? To my mind the 'baptized — at 5 or 6' is almost decisive. And I think I recollect his writing to Bishop Bagot about some baptism.[2]

Very truly Yours John H Card. Newman

TO ANNE MOZLEY

Dec 1. 1885

My dear Anne Mozley

Day goes after day, and I don't write to you. I have so many things to do, and my fingers are stiff. I have left out of my letters to Keble all about my looking towards Rome from the time I told him of it, May 1843[3] The account of Bowden in letters of 1843 is very touching. I think you should let me have my letter to my Aunt, since you can't use it yourself.[4]

I want very much to know how you are — and whether you have regained your strength

Yours affectly John H Card. Newman

TO ANNE MOZLEY

Dec. 3 1885

My dear Anne Mozley

We have this morning had a telegram from Autun with tidings of Maria Giberne's death.[5] It was from an Apoplectic seizure. She had within the week written a clever crique on Emmeline Deane's portrait of me.

I am sorry I misled you. When Fr Neville returned from Barrow, he

---

[1] Pusey presented Newman with a copy of the Benedictine edition of the works of St Gregory the Great, in thanks for the conditional baptism of his wife. The inscription in the first volume and Pusey's letter of thanks on Easter Sunday, gummed into it, speak of the benefit conferred, and Newman's 'gentle tender kindness' the previous day.
[2] On 24 Nov. Liddon thanked Newman for his letter of 23 Nov. 'It is a real help to me to have been able to see my way, through your assistance, to a conclusion'.
[3] On 17 Nov. Newman sent Miss Mozley letters of his to John Keble.
[4] See next letter.
[5] Miss Giberne died on 2 Dec.

reported to me that you had told him[1] you had an interesting letter of mine to my Aunt (found I suppose among her effects) which you were perplexed what to do with — as you could not, as an Anglican, consistently publish it. This is the letter I asked for[2]

I trust you will not overwork yourself

I cannot be sorry at M. Gibernes death. She had had for near 30 years a life of penance, and her friends, who faithfully corresponded with her, were going or gone — her great friend, Lady Georgina Fullerton, lately

Yrs affectly J H Card Newman

TO OSMUND AIRY

Dec 5. 1885

Dear Sir

I am sorry I have not been able till now to answer your letter.

Some of our Fathers will, I believe, send donations to the charitable object which was the occasion of it. For myself, I send you the inclosed cheque, if you will kindly take charge of it[3]

Very faithfully Yours J. H. Card. Newman

TO GERALDINE PENROSE FITZGERALD

Decr 5. 1885

My dear Child

You need not have sent your 5/ but I have a good case of almsgiving for it. I am glad to see a favourable review of you in the Saturday Review[4]

And I truly rejoice in your Mother's improvement. I said Mass for her without delay; the Holy Sacrifice gains benefits for us 'ex opere operato', whatever the personal worth of the celebrant

Yrs affectly J H Card. Newman

---

[1] 'that you had told him' — the words are written twice in the autograph.

[2] Anne Mozley replied on 5 Dec. that the letter was one Newman wrote to his aunt Elizabeth Newman in 1845. Anne Mozley did not know where it was. She continued: 'It brought heavy news to her, but I have always looked upon that letter as an instance of the alleviation that tenderness and affection can bring to any blow. I called upon her on my return from a long absence and she wished to show me the letter "It is very sweet" she said She looked about among portfolios in vain   It was *close* at hand in her work basket and constantly no doubt read over. It was a pleasure to have been in your mind at such a time'. See also *Moz.* II, pp. 491–2 and last note to letter of 9 Oct. 1845 to Mrs John Mozley.

[3] Airy wrote as Chairman of the Committee for providing cheap dinners for the children attending the elementary schools of Birmingham. A 'good and sufficient dinner' was provided at ½d. a head, and those who could not afford this were helped by a charitable fund. Fifteen thousand dinners were provided each week, about half of them free.

[4] This was a review of *Oaks and Birches*, a three volume novel by Miss Fitzgerald, who used the pseudonym 'Naseby'. The *Saturday Review* (28 Nov. 1885), pp. 719–20, described it as 'a really brilliant novel', and ended by saying 'it is an unusually clever book, though it must be read for the characters rather than the story.'

Dec. 5. 1885

Dear Sir

I had a great respect and love for Mr Ellacombe, and, though I had not seen him for so many years I felt that in his death I had lost a friend.[1] And I would gladly take part in a memorial to him, but I am obliged to abstain from a mode of perpetuating his memory, which is most natural, obvious, and even necessary to you and to those who think with you in religion, but which would be inconsistent in me to recognise.

I am sure you will understand me, though you may not agree with me, and am

Dear Sir Your faithful Servant John H Card Newman

The Revd J. L Gibbs

Decr 6. 1885

My dear Fr Stanton

Sister Mary Pia, had been in retreat and had renewed her vows.[2] She was very happy, and took part in the recreation with much gaiety, to use the Bishop's word. Then she wrote a letter to Mr Fullerton, and went either to her work room or to her cell. She was found on the floor with her face downward insensible and bleeding. This was about 4 o'clock. She remained in that state till 7 o'clock next morning, the 2nd, when she died.

Her letter to Mr F. was like any other letter, without any appearance of illness, of weakness and confusion. I think she spoke of some pictures which she was engaged upon and her handwriting was quite as usual.[3]

You kindly ask after my health. I have nothing the matter with me, but I am feeble. My eyesight is failing me, and my organs of speech, and my hearing, and my writing fingers, my knees and my ankles; so that at any time some part of me might give way, or have an accident. I have had several falls — I walk, read, write, speak at a snail's pace, and my mind gets soon confused, especially my memory. Thus I may call myself emphatically in God's hands, unable to move day by day except He wills it.

I pray for all your Fathers the best and fullest blessings of the coming Sacred Season and am,

My dear Fr Stanton Yours affectly
John H Card. Newman

The Rev Fr Stanton

[1] Henry Thomas Ellacombe died on 30 July 1885 aged 95.
[2] Stanton thanked for a telegram from Newman announcing Miss Giberne's death.
[3] Newman had also sent a telegram to Alexander Fullerton, who in return forwarded Miss Giberne's last letter. This had reached him only an hour or so before Newman's telegram.

TO PERCY WILLIAM BUNTING

Decr 10. 1885

My dear Sir

I thank you for your offer, and would gladly avail myself of it, if I intended to continue my remarks on Principal Fairbairn.[1] I do not see the need, and I am too busy, to do so. What I intend to do is to append a few notes to my article in the Contemporary of October, when published as a Pamphlet, which would only fill a page or two. If in the event they grew in bulk, which is not likely, then I must take my chance whether in some future number of the Contemporary you could admit them conveniently[2]

I am, My dear Sir, Yours very faithfully

John H Card. Newman

P. W. Bunting Esqr

TO LORD CHARLES THYNNE

Dec. 10th. 1885.

My dear Lord Charles,

I congratulate you sincerely on the special love which our Lord is showing you in calling you so near to Himself.[3] I said Mass for you, and, if I write but a short letter, it is because I am losing the use of my fingers. How sad is the death of your nephew. I will not forget him in my prayers.

Most sincerely yours, J. H. Card. Newman.

The Lord Charles Thynne.

P.S.   My kindest remembrances to Charlie [Thynne].

[1] Newman published in the *Contemporary Review* for Oct. his defence against Fairbairn's attack. See letter of 9 Sept. to Bunting. Fairbairn replied in the same *Review* (Dec. 1885), pp. 842–61, 'Reason and Religion', reprinted in his *Catholicism: Roman and Anglican*, pp. 205–36.

[2] Early in 1886 Newman reprinted *The Development of Religious Error*, his article of Oct., as a separate pamphlet. At the end of Feb. 1886 he printed but did not publish Notes on Fairbairn's reply of Dec. These Notes 'On Scepticism used as a Preparation for Catholic Belief' Newman sent privately to Fairbairn, Bunting and others. See letters of 4, 9, 16 and 17 Feb. 1886 to Lord Blachford, 1 March 1886 to Hutton and 6 March 1886 to Bunting.
   In 1890 Newman included both his article of Oct., and his 'Notes' in *S.E.*, pp. 69–89 and 90–107. Both are reprinted in *The Theological Papers of John Henry Newman on Faith and Certainty*, pp. 140–57.

[3] See letter of 1 Nov. to Lord Charles Thynne.

Bm Decr 11. 1885

Dear Mr Palgrave

Thank you for your very kind letter and beautiful gift.[1] The only return I can make is to wish you and yours a very happy Christmas.

Most truly yours John H Card. Newman

I congratulate you on your election at Oxford. Excuse a short letter. I cannot write without pain.[2]

TO THE SUPERIOR OF THE VISITATION CONVENT AT AUTUN

[15 December 1885]

I write to you, Reverend Mother, to condole with you and your Community on the loss you have sustained in the death of your dear Sister Mary Pia This at the moment is an extreme trial, especially when we consider the shock which was caused and its suddenness and other circumstance.[3] Bearing this in mind, I have offered the Holy Sacrifice on this morning, the Octave of the Immaculate Conception for you all, feeling a great sympathy for you invoking in your behalf the powerful intercession of the Blessed Virgin, so dear to you and to her

But I trust your 'sorrow will soon be turned into joy'. Heaviness endures for a night, but joy comes in the morning.[4] You have another Sister in heaven to pray for you, and to aid you in your journey to the land of rest and gladness. You have for 25 years given her a shelter and a home, while she was on earth, and she will not be ungrateful to you for your [care], but will do her part in securing you an eternal habitation and home for you in heaven

I cannot close this letter without thanking you for the great care you have taken to inform me without delay of the death of one in whom I was so much interested, and for whom I had so true and deep an interest.

I send you and all the inmates of your Monastery my fullest blessing and am

---

[1] *The Life of Our Saviour: Illustrated by twenty-four Chromolithographs from Italian Paintings, specially prepared for this Work*, published by the National Society in 1885.
[2] Palgrave was in 1885 elected Professor of Poetry at Oxford.
[3] See letter of 6 Dec. to Stanton.
[4] *John* 16:20; *Psalm* 30:5.

TO MARGARET DE LISLE

Decr 16. 1885

Dear Miss de Lisle

Thank you for your letter. How can I doubt that your Father and other dear ones who have been taken hence, have a share in the mercy which has been shown you. Did I say this before? I ought to have[1]

With my best Christmas Blessing, also on Rev Mother and the community,

I am, Most truly Yours John H Card. Newman

TO JOHN HENRY METCALFE

Birmingham Decr 16. 1885

Dear Sir

I lose no time in answering your letter, and parcel, hoping you will excuse my delay in opening it. I thank you for your kindness in sending me so acceptable a present. The arms are what I received; the motto I took, as necessary, on the spur of the moment.[2]

Thank you also for your interesting letter and the photogram.

Excuse the bad writing of an old man.

With my best Christmas greetings and wishing you all blessings

I am, dear Sir Very truly Yours
John H Card. Newman

J. H. Metcalfe Esqr

TO AN UNKNOWN CORRESPONDENT

Dec 16. 1885

Dear Sir

Any Saint's life and works must be interesting and useful. I wish I could give you advice, I trust God will finish and carry you through it. I gladly give you my blessing

Very truly yours John H. Card. Newman

TO J. R. BLOXAM

Decr 20. 1885

My dear Bloxam

All best Christmas blessings to you

Beware of any who come to you, asking questions about me[3]

Yrs affectly John H Card Newman

[1] This refers to Miss de Lisle's vocation as a Franciscan nun.
[2] See letter of 25 April 1879 to A. W. Hutton. Metcalfe sent a copy in colour of Newman's arms, with his motto underneath, which is still in Newman's room.
[3] Bloxam, who had written to Neville on 17 Dec. that he was trying to obtain 'John

TO LADY SIMEON

Decr 21. 1885

My dear Lady Simeon

I wish you and Queenie [Catherine Simeon] all the blessings of this sacred Season but I have nothing to write about. In a few weeks I suppose I shall make a pamphlet of an Article which I published some months back in the Contemporary Review, in defence of myself against criticisms of Principal Fairbairn. I printed some copies for friends at the same time, but did not send you a copy, as it was not one which you would care to see, though I thought of you.[1]

I have lost the use of my fingers, or I would write more. Certainly I am losing strength.

Yours affectly John H. Card. Newman.

The Honble Lady Simeon

TO R. BOSWORTH SMITH

[22 December 1885

Thank you for your pamphlet with the accompanying letter.[2] It is bold and powerful, with certain grave drawbacks. I agree with you in its main principles; but I grieve for Gladstone with a tenderness which I do not recognize in you. (He has never prospered in any true sense of the word, since in 1874 he attacked wantonly the Holy Roman Church and the Holy See, in the person of Pius ix.) I grieved deeply when, after giving out (as I understood him) that he was retiring from political life or at least from all conflicts, he re-appeared on the public stage. Of course he had reason of which I can know nothing.

As to the Church of England, I have no wishes just now for its destruction. I should rejoice to fancy the possibility of its reconciling itself to that Holy Catholic Church, whose boast it is that it concedes nothing; but I should not wish to purchase even the power and popularity of the Anglican Church at the

Oldcastle's' 'Life and Letters of Cardinal Newman, with notes on the Oxford Movement,' replied on 22 Dec., 'No one has applied to me for any information respecting you, and I should consider any such application an impertinence, unless, what is not likely, it came sanctioned by you — and then I could give nothing but what has already appeared in print; *not* private and sacred communications.'

Anne Mozley wrote on 23 Dec. to Newman: 'I have no doubt you have written to Dr Bloxam about the person called Meynell of whom I am not likely to hear.

Dr Bloxam would need your warning as he might be liable to fall a prey to any body expressing admiration and regard for your name.

The feeling must be very unpleasant of people prowling about to get information of ones past history, though your past is pretty well before the world already'.

[1] See letter of 9 Sept. 1885 to Bunting.

[2] On 21 Dec. Bosworth Smith wrote to Newman enclosing a copy of his pamphlet *The Reasons of a Layman and a Liberal for opposing Disestablishment. Three Letters to the 'Times' and one to Mr. Gladstone,* London 1885. At the General Election in Nov. 1885 the radicals in the Liberal party were campaigning for the disestablishment of the Church of England. Gladstone contented himself with saying that the question was not at that time 'mature'.

price of surrendering one jot or tittle of Catholic Roman teaching The Bishop of Durham[1] with you speaks of the Disestablishment of the Ch of E as a great national sin. No — that sin was committed three centuries ago, when the State sent the true Church the right about and installed the Anglican in her place.

J H N

TO EMILY BOWLES

Christmas Eve 1885

My dear Child

Thank you for your long letter. I rejoice to find that Frederic [Bowles] is such a support to you, and you to him. You have indeed had severe trials this year past. Christmas Day was the death day of my last sister, on the year ⟨1879⟩ I returned from Rome. I will not forget your wish

I am much weaker than this time year, but, as far as I know have nothing the matter with me. The two last Christmases I have had most kind and gratifying messages from the Holy Father.

I send you and your brother my blessing, as Christmas calls for it

Yours affectly John H Card. Newman

TO LADY SIMEON

Christmas Eve 1885.

My dear Lady Simeon

I will gladly send you my Pamphlet – but it will be some time before it is out.[2]

Yours affectly John H. Card Newman

TO THE MISSES BOWDEN

Christmas 1885

My Blessing
on you and on your Sisters

J. H. Card. Newman

TO JOHN O'HAGAN

Dec. 27. 1885

My dear John O'Hagan

It is a great comfort amid the sad events of life, and so many dying off, to have such a letter as yours. I can't help saying so, tho' you don't ask an answer from me.

---

[1] J. B. Lightfoot.
[2] See letter of 10 Dec. to Bunting.

I thank you and your wife with all my heart, and send you my Christmas blessing, and am Ever affectly Yours

John H Card. Newman

TO LORD BLACHFORD

Dec. 28. 1885.

My dear Blachford

I send you and Lady Blachford the best wishes of this sacred season, tho' the prospect of a New Year, always awful, is now almost painful. All we can do, is what you are able to do more than I, is to look forward hopefully as if things will turn out better than they promise. But when was a demos other than a tyrant? and what means the infatuation of educated men, who understanding that autocrats, kings, republics, and other forms of power all require a drag or regulator, think that a Demos can do without one?

I am deeply grieved to think that Gladstone is the author of this revolution. What a sad ending of a great career![1]

Of course you have seen Denison's pamphlet. Could he have any warrant or justification for making Mrs G. say what she says in her invective?[2]

My fingers re-act strangely on my brain — and because they are slow and perverse, so I mis-spell and omit my words or repeat them.

Yours affly J. H. Card. Newman.

TO ALEXANDER WHYTE

Decr 31. 1885

My dear Dr Whyte

I am very glad that you give me the opportunity, (as you do by your gift of Mr Macintosh's volume,)[3] of wishing you a happy new year, which I do with all my heart

Your recommendation will go very far in making me take an interest in it — but you must recollect my age. I read and write very slowly, and the day is

[1] The first general election after the third Reform Act of June 1885 had just been held. Gladstone was about to split the liberal party over Home Rule.

[2] George Anthony Denison, *Mr. Gladstone, with Appendix containing the accumulated evidence of Fifty-five Years, a Retrospect and a Prospect*, second edition, London 1885. Newman's copy is inscribed 'H.E. The Cardinal Newman from George Anthony Denison Decr. 22. 1885'. On p. 39 it was stated that Mrs Gladstone had recently said, 'Oh, William knows he is the only man who can govern England'.
On 29 Dec. Lord Blachford replied, 'I have not seen G. Denison's pamphlet. I feel great difficulty in taking any thing from him as really quite serious.'

[3] Whyte sent Robert Mackintosh's *Christ and the Jewish Law*, London 1886, explaining that it was by a young friend of his.

ended, ere it has well begun. And, though I do so little, I am soon tired, and am always ready for the indulgence of a sound sleep.

I hope you will allow it, if I send to you and to all who are dear to you my Christmas blessing

Most truly Yours, J H Card Newman

TO MR BOYD

[End of 1885?]

Cardinal Newman understands how painful must be the doubt which led to 'Mr B.''s writing; and how very serious is the step which has been the consequence of that doubt

He feels, however, he has no office or position justifying his interference in a matter which for various reasons specially belongs to the confessional.[1]

TO JOHN HARDMAN, JUNIOR

[End of 1885?]

Dear Mr Hardman

Will you kindly place the inclosed cheque to the credit of the Fund for the Cath. Poor Law Schools, as a donation from me to the Charity.

TO MISS PANTON

[End of 1885?]

Cardinal Newman is very sorry that Miss Panton has been put to trouble. He has no recollection whatever of having received a card from her, but he receives so many letters and his memory is so tried by them, that he cannot say more or less than he has above said

TO AN UNKNOWN CORRESPONDENT

[End of 1885?]

My dear Sir

I fear I can say nothing satisfactory to you on your deeply anxious question, because I do not know you. The answer to it depends on the particular case, upon the person who is the subject of it. I should advise one man one way, another the other.

[1] Newman erased the rest of his draft: 'As to Mr Boyd's reference to "intention" the Cardinal cannot do better than transcribe St Alfonso's words (Homo Apost. t 3 App. 3. n 18) "Praeter actionem (Hom. Apost. two Tract 14. n. 2.) "Minister"'
Both these passages speak of the 'intention' required in the administration of Sacraments.

What is certain is that you ought to act on a conviction of the divinity of the Catholic Roman Church, if you are to join it — by conviction, I mean on the ground you are sure on good reasons that it comes from God. The time it takes thus to be sure varies with the individual. A miracle, our Lord's actual voice, would be a warrant for a prompt assent; an argumentative inference may take years to ripen into certitude St Paul was converted suddenly — St Jerome and other Fathers after long consideration. The unlearned may be helped on slowly or quickly by aids not given to those who have greater natural opportunities.

Again individual minds differ. Some are more likely to waver in their convictions than others. Some are so clear as to their duty that to put off reception would be acting against grace and provoke [?] a withdrawal of it. In consequence one man requires a longer probation than another, and without knowledge of the person in question it is impossible to decide whether he should be received at once or to wait.

I say all this, in order that you may see why I cannot much as I wish it decide for you. Of course I *wish* your conversion *now*; but as to what your duty is, I can only say that in some cases I should agree with a father who urged his son to put off his reception, and in another case I should not

JHN

TO AN UNKNOWN CORRESPONDENT

[End of 1885 ?][1]

Dear Sir,

You must excuse a short letter, as I have lost the power of using my fingers in writing. I understand you to wish me to tell you the strongest book I know in exposition: first of the *idea* of the Catholic Church, and, next, of the position and aspect of the Anglican Communion relatively to that idea. Now, I am obliged to confess that I am the worst person you could have come to for an answer to your question. No one can have read less of Catholic English history than I have. Of course, I feel this to be a great loss and disadvantage, but not without some excuse, for I have so little leisure and so many interruptions. My second remark is that your question opens too large a field to be traversed in one book. But if I must name one which is most likely to meet your requirement, it would be Mr. Allies's *Per Crucem ad Lucem*,[2] an argument in two volumes going into details. As I have written so much on the subject myself, I naturally asked myself whether I could refer to any of my own volumes, which would be useful to you. But I have written nothing professedly on the Church, though many incidental trains of thought here and

---

[1] This letter, printed in the *Weekly Register* (16 Aug. 1890), p. 212, was there said to have been 'written by Cardinal Newman a short time back to a Birmingham gentleman'.
[2] London 1879.

there to your purpose occur, and though I do not recollect what I have written. The argument which I rely upon most is, 'The Church is more than a family,' as Anglicans make it, 'but a state or kingdom' which has jurisdiction, which a mere patriarchal body has not. An apostolical succession does not constitute a *state*, which is the Scriptural 'idea' of the Church. I have touched upon it in *Essays* (Longmans), volume 1, p. 220, volume 2, pp. 90–100.[1] But what is I think to your purpose is in my *Difficulties of Anglicanism*, volume 1, part 1. Lectures 1–6, pp. 1–127.[2] As I have an odd copy, if you will let me I will ask your acceptance of it.

Your faithful servant, John H. (Card.) Newman.

P.S.   Since writing the above I have thought of Dr. Bagshaw's *Credentials of the Catholic Church* (Washbourne, Paternoster Row).[3] It is spoken well of on all sides. The only doubt I have as to its answering your purpose is that so much of it is *à priori* reasoning. It is an octavo or duodecimo of three hundred pages.

TO GEORGE T. EDWARDS

Jany 1 1886

Dear Mr Edwards

I wish you a happy New Year, in the best sense of the words and it is the obvious and only return I can make for your kindness. I cannot send you a letter so interesting as that which has just come to me, both because I remain here without occurrences and because, if I had them, my fingers would not without pain and effort enable me to record them[4]

What every serious mind is occupied with is, I suppose, what you touch upon, the state of public affairs There are so many grave questions which require an answer — but the fortunes of the Church of England is the subject which tries me most. How great the temptation is to buy off the enemies of its temporal establishment by the sacrifice of what remains to it of true doctrine! But here is it that the ways of Providence are inscrutable, and what seems worst for religion may turn out to be 'Via prima salutis quod minime reris'.[5] But I must not occupy your time longer

Very sincerely Yours John H Card Newman

G T Edwards Esqr

[1] The references are to the fifth, 1881, and later editions. Longman took over *Ess.* I and II in 1885.
[2] The sixth lecture in *Diff.* I ends at p. 196 and Part I at p. 227.
[3] London 1879.
[4] Edwards wrote on 31 Dec. and described among other things meeting Cardinal Manning in London.
[5] *Aeneid* VI, 96–7.

TO LOUISA ELIZABETH DEANE

January 11. 1886

My dear Louisa,

I have felt how good you were in writing to me — but my fingers are too stiff to be able to answer you. God be with you. I hope your husband does not feel this severe weather. Do you recollect Maria Giberne? How very few remain whose names are associated with hers. She died lately.

I think I cannot mistake in fancying I have lost ground this last year.

My kindest remembrances to your family circle

Yours affectly John H Card. Newman[1]

TO FRANCIS WOODGATE MOZLEY

Jany 11 1886

My dear Frank

I shall be glad to see you any day you name, except from 1.30 and 2.30 when I dine

Yrs affly J H Card. Newman

TO CHARLES LINDLEY WOOD, VISCOUNT HALIFAX

Jany 15. 1886

My dear Lord Halifax

Ever since your first present of game came (now I have to thank you for two) I have much desired to write to you, but besides greater difficulties of my being so old, my fingers will not write without something like pain

I did not see at the time in the Papers the great loss you had sustained, and, if I may say so, without taking a liberty, I really felt it personally.[2] Your dear Father was always connected in my mind with the Oxford Examination Schools, and my own anxieties, hopes and fears, when the time of my own trial was coming on. I was in the Schools, on the crowded benches, when he was under examination, and I think there was a general satisfaction on his success without men knowing him[3]

One looks back with a sad pleasure on the days of youth, when one is receding from them, and though I never can be said to have known your

---

[1] When Mrs Deane replied she asked for a copy of *Callista*, a copy of which Newman had already given to her daughter Emmeline.

[2] The first Viscount Halifax died on 8 Aug. 1885.

[3] Lord Halifax, then Charles Wood, was at Oriel College and took a double First in 1821. His son replied on 20 Jan., 'My dear Father never spoke of your Eminence's name, which he often did [,] without the greatest interest, and appreciation.'

Father personally, there have been several accidental circumstances which have kept him in my memory, chiefly my great love for your Uncle.[1]

It is not ever too late to send a blessing   I send you one now, tho' Christmas is gone

My dear Lord Halifax Most truly Yours J H Card Newman[2]

TO THE EDITOR OF THE PALL MALL GAZETTE

Jany 16. 1886

Cardinal Newman is sensible of the compliment paid him by the Editor of the Pall Mall Gazette in asking of him a list of classical English Authors, but he is obliged to decline it, as feeling that he is not equal to the work.[3]

TO HENRIETTA WOODGATE

Jany 23. 1886

My dear Child

I am very glad to have a letter from you and to hear about you all — though I am sorry to say I am losing the use of my fingers and cannot write more than these few lines. I was glad to hear about you from the two Bellasises, who were pleased to meet ladies who knew me. With all kind thoughts of your Mother and Sisters

I am ever affectionately Yours
John H Card. Newman

TO WILLIAM CLIFFORD, BISHOP OF CLIFTON

Jany 25. 1886

My dear Lord

It was very kind of you to write to me — he was a most saintly man.[4] I have known him for 50 years, and was shocked to hear the news of his death. And there are so many deaths of my contemporaries younger than me, that it is a 'memento, homo, quia pulvis es etc'.[5]

[1] S. F. Wood.

[2] Lord Halifax replied on 20 Jan., 'there is no name that has ever been more to me, ever since I can remember — and as years have gone on — it has only seemed to grow greater, than that of Cardinal Newman — Your Eminence will forgive me for saying so much — for indeed it comes from my heart. We can never repay Your Eminence for all you have done for England, or be sufficiently grateful for having been permitted to see an ideal which has never disappointed those who have had the great happiness and blessing of coming under its influence.'

[3] The acting editor of the *Pall Mall Gazette* wrote on 13 Jan. asking Newman to join its 'Best hundred books' symposium. Sir John Lubbock had recommended those 'necessary for a Liberal Education'.

[4] Archbishop Errington died on 19 Jan. Bishop Clifford wrote on 22 Jan., 'He always had a great veneration for your Eminence and I know you highly valued his stirling [sic] qualities'.

[5] *Genesis* 3:19.

A great gain for him, but what a loss, especially for *you*. Of course I said Mass for him at once — and I hope to do so tomorrow. I am losing my power of writing.

Your affectionate Servant in J Xt   John H. Card. Newman

The Rt Rev The Bp of Clifton

TO WILLIAM PHILIP GORDON

Jan 31. 1886

My dear Father Philip

A good lay brother is a rare acquisition and a great loss. I said Mass for him this morning. We shall give him three Masses apiece[1]

Yours affectly John H Card. Newman

P.S.   I have addressed you, not knowing whether or not you were now Superior[2]

TO LADY HERBERT OF LEA

The Oratory Febr 1. 1886

My dear Lady Herbert

I am very glad to have the Life of the great Bishop and in your sending it to me I have an additional instance of your kindness to me.[3] Excuse my bad writing I am losing the use of my fingers, at least so far

Most truly your Servant in J.X.

John H Card. Newman.

TO MRS CORNISH

Birmingham, Feby. 2. 1886

Dear Mrs Cornish,

It is a very kind thought in you to send me Mr Copeland's letter to your dear husband, my intimate friend and much loved Charles Cornish.[4] I have always felt it sad that it was not given to me to see again the latter as I saw

---

[1] Brother Philip Ryan died 28 Jan. He had attended on Newman when he stayed at the London Oratory in June 1881. See letter of 17 July 1881 to Stanton.

[2] Gordon remained Superior until 1889.

[3] F. Lagrange *Life of Monseigneur Dupanloup, Bishop of Orleans*, translated from the French by Lady Herbert, two volumes, London 1885.

[4] Mrs Cornish's son, also Charles Cornish, sent Newman at her request a letter from Copeland to Charles Cornish, who died in 1870.

Copeland. I return the letter so full of interest. I am obliged to be short, as my fingers are stiff   I send you my blessing

Yours most truly, John H. Card. Newman.

I mention Charles Cornish's name in my daily prayers.[1]

Dictated letter   The Oratory, Birmm Febr 4, 1886
My dear Blachford,

I begin with hoping that you will let me *dictate* a letter which I call *Private*. I think you can advise me.

In the May and December Numbers of the Contemporary Dr Fairbairn has two severe articles to the effect that I became a Catholic as a refuge from scepticism. In October I published an answer to the May Article in the same Review, and my question is shall I also answer his second (December) Article.

I have written an answer and it is ready for the press, with the purpose of appearing in the Contemporary next month (March).[2]

At the last moment to [I] soliloquise as follows, — 'You are acting unworthily of your age and your station. You have made your protest in October; that is enough. If you write again you will be entering into controversy. You yourself know better than any man else that your submission to Rome was not made at all as a remedy against a personal, nay, or against a controversial scepticism. It is only a matter of time for this to come out clear to all men.'[3]

I feel this deeply, it would require a very brilliant knock down answer to Dr F. to justify my giving up my place 'as an emeritus miles' and going down into the arena with a younger man. The only shade of reason for my publishing it is that I wished to say in print that in past years I had spoken too strongly once or twice against the argument from final causes.[4]

I would send you the Article (which I have printed for my own purpose);

[1] On 20 Feb. Mrs Cornish replied, 'I so much wish I could tell you about him, and how his love and trust and value for you never failed'.

[2] See letter of 10 Dec. to Percy William Bunting.

[3] Lord Blachford replied on 5 Feb., 'I am quite distinctly of opinion . . . that any more argument on your part would seem fussy — as if you had more solicitude about the matter than it deserved . . .'

[4] Blachford replied, 'As to the argument about final causes — no doubt what you say has weight. But three lines would set you right there — three lines implying that this modification of your old views was the only matter that you cared to notice in Professor F's. rejoinder.

I am glad you think more highly than it was the old Oxford fashion to think about the argument from final causes. It is to me quite overwhelming from its combination of breadth and minuteness — of course it does not prove *perfection* of power or wisdom or goodness, (if indeed it does not tend the other way) but it lands you so firmly on the threshold of religion.

Am I right in remembering that in one of our after-chapel walks under the wall of Merton Gardens I said that if I were to choose a heresy I would be a Manichee — while you inclined to some thing in the nature of an *anima mundi*?' See letter of 6 Feb. to Blachford.

it makes about seven pages of the Contemporary, if you wish to see it. There is nothing in it of doctrine. Only every day is valuable if it is to come out in March.

Yours affectionately J. H. Card. Newman

Lord Blachford

TO LORD BLACHFORD

The Oratory Birmm Febr 6. 1886

My dear Blachford

Your prompt answer has just come. I don't forget your eyes or that you may have to trouble Lady Blachford.[1]

Principal Fairbairn is a great man among the Congregationalists and is said to be the prospective head of their new College at Oxford.[2] At the beginning of my first (October) Article I said *the* reason of my answering him was for the sake of my friends, who would wish to know how I viewed his criticisms. Catholics are very sensitive about giving scandal, and what I wrote was not a refutation of him, but an explanation in addition to what I published years ago in the Apologia. His line of argument was that I did not know myself, but that he, as a by-stander knew me better. This assumption I did not notice but employed myself in filling up the lacunæ as I called them of what I had already written. Hence I entitled the paper 'The Development of Religious Error' in illustration of the latter part, the 6th, of the Apologia I aimed at showing as an instance that to relinquish the doctrine of future punishment was to unravel the web of Revelation.

This involved my notion of the word Reason and gave rise in his second (December) Article to his arguing that my definition of Reason was utterly sceptical as disconnecting Reason with Truth. To refute this charge about my sense of Reason is the main subject of my second Article which I am now sending to you.

I should add that in a Postscript to my first Article I made fun of Dr Fairbairn saying that my view of Reason was 'impious.[3]'

I am afraid I do not retire from what I said about final causes so much as I led you to think.

I have omitted to say that if I did not insert the Article in slips which I send you, I should leave it for my Executors to do what they will with it.[4] This

---

[1] At the end of his letter of 5 Feb. Lord Blachford suggested that Newman should send him his proposed article.

[2] Fairbairn, who was Principal of the Congregationalist Airedale Theological College, Bradford, became the first Principal of Mansfield College, Oxford, in 1886.

[3] This postscript at the end of the article in the *Contemporary Review* (Oct. 1885), pp. 466–9, although included in the pamphlet reprints, is omitted from *S.E.* It is published here for the first time in Appendix I.

[4] It was printed in *S.E.*, pp. 90–107. It is also in *The Theological Papers of John Henry Newman on Faith and Certainty*, pp. 149–57. Final causes are the last point considered.

is an additional reason for feeling indifferent about its being published now. I say this to show what reason I have to be indifferent whether it appears in the Contemporary or not.

Yours affly John H. Card Newman

Lord Blachford

P.S.   I have sent you a great deal to read. Begin with the slips, I think they will be enough for your purpose.[1]

TO ANNE MOZLEY

Feb 8. 1886

Dear Anne Mozley

You had better keep the private books till you feel sure you shall not want them more. If it is a gain to you to consult Dean Church on the use you are making of any passages in them, do so. I don't know why I should be unwilling that he should see any part of them[2]

Mrs Borlase has returned two books of Keble's and other letters of the date of 1836. You ought to see them but I will not send them to you, till you tell me

Yrs affectly J H Card Newman

TO LORD BLACHFORD

Febr. 9. 1886.

My dear Blachford

Many thanks for your pains and promptness. I go by your judgment absolutely, and I *agree* with it. Sir J. S's view is quite coincident with my own, as are also your comments upon it.[3] Also I fully feel this, viz. that Dr Fairbairn's Article is simply puzzleheaded, that it does not require answering.

The only point I feel is the chance of scandals i.e. putting myself out of line with Catholic thought. A very clever and learned theologian, has just

---

[1] Lord Blachford replied on 8 Feb., in a letter dated 9 Feb., that after reading Newman's articles, he still held his 'first-sight opinion'. He could not judge about scandal to Catholics. 'You must take me as representing the general public.'

[2] Anne Mozley wrote on 18 Jan. 1886, 'I rely on the Dean's advice to guide me in the "Movement" on many points.'

R. W. Church was also in communication with Newman about his book *The Oxford Movement*. On 3 Feb. he wrote to Newman, 'I ought to have acknowledged the registered packet which arrived safely'.

[3] Lord Blachford wrote on 8 Feb., 'Old Sir James Stephen used to say that when, in any controversy, you had read what special pleaders call (1) the declaration (2) the answer and (3) the reply you had got at all that you were likely to know . . .' Lord Blachford added, 'it appears to me that having once established your case to your satisfaction, you rather injure your position by shewing any solicitude to have the last word'.

been defending me with great eulogy in the Contemporary against Dr Fairbairn, acknowledging at the same time that I sometimes say startling things. It is not very long since he wrote an unfavourable critique upon something I said, and from his reputation I think he will do me a great deal of good.[1]

His writing a panegyric on me in the Contemporary *removes any necessity of my answering Dr Fairbairn in that publication*, but the question of pleasing Catholics remains. Certainly, I am *not* dreaming of asking you about a question of 'scandal' — but the question I am going to propose to you remains.

I am not going to extort an answer from you, or to evade your decision. Nor did what I am going to suggest to you come into my head when I wrote to you, or till an hour ago — and now I want your straight forward answer, and if you answer in the negative I shall take it without haggling

In October when my Article appeared, I wrote to the Editor to say that I proposed to keep the copyright and to publish it in the shape of a pamphlet at the end of three months (January 1.)[2] He answered quite accepting it — and in the shape you saw it I had 500 copies struck off. They are not yet published, being delayed by my bother about answering Dr F's second Article of December. Meanwhile, when the Editor asked whether he should reserve a place in his Review for an answer from me to Dr F. I told him I did not see my way to accept his offer. And, I contemplated answering Dr Fairbairn in longish Notes appended to the pamphlet as you read it.

That plan of Notes at length I gave up, and resolved on writing an Article in the Contemporary for March, as you saw it in *slips*, and now my question whether your judgment (and *my* judgment) against an *Article* will lie against *Notes*, embodying the *Slips* and as appendages to the Pamphlet which was to have been, and is still to be issued.

(Lest it should perplex you, the Slips are printed by *my* printer, not the Contemporary's)

Ever Yrs affly J. H. Card. Newman.

TO LORD BLACHFORD

February 16th. 1886.

My dear Blachford,

Thank you for all your trouble which I trust has not been fruitless. I have cut up my slips into Notes and am appending them to the Article which has appeared in the Contemporary.

But I am *publishing nothing*. I am leaving it all for my executors to do what

---

[1] See letter of 4 Nov. 1885 to William Barry, who had criticised Newman's views on Inspiration. See first letter of 14 June 1882 to Bittleston.
[2] See letter of 5 Nov. 1885 to William Percy Bunting.

they will with unless something extraordinary should occur sooner, to call for what I have written. Anyhow there shall be no arena in any Review as if I were a Gladiator. In thus speaking I must not be supposed to speak disrespectfully of the Editor of the Contemporary, from whom I have received great civility.

Is not to-day your Mother's Anniversary? I always so consider it, thinking of her with great respect and kind remembrance.[1]

Yours affectionately, John H. Card: Newman.

TO LORD BLACHFORD

Febr. 17. 1886

My dear Blachford

I beg to teaze you with one more question.

Do you see anything objectionable in my writing on a copy of my *Notes* *'not published'* and sending it from me to Fairbairn.

It would enable me to send them to certain friends for whose sake I wrote them, without seeming cowardly and underhand.

Yours affly J. H. Card. Newman

P.S. It would not throw me back into the 'arena', which I certainly *won't* be.[2]

TO P. J. RYAN, ARCHBISHOP OF PHILADELPHIA

Febr. 17. 1886

My dear Lord Archbishop

It is a great gratification to me to receive from your Grace so kind a letter.[3]

I inclose what your friend asks for. I wish it were better written, but I am losing the use of my fingers

Begging your good prayers for an old man, I am

Your Grace's faithful Servant John H Card. Newman

The Most Rev The Archbp of Philadelphia

---

[1] Lord Blachford's mother died on 16 Feb. 1872.

[2] Lord Blachford replied on 19 Feb., 'The only objection that I see to sending your slips to Dr Fairbairn, is that he may make garbled extracts from them.' Newman sent Fairbairn his answer to the latter's second article. See letter of 12 March to Lord Blachford.

[3] Archbishop Ryan wrote on 4 Feb. asking for Newman's autograph for a lady whose letter he enclosed.

Febr. 18. 1886.

My dear Louisa,

I wish you to accept from me the work of a friend of mine, taken from the Roman catacombs. If the post brings nothing to the contrary, I shall take for granted you are at home, and send it to you.[1]

Yours affectly John H. Card. Newman.

TO J. SPENCER NORTHCOTE

Feb 18. 1886

My dear Provost Northcote

I thank you for the copy you have sent me, and Canon Brownlow, of Palmer's Catacombs. They make a splendid volume. I purpose to send them to Archdeacon P.[2]

Most truly yours John H. Card. Newman

I am losing the writing power of my fingers

TO ROBERT J. BLAKE[3]

Febr. 21 [1886]

My dear Robert

Thank you for your very kind remembrance; and for the Newspaper, which was very welcome.

If any thing brings you this way, don't forget to call on us

Yours affectly John H. Card. Newman

TO THOMAS WILLIAM MORTON, S.J.

Feb 24 1886

My dear Fr Morton

I thank God for sending to me your wonderfully kind letter.[4] I am losing the use of my fingers and can write very little.

---

[1] Louisa Deane wrote on 1 March to thank for W. Palmer's *Early Christian Symbolism*, edited by J. S. Northcote and W. R. Brownlow, London 1885.

[2] Archdeacon Edwin Palmer wrote his thanks on 19 Feb.

[3] This the most probable attribution of the note.

[4] Morton, son of Thomas Naylor Morton who was received into the Catholic Church by Newman on 7 Sept. 1853, see letter of that day to St John, wrote on 20 Feb. from Stonyhurst to congratulate Newman on his birthday: 'It is gratitude which forces me to write.

Thirty two years ago my father, a Protestant clergyman at Devizes, was in doubt and difficulties. . . . He sought you out at the Oratory for light and guidance. He found you and

My vision in memory is Ham. It is (opposite to Twickenham) where I lived as a little child, and which I dreamed about when a school boy as if it was Paradise. It in *great measure* is the original of the Chapter in 'The Office etc.' Mozley is very incorrect – Jennings is no authority.[1] I could fill a small volume with my recollections of Ham.[2]

Many, many thanks for the prayers you have got for me.

Most truly Yours John H. Card. Newman[3]

TO GEORGE T. EDWARDS

Febr. 25. 1886

My dear Mr Edwards

One trouble of old age has come on me a growing difficulty of writing from feebleness of fingers. This I mention, if my answer to you is not duly responsive to your kindness, but this feebleness of fingers affects my brain, so that I cannot say what with all my heart I want to say. I recollect Southhouse — and am thankful and surprised to find I had an opportunity so rare at Oxford of saying a religious word to an undergraduate. And I know that before I became Tutor I resolved with God's help to resign the office if I could not make it a pastoral one, and that for this reason I did in the event actually resign it. If you see Southhouse say everything kind from me to him.[4]

As to Mr Braithwaite I am not surprised, alas, at his lapse. He seemed to me to have no *root* of religion in him.[5] It is a common spiritual malady just

God vouchsafed that you should lead him to the Faith. Since then he has continued an excellent Catholic and has been blessed in having his eldest daughter a nun at Handsworth, hard by the place of his conversion, and myself his eldest son, a member of the Society of Jesus. As I grew up he instilled in me a grateful love of you . . .

From the time that I first read your "Lectures on the Present Position of Catholics in England", which was the first of your works I was capable of understanding, your writings have furnished me with an inexhaustible source of genuine pleasure . . .

During my noviceship at Roehampton it was my delight to visit the places associated with your early years — Ealing and Norwood and Twickenham and Bloomsbury Square where I had read you spent the days of your boyhood. Over and over again, but always in vain, have I tried to identify the scene of the chapter on "Discipline and Influence" in the "Office and Works of Universities", until at last I have almost become persuaded that it must be fictitious.' *H.S.*, III, pp. 60–3.

[1] In his 'thirst for knowledge' of Newman, Morton had read T. Mozley's *Reminiscences chiefly of Oriel College and the Oxford Movement*, and *Cardinal Newman* by H. J. Jennings.

[2] cf. letters of 13 and 17 July 1853 to Henry Wilberforce.

[3] Morton did not remain with the Jesuits, but after being a schoolmaster, was ordained priest in 1904. He worked at Bristol and Wells until 1919, when he moved to Winnipeg and became Rector of the Cathedral parish.

[4] Edwards wrote on 20 Feb., 'When near Southampton lately I was spending a little time with an elderly clergyman, Mr Southouse, living in retirement on his property, but without any parish or preferment. The name of your Eminence was mentioned, when he said "I have a very grateful recollection of Cardinal Newman, for he was Dean of Oriel when I was there, and he was the only man at the College who ever spoke to me about my soul" —' George Wrenford Southouse, at Oriel College 1831–5, was Vicar of Shanklin 1854–81. He wrote on 3 March and asked to be remembered still in Newman's prayers.

[5] Later, on 31 Dec. 1886, Edwards wrote, 'I wish I could tell your Eminence any thing good of Mr Braithwaite whose sad lapse I named to you, but to all human appearance he seems to have made "shipwreck of faith and a good conscience" — His poor mother still survives, but deeply sorrowing over her only son . . .'

now; it is the exercise of the intellect when the moral and spiritual nature is dead; but I believe that, viewed abstractedly by the intellect only there is no alternative between belief in the Catholic Church and infidelity though I should never tell a man to become a Catholic *in order* to crush his doubts. But I am on a subject which requires more words than my fingers will let me write

Thank you for your kindness

Most truly yours John H Card Newman

TO ALEXANDER FULLERTON

Febr. 25. 1886

My dear Mr Fullerton

Thank you much for sending me a letter so interesting from its relation to dear Lady Georgiana. I pray God that a work so happily begun may be accomplished as it promises to be.[1] I have lost almost my power of writing, and this feebleness of my fingers so acts upon my brain that I cannot form sentences, nor even spell. The doctor does not think much of it, but it is very uncomfortable.

You may be sure that any thing you have to tell me when you get to Rome, I shall receive with much gratitude

Very truly Yours John H Card Newman

TO GERARD MANLEY HOPKINS

The Oratory Febr 25. 1886

My dear Fr Hopkins

I have read your letter with much interest, both the sad part and the reference to your intended analysis of old Homer.[2] Alas, I can not send you more than a few lines in answer, for I am losing the use of my fingers and do not write except with difficulty. My birthday, then, I fear is more clouded in prospect of the future to me than my doctor will allow on his own part

Any how, I want your good prayers and I am sure I shall have them in my necessity

Very sincerely Yours John H. Card. Newman

[1] This refers to Mrs Craven's *Life of Lady Georgiana Fullerton.* cf. letter of 17 Nov. 1885 to Fullerton.
[2] Hopkins had to postpone his work on Homer and died in 1889.

Feb. 26. 1886.

My dear Allies,

Thank you for your most affectionate letter. Have I told you I am losing the writing power of my fingers? It puzzles my brain and hinders me forming sentences. The doctor does not make much of it.

Thank your wife and daughter for their messages. I hope the latter has finished her hard work.[1]

Ever yrs. Affly John H. Card. Newman

Febr 28. 1886

My dear Child

I am very much concerned to be told of your serious illness. I trust you are now quite well. I am losing the use of my writing fingers. You did not tell of the fate of Milton Hill. I suppose it is still in suspence.[2]

Stevie Simeon I know is married, but my memory is now so weak, that I had forgotten that Edmund was.[3]

Thanks for your congratulations   God bless you

Yrs affly J H Card. Newman

Private   March 1. 1886

Dear Mr Hutton

I have just been reading your article upon me in this month's Contemporary and you will understand, without my saying it what gratitude I feel to you for it.[4] Feeling this deeply, still I simply cannot believe that it is not coloured by your own kind mind, and it is more than I can bear.

But you must not think there is even a shadow of dissatisfaction that went with my reading it except of course that of the 'vanitatum omnia vanitas'.[5]

---

[1] Mary Allies had just finished *Leaves from St Augustine*.
[2] Milton Hill was the home of the Bowles family near East Hendred, Berkshire.
[3] Stephen Simeon was married in 1885 and Edmund Simeon in 1883.
[4] R. H. Hutton, 'Newman and Matthew Arnold, I Cardinal Newman', the *Contemporary Review* (March 1886), pp. 327–54, reprinted in *Essays on some of the Modern Guides of English Thought in Matters of Faith*, London 1887, pp. 47–97. Hutton described Newman's style and its relation to his profound convictions. At the end he remarked that 'for eighty-four years Newman has lived amongst us as though he had no continuous city here, and comparatively early in life he became aware that this was his destiny', yet 'The tenderness of his heart is at least as unique as the detachment of his soul from earthly interests'
[5] *Ecclesiastes* 1:2.

But so much I say to introduce the special thanks which I have to say upon it.

I can't help fancying you are in your latter pages generously defending me against Dr Fairbairn, wishing perhaps to supersede the need of my writing any thing more in my own defence in answer to his second paper last December, and this thought leads me to say the following:—

Last month I did write some pages on the subject for the Contemporary; but when I was about to send them to the Editor I said to myself 'Is it not after all infra dig. to descend into a public arena, like a gladiator at your age?' I felt this so vividly, that I put the question to Protestant friends, who saw more of the world than I do, and they decided that it would be a mistake for me to publish any thing more, I shall act on their judgment as to publishing. But I shall send to Dr Fairbairn what I have written telling him it was not to be published.

I am obliged to send it to certain friends, who were a little perplexed by Dr F. and I could not do this, without sending it to him also. But it will not be published in my lifetime if afterwards.

I shall send you a copy — but not for any notice, but as to a private friend.[1]

I am losing the use of my fingers for writing.

Most truly Yours John H Card. Newman

I wonder whether you will be able to understand this letter.

TO PERCY WILLIAM BUNTING

March 6. 1885 [1886]

My dear Sir

I have not forgotten your kind offer to give me a place in the Contemporary Review for remarks on Dr Fairbairn's answer to me.[2] I did write some pages, but before sending them to you, I thought I would ask some non-Catholic friends whether I should publish them or end (as far as I was concerned) the controversy.

They were decided in their judgment that I should content myself with the protest which appeared in October in the Contemporary

Thanking you then for the interest you showed in the matter, I have determined not to avail myself of it; but, as I have had some copies struck off

---

[1] See letter of 10 Dec. 1885 to Bunting. Hutton replied on 2 March that he had hoped his article would make it unnecessary for Newman to answer Fairbairn's further criticisms in the *Contemporary Review* for Dec. Hutton agreed with Newman's friends that he was wise in not returning to the subject.

[2] See letter of 10 Dec. 1885 to Bunting.

not for publication, I take the liberty of sending you one of them, but not as to the Editor.[1]

I am, My dear Sir, Very truly Yours

John H Card. Newman

I hope you will be able to read this. My fingers are losing their power of writing

TO WILLIAM BARRY

Mar. 8 1886

Dear Dr Barry

I thank you for your powerful and seasonable article, and return it.[2] I *think* I told you I was losing the use of my fingers, and this obliges me to be short, but on any of the subjects which you speak of writing to me about, I shall be glad to hear from you — but I am sorry to say that the feebleness of my hand leads to confusion of my head, and thus I have a difficulty in considering difficulties over and above what is intrinsic to them.

As to your Article, it is one from which cultivate[d] minds, Catholic and Christian may profit much — the only point on which more might fittingly be said is the Anglican Church. Its 'broad' portion lies on its laity, though great numbers of them are heartily attached to it with a 'broadness' which is rather an acceptance, however vague, and a belief in the authority, of its teaching, than a conscious and intentional latitude. In its clergy I think there is very little of broad Church   I cannot go on.

The moral strength of the Anglican Church is the strength of possession. It has never been ousted from its old Catholic home. It looks forward with de Maistre to be the unitive principle between itself, Rome, and Greece. And recollect, being English, it does not go by logic. I have not brought out all that I wanted to say

Very truly Yours John H Card Newman

---

[1] Bunting replied on 8 March about the Fairbairn controversy: 'I think the misunderstanding arises from differences of mental constitution, training, and — not a little — period.
I am very much obliged by your courtesy and cherish warmly the recollection of the interview which you kindly gave me some years ago.'

[2] Newman sent his private reply to Fairbairn, and Barry in return on 7 March sent his article 'The Church and the World', the *Fortnightly Review* (Feb. 1886), pp. 184–99. Its theme was that Liberal Protestantism could not preserve Christianity. 'Its leading men are those who believe less and less.' The Catholic Church was the only sure defence.

March 8. 86.

Mr Mac Corry has misunderstood Cardinal Newman. He had no intention of buying any copies of Mr Mac Corry's work, especially since, if the case is that it is not yet written ⟨as he learns from Mr Corry's letter⟩[1]

TO LORD BLACHFORD

March 11. 1886

My dear Blachford,

I was very much pleased to have your letter, and did not expect it. I hope I have not been unjust to Dr Fairbairn but I don't see how I can have been and no one tells me I have. Your three analyses of his meaning are very clear, and the third probably is the true one, but I cannot make him out.[2]

I was shocked at your remark about A[cland] I thought it was *Kant*, not Coleridge, whose great words were 'Reason and Understanding'.[3] They were words which (then *as now*) I could not understand, and I considered I had done enough to dispense with *Kant*'s sense of 'Reason,' whatever it was, by my quotation from Sir W. Hamilton.[4]

I am startled at my writing, all of a sudden, so much better to-day; can it *possibly* be, because yesterday for the first time my fingers were galvanized?

Yours affly John H. Newman.

[1] McCorry wrote from Salford on 15 Jan., enclosing a copy of Part 1 of his pamphlet *The History of the Irish Papal Brigade* 'by Joseph McCorry, The First Volunteer', and asking for a donation towards the printing of the second part. This letter Newman endorsed 'asked for Bishop and clergy's sanction'. Newman's reply was kind, and McCorry wrote again on 24 Jan. and 6 March, apparently expecting him to buy copies, Part II being as yet unwritten.

[2] Lord Blachford wrote on 9 March to thank Newman for his notes in answer to Fairbairn's December article in the *Contemporary Review*, and to say he had 'roasted the Professor pretty sufficiently'.

Lord Blachford continued: 'I have been labouring to conjecture what are the ideas floating in his head to which he seems to give so unfortunate an expression.

It seems to me that if he disentangled his own notions from the phrases in which he loses himself, he would probably find that he considered himself as standing up for the rights of intellect against those of authority (which, of course, may be equally founded on intellect) next for reason against instinct — i.e. reasoning analysed and developed against reasoning unanalyzed and thirdly as contending against the assumption of first principles not admitted by what he would consider a legitimate representative of the judgment of mankind in general.

And these championships, I imagine, condense themselves in his mind into the extremely irrelevant contention that an author must be philosophically sceptical who contends (1) that conclusions require premises — (2) that the faculty which draws conclusions is a different faculty from that which recognizes fundamental premises.

[3] Lord Blachford wrote, 'I am rather amused at your magnificent ignoration of Coleridge's "Reason and understanding" terminology. Poor Acland — what would he say at being thus unceremoniously ignored.

As early as 1832 he was talking of nothing else'. See *Moz.* II, p. 39.

[4] In his Notes replying to Fairbairn's article in the *Contemporary Review* for Dec. Newman quoted Sir William Hamilton, 'Nothing can be more vague and various than his (Kant's) employment of the word (Reason) . . . but even in his (Kant's) abusive employment of the term, . . . no consistency was maintained.' (*Hamilton on Reid*, Note A, v. 7). *S.E.*, p. 95; *The Theological Papers of John Henry Newman on Faith and Certainty*, pp. 151–2.

TO LORD BLACHFORD

March 12. 1886

My dear Blachford

You will join in my pleasure at receiving the inclosed.[1]

I meant by ἐπιστήμη that it was a collection of conclusions implying or involving the acceptance of the subjects of νοῦς.[2]

I have just heard from Hutton of the Spectator. He says 'I cannot help thinking that your terminology is more convenient than Kant's, though we rather lack an English word for νοῦς I think your reply to Fairbairn really touches the very root of the matter.'[3]

Yours affly J. H. Card. Newman

TO RICHARD HOLT HUTTON

March 15. 1886

My dear Mr Hutton

Your letter was very acceptable to me and pleasant. You defended my notion what 'Reason' might be considered as I should not have ventured or fancied defending it myself for I am deeply conscious I am no metaphysician[4]

I have another great satisfaction. I sent Dr Fairbairn my new answer to him. He seems to have taken my act very kindly as 'courteous' — which was

[1]This was a letter from Fairbairn: Airedale College, Bradford March 11/86
Your Eminence
I desire to thank you very cordially for your courtesy in sending me the paper on 'Scepticism used as a Preparation for Catholic Belief'.
It will be my duty to weigh carefully its varied criticisms and elucidations and I gladly recognise its fair and judicial tone even where unable to admit the correctness of its views or the relevance of its arguments.
I remain, Your Eminence Your very obedient Servant
A. M. Fairbairn.
[2] Lord Blachford asked, 'have you a purpose in leaving out ἐπαγωγή [induction] as ministering first principles for reasoning to act upon?'
In his Notes in answer to Fairbairn's second article, Newman said: 'There is a faculty of the mind which acts as a complement to reasoning, and as having truth for its direct object thereby secures its use for rightful purposes. This faculty, viewed in its relation to religion, is, as I have said, the moral sense; but it has a wider subject-matter than religion, and a more comprehensive office and scope, as being "the apprehension of first principles", and Aristotle has taught me to call it νοῦς, or the *noetic* faculty.' In a footnote Newman added: 'ἐπιστήμη, Aristotle's second faculty, conversant with necessary truth, answers well (analogically) to Reason, as I am considering it.' *S.E.*, p. 97; *The Theological Papers of John Henry Newman on Faith and Certainty*, p. 153.
[3] Letter of 11 March.
[4]Hutton wrote on 11 March that 'the delight to me in your books has always been that the sacramental view of all divine things has been so deeply rooted in you, that for you, without evading the indications of human weakness, the *natural* point of departure has always been that which best explained the divine aspect of human phenomena — but to treat your *mind* as sceptical because you follow so clearly the windings of the sceptical reasoning seems to me a most singular perversion of the truth'.

enough to enable me to write to thank him for his letter.[1] And thus, although I suppose he will use his right to reply, I don't expect anything from him of an unpleasant character.

My dear brother Frank.[2] I sometimes could have cried on reading his old letters of 50 and 60 years ago — He was a thorough going Evangelical, or rather I should say deeply and fervently a Christian, except there was just one thing which he revolted from more than he loved Our Lord, and that was the Sacramental principle. Now his religion seems to me as superficial as it was then deep.

How can you fancy I am not sensible, or rather very sensitive of your sympathetic interest in what I have written? only, since I cannot think I am worthy of it, it frightens me. I hope I am intelligible

Yours affectly John H Card. Newman

R. H. Hutton, Esqre

TO CHARLES J. STEWART

March 15. 1886

My dear Stewart

Thanks for your letter. Excuse a short answer, as I write with an effort. No books have yet come, which I cannot account for without your correspondent's act in it

Yours affectly J. H. Card Newman

TO SIR GEORGE SHERSTON BAKER

March 17 1886

Dear Sir Sherston

I have a great opinion of your energy and perseverance in any work you take in hand, and I doubt not the same qualities will distinguish you in your progress in duties which the profession of the law will open upon you.[3] I heartily wish you success and am very truly yours

John H Card Newman

Sir Sherston Baker Bart

P.S.   I am losing the power of using my fingers in writing.

---

[1] See letter of 12 March to Lord Blachford.
[2] Hutton wrote, 'I imagine your brother Frank, for instance, with an originally very religious nature, to have had a sceptical turn of intellect . . .'
[3] He was appointed Recorder of Helston in 1886.

March 20. 1886

Dear Canon Glover

I feel the honour which the Chapter of Leeds does me in the information you gave me in your letter of this morning, and I assure you I feel that 'warm sympathy' in its object which you rightly expect of me.[1]

I do not think, however, I could go beyond the expression of this sympathy without more of personal acquaintance with your good Bishop than it has been ever my lot to enjoy, or without feeling myself out of place and spoiling the significance of the affectionate and gracious act which you are proposing. I am sure you will understand me, and gladly giving you my blessing I am

Your faithful Servant J H Card Newman

Very Rev Canon Glover

Mar. 24/86.

My dear Allies

I thank your daughter sincerely for her beautiful present.[2]

It is the fruit of a most happy idea. She has pitched upon the only way, if there be any, of making St Augustine known in England.

Yours affectly John H. Card. Newman

March 25. 1886

My dear Dean

Many thanks.[3] I am going up to the Duchess [of Norfolk's] Requiem Mass on Monday. How I am to get thro' it, I can't tell. I hope I shall not be using your house as an Infirmary — I am, not ill, but so weak and sleepy.[4]

Ever yrs affly, John H. Card. Newman

[1] Glover wrote on 19 March as secretary and treasurer of a fund on behalf of Robert Cornthwaite, Bishop of Leeds for the 25th anniversary of his consecration as a bishop, saying 'The Chapter hopes that our desire to do honour to our Bishop will meet with your Eminence's warm sympathy.'

Cuthbert Butler, *The Vatican Council*, London 1930, I, p. 206, describes Cornthwaite as 'an extremist of the Manning type'.

[2] *Leaves from St Augustine*, sumptuously bound. See letters of 10 Oct. 1885 and 2 April 1886 to Allies.

[3] Newman had asked to stay with Dean Church, who wrote on 25 March 'As I telegraphed, we shall be delighted to have you, and you are very good to come. We are very quiet.

Please let me know if there is anything you would like seen to.'

[4] On 26 March the Duke of Norfolk invited Newman to stay at Norfolk House on days before the Requiem Mass, which began at 10 am. on Monday 29 March. There is a draft of

TO CHARLES BOWDEN

March 26. 1886

My dear Charles

I have accepted the Duke's wish that I should be present at the Requiem Mass on Monday. Perhaps your mother will be in Church, and I could see her after the function. At all events I hope she will let me call on her after it. I have wished all through the winter to call to see her, feeling my great age and feebleness, but the severe weather has hindered me

Yours affectly John H Card. Newman

TO WILLIAM PHILIP GORDON

Mar 26. 1886

My dear Fr Gordon

Fr Neville has already told you of the Duke's invitation made to me, to the Requiem Mass on Monday — I hope I shall not by coming put out any arrangements you had made. Fr N. [Neville] wrote directly, but I fear the letter did not go by the first post. I shall lodge at Dean Church by an engagement of some months. I propose to come from the Deanery with my Cardinal's belongings on, so that I shall be ready for the function by 10 o clock.

Yours affectionately John H Card. Newman

TO AN UNKNOWN CORRESPONDENT

March 26 1886

Dear Sir

I know how much cause there is for pain and disapproval at what is going on in Ireland, but I am not in a position to allow me to interfere in what is going on there.

And my fingers write with so much effort and pain, that I hardly manage to write you these few lines.

Very truly Yours John H. Card. Newman

Newman's telegram in reply: 'Many thanks, but I go to Dean Church. I engaged with him six months ago. I have not been there since I was a Cardinal. I return here Tuesday.'

Newman stayed from 28 until 30 March. On 7 April Dean Church wrote to E. S. Talbot, Warden of Keble College: 'I dare say you have heard we had three days of the Cardinal. He was so bright, so kind, so affectionate; very old and soon tired, but also soon refreshed with a pause of rest, and making fun of his old age. "You know I could not do an addition sum." Anyhow he was quite alive to all that is passing round him, though cautious and reticent, as he should be. But the old smile and twinkle of the eye, and bright, meaning εἰρωνεία, are all still there, and all seemed to belong to the old days'. *Life and Letters of Dean Church*, edited by Mary C. Church, London 1894, p. 321.

TO PETER LE PAGE RENOUF

Mar. 27. 1886

My dear Renouf   *Private*

I rejoice to hear of your merited appointment, and I wish my fingers were in a better state to express, as I should like my sense of its fittingness and the advantage which Archeology will derive from it.[1] But I fear you have heard very mistaken accounts of my temporal possessions. I would gladly do any service to you, if it were in my power — but I have not a shilling of income from Rome. I have not a shilling in English or foreign funds. I am bound up with the Oratory here, so that its wants are my wants — our school has never paid its way, and, beyond an annuity, could promise not a part of so large a sum as £750, and I am near my end, and would not leave on my representatives so great a burden

I am sure you will pardon me in writing you what you may read as an abrupt answer, but my hand obliges me to be brief

Yours affectly J H Card. Newman

TO MRS J. W. BOWDEN

Sunday [28 March 1886]

My dear Mrs Bowden

It is so fast to ask you to see me after the function.

The Duke may ask me to luncheon and he has been so kind I do not know how I could refuse him

Yours affectly John H Card Newman

TO WILLIAM CLIFFORD, BISHOP OF CLIFTON

March 30. 1886

My dear Lord

Have you any of your valuable letters dated 'Woodchester, March 24 1886' to spare?[2] or *will you allow* me to reprint some copies of these for my friends?[3]

Your Lordship's Very sincerely John H Card. Newman

The Rt Rev. The Bp of Clifton

[1] Renouf was appointed Keeper of Egyptian and Assyrian Antiquities at the British Museum in Jan. 1886.

[2] On 10 March Edward Bagshawe, Bishop of Nottingham, issued a circular letter in which he prohibited Catholics in his diocese from belonging to the Primrose League, a Conservative society founded in 1883, of which the Marquis of Salisbury was the first Grand Master. The Bishop's act caused a sensation. On 23 March Bishop Ullathorne wrote to Newman that he had tried in vain to persuade Bagshawe he had exceeded his powers. Ullathorne had then urged Cardinal Manning to appeal to the Holy See, which he did.   [*cont.*

TO T. W. ALLIES

The Oratory Ap. 2. 1886.

My dear Allies,

I am very sorry to send you a letter which may seem to you ungracious.[1]

For many years I have been obliged, by the difficulty of drawing the line, to withhold leave to writers to use my words (with my consent) at the beginning of their books. It was very distressing so to treat what was really a compliment to me, still more to do so in the case of near friends and highly esteemed writers whom I but partially knew. And, if I now did otherwise, I think I should hurt them much.

I hope you will take this into your mind and forgive my apparent unkindness.

Yours affectly John H. Card. Newman

TO WILFRID WILBERFORCE

April 2. 1886

My dear Wilfrid

Every thing you write is like yourself and makes a reader love you.

And no one can like such undisciplined language as that to which you draw attention.[2]

For myself I wish to adhere to the chair of St Peter — and the Holy See has said or implied enough to make me feel that a Protestant Mr Parnell is not a leader or representative whom he would like me to recognize.[3]

Yours affectly John H. Card. Newman

Bishop Clifford's letter laid down that in his diocese Catholics were free to join the Primrose League. Leo XIII had been urging them to take an active part in politics and the League was not secret but a loyal and patriotic association. Bishop Clifford's letter was printed in the *Weekly Register* (3 April 1886), p. 437. On the same page was another circular letter from Bishop Bagshawe, saying that he should have consulted the Congregation of Propaganda before acting, and that he now withdrew his prohibition of participation in the Primrose League.
[3] Bishop Clifford replied on 2 April that he had only a few copies left of his letter of 24 March, and told Newman he was free to reprint it.

[1] Allies asked on 1 April whether the publisher might advertise words from Newman's letter of 24 March about Mary Allies's *Leaves from St Augustine*.
[2] Edwin de Lisle, who lived in the diocese of Nottingham, had written a letter of strong protest to the *Observer* at his bishop's prohibition of the Primrose League. See letter of 30 March. Wilfrid Wilberforce then wrote de Lisle a letter of remonstrance, saying that he, Wilberforce, was a member of the British Home Rule Association, and that it was lawful to appeal to Rome against one's bishop, but not to defy him. On 23 March Wilberforce sent Newman a copy of his letter to de Lisle, saying that he was also sending it to the newspapers, but had little hope of its being published. It appeared only in the *Weekly Register* (27 March 1886), p. 404.
[3] Wilberforce thanked Newman for his 'kind note', and maintained that in belonging to the British Home Rule Association he was 'by no means recognizing the leadership of Mr Parnell'.

TO JOHN RICKARDS MOZLEY

April 3. 1886.

My dear John

Your letter interested me much, tho', my fingers being so weak, I can only reply briefly.[1]

My own conviction is that the Roman See, viewed as an historical character, has on the whole acted a largely beneficent part towards mankind, though its individual agents may, as men, be criticised. But I cannot write more. Thank you for your letter.

Yrs afftely J. H. Card. Newman.

TO WILLIAM BARRY

April 4. 1886

Dear Dr Barry

I am very sorry to hear of your accident; and, though not from an accident, but from old age, I am sorry to say about myself I am losing the use of my fingers in writing. This affects my power of putting down my thoughts on paper in a way which I should not have thought possible — but, if you will take this into account, I will do my best to remark on any questions you ask me[2]

Very truly Yours J. H. Card. Newman

TO WILFRID WARD

Apr 5 1886

My dear Wilfrid Ward

I was glad to have your letter. Principal Fairbairn sent me a civil answer in acknowledgment of the remarks on his second Article, which I had printed, not published. This was a great satisfaction to me.[3] When you were here, I intended but forgot to ask you whether there was not to be a new Edition of The Wish to believe.[4] I got through the expedition to London far better than might be expected but I am very weak.

Yours affectionately John H Card Newman

[1] J. R. Mozley made a note before copying out this letter:
'The following letter was in answer to one in which I had tried to express the debt due to the Papacy of the early part of the middle ages, which in letters previously written I had not sufficiently acknowledged.'

[2] Owing to his accident Barry did not acknowledge Newman's letter of 8 March until 29 March. He wished to consult him about the dialogue he was preparing on the difficulties against Catholic doctrine felt by thoughtful people.

[3] See letter of 12 March to Blachford.

[4] Ward replied on 11 March that it seemed unlikely that there would be a second edition of his The Wish to Believe. The first edition was a thousand copies. See letter of 16 March 1885 to W. Ward, who paid his second visit to Newman on 26 March 1886, his first having been on 30 Jan. 1885.

Private   April 7. 1886

My dear Emly

The compliment has been paid me of making me an Hon[or]ary member of the 'Royal Irish Academy' Please, tell me something about it — Catholics and Protestants, I suppose   A very kind letter came with the diploma[1]

Yours affectly J H Card. Newman

TO ALBANY JAMES CHRISTIE, S.J.

April 12. 1886

My dear Fr Christie

I gladly welcome your promise to send me your book; it has not yet come; publishers are slow[2]

Thank you for the kind words which accompany your notice of it.

This day is the 64th anniversary of my becoming a fellow of Oriel

Yrs affly J H Card. Newman

TO EDWARD PERCEVAL WRIGHT

April 12. 1886

Sir,

I feel the great honour done me by the Royal Irish Academy in electing me one of its honorary members in the Department of Politics Literature and Antiquities.

I beg to acknowledge the safe arrival of the Diploma of membership, which you have sent me, and the courteous and kind words with which you accompany it.[3]

I am, Sir, Your faithful Servant
John H Card. Newman

Ed. Perceval Wright Esqr etc etc

TO THE DUKE OF NORFOLK

April 14. 1886

My dear Duke of Norfolk

Of course I am very glad to receive so kind a letter under your hand, but it was so great though sad a pleasure to be allowed to take part in the last

[1] Lord Emly replied on 11 April: 'The R. Irish Academy is a most distinguished body composed of all the men most distinguished in literature and science, Catholics and Protestants alike. . . .
. . . Wordsworth was, as you have been elected a member'.
[2] *The End of Man*, London 1886, a poem in four books.
[3] Wright, Professor of Botany at Trinity College, Dublin, acted as secretary to the Royal Irish Academy, 1874–7, 1883–99.

duties of the late Duchess, that it needed no thanks for my thus professing my reverence and grateful attachment towards her memory

I am Your Grace's faithful & affect Servant
John H Card. Newman

His Grace The Duke of Norfolk E M. KG:

TO R. W. CHURCH

April 16. 1886

My dear Dean,

If I had had my wits about me, when I was with you,[1] I should have saved myself the trouble of many words and those after all but insufficient. I must be abrupt, for each word is some pain to my fingers.

It should be settled at once, while Anne Mozley and I are alive. We are not likely to quarrel, but her as well as my representatives, when we are gone may be many. I hope you will not refuse to arbitrate between us, nay more, to interfere, for I don't anticipate she would receive a movement on your part otherwise than as kind. Of course you might mention my having set you in motion, if you wish. I think a delay would be a pity.

First — as to our main position. Do I, as the owner of the various papers, I have put into her hands, employ her, as Hope Scott's representative employed and paid a man whom I recommended to them?[2] or is she an independent authoress, who has applied to me for information, as Sir John Coleridge (I suppose) did a kindness to Keble's family and friends in undertaking for them a Memoir of Keble? or is it best to put such views altogether aside, and for A.M. and me to go halves?

Here comes in the question which of us two is it employs printer and publisher? on *this* the foregoing questions seem to depend. As the Memoir is not to be published till after my death, and as the MS, as her writing will remain all along in her possession, this seems to show that the property of the work should be considered hers.

Or should the work, as a property, be given to one or two (quasi) trustees?

Perhaps I have said enough to open the question. But there is a collateral point which I ought to have determined before I sent her my papers. Among other documents I sent her a sketch of my life up to 1833.[3] I hope it is not too late to say what follows – this Memoir addressed to Ambrose St John, I wish to be used without curtailment (excepting made with my leave) — not refusing *interpolations* of A.M.'s own, in *illustration* etc. If she only used it merely as a source of information without quoting it *verbatim* and in its *entireness*, I should like to have it back, without denying her such use of it as she wishes to make, though she does not include it bodily in the Memoir.[4]

[1] For Newman's visit see letters of 25 March to Dean Church and 4 May to Lady Simeon.
[2] Robert Ornsby. See letter of 10 Dec. 1877 to Mrs Maxwell-Scott.
[3] See first note to letter of 14 Jan. 1885 to Anne Mozley.
[4] Dean Church wrote on 31 May 1886 that Anne Mozley intended to print the Memoir in

I think I have said enough to explain what it is that I want settled, and I hope I am in no way inconsiderate to A.M. or you.[1]

Yours affly J. H. Card. Newman

TO RICHARD ACLAND ARMSTRONG

April 25, 1886.

Dear Rev Sir,

I am glad to receive from you a volume so very able and serviceable in proof of the great subject of which it treats, impressing upon me the important and happy contrast which exists between the modern bodies which are external to the Catholic Church and those of primitive times, so that, whereas no Catholic would think of having recourse to Gnostic or Manichee in the conflict with unbelief, members of sects who are nevertheless in certain grave errors, as we think, are, as we rejoice to believe, not external to divine grace and the gradual leadings of divine mercy, and can be welcomed as aids in the defence of divine truth.[2]

I am sure you will let me say this, from the sympathy you feel in Catholics, tho' you stand apart from us, and I *must* say *it*, lest, while thanking you for what you have done so well, I seem to bear with passages in your book, which could not but seriously pain me.[3]

That God may visit you with a special Easter blessing and bring you into the perfect truth, is the sincere prayer of

Your faithful Servant John H. Card. Newman

P.S.   Excuse my bad writing, I am losing the use of my fingers

extenso. The only excisions were those of Newman, now printed in *A.W.* See second note to letter of 19 Feb. 1885 to Anne Mozley.

[1] Dean Church was ill, and did not reply until 9 May: 'As to the general position: I don't think that either Hope-Scott's biography, or Keble's, is on all fours with this case. In the greatest confidence, as between friends, you communicate to her generally what you wish done, and supply a mass of materials; and she, quite entering into your wish, undertakes to do her best with them, as she thinks best, subject to any conditions or wishes of yours — one of these conditions being that the work is not to come under your eye. It is more of a *joint* work than either of the two which you mention.' Church thought that Newman's and Miss Mozley's interests in the work were equal, but that she should have the copyright and make the arrangements for publication. See also letter of 11 May to Church. Later correspondence shows that Newman declined for his representatives any share in the profits of the work.

[2] On 22 April Armstrong sent '*With the Author's profound respect*', a copy of his *Man's Knowledge of God*, London 1886, hoping that Newman would agree that it contained 'common ground, not unimportant, for all devout believers in God'. Armstrong, who was a Unitarian, gave the reasons 'on which my own theism practically rests'. These included 'The Witness of Conscience', the heading of a chapter in which he quoted, p. 43, the passage from Theodore Parker on the conscience of a child, which Newman transcribed in *The Philosophical Notebook*, Louvain 1970, p. 50.

[3] Although Armstrong's book was very sympathetically written, it contained such sentences as 'We look neither, with some of our Protestant neighbours, to the merits of Christ to save us, nor, with our Catholic countrymen, to the mystery of the Eucharist to unlock for us the gates of heaven'. p. 150.

TO ALFRED PLUMMER

April 26. 1886

My dear Dr Plummer

Thank you for your new volume — which is full of interest to me[1]
I am losing the use of my fingers, and therefore must be abrupt.
Does not Basilides, as early as A D 120 quote St John's gospel?[2]

Yours faithfully & affectly J.H. Card. Newman

TO JOHN EDMEADES COLYER

April 29. 1886

My dear Sir

I do not like to answer so grave a question by letter, and the more so because, losing as I have for writing purposes the use of my fingers, I am obliged to be brief.[3]

However, if under the circumstances I must answer I can only say that I consider the Orders of the Church of England to be not more than probably valid, that is doubtful, not reliable, not safe. And it is a principle in Catholic theology that in the administration of the Sacraments 'non potest minister uti opinione probabili aut probabiliore, de Sacramenti valore, sed tutiores sequendae sunt aut moraliter certae.'[4]

TO ALFRED PLUMMER

April 29/86

My dear Dr Plummer

I am ashamed at having given you the trouble to write. It was my fingers which led me so to mislead you

Yrs affectly John H Card Newman

But I am very glad to have your detailed statement

[1] *The Epistles of St John*, Cambridge 1886, in the series 'Cambridge Greek Testament for Schools and Colleges'.

[2] On p. xxvii Plummer referred to the important evidence of Basilides for the authenticity of the Fourth Gospel. On 28 April Plummer replied with quotations from Basilides in Hippolytus's *Philosophumena*, and concluded 'The use of the Fourth Gospel by Basilides, even if it stood alone, would almost suffice to prove that the Gospel was written at a time when S. John was still alive.'

[3] On 27 April Colyer, who described himself as 'a priest of the Church of England and Proctor in Convocation for the Archdeaconry of Macclesfield', and who had been Vicar of Iffley for three years, when he became a friend of Mrs Crawley, asked 'for the quieting of a soul': 'The Orders of the Church of England, may they be relied on as a channel for the transmission of Divine Grace in your opinion?'

[4] St Alphonsus, *Homo Apostolicus* I, Tract I, Cap. iii, §25, Malines 1842, p. 12.

April 29, 1886.

My dear Lady Simeon

I have wished to write to you, but I cannot write without effort, and it affects my forming sentences and spelling. I *hoped* to see you after the Requiem Mass, though I feared lest, in your kindness, you would not let me. I was only one whole day in London.

I feel what you say about changing your house — God be with you and Queenie.[1]

Ever yrs affly J. H. Card. Newman.

April 29. 1886

My dear Aubrey de vere

If my fingers allowed of it, I should like to send you a long letter to express the pleasure, surprise, and instruction I gained from your approval or at least encouragement of what I have written in answer to Dr Fairbairn. You see in my defence of myself what I was too engaged in my own defence to see, and I am too glad to believe that I have written what may have a value in itself as well as be good as an answer to a critic.[2]

I am obliged to stop, for the difficulty in *writing* bothers my brain — and I can, not only not make sentences, but hardly spell, or at least write the right words.

As far as I have a right to speak, I follow you in your terrible fear about Irish matters

Yours affectly John H Card. Newman

May 4. 1886

My dear Lady Simeon

I shall be truly glad to see you, whenever Birmingham lies in your way — but give me notice, if possible, lest I be at Rednall. It will be no trouble to me

---

[1] Catherine Simeon.

[2] On 21 April de Vere thanked for the Notes in reply to Fairbairn's article in the *Contemporary Review* for Dec. and added that he had re-read Newman's first essay on 'The Development of Religious Error': 'I was much struck by what you said as regards the action of the Reason *taken by itself*, and its action when working in vital union with those higher sources of Inspiration by which its working was always intended to be guided.' It reminded de Vere of an analogy used by Coleridge, as though denying that the eye could see, because, if extracted from the head, it could no longer reflect objects.

to come here, if I know beforehand. On the 26th we commonly entertain the priests of Birmingham. Our lady friends, the mothers chiefly of our boys, are so kind as to come about July 20th, at our breaking up. We are sadly distressed since the morning at the serious illness of George Pereira, the eldest son, which must be a great blow to his mother, who had last year to nurse him through his serious accident in the hunting field. She has been a great friend to us.

I was only one whole day in London; I came on Sunday evening and returned mid-day on Tuesday.[1] I was not at Arundel; and it was an engagement of some standing that, (on matters of business,) my visit was to be to Dean Church. I wished to see his daughters, who had grown up almost, since I had been with him. I did not have your card till my visit to him was over.

My difficulty in writing has a curious effect on my brain — you must pardon my mistakes.

Yours affectly John H. Card. Newman

TO CHARLES JAMES LONGMAN

May 8. 1886

Dear Mr Longman

Messrs Ballantyne tell me that they printed nothing for me from stereotype plates nor, excepting the second edition of Gerontius,[2] is there any stereotype of any book with Messrs B and O [Burns and Oates] or Messrs Pickering

I ought of course to have all my stereotype plates insured — Will you advise me in the matter

J H N

TO JAMES CRAWFORD BREDIN

Rednal May 10. 1886

Dear Sir

My hand is so weak I cannot send you many words in answer to your letter.

You describe very vividly the trials you have had in religious inquiry, which have been the experience of so many

I know but one course to recommend tho' I feel it a difficult one — to resign yourself *patiently* and *unconditionally* to Almighty God, to ask His teaching, and to persevere in waiting for it. It is a tedious, forlorn course. But I believe in its success, when pursued — but few inquiring can be found to place

---

[1] See letter of 25 March to Dean Church.

[2] Newman wrote on 4 May: 'Card. Newman will be much obliged by Messrs Ballantyne informing him what stereotype plates they have of his, and the date when they first came to them.'

themselves even for a time *unreservedly* into the hands of a superior Power, and few are *constant* in such renunciation of self

As to the reports about myself which you mention, they are utterly unfounded. I never had even the temptation to disbelieve the infallibility of the Pope in matters of faith and doctrine — tho' I did not wish the doctrine to be made a dogma, *necessarily* to be believed by every Catholic. This was what the Catholic popular papers succeeded in getting defined. I believed it to be *true*, but not an article of Christian *faith*. *Now* I believe it as an article of faith.

With my best wishes and prayers for your becoming free from your present difficulties, and becoming a good Catholic, I am, dear Sir,

Sincerely Yours John H Card. Newman

TO CHARLES BOWDEN

Rednall May 11. 1886

My dear Charles

I have been going to write to you or to Emily about the 'Life of Hilde-brand'[1] but I wished to have more to say, and I have been doubting whether to write to you or to her, thinking that perhaps you may not have as much leisure time as she has. Will you let her see this letter.

Of course the only reason I don't send it to your Mother is lest I should needlessly trouble her.

I am losing the use of my fingers, and this is a difficulty in my bringing out all that I would say in this matter.

It is to me a great pity that so good and useful a book should not be. There is very little to correct in it, and reviewed as a whole the book is a great histori-cal argument in behalf of the divinity of the Catholic Church, and tho' from love of the Author one grieves to think it is not in all aspects Catholic, yet it is more likely to bring Protestant readers near the Church than if it were a Catholic work, and it has in consequence a rhetorical power which a Catholic historian will not be able to command in England. There are two sides to every question — but for myself I think only really strong arguments will avail against the republication.

There is one such strong argument. After I had mentioned the subject to your Mother the other day, I wrote to Messrs Longmans in Paternoster Row, who I thought would be kind enough to give me advice. I recollected that my 'Palmer's Journal to Russia' had not sold — and Mr Longman certainly gave it his distinct opinion that a book nearly 50 years old would not sell. And he spoke of a *Series* of histories which he was bringing out, and a life of St Hildebrand was to be among them. What this is worth, however, requires thought.

---

[1] *Life and Pontificate of Gregory VII*, London 1840, by their father, J. W. Bowden. See letters of 16 May to Bowden and 30 May to his mother.

As to corrections or explanations I don't see there need be [more than] three Notes.

(1.) On the Introduction and Chapter 1

(2) On the Decretals *backing up* what the book says of them.

3. On Cardinal Baronio's account of bad Popes, which many recent writers say is unfair.

Yours affectly John H Card. Newman

P.S. Thank Fr Rowe for his pamphlet; I shall write to him in a day or two.[1]

TO R. W. CHURCH

Rednall May 11. 1886

My dear Dean

I am very much rejoiced to find you so much better, and that you are going, or have gone, to Blachford.

I will write soon at length; at present I have but this to say for settlement of arrangement.

The copyright of *A.M's* [Anne Mozley] *book* does not involve the copyright of *my letters?* The *use* (being with my leave) of the letters does not involve their *possession* (as property) I have had some anxious questions on this point as regards Lilly's 'characteristics' and Mr Meynell's 'John Oldcastle.'[2]

Dean Church

TO JAMES STEWART

Rednall May 12/86

My dear Stewart

I am obliged to seem ungracious by not consenting to the leave asked of me by your friend.[3] From the impossible [sic] of drawing the line, I have been

---

[1] Rev. J. B. Rowe, of the Oratory, *Unnecessary Schools: A Letter to Sir Charles Russell, Q.C., M.P.*, London 1886. Rowe sent his pamphlet on 6 May, explaining that it was about the working of the 1870 Education Act. This was being interpreted as giving an exclusive right to School Boards to establish new schools, instead of the duty of supplementing voluntary schools.

[2] The copy ends here. For Lilly's *Characteristics from the Writings of John Henry Newman* see the letters of June. Aug. Sept. 1878, and for 'John Oldcastle' those to W. Meynell of Sept. 1885 and J. G. Cox of Oct. 1885. Newman made a rough draft: 'The copyright of the Book which she is engaged upon, as it stands, whether as a MS or as a publication is absolutely the property of Miss Mozley.

This however does not give her any right in the property of hitherto private or unpublished papers and letters of Cardinal N which, by loan from him she has in the aforesaid book quoted, referred to or in any way used.'

Dean Church replied on 13 May: 'Of course A.M. could have no copyright in your *letters*. The only question would be how far she might use them; i.e. make extracts, if so be, — *you not having seen* what use, or what extracts she has made.' See also letter of 16 April to Dean Church.

[3] The leave must have been to publish a letter of Newman's commending a book.

139

declining constantly for years to give it even to very intimate friends, and often it causes me pain, for it (I fear) pains them. It would still more if given to strangers, tho' not to them.

I am, My dear Stewart

Yrs affectly John H Card Newman.

TO J. R. BLOXAM

May 14/86

My dear B

An hour after you went today, I saw what a stupid mistake I had made[1]

In 1821 Jelf and Plumer were elected Probationers   1822 Ottley and I   In 1823 Pusey and Churton

Yrs affly J H N

TO WILLIAM HOBART KERR, S.J.

[14 May 1886][2]

You and your brother have done me a great kindness in sending me the   [3]
not only from my loving gratitude towards your Father and Mother, but for the sake of her [your] sister also. I never saw her (as far as I know) but once, and then she made a great impression on me. It was on a Sunday in the summer of 1863 when Lord Henry [Kerr] called ⟨was so good as⟩ at the Oratory with her. I was overcome by her appearance she was handsome and winning — and I said to myself some words such as 'Here is a grand lady fitted only [to] take her place in the world!' I was overcome still more some time afterwards to hear she was going into religion. I was dumb, and have ever since thought of her with extreme interest and reverence.[4]

Now they are all gone to their rest. Your father mother Francis [Kerr] and your Sister. I began to name your Sister in my Memento but could not go on with it. I always name Lord and Lady Henry and especially dear Francis whom your Mother for 30 years has urged upon me not to forget.

Since writing the above I have looked into the Life whether the date of summer 1863 came into it, and was touched to find it there[5]

---

[1] This concerned the date of W. R. Churton's election as a Fellow of Oriel College. See the account of Bloxam's visit in *Newman and Bloxam*, pp. 225–6, and cf. letter of 28 May 1886 to Herbert Warren.

[2] On 12 May W. H. Kerr sent on behalf of himself and his brother Henry Schomberg Kerr, S.J., *The Life of Henrietta Kerr*, edited by John Morris, Roehampton 1886.

[3] Newman left a blank space here in his draft.

[4] See letter of 26 Aug. to St John for this visit of Henrietta Kerr.

[5] *The Life of Henrietta Kerr*, pp. 75–6

TO W. S. LILLY

May 15, 1886.

My Dear Lilly,

Thank you for letting me see this. It seems to me one of the best things you have written.[1]

At the same time, I am not sure that you have sufficiently disengaged Liberalism from Liberty. Taking human nature as it is, how shall we *practically* separate the one from the other? Are we not obliged to look for some external calamity, physical, social, or political, such as the Deluge, or a rising of the masses, as doing for the human race what truth and reason, conscience and στοργὴ,[2] will not succeed in doing?

Yours very truly, John H. Card. Newman.

TO CHARLES BOWDEN

May 16. 1886

My dear Charles

I quite feel you should not hurry the matter; nay, it should for the present lie by, till your Mother has a clear view. And don't do any thing which would seem to oblige her to make up her mind. If I had been the cause of teasing her, I should be extremely vexed.[3]

I need not say more just now. Don't let her think that I am set upon it. I have all along thought she might not like it

Yours affectly J. H. Card. Newman

TO ROBERT WHITTY, S.J.

May 17/86

My dear Fr Whitty

Of course we can give you a bed, supposing you can stop for it[4]

Yrs affly J H Card. Newman

TO JAMES CRAWFORD BREDIN

May 21. 1886

Dear Mr Bredin

The soul is like the body; — different medicines suit different persons. I think there is just a chance of one or other of my Sermons, if you read this or that, being useful to you. So I shall ask you to accept a copy from me.

---

[1] Lilly added a footnote: 'The remarks of mine on Liberty, which the Cardinal had before him, were published three years later in chap. ii of *A century of Revolution*.' London 1892.
[2] 'affection'.
[3] See letter of 11 May to Bowden, who wrote on 16 May that he wanted his father's *Life Gregory VII* to be republished but 'Mama is, however, not very decided in her mind as to wishing the publication for various reasons'.
[4] Whitty hoped to call on Newman on his way back to Stonyhurst from Rome.

I hope I do not rightly understand you as if at once becoming a Catholic. You must gain the gift of faith first[1]

TO JAMES CRAWFORD BREDIN

May 23 [?] 1886.

Dear Mr Bredin

I had a fear lest you had misunderstood my words and were thereby moving too fast.

The sermons I send you have been the means of leading inquirers into the Catholic Church. So I thought they might be useful to you.[2]

TO OWEN DICKINS

May 28. 1886

Dear Sir

I am very sorry to have to answer you that I have very few personal friends either here or abroad; and those who honour me with their friendship are not men of secular influence. If you have heard the contrary, it is from strangers who from kindness towards me have indulged their fancy without foundation in fact. I have no one to write to; I am utterly unable to act, especially at my very advanced age, sorry as I am to have to say so[3]

TO JAMES GIBBONS, ARCHBISHOP OF BALTIMORE

May 28. 1886

My dear Lord Archbishop

I return to your Grace my warmest thanks for the splendid present you have made me in the copy you send me of the Acta et decreta of the Third Plenary Council of Baltimore, a copy, not only splendid in its outward accompaniments, but, which, over and above its value and interest in itself,

[1] The conclusion has been cut out for the signature.

[2] Bredin left a note: 'I received at the same time as this letter a copy of some sermons selected from the "Parochial and Plain Sermons" and edited by an English clergyman. — I never again heard from the Cardinal except once in 1887, which letter is at present in Fr McArdle's hands.'

In Feb. 1887 Bredin wrote a long letter about his religious position. Towards the end of Feb. 1888 he was received into the Church by Fr McArdle, a priest at the English Martyrs Church, Tower Hill, London, and wrote his gratitude to Newman.

[3] Dickins wrote on 28 May from 19 The Albany, Albany Road, Camberwell, 'to entreat you to use your powerful influence to procure me some kind of occupation at home or abroad'. He considered himself well qualified to be manager of a large estate, having had such experience in Spain. He was now forty-five and had four young children to provide for.

Dickens began by saying 'Although personally unknown to you, you will probably remember that we are closely related — your mother and my father's mother being sisters.' They were half-sisters. Newman's grandfather Henry Fourdrinier married a widow, Jemima Manning, née White. By her first husband she had one son, who died abroad, and one daughter, Minerva, who married John Dickins. Their son Frederick Owen Dickins was the father of Newman's correspondent.

witnesses to what Holy Church has already done in your great cities, and presages what she will do in the vast spaces of which those cities are the centres, thus fulfilling the anticipations of Saints four centuries since, that in the bad days which threatened for Christianity, the new world, then recently discovered, would redress the balance of the old.

Let me add that the inscription, with which you have graced the volume, gives it to me a personal interest, as perpetuating your act of kindness to me, when it takes its place, after I am gone, in the Library of the Oratory.[1]

Your Grace's faithful Servant John H Card. Newman

His Grace, the Archbishop of Baltimore

Excuse my bad writing. I am losing the use of my fingers.

TO T. HERBERT WARREN

May 28. 1886

Dear Mr President

Your ready acceptance of the small book I ventured to send you bore out what my friend, Dr Bloxam, said of your kindness when he would encourage me to make trial of your kindness. You have far more repaid me for my boldness in the Papers you sent me, about Magdalen College and Magdalen men, which renews at the present date the interest and respect which I felt in former years for the College of Dr Routh, Dr Johnson, Dr Mozley, Dr Bloxam, Mr Frank Faber, and many others of its members, on whose memories I gladly dwell.[2]

I am losing the power of using my fingers in writing, and must beg you to excuse an abrupt letter

Most truly yours John H Card. Newman

The President of Magdalen

TO MRS J. W. BOWDEN

May 30. 1886

My dear Mrs Bowden

I am so grieved to have to give you a moment's pain —[3] and think it so kind in you to have written yourself to me.

---

[1] In the copy of *Acta et Decreta Concilii Plenarii Baltimorensis Tertii*. *A.D. MDCCCLXXXIV*, Baltimore 1886, sent him was a dedication 'To his Eminence John Henry Cardinal Newman with the profound regards of James Gibbons Archbishop of Baltimore May 3rd 1886'.

[2] Newman sent a copy of *Lyra Apostolica* to Warren, who in return sent an address to his pupils given as a Magdalen tutor and *In Memoriam. Rev. Frederic Bulley, D.D. President of Magdalen College, Oxford. Rev. Thomas Henry Toovey Hopkins, M.A. Fellow of Magdalen College, Oxford*, signed T.H.W., and reprinted from the *Oxford Magazine* (21 Oct.), 1885.

[3] As to the republication of her husband's *Life of Gregory VII*, Mrs Bowden wrote on

I have nothing to say except to thank you for your kindness and to beg your and Emily's prayers for one who is so near his great change

Yours affectly John H Card. Newman

May 30. 1886.

Dear Mr La Serre,

I always take an interest in you, as feeling how much we got attached to you years ago, when you taught French in our School.

And I am glad to hear that you have the prospect of an engagement in London[1]

Very truly Yours John H. Card. Newman.

May 30. 1886

My dear Dean Plumptre

I know little enough of Dante — but I have habitually thought it enough to fancy that Ozanam etc looked at his doctrinal belief, and the other party to his politics and experience of Roman matters.[2]

However, there is a great German work by a writer whose name is something like Hettinger, now in course of translation by Father Bowden of the London Oratory, which I would enquire about, if you wish.[3] I know nothing about the Dedication – but as 'a cat may look at a king' I suppose M. Vaullot [Veuillot] might write a letter to Pope Pius about a question of *fact*. If it is a form of doctrinal profession accepted by the Pope, it is a more serious matter

Very truly yours John H Card. Newman

The Very Revd the Dean of Wells

29 May, 'it would be very much against my own and Emily's feeling'. See letters of 11 and 16 May to John Bowden.

[1] La Serre had come to 21 Bedford Gardens, Kensington, and offered tuition in French of every description. His prospectus of 15 June included testimonials from old boys of the Oratory School, and was headed by one from Newman: 'The Oratory, June 8th 1886.

Professor Henri La Serre was for many years Resident French Master at the Oratory School, where he fulfilled his duties to our complete satisfaction.

His knowledge of the French and English tongues eminently qualifies him for a teacher, whilst his skilful method goes far towards enabling students to master the difficulties of the language.

John H. Card. Newman.'

[2] A.–F. Ozanam, *Dante et la Philosophie Catholique au treizième siècle*, Paris 1840.

[3] Franz Hettinger, *Dante's Divina Commedia : Its scope and value*, translated and edited by Henry Sebastian Bowden, London 1887.

TO J. SPENCER NORTHCOTE

June 1. 1886

My dear Provost Northcote

I was very unlucky in having gone to Rednall yesterday by appointment on important business, when you called

I will gladly, do what you wish, if you will tell me more what you wish, I referred you in my letter of Sunday to my Dedication. Also I think I wrote one or two Addresses of which I have not copies. Also there is a passage in my Apologia page 271[1]

Something in past years will be best — for at my age there are some things which I can do, and some things which I can't; and I should be deeply grieved and mortified, if I could offer you nothing but what was cold and flat. One can't praise a man whom one admires and reveres as much as one does the Bishop

My handwriting reminds and warns me that my brain is not much more at my command than my fingers

Yours most truly John H Card. Newman

TO J. SPENCER NORTHCOTE

June 2. 1886

Dear Provost Northcote

I do indeed, with all my heart, join in the Address of congratulation, which, I believe, you are sending to the dear Bishop on the completion of the 40th year of his episcopate, and I hope that the chapter and clergy will allow me to unite my name to theirs in their pleasant and dutiful act.[2]

I recollect the day of consecration well. His Lordship had most kindly invited me and my intimate friends to the sacred rite, and after it he did me the special favour of making me acquainted with that holy woman, Mother Margaret Halloran [sic].[3]

Not long after the Oratory took its start in England, and special relations were created by the Holy Father's Brief between its Fathers and the Bishop of Birmingham, and the experience of the long series of years which have followed has filled me, as you may well understand, with the affectionate and

---

[1] See next letter. 'did I wish to point out a straightforward Englishman, I should instance the Bishop, who has, to our great benefit, for so many years presided over [this Diocese]' For Newman's dedication to Bishop Ullathorne see *Diff*. I, and for the Addresses, that for his episcopal Silver Jubilee Volume XXV, Appendix 1, and for his golden jubilee as a priest, letter of 23 Sept. 1881 to him.

[2] There was no formal Address from the Clergy. In the middle of June Newman called on Ullathorne at Oscott College. The latter wrote: 'He came alone, was very feeble, and glad of an arm along the gallery; but cheerful, gentle, and affectionate.' *Butler* II, p. 277.

[3] See diary for 21 June 1846.

grateful recollections, which so holy and kind a Superior could not fail to impress upon me.

This letter but feebly expresses what I would say — but I am losing the use of my fingers, and, strange to say, this confuses and impedes my use of words

I am, My dear Provost, Yours most sincerely

John H Card. Newman

The Very Rev Provost Northcote

TO CHARLES LATIMER MARSON

June 3. 1886

Dear Sir

I thank you for the kindly way in which you speak of me, and would be of service to you, if I could be.

But I have no experience enabling me to give you advice, and think you should know more of the doctrines and usages of the Catholic Religion, before taking the step of professing it[1]

Yours truly John H Card. Newman

TO ROBERT WHITTY, S.J.

June 3. 1886

My dear Fr Whitty

I had already ordered for myself the Life of Lucas, but rejoice to have it as the gift of his brother.[2]

I hope you will watch the proceedings of the Anglican body, as time goes on.[3] You should not ignore the Guardian   In yesterday's Number there is a noteworthy speech of Lord Halifax, in behalf of Catholic union. It shows the *yearning*, of the High Church for Unity, which may lead to much beyond itself.[4]

---

[1] Charles Marson, the Christian Socialist, had just moved from being a Broad Churchman to an Anglo-Catholic. See the article on him by M. B. Reckitt, in *For Christ and the People*, London 1968, edited by Reckitt, where this letter is quoted, p. 98.

[2] *The Life of Frederick Lucas, M.P.*, by his brother Edward Lucas, 2 vols., London 1886. See also letter of 23 July 1884 to Whitty.

[3] On 12 May Whitty wrote from Turin of his last audience with Leo XIII who spoke of the disposition of the English people generally towards the Catholic Church, and was greatly pleased on being told that Newman's elevation to the Cardinalate was one of the reasons for good feeling. Whitty added: 'The Pope kindly asked me to write a brief statement for him and this I have done. I am anxious to tell you what I have said. I do not mean to speak to any one else in England but yourself upon it. At least I cannot enter into the subject fully with any one else.'

[4] This was Lord Halifax's address on 27 May at the annual meeting of the English Church Union, of which he was President, the *Guardian* (2 June 1886), p. 829. He spoke on the Re-union of Christendom: 'Certainly no portion of the Catholic Church has undergone such considerable changes as the Church of England during the last four centuries; and, if so, ought we not to be more ready to correct our faults, and to welcome any opportunity of drawing nearer to those with whom we have so much in common.' Lord Halifax pointed out what an excuse for unbelief Christian divisions were, and continued: 'It has been well said by one belonging to the Roman communion, who has laboured much for peace (Cardinal Newman), that the

What you say about the German questions is very anxious — but the present state of Ireland leads one to ask whether troubles do not or may not arise, tho' of a different kind, where a Veto does not exist. Can any thing be more dreadful that [sic] civil war with its demoralization? You know me too well to think I am an Erastian

Yours affectly J. H. Card. Newman

P.S. The *education* of Priests is a different question. Have you a good warrant for what you say?

TO CATHERINE ANNE BATHURST

June 6. 1886

My dear Child

My writing days are past. Thank you for your affectionate letter. I do not attempt a, b, c, without effort and some pain

Yours affly J H N

TO MRS F. J. WATT

June 7. 1886

My dear Child,

It is not that I don't think of you and yours, or of your mother, or of Philipine [Watt], and you must tell them so, and thank them as well as yourself in my name for their good prayers for us on St. Philip's Day — but I cannot write without effort and distress, and you must not expect me, half way as I am from 80 to 90, to write letters.

God's blessing on you all. I thank Him for being so good to you.

Yours affectionately, John H. Cardinal Newman.

TO T. W. ALLIES

Jun. 14. 1886.

My dear Allies,

I wonder whether I have been so rude as not to answer Mary's question about the two Treatises of Athanasius before the Arian controversy.[1] I think them beautiful works, but it may be a fancy of mine, but, if I must hazard a view, I should doubt their being sufficiently interesting except to scholars.

I wanted to ask you a question, which, alas, has slipped out of my head.

celebrated phrase 'Securus judicat orbis terrarum,' was not so much an inference from principles, as an appeal to visible facts. St. Augustine hardly needed to argue for an undivided Church, when he could point to an undivided Christendom.' If Anglicans recognised appeals to the Privy Council from the Archbishop of Canterbury, surely they should prefer appeals to a Christian bishop, Leo XIII.

[1] Mary Allies was thinking of translating these treatises of St Athanasius.

I hope to send you or the Committee, for you, I think represent it, some books, if you will accept them for your new public library.[1]

Yours affectly J. H. Card. Newman

TO J. R. BLOXAM

June 15. 1886

My dear Dr Bloxam

I shall be truly sorry to have had a chance of meeting your President[2] and to miss it, but, alas, I shall be at Rednall a good deal in the weeks in prospect, and, since it will be partly on matters of business, I cannot say *when*. It would be a great pleasure to see him

Yours affectly J. H. Card. Newman[3]

TO N. J. CASAS

(in substance)   [15 June 1886]

Dear Sir

I thank you for the compliment of translating and for expressing your purpose of submitting your translation to the Archbishop[4] Of course you will have some guarantee also for the literary accuracy of the translation. My reason for your offering the Translations to a publisher, whether English or not, is, lest you should have a great expense thrown on your hands.

I can have no objection, certainly not, to Mr E Walford's proposing to advertise. I have objections of various kinds to your translating my Notes on Athanasius and the two volumes Via Media.[5]

TO ALBANY JAMES CHRISTIE, S.J.

June 15. 1886

My dear Fr Christie

I am very sorry to have given you perplexity and the trouble of a letter. And I should yet have been very sorry if that letter had not been shown me.

---

[1] Allies was trying to found a library in the rooms of the Catholic Union, at 10 Duke Street, St James.

[2] Of Magdalen College, Herbert Warren.

[3] Neville wrote to Bloxam on 15 June, 'The Cardinal . . . has been preaching these ever so many Sundays at the High Mass'.

[4] Casas wrote from 68 rue Jouffroy, Paris, that he had translated but not yet published *Dev., Ess.* I and II, *H.S.* I–III into Spanish. He proposed to translate *Ath., Call., D.A., Jfc., G.A., Mir., Idea* and *V.M.* The translations would be submitted to the Archbishop of Santa Fé before publication.

[5] Casas replied on 17 June that he would comply with Newman's wishes, but made no specific mention of this point. None of his translations were published.

The book came all right, if I had but been patient. It is a beautiful book, and most persuasive if a sick soul is to be won over without effort to meditate. The ternary metre is like the chime of bells from a Church Tower, praising and proclaiming Father, Son, and Holy Ghost[1]

Yours very sincerely John H Card. Newman

TO WILLIAM PHILIP GORDON

June 15. 1886

Dear Fr Superior

Burns and Oates have sent me the inclosed for correction   Perhaps they have also sent it to you. In case they have not I send it to you for any corrections of the statements about the London House

We have made on the Paper our corrections of what related to *us*. If you make any corrections which concern you, and then send it back to me, I will send it on to Burns and Oates *for a revise*.

I am writing to them to explain the cause of my delay in answering them

Yours affectly John H Card. Newman

TO T. W. ALLIES

June 10. [16] 86.[2]

My dear Allies,

The idea of extracts from St. Bernard is a very good one, but should you not see first how St. Augustine sells?

Yrs affly John H. Card. Newman

TO MESSRS GILBERT AND RIVINGTON

Rough Copy — June 14 1886 June 16 1886

Cardinal Newman is glad to receive from Messrs Gilbert and Rivington the list of the Stereotypes which they have in their keeping for him.

But there are two questions with which he must trouble them.

1. He believes the stereotype of 'the Arians' to belong to the present Firm of 'Pickering and Co.' At least, the copyright of the work is theirs — he is writing to them on the subject.

2 If as Messrs G and R consider the stereotype of the 'University Sermons' is his, then also is that of the 8 vols of 'Parochial and Plain;' also of 'Sermons on the day' 'Selections of Sermons' and of 'Lectures on Justification.'

Yet he does not recollect ordering stereotype for any of these twelve

[1] See letter of 12 April to Christie.
[2] On 15 June Allies thanked Newman for his letter of the previous day and said that his daughter Mary was planning a work similar to her *Leaves from St Augustine*.

volumes, though he did make corrections in the third Edition (1872) of 'University Sermons.'[1]

TO T. W. ALLIES

Jun. 20. 1886.

My dear Allies,

By a great misunderstanding for which, if it is my fault, I am very sorry, Wilfrid Ward, as I have just heard from him, has introduced a letter without my knowing into the Preface of a pamphlet which he has just published.[2] This has greatly annoyed me, I mean, annoyed me that I should have not spoken more clearly. I thought he meant to state I agreed in his opinion of Messrs. Spenser's and Harrison's theories, — not that I allowed a concret [?] letter of mine to be published. What he goes on to tell me is as follows:—

'The letter got quite without my knowledge into some of the papers a few weeks back. Mr Meynell, who, as the manager of the Burns and Oates firm sees the proof sheets, copied the letter and sent it to the Athenaeum, whence it was copied into other papers.'[3]

Yours affectly John H. Card. Newman

TO MESSRS BURNS AND OATES

June 21 [1886]

I am surprised to be told that your corrector of the proofs has without leave been publishing in the Athenaeum a letter of mine, which he found in the course of his confidential duties   Such a breach of propriety I have not met with but once in 50 years, viz in 1838[4]

J H N

TO WILFRID WARD

June 21. 1886

My dear Wilfrid Ward

I wish my fingers and my general feebleness allowed me to say how touched I was by what you told me, in relation to myself, about Mr Lionel Tennyson,

---

[1] cf. letter of 8 May to Longman.

[2] *The Clothes of Religion*, A Reply to Popular Positivism, London 1886. See letters of 21 June to Burns and Oates and to Wilfrid Ward.

[3] This is a quotation from W. Ward's letter of 19 June. Allies replied on 26 June: 'When I saw the quotation of your letter I felt sure that some such misunderstanding as you describe had caused it to be published.' See letter of 2 April 1886 to Allies.

[4] Burns and Oates replied that they were informed by Wilfrid Ward that the letters from Newman quoted in *The Clothes of Religion* were published with Newman's sanction, and added, 'An advance copy [of Ward's book] went (in accordance with the custom common with us) to the Editor of the "Athenaeum"; who has made use of it, which it was obviously open to him to make.' See next letter, to Wilfrid Ward.

and how very kind I think it in his Father to wish me to be told of it.[1] It is remarkable and cheering, as leading to the thought that the agnosticism of Englishmen is in many or most Englishmen only skin deep, and that, as careless Catholics in so many instances at the last send for a Priest so, when the awful future is immediately before many a sceptic, he sees what that future really implies and *to whom* he must look.

I have sadly misled you. I never meant that I could consistently acquiesce in a letter of mine being printed bodily. I dare say when I see it in the context it will not be what Mr Meynall has made it to be by his impertinence.[2] I have been obliged to decline what I feel really to be great honour on the part of friends from the difficulty of drawing the line. This I have done to an intimate friend within the last several months.[3] I am writing to Burns and Oates on the subject. Please, don't think me fussy

Yrs affectly J H Card Newman

TO CHARLES NATHANIEL ROBARTS

[22 June 1886]

Dear Sir

With Catholics to fast is understood to mean as its primary condition to have only one meal in the day (24 hours); but abstinence means abstaining from flesh meats and strictly speaking from eggs and milk, and is included in the notion of fasting, though separable from it[4]

TO WILFRID WARD

June 23. 1886

My dear Wilfrid Ward

I ought to have thought that you might mean 'putting into print'[5]

Of course I cannot bargain that any words I happen to use shall not be put into print; but it is often so ungracious, when leave is asked, bluntly to say No,

---

[1] Wilfrid Ward wrote on 19 June: 'I saw Lord Tennyson yesterday who told me that his son Lionel, who lately died on his way back from India, asked a few hours before his death that "Lead kindly light" should be read to him. It seemed to help him to pray, his wife said, more than anything else. Lord Tennyson seemed to wish that you should know this. I was especially glad as Lionel, whom I knew well, was *apparently* something of a sceptic during his life. But this seems to show that religious influences had still a hold on him.' On 22 June Ward added: 'Lionel Tennyson repeated three times the words "far from home" when his wife reached them, on the day of his death, in reading your hymn.'

[2] See the quotation from Ward's letter in that of 20 June to Allies. In the preface to his *The Clothes of Religion*, London 1886, p. xix–xx, Ward printed Newman's letter of 3 Aug. 1884 in commendation of the article which gave the book its title.

[3] See letter of 2 April 1886 to Allies.

[4] Robarts, who was Chaplain and Precentor at Christ Church, wrote on 21 June from St John's College, asking Newman to settle an argument which had arisen in the common room.

[5] Wilfrid Ward wrote on 22 June, 'I feel that I should have understood more clearly what you sanctioned.'

(as I had to do on a post card only yesterday)[1] that the only relief to my mind is being *consistent to a rule*. And your quotation did not after all strictly come under the rule because it was only a reference to an *opinion* of mine not to a criticism or favorable judgment on your book

Of course I was very much pleased by the words you used of me[2]

Yrs affectly J H Card Newman

P.S.   I wonder whether I have expressed myself intelligibly.

The Oratory, Birmingham June 23. 1886

Dear Canon Wenham,

I believe you have two objects in working the St Anselm's Society, one of which you have pretty well succeeded in, advertising Catholic books, and next in selling them at reduced prices, for which, in order to carry it out, you want pecuniary means.[3]

Mr Newdigate, who has lately called on me, has for his object this very undertaking, the collecting of pecuniary means.[4]

He seems to say that he contemplates finding the means for bringing into exercise a Society such as St Anselm's; this interests me very much. Should I take a liberty in asking you what is your annual expense — e.g. a London shop etc? and what chance you would have of purchasers did you sell books at half price.

Yours very Sincerely John H Card Newman

The Oratory Birmingham June 27. 1886

My dear Wilfrid Ward

You are taking much more trouble than I like.[5] What is done cannot be undone and I am very unwilling and don't wish you to with draw my letters. You have paid me a compliment in inserting them. Two friends to whom I

---

[1] This was in reply to Herbert Duke, who wanted to quote Newman's letter in commendation of lectures on the Church which he was about to publish.

[2] Ward wrote out what he had said when quoting Newman's letter of 3 Aug. 1884 in the *Clothes of Religion*: 'I may quote words of approval from one whose approval on such a subject, both as to the matter and as to the manner of controversy, is a greater reward to me than that of any other person now living.'

[3] St Anselm's Society existed for the diffusion of good books.

[4] See letter of 1 Aug. to Alfred Newdigate.

[5] Wilfrid Ward wrote on 25 June a letter marked *Private*, that he had written stopping the appearance of Newman's letter about the 'Wish to Believe', (see letters of 4 and 20 Dec. 1884), which he had meant to quote in *The Clothes of Religion*. Ward continued:
'I am most annoyed to find it is now produced in the Tablet, and as Mr Cox knows that you had been displeased at these appearances I am quite at a loss to understand his doing this without speaking to me. It comes again from a proof sheet. . . . The fact is that Cox and Meynell are now at the head of the firm of Burns and Oates and do these things recklessly to push the books they publish. All I can do now is to stop its appearance by cutting it out and explain in a few lines to the Tablet . . .'

refused the same thing as you asked me quite lately have written to me that they quite understood my reason for declining and one said he understood how Wilfrid Ward's quotations by mistake got into the press.[1]

Yours affectionately John H Card Newman

Wilfrid Ward Esqre Junior Carlton Club.

TO HENRY O'BRYEN

The Oratory, Birmingham June 30. 1886

My dear Rt Revd Monsignor O Bryen,

I am grieved I must anticipate a disappointment of the visit which you propose officially to make me on Saturday next. A week ago I had an accident which still confines me to my bed. I do not dare to hope that by Saturday next I shall have ventured down-stairs, but it is only my incapacity to receive your visit which will hinder me from availing myself of so great a pleasure and honour.[2]

Your faithful servant John H. Card. Newman

To the Rt Revd Mgr O Bryen.

TO CARDINAL GIBBONS, ARCHBISHOP OF BALTIMORE

Birmingham Luglio 1886

Eminentissimo e Reverendissimo Signore Mio Osservandissimo

I distintissimi meriti, di cui va adornar l'Eminenza Vostra non potevano non esser presi in particolare considerazione dal Santo Padre, il Quale, come apprendo dal pregevole Suo foglio, nel Concistoro del 7. Giugno pto tenuto nel Palazzo Apostolico Vaticano, L'annoverò fra i Principi di Santa Romana Chiesa. Laonde è mio preciso dovere di far Lene i più sentiti rallegramenti, aggiungendo che vivo sicuro, che il Gregge affidato alle paterne pastorali Sue cure esulterà per cosiffatto Suo innalzamento allorquando consideri che Sua Beatitudine con tale atto di Sovrana Clemenza non solo a Lei ma a Baltimore tutta ha voluta rendere il più grande segnalato onore.

Nel baciare a Vostra Eminenza umilissimamente le mane, mi gode l'animo di dichiarmi col più profondo ossequio.

Di Vostra Eminza Umilm̃o devm̃o Serviore

Giov. E. Card Newman[3]

Sigr Cardle Giacomo Gibbons
Arcivescovo di *Baltimora America*

---

[1] See letter of 20 June to Allies. Ward wrote on 30 June to thank Newman 'for the kindness of your last letter'.

[2] O'Bryen was the papal envoy or ablegate to Canada. He arrived in London towards the end of June.

[3] Only the last words and signature are in Newman's hand. James Gibbons was made a Cardinal on 7 June.

TO LADY SIMEON

The Oratory, Birmingham.
July 5. 1886.

My dear Lady Simeon

I have had a fall but am getting better. I do not like not to tell you so. I really have nothing more to say.

Yours affly John H. Card. Newman[1]

The Honble Lady Simeon

TO LADY SIMEON

July 7. 1886

My dear Lady Simeon

I will gladly see you and Q[2] — any time next week except about 2 o'clock, my dinner hour. I am not yet down stairs, but I trust I shall be next week. Thanks for your prayers.

I trust I have escaped a shock. I was kept in bed for above a week.

Yours affly J. H. Card. Newman.[3]

The Honble Lady Simeon

TO MESSRS GILBERT AND RIVINGTON

Copy   July 15. 1886

Cardinal Newman believes that this letter will not give Messrs Gilbert and Rivington the trouble of an answer.

He understands (in consequence of the question he asked on the second page of his letter of the 13th and their answer this morning)[4] that they have in their keeping stereotype plates of 'Difficulties' volume 2

---

[1] This letter was dictated but signed.

[2] Catherine Simeon.

[3] Neville wrote on 12 July: 'The Cardinal has asked me to say that he will be very glad to see you on Thursday and he will be at your service between 2.30 and 5 any time or times you would like. His Eminence bids me also remind you that Thursday is your own naming so that you must not be afraid to put off till Friday should Thursday be wet, or for any other reason, for Friday will be equally convenient to him.

I am glad to say that the Cardinal is not at all the worse for the fall. There is stiffness and some pain still, and there will be for perhaps a fortnight longer, but apart from that, he is, the doctors declare, remarkably well and in better condition than for several years past. I suppose that the rest has been good for him, but he intends this to be the last day in his room. I have nothing to say about the cause of his tumble except that he says he overbalanced himself, — it was a very bad fall.'

[4] Gilbert and Rivington wrote on 14 July that they had no stereotype plates of *Diff*. I.

He has wished to know this as necessary previous to having all his stereo-types insured[1]

THE GENERAL LIFE AND FIRE OFFICE

July 19. 1886

Cardinal Newman would be glad to ensure against fire and other accidents the stereotype plates of his publications.

He would be obliged to the Directors of the General Life and Fire Office to inform him whether he can ensure with them and on what terms.

The plates are in the vaults of Messrs G and R [Gilbert and Rivington] 50 St John's Square Clerkenwell

TO CHARLES JAMES LONGMAN

July 21. 1886

My dear Sir

I acted on your letter in May at once as regards the insurance of my stereo-types, though it has taken time to receive the letters I inclose and on which I should ask the favour of your advice.

First I found that the stereotypes of those volumes which had been in the hands of Messrs Pickering and are now in your hands while they were with them have been ensured at the 'General Fire Insurance Co'

Next besides the stereotype plates of my volumes which I mentioned to you, I find [I] have plates of 'Difficulties' volume 2 which I mentioned to you last year — so that I am already prepared with plates of one of the three volumes which according to our agreement I have to furnish you with when a new edition of any of the three is wanted

And now I have this morning received from the Fire Insurance Co the following answer to my application (as to the insurance of my stereotypes,)

---

[1] On 15 July F. von Hügel wrote from Hampstead:
'My dear Cardinal Newman,
 It is indeed kind and generous of you to do so much more than I ever hoped or thought of, for a work so entirely unconnected with your own, as is that of Fr Ferrigno. Allow me to thank you very warmly both in his name and my own. I have forwarded the cheque to him, and the envelope as well, as the words on it may well encourage, and indeed practically help him, in his somewhat discouraging undertaking.
 I hope it is not impertinent if I here make for myself an opportunity of saying how warmly I admire, how proud I feel, of the Duke of Norfolk's attitude and conduct during this anxious and sad political crisis. The sight of the union of love of Church and love of country *ought* to be common, but it is not: it is doubly refreshing to see it in the social head and leader of English Catholics, and although he is, of course, alone responsible for his actions and possibly quite original in some of their details, yet the inspiration and the temper of mind I may, perhaps, without presumption, trace back to Edgbaston and to yourself.'
 During the general election the Duke of Norfolk had condemned the National League in Ireland, and the proposal to give in to it as a surrender of principle in which Catholics could not have a hand. *The Times* (1 July 1886), p. 10.

which I do not understand, except that they seem unwilling to insure them.

Might I ask you whether I should apply elsewhere and to whom?

You say it would cost £900 to replace the plates which are in the hands of Messrs G. and R. [Gilbert and Rivington]

To Messrs Longmans

TO MISS LAURA SMYTH

[22 July 1886]

Cardinal Newman readily sends his blessing upon Miss Smyth's excellent undertaking.

Should he need any vestments for the Altar or Choir, he will not forget the high testimonials she sends him. He is not in want of any at present.

Perhaps she will be so good as to send him a list of the articles on sale ⟨she provides⟩ and a scale of prices.[1]

TO EDWARD BELLASIS

July 24. 1886

My dear Edward

My head and hand are so weak, that I am not fit to write letters. I find I owe you on account of the   [2]. So I inclose you a cheque for a small sum, if you will take of it what I owe you, and, if there is something over, let them at your *discretion* have it.

I never acknowledged your very learned Paper. The Oratory will gladly receive it[3]

Yrs affectly J H Card. Newman

TO CLARA CHANDLER

August 1. 1886

My dear Clara

I congratulate you with all my heart on having won so good a fellow as Henry, and I congratulate him on having found a lady so certain from what he says of you to make him happy.

Accept this rude welcome — I cannot send you such as I should like to send

---

[1] Miss Smyth wrote on 21 July that she had recently lost all her means of support and hoped to make church vestments for a living.
[2] The name of the family, who were the recipients of Newman's alms, is illegible.
[3] A note by Bellasis shows that this was his *The Machells of Crackenthorpe*, Kendal 1886.

you — but for a year past I have lost my power of writing, and I have lately had a bad fall

Harry gives me hopes of seeing you here. I rejoice at the prospect[1]

Yours affectionately John H Newman

TO ALFRED NEWDIGATE

Aug. 1. 1886

My dear Mr Newdigate

I write with such difficulty, that I am obliged to be abrupt – not to say rude Pardon me.

I would gladly in my small way give my name among others to a brief list of donations made to bring down the price of religious books, but I could not take a part in a limited liability company, or any plan involving commercial engagements. Such a list of donors would not interfere with a company, though, excuse me if I say, I should grieve at your giving your private property to it[2]

Very truly Yours John H. Card. Newman

TO THE SECRETARY OF THE CATHOLIC YOUNG MEN'S SOCIETY OF
GREAT BRITAIN

August 2nd, 1886.

My dear Mr. Quinn,

I am very sorry I am too late in sending to your annual Conference the assurances of my kind thoughts, my interest in your great work and my blessing.

Also my sympathy with your members on your loss of your founder, whom I knew.[3]

[1] Clara Chandler was engaged to Henry Williams Mozley, Newman's nephew, and they visited him together on 16 Aug. 1886. On 17 Aug. She wrote to Fanny Mozley: 'What a wonderful face his is. I don't think any photographs give one any idea of what it really is. He was so *very* kind that it was impossible to feel alarmed, and it was so delightful hearing him talk. He remembered my great uncle the Dean [George Chandler, Dean of Chichester 1830–59] very well, and spoke of him as having been a leader in Church matters in those times. He insisted on our having tea and pouring it out himself. Harry thought him looking a good deal aged and looking weaker, and he was a little deaf, but Harry was amused at his turning round on him when he was telling me to speak a little louder and saying "I can hear her very well, much better than you."! It was when I was thanking him for a little brooch he gave me which belonged to his grandmother, and which has her hair in it. Was it not very kind of him? I shall prize it more than anything. He said he had given Edith [wife of John Rickards Mozley] a pin and would like to give me something. He seemed very much interested in hearing of you all and asked at once a great deal about Aunt Anne's [Mozley] accident – also about Jane's [Mozley] plans. We stayed there nearly an hour.'
[2] Newdigate had founded in Leamington in 1875 the Art and Book Company, in order to spread religious books. He was now, as he wrote on 23 July, proposing to enlarge the Company. See also letter of 23 June to Wenham.
[3] This was Richard Baptist O'Brien, who died on 10 or 11 Feb. 1885. He had been Professor of Theology at All Hallows College, Drumcondra, when Newman was in Dublin.

I must ask you to excuse a short letter, not only on account of my age, but I have also lost the power of using my fingers for writing, that is, without difficulty, and am otherwise disabled just now.

Very truly yours, John H. Cardinal Newman.

Aug. 9. 1886.

Dear Mrs Keon,

Thank you for the Ode. Dear Mr Keon had splendid literary talents. I was in London just for 5 hours! I have lost my powers of writing.

Very truly Yours John H. Card. Newman.

Mrs Keon

Aug. 25. 1886

Dear Mr Longman

I should be very glad to put, as you propose the insurance of the stereotype plates into your hands.

Did I understand you rightly in your letter of July 22 that Messrs Ballantyne have got stereotype plates of 'Difficulties' volume 1. I wrote to them May 4 to ask them 'what stereotypes they had of mine, and the date when they first came to them' They answered May 8 that 'they printed nothing for me from stereotype plates.' If they are mine, should I not ask for them to be [sent] to Messrs G and R [Gilbert and Rivington]?

As I am writing, I will ask, unless it is against your rule or the custom, when a new edition of any one of my volumes is wanted, for a copy of the immediate last edition to be sent me. I am likely to correct very little, but sometimes the last edition had corrections in it, and the printer not knowing this has used for the new edition some old copy

Very truly Yours J H N

Aug 30. 1886

My dear Lord Braye

I shall be very glad to see you any day you will kindly name. My only engagements at present are this day week from 3 to 5, and my time for dinner which is 2.

Very sincerely Yours John H Card. Newman

The Lord Braye

TO ALFRED NEWDIGATE

Aug. 31. 1886

My dear Mr Newdigate,

You must excuse my abruptness, but my fingers will not bear my words.

The first point is to get the £5000. Is this possible either commercially or from Catholic zeal? Next, you say that your attempt has *already* succeeded in the years past, I should very much like to have proof of this. I am afraid you must [1] your leave to say that I cannot help being sceptical about it. Then I cannot help being alarmed in your having invested your own money to your good work.[2]

May I add that I do not understand what are the relations of your plan to that of the Bishop of Salford.[3]

Very truly yours John H Card. Newman

TO AN UNKNOWN CORRESPONDENT

Aug 31. 1886

Dear Sir

I should like to express to you more at length the compliment I feel to be conveyed in your letter, but I have lost command over my fingers and cannot write without an effort.

I have never acted as a critic towards my own works, and have very seldom re-read them except when a new edition was called of them — and then I altered what happened to catch my eye as faulty. I fear I have very little to say about what I have written than this

Very truly Yours John H Card Newman

TO BISHOP ULLATHORNE

Edgbaston Septr 1, 1886.

My dear Lord,

How good God has been to me in giving me such kind friends! It has been so all through my life. They have spared my mistakes, overlooked my defects, and found excuses for my faults.

God reward you my dear Lord for your tenderness towards me, very conscious as I am of my great failings. You have ever been indulgent towards

---

[1] Word illegible.

[2] In reply to Newman's letter of 1 Aug. Newdigate proposed that his company should pay only a limited dividend, and the rest of the profits be used to produce cheaper religious books.

[3] The Catholic Truth Society was founded in 1884, with Herbert Vaughan, Bishop of Salford, as its first President.

159

me; and now you show me an act of considerate charity, as great as you can, by placing my name at the beginning of the last work of your long life of service and sacrifice.[1] It is a token of sympathy which, now in my extreme age, encourages me in the prospect of the awful journey which lies close before me.

Begging your prayers, I am, my dear Lord, Your affectionate servant,

John H. Card. Newman.

TO AUBREY DE VERE

Sept. 2. 1886

My dear Aubrey de Vere

I rejoice to hear that we are to see you on the 6th

Yours affectly John H Card. Newman

TO LORD BRAYE

Sept 3. 1886

My dear Lord Braye

I hope you will excuse a short letter, which may seem sententious and abrupt. But I cannot write much.

On the one hand, the difficulty of a representative of the Holy See coming to England arises from John Bull, and from political parties as well as religious. On the other hand, the difficulty of an Englishman or Irishman going to Rome is that it will seem to be a move against the just influence of the Bishops.

I think it would be necessary for your friends to be well up in the history in the last three hundred years of the relations between Rome and these Islands. And they ought not to mind trial and temporary discouragement.

I don't write as if feeling I knew much about it, but I rejoice to be told of a beginning, and don't like to seem to be unmindful of your kindness in coming over here yesterday[2]

Very sincerely Yours John H Card. Newman

The Lord Braye

[1] *Christian Patience*, London 1886, contained a dedication to Newman:
'I do not forget that your first public appearance in the Catholic Church was at my consecration to the Episcopate, and that since that time forty years of our lives have passed, during which you have honoured me with a friendship and a confidence that have enriched my life. Deeply sensible of the incalculable services which you have rendered to the Church at large by your writings, and to this Diocese of your residence in particular by the high and complete character of your virtues, by your zeal for souls, and by the influence of your presence in the midst of us, I wish to convey to you the expression of my affection veneration, and gratitude, by the dedication of this book to your name. . . .'
Ullathorne inscribed Newman's copy 'with the affectionate regards of the Author'.

[2] Lord Braye was one of those who urged, especially in view of the situation in Ireland, that there should be an official channel of communication between the British Government and the Holy See. See letters of 20, 23 March, and 26 April 1887 to Lord Braye.

Sept. 6. 1886

My dear Dean of Salisbury

It is extremely kind of you to send me Professor Shairpe's Essays, and I wish I could express how glad I am to have it from you.[1] I only once had a sight of him, but for years I have had deep sense of the debt I owe him for his most favourable and sympathetic criticisms on me. I was grieved and saddened to hear of his death – and shall ever keep him in affectionate remembrance.[2]

Excuse my bad writing. I am losing the use of my fingers.

Most truly Yours John H. Card. Newman

The Very Rev. The Dean of Salisbury

Sept 8. 1886

My dear Lord Braye

I was very careless in not writing 'private' upon my letter. I quite sympathise in your movement and wish it success – but there are objects which at the present time are far more interesting to me, and more necessary   Such, for instance, is what is called in the Anglican Church 'the Christian Knowledge Society' nor could I, by recommending the measure you are advocating, do anything which might throw the foundation of such a Society into the shade.[3]

I would write more if my fingers allowed me

Yours very truly John H Card. Newman.

Thank you for the venison. Thank you for the Telegram

The Oratory, Birmingham Septr 18. 1886

My dear Canon Liddon,

I send you (please return) Dr Schaff's papers. You are quite right in saying that his plan is not a Catholic one. I had strangely been misled by my faulty interpretation of his words but I conceive I am right in saying that Dr Bright

[1] On 1 Sept. Boyle sent the 4th edition of Shairp's *Studies in Poetry and Philosophy*, London 1886, to which he had contributed a Preface. On p. X, Boyle said of Shairp: 'During the last years of his life the Sermons of Newman, which will ever remain among the masterpieces of English Divinity, were constantly in his hands . . .'
The new edition contained a chapter on Thomas Erskine.
[2] Shairp died on 18 Sept. 1885. He had met Newman at Trinity College, Oxford, in May 1880. See letter of 21 Nov. 1881 to him.
[3] See Newman's correspondence with Alfred Newdigate. A note on this letter to Lord Braye says that his 'movement' was the formation of a small Catholic association, the XV Club, which, he hoped would take up questions such as that of diplomatic relations with the Holy See.

was asked to take part in the plan and that Mr Walter Smith gave his leave. I have pencil marked both facts.[1]

As to the quarto book of letters chiefly transcripts from Keble's letters in 1836 there are only six letters of his in it. There is another quarto book which is made to precede it but not any one letter of Keble's is in that volume.

The subjects of Keble's letters are:–

Edition of Hooker

Consequences of Burton's death

Establishment men at Winton

The Pusey Theological Society (his paper in)

Hurrell Froude's Remains

The Library of the Fathers (the Archbishop not to be landed in a dedication of them)

The Archbishop comes to Sir Wm Heathcote's

Keble's Visitation Sermon. Under these circumstances seeing so few are from Keble I have a scruple about sending them till I hear from you.

I am, My dear Canon Liddon Most truly Yours

John H Card Newman[2]

TO ANNE MOZLEY

Sept 21. 1886

My dear Anne Mozley

I have been confined for a week and more to my room and bed, — the doctors prohibiting me to talk or to write on any thing which might interesting me. They were dismayed thinking me next door to death. I was much pleased by your new niece, but cannot write.[3]

I shall ask you soon to receive for half an hour Fr Neville. He could bring back some books, e.g. Hope Scott's Life[4]

Ever Yrs affly J H N

TO ALFRED NEWDIGATE

The Oratory Birmingham Sept. 21. 1886

My dear Mr Newdigate,

I trust Fr Neville has explained my silence. I have long had an intense wish that English Catholics had what answers to a 'Christian Knowledge

---

[1] Philip Schaff was about to begin his *A Select Library of the Nicene and Post-Nicene Fathers of the Christian Church*, fourteen volumes, Buffalo 1886–9. For this he made use of the Oxford 'Library of the Fathers', having come to an arrangement with Walter Smith, who represented Pusey's trustees. Schaff was a liberal evangelical, and his Library was not, as Newman thought, a Catholic one. See letter of 23 Sept. to Cardinal Gibbons.

[2] This letter was written by Neville, except for the signature.

[3] See letter of 1 Aug. to Clara Chandler.

[4] Anne Mozley replied affectionately on 22 Sept. and proposed that Neville should come early in Oct.

Society'. I cannot do much or more than a very little but I hope you will allow me to do what I can, for instance, could I help your connexion with the Bishop of Salford whatever it may be, or could I help in your plan of a migratory shop, or could I offer you anything to enable you to sell cheaply my own volumes.[1]

Very truly Yours[2]

TO H. P. LIDDON (I)

Sept 22. 1886

My dear Dr Liddon

You will, I trust, forgive me if in the following letter I seem to you inconsistent.

I fully thought that the book which Copeland recommended to you was a collection of *Keble's* letters of whom you were a confidential friend And therefore I sent for it, with the intention, if you wished it, of sending it to you[3]

But I find the collection which Copeland spoke so highly of was a lot of letters from friends of mine, but, though of Copeland's, not I think of yours, and a scruple has risen in my mind, whether I have a right to show them, in the life time of the authors to others.

I have no notions of their contents myself, not having read a word of them

I know I ought to explain how I let Copeland see them, and am so ungracious to you – but this I cannot do for various reasons.[4]

However, if you ask me any question which you have reason to think the Letters will answer, I will do my best to answer them

Very sincerely Yours John H Card. Newman[5]

TO H. P. LIDDON (II)

Sept 22 1886

My dear Dr Liddon

I am too feeble to write you a proper letter. I return with thanks the two letters.

Yrs very truly J. H. Card. Newman

[1] See letter of 31 Aug. to Newdigate, also that of 29 Sept. to him. Neither the Catholic Truth Society nor Wenham's St Anselm Society felt able to open Catholic bookshops.
[2] This letter was dictated but not signed.
[3] See letter of 18 Sept. to Liddon.
[4] See letter of 14 June 1869 to Copeland.
[5] The whole of this letter is autograph.

Birmingham Sept 23. 1886

Emo e Rmo Sig. Mio Ossmo

My dear Cardinal Archbishop,

This requires no answer. It is occasioned by the confusion of head which has led me to suppose that Professor Schaff was a Catholic. Of course I shall take the first opportunity of informing him of my mistake, but I do not at present know his address.

I am writing apropos of Dr Schaff's project of translating the Fathers which I strangely fancied was an undertaking of the American Church and to which in that light, I am sorry to say, I have given countenance in a letter to him.[1]

Kissing your Eminence's Hand I am di Vostra Eminenza

Umo Devmo Servitore Giov. E. Card. Newman[2]

A sua Eminenza Il Cardinale Gibbons Baltimore

The Oratory Birmingham Sept. 29th, 1886.

Dear Mr. Newdigate,

I am too feeble even to dictate, but I am too deeply interested in some such scheme as you propose. I think the papers and the programme of the Catholic Truth Society are excellent. I am rejoiced to see it is under the patronage of the Cardinal Archbishop and the Bishops. I think it is good as far as it goes, but I wish it to go much further.

It ought to be *bona fide* a Society. Its object should be to lessen the price of popular Catholic books and to promote the issue of original pamphlets so necessary for the time. I see you will require an annual subscription of ten shillings. Any parish priest, I conceive, would be able to raise a larger sum than this for so good an object. Of course many ten shillings are requisite even for one local store or shop, but I do not forget that the experiment must begin in one place, e.g. Manchester, and supported by a larger sum than a few ten shillings.

For myself, to illustrate what I mean, I would gladly offer for some one such local store twenty pounds *on the condition* that another twenty pounds was raised by others to meet it whether in larger or smaller sums.

I am so little able to correspond, will you let Father Hunter and Mr

---

[1] See letter of 18 Sept. to Liddon. In the Preface to his first volume Schaff said that Newman had expressed a kindly interest in the enterprise and wished it success. In April 1887 Newman bought thirteen volumes of Schaff's *Nicene and Post-Nicene Fathers*.
[2] Only the conclusion is in Newman's hand.

Connelly see this letter with an apology from me for not writing direct to them,[1]

I am, Yours very truly John H Card Newman

P.S. I willingly grant leave to Mr Connelly to use my three passages but he will have to get Messrs Burns and Oates' also.[2]

TO LORD BLACHFORD

Oct. 1st. 1886.

My dear Blachford,

I have been continually hoping to have a letter from you, feeling however, that neither of us had anything to write about. Unless indeed you were ill, which I feared, in spite of my own age being such as to make it illogical in me to fear for one so much younger. Also tell your sisters I have thought again and again of them, and am very sorry to find that, in spite of Devonshire air.

When one may not converse, or correspond, or read, nothing is left to one, but to think – this, to tell the truth, my medical advisers wished me not to think, if the subject interested me, I do not wish repeated what I feel came from their keen anxiety about me, but they spoke as if the next beat of the pulse might open the path, might be the first step, to death, and indeed it does seem likely that I shall suddenly fall off into some defect and fatal disorder.

The partridges will be very welcome, they are recommended me. So are pheasants in [season][3] My hand won't write more.

I congratulate you and Lady B. on the anniversary.[4]

My kindest thoughts to the Dean[5] and to your brothers and sisters,

Yours ever affectionately, John H. Card: Newman.

P.S. Noon Oct. 1st. I rejoice at their safe arrival. Tell the Dean that Father Neville is going to trouble him with a line soon.

What a cruel accident poor Wilson's son is suffering from.[6]

My Doctors don't seem likely to think my 3rd edition of Athanasius (on which I am employed) dangerous to me. However I have not asked them. I bore in mind the case of the great Ch: Ch: [Christ Church] Scholar, who,

[1] See letter of 6 Oct. to Sylvester Hunter, S.J. He and J. Connelly, Canon of Southwark, were active members of the Catholic Truth Society.
[2] The Catholic Truth Society wished to publish cheaply extracts from certain of Newman's works. Burns and Oates wrote on 6 Oct. to William Cologan, secretary of the Society, refusing permission for 'extracts from works, the copyright of which we have secured'. See letter of 8 Nov. to Burns and Oates.
[3] Lord Blachford wrote on 1 Sept. that he was sending Newman partridges and would send pheasants.
[4] Lord Blachford was married on 29 Sept. 1847.
[5] Dean Church was staying with Lord Blachford.
[6] Lord Blachford explained on 4 Oct. that R. F. Wilson's son had, after a skating accident, lost his reason, and eventually died.

when he found the corrupt passages of Aeschylus too exciting, was accustomed in relief, he said, to have recourse to the Tracts for the Times.[1] Don't suppose my Doctors are not good, religious men, for they *are*.

TO ALFRED NEWDIGATE

The Oratory, Oct. 4. 1886

My dear Mr. Newdigate,

Your letter has interested me very much but I don't think it could be sent to the Tablet without various preliminary acts.[2]

I could not let it go without having first explained your act to the 'Truth Society'. This will take some little time. Next I could not prudently take part in a scheme which you put forward as aiming at the conversion of the English nation. What I should aim at would be the improvement and benefit of ourselves. Then again I should be ashamed to imply (though you try to avoid it) that £20 or £40 would support a Catholic bookstore in any part of England. Here I must express what I have said to you several times that I am simply in the dark as to what it would cost and only see that £20 or £40 looks absurd.

Excuse this freedom.

Very truly yours J H N

TO HENRIETTA WOODGATE

Octr 4. 1886

My dear Henrietta

Certainly I have been alarmingly ill but I am very much better now, as I am thankful to say.[3] The doctors tell me that I have the prospect of getting through the winter well but they won't let me see friends. Love to all of you

Yours affly John H Card Newman

TO LORD BLACHFORD

October 5. 1886.

My dear Blachford,

When our Cook first saw your partridges, she cried out 'O how lovely' What will happen, when the first fruits of October makes its appearance!

---

[1] William Linwood. See letter of 5 Oct. to Lord Blachford.
[2] Newdigate sent the draft of a letter dated 30 Oct. which he proposed to send to the *Tablet*. It outlined the plans for his own society for opening Catholic bookshops, and said 'Cardinal Newman not only shows very great interest in the object, but gives practical effect to it by offering £20 for one such . . .' See letter of 12 Oct. to Newdigate.
[3] Henrietta Woodgate wrote on 3 Oct. to enquire after Newman's health.

I had not heard of the death of young Wilson.[1] Such sad events inflict upon one what I hope is not a wrong pessimism. In 2 of his plays Terence introduces the fear 'ne aut filius alserit aut usquam ceciderit,' 'peregre rediens aut filii peccatum, aut uxoris mortem, aut morbum filiae.'[2] Of course this carried our powers too much, for we cannot with Timon[3] leave human kind — but at times it is a keen and irresistible thought. I recollect, on the loss of my dear sister[4] shortly before I knew you, how my mother would not leave off gazing on her portrait — and I always have thought that she was going in fancy through the prospective sorrows and trials of her life, had she lived.

As to hobbies, doubtless I have mine as well as another, but you have not quite hit on mine. On publishing my Apologia, strangers asked me for a list of my publications. I think I attempted one in the second edition, and I soon found I could not stop short of some arrangement, yet the greater part of what I have written, is caused by *occasions* which needed putting together — and one hobby I will confess to is a love of order, good in itself, but excessive.

But I don't go on; in order to spare your eyes and to mortify my egotism.

I will but say about Athanasius that my second edition arose from my wish to make it as different from that in the Library of the Fathers as I could to meet Pusey's generosity, and that my plan was spoiled by my being called to Rome for the Cardinalate. I have stated and apologised for this in my Advertisement.[5] I shall not live for the proof sheets of edition 3.[6]

Yours affectionately, J. H. Newman.

The pheasant is come. My Greek friend was Linwood.
P.S.   Thank your sister for her most welcome letter.

TO SYLVESTER HUNTER, S.J.

Birmingham Oct 6. 1886
Dear Very Rev Father

Excuse my bad writing. I think I saw a letter of yours to Mr Newdigate lately, which suggested to me the idea of two such good Societies yours and what he contemplates being united.[7] Is not a 'Society for the support of shops for the sale of Catholic books' very desirable. I know how much the 'Truth Society' is doing — would not such enlargement of it in the way I speak of be of great service to it?

---

[1] See letter of 1 Oct. to Lord Blachford, who thinking of the man's father, R. F. Wilson, wrote 'Certainly paternity has a good deal of suffering to set against the blank of childlessness', which was his own state.

[2] *Adelphi*, I, i, 11–12; *Phormio*, II, i, 13–14.

[3] The Cynic philosopher.

[4] Mary Newman died on 5 Jan. 1828.

[5] Lord Blachford wrote on 4 Oct. 'I am amused at your taking refuge in Athanasius as a light relaxation.'

[6] This was published in 1887.

[7] See letter of 29 Sept. to Newdigate.

Alas, I can take little part in a plan which has been so much in my mind ever since I have been a Catholic but I would give such support as I could, as I told Mr Newdigate[1]

Excuse me and believe me   Your faithful Servant

J. H. Card. Newman

The Very Revd F Hunter S J

TO LORD BRAYE

October 8 1886

My dear Lord Braye

Excuse my abruptness. I must use as few words as I can.

In a day like this, combinations of zealous Catholics will be formed — but there is always the chance of collisions. Your Society is as little likely to hurt others, as any can be. I rejoice in its existence — tho' I fear it will have great trials. But trials have their great advantages.[2]

I am too old and weak to take up any work. If I did it would be an association such as the Truth Society, to be worked by local Catholic shops in great towns. It would require money I can't write more

Most truly Yours J H Card. Newman

TO ALFRED NEWDIGATE

Oct. 12. 1886

Dear Mr. Newdigate

I have been too ill to write to you

I will gladly do my part in the good work you propose

But I mark a confusion about one important matter. I thought you were in such sense connected with Truth Society that you came under the sanction of the Cardinal Archbishop and Bishops.

Since this is not so, I think the time cannot be said to have come yet, for me to give my name as Cardinal to your undertaking.

I must ask you neither in the Tablet or elsewhere to introduce my name, tho' (if it is worthwhile) of course you might mention the offer you have had of £20.[3]

Very truly yours John H Card. Newman

---

[1] Hunter replied that he thought Newdigate's and the Catholic Truth Society could work best side by side, the latter publishing and the former distributing.

[2] See letter of 8 Sept. to Lord Braye.

[3] Newdigate sent out a circular in Nov., without mentioning Newman. See letter of 4 March 1887.

TO BARTHOLOMEW WOODLOCK, BISHOP OF ARDAGH

The Oratory, October 25th. 1886

My dear Lord,

Thank you for the Paper you sent me and which I now return. Of course I take great interest in what is going on and I only wish it was in my power to give an opinion on any of the subjects which it opens.

I am no judge of details, and even if I was, the questions to which they lead have so changed in the last thirty years, and the principles which they involve, that I am unable to handle them.

All I think I can express strongly is, that the standard of examinations should be as high in our Universities as it is in other Academical Institutions of the day.[1]

TO WILLIAM BARRY

Oct. 28. 1886

Dear Dr Barry

Thank you for sending me your very impressive Sermon I read it with much interest.[2]

Very truly yours John H. Card. Newman

TO MRS TIMOTHY SULLIVAN

Oct. 30. 1886.

Madam

You have thought, I fear, my silence very rude, when you had written to me so interesting and important a letter, and so it would have been if there had been no good reason for it. But I have one which I am sure your charity will accept. I have been seriously ill and could do nothing, and even now write with difficulty.

I am not fond of bazaars, but when the one you refer to is over, I will gladly ask to be allowed to show, even in a small way, my interest in your most excellent object.[3]

I am, Madam, Your very humble servant

John H. Card. Newman

The Lady Mayoress Dublin.

[1] A note on the copy says 'The remainder is cut off.'
[2] *In Memoriam*, Sermon preached at St Peter's Church, Leamington, on 15 June 1886, at the funeral of Nicholas Selby du Moulin-Browne, Birmingham 1886.
[3] Mrs Sullivan was Lady Mayoress of Dublin 1886 and 1887. She was collecting money for the Sacred Heart Home, on anti-proselytising institution, of which she was the first President.

TO ALFRED NEWDIGATE

Nov. 4. 1886

My dear Sir

Will you kindly tell me whether you have a recognised *shop* any where, where in [sic] might send some books for sale?

You know how much more interesting I should find it (and others also, as I think) if it was in larger place like Manchester than if at Leamington[1]

Very truly yours John H Card. Newman

A. Newdigate Esqr.

TO MESSRS BURNS AND OATES

[8 November 1886]

Cardinal Newman thinks it right to bring the following matter before Messrs Burns and Oates

In declining to give leave to an applicant who desired to insert in a tract quotations from a volume of his Sermons published by them they use the following words

'it will never do for us to multiply cheap issues of extracts from works, *the copyright of which we have secured*'[2]

The Cardinal wishes to know from them whether they include in this statement any work of his of which they consider themselves to possess the copyright. The purchase of an edition is no purchase of a copyright[3]

TO A. REEVE[4]

8 Nov 86

Dear Sir,

Thank you for your kind and most welcome letter. I return your rosary blessed. Excuse a short note, but I write with difficulty.

With my blessing on yourself, most truly yours,

John H. Cardinal Newman.

---

[1] Newdigate replied on 5 Nov. that the Art and Book Company of Leamington had no shop in Manchester or any large town, but at Oxford Fr Parkinson S.J. was anxious to improve a shop he had been instrumental in starting. Newdigate thought that would be an excellent place for Newman's purpose.

[2] See postscript to letter of 29 Sept. to Newdigate.

[3] Burns and Oates replied on 9 Nov. that Newman had parted with the copyright existing in certain editions of his works, for which he received a royalty.

[4] Newman's correspondent was an American.

TO MESSRS BURNS AND OATES

Copy of sent   Nov 11/86

I cannot think it allowable in you to say that you have for long time or short, or for any time whatever, the copyright of any books of mine, considering such a statement to be at variance with the fact. It is as incorrect thus to speak, as if a tenant who had a lease on land, were to tell his landlord that he possessed the freehold.

I am obliged therefore to protest against it.[1]

J H N

TO GEORGE CORMACK

Nov 11 [1886]

Dear Rev Father

I gladly send you and the attendants on your Mission the blessing you ask me for, and cannot but be sure that blessings from on high have already accompanied so good a work[2]

Excuse my difficulty of writing

and believe me to be Your faithful Servt

J H Card. Newman

TO NICHOLAS DARNELL

Nov 12th 1886.

My dear Fr Nicholas

I am not a good scribe just now, but I have been thinking of you ever since I heard so poor an account of you from R Bellasis, that you had left your work in the North and were constrained to be all but idle at Clifton.[3]

I can fancy how this may try you and have been setting my brains to work to find how I could show you my sympathy. I can find nothing better than to ask your acceptance from me of my publication of Mr Palmer's Russian Journal which it is possible you have not seen and which will at least show I do not forget you.[4]

Yours affectionately John H Card: Newman

[1] Burns and Oates replied on 13 Nov. that they had secured the exclusive use of the copyright of such editions of Newman's works as they printed at their expense. He replied on 14 Nov.

[2] The Rosminian Father Cormack with companions was giving a mission at St Peter's Birmingham.

[3] Darnell had retired from his parish at Haydon Bridge, Northumberland, and was living at the Clifton Wood Convent.

[4] Darnell replied on 15 Nov., 'how utterly unworthy I feel myself of your great condescension and goodness in admitting me to occupy a place in your thoughts for a single moment — one who has been worse than unfaithful to S. Philip and yourself, and so long estranged from your salutary influence and your happy home.' cf Volume XX.

On 18 Nov. Darnell acknowledged William Palmer's *Notes of a Visit to the Russian Church*, in which was written 'With the affectionate regards of John H Card. Newman'

[14? November 1886[1]]

The first law book I have consulted says ⟨p 92⟩ 'Copyright — the right of an author to print and publish his own original work, exclusively of all other persons.'[2]

What you considered you had purchased from [me] was, as you said, a royalty.

I find a royalty and a royalty is a pro rata payment to a grantor or lessors, on the working of the property leased or otherwise on the profits of the grant or lease. The word is especially used in reference to mines, patents and copyrights[3]

I am startled in your claiming the copyright in my works instead of their use.

The transaction is not completed as regards the two volumes of Sermons. I am quite ready on my part to put an end to this engagement

J H N

TO JOHN HARDMAN, JUNIOR

Nov. 16. 1886

My dear Mr Hardman

I am glad that your Father's good deeds are not to be left unrecorded.[4] He was truly noble and loyal as a Catholic and a friend. I never forget in my prayers the good and kind men who supported me against Dr Achilli, and your Father was one of the foremost. Excuse a short letter, for I write with trouble

Yours most truly John H Card. Newman

TO EDWARD HAYES PLUMPTRE

Nov 17. 1886

My dear Dean Plumptre

I must ask you to excuse these few ill written lines to thank you for your very kind present and to congratulate you on the important work which is conveyed to me in it.[5] I am quite astonished at the quantity of labour, to say nothing of higher qualities, which the volume betokens, and although much labour is, often, I know, pleasant labour, it implies much anxious thought and

---

[1] This draft is undated and was perhaps not sent.
[2] Herbert Newman Mozley and George Crispe Whiteley *A Concise Law Dictionary*, London 1876, p. 92.
[3] ibid. p. 388.
[4] Presumably the notice in *Gillow III*, pp. 131–3.
[5] *Commedia and Canzoniere of Dante Alighieri*, Volume I, London 1886.

perseverance, especially as it embraces verse and prose   I am glad I have the prospect of seeing you next month, and, as I hope, Mrs Plumptre.

I am, dear Dean of Wells Most truly yours
John H Card Newman

TO LADY SIMEON

November 18. 1886

My dear Lady Simeon

I have long wished to write to you, but to write is a trouble.

I have wanted to know whether the sojourn abroad was a success — also to assure you, that, in consequence of what you said to me, that I have thought much about dear Q . . ., and said many prayers for her.[1]

Yours affly J. H. Card. Newman.

The Honble Lady Simeon

TO LORD BLACHFORD

November 23/86.

My dear Blachford,

Thanks to your munificence, I have in prospect of my dinner a snipe, a woodcock (and November 22nd.) a pheasant.

You must not despise our cook — we have had a female artiste now since we have had a boys' school and an additional house for women servants. As to the Maxim you mention, she had great pity on my peculiarity, tho' my reading from a boy has made it apply to wild ducks. 'Take them through the Kitchen and take care they don't go too near the fire.'[2]

The last accounts relieve my anxieties about Church. I hope the invalids are better, but it is unusual weather everywhere — Here we have had candles all day and I can't see to read even with them.

Yours affectionately, John H. Card: Newman.

TO EDMUND STONOR

Nov. 26. 1886

My dear Monsignor Stonor

I want to ask of you the favor of offering my Obolus to the Holy Father. I have lost the power of writing so what I propose to do, in sending to you my

---

[1] This refers to Catherine Simeon. See letter of 3 Nov. 1887 to Emily Bowles.
[2] Lord Blachford wrote on 17 Nov. wondering whether Newman had the cook of a Cardinal or merely of an Oratorian, and added: '. . . if I remember right, you would not like a snipe roasted after the fashion of an epicure — i.e. carried through the kitchen and allowed to look at the fire *in transitu.*'

cheque, is to send also a few lines to him such as Leoni xiii Beatissimo Patri, Augustissimo, Sapientissimo, ego, servus et creatura ejus etc etc.

Please to tell me if such a form of Address in conveying an Offering is so unusuall as to be impossible. I much fear that a decently written letter I am too feeble to send, but I *could* write one or two lines, such as I describe

Very truly Yours John H Card Newman

TO ANNE MOZLEY

Nov 28/86

Dear Anne Mozley

Fr Neville returned much pleased by his visit, and charmed with his dinner.

Lord Blachford is substantially right about Cumberland.[1] I think he came to an evening party at our house. My Father's partial love for me led to my *reciting* something or other in the presence of a literary man. I wish I could think it was 'Here Cumberland lies' from Goldsmith's 'Retaliation,' which I knew well as a boy.[2] The interview ended by his putting his hand on my head, and saying 'Young gentleman, when you are old, you can say that you have had on your head the hand of Richard Cumberland.'

I think you have got somewhat off the lines about the Arnold correspondence as if I knowingly had put it aside. My principle was to send you all the letters I had. Twenty years ago I burnt lots of letters, keeping what was worth keeping in the large quarto books. I think they go down to 1835. I then began 1836 in the roan books. I have never, I think read a line of them since 1860 when I collected and finished them. But now, when you were kind enough to make your most valuable offer, I professed and acted on the principle of sending you *all* I found, and that in order to give you 'elbow room.' I sent you all I found, not indeed simply for publication, but that this was to be the *rule*, viz. that *your discretion* should decide, and this I thought was the use of Dean Church that, when you were in doubt, you would have some one to consult[3]

But now you speak as if I had kept the correspondence back. No such thing. I am not sure that it survives. Dr Stanley asked for it when he wrote

[1] Richard Cumberland, the dramatist. Anne Mozley wrote on 24 Nov. that she had heard from Lord Blachford the story Newman now recounts. *Moz.* I, pp. 17–18.
[2] Cumberland's epitaph in 'Retaliation', 61–78, begins:
'Here Cumberland lies, having acted his parts,
The Terence of England, the mender of hearts . . .'
The Poems of Thomas Gray, William Collins, Oliver Goldsmith, edited by Roger Lonsdale, London 1969, pp. 751–2.
[3] On 21 Oct. Anne Mozley wrote that she had shown Dean Church the two books containing Newman's Early Journals. See letters of 13 and 18 March 1885 to Anne Mozley, to whom Church spoke 'of his great interest in the two books.' She wrote, 'I cannot over-estimate his value as an adviser'. She also wrote: 'You have I know seen some papers of his the Dean's on the Movement he has let me read them — He is *the* man to do the subject justice, and what feeling it wakens in him'.

Arnold's Life, but sent it back without using it. If I find it, you shall have it —
but I doubt if it tells much against Arnold, but then it is a *private* letter, and I
have no leave, no right (even by the law?) to publish it.[1] Hampden's letter,
which I sent you in the Dublin Review, I consider public.[2]

Yrs affectly John H Card. Newman

TO EMMA TYNDALL

Nov 28 1886

Dear Madam

I am sorry to say I cannot answer your letter as I have lost the use of my
fingers for writing This must be my excuse, which I am sure you will
kindly accept.[3]

Yours very truly John H Card Newman

TO WILLIAM PHILIP GORDON

Nov 30/86

My dear Father Superior

We are very sorry for your loss, especially as so sudden, and sympathise
with you. We have begun to say the Masses.[4]

Excuse so brief a letter, but I write with any effort [sic]

Yours affectly John H Card. Newman

TO EDMUND STONOR

Dec. 4/86

My dear Monsignor

I inclose a letter for the Holy Father, and a cheque for £20 sterling   I hope
he will be able to read the first. It is my very best.

Many thanks for your letter

Most truly Yours John H Card. Newman

[1] Anne Mozley wrote on 26 Nov. about Newman's correspondence with Thomas Arnold in
1833, which she thought he 'intentionally withdrew'. On 2 Dec. she explained that she was
seeking a letter from Newman to Arnold 'that Froude found amusing'.

[2] See letters of 4 and 7 Aug. 1871 to Henry Wilberforce.

[3] On the blank page of the autograph is written:

'A medium was controuled by the spirit who alledged to be Cardinal Piero-Choun[?] who
implored me to obtain leave from Cardinal Newman that the medium should have an audience
with the latter and the former would again controul him, and receive his confession

This note to me is a strange inconsistent reply to this request

Emma Tyndall'

[4] Francis O'Carroll, a priest of the London Oratory, had died.

TO AN UNKNOWN CORRESPONDENT

Dec. 7. 1886

May the Blessed Mary
be your Protection and Comfort
this day and all days
till she welcomes you
to the eternal Home
above.

J. H. Card Newman

TO MESSRS BURNS AND OATES

To Messrs Burns   Dec 10. 1886
Gentlemen

I wish you to be good as to order of Messrs Gilbert and Rivington for the
four volumes, which came to you from Messrs Pickering, new Title Pages,
substituting in them your name for the name of Messrs Pickering

While requesting you to do this, I think it right to add, that my mind is
not yet made up as to the publication of these four volumes, when the present
editions have run out

J H N

TO ANNE MOZLEY

Decr 10. 1886

My dear Anne Mozley

The inclosed has been sent me by the nephew of Dean Lyall. I send it you
on the chance of your wishing to see it[1]

Yrs affecty J. H. Card Newman

TO ALFRED HENRY SPURRIER

Dec. 11. 1886

I wish the state of my fingers allowed me to write a sufficient, or at least a
readable answer to your question. I must be abrupt, because I must be short.

Who can have *dared* to say that I am disappointed in the Church of Rome?
'dared,' because I have never uttered, or written, or thought, or felt the very

[1] This was a copy of Newman's letter of 16 July 1842 to W. R. Lyall, *Moz.* II, pp. 399–400,
on how the only theory on which the Church of England can stand is that 'the present state of
the Church is like that of an empire breaking or broken up'.

shadow of disappointment. I believe it to be a human institution as well as divine, and so far as it is human it is open to the faults of human nature; but if, because I think, with others, that its rulers have sometimes erred as fallible men, I therefore think it has failed, such logic won't hold; indeed, it is the wonderful anticipation in Our Lord's and St Paul's teaching, of apparent failure [and real] success in the times after them which has ever been one of my strong arguments for believing them divine messengers.

But I can't write more. One word as to your next page. Faith is a divine gift. It is gained by prayer. Prayer must be patient and persevering. I have not strength to explain and defend this here. God bless you.[1]

TO R. BURTON DINZEY, JUNIOR

Dec. 19. 1886

Dear Sir

I would gladly comply with your request, which I feel to be a very kind one — but my fingers are too weak to allow of my writing out the Verses without effort and pain[2]

I have been obliged to say to many others what I say to you now, that I am *unable* – Recollect how old I am – close on 86

May you and I and all of us be led on into the rest proposed for the people of God[3]

Most truly Yours John H Card. Newman

TO BARTHOLOMEW WOODLOCK, BISHOP OF ARDAGH

Decr 19. 1886

My dear Lord

You ask of me a very small favour, and I seem, I fear, very ungracious in refusing it.

The truth is I have for many years done the same incivility to dear friends and to personages in authority and you are both   So I must beg you to be merciful with me.

---

[1] Spurrier wrote in Feb. 1887, to say that he had prayed as Newman told him, and was about to be received into the Church. He seems to have begun studying for the priesthood, since he was at the Gregorian University in Rome, but then went to the London Hospital, and eventually became Health Officer of Zanzibar.

[2] Dinzey was an invalid and asked for an autograph, and a poem in Newman's writing. Newman also sent an early photograph, writing 'I have none of the recent photographs'.

[3] Dinzey lived at Saint Bartholomew, in the Dutch West Indies, and his father wrote on 21 Jan. 1887: 'Please accept of my heartfelt thanks for so kindly replying to the request of my son, and especially so for your Holy Wish that he might be among those led on into the rest prepared for the people of God.

God grant that that wish was answered in Heaven – for even while it was being expressed my dear son's spirit was preparing to depart from its earthly abode, and passed away two days afterwards – I trust into "that rest", led on by the Spirit of that beautiful Hymn, of which he was so fond . . .'

When the Bazaar is quite over. I shall ask you to accept an offering for the undertaking to St Patrick and St Mel[1]

Yours affectionately John H Card. Newman

I have lost the use of my fingers for writing

TO LORD CHARLES THYNNE

Dec. 21. 1886.

My dear Lord Charles,

I have not forgotten your wish all along, and I rejoice and am thankful that it is so happily accomplished. What a great gift you must feel it to be.[2]

Excuse so brief a letter but I have lost, I fear, the use of my fingers for writing.

Most truly yours, John H. Card. Newman.

The Lord Charles Thynne.

TO CATHERINE ANNE BATHURST

Decr 27. 1886

My dear Child

I rejoice you are so prospering, and gladly, in answer to your wish, and in return for your prayers, send you my blessing.[3]

I cannot write more, for I have lost the necessary use of my fingers.

Did you get a little pamphlet from me in answer to a Congregational Divine, a year ago?[4]

Yrs affecly J H Card Newman

TO CATHERINE BOWDEN, SISTER MARY ALBAN

Dec 27. 1886

My dear Child

I am sure you and your Sisters about you will excuse me, if I am brief. I cannot write without pain and effort

But at least I can thank you for your prayers for me, and can congratulate you all on the Festival, and send you, as I do, my blessing.

Yrs affly J. H. Card. Newman

---

[1] The bazaar was presumably in aid of St Mel's College, Longford.
[2] Lord Charles Thynne was ordained priest in Rome in Dec.
[3] Catherine Bathurst wrote on 26 Dec. that in the course of the year she had opened a preparatory school for boys at Shoreham.
[4] *The Development of Religious Error* in reply to A. M. Fairbairn, reprinted from the *Contemporary Review* (Oct. 1885).

TO WILLIAM PHILIP GORDON

Dec. 27. 1886

My dear Fr Superior

Do you think I have any chance of prevailing on the Duke to be President of the Birmingham Triennial Festival in 1888? I have been asked by a prominent person to ask him — but shall not think of doing so, if the application is not likely to be successful. I inclose his letter.[1]

With best wishes and congratulations on the Great Feast to you and yours

Yours affectionately John H Card. Newman

TO ALEXANDER FULLERTON

Decr 29. 1886

My dear Mr Fullerton

It is very kind in you to write to me to tell me of the progress of your religious yet anxious work. Thank you for doing so. And I rejoice to hear your account of Mrs Craven's progress.[2]

I pray that the fairest and best Christmas blessings, may be given both to your works and to hers. I cannot use my fingers for writing, and must beg you to excuse this unworthy letter

Most truly Yours J. H. Card. Newman

TO W. S. LILLY

[1887?]

My dear Lilly

Pray pardon my silence. I have been wanting to write to tell with what great pleasure I have read your proof.[3] It is a remarkable result of Darwin's work. But the more I was pleased, the more I was frightened as you proceed to express your belief that the first men had tails. I think this temerarious. I can hardly write, my fingers are so weak. That is why I have written so little to you of late

Most sincerely yours J. H. Cardinal Newman.

[1] The Duke of Norfolk accepted. See letters of 10 Jan. to the Duke and 29 Jan. 1887 to Gordon.
[2] With her life of Lady Georgiana Fullerton.
[3] The proof of chapter iii of *A Century of Revolution*, 'The Revolution and Science'.

TO WILLIAM ROBERT BROWNLOW

Jany 3. 1887

My dear Canon

Receive my best thanks for your affectionate letter. It is very kind in you to send it. I wish I could send you a suitable answer — but I have lost the free use of my fingers

Continue your prayers for me and believe me to be your[s] gratefully and affectly

J. H. Card. Newman

TO JOHN GELLIBRAND HUBBARD

[3 January 1887]

My dear Sir

I fear I must consider myself to have acted uncourteously towards you — but I am very sorry to think so, and beg to assure you that such conduct was as far as possible from my intention, and that I wish hereby to apologize with all my heart for having laid myself open to an act so inconsistent with the habitual respect and good will with which I think of you. Do write me a line to say you accept this my very sincere sorrow at having seemed rude to you[1]

TO WILLIAM KNIGHT

Private   January 7. 1887
My dear Sir

Neither my fingers nor my eyesight allow me to express in writing the debt of gratitude which I owe to the late Principal Shairp for the kindness with which he has so many times spoken of me in his publications, nor the deep sorrow with which I heard of his death. My hitherto unfulfilled wish to comply with your request on this point has been a trouble day after day, amid my existing engagements, but it could not be helped — I am too old to be able to do a thing because I wish it.[2]

[1] Hubbard, who was an M.P. and an extreme High Churchman, was engaged in controversy about Apostolic Succession and Anglican Orders. Sentences attributed to Newman casting doubt on their validity, had been quoted on the subject by H. Arnold Thomas in 'Position of Congregationalists', the *Nonconformist* (2 Dec. 1886), p. 1163. Hubbard asked Newman where they were to be found. Newman's reply is not extant, but the quotations came from *Ess.* II, pp. 76 and 85. The acknowledgment of Newman's reply was delayed, hence his letter.
    Hubbard answered on 4 Jan. that he did not think Newman either had acted or could act discourteously. He wrote again on 10 Jan. to thank for copies of *Ess.* I and II.
    [2] Knight wrote from the University, St Andrews on 9 Dec. 1886 to ask for Newmans' reminiscences of Principal Shairp for the book he was preparing, *Principal Shairp and his Friends*, London 1888, saying 'There was no religious Teacher and Guide of our time to whom he looked up, with greater veneration, and sense of indebtedness, than to you; and, in a

But passing by my personal feelings, I lament the Principal's loss to us on a more serious account. In this day of religious indifference and unbelief it has been long my hope and comfort to think that a silent and secret process is going on in the hearts of many, which, though it may not reach its limit and scope in this generation or the next, is a definite work of Divine Providence, in prospect of a state of religion such as the world has never yet seen; issuing, not indeed in a millennium, but in a public opinion strong enough for the vigorous spread and exaltation, and thereby the influence and prosperity of Divine Truth all over the world. The world may not in the Divine Decree last long enough for a work so elaborate and multiform. Or without indulging in such great conceptions, one can fancy such a return to primitive truth[1] to be vouchsafed to particular countries which at present are divided and broken up into a hundred sects and at war with each other.

I am too tired to go on — and therefore I must beg you not to consider this other than a private letter. I ought not to have begun what I cannot finish — especially since I have not brought home what I have been saying to the subject of Principal Shairp.

Very truly Yours J. H. Card. Newman

P.S. Fr Neville is confined to his room, not to say his bed, with a bad, with a bad cold. I think you will take this instead of his writing.[2]

TO THE DUKE OF NORFOLK

Jany 10. 1887

My dear Duke of Norfolk

I trust I am not unmindful of the many important calls upon your Grace's time and thoughts, when, as you will see by the inclosed letter formally addressed to you, I am myself acting the very part which I know must be so trying to you.[3]

I am led to write to you by the service I shall be indirectly doing to the Birmingham Oratory by a step which will gratify the applicant for whom I write in a matter, as to which they have a great pride and historic interest; and not only so, but which also will continue and increase the good will already felt

memorial-portrait of him (just hung on our College walls) a volume of your Sermons is represented as lying on a table, along with the Poems of Wordsworth.'
For Shairp's published remarks about Newman, see letters of 6 July 1877 and 25 Nov. 1881.

[1] See letter of 19 Nov. 1887 to Knight, in which Newman asked for these two words to be altered, when he allowed this private letter to be published, in *Principal Shairp and his Friends*, p. 387.
[2] This letter was written entirely by Newman. Knight replied on 10 Jan. 'Your very kind letter was a ray of light to me', and hoped 'if the subject of that preparation going on by a silent and secret process, for a state of Religion such as the world has not yet seen, recurs to you', Newman would dictate his thoughts.
[3] The enclosure was an invitation to the Duke of Norfolk to be President of the Birmingham Triennial Musical Festival in 1888. See letters of 27 Dec. 1886 to Gordon and 14 Jan. 1887 to the Duke.

towards us by the local musical world, which is a special power in Birmingham, and with which through our two Fathers Bellasis we are on excellent terms.

There is another consideration which occurs to me; it is this — Though politics and religion are prohibited and impossible in a musical undertaking, it is impossible too, that the sight of your Grace should fail to inspire friendly thoughts both towards yourself and towards Catholics, a consideration not to be overlooked in a place and time in which lately there has been so much modification of opinion

However, I leave the whole question to your better judgment, and am, My dear Duke

Your faithful & affecte Servant John H Card. Newman

P.S. Excuse my bad writing

His Grace The Duke of Norfolk E M   K.G.

TO JAMES PATRICK MUIRHEAD

[11 January 1887

Dear Sir

I thank you for the compliment you pay me in translating my Verses; and it is a pleasure to know you think them worthy of so happy a rendering[1]

TO THE DUKE OF NORFOLK

Jany 14. 1887

My dear Duke of Norfolk

I am sending off your letter to Mr Jaffray.[2] It is strange if it does not much please him — both in your acceptance, and your mode of accepting   I feel its kindness towards myself

Yours affectly John H Card. Newman

TO THE DUKE OF NORFOLK

Jany 17/87

My dear Duke

The inclosed letter so pleases me, that I am led to think it will please you. Pray burn it[3]

Your affectte Servant J H Card. Newman

The Duke of Norfolk E M

---

[1] Muirhead had translated 'Lead, kindly Light' into rhyming Latin, in *Blackwood's Magazine* (Jan. 1887), p. 80.

[2] John Jaffray was Chairman of the Committee of the Birmingham Musical Festival.

[3] This was the letter of thanks from the Musical Festival Committee. See letter of 29 Jan. to Gordon.

TO MRS EDWARD BELLASIS

Jany 18 1887.

My dear Mrs Bellasis

I have ill requited your kind and welcome letter, by my letting weeks pass before I answer — yet I have something to say in explanation. It is very well for your dear sons to give you a flourishing account of me, but that is the good, and (thank God) the happy and a true side of the picture – but not the whole. Now, so it is, that my fingers will not write without pain to me, and my eyesight will not act by candle light and we have scarcely any sun since the year began. Hence I have been obliged to sit quiet for hours, doing nothing and having plenty to do, especially in the matter of letter writing

I am sure you and Clara [Bellasis] will pity me under such circumstances. I could not indeed have a lighter trial, but I think it sufficient to save me from incurring the charge of ingratitude to your kindness, which I should otherwise incur

It is not too late to wish you a happy new year and to send you and Clara my blessing

Yours affectly J. H. Card. Newman

TO LAETITIA COLE

Jany 18. 1887

My dear Miss Cole

You must think it very rude in me not to acknowledge your kind and welcome letter with its inclosure before now. It has been owing to my failing eye sight, which not even three candles enable to read, and to my failing fingers which get tried before I have written half a dozen words, and, strange to say, are beginning even to spell wrongly.

Under these circumstances, it is not very likely that I should, as you suppose, be writing my Life, and the thought indeed has never come into my head nor is likely to do. I suppose compositors and the like, finding it necessary to fill up their pages, are obliged to say something, and say what they think likely to be the fact, tho' they are not sure of it

With my best respects to your Mother

I am, Sincerely Yours John H Card Newman

My dear Mr Palgrave   Jany 18. 1887

Your letter was a very kind one, as yours always are, and it is always pleasant to me to be reminded of your dear Father, whose words gave me so much encouragement, when I was in literature a beginner.[1] I gladly give permission for your use of my small compositions, but it would be civil to ask Messrs Rivingtons if they have any hold in law on any of them.[2]

Your excellent undertaking in pictures is one which Hope Scott began (say) 50 years ago. It failed — Times are different now.[3]

I shall be glad to receive from you the Christmas print[4]

Most truly yours John H Card. Newman

F. T. Palgrave Esq

P.S   Your beautiful gift has come. All who have seen it admire it much.[5]

[1] See letter of 15 July 1866 to Palgrave.
[2] Palgrave asked permission to include some of Newman's poems in his *The Treasury of Sacred Song*, Oxford 1889. See pp. 282–301. Palgrave presented a copy of *The Treasury* on 8 Oct. 1889.
[3] See letter of 11 Dec. 1885 to Palgrave.
[4] Palgrave sent one of the series of prints, an 'Adoration' taken from a fresco of Gaudenzio Ferrari.
[5] In Nov. 1887 Palgrave was in Birmingham, and described, in his Journal, a visit to Newman: 'I was allowed an interview with Cardinal Newman at the Oratory. There sat that aged man with his snow-white hair; he rose and thanked me for coming and for caring for him with a sort of young child's gracious simplicity. He was much changed, of course, since I had last seen him many years ago: the look of almost anxious searching had passed into the look of perfect peace. His mind was not only bright as ever, but with the cheerfulness and humour of youth. He talked of his old Oxford days . . . Then of [Dean] Church, 'whom no one could know without loving'. He spoke of his voyage long ago in the Mediterranean; how little he had, however, seen of Italy. We talked of Rome, of Varallo, when he at once recalled the Gaudenzio 'Nativity' which I sent him last Christmas. He went on to speak of Creighton's 'Papacy', and the Renaissance and its evils in high places; and he broke out, with a bright smile of tenderness: 'How wonderful was the revival of the Church soon after under Loyola, St Philip Neri, San Carlo Borromeo!' Then he spoke of Tennyson, and said that in poetry one went back to what one knew in youth. I said Wordsworth perhaps — at which he smiled, and quoted the first stanza of the parody in the 'Rejected Addresses,' ending with
                              And burnt off half its nose.
He went on to say that Scott had been his favourite, and alluded playfully to his age (eighty-seven in January next) as a reason why he read less than he would have liked. He thanked me again for what he called my kindness in caring to see him. This great and perfect humility was almost overwhelming in its strikingness. No wonder he looked up with reverence to the two Borromei, whom he mentioned with special admiration. What a strange and beautiful union of the saint and the poet! His voice has much of its old strange sweetness, such as I heard it at Littlemore in my Oxford days – how far off for both of us!' Gwenllian F. Palgrave, *Francis Turner Palgrave*, London 1899, p. 202.
   The first four volumes of Mandell Creighton's *A History of the Papacy during the period of the Reformation* were published between 1882 and 1887. Newman quoted the second stanza of 'The Baby's Debut' from *Rejected Addresses*, Papa gave presents, to Jack a top, and to his sister who was younger, a doll of wax:
                    'Jack's in the pouts, and this it is, —
                    He thinks mine came to more than his;
                         So to my drawer he goes,
                    Takes out the doll, and, O, my stars!
                    He pokes her head between the bars,
                         And melts off half her nose!'
James and Horace Smith, *Rejected Addresses*, twenty third edition, London 1852, p. 10.

January 20. 1887

My dear Blachford

I am much grieved at your account of dear Wilson.[1] He took an impressive leave of me, when he last was here — but that was several years ago and I think his illness must be more recent. It is sorrowful enough to lose a friend — but to have to know by a definite and extraordinary blow, time uncertain, is an increase to one's distress. I shall write him a line or two.

I am on the whole wonderfully well, tho' I write and see less easily — and walk with some difficulty. My fall in June cost me two inches in my height — though between June and September I went to London and back, made a call at Rednall and preached a sermon — but then came a relapse which no one professed to understand, and since that I cannot speak with confidence.

I have been keeping in mind your birthday which I think is on the 31st the day I was had up in /53, to be rowed by the Queen's Bench.[2] Did you not tell me that Lady Blachford's was the 21? As I am writing I shall ask you and her to accept my congratulations by anticipation, as I am not secure of my memory, when the right day comes.

The game was a great treat and I ate it all myself — the pheasants superb.

I have not yet learnt what Lord Ildsleigh's (I can't spell it) 'mortification' was; was it from Lord Randolph Ch' [Churchill] or having to give up the Foreign Office? but few people could keep from revering such a man as he was and being touched at his death.[3]

Ever Yrs affly J. H. Card. Newman

P.S. You must be, as I am, very anxious about Church.

Jany 21. 1887

Dear Sir

I thank you sincerely for the gift you send me of M l'Abbé Maillard's Translations. Also I ask your kindness to convey my thanks to himself also. I will make a point of bringing it before the notice of the Rev. Prefect of the Oratory School

I am, Your faithful Servant John H Card. Newman

G. F Engelbach Esq

[1] Lord Blachford wrote on 14 Jan. that R. F. Wilson was dying of cancer.
[2] See diary for 31 Jan. 1853. Lord Blachford was born on 31 Jan. 1811.
[3] Lord Blachford wrote: 'How very pathetic that a life so useful and distinguished as Northcote's should close in such mortification!' Sir Stafford Northcote, Earl of Iddesleigh, was removed from the office of Foreign Secretary against his wish. He learned on 4 Jan. from the newspapers that his offer to resign had been accepted. He died at 10 Downing Street on 12 Jan., just after he had taken leave of his staff.

TO GEORGE T. EDWARDS

Jany 22. 1887

My dear Mr Edwards

I thank you sincerely for your kind greetings on the New Year. I should have written in answer long before this, except that I have lost the use of my fingers for writing, and cannot attempt it without effort and pain.

I wish I could write more. I read the small publication called 'Stepping Stones' with great interest and pleasure, and should have liked very much to have made some remark upon it.[1] But so many books come to me, that I cannot be sure it was your kind gift. And this moment I fear I have mislaid it, and my eyesight is so bad that I cannot at will find it

Very truly Yours John H Card Newman

P.S. I have found Stepping Stones a very striking paper and *full of promise* — but the authoress is not a Christian. She wants *faith*, in order to it. 'By grace are ye saved *through faith*' and, I do not recollect tokens of a true sense of sin

TO WILLIAM PHILIP GORDON

Jany 29. 87

My dear Fr Sup.

I ought to have written to you before now, as I do now, to thank you for your trouble, which has quite done for me what I wanted. The Duke at once accepted the application of the Committee, and in so generous a way as to please them much.[2]

Yrs affly J H Card Newman

TO THE HON. MRS MAXWELL-SCOTT

Febr 19/87

My dear Mamo

I must ask you to wait a few posts before you write to Burns and Oates.[3] I have found them trying to *get a hold* on my works, and tho' I can agree to

[1] On 31 Dec. 1886 Edwards sent Newman a paper by Sir James Stephen's youngest daughter Caroline Emelia, 'as I know your sympathy with all who had had to struggle with doubt and unbelief. She has passed through deep water and her "Stepping Stones" is a touching history of her inward striving'. Edwards added, 'I occasionally hear from her and she has named you as a friend of her father's.' Caroline Stephen joined the Society of Friends in 1879.

[2] See letters of 27 Dec. 1886 to Gordon and 10 and 17 Jan. to the Duke of Norfolk.

[3] Mrs Maxwell-Scott wrote on 10 Feb. asking to be allowed to reprint for Scotland Newman's sermon on her father, 'In the World but not of the World', *O.S.*, pp. 263–80. 'So many people knew him, or knew of him and I am assured that if they had opportunities of knowing more of him and his conversion, it might bear fruit ...'

Newman told her to write to Burns and Oates, who gave permission for the cheap reprint provided that Newman approved. This she explained in a letter of 18 Feb.

their letting *me* print a small edition of the Sermon, I cannot let *them* print it. Besides, Murray would, if so, have to be asked.[1] So please, *wait* a bit

Yours affectly J H Card Newman

Turn over

P.S.   Would it be against your wishes if the copies which I sent you were for distribution and not for sale

TO LORD BLACHFORD

Feb 23. 1887.

My dear Blachford,

I have long kept your brother in law in mind and wondered how he was.[2] I should have asked you, had I not felt that, from the nature of the complaint, there would be nothing to tell me, except that it was a time for patience and suffering, and so your letter shows me it has so been out of the common. When it is right to do so, say for me what is kind to your sister.

I suppose I have a touch of the same complaint, (I have long thought I should) not only because my brother as I has lost the use of his fingers for writing but because like Mr L. [Legge] in a way I have lost the use of my language, cannot speak sentences, and cannot recollect the names of my friends in this house, and even the above is a sort of agony because I cannot bring out the right name. This applies even to my speaking of W N [Neville] — except more commonly I call him by mistake Ambrose.

Thank you and your wife and your sister for their congratulations on the 21st. Church has been very good in writing his good wishes. His daughter Mary says he has got over his low spirits. My own experience is that the continental weather is as capricious as ours, yet you may indeed, but cannot be sure of falling on a good season, and a bad season is very bad.

Horace, (who I trust has seen the end of your cold) to me, is the complement of St Paul and St John. He is most touching from his contrast to the new life of faith. Poor Horace — not more than 56 I think, when he died. 'Lusisti satis, edisti satis, atque bibisti; tempus abire tibi est' etc[3] How unspeakably sad.

Yours affly J. H. Card. Newman

---

[1] See letter of 26 Feb. 1887 to Burns and Oates, and cf. that of 11 Nov. 1886 to them.

[2] Lord Blachford wrote on 21 Feb. that the husband of his sister Marian, had just died. He had long suffered from paralysis.

[3] *Epistles* II, ii, 214. Lord Blachford wrote that he had been laid up with a bronchial attack, but was now able to watch the birds and deer and rabbits from his window. 'I think I keep in mind what even Horace tells us, and what such a place as this is always recalling 'neque harum quas colis arborum" etc – If he would but have left out the "invisas"!'

'neque harum, quas colis, arborum
Te, praeter invisas cupressos,
Ulla brevem dominum sequetur.' *Odes* II, 14, 21–4.
Lord Blachford was childless. Cypresses were the symbol of funerals.

TO H. P. LIDDON

Feb. 23. 1887

My dear Canon Liddon

Your very kind and welcome letter makes me feel, that, tho' I answer in few words, you will understand me to be as pleased and as grateful for them as if I used many.

I hope you still feel the benefit of your foreign excursion, and that especially as increasing your strength for the anxious [work] which engages you[1]

Very sincerely Yours John H Card Newman

TO ALFRED PLUMMER

Febr. 23. 1887

My dear Dr Plummer

I thank you for your fresh kindness with all my heart

But, as I was told that Mr Creighton's series was not to be controversial, it made me sad that, even at p xiii your book begins upon 'Roman Encroachment'.[2]

God bless you

Yrs sincerely J H Card Newman

TO MRS F. J. WATT

February 23rd. 87.

My dear Child,

I am always thinking and praying about you. But I cannot write — without effort and difficulty. I am glad you are going near Bournmouth.[3]

My blessing on your children,

Yours affectionately, J. H. Cardinal Newman.[4]

---

[1] The biography of Pusey.

[2] Alfred Plummer, *The Church of the Early Fathers, External History,* London 1886, in 'Epochs of English Church History' edited by Mandell Creighton. Newman is referring to the table of contents for Chapter VI, 'The Churches in Italy', still to be found in the eleventh impression in 1905: 'Early Christianity Greek and uncentralised — Roman Christianity Greek in origin — Epistle of Clement — Epistle of Ignatius to the Romans — Visits of Hegesippus and Polycarp to Rome — Episcopacy in Rome promoted by heresy — Martyrs among the Bishops of Rome – Obscurity of the early Bishops — Nature of the appeals of Irenaeus and of Tertullian — First Roman encroachment; Victor and Polycrates . . .'

[3] Mrs Watt's daughter Margaret wrote on 19 Feb. reminding Newman that he had baptised her soon after her birth, seventeen years earlier, and saying that her family were hoping to move closer to Bournemouth.

[4] On 23 Feb. Newman sent a lithograph to Bernard Hennin: 'I regret to say I am too old to attempt to answer letters.'

Febr. 24. 1887

My dear Mr Edwards

My difficulty in writing breaks my thoughts and my feelings, and I not only can't say what I wish to say, but also my wishes themselves fare as if a dish of cold water was thrown over them.

I felt your letter, as all your letters, to be very kind to me and I feel very grateful to you. I don't know why you have been so kind, and you have been so more and more.[1]

I will not close our correspondence without testifying my simple love and adhesion to the Catholic Roman Church, not that I think you doubt this; and did I wish to give a reason for this full and absolute devotion, what should, what can, I say, but that those great and burning truths, which I learned when a boy from evangelical teaching, I have found impressed upon my heart with fresh and ever increasing force by the Holy Roman Church? That Church has added to the simple evangelicism of my first teachers, but it has obscured, diluted, enfeebled, nothing of it — on the contrary, I have found a power, a resource, a comfort, a consolation in our Lord's divinity and atonement, in His Real Presence, in communion in His Divine and Human Person, which all good Catholics indeed have, but which Evangelical Christians have but faintly But I have not strength to say more.

Thank you for the beautiful edition of the New Testament. I have a great dislike to heavy books

Very sincerely Yours, John H Card. Newman

Febr. 24. 1887.

With all my heart
I send you and Queenie
my Blessing[2]

[1] Edwards sent a New Testament, Authorised Version, in large print, and divided into four parts, to make each lighter to handle. He had visited Newman a fortnight before, and on 19 Feb. wrote: 'I venture also to hope that amid the sad divisions of our English Christianity you regard the English Bible as a not unimportant bond of Union among a large number of those, whom, though you cannot regard as fellow Churchmen, yet I know you regard as fellow Christians. William Wilberforce once said, "if we cannot reconcile all opinions, at least let us try and unite all hearts", and your Eminence, living in the loving regard of many English Christians has shown how practicable it is to have much of the latter, where corporate unity is unattainable'.

[2] Lady Simeon wrote on 21 Feb. for Newman's birthday, and asked his blessing.

My dear Mr Wegg Prosser

Your letter is a very kind one, and I thank you for it.[1] I wish I could write a fitting answer to it. But at my age I have neither the brain nor the command of fingers, so as to use the words proper to express the gratitude for the kindness you show me in keeping me in mind – and I can but ask you to take the will for the deed

Most truly Yours John H. Card Newman

TO MESSRS BURNS AND OATES

Febr 26? [1887]

Card Newman begs to inform Messrs B and O that Mrs Maxwell Scott has asked him to consent to the publication by itself of a cheaper edition of his Sermon on Mr Hope Scott, her father

As the Sermon in question has already been published by Mr Murray, he conceives no permission is, strictly speaking, necessary, but the Cardinal has no difficulty to her proposal, provided Messrs B. and O. consent that *he* should publish the volume and pay for the prints[2]

TO THE HON. MRS MAXWELL-SCOTT

Febr 27 1887

My dear Mamo

In the course of the last week I have written *twice* to Burns and Oates, but have had no answer from them.

I will let you know as soon as I hear

Yrs affectly J H Card. Newman

TO MESSRS BURNS AND OATES

Febr 28/87

As Cardinal Newman does not hear from Messrs Burns and Oates to the contrary, he considers they have no difficulty to the proposal in consequence of Mrs Maxwell Scott's wish that he should provide them with a small issue of his Sermon on Mr Hope Scott to sell for him on commission.

[1] Wegg-Prosser sent birthday wishes.
[2] See letter of 19 Feb. to Mrs Maxwell-Scott. Newman's sermon was Appendix I in Robert Ornsby's *Memoirs of James Robert Hope-Scott*, published by John Murray in 1884.

Accordingly, he is writing to her by this post to ask how many copies she will require for its sale in her neighbourhood   He will limit the copies printed to that number

J H N

TO THE HON. MRS MAXWELL-SCOTT

The Oratory 28 February 1887

My dear Mamo

Since Burns and Oates are still silent, I am writing to them to say that I suppose silence gives consent;[1] and that I am writing to you to know how many copies you will require for your purpose. Will you let me know.

Yours affectly John H Card Newman

TO LORD CHARLES THYNNE

Feb 28th. 1887.

My dear Lord Charles,

While I thank you and the Duchess for the very kind remembrance which her Grace and you have made of my birthday, I have an opportunity to express how much I rejoice and sympathise in the Providential dispositions which have made you a Priest and have taken you to Ditton Park.[2]

God be praised for events in various ways so happy. With my Blessing on you and the Duchess.

I am, most truly yours, J. H. Card. Newman.

The Ld Chs Thynne

TO BARTHOLOMEW WOODLOCK, BISHOP OF ARDAGH

Febr 28. 1887

My dear Bishop of Ardagh

It is very kind in you to send me your Pastoral and I have read it with much interest. I only regret that, having almost lost the use of my fingers, I cannot make a suitable return to you.

I hope you do not suffer from the weather, which is considered severe here

Yours affectionately John H Newman

[1] See letter of 2 March to Burns and Oates.
[2] Lord Charles Thynne was now chaplain to his sister the dowager Duchess of Buccleuch at Ditton Park, Slough.

TO CHARLES BOWDEN

March 1. 1788

My dear Charles

I am very glad to have so valuable and opportune a work from you and Emily [Bowden]. What I have already read of it, is most interesting.[1]

Have you got leave from Burns and Oates? They are stiff about letting quotations from me being made. Unluckily I have let them purchase an edition of my volumes quite lately. Mr Brittain will tell you.[2] Does not B N C spell this word with one *n* now? As if being King Alfred's 'Brewery House'[3]

Yrs affectly J H Card Newman

P.S. I am glad to hear so good an account of your Mother

TO W. A. GREENHILL

March 1/87

My dear Dr Greenhill

I am very glad to answer you, though I write with difficulty

I don't think I made any innovation of ritual at St Mary's down to a surplice for preaching in.

I found the stationary communion with its napkins or table cloths, as you recollect it, and so I left it. Hawkins, my predecessor, I have heard say again and again that it was a remnant of Puritan times. He spoke as recollecting two previous Vicars, James and Bishop. Bishop was Vicar for, I think, 20 years.[4] I believe the custom was from time immemorial, as far as Protestants are concerned. Kindest remembrances to Mrs Brine

Most sincerely Yours John H Card. Newman

I regret to say I am too old to attempt to answer letters

[1] This was presumably Emily Bowden's *Life and Martyrdom of the Holy and Glorious Martyr, Cecilia, and those who were with her, SS. Valerian, Tiburtius and Maximus*, London 1887, translated from their Acts. Charles Bowden gave the *Nihil Obstat*.
[2] James Britten was the secretary of the Catholic Truth Society, which had been unable to print extracts from Newman's works. See letter of 11 Nov. 1886 to Burns and Oates.
[3] Brasenose College, Oxford, was originally Brazen Nose Hall.
[4] William Bishop was Vicar of St Mary's, Oxford, from 1810 to 1819, and William James until 1823, when he was succeeded by Edward Hawkins.

TO MRS JOHN RICKARDS MOZLEY

March 1. 1887

My dear Edith

I shall rejoice to see you on Saturday at 3

Thank you for the good news of Aunt Anne. I have been very impatient to hear about her

Yrs affly J H Card. Newman

TO HENRY SEBASTIAN BOWDEN

March 2. 1887

My dear Sebastian

Your interesting volume has come, and I am very glad to have it.[1] I do not know Dante so well as to have an interest in him for his own sake, but, tho' I know that many great, wise and eloquent men do become Christians, I feel with most men that it is unnatural that genius should be dissociated from religion and instinctly [sic] wish it proved that such as Dante should be pupils of St Thomas. Therefore we are much indebted to those who give us reasons for thinking that what is in itself so fitting and natural is really a matter of fact.[2]

But my fingers will not let me write more

Yours affectly John H Card. Newman

TO MESSRS BURNS AND OATES

March 2. 1887

By the same post that brought your letter this morning I received a letter from Mrs Maxwell Scott begging me to act for her in this matter.[3] Acting on this request of hers and repeating what I have said before, I mean to take the whole expense of the Sermon struck off upon myself. My only question is what is to be the retail price of single copies without regard to there being a

[1] Dante's *Divina Commedia* from the German of Franz Hettinger, edited by H. S. Bowden, London 1887.

[2] Bowden wrote on 1 March, 'Whatever the poet's faults, he was first and always Catholic.'

[3] Burns and Oates said on 1 March that they had asked Mrs Maxwell-Scott how many copies of Newman's sermon she wished printed, and suggested five thousand. Mrs Maxwell-Scott wrote on the same day to Newman: 'I don't understand Messrs Burns proceedings at all. *Without hearing again from me*, they sent me last week an estimate' for a cheap edition. 'I have not answered them and shall not, unless you bid me tell them that I leave the whole matter in your [Newman's] hands.'

profit to me, and without interfering with the sale of the whole volume. My own proposal is for me to print one hundred copies at such price as you determine

TO THE HON. MRS MAXWELL-SCOTT

2 March 1887

My dear Mamo

| You shall have no more trouble in the matter. If all is well you shall have 100 copies of the sermon from me, as you wish. |

Yours affectly John H Card Newman

Mrs Maxwell Scott

P.S.   I grieve to hear of your bad cold — but I rejoice to find you have heard from New York[1]

TO MISS EMMELINE DEANE

March 3/87.

My dear Emmeline

It would be a great pleasure and favour to me to be painted by you. These are not idle words, and I should rejoice to see you. But my time is not my own. It is not now my own, as if I were young — and I have much to do, and have no certainty when the supply of time will cease, and life end.

You may recollect the histories of St Bede and St Anselm. They were each of them finishing a great work, and they had to run a race with time. Anselm did not finish his — but Bede just managed to be successful. Anselm was 76 — but Bede was only 62. I, alas, alas, am 86.

What chance have I of doing my small work, however much I try? and you lightly ask me, my dear child, to give up the long days, which are in fact the only days I have!

The only days I have, because it is my misfortune not to be able to read by candle-light, and at this very time though March has begun, I am anxiously waiting day by day, though as yet in vain, for the morning light to be strong enough to enable me to say Mass without the vain attempt to use a candle.

I must add that now for two years I have lost the use of my fingers for writing, and am obliged to write very slowly in order to form my letters.

It is all this which hinders my saying categorically 'yes' to your kind, and, to me, welcome question

But I will say this — I am labouring to carry two volumes of St Athanasius

[1] Her husband was in America.

through the press — I fear this will take at least half a year — this must be — but I know no excuse, if it suits you, why you should not write again to me then, if I am then alive.[1]

Yours affectly John H. Card. Newman

Miss Emmeline Deane.

TO GERARD MANLEY HOPKINS

March 3. 1887

Dear Fr Hopkins,

Your letter is an appalling one — but not on that account untrustworthy. There is one consideration however, which you omit. The Irish Patriots hold that they never have yielded themselves to the sway of England and therefore never have been under her laws, and never have been rebels.[2]

This does not diminish the force of your picture — but it suggests that there is no help, no remedy. If I were an Irishman, I should be (in heart) a rebel. Moreover, to clench the difficulty the Irish character and tastes is very different from the English.

My fingers will not let me write more

Very truly Yrs J. H. Card. Newman

TO MESSRS BURNS AND OATES

Mar. 4/87

Messrs B and O by their silence in answer to Card Newman's question, seem to imply that Mrs Maxwell Scott's separate copies of his Sermon on her Father's death, will not, whether at a high or a low price interfere with the sale of the volume in which it is found. Also, he observes that they are silent as to his proposal that they should sell the Sermon on commission for him

In consequence he intends to print for Mrs Maxwell 100 copies of it, and shall send them to her direct.[3]

P.S. Card Newman has given 100 copies of Sarra to the Catholic Truth Society[4]

[1] Emmeline Deane painted Newman's portrait in oils during March 1888.
[2] See letter of 19 Dec. 1881 to William Walsh. Hopkins was in Dublin, Professor of Classics at the Catholic University College, which was under the care of the Irish Jesuits.
[3] The question Newman wished answered was whether Burns and Oates objected to his publishing Hope-Scott's funeral sermon. Their letter of 3 March merely said that the lowest price at which a hundred copies could be sold was one shilling each. Burns and Oates wrote on 7 March accepting Newman's arrangements.
Mrs Maxwell-Scott wrote at the beginning of April to thank for the copies of the sermon
[4] Domenico Sarra, *The Doctrine of Indulgences explained to the Faithful*, translated by Ambrose St John, London 1868.

TO ALFRED NEWDIGATE

March 4. 1887

Dear Mr. Newdigate,

Will you tell me how your circular to the Clergy has succeeded — also, the Joint Stock Society Limited, which you spoke of[1]

When are you likely to claim my offer of £20?

Very truly yours John H Card. Newman

TO FREDERICK GEORGE LEE

Mar 11. 87

I regret to say I am too old to attempt to answer letters

Thank you very sincerely for your Pamphlet on the Art of the day. Also for your Edward vi[2]

I write with difficulty

J H N

P.S.   Best Remembrance to your Wife and son

TO JEREMIAH MACVEAGH

March 16. 1887

Dear Sir

I beg of you the kindness to convey to the members of St Patrick's Celtic Union my thanks for their congratulations upon the recurrence of my birthday.

I wish also to express my warm sympathy in their zeal for the promotion of the study of the Celtic language, its literature and history, the object for which the Union was founded.[3]

I have the honour to be

Your faithful Servant, J. H. Card. Newman

[1] See letter of 12 Oct. 1887 to Newdigate, who sent out 1500 circulars, to which he received 49 replies. Of these 15 said their wants were sufficiently supplied and 31 wished for a religious shop. In his letter of 7 March 1887, Newdigate said that his Art and Book Company and the Catholic Truth Society were opening a joint depot in London.

[2] F. G. Lee, *Immodesty in Art: an Expostulation and Suggestion . . .* , London 1887; *King Edward the Sixth: Supreme Head: An Historical Sketch*, London 1887.

[3] MacVeagh, Honorary Secretary of St Patrick's Celtic Union, writing from 126 York Street, Belfast, sent a copy of a resolution congratulating Newman on his birthday. It was 'unanimously and enthusiastically' adopted at the recent weekly meeting. The Celtic Union was founded 'to promote the study of the language, literature and history' of Ireland. See second note to letter of 14 March 1855 to Edward Caswall.

TO LORD BRAYE

March 20. 1887

My dear Lord Braye

I am very desirous to know how your Association is faring as regards its object. You at one time, at Lord Salisbury's suggestion, thought of bringing your wishes before the House of Lords — I have not found any confirmation of this in the Papers. Would you, at your leisure, kindly inform me how things stand?[1]

Most truly Yours John H Card. Newman

The Lord Braye

TO HENRY JAMES COLERIDGE

March 20. 1887

My dear Fr Coleridge

I have not written to you because I thought you had nothing pleasant to tell me. I now write to say, that I never forget your Brother day after day, and to express a hope that your great trial does not affect your health.[2] Excuse my bad writing

Yours affectly John H Card. Newman

TO RICHARD A. ARMSTRONG

March 23. 1887

My dear Sir,

Your question requires an answer from me, but overleaf you will see a notice, which I fear I must act upon.[3] Also my difficulty of writing forces me to be obscure.

What I have written about Rationalism requires to be expanded. If you will let me be short and abrupt, I would contrast it with *faith*.[4] Faith cometh

---

[1] See letters of 3 and 8 Sept. 1886, 23 March and 26 April 1887 to Lord Braye.

[2] Lord Coleridge married in 1885 as his second wife, Amy Augusta Jackson, daughter of Henry Baring Lawford. Her first marriage, at Gretna Green, was declared null by English law. She was accepted in society, partly because her history was not known, but she was not accepted by those who felt a repugnance to such tampering with matrimony, nor by those who did not admit in the State power to declare invalid a Christian marriage.

In 1892, after Newman's death, H. J. Coleridge wrote a memorandum to the effect that Newman's kindness and courtesy towards his brother and the second Lady Coleridge should not be construed as giving approval to their marriage.

[3] This was the lithographed sentence: 'I regret to say I am too old to attempt to answer letters.'

[4] Armstrong wrote on 22 March thanking for Newman's letter of 25 April, 1886, and asking enlightenment on his understanding of the term 'Liberalism'. Referring to the 'Biglietto Speech', *Add.* pp. 61–70, Armstrong wrote: 'I entirely understand and cordially concur if the reference be exclusively to the careless tolerance which arises from personal indifference to

by hearing,[1] by the *Word of God*. Rationalists are those who are content with conclusions to which they have been brought by reason, but 'we are saved by faith,'[2] and even in cases and persons where true conclusions can be arrived at those conclusions must be believed on the ground that 'God has spoken.'

A man may be a true and exact theist and yet not have faith. What he lacks in order to faith is the grace of God, which is given in answer to prayer.

I have written as much as my fingers will write, and more perhaps than you can read.

Most truly Yours John H. Card. Newman.

P.S. Liberalism is the *development* of Rationalism. It views faith as a mere *natural* gift, the like and the consequence of reason and the moral sense; and by reason and the moral sense he estimates it and measures its objects. A man soon comes to be satisfied with other men, though they ignore faith and its objects, provided they recognise reason and the moral sense. This is Liberalism.

TO LORD BRAYE

March 23. 1887

My dear Lord Braye

You must not measure the sympathy I feel in your trials by the length of this letter, for I am sorry to say that the feebleness of my writing powers increases.

I truly sympathise in what you tell me now, but the worst action for your cause would be to show in public, in the House of Lords, or by the Press, any displeasure with the Bishops. I think you cannot disagree with me in this. You have taken in hand a very difficult question: you have to educate and convert men to it. Is it a wonder that it requires time and labour? How did men like Wilberforce make their [way] except by patience and perseverance?

These characters of mind are the more necessary in a work like yours, because it is so little popular. The English people start from any intercourse

truth and the lack of desire for any religious conviction. But I have been bred in a school in which Liberalism is regarded as something other than that, and I have understood Liberalism in religion to mean that attitude of mind in which the individual, though profoundly convinced of the truth of certain propositions in religion and clinging to them with intense and grateful loyalty, nevertheless is wholly without resentment against those who have been led by reason and by conscience to hold other propositions, would encourage them to continue to make reason and conscience the instruments of their thought, and is able to enter into full brotherly co-operation with them on all matters in which there still is a sufficient basis of agreement' Armstrong went on to instance *Apo.* as embodying Liberalism in this sense, and asked whether he was right in thus understanding, or whether the sentiments of *Apo.* and of Newman's earlier letter to him were 'in reality merely courteous and urbane, but were never intended to represent the kind of tolerance which I have identified with Liberalism'. Newman endorsed the letter 'answered at once'. Armstrong replied on 25 March promising to ponder Newman's letter 'earnestly and, I hope, prayerfully'.

[1] *Romans* 10:17.
[2] *Ephesians* 2:8.

with Rome, as from an enemy, a traditional foe. They prefer Mahomet[an]ism to Popery. What one has to do is conciliate, and to speak against our own rulers and authorities is to make for us fresh enemies where we look for friends.

Every man has his own work – it would be absurd if I pretended to suggest any work to you, nor could I even dream of it. But are there not Catholics such as Lord Ripon who could give you the advantage of his experience, and do for you that which with the best will in the world I am [not] able to do?

Any how, don't despair. God has some purpose for you. Ask Him to show it you May He ever be with you

Most truly Yours J H Card Newman

TO CHARLES LORAIN

24 March 87

Cher et Révérend Père

Je garde le plus reconnaissant souvenir des bontés que m'a témoignées le chanoine Lorain en 1846. Souvent depuis cette époque j' ai cherché à savoir de ses nouvelles, s'il vivait encore ou si nous l'avions perdu. Je n'ai malheureusement rien à dire de ma visite, sinon la vive impression que m'ont laissée les marques d' affection dont j'ai été l'objet de la part des Français et l'attraction que j'en ai ressentie en retour.[1]

Tout votre et en toute sincérité

J. H. Card. Newman

PAPER ON SECRECY IN VOTING

March 25. 1887

I wish to make an observation on a question asked me at the last Congregation.[2]

I was asked whether I considered that a Father voting in Congregation was bound to secrecy as to his vote. I answered that he was not bound, and I should say so still; but, having to answer suddenly, I did not bring out my full meaning.

I answered the abstract question, but viewing it practically, there are various reasons which deprive a voter of his liberty of speech. E.g. What is meant by voting by the medium of a ballot box except ⟨there is intended⟩ a rule of secrecy? and how can that rule be broken, without the serious risk of indirectly revealing the vote of another, or again of giving an absolutely false

---

[1] Lorain was preparing his *Vie de M. l'Abbé Lorain*, Dijon 1888. For Newman's visit to Hilaire Lorain in Sept. 1846 see Volume XI.

[2] At the meeting of the 'Deputies' on 21 March, the minute book of the Oratory records: 'The Father read a short Paper on the lawfulness or unlawfulness of any Father making known to other Fathers the way in which his vote might be given in the Ballot Box, whether for or against'.
The only recent votes taken appear to have concerned minor financial matters.

impression of what another's vote has been? Secrecy, again, hinders the formation of parties in the body. It has in consequence ever been the rule of the Congregation.

As to myself and my vote of the other day, this I know well, that no one, from anything I then said in Congregation could possibly tell, whatever he might fancy, which way my vote went on that occasion, whatever view I might hold about the obligation of the rule of secrecy.

TO C. H. HOPE

March 26. 1887

Cardinal Newman does not feel called upon to answer ⟨enter into⟩ a question which the questioner introduces by affirming that it cannot be answered. Nor does he conceive the ancient Patriarchates of Antioch and Alexandria necessary for the present claims of the Pope. When Mr Hope goes as far as the early Fathers undeniably do go in proof of the Pope's claims perhaps he will see his way to go further.[1]

TO LORD BLACHFORD

April 2. 1887.

My dear Blachford,

Some weeks ago you were amused at learning from me that I was engaged on a third Edition of the Treatises of St. Athanasius; and you were led in consequence to enquire whether it was not possible to suggest a philosophical reason for my act by putting me and the Bishop of Chester into one category, as lovers of Printers Proofs.[2]

As to the Bishop, in his case 'habes confitentem reum',[3] as to me, I send you the Advertisement to my second, and now to be reprinted in the forthcoming 3rd. edition of my volume, if you won't mind the trouble of it.

I am going through the work again from a deep sense of its imperfection. I am writing against time. St. Bede and St. Anselm both wrote against time, in a like case. St. Bede was granted his wish; St. Anselm, I think, was not. St.

---

[1] Hope, an Anglican clergyman wrote on 25 March from Long Stratton Rectory, Norfolk, 'partly to satisfy myself, and partly through the urgency of a gentleman of your communion now staying at my house', asking for any authority, previous to the Council of Nicaea or at least previous to Chalcedon, for the supremacy of the Pope, since papal actions towards the Patriarchs of Antioch and Alexandria did not sanction it; and concluding that, from his own reading of history, 'a supreme papacy is worse than useless . . . I should much like to convince my friend on a point, on which I am very little doubtful'.

[2] Answering the postscript to Newman's letter of 1 Oct. 1886, Lord Blachford wrote on 4 Oct., 'I am amused at your taking refuge in St Athanasius as a light recreation.

Have you seen . . . the Bishop of Chester's (Stubbs') Lectures on Medieval and Modern history? — The first sentence of his preface caps pretty well your story of the Ch. Ch. [Christ Church] scholar.

"If I am asked" he says "what is my reason for printing these lectures I might be at a loss for an answer. . . . It may be that they owe their present form to the fact that the *love of correcting proof sheets* has become a leading passion with the author."'

[3] Cicero, *Pro Ligario* I, i.

Bede was a little past 60. St. Anselm a little past 70. What prospect have I at 86? However, the new Edition has gone to Press.

Sometimes I think I am slowly going downhill but I can't tell. My liability to fall is my great danger. I began in 1880 with breaking my ribs. In the last year I have lost 2 inches in my height, without counting loss of uprightness.

The Duchess of Norfolk is dying. It will be a grievous blow to the Duke. He is a specially domestic man, and his wife has been his life. I have known him since he was a child of 5 years old at Abbotsford,[1]

Yours affectionately, John H. Card: Newman.

TO THE HON. MRS MAXWELL-SCOTT

Good Friday [8 April 1887]

My dear Mamo

I ought to have told you I sent you the Sermons about 10 days ago I hope you got them safely[2]

Yrs affly J H Card. N.

TO THE DUKE OF NORFOLK

April 12. 1887

My dear Duke

There is but One able to support you under your heavy trial — and He will
We hope to do our part. We had said many Masses for the dear Duchess before the end came — and now we hope, every one of our nine Priests, to say three for her

Yours affectly John H Card. Newman

TO LORD BLACHFORD

April 14. 1887.

My dear Blachford,

May all the best blessings of Easter come on you and yours.

I always associate your dear sister Marian with Beethoven's music in which she let me accompany her so long ago.[3]

My main reason, I think, for my sending you my Advertisement was that I thought you would like to read it, as I think you did.[4]

Ever yours affectionately, John H. Card: Newman.

---

[1] See letter of 7 Jan. 1853 to J. J. Gordon. The young Duchess of Norfolk died on 11 April 1887.

[2] See letter of 4 March to Burns and Oates.

[3] After the death of her husband Henry Legge, Lord Blachford's sister was leaving her house at Blackheath.

[4] In returning the advertisement for the third edition of *Ath*. Lord Blachford wrote: 'It is touching that you should have begun and ended your literary career with Athanasius. . . .'

TO FANNY MOZLEY

April 14 1887.

My dear Fanny Mozley

I am anxious to hear how your Sister is going on. Will you be kind enough to send me a few lines about her.[1]

Yours most truly John H. Card. Newman

TO ALFRED NEWDIGATE

April 14. 1887

Dear Mr. Newdigate,

I am glad to conclude from your letter that you have been able to raise £20 to meet mine: Am I right?

Also I am interested to find you have a Committee. May I see the names? is it distinct from the Committee of the Truth Society? and from St. Anselm?

Perhaps you cannot answer me on these points at once. I will write again, if you[2]

Very truly Yours John H Card. Newman

TO WILLIAM PHILIP GORDON

April 15 [1887?]

Dear Fr Superior

I shall not be surprised if you cannot supply Sir Maurice O'Connell's request but I do not know what else I can do for him, than give him the chance

Your affly John H Card Newman

TO H. P. LIDDON

April 18. 1887

My dear Canon Liddon,

I hardly can suppose you are not abundantly supplied with letters of Dr Pusey's, but, as the inclosed is more discursive from most of his, I send it you,

---

[1] Anne Mozley had had an operation on one of her eyes. Her sister Fanny replied reassuringly to Newman on 15 April and she wrote herself on 4 May.
[2] The sentence is not completed. See letters of 23 June 1886 to Wenham and 29 Sept. 1886 and 4 March 1887 to Newdigate.

asking you, if you do not want it, to burn it.[1] I suppose there is nothing to tell about the Dean[2]

Yours very truly John H Card. Newman

TO WILFRID WARD

[18 April 1887]

I wish my hand and my brain let me answer your question by Fr Ryder. And how, putting this difficulty aside, can I answer it, when I live so entirely out of the world

As to whether a protest of the Catholic laity against the state of things in Ireland is expedient, depends on whether it is largely signed

Whether largely signed depends on whether the English ecclesiastical authorities do not interfere with it.

Again, can it be largely signed without a statement of principles and an agreement in arguments, and, though on the whole Liberals and Conservatives are agreed in spirit are they so agreed as to be able to put forth a joint case in writing

Is there not some prospect of the Holy See interfering and is it not *better* to wait to see if it does and what it says[3]

TO LORD BRAYE

April 26. 1887

My dear Lord Braye

I don't know how we can assume what the Pope's wishes are on the subject, till we know more about them.[4] My memory goes to this, that a Bill

---

[1] Liddon replied on 19 April that Pusey's letter was 'valuable in many ways', because 'the reference to your "Arians", is a distinct contribution to the history of Dr Pusey's theological mind; indeed I do not remember his referring to the "Arians" in any other letter, though he used to talk much of the value of this book, when we were arranging the subjects for the Oxford School of Theology – ten years ago. Nor, at this early date, is there any other so explicit reference to the first volume of the "Parochial Sermons" – at least, so far as I know.' Pusey's letter of 11 April 1834 is in Liddon's *Pusey*, I, 289–91.

[2] Liddon replied that Dean Church was about to return from abroad in better health

[3] Wilfrid Ward, who was in touch with Ignatius Ryder on the matter, wrote from the Junion Carlton Club on 19 April to thank Newman for his letter. This was the period of the 'Plan of Campaign' when Irish tenants were organised as a body to treat with their landlords as to rents, and it led to widespread evictions. Ward wrote of 'the very strong public feeling which I see on all sides of scandal at the action of the Irish Archbishops and clergy and of wonder that the Pope does not at least institute an enquiry. . . . As far as I can hear the Pope has no sufficient information on the loyalist side, showing the *necessity* of interference'.

See also letter of 28 Sept. 1887 to W. Ward.

[4] Lord Braye wrote on 22 April about his plans for the establishment of diplomatic relations between Great Britain and the Holy See:

'I have heard from Lord Spencer he is all "pro" the project, so is Lord Lytton whose letter the Duke of Norfolk sent me some two months ago. I saw the Bishop of Northampton [Arthur Riddell] a few days since. He assures me that not only he himself but most or all of the other bishops are in favor. What however is the use of all this if no one moves . . .'

recognising the Pope passed the second reading in the Lords about 40 years ago, but an amendment of Lord Eglington's made it impossible for the Pope to accept the Bill, and so the attempt dropped.[1] One ought to know what the Pope thinks after so long an interval. Again they say that both Liberal and Conservative Governments have lately declined to communicate with him about the state of Ireland —[2] we might from not knowing how things stand be acting disrespectfully towards him if we addressed *him* — and sending the proceeding in Parliament to him would have a directness which speakers in Parliament would not have

Very truly Yours John H Card. Newman

TO LORD BRAYE

not sent   [towards the end of April 1887?]
My dear Lord Braye

Excuse an abrupt answer to your letter of this morning

But it would be a great fault to be abrupt with the Holy See, and therefore I think a move in Parliament, which you propose, or some such introduction seems to me necessary as a first step to prepare the Pope for determining his own wishes   Pope was treated ill, I think by Lord Eglington ⟨the Upper House⟩ 40 years ago — and in consequence the Holy See never accepted the proposal of the Government, and you must not take it for granted that this rudeness is condoned at Rome.

I don't see then that you can move in England without preparing the way by previous steps it [in] Rome, and what they should be, it is not easy to say.

I will set down one instance, as an illustration of the difficulty.

Great Britain and Ireland are under Propaganda, and Propaganda has powers (which the Pope of course might recall, if he would) but which deprive him of acting till they actually are recalled. I know a case in which, when the Pope had signified his intention of making an important ecclesiastical appointment, the Cardinal Prefect of Propaganda drew himself up in his chair and said 'That appointment is not made, it rests with me.'[3]

I don't think you can get on without the Cardinal Archbishop, and I am not sure that the necessity of your step will not force itself upon him

---

[1] The Diplomatic Relations with Rome Act of 1848, contained an amendment proposed by the Earl of Eglinton and carried in the Lords on 18 Feb. 1848 by 67 votes to 64, that the papal nuncio to Great Britain must not be 'in holy orders of the Church of Rome' nor 'a Jesuit or member of any religious order, community, or society of the Church of Rome, bound by monastic or religious vows'. The Bill passed the Commons in Aug. and received the Royal Assent on 4 Sept. 1848, but remained a dead letter. See Bernard Ward, *The Sequel to Catholic Emancipation*, London 1915, II, pp. 191–204.

[2] Cardinal Manning objected to a layman such as Lord Braye meddling in these matters. He wrote at this period to Herbert Vaughan, that he had been in touch with the Liberal and with the Conservative governments. 'All alike refused to intervene. They held the matter to be purely ecclesiastical and therefore external to the sphere of Government.' J. G. Snead-Cox, *The Life of Cardinal Vaughan*, London 1910, I, pp. 466–7.

[3] This refers to the proposal in Nov. 1847 to appoint Wiseman as Archbishop in London.

TO ALFRED NEWDIGATE

April 26. 1887

Dear Mr Newdigate

I have no objection to an itinerant shop, if the Committee prefer it to a local

Very truly yours John H. Card. Newman

TO LORD BRAYE

April 27. 1887

My dear Lord Braye

I don't want to trouble you with a needless letter — but I write a line to say that difficulties are not removed by what Lord Lytton writes —[1] I thought that Lord Eglinton's amendment against the Pope's sending an ecclesiastic was carried. If so, the amendment, while it stands, hinders Diplomatic Relations, for a Cardinal cannot submit to such an insult to the Pope

But excuse me — 1 don't wish to argue

Very truly Yours
John H Card. Newman

TO J. G. SNEAD-COX

The Oratory, Birmingham. April 27, 1887.

I am very sorry, but I am obliged to say that I shrink from your proposal.[2] I could not have the face to send my writings to the Holy Father; and the offence, as I should consider it, would be increased if I had them, as I must in that case have done, bound in a costly fashion. I am what I am. I might be

[1] Newman was answering Lord Braye's letter of 27 April, which quoted Lord Lytton, who seemed to think the Eglinton amendment had been repealed.
    Lord Braye went on to say that when he was in Rome in 1883 he formed the opinion that Leo XIII was very anxious to have diplomatic relations with Great Britain. 'There can be little doubt that Cardinal Manning thwarted the scheme.' Lord Braye concluded, 'But should your Eminence lend your mere name to the measure I believe the issue would be very materially advanced.'

[2] Cox wrote on 25 April that he was to announce before the end of the month in the *Tablet*, of which he was editor, a scheme to mark the sacerdotal golden jubilee of Leo XIII by presenting him with all the books written by English Catholics during the previous fifty years. Authors would be invited to present their own works. The idea had been welcomed by Cardinal Manning. Newman was asked for his approval and for 'a few lines for publication'. See letters of 8 May and 23 June to Bishop Ullathorne, also those of 26 May to Paul Strickland and 12 June to R. F. Clarke.

worse; but certainly I might be much better. Excuse a short letter, but I do not use my fingers without pain.[1]

Very truly yours John H. Card. Newman.

TO MALCOLM MACCOLL

April 27. 1887.

Dear Canon MacColl,

I am glad that the negligence of the London Booksellers allows me to ask your acceptance of the volume which contains the μία φύσις σεσαρκωμένη[2] Burns and Oates have it always on hand, and it is advertised in every copy of every volume of mine, whether theological or not.

It is an old complaint that bookshops save themselves trouble by saying that books are out of print. I am glad of this opportunity of hearing from you and writing to you, so this neglect is my gain.

Did not poor Palmer die suddenly?

Very truly yours, John H. Card Newman.

TO AUGUSTA THEODOSIA DRANE

May 4. 1887

My dear Mother Provincial

I direct to you at Stone, in the hope and trust that the anxieties are over which took you from home.[3]

I write to you in anticipation of tomorrow, in the name of all of us, assuring you of the earnestness of our good wishes for you all, and our prayers for you.[4]

---

[1] Neville wrote later about this letter: 'The Cardinal was, in fact, habitually ashamed of himself that he had ever written against the Catholic Church, and he could not, to use his own words on the subject, *commit the presumptuous impertinence* of sending as a present books of his own, which, however free from objection they had become, had originated in, and still bore testimony, through the corrections made in them, to his Protestant hostility towards the very person officially to whom they would be sent. On this point he was very sensitive

Compliance being impossible to him, he wished to explain himself . . . The object of the letter was, however, so entirely misapprehended that no explanation could be made; indeed he met with rebuff rather than with encouragement to explain . . .'

Newman's unwillingness to have his works presented to the Pope was of long standing. See letter of 30 Nov. 1879 to Allies.

[2] MacColl wrote on 25 April from Ripon, where he was canon in residence, asking for the volume containing Newman's essay on St Cyril's formula, *T.T.*, which the London booksellers had been unable to supply.

In the copy of Newman's letter the space for the three Greek words has been left blank. When the letter was printed in *Malcolm MacColl Memoirs and Correspondence*, edited by G. W. E. Russell, London 1914, p. 307, the words 'Dream of Gerontius' were inserted.

[3] At the end of 1886 she had had to visit a sister of hers in Devon who was dying.

[4] Feast of St Catherine of Siena.

We know how much we owe to you for your prayers for us and have continually to praise God for His mercies to us in consequence

Especially I myself wonder at His goodness towards me, and feel how much I am indebted to the prayers of my friends. Whatever trials I may, in God's loving wisdom have to meet before the end, the gentleness with which He now deals with me is most wonderful

With my blessing upon all of you

I am, Your faithful and affectionate servant John H. Card. Newman

TO BISHOP ULLATHORNE

May 8. 1887

My dear Lord

I was surprised some days ago to have a letter from Mr Cox of the Tablet to the effect that it had been determined, he did not say by whom, to present to the Holy Father, as a Jubilee offering from English Catholics the works they have published during the last 50 years.[1]

I say then to your Lordship, as a point on which I feel very strongly and not liking to leave you in ignorance of it, that never could I take part myself in such a measure. Writing, as I ever have written, not with authority or official position, and deeply conscious of my own insufficiency, I could not presume to take a step which is repugnant to my very nature. Others are differently circumstanced; they have not handled religious subjects, or they speak authoritatively.

All this I have signified to Mr Cox

Your faithful and affectionate Servant J H Card. Newman[2]

Excuse my bad writing
The Rt Rev. The Bishop of Birmingham

[1] See letter of 27 April to Cox who did not say who had originated this scheme or in whose name, apart from his own, he was writing.

[2] Bishop Ullathorne replied on 9 May that all he knew about the proposed presentation was contained in a letter from Herbert Vaughan, Bishop of Salford, 'As I was not at the Low Week meeting of the Bishops'. Vaughan, who owned the *Tablet*, wrote: 'I am going to get up through the Tablet a present to the Pope of a copy of all books published in England by Catholics during the past 50 years. The Cardinal [Manning] and those of the Bishops whom I have seen about it, greatly approve. Will you kindly let me say that the scheme has your Lordship's approval also.'

Ullathorne continued: 'I gave a general approval, though it would not have been the offering I should have thought of. For I saw it would be difficult to draw a line, and there is a good deal of matter printed which would scarcely be worthy of being offered to the Pope; not that I should include anything in that category which you have written. For your works are constantly being quoted, and justly so, for standard thoughts and illustrations. I have this winter read them nearly all through in order of their publication, and that with an ever growing pleasure. But it must be a matter for individually [sic] judgment and feeling whether an author chooses to offer his works in homage to the Sovereign Pontiff or not.'

TO MALCOLM MACCOLL

May 11. 1887

My dear Canon MacColl

I hope my book got to you — I sent it a few days after my letter   I directed it to you at Residence, Ripon.

Yours very truly J. H. Card. Newman

TO POPE LEO XIII

May 15 [1887]

Il Duca di Norfolk e si interamente conosciuto alla Vostra Santita, che non ha bisogno Ella delle lettere da me intorno di lui; ma mi gode molto che l'umiltà del medesimo mi apre questa opportunità d' esprimere alla Vostra Santità l'affezione e stima che porto a lui.

L'ho conosciuto da fanciullo, e posso assolutamente asseverare *come* semplice, *come* profonda è la di lei aderenza e divozione alla Chiesa Cattolica, *come* geloso è il Duca d'assicurare l'esaltazione e la propagazione del Cattolichismo. Ecco il vero ed il solo motivo che lo porta ai piedi di Vostra Santita. Non è politico, no, ma collocato da Providenza in alto luogo sta in mezzo di molti e larghi gradi ed ordini del populo nostro, e, per questa causa, il di lui testimonio in una questione di religione e importante [?][1]

TO HENRY GEORGE WOODS

Birmingham May 16. 1887

My dear Mr President

I am ashamed to return year after year so ungracious an answer to your and the Bursars' invitation of me to the Gaudy. But I fear I have too true an excuse for declining it.

I am now of a great age, and though I am thankful to say I have no ailment, I am so feeble that I am always in danger of falling, and have in fact had some bad falls. In consequence I have a difficulty in walking Be sure I do not forget my old and dear College, when Trinity Monday comes round.

Excuse my bad writing, but my fingers write with difficulty

Most truly Yours John H Card Newman

The Rev The President of Trinity College

[1] The Duke of Norfolk no doubt intended to give his view of the harm done to Catholicism by the 'Plan of Campaign' in Ireland, but it was publicly denied that he went to Rome to discuss the matter of diplomatic relations with the Holy See. The Duke wrote on 31 May: 'It happened to be most opportune that I had such a letter to leave with the Holy Father to show him all I had said was said from a Catholic point of view.'

On 3 June it was announced that a special delegation had been appointed to convey the Pope's congratulations to Queen Victoria for her Golden Jubilee, celebrated on 21 June.

TO FELIX TAYLOR

May 20. 1887

Dear Sir

I hope you will excuse my not answering your letter. I cannot write without pain and effort.

Yrs very truly J H Card. Newman

I regret to say I am too old to attempt to answer letters

P S I have not met i th Fathers any thing to throw light upn your questn[1]

TO AN UNKNOWN CORRESPONDENT

May 20. 1887

My dear Sir

I have received with pleasure your Poem on the Deus homo and thank you for it

Very truly Yours John H Card. Newman

TO HENRY HARRIS

May 23. 1887

Dear Mr Harris

I began a Letter to you immediately on receipt of your excellent Book on the Atonement,[2] but I was obliged to leave off as I am now suffering from a sad though not severe trial. My fingers will not write from weakness. I can't make my letters distinctly. I write a few lines and then knock up, and what I write is with pain and effort, and the effort affects my head. This is [my] apology.

Yours very truly John H. Card. Newman.

TO BISHOP ULLATHORNE

May 23. 1887

My dear Lord

I find no letter of invitation has been sent from this place to your Lordship for our feast on the 26th. You will I am sure understand that the omission was an accident, arising from our belief that you had not yet left your winter quarters at Oscott. Will you kindly take this letter as our apology[3]

Your Lordship's affecte Servt John H Cardinal Newman

[1] Taylor was a third year student at Manchester New College, London.
[2] *The Scripture Doctrine of the Atonement and its Place in the Christian System*, London 1887.
[3] Bishop Ullathorne replied on 23 May that the Oratorian Fathers probably knew that he was still away at Oscott, waiting for milder weather.

TO KENELM VAUGHAN

May 25 1887

I gladly send you, as you ask, my blessing on the good work ⟨house⟩ of expiation and prayer, and most heartily invoke God's blessing on so good a work[1]

JHN

TO PAUL STRICKLAND

May 26/87

To the Secretary of the Executive Committee
Dear Sir,

Fr Ryder has shown me your letter to him and I am glad to receive the information it gives me on responsible authority of the appointment of an Executive committee for the furtherance of 'Great Britain's Jubilee Offering to the Pope', that offering, I believe, mainly consisting of Catholic literature.[2]

Nothing certainly could be more acceptable to the hearts of English Catholics than a Memorial of their deep devotion to the Holy Father, and I wish, in answer to your inquiry I could propose to take part in it; but I fear, to my great pain, that I am obliged distinctly to say that I never can consent to apply to the purpose you name the volumes I have written, volumes most of which are on theological subjects, and very few have been submitted by me to ecclesiastical revision. My wonder is how any one could expect it of me. How can I in decency offer such works to the Pope, whatever mixture of truth after all there may be in them, and whatever controversial force or intellectual merit? Such an act would be repugnant to my primary ideas of merest pro-

---

[1] Kenelm Vaughan wrote on 24 May from the House of Expiation, 28 Beaufort Street, London S.W., 'I have the pleasure, in the absence of the Rector, of sending you the accompanying report of our humble beginnings of the work of Expiation, together with a print of our badge' and asking Newman's blessing and prayers for the work.

[2] After Newman's letter of 27 April to Cox, Strickland had been appointed Secretary of the Committee for the Jubilee Offering to the Pope and his office was set up in the London Oratory. He sent a printed circular to Newman dated 'May', and signed by Cardinal Manning, in which the latter explained and commended the scheme; and a printed slip was enclosed which read, 'The Executive Committee of the Jubilee Offering of Great Britain begs to submit the enclosed document to your notice, and to invite you to allow your name to stand as proposed on the General Committee. Kindly address your reply to His Eminence The Cardinal Archbishop of Westminster, Archbishop's House, Westminster London.' The Executive Committee were, Manning, R. F. Clarke, S.J., J.G. Cox, William Gordon of the London Oratory, and Wilfrid Meynell. There was apparently no covering letter. Newman did not reply.

On 24 May Strickland wrote to H. I. D. Ryder, 'I am directed by the Executive Committee of Great Britain's Jubilee Offering to the Pope, to ask you to kindly assist us in obtaining the name and favour of Cardinal Newman for the Committee, or at least an intimation of His Eminence's willingness or unwillingness to afford his co-operation. The committee feel, that the absence of His Eminence's name might give rise, in some minds, to the conjecture that His Eminence's co-operation had not been sought: and the only method of correcting the misapprehension now available — that of announcing that no reply has been given by His Eminence to the Committee's Circular — seems hardly a suitable one.'

priety, and this I signified some weeks ago, as far as the occasion admitted, in answer to the informal intimation, solitary as well as informal, that the plan which has been ultimately adopted was in contemplation. I wrote in reply that I hadn't *'the face'* to commit myself to such an act.[1] I expected my letter would have been answered, in which case I should have written again, but an informal statement was sufficient on my part for an informal question.[2]

J H N

TO T. W. ALLIES

May 27. 1887.

My dear Allies,

I am ashamed of myself not having thanked you for your book,[3] but I can in fact explain my omission. I ever kept it in mind that I had not answered what I so much valued, so much that, when I wrote last Friday it was because I felt the debt which lay upon me, but as I took up my pen, I forthwith forgot one principal cause of my writing, being carried off by the subject of Low Week.[4]

But, alas, my weakness of memory shows itself continually now. What I wish to say I forget before my interlocutor has finished what he is saying, nay I begin sentences and cannot complete them from forgetfulness. This has been one cause of my leaving off preaching — a fear that I should find myself left in the lurch by my memory.

But the immediate cause of not acknowledging your volume was this, that I literally cannot read except by sun light, and have been unable to say Mass till the sun rose earlier.

---

[1] See letter of 27 April to Cox. He was now a member of the Executive Committee headed by Manning.

[2] Strickland replied on 2 June that he would place Newman's reply before the Executive Committee, and added: 'Meanwhile, I would venture to say that the nature of the Committee's application, has been slightly misunderstood. They did not take it upon themselves to ask for a contribution of your Eminence's Works, but, that they might place your Eminence's name on the general committee.' He went on to say that 'The approval of the Holy Father for this particular offering was expressed, before the public announcement was made . . . The idea is to have in Rome, in some place to be assigned by His Holiness, a complete library of English Catholic Works, accessible to English students and visitors.

If your Eminence could have associated your name with this offering, by allowing it to stand on the Committee, that association would have been very welcome.' In a postscript Strickland added: 'Of the informal invitation alluded to the committee has no cognizance; it was no doubt sent, when the offering was proposed to be made by the Tablet alone, and before it was adopted by the Bishops.' In fact, not only was Cox a member of the Executive Committee, but his invitation of 25 April, which Newman answered on 27 April, was sent out after the Low Week meeting of the Bishops, and with Cardinal Manning's approval.

In June a second printed circular was sent out, similar to the one in May, but with Newman's name omitted from the Committee, and Wilfrid Ward's added to the Executive Committee. It included a printed form for entering donations of money and books.

[3] *The Throne of the Fisherman*, London 1887. Inscribed 'His Eminence Cardinal Newman from the Author March 4 1887.'

[4] This letter is not to be found.

I have read hardly more than your 'Table of Contents', but that has made me think it is one of your best volumes.

I have not forgotten you at Mass since I saw you.

Yours affectly J. H. Card. Newman

TO H. P. LIDDON

May 27/87

Dear Canon Liddon

I nearly agree with you. My impression is that the Theological Meetings began about 1836 and ended in consequence of Number 90. There is a note upon them in Apologia p 389 edit 1886[1]

Harrison would have been the man for those years. Perhaps you made use of him

Yours very truly John H Card. Newman

TO HENRY BEDFORD

June 6th. 1887.

My dear Professor Bedford,

Thank you for your kind and welcome letter.[2] I am, however, very sorry to say I cannot thank you fittingly as I have almost lost the use of my fingers for writing.

With my best blessing,

Yours affectionately, John H. Card. Newman.

TO HENRIETTA WOODGATE

June 6. 1887

My dear Child

I was very glad to have your letter, though I can thank you in only a few lines as my inability to use my fingers in writing increases on me — After attempting a few lines they knock up. Fifty seven years ago in the month of

[1] Newman appears to have given a mistaken reference. Liddon wrote on 26 May: 'Do you remember when the "Theological Society" ceased to meet at Dr Pusey's House? Its first meeting appears to have taken place on Nov. 12 1835. And the last list of papers that I can find are those for Act [Summer] Term 1841: the last paper being Mr Keble's on the Mysticism of the Early Fathers, part 2.

Am I right in thinking that Tract 90, and the controversies which followed it, brought the Theological Society to an end?'

See Liddon's *Pusey*, I, pp. 332–42.

[2] Bedford wrote on 25 May for the feast of St Philip 'to relieve my own heart of some of the gratitude it owes especially to St Philip for his gift of you to the Church'.

June I rode twice through your (new) country, from Oxford to Brighton and from Brighton to Oxford and was much struck and pleased with its wild and free healthiness. I cannot write more to explain myself. Let me hear from you, when you have any thing to tell me[1]

Love and blessing from me to all of you

Yrs affectly J. H. Card. Newman

TO CATHERINE ANNE BATHURST

June 9 1887

My dear Child

I cannot write without effort and pain — I cannot read except with sunlight — so I am a very bad correspondent.

All then I can do is to pray for you at the right times and to have you in mind and this I will try to do

Yours affectionately J H Cardinal Newman

TO RICHARD FREDERICK CLARKE, S.J.

June 12. 1887

Private
Dear Fr Clarke

I am sure I may ask of you a favour. If it is a great one, or one which is a trouble to you, I can but say that I am not likely to be asking any one for favours long, and those who are kind enough to think that by my writings I have done some service to the cause of religion among us, may not be unwilling to assist me in a matter in which those writings are concerned.

A member of your executive Committee has, without my knowledge or consent, advertised his presentation of my books, as a jubilee offering of his own to the Pope.[2] I beg of you, and I trust I may without presumption beg of others of your committee, to prevent this offering of this gentleman from being included in the number of those offerings which go from the Committee to Rome. It would be a misleading step, if allowed, which would pain me much.

---

[1] Mrs Woodgate and her daughters had just settled in a new home at Crowthorne, Berks. For Newman's journeys see *Moz.* I, pp. 229–30, and 232.

[2] In the *Weekly Register* (11 June 1887), p. 739, there was a list of authors who had presented their works for the Pope's Jubilee Offering. After it came 'The Works of Cardinal Newman (Have been presented by the Editor of the Weekly Register)' i.e. Wilfrid Meynell. Fr Faber's Works were presented by the London Oratory.

Of course I mean nothing disrespectful, by this request, to the contributors to the Jubilee offering, of whom many are near and old friends; but what is a plain duty in their case is not a duty in mine

I trust I shall receive a favourable answer from you; any how an answer let me have[1]

I am

TO WILFRID WARD

June 17 1887

My dear Wilfrid Ward

I feel much the kindness of your words about me in the Address to the Pope, and am much pleased to have them introduced. God is very good to me.[2]

Yours affectly John H Card. Newman

TO JOSEPHINE HOPE

June 21. 1887

My dear Josephine

I should like to send you a long letter, but my fingers won't write, and I fear you will not be able to read this attempt.

I like your book extremely.[3] It has great merits. You have hit off your characters very well. Few Catholics have described so well a pious dissenting Evangelical. And in her way Fanny is as good as Bessie. And the contrast of motives (each supernatural) which led the two into the Church is excellently brought out.

You are somewhat ambitious in your sketch of Staples — but it is good as an imagination, which requires filling out

There is perhaps too much *direct* teaching and preaching in the Tale, though perhaps it could not be helped. You have referred to Bishop

---

[1] Clarke, who was himself a member of the Executive Committee, replied on 15 June that Meynell's move was not sanctioned by the Committee. 'I knew nothing of it until I saw it announced in the Tablet'. Others shared his regret at the way Newman was treated. However, Clarke had got in touch with Meynell, who sent him a note on 14 June, 'I shall ask the Committee to allow me to withdraw the offer to give Cardinal Newman's works'.
See also letter of 28 June to Clarke.
[2] Ward sent the address to the Pope which he had drawn up at the request of the Council of the Catholic Union on the occasion of his Jubilee, and explained that it contained a reference to Newman. This said: 'we in this country have special reasons for gratitude to the Holy Father. The elevation to the sacred purple of many members of English-speaking races, and above all, of one whose name is specially dear to us all — John Henry Newman — is a great honour done to our country'. See the *Weekly Register* (11 June 1887), p. 757.
[3] *In the Way*, London 1887, a short religious tale which gives some idea of the Sussex country and the Sussex poor of that date.

Hay once; I think it would have been more prudent, if at the foot of the page you had here and there said 'Vid. Bishop Hay', 'vid. Fr Faber', or the like.

Now my dear Child, I hope this criticism will not frighten you. If I was not pleased with your work, if I did not think as likely to do glory to God, if I did not love you and take an interest in you, I should not have written. You must not be startled at my abruptness, that arises from the effort and trouble with which I write.

I always have you and your sisters and brother in my prayers

Yours affectly J. H. Card Newman

TO BISHOP ULLATHORNE

Birmingham June 23 1887

My Lord

I have reason to believe that my publications during the last fifty years are likely to be sent to Rome, as if from me, and as a portion of the Offering to be made by British Catholics, to the Holy Father on occasion of his Jubilee.

This proceeding is, I suppose, meant for a compliment to me, but, considering that the greater part of my writings belong to a period when I was a Protestant, and that the rest are without such ecclesiastical revision as could make them of authority, I should be strangely constituted if I could take pleasure in their being presented to the Sovereign Pontiff.

My purpose in writing to your Lordship is, not to trouble you with the necessity of an answer on a personal matter, but to record my judgment upon the inconsiderate act of an anonymous person, committed, not only without my sanction, but in spite of a distinct protestation.[1]

Excuse my inability to use a pen.

I am, My Lord Your Lordship's faithful Servant
John H. Card. Newman.

The Rt Revd The Bp of Birmingham

[1] Meynell persisted in presenting Newman's works, but anonymously. See letter of 28 June to Clarke and Meynell's own admission in the *Athenaeum* (23 Aug. 1890), p. 258. Hence Newman wrote this formal letter to Ullathorne, in addition to that of 8 May. Newman now at the end of June sent similar formal letters of protest to Cardinal Manning and to the Bishops of Liverpool, Shrewsbury, Clifton and Newport. For Manning's reply see letter of 4 July to him. The Bishops replied expressing regret at the inconsiderateness shown towards Newman.

TO EDWARD BELLASIS

June 24. 1887

My dear Edward

I write with much effort and some pain, which hinders me from being otherwise than abrupt and often difficult to understand

I rejoiced greatly at your Papers. They are an unexpected boon. Alas, that they were, or could be, longer; but differences of view soon showed themselves (PRIVATE) between Sir John Acton with others, and my special friend, your dear Father.

I saw nothing in them to be changed. May I see the Papers in *Proof*? I saw nothing to alter[1]

Yrs affly J H Card. N.

TO ALFRED HENRY MILES

June 24/87

Cardinal Newman has no difficulty in allowing three out of his four sets of Verses which Mr Miles names to appear in 'Poets and Poetry' but 'the Dream of Gerontius' seems to him too large a composition for Mr Miles's purpose

Has Mr Miles got others as long?[2]

TO R. B. GODOLPHIN OSBORNE

June 24. 1887.

Dear Father Godolphin Osborne,

Thank you for the high compliment which the officials and members of the Oratorium Parvum have done me in presenting my writings to her Majesty. It has gratified me much. I only regret, and ask you to pardon the inadequate words and penmanship in which I make my acknowledgments. I have lost the use of my fingers, yet think it better, in expressing my thanks, to be my own amanuensis, however poorly, than to use the aid of a friend.[3]

I am, my dear Fr Osborne Your faithful Servant

John H Card. Newman

[1] This refers to Bellasis's eleven page appendix to the annual report of the Oratory School Society, *A Contribution towards Oratory School Annals, by an ordinary member of the Oratory School Society. The Year 1858*, Westminster 8 July 1887. The paper dealt chiefly with events in the first three months of 1858, when the Oratory School was being planned.

[2] Miles was preparing *The Poets and Poetry of the Century*, the tenth volume being *Sacred, Moral, and Religious Verse*, London 1897. He included seven of Newman's poems, 'Opusculum', 'Nature and Art', 'A Thanksgiving', 'Moses', 'Humiliation', 'David and Jonathan', 'The Pillar of the Cloud'. Also the second part of *The Dream of Gerontius* and 'Praise to the Holiest'.

[3] See letter of 24 July to Osborne.

TO FANNY MOZLEY

June 27 1887.

My dear Fanny Mozley

How is your sister Anne? just one line. It is so long since I heard about her[1]

Yours affectly John H Card Newman[2]

TO RICHARD FREDERICK CLARKE, S.J.

[28 June 1887][3]

In my acknowledgment of this letter on June 28 I said

So I am to be sacrificed, that the Jubilee Offering, decided on without any act of mine in it may look well.[4]

TO CHARLES JAMES LONGMAN

Bm July 2. 87

Dear Mr Longman

I have no thought and no chance of publishing an autobiography. I have never liked such work, and now my increasing infirmities make such an attempt impossible; especially my difficulty in writing[5]

[1] Anne Mozley herself replied on 30 June that she was quite well.

[2] On 6 Aug. 1887 Anne Mozley wrote to Newman, who seems to have expressed uneasiness at a visit to his brother F. W. Newman by his niece, Jane Mozley: 'I fully believe that Mr F Newman (bearing Jemima in mind) would never speak to Jane of his sceptical opinions and I am sure (she is so like her mother on such points) that he could have no influence. Nor would she run the risk of twice hearing what would distress her and drive her to some strong protest.

Can any one be "intimate" with a person whose mind is so made up of "hobbies" as to be incapable of taking in the thought of other minds? Can such a person have influence?'

[3] After receiving Clarke's reply of 15 June to his own letter of 12 June, Newman later wrote again and sent a telegram. Clarke replied on 27 June: 'I have reason to believe that though Mr Meynell has withdrawn his gift some anonymous donor will present your Eminence's works to the Memorial Library.' He feared he might not be able to prevent this, and added 'the Memorial without your Eminence's works will be like a Crown without the central gem. But I would sooner see the Memorial fail than be wanting in my duty, or even in any sort of courtesy to one who has so many claims on me as your Eminence'.

[4] On 2 July Newman began drafting a letter on how 'the word of an anonymous person is worth nothing', and asking 'on whose authority?'

[5] Longman wrote on 1 July that he had seen a paragraph in a newspaper stating that Newman was going to publish an autobiography. 'Such paragraphs are frequently pure inventions, but if there should be any truth in this one I need hardly say what pleasure we should have in undertaking the publication.'

George Lillie Craik also wrote, on behalf of Macmillan, on 30 June: 'It is stated in the St James's Gazette that you are about to publish a volume of Autobiographical Reminiscences', and asked to be allowed to bring it out. Macmillan was to publish Dean Church's 'book on Oriel College', i.e. *The Oxford Movement*, 'and there is a natural congruity in the two books'. See also letter of 4 July to Cardinal Manning.

If you would allow me to ask you to let me speak to you *in confidence*, I would say that I have put all my papers and copies of letters up to 1845 in the hands of a great friend, a Protestant, making no conditions, (as to pecuniary matters etc) except that I am not to see the resulting work and it is not to be published in my life time.

In 1874 I wrote a sort of sketch or skeleton to connect the successive events together But I made the property over, as a point of honour, to my friend.

I will mention my wish that you should have the engagement, but I cannot do more than recommend.[1]

I am on a very different work — the new edition of my translation of Athanasius — if I live.

Very truly Yours John H Card. Newman

TO R. W. CHURCH

July 3. 1887

I was very glad to receive your letter, for I feared the heat of London was telling upon you, and the Papers said nothing of you good or bad.[2] For myself, though I have no complaint, 'senectus ipsa est morbus,'[3] showing itself in failure of sight, speech, joints, hearing.

TO H. P. LIDDON

July 3. 1887

My dear Canon Liddon

I am sorry not to have found in my Diary any thing to the purpose of your question

I find I went over to Holton on St Bartholmews Day 1836; that I slept there and returned the next day to Oxford[4]

My impression has ever been that Pusey was anxious to bring Mr Tyndal(?) who was a mild evangelical on a better understanding with me[5]

Very truly Yours John H Card. Newman

[1] Newman wrote to Dean Church, who replied on 13 July, 'I thought it best to communicate to Miss Mozley what you understood and what you wished about the book. She is very grateful for the proposed arrangement: she has hitherto published with Rivingtons; but she entirely falls in with your suggestion about Longmans,' who published *Moz.* I and II in 1891.

[2] At the end of June, Dean Church wrote about his recent travels in Italy.

[3] Terence, *Phormio*, IV, i, 9.

[4] See diary for 24 Aug. 1836.

[5] Pusey was staying with his mother at Holton Park, Oxfordshire. 'The idea of a Library of the Fathers seems to have taken definite shape during a visit which Newman paid to Pusey at Holton Park on August 24th, St Bartholomew's Day, 1836. Pusey was anxious to bring about a meeting between Newman and Mr. Tyndale, the clergyman of the parish, who held very Low Church opinions; so Newman dined and slept at Holton, returning to Oxford the next morning'. Liddon's *Pusey* I, p. 420. T. G. Tyndall was Rector of Holton.

TO CARDINAL MANNING

The Oratory, Bm July 4, 1887

My dear Cardinal,

Will you kindly tell Mr Arnold while I thank him for the compliment he pays me, that I neither have nor have had any intention of writing in any shape autobiographical Reminiscences which is a line in literature beyond me[1]

Thanking you for your notice in another matter[2]

I am My dear Cardinal Yours affectly

John H. Card. Newman

His Eminence The Card. Archbp

TO WILFRID WARD

Jul 4. 1887

My dear Wilfrid Ward

I wish you to see the *point of view* from which I have written about inspiration. May I trouble you to let me have the inclosed paper again.

Yours sincerely John H Card. Newman

MEMORANDUM

July 4. 1887.

My eyes do little for me now in the way of reading and my fingers still less for my writing.

In what follows I can only speak under correction, but, as far as I see as regards the relation of Scripture history to science a great question awaits its solution from the Holy See. What the solution is to be I have at present no opinion of my own. I, with the rest of the world can but wait for it.

It is a question on which we cannot reasonably expect an infallible decision till the sense of the Scripture enunciations is known for certain. Meanwhile a opportunity has offered I have earnestly pressed authors who think with the writer in the XIXth of July 1887 to commit themselves to a statement of

---

[1] Manning wrote on 3 July, 'I cannot refuse to send you the inclosed note from Mr Edward Arnold, Grandson of Dr Arnold: but I can anticipate easily your answer.'

Edward Arnold wrote on 30 June to Manning about Newman's supposed reminiscences, asking for a line to him 'enabling me to propose to His Eminence the possibility of making "Murray's Magazine" the vehicle of publication in the first instance?'

Edward Penrose Arnold-Forster, eldest son of William Arnold, was left an orphan in 1859, and adopted by his uncle William Edward Forster, the Liberal Statesman who had married Thomas Arnold's eldest daughter.

[2] Manning's letter continued: 'Your letter on the subject of your works will, I fear, disappoint many friends but I do not venture to express any wish or judgment contrary to yours, I only wish that yours were in conformity with ours. The collection will be capitally incomplete without your Catholic works which ought to come first.'

propositions in which they consider it has already been proved that Scripture and science are for certain at variance. Surely it becomes us to imitate the Church's patience, not rudely to attempt to force the hand of authority, but to *prepare the way* for a final decision *by collecting points* which may or may not be taken up in it.[1]

I will set down from my Article suggestions of this kind on one side or the other: e.g.

I Page 4. 'These two Councils decide that the Scriptures are inspired, and inspired throughout, but not inspired by an immediately divine act, but through the instrumentality of inspired men; that they are inspired in all matters of faith and morals, meaning thereby, not only theological doctrine, but also the historical and prophetical narratives which they contain, from Genesis to the Acts of the Apostles; and lastly, that, being inspired because written by inspired men, they have a human side, which manifests itself in language, style, tone of thought, character, intellectual peculiarities, and such infirmities, not sinful, as belong to our nature, and which in unimportant matters may issue in what in doctrinal definitions is called an *obiter dictum*. At the same time, the gift of inspiration being divine, a Catholic must never forget that what he is handling is in a true sense the Word of God, which, as I said in my Article, 'by reason of the difficulty of always drawing the line between what is human and what is divine, cannot be put on the level with other books, as it is now the fashion to do, but has the nature of a Sacrament, which is outward and inward, and a channel of supernatural grace'[2]

II. Page 12. 'Are we to conclude that the record of facts in Scripture does not come under the guarantee of its inspiration?

We are not so to conclude

For this plain reason — the sacred narrative, carried on through so many ages, what is it but the very matter for our faith and rule of our obedience? What but that narrative itself is the supernatural teaching, in order to which inspiration is given? What is the whole history, traced out in Scripture from Genesis to Esdras, and thence on to the end of the Acts of the Apostles, but a manifestation of Divine Providence, on the one hand interpretative, on a large scale and with analogical applications, of universal history, and on the other preparatory, typical and predicative, of the Evangelical Dispensation? Its pages breathe of providence and grace, of our Lord, and of His work and teaching,[3]

---

[1] Wilfrid Ward had evidently called Newman's attention to Mivart's article 'The Catholic Church and Biblical Criticism', the *Nineteenth Century* (July 1887), pp. 31–51. Mivart thought the conflict between the Church and science was now over, and hoped for a further transformation of opinion which would remove the conflict with historical criticism. He took a broad view of Inspiration, spoke with approval, pp. 47–8, of Newman's article 'On the Inspiration of Scripture' in the *Nineteenth Century* (Feb. 1884), and made quotations from his 'Postscript', ending with 'Inspiration of Scripture in *omnibus suis partibus* is one thing; *in omnibus rebus* is another'. *S.E.*, p. 62. He said that Newman would be much more radical but for his ecclesiastical position. See letter of 11 July to Wilfrid Ward.

[2] This is a quotation from Newman's 'Postscript' to his Inspiration article, *S.E.*, pp. 40–1.

[3] The quotation, unfinished, is from the Inspiration article, *S.E.*, p. 11.

TO CHARLES MICHAEL BERINGTON

July 7. 1887

Cardinal Newman is very sorry to hear from Mr Berington of Mr Parsons'
death, the news of which took him by surprise[1]

He hopes he will be so kind as to convey the Cardinal's most sincere condolence to Mrs Parsons, and to assure her that it is his purpose to say Mass for
her husband to-morrow morning.

TO AUBREY DE VERE

July 10/87

My dear Aubrey de Vere

I congratulate you on your new volume, and wish I could write about it as
much as I should like to do.[2] The putting the Legends into verse, as you have
done, is a happy idea

I regret to say I am too old to attempt to answer letters   Also, I should
like to have heard where you stand in politics. I have not heard from Emly for
an age   How comes your name not to be among the signatures of the Irish
Gentlemen, the O Conor Don's and the rest?[3]

Yours affectly J H Card Newman

P S   Your St Jerome's death is beautiful

TO MESSRS BURNS AND OATES

July 11. 1887

Received from Messrs Burns and Oates the sum of £80.7.1 due to me
from them at this time by sale of my publications

J H N

In answer to Messrs B and Oates question a few weeks ago as to a new
Edition of his Volume of Verses, Cardinal Newman has to observe that he has
no encouragement to continue any business relations with a publishing Firm,

[1] Berington wrote from Little Malvern Court on 6 July, to announce the death on 5 July of
Daniel Parsons, who went up to Oriel College in 1828. A few days before his death he had said
of Newman, 'how well I remember his giving me my first lesson in Logic; how things have
changed since then'.
[2] De Vere sent his *Legends and Records of the Church and the Empire*, London 1887, which
included a poem 'The Death of St Jerome'.
[3] There follow four words, perhaps 'Are [you] patient of such matters'. De Vere was
strongly opposed to Home Rule. The loyal address to which Newman refers was that of Irish
Catholics in London to the Queen on her jubilee. De Vere was in Ireland at the time and had
not heard of it. It was signed by Lord Emly, the O'Conor Don and many others.

which profess to consider a royalty of an edition of a volume equivalent to the possession of the copyright[1]

J H N

TO WILFRID WARD

July 11/87

I regret to say I am too old to attempt to answer letters
I am too old for controversy.[2] If I am patient my words will explain themselves. I have not read Dr M's [Mivart] article[.] I have ever maintained the 'pietas fidei'.[3]

Yours affly J. H. N.

TO L. J. STAFFORD

July 14. 1887

I regret to say I am too old to attempt to answer letters and I wish I could send Mr Stafford a better Autograph than this.

John H Newman

TO MISS LOUISA DEANE

The Oratory July. 15. 1887

My dear Louisa

Fully as I know all of you must have been prepared for your great loss, that, (I know too) has not, and will not, destroy the suffering, especially to your dear Mother. Tell her how much I feel for her, and that I have not forgotten to think of her, when I have gone into our private Chapel.[4]

With my love to all of you,

Yours affectly John H. Card. Newman

---

[1] Messrs Burns and Oates wrote on 15 June that their edition of *V.V.* was nearly exhausted and asked instructions for a new edition. See letter of 11 Nov. 1886. To the present letter they replied on 14 July, that they believed they were protecting Newman's interests, and they were desirous of continuing to publish his works.

[2] In reply to Newman's letter of 4 July and its enclosure, Ward wrote on 10 July: 'I feel that Dr Mivart has gone in the teeth of the advice you give in your memorandum, while he has burlesqued the careful and guarded suggestions you make in your article . . . he adopts with acknowledged ignorance of the value of the evidence adduced the theories (in substance) of the rationalistic critics of the Bible who treating it as a merely human book reason from assumptions which a Catholic wholly denies'. Ward went on to describe Mivart's article as violent. See also Jacob W. Gruber, *A Conscience in Conflict, The Life of St. George Jackson Mivart*, New York 1960, pp. 171–5.

[3] Ward wrote again on 20 April 1888: 'We have been to attend the Catholic Congress in Paris which gave us an interesting opportunity of learning the feeling in French Ecclesiastical circles on some of the matters which have been troubling us in England. Dr Mivart's Article appears to have startled them a good deal, and I was pleased to find that there is a strong sense of the difficulty and importance of the question of Scripture Inspiration, and that the abler men (as far as I could hear) are opposed to anything like a narrow view on the subject, tho' they are shocked at the wholesale surrender of Dr Mivart and at his language'.

[4] Louisa's father, J. B. Deane, died on 12 July.

TO LORD BLACHFORD

The Oratory, July 18th. 1887.

My dear Blachford,

Is it not audacious in me to send you a short and empty letter and to expect one of decent dimensions from you — but I write for the chance, the poor chance I fear, of your having something consolatory about Wilson,[1] and I am glad to show you my best penmanship, tho' it will not last for very long.

I cannot help thinking that I am gradually declining — but the Doctor will not allow it. I have no *internal* feeling of weakness, as some people have, giving them the imaginative impression that death is at hand — but I am sadly feeble, with the apprehension I may make a false step and break a bone at any moment.

I don't like the account of Church at all – but as to you he says you are most flourishing —

What is your view of politics? I don't see your name in the London Papers. Is the English Constitution to weather the storm? Wasn't Lowe right in saying 'We must educate our masters'[2] yet Gladstone is a phenomenon he did not contemplate.

Ever yours affectionately, J. H. Card: Newman.

TO G. WASHINGTON MOORE

July 23 1887

I regret to say I am too old to attempt to answer letters

And I am obliged to say that Mr Moore's application must be subject to this rule

J. H. Card Newman[3]

TO R. B. GODOLPHIN OSBORNE

July 24, 1887.

My dear Fr Osborne,

Your letter and enclosure of this morning were most acceptable to me. I was truly gratified by her Majesty's message and by the kindness of Sir H. Ponsonby's conveyance of it.[4]

Express to the Brothers of the Oratory my intimate sense of their

---

[1] See letter of 20 Jan. 1887 to Lord Blachford.

[2] This is the popularized version of the words of Robert Lowe, on 15 July 1867, when the second Reform Bill was passed: 'I believe it will be absolutely necessary that you should prevail on our future masters to learn their letters.' The political storm was caused by the Irish question.

[3] This letter with its stamped but uncancelled envelope, was apparently not sent.

[4] See letter of 24 June to Osborne. Sir Henry Ponsonby wrote to Fr Osborne from Windsor Castle on 16 July: 'The Queen has received with much pleasure the beautiful present of

affectionate thought of me, and my regret that my fingers will not allow me to write my thanks in better style.

Very truly Yours J. H. Card. Newman

The Revd Fr Godolphin Osborne

TO THE SECRETARY OF THE CATHOLIC YOUNG MEN'S SOCIETY OF GREAT BRITAIN

[July 1887]

Dear Mr Quinn,

I congratulate your society upon your approaching anniversary meeting, and rejoice in the ever enlarging prospects of its good work. In a day when the attractions of the world have an unusual strength, it is one of the greatest consolations to know that there are those who, with a simple and winning earnestness, are lifting up against them the old and noble standard of truth and duty. I gladly send you and the society my blessing, and am your faithful servant,

J. H. Cardinal Newman.

TO CARDINAL RAMPOLLA

Birmingham 2 Agosto 1887

Eṁo e Rṁo Sig Mio Ossṁo

Ho ricevuto con profonda riconoscenza il dono di Sua Santita, essendo quattro medaglie pel grazioso mezzo di Vostra Eminenza; e Le bacio umilissimamente le mani che mi hanno trasmesse

Di Vostra Eminenza

All' Eṁo Reṁo Sig Cardinale
Mariano Rampolla Segretario di Stato[1]

TO EMILY FORTEY

The Oratory, Bm Aug 4/87.

My dear Child,

I recollect you perfectly well.[2] I shall be glad to see you next week, except between 1.30 and 2.30   But you must let me know[3]

Yours affy J. H. Card. Newman

the works of Cardinal Newman, which has been offered to Her Majesty by the Brothers of the Oratory — and I am commanded by Her Majesty to request that you will convey the Queen's best thanks to them for their good wishes, and for this gift.'

[1] Rampolla was made a Cardinal in March 1887 and then appointed Secretary of State.
[2] Emily Fortey wrote on 3 Aug., 'I am one of those happy souls who owe their conversion principally to the influence of your life and writings — as far as human causes can be assigned for conversions. . . . It was in the summer of 1882 when I was a girl of 16 that I first wrote to you, and your kind answer encouraged and strengthened me during the two years of weary waiting that I spent before my father gave me permission to do what I wished. Then when I was on the eve of being received into the Church I wrote to you once more to beg your Blessing, which you sent me on Oct: 4th 1884, the very day that I became a child of the Church.

TO R. W. CHURCH

Aug 7. 1887

My dear Dean

My first thought on finding I must go to London, was whether I could make it an opportunity for seeing you, and I feel how good you are in telling me there is no difficulty on your side and that you could take me in at the Deanery[1]

But I grieve to say, that tho' Ogle were to say, as perhaps he would, that I could go to you, I could not do so. No one but myself knows how shaky I am and with what difficulty, nay pain I walk a few paces, how want of strength, and of memory, hinders me from conversing and what uncomfortable ailments they are which, as being too small or for other reasons, I could not explain to another. So I must say no to you, and you must not think me ungrateful

I should like to write more, but cannot

Yrs affectly John H Card. Newman

I mean to go and to return the same day[2]

TO BISHOP ULLATHORNE

Aug. 11. 1887

My dear Lord

Your Circular has made us here very sad.[3] Yet if any one has a claim to be released from his long service to the Church, and to receive his reward, it is you.

[See letters of 6 July 1882 and 3 Oct. 1884 to Emily Fortey.]
   Now there is one thing left; it has been one of the greatest desires of my heart to see you, and thank you in person for your goodness to me and receive a blessing from your own lips. . . . I know that I am asking a very great favour; I can dare to ask because I am one of your children. I want to see your own face instead of pictures, and hear your own voice instead of reading your books. If you must refuse me I shall come home sad, but I beg you to grant me this great favour for the love of our Lady and of St Philip. Now I know you cannot refuse me!'
   [3] Newman sent Emily Fortey a telegram on 5 Aug. 'I leave here early next Wednesday therefore come before Tuesday afternoon.' The visit was on Monday 8 Aug.
   When Emily Fortey wrote on 16 Aug. to thank for her visit, she said: 'It seemed almost as if you could see into my soul and read there all my inconstancy when you gave me the word "perseverance" for my whole life. I will try to learn your lesson.'

   [1] J. W. Ogle had told Church that Newman might be in London on 10 Aug.
   [2] Newman went to London again on 17 Aug. to see an oculist and called upon Dean Church.
   [3] This was a circular announcing Ullathorne's retirement as soon as a successor could be appointed. He was partly paralysed.

I said Mass for you yesterday and trust my strength will allow me to repeat the pleasant duty again and again

Your faithful & affecte servant John H. Card. Newman[1]

TO JOHN WILLIAM OGLE

Aug 12./87

My dear Dr Ogle

I have to thank you and Sir William Bowman for the trouble you are both taking about me.[2] I don't see anything likely to prevent my coming to Town next Wednesday the 17th, and, as far as I am concerned, I accept the appointment — I suppose at 12 oclock

Yours sincerely J. H. Card. Newman

TO MISS LOUISA DEANE

Aug. 12. 1887

My dear Louisa,

I hope you can give me a good account of your Mother. Any thing you can tell me about yourselves will of course be deeply interesting to me.

Yours affly John H Card. Newman

TO JOHN McLAUGHLIN

August 12. 1887

Dear Fr Mac Laughlin

I have been reading your book, since it came to me, with great interest and pleasure, and pray and trust it may achieve that success which you desire for it and which it deserves.[3]

Very truly Yours John H. Card Newman

TO THE EDITOR OF THE CAMBRIAN

The Oratory, August 24th, 1887

Sir

I feel the compliment paid me in the insertion of a Translation of my verses, 'Lead, kindly light,' in *The Cambrian* newspaper.

---

[1] For Ullathorne's visit on 18 Aug. when Newman asked for his blessing, see *Butler* II, pp. 283–4.

[2] Sir William Bowman was the leading ophthalmic surgeon in London, at 5 Clifford Street.

[3] *Is One Religion as good as another?* London 1887. McLaughlin had consulted Newman about his book, and paid a visit to the Oratory on 25 April. He wrote on 1 May about 'the extent and the degree, your writings and example influenced the conversion of the multitudes of persons whom I received into the Church during the twenty-two years of my missionary life.'

In answer to your question, I can but say that it consists of *three* not *four* stanzas, and the fourth (to use your words) is not 'authentic' but 'an unwarranted addendum by an other pen.'[1]

Excuse my bad writing.

Your faithful servant, J. H. Card. Newman

TO MRS JOHN HUNGERFORD POLLEN

Aug. 27. 1887

My dear Mrs Pollen

I have wished to send you a letter of thanks for your sadly interesting and long letter, ever since I received it. But I don't like now to inflict on friends the 'pot hooks and hangers' which are the highest sort of writing to which I attain. I am glad to find Antony's account of the   [2] so good

Most truly yours John H Card. Newman

TO AN UNKNOWN CORRESPONDENT

Aug 30. 1887

To A B

The cause of your friend's distress is one of those special facts, which illustrate what I have in various publication so strongly insisted on, that in logic there is no resting place between Catholicism and Atheism and Atheism,[3] and in particular that Theism is not tenable as a safe half way house between two extremes.

All religion is a call on us for Faith; and there are fewer such calls on us, or at least not more or heavier, in revealed religion than in rationalistic.[4]

Evil and the origin of evil is the fundamental trial of Faith.

This is one of the pregnant meanings of 'Lead Kindly Light' The moral is contained in the words 'One step enough for me'. Beyond that one step is the province simply of Faith.[5]

---

[1] The editor of the *Cambrian*, S. C. Gamwell wrote from Swansea on 22 Aug. that he had published a Welsh translation of the three verses of 'Lead, kindly Light' in his newspaper. Hence a controversy had arisen as to whether there was not a fourth verse. Gamwell asked whether it was authentic.

Newman's reply was widely noticed in the newspapers. The additional verse was by E. S. Bickersteth. See letter of 20 June 1874 to Bickersteth.

[2] Words illegible to the copyist.

[3] Sic. See *Apo.*, p. 198 and *G.A.*, p. 495.

[4] Here a passage is crossed out in the draft: 'P S (If, to soothe the perplexed rationalist, we make a supposition (quite out of the rationalistic line) we might conjecture that the brute creation were spirits in a penal state for sins committed in a prior state of existence.)'

[5] The following is crossed out in the draft: 'To attempt to go beyond it by our Reason is like a schoolboy going out of bounds; it is like going into a wild desolate hopeless region, "ad terram tenebrosam, ad terram miseriae, ubi umbra mortis et nullus ordo, sed sempiternus horror", if man presumes to take it into occupation.' *Job.* 10: 21–2.

227

TO JOHN BRAMSTON

August 30. 1887

My dear Dean

For it is the only title I now know you by, since I heard of your resignation of your office. I have all along thought of you as one of my old and cherished friends, and now I rejoice to hear from you and to receive your present. I have lost the use of my fingers for writing, and am obliged to leave off abruptly but you must not think, because I don't show it, I don't think of you day after day.

Yours affectionately, John H. Card. Newman.[1]

TO R. W. CHURCH

Sept 1/87

My dear Dean

Knox had so fully *nothing* to do with the movement, that I even forget what allusions we at any time have made to him in print.[2] He wrote strongly about the Eucharistic *Gift* I think, and I maintained that a gift required what he did not grant, a keeper. We were glad to have him as far as he went, and I think used him — but he had no more to do with us than Hampden or Arnold

The Irish are always claiming English men and acts — the zealous poor used to call Oakeley 'O'Kelly', and an Archbishop has lately claimed St Boniface for an Irishman.[3] Professor Stokes is hardly worthy of notice; I looked through his article when it came out[4]

I subjoin a confirmation of what *alone* my memory goes to from my Essays vol 2

Yours affectly J H N

[1] See also letter of 8 Nov. 1887 to Bramston.

[2] Dean Church wrote on 31 Aug., 'A certain Professor Stokes has been writing in the Contemporary Review, August, about Alex. Knox. He writes to show that "Knox was the mediator or channel connecting Wesley with the Tractarian movement," and considers "Knox as the secret, unacknowledged, but none the less real fount and origin" of it.

It seems to me rather a large mare's nest, but of course my memory does not go back so far. But I always imagined that Knox was not much known or thought of in the early days of the movement, and that there was certainly nothing learned from him when it began. I can find no trace of his influence. Am I right in thinking that neither directly nor indirectly through Bishop Jebb, he had any thing to do with the early stages of the movement, or "transmitted" any thing — Wesley's, or any one else's, to the Oxford men?

Mr Stokes is very extravagant . . .'

The article of George Thomas Stokes, Professor of Ecclesiastical History at Trinity College, Dublin was 'Alexander Knox and the Oxford Movement', the *Contemporary Review* (Aug. 1887), pp. 184–205. See especially p. 195.

[3] See letter of 16 Nov. 1884 to W. R. Brownlow.

[4] Church replied on 2 Sept., 'I thought it must be a very great mare's nest' and said he had written to the *Guardian*, speaking out of his own knowledge. 'I should like to have called it *sans phrase*, a mare's nest: but I thought it would not be civil to a "Professor". He is not a wise man.'

The article in the *Guardian* (7 Sept. 1887), pp. 1337–8, 'Professor Stokes on Alexander Knox and the Oxford Movement', signed 'R.W.C.', said that Stokes's conclusion 'can only appear grotesque', and that the Tractarians found their doctrines in the English divines, and still more in the Fathers.

You must excuse my quoting a passage that is controversial

Where there is a true Succession, there is a true Eucharist; if there is not a true Eucharist, there is no true Succession. Now, what is the presumption here? I think it is Mr Alexander Knox who says or suggests that, if so great a gift *be* given, it must have a rite. I add, if it has a rite, it must have a *custos* of the rite. Who is the *custos* of the Anglican Eucharist? The Anglican clergy? Could I, without distressing or offending an Anglican, describe what sort of custodes they have been, and are, to their Eucharist? 'O bone custos', in the words of the poet, 'cui commendavi Filium Meum'.[1] Essays Critical etc Vol ii p 110. 1881.[2]

NOTE TO MEMORANDUM OF 4 DECEMBER 1881

Sept 11. 1887

As to the said annual income from my works, I forbid any part of it being lent or given for the purpose, use etc of a Grammar School carried on by the Fathers of the Oratory.[3]

J.H.N.

---

[1] Terence, *Phormio*, II, i, 57–8.

[2] This is a passage from the letter of 5 Aug. 1868 to H. J. Coleridge. See also *Ess.* I, pp. 269–71; *Apo.*, p. 97; *Moz.* I, 440 and 470, II, 93, 133 and 216. Also R. W. Church, *The Oxford Movement*, London 1891, pp. 28–9 and 128.

[3] A Catholic Grammar School was begun in Birmingham in 1858, which came to be known as St Chad's Grammar School, with as headmaster a priest of the diocese, John O'Hanlon. This school was in 1881 transferred to Erdington, to the Benedictines there. In 1886 the Benedictines decided to close their school, and Richard Bellasis with Paul Eaglesim began negotiations for its transfer to the Oratory. In July 1887 a meeting of the Birmingham clergy asked that the School should be reopened at Edgbaston at the end of the summer holidays, so that there might be no break in continuity. On 11 Aug. Bishop Ullathorne wrote to Eaglesim 'It gives me great satisfaction to know that the Oratorian Fathers are contemplating a Grammar School for Birmingham, and with the entire approval of the Reverend Clergy of the Town, and I hope with their cooperation, are taking active steps to realize their plan.'

There was no question of any grant from Government or City, and the whole expense of the School would have to be found from donations and the small fees paid for the boys. In May the plan was put before the Deputies, the Governing Body of the Oratory, and on 3 Sept. 1887 the following decree was passed by Congregation of the Oratory as a whole:

'Whereas Fathers Richard Bellasis and Paul Eaglesim inform us that, in accordance with the scheme they laid before the Deputies on the 16th of May last, they are now ready to open the Grammar School in the Oliver Road on the 19th day of this September, it was decreed by seven votes that we approve of their doing so, on the clear understanding that they take upon themselves all the pecuniary risk of the undertaking.

It was also decreed that each Father, being a Priest, should say a Mass, and those who are not Priests, should offer up a Communion, for its success.'

Newman was fearful of this new liability in view of the other commitments of the Oratory. The Minute Book of the Oratory contains this entry for 11 Sept. 1887: 'The Father wished it to be recorded (1) that the application to the Bishop for the establishment of a Grammar School was not made with his full consent and knowledge. [a draft by Neville adds 'nor had he seen the Bishop's letter concerning it.']

(2) That he did not wish anything published in the newspapers or elsewhere by which it might appear that the new School was established by us as a Congregation — it being the work of two zealous Fathers of the Congregation only. [According to Neville's draft Newman 'would contradict any statement if it had been published']

(3) That he would not allow any Congregational money to be expended on it.'

See also Newman's Memorandum of Dec. 1889.

On 28 Oct. 1895 the Oratory took upon itself the financial responsibility for St Philip's Grammar School.

TO EDMUND LAWRENCE HEMSTEAD TEW

Sept 24 1887

Dear Sir

I had a great affection for Mr Henderson[1]

I regret to say I am too old to attempt to answer letters I can neither write nor read writing

Yours very truly John H Card Newman

TO JOSEPHINE HOPE

Sept 28/87

My dear Josephine

What a very welcome letter you have sent me. I congratulate you and Wilfrid Ward with all my heart. I know enough of you both to be able to say this without impertinence. I send you my blessing gladly. My fingers will not write more.[2]

Yours affectionately John H Card Newman

TO WILFRID WARD

Sept 28/87

My dear Wilfrid

What a capital letter you have sent me. I rejoice to receive it, and send you gladly my congratulations and blessing.

I have neither eyes to see, nor fingers to write. So these few lines (are they lines?) are but an ungrateful return for yours and Josephine's

Yours affly J H Card. Newman

May I have a look at my letter which has got abroad?[3]

TO LORD BLACHFORD

Septr 30. 1887

My dear Blachford,

Your birds of the 28th have come.[4] And I thank you now for those before them, which I fear were not acknowledged.

---

[1] Tew, Vicar of Hornsea, had married a daughter of Thomas Henderson, who went up to Christ Church, Oxford, in 1820, aged nineteen. He was a Student there 1820–9, and held livings in Essex from 1831 until his death in 1861.

[2] Josephine Hope and Wilfrid Ward both wrote to announce their engagement.

[3] Ward in his letter of 27 Sept. said that an inaccurate reference to his visit to Newman, to consult him on the wisdom of English and Irish Catholics appealing to the Holy See in the Irish question, had appeared in the *Freeman's Journal*. See letter of 18 April 1887 to W. Ward. It was stated that Newman had expressed no definite opinion as to the 'Plan of Campaign'. Newman understood that it was a letter of his which had got abroad.

[4] Lord Blachford had sent more game.

I wish, alas, you may be able to read my acknowledgment in my hand writing.

Yours affly J. H. Card. Newman

TO MOTHER MARY LOYOLA

Oct 4/87

My dear Rev Mother

I shall rejoice to have your work, which is sure to be interesting, and thank you for the kind thought of sending it to me. It will be an important addition to our library.[1]

And I readily send you my Blessing for you and yours and all you ask for, and for the two Anglican Clergymen, and wish my fingers allowed me to send it you in better style

Mostruly [sic] Yours John H Card. Newman

TO RICHARD STANTON

Oct 4. 87

My dear Fr Stanton

I delayed writing thinking to save you the trouble of reading a second letter, but I won't delay longer. Thank you very much for your intention I am certain the book will be a very valuable one, and shall be glad to have it.[2] I have lost the use of my fingers — but this is the best letter I have written for a long time

Yours affecty J. H. Card. Newman

TO ROBERT SINKER

Oct 6/87

My dear Sir

I thank you for your sadly interesting letter, and for your kindness in your sending me its inclosure.[3]

I regret to say I am too old to attempt to answer letters, as they should be answered, but trust you will accept this acknowledgment, as being the best I can make you

Yours faithful Servant John H Card Newman

[1] *St. Mary's Convent, Micklegate Bar, York*, edited by Henry James Coleridge, London 1887.
[2] Stanton had compiled *A Menology of England and Wales*, London 1887, at the request of the English bishops.
[3] Sinker's letter is not to be found. He was a Hebrew scholar and wrote also bibliographical works. From 1865 to 1871 he was chaplain and librarian at Trinity College, Cambridge.

Oct 14. 1887

My dear Father Gordon

Your letter warning came last night, and I said Mass for Fr Keogh just now. And I have made known to our Fathers the novena[1]

My fingers won't write — so I am obliged to be abrupt

Yours affectly J H Card. Newman

TO FREDERICK GEORGE LEE

Oct. 17. 87

My dear Dr Lee

I hope you will not be scandalised at the disgraceful in which [sic] I turn to you my thank [sic] for your fresh kindness in sending me your new Volume.[2] But I am gradually losing the use of my fingers, and cannot read my own writing

I want to ask you an additional favour. I want to gain your permission to let me insert in my 'Occasional Verses' the lines of my Birthday which you me [sic] the honour of inserting in your 'Lyrics of Light and Life'[3]

With my affectionate remembrances of your wife and son

I am, most truly Yours John H Card Newman

TO WILLIAM KNIGHT

Oct 20/87

Professor Knight

has sent all the letters except the last from me to himself.[4] In your explanation of my letter to you in the beginning of this year I wish that for 'primitive Church' you will put 'the Church to which he himself now belongs'.[5]

I wish very much to see the original of that fragmentary letter to which your foregoing note is to be appended

---

[1] Edward Keogh of the London Oratory died on 29 Oct. 1887.

[2] Lee sent his *Reginald Pole*, London 1888, inscribed 'To His Eminence John Henry, Cardinal Newman etc etc etc With the Author's respectful regards. Lambeth: October, 1887'.

[3] This was 'My Birthday' (1819) in Lee's *Lyrics of Light and Life*, London 1875, p. 6, *V.V.*, p. 5. See letter of 13 March 1874 to Mrs F. G. Lee. Lee replied on 18 Oct. that the poem 'was regarded only as a valuable loan.'

[4] See letter of 7 Jan. The whole of this present letter is in Neville's hand.

[5] Newman had spoken of 'primitive truth' not 'primitive Church' in his letter. There was no alteration made when Knight printed it in *Principal Shairp and his Friends*, but he preceded it with a note at p. 386: 'It was originally a private letter; and in consenting to its publication now, the Cardinal asks me to add that nothing in it is to be taken as implying that he considers that there is any other refuge for the spirits of men than the Church to which he now belongs'

Oct 27. 1887

Cardinal Newman would be obliged by Messrs Burns and Oates sending him the remaining copies of Messrs Pickering's edition of his 'Athanasius' volumes 1 and 2, and charging them to him. By their account last June there were then 18 copies still on hand, and the selling price 7/6 a volume, though some copies, he supposes, have been sold since June.

He has already told Messrs Burns and Oates that he proposes to commit to Messrs Longman a new edition of his 'Verses' including the 'Dream of Gerontius' on which as a separate publication Messrs Burns and Oates have at present a royalty edition[1]

TO WILLIAM KNIGHT

The Oratory, Birmingham October 28. 1887

Dear Sir

I know that the printers are slow and I may be impatient, but I think you should be aware that the proofs of my letters including the fragmentary one have not yet come to me.

I am rather anxious on the subject because they were private letters not written with any view to publication

Excuse this trouble which I am giving you and

Believe me to be Very truly yours
John H Card. Newman

Professor Knight

TO EMILY BOWLES

Nov 3. 1887

My dear Child

Thank you for your interesting letter, which I was very glad to receive[2] I wish my fingers would write now

Yours affectly J. H. Card. Newman

---

[1] See also letter of 17 Dec. to Burns and Oates.

[2] In a letter of 27 Oct. Emily Bowles described her visit to the home for girls established by 'Mary Simeon at Eastleigh — and was delighted to see her as a true mother to her 35 little girls — *all* rescued from brutal outrage and houses of sin. . . . It was good to see the little ones washing and ironing and laughing as if a sponge had been passed over their lives — and above all to see the change in Mary's face — *always* formerly restless, craving and sad, but now full of peace and happiness.' Emily Bowles went on to describe the wedding of Mary Simeon's half-sister Catherine on 25 Oct. to the Hon. Algernon Henry Grosvenor, fourth son of Lord Ebury, 'in the midst of a brilliant throng of guests — Duchess of Westminster, Eburys, Grosvenors, Clarendons, Colvilles and what not . . . the crowd of "upper ten" was great'.

TO WILLIAM KNIGHT

Nov 3 1887

My dear Mr Knight

You need not fear my corrections. As far as I recollect, I only know of three epithets which I shall wish to make on my second letter apropos of the Roman Church But you must let me propose them to you. I make them for the sake of appositeness[1]

Very truly yours J. H. Card. Newman

TO JOHN BRAMSTON

Birmingham. Nov 8, 1887

My dear Dean

Though I have had your kind present close to me ever since it came, and have thought of you again and again, I have not been able to determine whether I have acknowledged it in writing to you or not.[2]

And so at length, I resolve to write an unreadable letter rather than run the chance of seeming ungrateful to you.

So God bless you always

Ever yours sincerely J. H. Card. Newman

TO CHARLES WELLINGTON FURSE

Nov 11/87

My dear Canon Furse

I shall be very glad to see you and your daughter on Monday and grieve to hear from [you] of your great loss

Ever Yrs J H Card Newman

TO HENRY JAMES COLERIDGE

Nov 13. 1887

Private

Dear Fr Coleridge[3]

I am obliged to answer a question which somewhat puzzles me. Is our Lord's '*Miraculous* conception' a Catholic phrase? If so, how does its sense

---

[1] See letters of 20 and 28 Oct. to Knight.
[2] See letter of 30 Aug. to Bramston, who on 11 Nov. spoke of how already Newman's first letter 'had caused me sincere joy in the remembrance of past friendship'.
[3] This letter is in Neville's hand, except for the last paragraph, in which Newman apparently summarises Coleridge's reply. There is no conclusion to the letter.

differ from the Blessed Virgin's Immaculate Conception? She was saved from original sin by a special grace anticipating it. Is that the way in which we also regard 'conceived by the Holy Ghost'? Is the privilege in the two cases the same? Does a gift of grace do for Mary the very same thing as God the Holy Ghost does for our Lord?

We say of St John the Baptist that he had the gift of the Holy Ghost three months before his birth. Would that gift if it had occurred six months earlier than it actually did have been the same as that which was the beginning of our Lord's Incarnation? Are our Lord, the Blessed Virgin and St John the Baptist instances in different degrees of the same thing? Is our Lady's freedom from original sin simply an indirect consequence of grace given to her in the beginning of her existence, or her Conception a Divine act identical in nature with that of the Holy Ghost in our Lord's instance?

If you could get me this answered of course I will keep silence whence that answer comes.

Answer The Holy Ghost wrought a miracle in Mary taking on Him the function of a father and *creating* what an earthly Father *makes* but in the Immaculate conception He did but [what] was a supernatural act, and not *grace*

TO EDWARD BELLASIS

Nov 34 [14] 87

My dear Edward

I was shocked yesterday to find you were gone without my knowing. I had looked out for a call from you and I now write these few old [?] lines, to express my sorrow as better than nothing

Yrs affectly J H Card Newman

TO WILLIAM KNIGHT

Nov 16/87

Dear Professor Knight

I have little doubt that it is my fault that you have not sent me the copy of my letters, for my memory is very bad. I think I have not thanked you for the letter of January 7 which your daughter has so kindly copied. I will send it back to you at once if you will let me have the others to compare with, since they were all written at different times I don't think you need fear my meddling with them[1] I am not able to write more

Very truly Yours John H Card Newman

[1] See letter of 3 Nov. to Knight.

The Oratory, Birmingham November 18th 1887

My dear Lord Selborne

I was glad to understand you to say that you thought of a Memoir of your dear brother.[1]

This has led me to enquire whether there are not still unpublished papers with me which may aid your object. My eyes and fingers are unable to determine this point for myself. Accordingly I have engaged Fr Eaglesim of this house to do what I cannot do myself.

My report to you from him is as follows:—

There is sufficient matter for an interesting account of his transactions with the Greek Patriarch at Constantinople. Also of his dealings with ecclesiastical authorities in Greece and Syria. There are Journals too in the same years as the above while he was in France.

Would you like these papers sent to you as specimens for your judgment upon what he has left behind him.

I should add that he has left also papers adverse in his perplexity to the Faith he ultimately adopted, but I do not conceive that you would include such first–thoughts in your Memoir.

My dear Lord Selborne Most truly Yours John H Card. Newman[2]

The Rt Hon The Earl of Selborne

The Oratory, Birmingham Novr 19. 1887

My dear Professor Knight

I fear that a letter I wrote to you immediately after you came here has miscarried; it was directed to you at Bath.

It was to say that one or two of my sentences might be more exactly expressed. I fear in consequence that I seemed inconsiderate to you.

---

[1] 'In 1887 I went . . . to Birmingham . . . I then saw Cardinal Newman, [on 27 Oct.] for the last time, at the Oratory, where he lived. He received my daughter Sophia and myself very kindly; we talked of old days, of Oxford and of my brother William, of whom he spoke tenderly: and when I mentioned the idea which was in my mind of writing some memoir of him, if time and strength permitted, he promised to send me a large number of William's journals and other papers, which were in his possession: this he did soon afterwards. He spoke also of Ireland, regretting what he understood, from the information which had reached him, to be the ill-success of Mgr. Persico's mission. He looked very frail and infirm; and I thought his end was near.' Roundell Palmer, Earl of Selborne, *Memorials, Part II, Personal and Political*, London 1898, II, p. 248. For his daughter's account of this visit see *Sophie Matilda Palmer Comtesse de Franqueville 1852–1915 A Memoir* by her sister Lady Laura Ridding, London 1919, p. 185. The Earl was about to go out to Rome and Newman gave him a message for Leo XIII. See Volume XXIX, Appendix I.

[2] Only the conclusion is in Newman's own hand. Lord Selborne replied that he would only wish to publish documents which had interest as showing the steps by which William Palmer reached his final convictions.

What I have been led to write to you about has reference to some words in the second of my letters to Professor Shairp, which I have now altered and return to you with the rest as well as the correction in my letter to you of January 7th viz the substitution of instead of 'primative truth' 'the Church to which he now belongs'

I am, my dear Principal Knight,

Yours Sincerely John H Card Newman[1]

TO POPE LEO XIII

[25 November 1887?]

Jam iterum, Beatissime Pater, Dei misericordia, me sospitem provehit usque ad Salvatoris nostri Festa Natalicia. Proinde quid faciam potius, quam his litteris, ut antehac hoc felicissimo tempore, profiteri Sanctitati Tuae et amorem meum et devotionem, et petere abs Te SS. Pater Benedictionem Suam Apostolicam necnon ut benigne accipiat humilitatis meae consuetum obolum . . .

TO WALTER DAVID JEREMY

Nov 27. 1887

I regret to say I am too old to attempt to answer letters On the subject of 'Lead Kindly Light' vid the Welsh Paper, the Cambria[2]

J. H. Card Newman

TO JOHN MURRAY

The Oratory, Birmingham Nov 30. 1887

Dear Sir

I do not see any difficulty in complying with your wishes as regards to my letters to Mr Rose, but I think it well to observe that Dean Burgon in his printed remarks upon them, with excellent intention, yet with a misunderstanding of the minute details of fact, leaves an impression on my mind somewhat different from that of my own words as contained in the Advertisement to the 'Arians' and in the 'Apologia' p.p. 25, 26.[3]

---

[1] Only the signature is in Newman's hand.

[2] See letter of 24 Aug. to the Editor of the *Cambrian*. On 18 Nov. Jeremy sent his translation into Welsh of 'Lead, kindly Light.' 'I composed it a few months ago after seeing two other translations in a Swansea Newspaper — the Cambrian . . . I have since seen two other Welsh translations, one of them being in a Unitarian Hymn Book. There is probably no other English Hymn of which *five* translations into Welsh have been attempted.' Jeremy was a Unitarian minister and then a barrister at Gray's Inn.

[3] Newman is referring to the account of the origin of *The Arians of the Fourth Century.* See J. W. Burgon *Lives of Twelve Good Men*, London 1888, I, pp. 165–7. On 28 Nov. Murray, who was the publisher, sent proofs of the pages on Hugh James Rose which contained letters written by Newman, asking for permission to publish.

Of course I am not going to insist on so minute a matter, but it suggests to me that perhaps there are parts which I have not seen of those letters which he has actually quoted which I should view differently from his view of them. Therefore do not think me over subtle or exacting if I ask to read the whole of the letters from which Dean Burgon quotes, as they may throw light upon what the Dean has actually printed.

Will you therefore kindly send me your letters (say for a post or so) and I will return them 'registered'.[1]

I am, Dear Sir, Your faithful Servant

John H. Card Newman

John Murray Esqr.

TO WILLIAM KNIGHT

The Oratory, Birmingham Decr 1. 1887

Dear Professor Knight,

You must not suppose that I write from any anxiety on my own account if two letters of mine have not reached you, but I fear they haven't, though I directed them both to St Andrews and to Bath.

If you have received them pray take no notice of this as I should not like to seem inconsiderate to your kindness. My first was immediately after your departure from here and my second on the 19th of November.

I am My dear Professor Knight   Hoping that I am not making up a mystery

Your faithful Servt John H Card Newman[2]

TO JOHN MURRAY

The Oratory, Birmingham Decr 2nd 1887

My dear Sir

I am obliged to you for your satisfactory letter,[3] but I fear I must encroach upon your interposition still further.

I hope that Dean Burgon will not object to let me see the intermediate portions of his (Dean Burgon's) writing which are (necessarily) comments on my letters, as well as my whole letters themselves.

Also I should like to see Mr Rose's letter to me which in fact is an interpretation of what I had written to him.

---

[1] Murray replied in a letter dated 30 Nov., sending proofs of further letters of Newman, which Burgon had quoted, and saying he would surely accede to Newman's request. To Burgon himself Murray wrote on 30 Nov. that Newman's letter was 'very civil, I conclude you will think proper to comply with his request'. See the letters in Dec.

[2] Only the signature is in Newman's hand. See also his letter of 26 May 1890 to Knight.

[3] See second note to letter of 30 Nov. to Murray.

And if I am not exorbitant I will ask for the dates.

I am very sorry to give you this trouble, but I don't see how I can help it.[1]

I am, Dear Sir, Your faithful Servant

John H. Card Newman

John Murray Esqre

P.S. Of course I recollect the case of Lord Ward v Copleston which at the time of its occurrence I followed with great interest. I am not aware that any thing has passed in a Law-Court changing or modifying the Judge's decision.[2]

TO ADOLPH PERRAUD, BISHOP OF AUTUN

Dec 3. 1887

Monseigneur

I send your Lordship my best thanks for giving me the striking Memoir of the striking man, whose earthly presence the Oratory has lost.[3]

I wish my eyes and my fingers could offer you an acknowledgment more worthy of your kind thought of me, but I know you will pardon this the best attempt of a very old man

I am, My dear Lord, Yr humble affecte Servant

John H Card Newman

His Lordship The Bp of Autun

TO JOHN WILLIAM BURGON

The Oratory, Birmingham Decr 4. 1887

My dear Dean Burgon

I thank you for the considerateness with which you have treated me in your Life of my dear friend Mr Rose, and I will be as short as I can in my remarks upon what you have selected, but you yourself have taken such pains with a history which you have felt to be interesting that you will understand the difficulty I have in returning the letters etc to you in a poor twenty four hours, nevertheless they shall go to you without much delay.

Yours very truly As far as my fingers will allow me to say so

John H Card Newman[4]

The very Rev The Dean of Chichester

[1] Murray replied on 3 Dec., 'I am to-day honoured by your second Letter, which I will [send] forthwith to the Dean as he alone can answer it.'

[2] See letter of 19 Aug. 1884 to Thomas Fisher Unwin. Murray wrote to Burgon on 3 Dec. that Newman's 'Postscript looks to me a little threatening'.

[3] Perraud had sent Newman a memorial card of Père Pététot, Superior-General of the French Oratory, who died in 1887. He had retired in 1884 and been succeeded by Perraud.

[4] This letter is in Neville's hand until 'As far as my fingers . . .'

TO JOHN WILLIAM BURGON

The Oratory, Birmingham Decr 5. 1887

My dear Dean

I have read with great interest the complementary matter, both yours and mine, which at my request you have been kind enough to send me, and as far as my portion of it is concerned I make no objection to your making such use of it as you wish.

I have thought it better to send this letter through Mr Murray as he is as much concerned in the publication of your work as you are yourself.

I am, my dear Dean Burgon Very truly Yours

J. H. Card Newman[1]

P.S. I think you may like to see the paper of remarks which I made on reading the succession of my letters and I therefore enclose it[2]

TO JANE TODD

For Dec. 8 1887

My dear Miss Todd

Don't fancy I don't think of you because I do not write[3]
But I can scarcely use my eyes or my fingers
I send you my blessing, and pray that all grace and peace [?] may be yours

Yours affectly John H Card Newman

TO ALFRED NEWDIGATE

Dec. 9 1887

My dear Mr Newdigate

I congratulate you in having success in so many, so cheap [?], so important, and such handsome little books [4] My only regret is that I cannot any

---

[1] Only the actual signature is in Newman's hand.

[2] This is not to be found but the drafts of some of Newman's remarks are preserved as Neville took them down. As to Newman's letter of 28 March 1831 to H. J. Rose, (Burgon, *Lives of Twelve Good Men*, I, pp. 165–6), Newman wrote: 'If the negotiation between Mr Rose and myself is given at all, the whole should be given   Please insert the *whole* letter'

Letter of 26 Nov. 1832, (op. cit. p. 167), 'I dont understand what the MS is here referred to'

Letter of 16 Aug. 1833, (op. cit. p. 194), 'What had I "penned"? The PS need not be printed' Burgon printed it in his second volume, pp. 309–10.

On 6 Dec. Murray wrote to Dean Burgon: 'I congratulate you on the thoroughly kindly letter of the Cardinal and I hope you will now write to him direct'.

[3] In a letter of 16 Nov. 1889 to Neville, Jane Todd explained that the first letter she received from Newman 'was in November *1850* in answer to some trouble I had about my general confession — since then he never failed to reply to all my tiresome letters — with gracious healing words . . .' Fearing that she was 'leaning *too much* on created help' she burnt them in 1859, made another holocaust in 1878, and burnt a few more later, sending Neville only this present one. She added that 'though the letters are no more — the many passages I can recollect come back and speak to me *now* . . .'

[4] Two words are illegible.

longer continue the offer of £20. *Life is uncertain,* but I inclose, *instead* of [1]
engagmts; an offering to your good work, a cheque for £5.
N.B. I am out of a cheque so I borrow a friend's
    With my blessing and prayer for you

Most truly yours John H. Card Newman

TO EDMUND STONOR

Dec 13. 1887

My dear Monsigor Stonor

Thank you. I inclose a letter from me to the Holy Father.

And a cheque on Messrs Plowden I can neither see nor write This must be my excuse to the Pope for my wretched writing[2]

Most truly Yours
John H Card Newman

TO E. K. CHAMBERS

Decr 15/87

Sir

I regret to say I am too old to attempt to answer letters

Your faithful Servt J. H. Card Newman

TO LORD BLACHFORD

Dec 17./87.

My dear Blachford,

I am always thinking of you, but know how very difficult it is for either for you or for me to find matter for a letter, not to speak of the difficulty of my writing and your reading.[3]

Poor Church! I feel for him deeply — such an addition to his troubles is overwhelming. Tell him whenever you write how grieved I am for him and his family circle.[4]

I am losing the use of my eyes.

Yours affly J.H.N.

P.S.   Thank you for the new flight of game.

---

[1] Two words are illegible.

[2] There is a note in Neville's hand: Birminghamiæ Jan 27. 1888
Ego Joannes Henricus Newman Cardinalis Diaconus Basilicæ S. Georgii Martyris in Velabro his litteris constituo amplissimum virum Reverendissimum Edmundum Stonor Canonicum Ecclesiæ S. Joannis Lateranensis, Procuratorem meum ut officio fungatur inducendi in Canonicatum supradictæ Basilicæ dignissimum Rectorem Monsignor Cæsarem Guismondi loco cujusdam nuper defuncti.'

[3] A note on the copy says that the whole of this letter was written by Newman.

[4] Dean Church's only son Frederick was seriously ill and died on 16 Jan. 1888, aged thirty-three.

Dec 17. 1887

The Cardinal begs to say that he has no intention of publishing a new edition of the 'Dream of Gerontius' with Messrs Burns and Oates and he would be obliged to them by their sending his stereotyped plates of the 'Dream' on application to Messrs Gilbert and Rivington.

He thanks Messrs B and Oates for informing him about the state of sale of Discourses to Mixed Congregations and Sermons on Various Occasions of which there are at present a royalty edition not stereotyped

TO CHARLES LONGMAN

[18 December 1887?][1]

To Messrs Longman

Dear Mr Longman

I am led to doubt whether you fully know my position as regards some of my books with Messrs Burns and Oates. They have incidentally told me that they have made some agreement about their publications with an American firm. Accidentally to know this fact is all the co-operation I have had in the matter excepting in a royalty edition which is now expired of the Dream. Does this affect my making any arrangement with you.

I should add that unexpired royalty *editions* are outstanding in the case of 2 volumes of Sermons and two Tales. This I shall have to provide — and must be met with the following provision

Nor are you aware as I think how many of my works are still unstereotyped viz the 2 volumes of Sermons, Loss and Gain, Callista, Athanasius

To set against these difficulties I should have nothing more than your purchase of the stock of the Arians and Athanasius You will see what great modifications this state of facts may make necessary in your proposal.

I should also add that unexpired royalty *editions* exist against 2 volumes of Sermons and 2 Tales

 of Mixed there remain 1150 copies

  Sermons on Various Occasions 1100 copies

I do not at present know what the number of the two Tales may be

TO EMILY BOWDEN

Dec 23 1887

My dear Emily

A happy Christmas to you and your Mother. I was shocked to hear of the accident she had had — but I heard at the same time that she had recovered

[1] This letter appears to give information mentioned in that of 17 Dec. It is entirely in Neville's hand.

I was most pleased to receive your letter Excuse this illegible scrawl — but neither will my fingers write, nor my eyes read

Yours ever affectly John H Card Newman

TO AUGUSTA THEODOSIA DRANE

[31 December 1887]

I am very sorry not to have written to you on St Johns day your letter was most welcome I send you the best Christmas blessings I wish you in return

Cardinal Newman[1]

TO HENRY WILLIAMS MOZLEY

[January 1888]

I regret to say I am too old to attempt to answer letters
My dear Harry

I wish y[ou] and Clare joy of the new comer. It is a good time and I wish him all it's blessings.[2]

Please direct and post the inclosed.

Yrs affly J H N.

P S   The relative position of the two names at least is wholly mine[3]   Thanks[4]

TO R. BAGOT

[10 January 1888][5]

I regret to say I am too old to attempt to answer letters[6]   I can neither read nor write, and I am sure this will excuse me with you

J H N

TO GEORGE T. EDWARDS

Jany 10. 1888

My dear Mr Edwards

Many thanks for your very kind letter. Your news of Mr Fisher's death made me sad, though I know we all must die, and believe that few, calling themselves Protestants are so well prepared as he was.[7] I may have spoken to

---

[1] This was a telegram sent in answer to a letter of 26 Dec.
[2] The reference is to the birth of John Henry Mozley on 28 Dec. 1887.
[3] This refers to the baby's names.
[4] For Newman's sermon on 1 Jan. about Leo XIII see *Ward II*, pp. 529–30.
[5] A note to the letter says 'received 11. January. R.B.'
[6] This sentence is lithographed, the rest written by Newman.
[7] Edwards wrote on 31 Dec. to say that John Cowley Fisher had died the previous Oct.

you sharply perhaps about some of his sayings, but it was against his logic and his positiveness against which I spoke, not in any unkindness towards him as an individual. May we meet in heaven.

My fingers will not write more

Most truly yours John H Card Newman

P.S.   I hope this winter is less trying to you at Red hill than last

TO LORD BLACHFORD

January 11. 1888

My dear Blachford,

Thank you for another pheasant.

I mean not to forget your and Lady Blachford's birthdays now in prospect, though I cannot rely on my brain or my fingers.

Yours affly J.H.N.

TO R. W. CHURCH

[22 January 1888]

My very dear C

I understand how your loss must pierce so tender a heart as yours
God be merciful to you and all of you and bless you[1]

J H N

TO ISAAC THOMAS HECKER

Jany 22 ⟨1888⟩[2]

Do you mean to say that; with all his faults, Wesley was not a man of faith

---

[1] Dean Church at Hyères wrote on 17 Jan. the news of his son's death the previous day.

[2] Newman made a memorandum before writing this draft letter: 'Jany 20 1888
Fr Hecker p 81 says God has created all men equal, and with equal rights, among these is liberty.
1 Is a man, in his nonage by right of creation free of his father?
2 Has a man, as a permanent right, freedom from his civil magistrate? has he a right, when he will, to rebel? Can rights of nature be otherwise than permanent?
Does this theory agree with Mr Lilly's in his article on the 1st principles laid down in 1789?' See W. S. Lilly 'The Principles of '89', the *Contemporary Review* (June 1881), pp. 944–70, reprinted in *Chapters in European History*, London 1886, II, pp. 196–247, attacking 'The Declaration of the Rights of Man'.
Newman was criticising Hecker's *The Church and the Age*, New York 1887, whose thesis was that 'The Principles of American Freedom are Catholic — Protestantism is opposed to them'. On p. 81 Hecker said: 'Human nature, as it now exists, is essentially good, and man naturally seeks and desires his Creator as the source of his happiness. Man has lost none of his original faculties and has forfeited none of his natural rights by Adam's fall, and therefore is by nature in possession of all his natural rights, and it is rightly said: "Among these are life, liberty, and the pursuit of happiness." "God has created all men equal" in regard to these rights, and therefore no one man has the natural right to govern another man . . .'

and better pleasing to God, than Washington? Why then should the successors of Washington be better Christians than those of Wesley?

What you call a maintenance of first principles and an instinct, I call pride and self will

TO HENRY BEDFORD

Jany 27. 1888

A Blessing for the new year on you and all your community with all my heart.[1]

J.H.N.

TO MRS JOHN HUNGERFORD POLLEN

[1 February 1888]

I am very sorry to say it is impossible[.] I cannot get my fingers to be less abrupt as[2]

All best blessings on you and yours

J H N

I regret to say I am too old to attempt to answer letters[3]

TO JAMES LAIRD PATTERSON

[6 February 1888][4]

My dear Bishop of Emmaus

I thank you for your letter and congratulate you and the parishioners on your new Patron. But a Martyr is a Martyr whether at Chelsea or Rochester and I cannot compare them. For this reason I cannot leave St John Bishop and Martyr out in the cold, in order to find a glorious shrine for St Thomas, Chancellor of England. And mayn't I say so about the Carthusians will [?] therein[?] too amid their cruel torments at Clerkenwell.

[1] Bedford lived at All Hallows College, Dublin.
[2] The rest is illegible. On 30 Jan. Mrs Pollen asked that her Oratorian son Anthony might accompany his father to Paris for the final profession as a nun of their daughter Anne on 11 Feb.
[3] This sentence is lithographed.
[4] Bishop Patterson on 5 Feb. sent Newman a circular aimed at spreading devotion to the English Martyrs. He had put above one of the altars of his church, St Mary's, Chelsea, a picture of Sir Thomas More, who was beatified in 1886.

TO ALEXANDER FULLERTON

The Oratory, Birmingham Febr 20. 1888

Dear Mr Fullerton,

I am glad of your news about the Life[1] and the Convent.

Pardon so short a letter because my fingers will not let me write

Most truly Yours John H Card. Newman[2]

P.S.   I grieve to have your letter about Cardinal Howard[3]

TO GERARD MANLEY HOPKINS

Febr. 24 [22] 1888[4]

You are one of those friends and well wishers, who have so kindly addressed to me letters of congratulation on my birthday, — letters which touched me much, and for your share in which I hereby offer you my sincere thanks.

With my Blessing

J H N

TO H. P. LIDDON

The Oratory, Birmingham Feb. 22. 1888

My dear Dr Liddon,

The 'Memorial' was Golightly's work but from the first I would have nothing to do with it.[5] I entreated Pusey not to be swayed by me but to act upon his own view. But I cannot be sure that there was not some compromise between me and Pusey though I cannot recollect it at all, that is I cannot fancy that I came into the plan of building a church to the Reformation. If any letter of his says so of course I cannot deny it. Down to this day I have not thought of it as a great event; I think rather that I have despised it.[6]

If you see Dr Bright pray thank him for his congratulations.

Very truly Yours John H Card Newman[7]

[1] Mrs Craven's Life of Lady Georgiana Fullerton, published in 1888.
[2] Only the conclusion and postscript are written by Newman.
[3] Cardinal Howard's brain was paralysed. He died in 1892.
[4] The postmark of this lithographed letter is 22 Feb. Only date, blessing and signature are in Newman's hand.
[5] In writing on 21 Feb. for Newman's birthday, Liddon added: 'I had meant to have troubled you about the 'Martyrs Memorial' [at Oxford. See Liddon's Pusey II, pp. 64–76], so far as to ask you whether its erection appeared to you at the time so much of an event, as it does in the retrospect, and in Dr Pusey's correspondence with Harrison and Bishop Bagot. You would remember that Dr Pusey, though pressed by Harrison, (who had then lately gone to Lambeth) and by Bishop Bagot, declined to support it in its original or Golightly form, as a memorial to the Reformers, but that he was willing to build a church in memory of the Reformation — a plan which Bishop Bagot discountenanced — but which you, who had kept quite clear of the earlier proposal did for a time sanction. . . . [The dots are Liddon's]
The subject does not seem to be noticed in the Apologia: and I find it difficult to decide what kind or degree of importance ought to be attributed to it'
[6] Liddon replied on 23 Feb., 'in a letter from Dr Pusey to Mr Keble dated Jan 29. 1839, I find the sentence, "N. gradually became against the plan", i.e. the later plan proposed by Dr Pusey of commemorating the Reformation or certain aspects or results of it, as distinct from Golightly's earlier plan of commemorating the Reformers.'
[7] Only the signature is in Newman's hand.

TO GEORGE T. EDWARDS

Febr. 24 1888

You are one of those friends and well wishers, who have so kindly addressed to me letters of congratulation on my birthday – letters which touched me much, and for your share in which I hereby offer you my sincere thanks.

With my Blessing J H N

TO ROBERT CHARLES JENKINS

The Oratory, Birmingham. Feb 26, 1888.

My dear Canon Jenkins,

I wish I could thank you for your letter satisfactorily and I wish I could respond to your kind and eloquent verses worthily in this acknowledgment that I make of them, but I cannot do so worthily because after all I am not worthy of them, but they show your warm sympathy with me.[1] An additional trouble to me is my being obliged to use an amanuensis but you will excuse me.

Very truly yours, John H. Card. Newman.

TO THOMAS LIVIUS

The Oratory, Birmingham March 10/88

My dear Father Livius,

Thank you for your very handsome book which is quite a present; and its contents are as worthy of its outside appearance as a present ought to be.[2] I am obliged to write by the hand of a friend – you will excuse it

I am Yours truly J H Card Newman

TO EDWARD ILSLEY, BISHOP OF BIRMINGHAM

March 19. 1888

My dear Bishop of Birmingham

Your Lordship's letter is as kind as it is welcome to me. I trust to say Mass for you on Thursday[3]

Excuse my bad writing

Your Lordship's faithful & affectte Servant J. H. Card Newman

---

[1] Jenkins sent a sonnet in honour of Newman's birthday.

[2] Livius sent a specially bound copy of his *S. Peter, Bishop of Rome; or, the Roman Episcopate of the Prince of the Apostles*, London 1888. The book was dedicated to Newman and Livius also inscribed this copy 'with the Author's respectful regards and congratulations February 21st 1888.'

[3] Bishop Ilsley, who had received the Brief appointing him Bishop of Birmingham on 18 March, wrote the next day to inform Newman, saying 'Knowing the kind interest your Eminence has taken in the matter of this appointment I feel it to be my duty to send you the earliest intimation thereof.'

TO WILLIAM LOCKHART

The Oratory, Birmingham Palm Sunday [25 March] 1888
My dear Lockhart

I was shocked and grieved at your letter. I had not heard of him for some time. I hope to say Mass for him tomorrow morning.[1]

You are so full of it that I suppose you hardly have the heart to speak of what I am very sorry to see in the paper.[2]

Yours affectionately J H Card Newman[3]
The Very Revd Fr Lockhart

TO WILFRID WARD

The Oratory Birmingham March 27. 1888.
My dear Mr Ward

The Cardinal bids me to say that though he knows well that he delivered the lectures in the years 1837, 1838 on the Prophetical Office and on Justification in Adam de Brome's Chapel he never has been clear how the fact stands as regards (Number 85) Wm P. Neville

April 4th. So far I got ten days ago when some one entering the room broke my answer to you till now.

I can say no more, after much research, in answer to your difficulty than that the Tract was *published* on St Matthew's day 1838, which you already know well enough, and I am afraid I must say that I have no clear view in what place I delivered them.[4]

I can do no more I am ashamed to say.

Yours affectionately J H N.[5]

TO THOMAS LIVIUS

The Oratory, April 11, 1888
My dear Fr Livius,

Though my eyes and my fingers will not consent to my writing about your work I send you a few lines from the pleasure which such parts of it as I have

[1] Lockhart wrote on this letter (which is only signed by Newman) 'In answer to my letter announcing Mr Oxenham's death. W.L.' Henry Nutcombe Oxenham died on 23 March. His sister wrote on 25 March, that the day he died Lockhart 'brought him Holy Communion and later on my brother asked for your words in the "Dream of Gerontius" and begged F. Lockhart to "go straight on" assenting to his remark "there was no one like Newman".'

[2] The decree *Post Obitum* of Dec. 1887, in which the Holy Office condemned forty propositions taken from Rosmini's works, was published towards the end of March. On 3 April 1888 Ullathorne wrote to Newman that he was 'surprised at the long delay' in condemning Rosmini's teaching.

[3] Emmeline Deane finished her second portrait (in oils) of Newman, on 24 March.

[4] *Tract 85*, 'Lectures on the Scripture Proof of the Doctrine of the Church', was reprinted in *D.A.* as 'Holy Scripture in its relation to the Catholic Creed.' Newman delivered these lectures also in Adam de Brome's chapel at St Mary's. See *Moz.* II, p. 257.

[5] Only the signature is in Newman's hand.

been able to master have given me. Especially I would dwell upon your remarks on Dr Lightfoots treatment of St Clement's Epistle. It is capital and most important, I mean the passage from page 462 to page 545, though I ought to read it more than once to presume to have an opinion upon it[1]

Excuse these few words and believe me

Your affte Servant J H Card. Newman[2]

TO JOHN OAKLEY

April 11. 1888

Cardinal Newman begs to send his respects to the Dean of Manchester and while he is sorry that the state of his eyes and fingers hinders his duly acknowledging the Dean's kind letter, he fears he cannot indulge the same regret that he is unable to read the Memoir which accompanies it; but he is sure that all that the Dean has written is in kindness, and begs to subscribe himself the Dean's faithful Servant[3]

TO MRS AUGUSTUS CRAVEN

Oratory, Birmingham Ap 17. 1888

Dear Mrs Craven,

I rejoice to be told that you have finished the work which I was so anxious you should undertake.[4] Though I expressed to you from the first how inadequate my critical powers are, or indeed any ones to handle such a subject, I knew enough what I have had to expect from you to feel a great encouragement in your kind wish that I should not forget you in my prayers, and I am glad that I have lived so long as to be able to send my blessing upon your work, that is to say, on a Memoir of Lady Georgiana Fullerton written by Mrs Craven.

Thank you for so great a favour, and excuse the imperfection of these lines which I am unable to write with my own hand.

TO THE HON. MRS MAXWELL-SCOTT

April 18/88

My dear Mamo

The Catalogue has interested me very much.[5] So of course in another way has your domestic news. That you should be near Wilfrid and his wife, it is

[1] See letter of 10 March to Livius, who, in Chapter XIX of his *S. Peter, Bishop of Rome*, pp. 462–506, discussed Bishop Lightfoot's views.

[2] Only the signature is by Newman.

[3] Oakley sent Newman a copy of his recollections of H. N. Oxenham, which occupied three columns and a half of the *Manchester Guardian* (31 March 1888), p. 5. Oakley, who signed himself 'Vicesimus', wrote appreciatively of Oxenham, whose friend he had been for thirty-five years. He spoke of Oxenham's devotion to Newman, 'his love and reverence . . . was unbounded'.

[4] Mrs Craven wrote on 14 April that her *Life of Lady Georgiana Fullerton* was soon to be published. She asked to be allowed to insert Newman's letter of 17 Nov. 1885 at the beginning of her book. It was printed there and also an extract from this present letter.

[5] This was a *Catalogue of the Abbotsford Curiosities*.

very pleasant to be told. But I do not understand quite whereabouts you and your husband are — not in the Isle of Wight?[1] and I wish you had told me something about Mary Kerr. Is she not, like you, an authoress?[2]

I do not deserve a long letter from you, still I rely on your being charitable
With all kind remembrances to your husband

Yours, My dear Mamo affectly J H Card Newman

TO H. P. LIDDON

April 22/88

Dear Dr Liddon

Thank you and Miss Pusey for your kindness.[3]
But you or she had prepared me for the event.
He was an old friend, tho' I did not know his children

Yours most truly J H Card Newman

TO LORD BLACHFORD

Birmm April 25/88

My dear Blachford,

Tho' Canon Liddon prepared me, it was a great and painful shock to me to read your notice of the new trouble which has come upon the Churchs.[4] How, for instance can they safely come home in this weather? What a trial in so many ways!

I don't think I have ever differed from you about Ireland, except perhaps I went further, as thinking simple separation better than a local Parliament.[5] Your mistake about me was, that, whereas I was *prophesying* what *would* happen, from the deep impression the state of Ireland made on me in 1851–1858, you took it for *agreement*.

In two points, however, I defended and defend them, not in their conduct or its expediency, but in their hatred of and violence towards England — Still

1. Why do we not give to them the same religious freedom and independence which we give to Scotland.

---

[1] Mrs Maxwell-Scott wrote on 17 April from 'Prior's Barton, Winchester.' She was living there with her family, having let Abbotsford for a few years. Wilfrid Ward and his wife, Mrs Maxwell-Scott's half-sister, were living at Freshwater in the Isle of Wight.

[2] This refers to Mary Monteith, the widow of Francis Kerr.

[3] A note on the envelope of Newman's letter says 'Rev. W. Pusey's death'. William, brother of E. B. Pusey, died on 19 April 1888.

[4] Perhaps the death on 30 Jan. 1888 of Church's great friend, the American botanist Asa Gray.

[5] See letter of 27 July 1885 to Lord Blachford.

2. What ground have we for utterly ignoring their claim to be under English law.

As to Home Rule it would destroy both themselves and us. You cannot have two supreme powers.

Yours affly J.H.N.

TO HENRIETTA WOODGATE

May 1/88

My dear Child

Excuse bad writing.

I shall rejoice to see you, except at 2, when I dine

Yrs affectly J H N

TO F. K. CARRITT

[3 May 1888]

My dear Sir

I thank you for your painfully interesting letter and I hope I may be allowed to express my sense of the forbearance which under very trying circumstances you have manifested. A blessing must come on both father and mother for conduct so temperate and self-restrained.[1]

You ask me about your son's prospect of becoming a priest. This depends on the bishops or monastic superiors, and they make no sudden decisions on such a question. There are three ways of becoming a priest with which your son ought to be acquainted. The 1st opening he would have (if he was considered to have a vocation) would be by the way of patrimony, that is, by his being able to maintain himself. The 2nd per paupertatem that is, his claiming to be a monk or regular, which would imply vows of obedience for life to the superior. The 3rd by giving himself to the service of a bishop also for life. In the two latter cases his education and board are provided by the bishops or superior. The normal age of ordination to the priesthood is 24.

I am afraid I cannot say more to simplify your difficulties. It is natural for your son to go to Cardinal Manning to whose diocese I suppose he belongs but if you have any special question to ask me I will answer it to the best of my ability

[1] Carritt, an Anglican, wrote on 2 May from 68 Southwood Lane, Highgate, to say that his son John Price Carritt, who was sixteen in Feb., had become a Catholic the previous year, while a schoolboy at Rugby. He had frequently visited the Passionists at Highgate near his home, and had been received by the Provincial, Vincent Grogan, without his parents being informed. They had accepted the situation, and their son now wanted to become a priest. Carritt wrote to Newman for advice, saying he was prepared to pay his ordinary expenses, but could neither afford nor was inclined to pay for his education as a priest. The son remained a layman.

TO EMILY BOWLES

May 4/88

My dear Child

I am sure I shall find your book very interesting and well worth reading Thank you for it by anticipation.[1]

I am expecting another (very different) work full of interest, Mrs Craven's

Yrs affly J H N

TO AUGUSTA THEODOSIA DRANE

May 5. 1888

My dear Mother Provincial

I wish I could write you and your's, such a letter as your great Festival requires.

But I can send you all my blessing, and this I do

Yours affecty John H Card. Newman[2]

TO EDWARD ILSLEY, BISHOP OF BIRMINGHAM

The Oratory, May 5, 1888

My dear Lord Bishop,

I hope you will allow us to have your presence as Celebrant at High Mass on Friday June the 1st.[3] in spite of my own absence.

For myself I hope also that this is not inconsistent with our meeting at luncheon after Mass.

Your faithful Servt John H Card Newman[4]

The Rt Revd The Bp of Birmingham

TO HENRY GEORGE WOODS

The Oratory May 9 1888

Cardinal Newman is very sorry to say he is obliged to decline the kind invitation of the President and Bursars of Trinity College, on account of the increasing feebleness of his health.

He thanks them for the kindness they have done him, and begs them to accept by anticipation his congratulations on the coming Festive Day.

The President and Bursars of Trinity College

[1] Emily Bowles, *Madame de Maintenon*, London 1888. Inscribed 'For, John Henry Cardinal Newman with the loving reverence of many years E.B. May 1888.'

[2] A note on the copy says this was the last letter received in Newman's own writing.

[3] For the celebration of the feast of St Philip.

[4] Only the conclusion is autograph.

May 12. 1888

Dear Rev Father

I am sorry to send you what seems an ungracious answer, but but it does not lie in my power even in a poor way to profit by the example which your subscription list sets me

And I am so weak in my sight, that I am, at least in the winter months, debarred from writing

I am obliged to throw myself on your kind consideration, which I am sure you will grant me

Very truly Yours J H Card Newman

TO JOHN HIGGINS
May 13/88

Many years ago a young man, I think of Rednall, assisted us in the care of our garden and field. I was pleased with him and gave him a mathematical work that I thought might be of use to him

He has today written to me to say his name was 'Higgins', and has asked[1]

I hereby readily give him a recommendation for the office of caretaker of Rednal Hill.

John H Cardinal Newman

TO R. W. CHURCH
May 15 [1888]

Copy
Confidential
My dear Dean

I write to ask you whether you know personally a good London sollicitor for a friend here, who has a reason for not making use of a Birmingham lawyer[2]

J H N

---

[1] This sentence is unfinished. Higgins wrote from Leech Green Lane, Rednal on 12 May asking for a recommendation. The book Newman had given him was John Bonnycastle's *An Introduction to Mensuration and Practical Geometry*, London 1816, with many later editions.

[2] Dean Church replied on 16 May, 'The Solicitor who does for me what I want is Dr Edwin Freshfield, of the firm of Freshfield and Williams. He is a personal friend, and the firm is one of the first in London.'

Freshfield wrote from 5 Bank Buildings on 18 May, 'I need hardly say that I think there is nothing the Dean of St Pauls could ask me to do that I would not do if I could.' He offered to visit Newman the following week. On 1 June he wrote to Newman, 'I have had your will and Codicils embodied in a new Will which is quite ready for your Eminence's Execution . . .' The will was signed on 5 June, with Edwin Freshfield and Lewis Mortimer, solicitor at the same address, as witnesses. It ran: 'This is the last Will of me John Henry Cardinal Newman of the Oratory Edgbaston — 1 I revoke all my former testamentary dispositions and I appoint the Reverend William Paine Neville, the Reverend Henry Aloysius Bellasis and Mr Anthony Cecil Hungerford Pollen all of the Oratory aforesaid to be Executors of this my Will — I bequeath to the said William Paine Neville absolutely the copyright of my publications and all my manuscripts long and short in my own handwriting or in that of others and such rights as I have by law in letters addressed to me by others and in my possession and in letters addressed to others by me whether in my possession or not — 3 I devise and bequeath all my real and leasehold property (if any) whatsoever and wheresoever unto and to the use of the said Anthony Cecil Hungerford Pollen absolutely subject as to leaseholds to the rents and covenants under which I may hold the same — 4 I bequeath all the residue of my personal estate (subject to the payment thereout of my funeral and testamentary expenses and debts) to the said William Paine Neville, Henry Aloysius Bellasis and Anthony Cecil Hungerford Pollen or such of them as shall be living at my death for their or his absolute use — In Witness whereof I have hereunto set my hand . . .'

Newman left private instructions about his property, some of the earlier ones becoming out of date, as when the firm of Longmans took over all his books. By a memorandum of 28 Aug. 1883 he made over annuities of £40 and £10 to John Norris and Paul Eaglesim respectively, to take effect at once.

Newman left a memorandum about his papers: 'March 12, 1882 I have left by will to Fr Wm Neville (besides my copyrights) all my *Papers*, including all letters which I have written or received; that is, *not* merely in trust for the *Congregation*, nor as a way of leaving them (indirectly) to the Congregation — but as *his own private* property, so that he may withold them, destroy the whole of them, or any part of them, or sell them, or give them away if he pleased. Only whatever money comes of them, whether from the sale of copyright, or from income by publication etc etc he is bound as well as the other Executors to spend it with them on the behalf of the Congregation. I have done this because he knows my wishes about them, as no other Father does. J H Newman' Newman then wrote 'Turn over' to the next page, for the connected memorandum which followed immediately: 'June 28 1884

Legally I suppose, the three joint Tenants to whom I leave my effects, (they are, as it happens, also my Executors) W. P. N, J. Norris, and H Lewis B. [Bellasis] are *owners*. But it has always been understood in the Congregation that they the Joint Tenants were but *nominally* owners, and must merely act as convenient instruments of the Congregation and not bonâ fide owners, since the law did not recognize the Oratory as a corporate body to whom property could be left. Here I am acting on another idea. Of course I am leaving what I leave for the benefit of the Oratory — but I wish my Executors and Legatees to be Trustees in such sense that they should, while they live, have a right to a discretion with reference to the *objects for which* they pay over any proceeds of my property.

John H Card. Newman

N.B. I have chosen my three executors on the principle of having as representatives the older, the middle aged and the junior fathers of the Congregation.

J H N Febr 12/88

As to my will and its bequeathments I wish its provisions put into the hands of my Executors together with an express understanding of their right to select the particular objects to which the proceeds are to be applied. Ap. 15 1889

(N.B. April 15.1889. Fr John Norris's name was omitted for accidental reasons of mine for that of Fr Anthony Pollen.)

John H Newman April 20 1889

Memorandum for my Executors

I leave the neat annual pecuniary proceeds of my published volumes to my executors and Joint Tenants for the use of the Oratory House buildings including the new Dormitory together with Rednall as these Joint Tenants think fit from time to time.'

Newman then mentioned a New South Wales Bond for £500 and a house worth £2200, which he also left to his executors 'for the use of the Congregation with this previso [sic]. viz. that it is in the first instance to be available as a guarantee from us to the Bishop for any candidate for Ordination who needs in whole or in part a Patrimony.

John H Card Newman The Oratory Dec. 23. 1889'

Newman also noted: 'March 7. 1888
Since I have been Cardinal, I have expended on the Oratory £4439 — Thus:—

	£
New Dormitory	700
Chimnies[?]	300
Rednall	1039
Debt to [A.W.] Hutton	1000
Debt to Fr Wm Neville	600
Debt to Fr Minister	800
	4439

As I could not meet this entire sum from my private resources at once, I threw a part upon

TO MRS FREDERICK GEORGE LEE

May 15/88

My dear Mrs Lee

Thank you for your kindness in writing to me, and give Ambrose my warmest congratulations on his intende[d] marriage. Most gladly will I say Mass for him and her on the day, if he let me know. I wish you and Dr Lee on the event also[1]

Excuse my bad writing — I have lost the proper use of my fingers

Most truly Yours John H Card Newman

TO FRANCIS WOODGATE MOZLEY (I)

The Oratory Birmingham May 15. 1888

My dear Frank,

Will you write to your Aunt Anne about the Lyra Apostolica

Yours affly J H N

TO FRANCIS WOODGATE MOZLEY (II)

The Oratory May 15. 1888

My dear Frank

Thanks for your letter I thought it best to let your Aunt Anne decide, and sent it to her. *She* has borrowed the autographs of them from me.[2]

Love to your wife and baby

Yrs affectly John H Card Newman

the future, on *a quasi* "Post obit" to be discharged gradually by the proceeds of my literary copyrights The proceeds of these copyrights I have left entirely to the Fathers and Congregation, but before they enter into any usufruct of them, they will have to pay, by means of them, the following sums for which I consider myself engaged to the respective persons named

		£	
(1)	Viz to Dr Jordan	100	
(2)	Dr Ogle (a present)	20	
(3)	Dr Blunt ditto	20	
(4)	Funeral expenses	300	
(5)	Decorations of St	300	(Alabaster)
	Philip['s chapel]		
(6)	[Thomas] Godwin, a *small* annuity		
(7)	Mrs Proscott (ditto)		
(8)	General Index, to my 36 volumes.		

J.H.N.'

[1] Mrs Lee's son Ambrose was married on 8 Aug. 1888 to Rosie Wallace, niece of W. P. Gordon of the London Oratory.

[2] According to a letter of 24 May from Anne Mozley, Frank Mozley wanted to see the 'Copy the Lyra was printed from'. Anne Mozley now lent is to him, with instructions to return it to her.

May 15. 1888.

My dear Aubrey de Vere

I wish my fingers could thank you better than this letter can for your Essays[1] I don't pretend to have read them properly, but I have any how got a great deal valuable and instructive from them, and thank you for what I have found so interesting and so new[2]

I wish I were not obliged to stop, and to ask you abruptly to believe me

Yours affecty John H. Card Newman[3]

May 16/88

My dear Mrs Lee

I certainly think I wrote to thank you and congratulate you on the news of the marriage of Ambrose — but, as I am assured by a friend that I have not, and shall be very sorry to omit my kind thoughts I write these almost illegible lines, begging you to excuse the feebleness of my fingers.

Yours afftely John H Newman

The Oratory May 18 1888

My dear Lord Archbishop

Thank you for the thoughtful kindness of writing to me.[4] I had day by day thought of the expected letter, and, before I opened yours of this morning, I said to myself, Here are the tidings at last.

Yet the severance of the duties of a long life must be a great trial to you as the many who love you will deeply feel

Your Grace's affectionate Servt John H Card Newman

The Oratory, Birmm May 26/88

My dear Louisa

I rejoice to find that in a difficulty connected with our school-boy's Latin Play in the coming July you may kindly assist us.

[1] *Essays Chiefly on Poetry*, volume 1, London 1887.
[2] Some of the pages on Wordsworth and on Henry Taylor have been cut.
[3] The whole of this letter is in Newman's hand.
[4] Ullathorne wrote on 17 May that by a Brief of 27 April he had been absolved from the See of Birmingham and made titular Archbishop of Cabasa.

We want scenery, that is, back scene, side scenes, and drop scene, and Miss Ellison has been kind enough, to my great pleasure, to speak to you in our behalf.[1] She tells me that you have a taste for such a line of painting and are not unwilling to help us. I will send you all particulars as to the measurements and subjects connected with the Play, together with an English version with notes of the Plot as soon as I know your address.[2]

You will like to know meantime what the stage measures and I will write it below. I believe that Moliere's 'Avare' is founded on the Play. The scenery comprises opposite to each other a rich man's house and the miser's. It might be a cottage on the one side and a magnificent house connected with the temple on the other,

Yours very affectionately J. H. Card. Newman.

P.S. The dimensions of the present Scenery

Drop Scene

13ft 6in high 17ft 7 in wide.

Back Scene

15ft 4 in high 20ft wide

The Stage is

23ft 6 in from front to back.

26ft 5 in from side to side

The Front of the Stage is 2 ft from the floor but I don't yet know what the incline is

Suggestion

I spoke of a temple, but an altar which a man can hide behind would be more suitable. The scene should be in the open air. Could you not avail yourself of Pompeii?

The slides of a magic lantern would help you so much for the side scenes.

As a background, trees, as you wish, may form one: foliage and rocks rising up towards Vesuvius.

Would it be well for you to send your carpenter to report to you of the size etc?

I have nothing to say about a drop scene. Is the expense considerable? Of course it would be on a roller.

Perhaps the altar should not be in the middle of the stage.

Yours affectly John H Newman

[1] Newman consulted Miss Edith Ellison of 82 Drayton Gardens, South Kensington, about a scene-painter for the *Aulularia of Plautus*, and she secured Louisa Deane.

[2] Newman sent Louisa Deane 'a munificent enclosure' for her work and invited her to the play on 24 July.

June 2 [1888]

My dear Mrs Lee

A dismal thought has come upon me that the letter which I inclose, having just found, missed the post.[1] Of course it was intended for you. Pray pardon me.

Very truly Yours John H Card. Newman

TO CLARA BELLASIS

June 7. 1888

My dear Clara Bellasis

I am deeply grateful for the great pains and anxious care which you and Mr Bellasis took for me last Monday night.[2]

And indeed the anticipation of such kindness, on your brother's suggestion, has been, after all, and still is, a pleasure as well as a pain:— for it was both a comfort and a service.

Excuse my bad writing but I cannot help it.

Yours affectionately John H Card Newman

TO ROBERT CHARLES JENKINS

June 7. 1888

My dear Canon Jenkins

I wish my hand writing equalled your your learning and diligence and success in the translation of the beautiful act of devotion which you kindly send me

Very truly Yours John H Cardinal Newman

TO HENRY JAMES COLERIDGE

June 26/1888

My dear Fr Coleridge

Your remembrance of me in sending me your translation of Lady G.F's life is most welcome and grateful to me.[3] I am cut off from writing and (partly)

[1] Perhaps that of 15 May. Mrs Lee wrote on 6 June, 'Your letters were all duly received.'

[2] This refers to Newman's visit to London on Monday 4 June. On 5 June he signed his will there. See letter of 15 May to Dean Church. On 6 June he visited F. S. Bowles at Harrow. The latter wrote on 8 June to Neville of Newman's 'loving condescension'. Bowles was so overcome that he 'could say nothing'. He continued: 'I should like you to tell him that I look upon his visit and blessing as a sort of plenary indulgence for all my offences against him for the last nearly 46 years, from the time that is in 1842 when I gave him much trouble as a useless and ineffective curate of his at Littlemore until this last June 6th 1888, when I could only make a fool of myself in his presence . . .'

[3] Coleridge wrote on 21 June that he was sending Mrs Craven's *Life of Lady Georgiana Fullerton*, London 1888, which he had translated and edited.

from reading and corresponding, and also from intercourse with friends, and thank you for the sympathy and edification which has been brought to me by the perusal of your Volume But I cannot write more

I hope you are better than of late

Yrs affly J H Newman

TO JOHN BRAMSTON

June 27. 1888

My very dear Bramston

I hear with great sorrow that you have been seriously ill.[1] What various reasons I have for this being a blow to me! You are one of my oldest friends. Indeed, except Lord Blachford, who came near you? My love for you began at Provost Copleston's dinner table in 1823.[2] I wish my fingers would write what my heart would say. Amid many changes of life you are one of those who have been constant to me. And it touches me to think that (as I believe) I am older than you, and ought to be nearer departure hence.

While I live, please God, you *shall never* be out of my mind, and, as I pray that God may have mercy on me, so may He have mercy on you.[3]

Ever yours affly John H. Newman

TO R. W. CHURCH

The Oratory, Birmingham. June 28. 1888

My dear Dean,

I think I have never seen Dr Trench but twice in my life. Blachford can tell you about the first time better, I believe, than I can. He came from Cambridge to see Oxford.[4]

The second time I saw him at the breakfast upon the consecration of Keble's new Church in 1841, when, together with Bishop Sumner and Archdeacon Dealtry he all but cut me. I had my compensation of becoming acquainted for the first time with dear Fr Ambrose St John.

[1] Bramston's daughter Mary wrote on 26 June to tell of his serious illness. She said that a letter from Newman 'would be a great comfort and help to him. He always keeps your letters in his pocket book, and looks on them as his greatest treasures: you are the only one of the friends of his youth left to him, and I think he has never felt for any one else what he has for you.'

[2] See letter of 25 March 1860 to Bramston.

[3] On 8 July Bramston thanked Newman, and spoke of his 'undeviating kindness.'

[4] Church wrote on 27 June to ask whether Newman was at the Hadleigh Conference in July 1833: 'I thought that neither you nor Keble were present there. But in Trench's Letters and Memoirs, just published (i. 143) he is said to have remembered taking a walk with you. — He was at the time Mr Rose's Curate.' This was *Richard Chenevix Trench, Archbishop. Letters and Memorials,* edited by the author of 'Charles Lowder' [Maria Trench], two volumes, London 1888. Neither Newman nor Keble were at the Hadleigh conference, where Trench was H. J. Rose's curate. Newman and Trench first met in the summer of 1835. See *Moz.* II, p. 128.

I know nothing of Trench's being at Hadleigh as curate or otherwise or strangely the history of the past has gone out of my mind.

In answer to your question I can say categorically that I was not at Hadleigh myself.

Yours affly J. H. Newman.

P.S. June 30/88 I have no recollection of ever having been at Hadleigh.

Or ever hearing that Keble was there. Or hearing that Dr Trench was Rose's Curate there. Nor of walking with him.

I arrived at Brighton from Dieppe July 8.; and, at p. 36 of my Apologia I imply that the Hadleigh meeting was prior to the 8th when I returned.[1]

Yrs affly J.H.N.

TO ALFRED PLUMMER

July 1/88

My dear Dr Plummer

I fear I have no intelligible answer to write to you in answer.[2] I doubt whether I have ever seen even the outside of Mr Darby's book,[3] but I *have* seen Dr Jebb on the Eucharist — and thought it good but incomplete.[4]

As to the subject of Justification, the only claims I have made for myself, is to have shown or to think I have shown that the difference between Calvinists and Arminians is *verbal* — the former maintaining that justification is an *act of God*, but the latter meaning by it a *state of a man's soul*.[5]

Excuse a short letter

Most truly Yours John H Card Newman[6]

---

[1] The Hadleigh meeting was held 25–9 July 1833.

[2] Plummer wrote on 21 June: 'Dean Darby of Chester sat next me at dinner one day last week. He is a nephew, I believe, of Alexander Knox. Certainly he possesses many of his papers, and he proposes to publish a selection of them.

Many years ago Bishop Wilberforce of Oxford said to Darby "It was Alexander Knox's, treatise on Justification which *first set Newman thinking* on the subject", not, as I understand, meaning that your Lectures on Justification owed anything to Alexander Knox, but that what he had written suggested the subject. Dean Darby was anxious to know whe.her there was any foundation for Bishop Wilberforce's opinion'. Plummer added that he was writing simply on his own, and at no suggestion of John Lionel Darby, who remarked that 'this question had nothing to do with the controversy recently raised in the *Guardian* by Professor Stokes.' See letter of 1 Sept. 1887 to R. W. Church.

[3] i.e. the book mentioned by J. L. Darby, the treatise on Justification in *The Remains of Alexander Knox*, four volumes, London 1834–7. The only work by Knox in Newman's library is *The Doctrine of the Sacraments*, London 1838, an extract from *The Remains*. In Newman's copy half the pages on the Eucharist have been cut, but none of those on Baptism, where Justification is treated. See also *Jfc.* p. vii, where Newman states he wrote without reference to Knox.

[4] The only work by John Jebb, Bishop of Limerick which Newman possessed was *Pastoral Instructions on the Character and Principles of the Church of England, selected from his former Publications*, London 1831. Newman acquired his copy in 1834. The pages on the Communion Office have not been cut. See also *Moz.* II, p. 216.

[5] *Jfc.* pp. ix, 182–4, and 382–404.

[6] The whole of this letter is in Newman's hand.

TO AUGUSTA THEODOSIA DRANE

July 13. 1888

My dear Mother Provincial

I shall be, I think, passing through Stone soon and wish to bid you and all of you, goodbye, before I go hence. I could not pay you a visit of much more than half an hour; but time is not the measure of such meetings and partings.

I wish to thank you for all the kindnesses which you and yours have done me in so long a course of years.[1]

Continue to pray for me

Yrs affectly John H Card Newman[2]

TO LADY SIMEON

July 27. 1888.

Copy

My dear Lady Simeon,

I fear you have thought me neglectful of your interesting letter of some months ago, but I cannot, of course, write private and familiar letters by the hand of another.

You will be sorry to hear that I certainly [am] much weaker than I was; also, though not as I hope worse in my hearing, my sight is very indifferent and makes me anxious, but you cannot be disappointed at being told of such short-comings at such an age. I made the tour of North Wales last week with the view of benefitting myself, not however with great success.

Excuse what I would make more interesting if I could. At least remember me kindly to your daughter.

Yours affectionately, John H. Card. Newman.[3]

TO LORD COLERIDGE

August 4, 1888.

My dear Lord Coleridge,

I could not help crying on reading the fresh instance you are giving me of your affectionate feelings towards me, and I pray God to bless you in accordance with your marvellous kindness.

I call it marvellous, because it is so much more than I am conscious I can

---

[1] Newman was on his way to North Wales. See next letter. For an account of Newman's visit to Stone on 16 July, abbreviated from a much fuller account by one of the nuns present, see *Butler* II, pp. 288–9...

[2] The whole letter is in Newman's hand.

[3] A note on the copy says that the first and last paragraphs were in Newman's writing.

claim, and which I can only try to repay, as I do, by keeping you in mind day after day.

I rejoiced to see Professor Shairp, before his (to me) painfully sudden, unexpected death.[1]

Yours affectionately, J. H. Card. Newman.

TO LORD BLACHFORD

The Oratory Aug. 6. 1888

My dear Blachford

Sir F. Doyle has left an impression on me for which I cannot account, very pleasant however since he is so great a friend of yours. I doubt whether I was in a room with him ever more than twice, and that as long as fifty years ago, yet in 1865 on his writing to me on the subject of the 'Dream of Gerontius' I could not help exclaiming to myself (if not to him) 'How like Doyle'! The remembrance of him has always been a pleasant thought to me. I need not say more to you.[2]

I was rejoiced at Miss Mozley being so pleased at the sight of us. Thank you for writing to me about it.[3]

Yours affectionately J H Card Newman[4]

TO THE EARL OF DENBIGH

23 Aug 88

Thank you for your Lordship for your friendly and welcome letter. We [I ?] shall rejoice to have your son with us [me ?] and hope nothing will turn up to interfere with an arrangement which we all shall desire Fr Norris will return home in a few days[5]

Excuse my bad writing etc.[6]

[1] Shairp died on 18 Sept. 1885. He and Newman met at Trinity College, Oxford, on 24 May 1880.

[2] Sir Francis Doyle died 8 Feb. 1888. On 11 June Lord Blachford wrote, 'Doyle has been my intimate friend for 61 years — a year longer than we have known each other.' For his letter to Newman see those of 26 Nov. 1868 and 12 Feb. 1869 to Sir Frederic Rogers.

Lord Blachford passed Newman's words on to Sir Francis Doyle's family, and his son Everard wrote to tell him 'how much your beautiful hymn "Lead kindly Light" comforted his dying moments'.

[3] Blachford noted on the letter, 'This was on occasion of the annual acting of a Latin play — in this case Plautus' Aulularia — altered for the purpose by the Cardinal. It seems to have gone off very well — I should have liked to have seen Plautus + Newman. B.'

[4] This letter was written by Neville and signed by Newman.

[5] Lord Denbigh wrote on 22 Aug. that he wished to place his youngest son Basil, aged fifteen, at the Oratory School. He had hitherto been at Downside, 'but I think a change of hand will do him good and urge him forward in his studies'. He wished to become a priest. Basil Feilding became a priest and distinguished himself as a chaplain in the South African War.

[6] On 28, 30 and 31 Aug. Newman was present at the morning performances of the Birmingham Musical Festival together with the Duke of Norfolk. Mendelssohn's Elijah was performed on 28 Aug., Handel's Messiah on 30 Aug., and Bach's Magnificat, Beethoven's C Minor Symphony and Berlioz's Messe des Morts on 31 Aug.

TO CHARLES JAMES LONGMAN

The Oratory Sept 5. 1888

Dear Sir

With respect to the terms to which you have had no objection in accepting from me, my only difficulty is that Fr Neville apprehends that by my having accidentally left out any mention of who is to pay for the printing I may have led you to interpret them differently from myself. But since you have let me make other suggestions instead of an engagement on commission, are you willing to place the Callista on a royalty basis?[1]

But how is this affected by the American arrangement?

Of course the work ought to be put into the printers hands without delay since there are no stereotype plates, so I ask, Have you any thing to say about the type etc

Yours very truly J H. Card. Newman

To C. J. Longman Esqre

TO LORD BLACHFORD

Septr 10 1888.

My dear Blachford,

Thank you for your account of dear Wilson. His wife has been kind enough to write to me.[2] I grieve to see the account of Claughton,[3] R. Palmer,[4] and Bramston. Did I tell you of Sir F. Doyle's kindness? nay, of Tennyson's?

I was pleased at what you said about Plautus, but you must know what a reverse side to him there is.[5] But he was better than those for whom he wrote.

J.H.N.

TO LAWRENCE DILLON

The Oratory, Septr 13. 1888

Sir,

I thank you sincerely for the proposal contained in your letter. It is indeed far more than a mere compliment on the part of the Chief Librarian to have

---

[1] Newman was continuing the transference of his works to the firm of Longmans, Green and Co. Burns and Oates informed him on 10 July that there only remained twelve copies of their royalty edition of Callista. Burns and Oates had made an arrangement with an American firm. See letter of 18 Dec. 1887 to Longman.

[2] On 23 Aug. Blachford wrote that R. F. Wilson had not long to live. Wilson's wife wrote the same news on 18 Aug., and said 'Will you of your charity think of him when you offer the Holy Sacrifice. . . . If it is not asking too much, one word of love and leavetaking from you would be exceedingly precious to him.'

[3] Thomas Legh Claughton, Bishop of St Albans.

[4] Earl of Selborne.

[5] Newman had sent Lord Blachford a copy of the *Aulularia*, and Blachford wrote, 'I had never read a line of Plautus and had no conception how good it was.'

my name associated in the mind of the public with such a man so revered, so keenly and bitterly mourned for, as General Gordon. And it is very gratifying to be told that it would be pleasing to his immediate relatives.

As to your question concerning an edition the first step must be to refer you to Messrs Longman in whose hands the publication lies.[1]

Yours faithful Servant J. H. Card. Newman

Laurence Dillon Esqre

TO R. W. CHURCH

Sept 16/88

My dear Dean

Yours proposal is too kind I must leave it to you to decide, whether I can, with propriety, accept it.[2]

Yours affectionately J H Newman

Is not this Pusey's anniversary

TO LAWRENCE DILLON

Sept 23. 1888

Sir

Thanking you for the interest you have taken in a matter which concerns myself I have come to the conclusion that under the circumstances I think it better not to prosecute it

Your faithful Servt J. H. N.

Laurence Dillon Esqre Alexandra Park, Manchester

TO CHARLES EYRE, ARCHBISHOP OF GLASGOW

The Oratory, Birmingham Sept 24/88

My dear Lord Archbishop

I shall read with great interest the historical paper you have so kindly sent me of the Ancient See of Glasgow and I thank you truly for it.[3]

My dear Lord Archbishop Yours faithful Servt
John H Card Newman[4]

His Grace the Archbp of Glasgow

---

[1] A copy of the *Dream of Gerontius* with General Gordon's markings (see letter of 7 April 1885 to Mary Murphy) had been presented to the Manchester Free Reference Library by Dillon, who, on 11 Sept. asked permission to publish it. Newman finally refused after reference to Messrs Longman, who considered the proposal commercially not desirable.

In 1892 Dillon printed but did not publish a paper *On General Gordon's copy of Newman's 'Dream of Gerontius'*.

[2] Dean Church's reply on 17 Sept. shows that Newman wanted to ask Freshfield, who had drawn up his will, to settle some matter for him.

[3] Archbishop Eyre published *Papers on the Old Cathedral of Glasgow*.

[4] Only the signature is in Newman's hand.

The Oratory, Birmingham Septr 26. 1888

Dear Mr Oates,

I thank you for the Prospectus of your charitable institution but I am sorry to be unable to aid it just now.

Very truly Yours John H Card Newman[1]

TO LORD BLACHFORD

Oct. 13. 1888.

My dear Blachford,

Your fresh present has come. As coming from one I have known so long, it comes with a special acceptableness and grace, though I owe the kindness of a similar thoughtful care of me to other dear friends. So don't think you need make a point of it.[2]

Yours affly J.H.N.

TO FRANCIS TURNER PALGRAVE

The Oratory Birmingham [16 October 1888]

My dear Mr Palgrave,

I have seen a notice in the papers of a loss which I feel must try you much, and which throws me back on old Oxford days with sad and affectionate remembrances.[3]

I think I did not know you or your brother personally but you were introduced to my thoughts by my acquaintance with your dear Father who was a kind critic of my first essays in writing as you have been in more recent years yourself.[4]

Excuse these lines by the hand of another which is my only way of writing.

Yours affecly John H Card Newman

Francis Palgrave Esqre

---

[1] Only the signature is autograph.

[2] Lord Blachford wrote again on 27 Oct. that he had sent 'a partridge and a woodcock (the first of the season) from Blachford.'

[3] Palgrave's brother, William Gifford Palgrave died on 30 Sept. at Montevideo. He was a Scholar at Trinity College, Oxford, 1843–7, and after obtaining a commission in the Indian Army, became a Catholic and then a Jesuit. He was a missionary in India until 1853 and then in Syria. In the middle sixties he left the Jesuits, entered the Consular Service and in 1868 married. He served in many widely separated parts of the world, ending as Minister-Resident in Uruguay, from 1884.

[4] Palgrave replied that he and his brother had never wavered in their love for each other, in spite of long separations. Also 'he looked back, through his whole life, with affectionate reverence to you and to the lessons which he received in youth from your writings'. Palgrave added that his brother, after leaving the Jesuits 'and passing through a dark and unsatisfying period of doubt, some four years since he sought and obtained from Rome full readmittance to the Church from which he had wandered for a while.'

The Oratory, Birmingham Oct 29th 1888

My dear Sir,

I have no property whatever in the Oxford translation of the Fathers. Canon Liddon is the most likely to give you available information on the subject.

I hope that my delay in answering your letter has not inconvenienced you.

Your faithful Servant J H Card Newman

TO LORD BLACHFORD

The Oratory. Birmm Oct 31. 1888.

My dear Blachford,

God bless you, ever and always[1]

Yours affly, J.H.N.

TO EMILY BOWDEN

[1 November 1888]

I send you my best blessing with all my heart

Cardinal Newman[2]

TO WILLIAM EWART GLADSTONE

[6 November 1888]

My dear Mr Gladstone

It is a great kindness and compliment your asking to see me.[3] I have known and admired you so long. But I cant write nor talk nor walk and hope you will take my blessing which I give from my heart

Yours most truly John H Card Newman[4]

[1] On 30 Oct. Neville wrote to Lord Blachford at Newman's request to say that he was ill. He had had a fall in the evening of 28 Oct. and suffered from shock and difficulty in eating, but was already improving.

On 5 Nov, his doctors, Ogle, Blunt and Jordan announced that 'his state is now so satisfactory that no further bulletin will be issued.'

[2] This was a telegram.

[3] Gladstone, who was staying in Edgbaston, wrote on 6 Nov. to Neville, to ask whether Newman was well enough to receive a visit, 'in case he should be altogether able, and also kindly disposed, to see me, I should hold myself in readiness at any time tomorrow, or in the forenoon of Thursday, to wait upon him.'

[4] The whole of the letter is autograph.

TO CHARLES GORE

The Oratory, Birmingham, Novr [14] 1888

Dear Mr Gore,

In the prospect of the Feast of St Edmund King and Martyr. Amen

I am bold to ask you to accept from me a picture of Keble made sacred by a relic of a Saint and Martyr.[1]

As the likeness of a very dear Friend, I welcomed it when received from dear Mr Richmond, and have gladly guarded it since that time.[2] But in spite of my personal affection for the original I have not thought I could consistently leave it to my brothers of St Philip Neri.

It has struck me from your own relation to my other and equally dear friend Pusey, that I may gain in your House in St Giles's place for the picture, and thus in our Lord's words you will be receiving 'the just in the name of the just, and a disciple in the name of a disciple.'[3]

Excuse me if I have said anything rude or unacceptable in this request.[4]

Believe me dear Mr Gore Most truly Yours

John H. Card. Newman[5]

TO FRANK MCGEDY[6]

Novr 20. 1888

Dear Sir

You will be glad hereby to be informed that I am recovered from my late illness

I subjoin my physician's testimonial

Your faithful servant John H Card Newman

His Eminence the Cardinal Newman is slowly recovering and we hope may be spared to his friends for a little longer space of years

Robert C. R Jordan M D

Nov 20. 1888

[1] The portrait of Keble was 'framed in oak from the tree in Oakley Park traditionally associated with the martyrdom of St. Edmund. So much confirmation of the tradition exists as that when the tree fell, in 1849, an arrowhead was found embedded in it.' G. L. Prestige, *The Life of Charles Gore*, London 1935, p. 80.

[2] See letter of 3 June 1883 to George Richmond.

[3] *Matthew* 10:41-2.

[4] Gore replied from Pusey House on the 'Eve of St Edmund', 15 Nov., 'However great the value which the picture of Mr Keble would in any case have had for us, it is increased tenfold by its having belonged to you and been prized by you and coming from you — and by its having attached the sacred relic of which you speak.'

[5] Liddon wrote to Gore: 'Indeed I do congratulate you and the Pusey House on such an acquisition and such a letter. It brings you within the lines of what I always think of as the heroic age. How the perfect and inimitable grace of courtesy which characterizes the Cardinal's writings survives — even the test of dictation!' Prestige, op. cit. p. 80.

[6] McGedy was Secretary of the Law Union Insurance Company, 126 Chancery Lane. Newman's letter was not sent.

TO POPE LEO XIII

[25 November 1888?][1]

Quot anni deinceps, ex voluntate Dei, Beatissime Pater jam restant mihi in posterum, — anni quando possum, ut hactenus, appropinquantibus Nativitatis Domini Nostri Jesu Christi festis diebus, Sanctitati Vestrae in mentem me revocare, gratulaturus de Festo, Benedictionem Apostolicam Festi causa petiturus?

Nescio prorsus; illud solum intelligo, grandaevus homo, et in intimo sensu meo praesens habeo, animam et vitam meam proximam esse et tanquam contiguam 'domui aeternitatis meae,' et hasce literas quas grati animi impulsu, ad Sanctitatem Vestram scribo forsitan esse meas ultimas.

At vivo adhuc; et dum vivo, ad Sanctam Sedem anno exeunte me verto, sperans fore ut Sanctitas Vestra benigne accipiat anniversarium meum obolum (libras 20 sterling, 500 francas) quem per manus Revmi Edmundi Stonor ante pedes Petri positum velim.

TO W. J. RIVINGTON

The Oratory, Birmingham, Novr. 25th. 1888

Dear Mr Rivington,

I thank you for the account of the long and laborious life of Mr William Rivington in the service of religion. Few men have the opportunity of pursuing a course so free from personal motives and interests. I am glad to have a notice which will perpetuate a record of such a man.[2]

Excuse so short an acknowledgment,

Your faithful Servant John H Card Newman

W. J. Rivington Esqr

TO LORD BLACHFORD

December 9. 1888

My dear Blachford,

I don't like to have such kind presents of game from you without acknowledging them.[3]

Yours affly J.H.N.

---

[1] There exists for 1888 also the set of formal Christmas letters to Sovereigns, dated as in former years 25 Nov., all signed by Newman, but not sent.

[2] William was a younger son of the publisher Charles Rivington, who died in 1831. He became head of the printing firm of Gilbert and Rivington, and retired in 1867. 'This gave him the leisure he needed for attending to numerous philanthropic schemes. After an active life he died in 1888'. *The Publishing House of Rivington*, edited by Septimus Rivington, London 1894, p. 46.

[3] Lord Blachford replied on 15 Dec., 'I hear that Ogle found you uncommonly alive about what is going on in the world. I wonder how you do it.' Lord Blachford said his own alertness was waning, though he was curious as to the future of 'the French Republic — the English constitution — the Eastern autocracies — with their tremendous armaments and infidel science. One seems to be finishing the second volume of a novel without the chance of getting a glimpse of the third.'

Dec 14/88

My dear Canon Liddon

Have you seen the account given in Dean Burgon's 'Twelve Good Men' of the Provost of Oriel election in 1827–28. He writes very kindly of me but I do not acquiesce in his conclusions. Pusey and I voted for Hawkins, not for Keble.[1] Do you care to see my letter written on the subject at the date of[2]

Yours most truly
John J H Card. Newman[3]

The Oratory, Birmingham Jan 7, 1889

Dear Mr Edwards

God has never failed me. He has at all times been to me a faithful God. I trust your prayers will do me good. They will carry me on to the end.

Yours most truly J. H. Newman[4]

Geo. T. Edwards Esqre

The Oratory Birmingham Jany 7. 1889

My dear Wilfrid

I grieve to read your letter, and as far as lies in our power we will join our prayers with yours.

My blessing on Josephine and the little child.[5]

Yours affectionately J H N

Wilfrid Ward Esqre.

[1] See J. W. Burgon *Lives of Twelve Good Men*, I, p. 404, and cf. p. 398.
[2] Liddon replied on 15 Dec. asking to see the letter to which Newman refers, evidently that of 19 Dec. 1827 to Keble. Liddon thought Burgon 'so intent upon making the best of his more intimate friends, that he is not able to retain a sense of historical justice or proportion'. See letter of 9 Jan. 1889 to Church.
[3] Newman made two attempts at the signature, the rest being in Neville's hand.
[4] Only the signature is autograph.
[5] This was Maisie Ward, born on 4 Jan. and not expected to live. She was out of danger by 9 Jan. and died in 1975.

The Oratory Jany 8. 1889.

Dear Ignatius

The Fathers will be very sorry to hear of your wish but for a long time you have had a right to exercise. They will lose a careful and conscientious parochus for their people. They may [sic] meet with as worthy a successor and I grieve for the cause of it.

Yours affectionately J H N[1]

TO R. W. CHURCH

The Oratory, Birmingham Jan. 9. 1889

My dear Dean,

You can make what use you will of the letter.[2] I send you also two memorandums.

Yours affly J.H.N.

The Dean of St Paul's

Memorandum

I did not write in antagonism to Burgon but only as to what I knew better than he did and about what he could know nothing.[3]

I recollect in defence of myself talking with Jenkyns as regards Keble and saying, 'What we wanted was not an Angel but only a Provost.'[4]

Jenkyns and I think Awdry were strikingly determined in favour of Hawkins from the fact that three Tutors Dornford, myself and Pusey all three voted for him though they feared he would not get on with his Fellows. (N.B. The other Tutors, Robert Wilberforce and Froude being friends of Keble's as a matter of course voted for Keble. My memory, I believe, bears me out clearly.)[5]

---

[1] Only the initials are autograph. Ryder wrote on 6 Jan. asking to be relieved of his office as parish priest, which he had held for thirteen years. He was suffering in his legs.

[2] This was a copy of Newman's letter of 19 Dec. 1827 to Keble, which Newman had just sent to Liddon. On 31 Dec. 1888 Neville sent it to Church, explaining that Newman said 'it hardly tallies with Burgon's account'.

[3] Dean Church wrote on 2 Jan. 1889, about Burgon's *Lives of Twelve Good Men*, 'he irritated me when I read his book, by his Olympian airs. He was a very affectionate fellow, but with no more real modesty than a modern Greek, and his presumption, when he was displeased, made him ill-natured and reckless.' Church added that as to the Oriel election 'he could know nothing about it of his own knowledge.' Church reviewed Burgon's book in the *Guardian* (23 and 30 Jan.).

[4] See postscript to letter of 29 June 1882 to Pusey.

[5] Keble retired from the contest and the actual election was unanimous. On 9 Jan. 1889 Neville wrote at the end of this Memorandum: 'The above was dictated for you by the Cardinal immediately after he had read your letter of Jany 2. 1889. His Eminence said that of course you might make what use you pleased of the copied letters . . .'

TO JOHN THOMAS WALFORD, S.J.

Jany 17/89

My dear Walford

My blessing on you and yours

J H Card. Newman

TO WILLIAM EWART GLADSTONE

The Oratory, Jan 27. 1889

Cardinal Newman begs to offer his best acknowledgements to those kind persons, friends and others, who have shown so intimate an interest in the state of his health during his recent illness[1]

The Rt Honble Wm Gladstone M.P.

TO BEAUMONT COLLEGE

[21 February 1889]

I rejoice to have their prayers and thank the community and boys. I gladly give my blessing and pray Almighty God may send a large one.[2]

TO AUGUSTINE FRANCIS HEWIT

The Oratory, Birmingham. Feby 28. 1889

My dear Fr Hewit,

I was very sorrowful at hearing of Father Hecker's death.[3] I have ever felt that there was this sort of unity in our lives, that we had both begun a work of the same kind, he in America and I in England, and I know how zealous he was in promoting it. It is not many months since I received a vigorous and striking proof of it in the book he sent me.[4] Now I am left with one friend less, and it remains with me to convey through you my best condolement to all the members of your Society.

Hoping that you do not forget me in your prayers.

I am, dear Fr Hewit Most truly Yours

John H. Card. Newman[5]

[1] This is printed, except for date and addressee in Neville's hand. Among those to whom this circular was sent, was Bishop Hedley.
[2] This was a telegram.
[3] Isaac Thomas Hecker died on 22 Dec. 1888.
[4] *The Church and the Age*, New York 1887.
[5] Only 'Yours' and the signature are autograph.

The Oratory. Birmm March 22. 1889

To Ld Blachford

I ever loved and felt attached to your home and family and think I can understand your and their sorrow.[1]

I once presumed to make a sonnet on its life.[2]

God bless you and yours

J.H.N.

March 21. 1889[3]

The Oratory, Birmm April 6. 1889

My dear Dean Plumptre

May the God of love and peace support you in this great affliction.[4] In answer to you I am not neglecting what is in my power, which is little enough, if only from my sense of the kindness with which both you and she have treated me. It is not often that such genuine tenderness has been shown me. I hope I shall not be ungrateful to you and her. Do let me hear from you again.

Yours affectionately J. H. Newman

The Very Rev. The Dean of Wells

The Oratory, Birmingham, May 5, 1889.

My dear Blachford,

I tried to write you a line, but the failure is no great loss.

Tell me how you are.[5]

Yours affectionately, J.H.N.

---

[1] Lord Blachford's youngest sister, Sophia, born in 1816 had just died.
[2] 'Home', *V.V.* p. 62, the first poem in *Lyra Apostolica*, written on 16 Nov. 1832 after Newman's first visit to Lord Blachford's family. *Moz.* I, p. 279.
[3] This letter was written on this day and corrected and sent off on 22 March.
[4] Mrs Plumptre died on 3 April 1889.
[5] Lord Blachford replied on 7 May that his health was breaking up.

TO AUGUSTA THEODOSIA DRANE

May 5/89

Dear Mother Provincial

I wish you and yours as great a blessing as the dear Archbishop has gained.[1]

Yours My dear Revd. Mother J. H Newman[2]

TO AMBROSE LEE

The Oratory Birmingham May 5. 1889

My dear Ambrose,

I am deeply grieved at your letter.[3] Of course I will do the most I can to assist you. Write to me again if you have anything to say. My most affectionate wishes to your Mother and Father.

Truly Yours J.H.N.

TO WILFRID WARD

I regret to say I am too old to attempt to answer letters

May 25 1889

My dear Wilfrid Ward

I very much fear that I am vexing you by not writing. I am writing to you every day and I trust you will have patience with me. Your book is a capital one, very able, and very kind to me personally.[4] Bear with me and believe me

Yours affectionately J H Newman[5]

TO HENRY SCHOMBERG KERR, S.J.

The Oratory Birmm May 29. 1889

Dear Fr Kerr,

Your concern for the poor Watt family is very kind.[6] I take advantage of it by sending you a cheque for £50 herein enclosed, to be disposed of as you think best in their behalf.

[1] Archbishop Ullathorne had died on 21 March.
[2] Newman also wrote to A. T. Drane on 12 April 'Almot sininc Octob. I have been lying on my oladege' [old age]
[3] See letter of 8 July to Lee.
[4] *William George Ward and the Oxford Movement*, London 1889.
[5] Only the superscription, signature and date are autograph.
[6] They now lived at Bournemouth, where Father Kerr was stationed.

My eyes will not let me write myself but I do my best by sending my kindest remembrances to 'Mamo' and your sister-in-law[1]

Yours most truly John H Card Newman[2]

TO HENRY SCHOMBERG KERR, SJ.

The Oratory, Birmm May 31, 1889

Dear Fr Kerr

I am ashamed of myself in being so thoughtless with you and I want to anticipate your answer to my cheque.

The case is this. Eleanor Bretherton (Mrs Watt) has been a penitent of mine from a child. When she was grown up she made a very foolish match. I have not felt called to assist her in her troubles, but now, when I feel less interest in the matter, I wish to do her a service as my last. Hence the cheque which I fear must give you trouble. Pray excuse me.

Yours most truly J H Card Newman

TO AN UNKNOWN CORRESPONDENT

The Oratory, Birmm June 21/89

Dear Sir

I congratulate you with all my heart on the great mercy which Almighty God is shewing you. I wish my age allowed me to have the favour of congratulating you in person and I hope you will allow me instead to write you these few lines of welcome.

Yours most truly John H Card. Newman

I regret to say I am too old to attempt to answer letters

[1] Mrs Maxwell-Scott and Mary, widow of Ralph Kerr.

[2] On 12 May Newman sent £100 for the West African Missions to Sir James Marshall, who had been Chief Justice in the Gold Coast. He replied next day, 'The personal interest which Your Eminence takes in these missions has had great weight with the Propaganda.'

The sum was to go towards the support of a British bishop in Nigeria, which Marshall thought to be too exclusively under French missionary influence. After the latter's death in Aug. 1889 and the withdrawal of William Kane, the first Puisne Judge in the Niger Territories, who left to become a Jesuit, Newman in March 1890 asked Neville to write to William Bellasis about his benefaction. Bellasis had charge of it and Newman, fearing it might not now be used as he intended, suggested it might be applied to another 'very important purpose'. In fact the £100, invested in Consols had doubled by the time Newman died, and was used to found a bishopric. See W. R. Brownlow, *Memoir of Sir James Marshall*, London 1890, pp. xi and 160.

TO LORD BLACHFORD

July 6. 1889

My dear Blachford

No — Church did not tell me   My own anxiety made me write to you. I never shall forget you[1]

J.H.N.

TO AMBROSE LEE

The Oratory, Birmingham July 8. 1889

My dear Ambrose,

I have been anxious for a long time to have some news of your Mother. Excuse this short letter written with a view to gain an answer from you about it.[2]

Yours affectionately J H N

Ambrose Lee Esqr.

TO AUGUSTA THEODOSIA DRANE

The Oratory July 21/89

Dear Mother Provincial

I have benefitted so much by your prayers at Stone that I think I may safely rely upon your kindness in making an intention of them in behalf of my eyesight which is at present a great penance to me. I have abundant blessings here and I add my blessing to you all.

Yours affectionately J H Card. Newman

The Mother Provincial, Stone

TO ANNE MOZLEY

Aug. 13 1889.

I am sorry to say my illness prevents my seeing you

J H N

TO W. S. LILLY

[September? 1889]

I am too old to write; I cannot hold the pen.

J.H.N.

---

[1] This refers to Lord Blachford's ill health.
[2] Mrs Lee died on 1 Sept. 1890.

TO LORD BLACHFORD

The Oratory, Birm Septr 6/89

My dear Blachford

Thanks for the partriges which are very acceptable. Also thanks for the account of yourself which allows me to take the favourable side. As to myself I am obliged to commit myself to the paradox to being just so well as is consistent with illness. Church also must be thanked for the relief he afforded me

Yours affly J.H.N.[1]

TO LORD BLACHFORD

The Oratory, Birmm Sept. 28. 1889

My dear Blachford,

Your letter of this morning added of course to the griefs which for a long course of years have gathered heavily upon my mind. And though I knew all along what must take place any how some day or other to the destruction of my tenderest memories, yet, I was not the more prepared for your very kind and distinct announcement when it came to me[2]

Yours J.H.N.[3]

TO CARDINAL PAROCCHI

The Oratory Birmingham Octr 2. 1889

My dear Lord Cardinal

Thank you for the interest you express in a case which is very dear to me, as is well recognised by the Passionist Fathers.

[1] On 18 Sept. Neville wrote to H. P. Liddon: 'The Cardinal says he would wish to see you, and he would be very sorry to check your coming, if you have anything of importance or even less than that to ask or say, and, if in that case you come, he would do his best to see you, tho' he could not talk to you for long. Otherwise, you had better not come. He wished me to be very careful not to hinder you coming in the case that I have named.

The doctors say he is very well and he feels so himself, but his weakness is very trying to him.'

[2] Lord Blachford wrote on 27 Sept., 'I ought to tell you that within the last two days, my doctors have told me plainly that I am not to recover.'

[3] On 29 Sept. Newman dictated a letter to Cardinal Manning, congratulating him on his part in the settlement of the London dockers' strike. Manning replied next day: 'Your letter of this morning is as grateful to me, as it was unlooked for: and I thank you for it very heartily.

I was rejoiced to see the other day the words you spoke in the Church about Giordano Bruno. They showed the old energy of days long past for both of us.

Do not forget me in your prayers. Every day I remember you at the altar. Believe me always yours affectionately

Henry E. Card. Manning.'

When the Papal Allocution, condemning the demonstration at the erection of a statue of Giordano Bruno in Rome, was read in the church of the Oratory on 14 Sept., Newman added words of his own in condemnation of the infidel declarations of which it had been the occasion. See the *Weekly Register* (21 Sept. 1889), p. 355. According to Neville, Newman's words were toned down by the person who read them out.

Certainly Fr Dominic of the Mother of God was a most striking missioner and preacher and he had a great part in my own conversion and in that of others. His very look had a holy aspect which when his figure came in sight in my circle most singularly affected me, and his remarkable *bonhomie* in the midst of his sanctity was in itself a real and holy preaching. No wonder, then, I became his convert and penitent. He was a great lover of England.

I grieved at his sudden death, and I thought and hoped he would receive from Rome the *aureole* of a Saint as is now to be.

Humbly and affectionately kissing your Eminence's hands, I am,

Your Eminence's most devoted Servant J H Card. Newman[1]

The Most Emnt and Most Revd Lord
His Emce Cardinal Parrochi, Cardinal Vicar Rome

TO LADY BLACHFORD

The Oratory Birmm Nov 5/89.

My dear Lady Blachford,

Thank you for having me in memory amid your sorrow for one who is still dearer to you than a life long friend. I am always thinking of him, and together with him of those who are so dear to him.

The last account, alas, is the gravest.[2]

Yours most sincerely J.H.N.

TO JOHN TRANT BRAMSTON

The Oratory, Birmingham, Nov 15, 1889.

My dear Mr Bramston

Up to this hour I have been thinking of your father day by day and night by night.[3] Now the end has come which I have been so waiting and associating with what is soon to happen to myself. May I be as safe as I believe and hope he now is.

Most truly Yours J.H.N.

P.S.   My fingers won't write.[4]

---

[1] Only the signature is autograph.
[2] Neville wrote on 4 Nov. to Mary Church:
'The Cardinal will be very glad indeed to see you and you need not fear that he will be wishing you gone. As to what you say about Lord Blachford, the Cardinal is quite prepared to hear the bad news which you have in mind, and you need not fear that it would hinder his seeing you. He has received the blow already viz when Lord Blachford gave him an account of himself which shewed that the worst must be expected. For a few days the Cardinal was thrown back very markedly by that news, but now it would not pain him to see you even if the bad news accompanied you rather it would be a relief to him.'
[3] Dean Bramston died on 13 Nov. His son, who was a master at Winchester College, sent the news.
[4] Towards the middle of Nov. Newman went out in the snow to act as a peacemaker in the case of the Catholic girls employed at Cadbury's chocolate works, who were obliged to attend

TO LADY BLACHFORD

The Oratory, Birmm Nov. 24/89

My dear Lady Blachford,

It was very kind in you to write your words so directly though on so sad a matter.[1]

I do not know why, but, as coming from you, it gave me a feeling of comfort which I needed. I pray that the blessing of God may come upon you and him and all dear to him. He is nearly the dearest as well as the oldest of my early friends.

Yours most sincerely John H. Cardinal Newman

TO EDMUND STONOR, ARCHBISHOP OF TREBIZOND

[End of November 1889]

I hope I am not offending against the etiquette of Archbishops or the special prerogatives of your own position[2]

The favour I would claim of you is a repetition of the service which you have so often and so kindly done me, in a word, I want to beg from you when Christmas comes your good offices to enable me to offer His Holiness my anniversary obolus, it being probably my last opportunity

In that case I would send the sum of £20 (crossed) to your name at Plowden's[3]

MEMORANDUM ABOUT ST PHILIP'S GRAMMAR SCHOOL

Thursday, Decr 1889.

I write a few words on an (to me) an anxious and important subject. It has been supposed that I have opposed myself directly to the scheme of the Grammar School.[4] The real fact was as follows. I did not like the plan and did not see how I could with least pain or want of tact oppose personally what zealous Fathers urged, and especially because money might be a difficulty to the plan. It became in consequence a happy thought that S. Philip had so

daily Bible instruction. See *Ward* II, pp. 534–5 and *Trevor* II, pp. 640–1. On 15 Nov. George Cadbury wrote from Bournville to Edward Hymers who had forbidden the girls to attend: 'I am obliged to you for your note and was about to answer it when Cardinal Newman called. My brother and I saw him and were charmed by the loving Christian spirit with which he entered into the question. He confirmed your views and we promised him that we would, if possible, find some way of meeting the difficulty without your flock suffering in any way.'

[1] Lady Blachford wrote on 21 Nov. that her husband died in his sleep at 6 a.m. that day.
[2] Stonor was made titular Archbishop of Trebizond on 11 Feb. 1889.
[3] The English bank in Rome.
[4] See at 11 Sept. 1887 notes to 'Note to Memorandum of 4 December 1881'.

insisted in the case of pecuniary expenses upon the 'habent possideant'[1]   I
said to them 'I grant leave on our well known rule, "habent possideant"'
Another similar pretext occurred to me out of the fact that Austin had been
allowed by us in about the year 1860, tho' against the Rule LXX to carry out
Miss Bathurst's orphanage without the Congregation on a plan like the
Grammar School.[2]

The plan of such a school did not please me, but I was not much against
it till to my displeasure I found the authors of it has joined secular priests in
taking an active part in it without me, and without me applied to Rome for the
Pope's blessing. To these reasons, the fear of our being entangled in money
matters before we knew where we were[3]

TO EMMA DERMEY

[December 1889]

Madam

In reply to your letter to Cardinal Newman written last Friday his
Eminence asks me to say for him as follows:— That he is too ill to answer your
letter but he refers you to a passage which you seem not to have observed
pp. 231–232 of Via Media Vol 2 Pickering. 1884.[4]

TO DR ROBERT JORDAN

[December 1889]

Thank you for your beautiful and touching lines but I hope you will not
think me unkind in saying that it is a sorrow to me that you have no part in
the greatest of the joys of this season.[5]

What can I do but send you and Mrs Jordan my Christmas bless[ing][6]

[1] St Philip would not allow his Oratorians to take vows like members of religious orders.
When some of them drew up a paper advocating that they should renounce whatever they pos-
sessed, St Philip wrote on the paper 'habeant, possideant'. G. Bacci, *The Life of St Philip
Neri*, London 1902, I, p. 115.

[2] St Philip's Orphanage was carried on by Austin Mills. Decretum LXX of *Instituta
Congregationis Anglicae Oratorii S. Philippi Nerii*, Rome 1847, restricted the activities of the
Congregation as such, lest it should be distracted from its primary work.

[3] The draft, in Neville's hand, is incomplete.

[4] Emma Dermey, staying at Holfield Grange, Coggeshall, Essex, asked enlightenment
about Newman's view of the Eucharistic presence of Christ as given in *V.M.*, ii, p. 228, note 6,
and quoted by Charles Gore, *Roman Catholic Claims*, 2nd edition, London 1889, p. 20, note,
to show that 'while it agrees very well with the ancient use of the Eucharistic mysteries, agrees
very ill with some modern practices, attractive as they are, connected with the Tabernacle and
the Monstrance.' (C. Gore, loc cit.). In *V.M. II*, pp 231–2 Newman shows that whether the
Real Presence is called 'local' with Bellarmine or 'non-local' with St Thomas, is a matter of
words.

[5] At the time of Newman's illness in the autumn of 1888 Henry Lewis Bellasis wrote on
31 Oct. 1888 to his brother Edward an account of how Newman had received the last
Sacraments in the presence of his Community. 'Throughout this time he did not speak at all.
But when all was over, he characteristically began to explain to Dr Jordan—who is a protestant
as you know — the meaning and object of Extreme Unction.'

[6] Dr Jordan had retired earlier in the year and left Birmingham. He wrote again on 20 Feb.
1890 for Newman's birthday, and sent him some cream.

TO R. W. CHURCH

The Oratory, Birmingham December 9, 1889

My dear Dean,

You have had domestic sorrows which I have not had, yet I rival you in many ways which equal yours. My memory runs back as yours cannot into a grave memento which comes vividly home to me. Do you recollect our walking together in 1841 to see the last from the top of the coach at Carfax of Hope-Scott when he was on his passage to Rome. I then felt strangely that in seeing Blachford I was seeing the last of a dear friend leaving me after a long friendship. I was losing in him the dear friend whom I had known so long. I never quite recovered that loss, but I think we have loved each other to the end in spite of serious obstacles. Your kindness will excuse these reminiscences.[1]

Ever yours affly J H N[2]

The Very Revd The Dean of St Paul's

TO JOHN EDWARD COURTENAY BODLEY

The Oratory, Birmingham Decr 26. 1889

Cardinal Newman is greatly pleased and flattered at Mr Bodley's letter, and the purport of it, but he is sorry to say that he cannot avail himself of Sir John Lambert's information. He is obliged to answer that he is now nearly 90 years, and the trials of that age, and want of sight, cut him off from taking part in so important a plan as he (Mr Bodley) suggests. The Cardinal is obliged to write this by the hand of another.[3]

J. E. C. Bodley Esqre

[1] Dean Church, who had kept Newman informed of the stages of Lord Blachford's illness, replied on 12 Dec., 'I knew what he was to me, and I knew that he must have been very much more to you, and that you had in a way lost him twice.' For the renewal of Newman's friendship with Lord Blachford see letter of 26 Aug. 1863 to Ambrose St John.

Four days before he died Newman wished that the ivory of our Lady and Child which Lord Blachford had given him and which hung over the mantelpiece in his room, should be sent to Cardinal Macchi, who had been so kind to him in Rome. Neville was to write to him and say 'that of all his friends his intimacy with Lord Blachford had been the very closest — that of all his friends Lord Blachford was the most gifted, the most talented and of the most wonderful grasp of mind — and he valued him exceedingly — that though people had been used to say that his most intimate friend was Hurrell Froude, it was not so, for close though that intimacy was, it did not approach to his intimacy with Lord Blachford [who] had been his pupil at Oriel, and he had prepared him for his examinations. It was then that their friendship began, and when Lord Blachford also became a Fellow of the College, they were more and more drawn to each other, and there was no secret of the one from the other. To Lord Blachford it was that the Cardinal first disclosed the first dawning upon him of the vision of Rome, most misty, most vague, so doubtful though it was. He only just touched upon it, but with this disclosure the intimacy departed and the oneness between them came to an end.'

[2] Only the initials are autograph.

[3] Bodley was Secretary to the Royal Commission on the housing of the working classes, 1884–5 and the author of three reports on England, Scotland and Ireland. Sir John Lambert devoted much of his life to matters of poor law and sanitation, and was secretary of the Local Government Board from its beginning in 1871 until 1882. He was made a Privy Councillor in 1885. Bodley travelled in South Africa, America, and Canada 1887–9, and then settled in France.

TO A. B. GROSART

The Oratory, Birmingham. Decr 26 1889.
Cardinal Newman begs to thank Mr Grosart for the present of 'Three Centuries of Hymns' and he heartily wishes to Mr Grosart the blessings of the Christmas Season.[1]

TO MALCOLM MACCOLL

The Oratory, Birmingham Dec 29. 1889

Dear Mr McColl,

Thank you for the loan of your Reviewer's important criticism which I return. But however careful and praiseworthy the discussion has shown itself, I feel myself obliged in my present state of eyesight and at near 90 to limit myself to the protection of St Athanasius as sufficient, not to speak of St Augustine, and St Thomas, who also say, I think, that the 'Primogenitus' is a word relating to nature, not to office. It is a way with heretical teachers like the Audians [Arians?] to try to appeal to great authorities[2]

With the good wishes of the season

J.H.N.

TO MALCOLM MACCOLL

The Oratory, Birmingham. January 16/90

Dear Canon MacColl,

I have always felt the flattering words you have used of me and I acknowledge them still.

Yours very truly, J. H. Newman.

The Rev. Canon MacColl.

TO GEORGE T. EDWARDS

The Oratory, Birmm Jany 29/90

My dear Mr Edwards[3]

Accept my tardy Christmas greetings and good wishes to you for fulness in faith, hope, charity, gladness, and peace; for the blessings of Holy Church, and of Gospel gifts, for the Communion of Saints and the Life Everlasting.

I shall venture to send you what I may call my Creed overleaf.

Yours most truly J H N

[1] Alexander Balloch Grosart's *Songs of the Day and Night; or Three Centuries of Original Hymns for public and private Praise and Reading* . . . printed for private circulation, Edinburgh 1890 [1889].
[2] See *Ath.* II, pp. 459–62, and see also *T.T.*, pp. 205–7.
[3] Only this word and the 'J H N' are autograph. The rest is in the hand of William Neville.

My Creed

Soul of Christ, be my sanctification;
Body of Christ, be my salvation;
Blood of Christ, fill all my veins;
Water of Christ's side, wash out my stains;
Passion of Christ, my comfort be;
O good Jesus, listen to me;
In Thy wounds I fain would hide,
Ne'er to be parted from Thy side;
Guard me should the foe assail me;
Call me when my life shall fail me;
Bid me come to Thee above,
With Thy Saints to sing Thy love,
World without end.   Amen.[1]

TO EDWARD HAYES PLUMPTRE

The Oratory, Birmingham Jany 29/90

My dear Dean,

I continually think of you though I can do nothing more. And now I write, not as if I could be a help to you, but merely to assure you that I do not forget you. May God give you his best blessings.

Yours affectionately, J H N.[2]

The Very Revd The Dean of Wells

TO EDWARD BELLASIS

The Oratory, Feby 21. 1890

Thank you for your birthday letter and present.

J H N[3]

Edward Bellasis Esqre

TO THE MISSES BOWDEN

The Oratory. Feby 21. 1890

Thanks to you all from my heart for your goodness.

J H N

The Misses Bowden

---

[1] This is Newman's translation of the Anima Christi, made about 1854. *M.D.*, p. 352.
   Edwards thanked Newman on 21 Feb. for his 'Creed': 'I rejoiced to notice as I read it, how Christ was the Alpha and Omega of it all, and I could not help feeling that if all creeds and confessions were couched in similar language, there would not be so many sad separations, on earth, among those who bear the name of Christ.'
[2] A note on the copy says 'written by an amanuensis'.
[3] Only the initials are autograph in this and the letters that follow.

TO EMILY BOWLES

The Oratory, February 21, 1890

My best thanks to you. I often think of you when I put on my ring.

J H N

Miss Bowles

TO H. P. LIDDON

The Oratory. Feby 21. 1890.

In spite of what you say I cannot refrain from thanking you for so thoughtful a letter.[1]

J H N

Revd Canon Liddon

TO FREDERICK BAKER

The Oratory March 8. 1890

Cardinal Newman's Compliments to Mr Baker and in answer to the two letters received from him he begs to say that he has no information to give on the subject of them and that he had no knowledge of the proceedings of the Bishop of London.[2]

To Mr Fredc Baker Malvern House Swansea.

TO LORD CHARLES THYNNE

The Oratory, Birmingham March 10, 1890

My dear Ld Charles Thynne

I have had you in mind almost ever since I heard of your happy destination, thinking of you with a sort of sad and almost keen sense of the intensity of my contrast to you who have had given you those great privileges which I have not myself.[3]

---

[1] Liddon sent good wishes for Newman's birthday. On 22 Nov. 1889 Neville wrote to Liddon: 'The Cardinal has borne in mind that some time back you said you might be coming this way towards the end of the year. He wishes me, therefore to prevent the chance of disappointment by saying that if you will give him a little notice he would hope to be at your service.'

[2] Baker asked if it was true, as the Bishop of London was reported as saying, at the trial of the Bishop of Lincoln, Edward King, reported in the *Church Times*, (14 Feb. 1890), that when Newman became Vicar of St Mary's, Oxford, it was the custom to sing 'Glory be to Thee, O Lord' before the Gospel.

[3] See letter of 28 Feb. 1887 to Lord Charles Thynne, who wrote on 8 March to congratulate Newman on his birthday and to thank him 'for all you have been to me and mine'. He added that he was saying Mass daily for his sister the Duchess of Buccleuch, whose chaplain he had become. Newman had said mass for what proved to be the last time on Christmas Day 1889, and was trying to learn more or less by heart from a missal for the partially blind, in the hope of saying mass again. See *Ward* II, pp. 532–3.

May God bless you and your Sister, to whom I send my best remembrances in that gift of sight which for great reasons, though I know them not, is no longer mine.

Yours affly J.H.N.

P.S.   And how is Lady Kenmare?[1]

The Revd Ld Charles Thynne

TO AUGUSTINE FRANCIS HEWIT

The Oratory, Birmingham March 15, 1890

Dictated

Dear Fr Hewit,

In answer to your letter I am glad to be told what is so interesting to me viz. that the Life of Fr Hecker is in preparation.[2] I had a great affection and reverence towards him and felt that which so many good Catholics must have felt with me on hearing of his illness and death. I wish, as you ask me, that I could say something more definite than this of his life and writings, but my own correspondence with friends, and especially the infirmities of my age, hinder me and make it impossible for me to venture upon it. This, alas, is all that I have left me now by my years towards the fulfilment of welcome duties to the grateful memory of an effective Catholic writer (I do not forget his work in England) and a Benefactor, if I may use the term, to the Catholic Religion, whose name will ever be held in honour by the Catholic Church.

Yours Most truly J H N

TO EDWARD ILSLEY, BISHOP OF BIRMINGHAM

The Oratory, Birmingham March 15. 1890.

My dear Lord Bishop,

We are much pleased and gratified to find that we are to have two days in the week for the Theological Lectures, and we shall wait cheerfully for your convenience as to the commencement of them. We know how much trouble the arrangement must have cost you.[3]

Yours most truly, J H Card Newman

The Rt. Reverend The Bp of Birmingham

---

[1] Lord Charles Thynne's only daughter Gertrude was the wife of the Earl of Kenmare.

[2] This was Walter Elliott, C.S.P., *The Life of Father Hecker*, New York 1891, which first appeared serially in the *Catholic World*, 1890–1. For a criticism of this biography see Vincent F. Holden, C.S.P. *The Yankee Paul*, Milwaukee 1958, p. 419.

[3] Bishop Ilsley arranged that Victor Schobel, professor of theology at St Mary's Seminary, Oscott, should give lectures on dogma twice a week until July at least, to the young Oratorians.

TO EDWARD ILSLEY, BISHOP OF BIRMINGHAM

March 17, 1890

My dear Ld Bp

I herewith enclose you £50 as a first instalment of what I conceive will be due for the Theological Lectures. I will anticipate a second instalment when July comes

Yours most truly J. H. Card. Newman

P.S. We thank you much for the service you have done us.

J.H.N.

Rt Revd The Bp of Birmingham

TO MRS KATE SYKES

The Oratory Birmingham March 22 1890.

Cardinal Newman thanks Mrs Kate Sykes for the Compliment she pays him and gives her his permission to print his 'Lead Kindly Light' in the Biography of her brother which she is about to bring out. The verses will be found correctly printed in Cardinal Newman's 'Verses on Various Occasions' published by Messrs Longman

Mrs Kate Sykes Cusetta, Chapel Allerton, Leeds.

TO AUGUSTA THEODOSIA DRANE

Dictated   The Oratory, Birmingham March 23, 1890

Dear Mother Provincial

Don't be pained that I do not write to you and yours. Strange to say I have no time. I pray for you all with all my heart, however badly. I have so many necessary letters to write about, so many papers, so many anxieties, so many prayers to accomplish, especially prayers in the Mass, so many ailments, though, thank God, not painful, for me to attend to, so many duties from the kind urgency of the medical men, and so on, that you would feel for me if you knew them.

The blessing of God be upon you all. I wish I could promise myself a visit to the dear Archbishop's grave.[1] Pray that I may be able. And now I pray again for every one of you

Yours, all, in the eternal peace of Jesus Christ. J.H.N.

The Mother Provincial Dominican Convent Stone

[1] Archbishop Ullathorne was buried in the chapel at St Dominic's, Stone.

TO HUBERT HUNTER PHELPS

Dictated   The Oratory, Birmm March 23/90
Dear Sir,

I have been much gratified by your letter.[1] I well remember your father and his friends and I thank you for having so interpreted his kindness towards me. May God bless you as he has blest me

Yours most truly J.H.N.

Revd H. H. Phelps The Vicarage, Congleton, Cheshire

TO BARTHOLOMEW WOODLOCK, BISHOP OF ARDAGH

Dictated   The Oratory, Birmm March 23/90
My dear Dr Woodlock,

I thank you for so faithfully remembering me after so many [long] a time in your present sphere As I cannot use my own hand pray accept what I wish was of a more affectionate nature in its character. I am looking forward with pleasure to the visit from you on your way to Rome[2]

Yours most truly J H.N.[3]

The Rt Revd The Bp of Ardagh

TO ANNE MOZLEY

Dictated   The Oratory Birmingham April 25 1890
My dear Anne Mozley

I hope you will not consider me unkind towards your generosity, but in very truth I have been thinking of your nephews and nieces, who have a right to occupy the first place in your mind. I am partly led to write this to you because my former letter may against my will, have seemed to you ungracious. Be not severe on my good intention.[4]

Yours affectionately J H N.[5]

[1] Phelps, who was Vicar of Congleton, wrote on 23 Jan., 'I have been extremely affected by reading the last edition of your Apologia. My father who was fellow and tutor of Corpus took his degree the year before you did and knew you and greatly admired your genius. . . . I earnestly pray through Jesus Christ that yours like my father's may be "the house not made with hands eternal"' (II *Corinthians*, 5:1)
William Whitmarsh Phelps took his degree in 1819 and was a Fellow of Corpus Christi College, 1822–4.
[2] Woodlock wrote on 21 Feb. for Newman's birthday and said he hoped to call, and to have 'the great advantage' of discussing with Newman the then state of 'our Catholic University of Ireland.' Woodlock came about 20 April.
[3] On 29 March Ignatius Ryder wrote to R. C. Jenkins, 'The Cardinal bids me say "It pleases and touches me to be borne so affectionately in mind"'.
[4] Neville added a note that Newman was very weak and 'in bed by the doctor's request.'
[5] On 26 April Wilfrid Ward wrote to Tennyson from Ushaw: 'I had a most interesting talk with dear old Cardinal Newman on my way from Ireland to this place. He talked about the Philosophy of Religion among other things, and about the line of thought in the "Ancient

Dictated   The Oratory April 29. 1890
Dear Mother Provincial

I send to you and yours my best blessing, and above all St Catherines, if I may venture to plead with her. I have had an accident which has shaken me soul and body,[1] and has been met only by such dear and faith-ful friends as have paid (paid is a bad word but never mind) me such persevering attention for so long. May God by means of their faithful help still avert evils from me.

Yours affectionately J H N

The Very Revd Mother Provincial Stone

[April or May? 1890][2]
My dear Dean,

I fear you have not, from your silence, a good account to give of yourself. I wish I could do more than send you my kindest sympathy.

Yours most truly J H N

Dictated   The Oratory, May 3. 1890.
My dear Emly,

This book was to have gone to you as long ago as last Christmas, as my answer to your kind card of that date, but various delays hindered it.[3] In now

Sage" which had struck me as running parallel with his own Grammar of Assent. He is feeble but very well and *very* keen, about all these great questions'. *Materials for a Life of Alfred Tennyson*, by Hallam Tennyson, n.d., IV, p. 253.

[1] Newman had a fall after Easter.
[2] Dated by Plumptre.
[3] This was a copy of *Stray Essays*, privately printed, Birmingham 1890, and contained the Inspiration articles and the answer to Fairbairn, with the reply to his second article, which had only been sent to a few people. See letter of 17 Feb. 1886 to Lord Blachford. Neville sent *S.E.* on 4 May, with a covering letter:
'The Cardinal sends you by this post a little book with a letter accompanying it, and I am to post another of my own by way of speeding his reaching you.
It is printed for private circulation but though the Cardinal sends you a copy he is not going to circulate it, because it has, he says, chiefly been for the pleasure of sending it you that he has printed it. No portion of the book is quite new, but there are important omissions, emendations, and additions, which you will regard with not the less favour as coming from his sick-bed. The latter portion of it is really as good as new for it never was sold and has been but very little seen. This is pretty much what his Eminence has been saying to me ("and which I might say") about it, but I must not forget that, besides saying he won't circulate it, he added that that must wait till he is gone, on which account you have my welcome to your being for a long time to come its sole possessor, though he does accuse me of pressing him to

sending you this private copy I wish to express my sense of its faults, and it gives me the opportunity to speak to you some words on a matter personal to myself.

You must have been almost hurt at my saying, when I saw you last year that my writings had been of no interest to me except for the moment, in spite of the forbearance and the intelligent welcome they had received from men of judgment and well-wishers. This is what a recent tradesman in his criticizing me called my cantankerousness, and I fear I have shown it too often, as, alas, I must have done in my answer to the application about Archbishop Trench, in which, I feel that, though I may have been just, I was not generous to his memory;[1] nay, as I must feel in respect to my recent remarks to my critics on my own theological works. It is as if I could not bear to be praised. Hoping my friends will forgive me this weakness,

I am, Your affectionate friend,

J H Newman

TO WILLIAM GREANEY

Dictated　　　　　　　　　　　　　　　　The Oratory, May 4, 1890
Dear Mr G

While I feel the Compliment paid me by your request I consider that what you ask of me are strictly personal gifts and such as are to be actually bequeathed by the receiver, and though I am quite willing that the kind things said of me, and done should be known at the proper time it would be a most serious pain and blow to me to have them intruded on the public during my life time. Therefore with every kind and grateful feeling towards the Catholic Truth Society whose zeal and energy I so much admire, I am obliged to ask your permission to return you an answer which will be of the nature of a disappointment to you. Still, different of course though the comparison is, I should as lieve think of exhibiting the Holy Father's letters to me, though of another kind, as expose to the gaze of the public, honours so special as those you request.

I am sure you will see the force of the difficulty which I have in answering you to the full but I will do what I feel I can and I hope will take it as a proof of my interest in the forthcoming Conference.[2]

With my best wishes and blessing I am My Dear Mr Greaney

Yours most truly J. H. Card. Newman

send it to so many others, "as if I wanted his last days to be spent in controversy and did not wish him to die in peace."

The doctor gives a very good account of the Cardinal in every respect, except his strength, which, though it is now rallying, has suffered much from a recent accident.'

S.E. has been published in *The Theological Papers of John Henry Newman on Faith and Certainty*, Oxford 1976.

[1] cf. letter of 28 June 1888 to R. W. Church.
[2] The letter of Greaney, who was Administrator of St Chad's Cathedral, is not to be found.

TO EDMUND STONOR, ARCHBISHOP OF TREBIZOND

Dictated   The Oratory, Birmingham May 8, 1890
My dear Archbishop Stonor,

I do not know how duly to express the surprise and pleasure with which I received your splendid and most holy gift. You will kindly understand this difficulty, which indeed I am too obviously showing, when you read this poor answer in return which my infirmities make so inadequate to the occasion. All that I can say is that you have now left with us a visible memorial, which my successors will feel even more keenly than I do myself, of these last twelve years in which you have been the chief aid of a poor being, and his sole resource, while bound by the various duties entailed on him by his position. This I have felt from the first, and now you increase the debt, but I hope you will accept this present expression of my feeling as my heartfelt acknowledgment.

I am My dear Archbishop Stonor

Your affectionate friend J.H.N.

TO WILLIAM DYKE ACLAND

Dictated   The Oratory, Hagley Road, May 10. 1890
Dear Captain Acland,[1]

Cardinal Newman has dictated as I give his words from his lips.

'Cardinal Newman rejoices at the thought that he is asked to see one of a

The Catholic Truth Society was holding a conference in Birmingham at the beginning of July, and asked Newman to lend material concerning himself for exhibition during it.

On 2 July, in the morning, Newman received an address from the Catholic Truth Society, sitting in the recreation room at the Oratory. He 'looked particularly well, and spoke in low but clear tones', as follows:

'My dear friends, — I wish, both in thought and language, as far as I can, to thank you, as I do very heartily. I thank you for your affection — it is the affection of great souls. You are not common people. I could say a great deal, but I will only pray that God may sustain and put His confirmation upon what you do. I give you every good wish. Your Society is one which makes us feel the sadness of the days through which we have passed when the Church wanted those assistances of publication which Protestants possessed in such abundance. I envied both the matter and the intention of those publications. It is a cruel thing that our Faith has been debarred from the possibility of lively action, but it was no fault of Catholics. They have been so pressed and distracted from the formation of any policy, that the Church has had to depend on only a few heads and the management of a few. This had been the cause of the absence of interest and popularity in publications among Catholics. But now there is no reason why we should not have the power which has before this been in the hands of Protestants, whose zeal, however, I have always admired. But the reward is at hand for us, and we must thank God for giving us such a hope. I may say of myself that I have had much sorrow that the hopes and prospects of the Church have shown so little sign of brightening. There has been — there is now — a great opposition against the Church; but this time, and this day, are the beginnings of its revolution. I have had despondency; but the hour has come when we may make good use, and practical use, of the privileges which God has given us. We must thank God and ask for his blessing and mercy. May he sustain you. God is not wanting if we are ready to work. I beg you to pardon and to forget the weakness of my words. I am content to pray for you and for your work. God bless you.' The *Weekly Register* (5 July 1890), p. 12.

[1] Captain Acland, R.N., was the eldest son of Henry Acland, Regius Professor of Medicine at Oxford.

family whom he has ever held in affection and memory, and his only difficulty in answering Captain Acland lies in his writing from a sick bed and in his present great weakness which incapacitates him from doing what he would wish, yet he cannot refrain for once to avail himself of so kind an opportunity

If Captain Acland will kindly give his card to our porter Fr Neville will bring him upstairs for a short visit if he (Captain Acland) will allow him (the Cardinal) to take that liberty with him'.

Yours respectfully, Wm P. Neville.

P.S. The Cardinal bids me add 'If you like to take your chance of seeing him this afternoon, 2 o'clock or thereabouts, would, he thinks, be a likely time.'

TO JOHN B. BAGSHAWE

The Oratory, Birmm May 14. 1890

Dear Canon Bagshawe,

I am grateful to you for another of your volumes and am pleased to find they carry with them the approbation and the suffrages of so many Catholic critics and readers.[1]

I am My dear Canon Bagshawe Most truly Yours

TO LADY MARTIN

The Oratory, Birmm May 14, 1890

Dear Lady Martin

I am pleased to receive your and Sir Richard Martin's most interesting Memoir of Don Bosco which I have not been slow to have read to me in behalf of the great works which he has so silently achieved.[2]

I am Most truly Yours J.H.N.

---

[1] Bagshawe evidently sent his *The Church; or What do Anglicans mean by the Church*, London 1890.

[2] This was Jacques Melchior Villefranche, *Life of Don Bosco, founder of the Salesian Society*, translated from the French by Lady Martin, London 1890.

In his last days at his own request, a Life of the Curé d'Ars was read to Newman, in which he took great interest. This was followed by this life of Don Bosco, Founder of the Salesians, but according to Neville, 'it had not the same interest for him. It lacked life and variety. He was always in good luck. Let him have a rebuff, it ever brought a tenfold harvest of good. There was a monotony in this to him, and the reading was broken off.' Edward Bellasis, *Coram Cardinali*, London 1917, p. 76.

Dictated   The Oratory Birmm, May 14/90
My dear Mr Ward,

I thought your present especially kind knowing you had so many things to weigh you down. May God give you a recompense according to your trial.[1] I began to read your translation without delay, and, as I expected found it arrested me at once. I should hope it must have a great circulation.[2]

With my best love to Richard [Ward] and to your daughter at home, and hoping they will give me some good news of yours and theirs. I am

Yrs Most truly J.H.N.

To Mr Francis Ward, 26 Hyde Pk St

The Oratory Birmingham Ascension Day 1890 May 15.
Dear Sir

Cardinal Newman asks me to write to you for him as follows:–

'I am too ill to write to you myself but I am much pleased as well as much edified at your touching sentiments and musical language'.[3]

I am Yrs respectfully Wm P. Neville

Wm J Haydon Yates Esqre

Dictated   The Oratory, Birmm May 19, 1890
Dear Sir,

Thank you very much for sending me your Edition of Latin Plays and the implied compliment which goes with the book.[4]

Most truly Yours, J.H.N.

The Warden of Keble College.

[1] Ward's wife died on 29 April 1889 and his daughter Eliza, wife of Charles Stanton Devas, died on 6 June 1889, aged 36, leaving nine small children.
[2] This was Maurice Chauncy's *The History of the Sufferings of Eighteen Carthusians in England*, translated from his Latin, London 1890.
[3] Yates, who wrote from West Green, Tottenham, sent some of his poems.
[4] This was a collection of plays of Terence and Plautus, with Wagner's text and Colman's translation, beautifully bound, 'as curtailed for acting at St Peter's College, Radley, Oxford 1885–8.' The volume was inscribed, 'For his Eminence Cardinal Newman from the Editor R J W with every feeling of respect. May 1890.'

TO LORD COLERIDGE

The Oratory, Birmm May 26/90

My dear Lord Coleridge,

It is only within the last few days that I heard read your to me most overpowering letter about my Oxford preaching and I can only say that affectionate and gravely sincere as it was it filled me with remorse and I may say dismay on account of its being so far from the true mark in point of fact.[1] I have through God's mercy my good points but I know well they do not involve any special scale of excellence, and I take such words as you have written as an earnest of the blessing which naturally comes upon the actions of a true and merciful man, as you are. Anyhow I can thank you heartily for such personal kindness towards me whatever criticism may be exercised by others upon it.

Yours most affectionately J.H.N.

TO WILLIAM KNIGHT

DICTATED   The Oratory, Birmm. May 26/90

My dear Professor Knight,

I am in course of having your book read to me and I take great interest in it in spite of the very friendly notices which occur in it, and which I feel I have no right to claim more than another. It shows your kindness and I thank you for it[2]

Yours very sincerely signed per pro Cardinal Newman

Wm. P. Neville.

[1] The first part of chapter XVII of William Knight's *Principal Shairp and his Friends*, London 1888, consisted of a paper specially written for the Memoir, by Lord Coleridge. He spoke of Newman pp. 413–15:
'But no notice of Shairp — no notice of any Oxford man of that period who took life seriously and gave himself the trouble to think — can omit that great penetrating influence, that waking up of the soul . . . which came to us week by week from the pulpit of St. Mary's, and day by day from the writings and the silent presence amongst us of that great man who still survives at Birmingham in venerable age, but with undimmed mental eye and unabated force of genius, a Roman cardinal in title, but the light and guide of multitudes of grateful hearts outside his own communion and beyond the limits of these small islands. . . . [Shairp] came under the wand of the enchanter, and never threw off, or wished to throw off, the spell. . . . I do not mean that he ever became in doctrine what is commonly called a High Churchman; Newman taught principles of life and action rather than dogmas, though no doubt he himself drew his principles from what he believed to be dogmatic truths . . .'
[2] William Knight, *Principal Shairp and his Friends*.

TO R. W. CHURCH

dictated   The Oratory, Birmm May 28/90
My dear Dean

I have to thank you for your considerate letter. The account of Mrs Legge is very sad. Catharine seems to be overliving them all.[1] Send as you have opportunity a few words of kindness to them. This must be a trying time for you; we hear nothing of your ecclesiastical troubles.[2] For myself I am astonishingly well. It may interest you to know that in matters of business I am getting intimate with the Longmans but I could not help being sorry for the disappearance of the name of Rivington.[3]

Yours affly J.H.N.

The Very Revd The Dean of St Paul's

TO FRANCIS RIVINGTON

The Oratory, Birmingham June 2, 1890
Dear Mr Rivington,

I received with much surprise your announcement so closely bearing upon my pleasant memories of the time as early as 1830 when I first knew your house and I cannot but feel regret at the dis-appearance of your time-honoured name[4]

I am, very truly Yours J.H.N.

Mr Francis Rivington Waterloo Place, London

TO FREDERICK BAKER

The Oratory, Birmm. June 3. 1890
Dear Mr Baker,

Alas yours is a very difficult case, and I feel with you entirely.[5]

My view of the matter is this:– Instead of following the inspired teaching

---

[1] These were Lord Blachford's sisters. Dean Church wrote on 11 July to announce the death of Mrs Legge. His last letter to Newman on 18 July said: 'I think you will be glad to know what comfort your note gave to poor Miss Rogers in her bereavement.' She herself wrote on 17 July, 'The few lines at the end seemed to give me strength now and for the future to bear any trials that the Almighty may in His Mercy and Goodness, please to send me.'

[2] From Feb. until Nov. 1890 Edward King, Bishop of Lincoln was being tried before the Archbishop of Canterbury for his ritualistic acts.

[3] See next letter.

[4] The publishing firm of Rivington came to an end in 1890.

[5] Baker, a fundamentalist, had been upset by Charles Gore's views on Scripture as contained in his essay 'The Holy Spirit and Inspiration' in C. Gore (Editor), *Lux Mundi*, London 1889, which claimed some support from Newman's article, 'The Inspiration of Scripture', the *Nineteenth Century* (Feb. 1884). Baker, who wrote on 17 May, referred in particular to p. 355 note 1, and p. 350 of Gore's article (15th edition p. 261 note 1, and p. 257), which he thought claimed Newman's patronage unfairly, and concluded 'This essay has troubled me much, the more so as it appears to claim you, at least partially, as a supporter.'

of the Catholic Church, you have thought in times of controversy you could have a faith short of it, and now, when clever men have arisen to hurt your religious sentiments, you are surprised to find it has failed you and that this is the result of your dependence upon private judgment. I can only advise you, as I have ever advised others in these days of difficulty, to have recourse to the Revelation of God, whatever it be, and there find your peace. If He has appointed a Prophet in His Church for His people, you must not set up another contrary to him. The Church is infallible because God has made it so.

You ask me 'Do you agree with Mr Gore?' I do not feel myself bound by the question. I leave it, either now or at another time to the Holy See to decide. I wait till the Holy Church has given its answer, and am not impatient if She delays.

Also, you say 'Is this the finale of the Oxford school which you and Dr Pusey founded seventy years ago to contend with Liberalism?' My answer which I am sorry is not also yours, is, that, it is the finale, because we are bound to go not by mere Reason but by Faith, which will be the safer in the long run, but to which apparently, you are not bound. Your contention is to go by Reason and not by Faith[1]

I am, dear Sir, Yours most truly J.H.N.

FROM W. WOOD

Clare Suffolk June 7th 1890

Dear Sir

I do not know the style in which I ought to address you but I am sure that you will forgive any informality that springs from my not knowing the usages of your people; especially do I think you will be ready to overlook any infringement of the outward laws of reverence due to your position when you know that I am writing this expressly to inform you, as I think it is my duty to do, how much I owe to you.

The question of whether I should acknowledge my spiritual debt has been on my mind for some months. I have at last decided it in the way that this letter shows.

And now I am at a loss to say what I feel towards you. Were it not for the perfect

---

[1] On 10 June Neville wrote to Wilfrid Ward giving Newman's opinion of Ward's article on *Lux Mundi*, 'New Wine in Old Bottles', the *Nineteenth Century* (June 1890) pp. 942–56, reprinted in *Witnesses to the Unseen*. Newman's message was: 'I think the argument of Lux Mundi is in substance the old story of Private Judgment. This does not interfere with the force of your work. Your article is excellent and most important.' See also Wilfrid Ward's 'Reminiscences' in *The Wilfrid Wards and the Transition*, pp. 182–3: 'I was in constant correspondence at this time with Cardinal Newman and visited him more than once. He was said to condemn *Lux Mundi*. But I found in conversation that he was still in the same position as he held in the days of Acton and Simpson's effort in the *Home and Foreign*. His sympathies were divided. He sympathised strongly with the desire to keep thought among Christians open minded and up to date. But he dreaded the liberalism and rationalism which he knew would introduce themselves under cover of this laudable endeavour. He desired to open a door to increased freedom and life in the Catholic schools but to do it very cautiously. He certainly thought that *Lux Mundi* as a whole was too liberal. But to myself he did not speak of it with unmixed reprobation. He rather treated it as an indication to be taken very seriously of the necessity of a strong plea within the Catholic Church for a frank recognition of the sober conclusions of biblical science, and a view of biblical inspiration compatible with complete frankness as to facts.' According to Neville, Newman remarked of *Lux Mundi*: 'It is the end of Tractarianism. They are giving up everything.'

confidence established by your writings I should leave unsaid what I want so much to say. But that confidence begotten in me towards you leads me to endeavour to say quite simply what is in my heart.

About four years ago I came by the first three volumes of your parochial and plain sermons and sometime afterwards I bought an odd volume of selected sermons adapted to the seasons of the ecclesiastical year. These sermons, with the hymn 'Lead kindly light' (so frequently sung by my congregation) are all that I have read of your writings. But — how poorly should I say it if I attempted to put down how much I have received from those four volumes. Surely it is right that I should tell you, if I could, how my life has been changed, how my spirit has been fashioned, how the mind that was in Christ Jesus has been communicated to me by the reading of your sermons.

If I were to allow in myself a perfectly free and natural expression of feeling I should say with a feeling of grateful tears about my heart — 'God bless you Cardinal Newman, God bless you!'

When I tell you that I am a minister of Jesus Christ to a congregation of those who are called 'Independents' you will know at once, much better than I know, what an ecclesiastical gulf divides me from you. These matters I fail to understand, and I have, I must confess, very little wish to understand them. I only know that I desire most sincerely to live the life of our Lord Jesus Christ, to do His will, to have His Spirit to take hold of my tasks and duties and carry them forward as He would have me, and I know that you have helped me as no one else has to be distinctively in aim and spirit, a Christian. Therefore I cannot see, notwithstanding our relative positions that I am doing anything but what is loyal to Him and what you will not regard as presumption at all in thus writing out of the fulness of my heart.

I feel that I have very inadequately stated my experience of benefit, but that precious and profound doctrine which you teach us viz: that the best part of the Christian life remains hidden, leads me to hope that from this very impoverished utterance you may be able to understand how rich and, I hope, lastingly rich you have made me in that inward life according to which we are accepted.

I am yours faithfuly and gratefully W. Wood

TO W. WOOD

Dictated June 8, 1890
Dear Mr Wood,

I wish to express my sense of gratification and thankfulness upon receiving your letter but I am too near my end to write to you. I am now in my 90th year. I pray God to bless you and bring you forward in the one faith of Jesus which He has given and taught to all his people. May we meet together above to praise God for his mercies shown to us so largely who are unworthy of them

Yrs with affte interest J.H.N.

TO FREDERICK BAKER

The Oratory, Birmingham June 14. 1890
Dear Sir

Cardinal Newman in answer to your letter received early this week has dictated for you as follows:–

Dear Sir

I wrote to you in private, not that I did not feel myself responsible for my acts when I am gone, but having no call to engage in controversy.[1]

J.H.N.[2]

Yours very respectfully Wm P. Neville

Frederic Baker Esqre

TO MRS LUCY WHITLEY

dictated   The Oratory, Birmm June 17 1890

Cardinal Newman feels the kindness of Mrs Lucy Whitley's interest in the authorship of 'Lead Kindly Light'. It was written by him on the Mediterranean June 16. 1833, in anticipation of his prospective duties on his return to England. He makes mention of it in his *Apologia* page 35. It has no other author.

To Mrs Lucy Whitley Baldhu Vicarage Scerries, Cornwall.

TO THE EARL OF ROSEBERY

The Oratory, Birmm June 24, 1890

My dear Lord,

I have just now found from the kind openness of a dear and zealous friend that you have written to him on the subject of my likeness.[3] This is a fresh instance of the gratuitous kindness which you are always showing me when you have an opportunity and which had again been brought home to me on occasion of the recent opening of the Library in the North[4]

Most truly Yours J.H.N

The Rt Honble, The Earl of Rosebery

[1] See letter of 3 June to Baker.

[2] Neville noted that this letter was 'not signed by the Cardinal because ill in bed'.

[3] Lord Rosebery had written to Neville that he was disappointed with the Millais portrait. His diary for 13 Aug. 1890 states: 'While at luncheon received a telegram from Father Neville to say that if I wished to see Cardinal Newman's remains I must come at once. So caught the 2.10 train. Arrived at the Oratory at 5. Met Father Neville who took me to the Church, then to the little sitting room and tiny oratory, where he produced a good portrait of the Cardinal which the Cardinal had proposed to give me when he heard I had been disappointed of Millais's, and had been over-ruled, I suppose, very naturally . . .' Lord Rosebery had been presented to Newman at Norfolk House, in May 1880. On 7 July 1885 he wrote to ask Newman to autograph a copy of *Apo*.

[4] This was perhaps a reference similar to that Lord Rosebery made when he opened a library at Whitechapel on 25 Oct. 1892. There, to show the peace of a library, he adapted Newman's apostrophe to Kingsley, in the first edition of *Apo*. p. 25, 'And now I am in a train of thought higher and more serene than any which slanders can disturb. Away with you . . . and fly into space'. Thomas F. G. Coates, *Lord Rosebery. His Life and Speeches*, London 1900, II, p. 624.

The Oratory, Birmingham. July 11. 1890
My dear Father Walford,

I feel very grateful for your most tender care and thoughtfulness and affectionate attachment towards me as shown by the splendid spiritual bouquet you procured for me on St Philip's Day and I thank yourself and the contributors for so great a mercy with all my heart.[1] I wish my want of power of showing my gratitude could be brought home to my many friends and true benefactors. You must, please, believe what I have not the opportunity or means of showing, and you will be too kind not to give me credit for it. You know I am sure how difficult it is to me to write or read and will excuse me.

Yours affly J H N

The Oratory, July 19. 1890
My dear Mother Provincial

I trust you do not think I forget you because I do not write. Your hold upon Mother Margaret and the good Archbishop keep me from this anxiety. Tell me that you do not forget me, and that I have the consolation of knowing that no selfishness of mine brings to me so great a deprivation   One thing at least I can report to you; the great comfort and consolation we have received in the Beatification of our Giovenale Ancina, the friend of St Philip.[2]

With my blessing to you and yours

Yours very affectionately J H N[3]

The Oratory, Birmingham July 20 1890.
Dear Lady Simeon,

It is not because I have not thought of you that I have not had you in my mind before me, but because my days are parcelled out by the necessities which my infirmities occasion.

Alas! as I fear, you are in the same case. I can only hope that your inconveniencies will create in you a kind sympathy in mine. I believe I have

---

[1] Walford was stationed at Manresa, Roehampton.

[2] Juvenal Ancina of the Roman Oratory, who became Bishop of Saluzzo, was beatified on 9 Feb. 1890.

[3] In this and the following letter only the initials were autograph.

nothing to tell you except how day after day I realise the trial of having nothing seriously to do, and I now at length write in the hope that I may gain the consolation of some information which your own sources may give me. Pardon this selfish letter and do not be angry with me.

Yours affectionately, J.H.N.[1]

TO SIR JOHN EARDLEY EARDLEY-WILMOT

The Oratory Birmingham July 31. 1890

Dear Sir Eardley Wilmot

Though I have not any very great influence in the matter I very gladly take part in a movement in which you are interested for the advance of the Industries of Ireland and I am sorry I have so long left your letter unanswered before sending you my name.[2]

Yours very truly

John H. Card. Newman[3]

TO THE SECRETARY OF THE CATHOLIC YOUNG MEN'S SOCIETY OF GREAT BRITAIN

The Oratory, Birmingham July 31 1890

Dear Mr Quinn

I thank you for your Notice of your Annual Meeting and the opportunity you now give me of taking part in this new anniversary of your excellent Institution by participating with your Archbishop in his blessing upon it.

Yours very truly J. H. Card. N.

Hon. Sec. Cath: Young Men's Socty

[1] On 9 Aug. Neville wrote to Anne Mozley an account of the end of term at the Oratory School: 'From the Friday before [Sunday] the 20th [July] till the close of Wednesday the Cardinal did everything, went through everything as in days of yore, excepting that he did not dine with the guests. He talked with comers nearly two hours in the early morning – received everybody in the cloister – gave the prizes and in the evening followed the play [*Andria*]. He had done more than this in Church the previous Friday and Sunday'.
   Newman also, as was his custom, gave a private farewell interview to those boys who were about to leave the Oratory School for good. One of these was James Dessain, father of the editor of these letters. Newman mistook him for a boy who had acted as the school sacristan, and to his embarrassment, gave him unmerited praise. After John Norris, the headmaster, had corrected the mistake, Newman smiled and said, 'Never mind, I dare say you have been a very good boy all the same.'
   [2] Wilmot wrote on 10 July, 'We are forming the London Council of the Irish Industrial League . . . The Committee would consider it an honour if your Eminence would allow your influential name to be added to the enclosed list . . .'
   Wilmot took a great interest in the development of Irish industries.
   [3] The signature is Newman's. Copies exist of a letter of 29 July or 2 Aug. addressed to H. de Burgh, said to be enclosing £5 for his appeal on behalf of the daughter of Thomas McNevin, the friend of O'Connell, but they are clearly forgeries.

The Oratory, Birmm Aug 2/90

My dear Grace,

Thank you for your wish to see me.[1] I embrace it readily and I will see you whatever day next week suits you for that purpose.[2]

Yours affectionately, J.H.N.

P.S. I am sometimes engaged with the doctor.[3]

Mrs Langford.

APPENDIX

POSTSCRIPT TO 'THE DEVELOPMENT OF RELIGIOUS ERROR'

P.S.[4]–This is all I think it necessary to set down in explanation of passages in my *Apologia*. As to my other writings, I can safely leave them to take care of themselves. Anyone that looks into them will see how strangely Principal Fairbairn has misrepresented them. But perhaps, for the sake of those who do not know them, it is my duty briefly to denounce the monstrous words which he has used about me.

His *organon* of criticism is the old 'Fallacy of the Leading Idea,' viz., that

---

[1] Grace Mozley, the only child of Newman's sister Harriett, had married in 1864 and emigrated with her husband to Australia. She was born in 1839 but Newman had not seen her since 1843, when his sister had broken off relations as he became more Catholic. Grace was now on a visit to England, staying with John Rickards Mozley and his wife Edith, who wrote on 1 Aug. that 'she would like very much to try and see you before she goes back to Australia. She is rather shy of proposing it . . .'

[2] Grace Langford replied on 5 Aug., 'My dear Uncle —

It is very kind of you to be willing to see me — I am staying at the Lakes with John and Edith Mozley and return to Cheltenham [where her father Tom Mozley lived] on Friday — but break the journey at Birmingham and hope to be with you some time on Saturday morning [9 Aug.] — should this be convenient to you.

My time is short in England as I sail for Australia in October.

Believe me Yours affectionately Grace Langford'

[3] Mrs Langford wrote a long account of her visit, 'He was very kind, holding my hand in his all the time. I was sorry I had kept my glove on. But I could not quite understand all he said to me. . . . He told me he had once seen me at the Oxford Observatory when I was three years old . . . He said Willie (my son) had gained good opinions and everyone had spoken well of him. He asked about my father's books. . . . At last he gave me, as he does to all visitors, a blessing . . .'

Afterwards Mrs Langford told Neville that she had 'met Maria Giberne at Rome and that she had nursed me through an illness, and had been one of the pleasantest recollections of my Roman visit.' As she left Neville gave her 'a small volume nicely bound of the Cardinal's earlier poems with his and my initials in his own hand.' He also gave her Newman's last message that 'I had touched him deeply by the way I had spoken of Maria Giberne.'

This was in the afternoon of Sat. 9 Aug. At 1 a m. on Sunday 10 Aug. Newman was taken ill. He died of pneumonia in the evening on Monday 11 Aug. 1890.

[4] This is the postscript to Newman's article in the *Contemporary Review* (Oct. 1885), answering A. M. Fairbairn. When he reprinted his article privately in 1886, this postscript was added. It is now published for the first time. See third note to letter of 6 Feb. 1886 to Lord Blachford.

of imagining to himself an hypothesis, by which he may proceed to interpret such phenomena of intellect as it pleases him to ascribe to me, and thereby to save himself the task of quotations, or any pains to which a conscientious critic would feel himself bound. In fact, though he professes to have read, or rather to have 'studied,' all my 'works, tracts, essays, lectures, histories, and treatises,' after all he has selected for adverse notice (over and above the *Apologia*) only some clauses in an Oratorian, and two sentences in a University Sermon.

As to what he considers my 'Leading Idea,' it is in truth an imputation as offensive to the feelings of a Catholic as it is preposterous in itself; it is that I have been and am thinking, living, professing, acting upon a wide-stretching, all-reaching platform of religious scepticism. This scepticism is the real key to my thoughts, my arguments, and my conclusions, to what I have said in the pulpit and what I have written in my study. I may not realise it, but I am 'a poet,' and 'it is the unconscious and undesigned' revelations of self 'that testify more truly of a man' (p. 663). This, he tells us, is his deliberate view, gained with pains and care, and on my part admits of no escape.

'It will be necessary,' he says, when starting on his search for it, 'to discover, if possible, Dr. Newman's *ultimate ideas*, or the *regulative principles* of his thought' (p. 663). Next, 'It is difficult, almost a cruel thing,' still a necessity, 'to attempt to reach the *ultimate principles* that govern his thought' (p. 664). 'Unless his *governing ideas* are reached, neither his mind nor his method can be understood' (*ibid*). Once more: only by holding certain points distinct 'can we get at those *ultimate principles* or *ideas* we are here in search of' (p. 665).

At last he has found the object of his careful searching: he quotes some half sentences from my *Apologia*, which he does not understand, accuses me of slandering the faculty of Reason (*supr.*, p. 7), asks how I come to do so, and then announces his discovery: 'The reason must be sought in Dr. Newman's *underlying philosophy*,' which is 'empirical and sceptical' (p. 667). From 'leading ideas' and 'fundamental principles' I have all through my life shrunk as sophistical and misleading, but I do not wonder that Dr. Fairbairn should like them, for they are to him, as I have intimated, of the greatest service. His 'underlying philosophy,' gained so carefully, enables him to dispense in his criticisms on me with quotations, references, evidences, altogether.

To this use he puts his 'Leading Idea' in the very next sentence after he has discovered it; and by the sole virtue of it he at once utters a sweeping condemnation of my *Grammar of Assent*, without any one quotation or reference to support him. Thus he writes: 'The real problem of the *Grammar of Assent* is, How, without the consent and warrant of the reason, to justify the being of religion, and faith in that infallible church which alone realises it. The whole book is pervaded by the intensest philosophical scepticism; this supplies its *motif*, determines its problem, necessitates its distinctions, rules over the succession and gradation of its arguments. His doctrine of assent, his distinction into notional and real, which itself involves a philosophy of the most empirical individualism, his criticism of Locke, his theories of inference, certitude, and the illative sense, all means the same thing' (p. 667). Not a shred of quotation is given to support this charge — not a single reference; but at the end of it, instead of such necessary proof, a sentence is tacked on to it, which after some search I found, not in the Essay on Assent, but in one of my Sermons written above thirty years before, taken out of its context, and cut off from the note upon it which I had added in its Catholic Edition.[1] Such is the outcome of Dr. Fairbairn's scrupulous care, that 'lectures and treatises should be chronologically arranged' (p. 663). Such above all is the gain of a 'Leading Idea,' and it is irresistible in the hands of Dr Fairbairn; it ignores or overrides facts, however luminous. The instance I have given is a strong one, but I will set down some others.

For instance: 1. When I have with warmth and strength of words denied that the alternative of atheism is my *only* argument for believing in the Catholic Church, and given evidence in contradiction of the charge, he answers, that it is *'certainly true,'* on the contrary, that 'I believe it is the only *real* alternative' (p. 664).

2. When I express my recognition of the 'formal proofs on which the being of God rests,' and 'the irrefragable demonstration thence resulting,' he says that my 'recognition must be criticised in the light of my own *fundamental principle*; it is to me entirely illegitimate' (p. 668).

3. He cannot help being obliged to quote me as saying that the 'unaided reason, when correctly exercised, leads to a belief in God'; still he boldly says of me that 'in my intellect, as I know it, in my reason, as I interpret it, I find no religion, no evidence for the being of a God' (p. 669).

4. When I say that I am a Catholic because I believe in God, and that Theism is attainable even under paganism (*Univ. Serm.*, p. 21), No, he answers, 'you really mean that you are a Catholic' only 'that you may continue a Theist' (p. 665).

5. And when I say that the Church's infallibility is 'far from' being the only way of withstanding 'the energy of human scepticism' (*Apol.*, p. 245), he answers that my 'position' will not 'allow me to hold that Theism existed without and independently of Catholicism' (p. 665).

6. 'Reason,' I have said in my *University Sermons*, 'when its exercise is conducted rightly, leads to knowledge; when wrongly, to error. It is able from small beginnings to create to itself a world of ideas. It is unlimited in its range. It supplies the deficiency of the senses. It reaches to the ends of the universe, and to the throne of God beyond them. Also, it has a power of analysis and criticism in all opinion and conduct; nothing is true or right but what may be justified, and, in a certain sense, proved by it; and unless the doctrines received by faith are approvable by Reason, they have no claim to be regarded as true' (pp. 182, 206, 207, 256). How carefully he has 'studied' my writings!

[1] *U.S.* p. 194, note 9.

The account *he* gives of their teaching about Reason is this: 'There is another and still deeper difference – *the conception of the Reason*. . . . Dr. Newman's language seems to me often *almost impious*' (p. 673).

Such are the convenient uses to which he puts his fundamental principle. No wonder he gratefully recognises and records the service which his fundamental principle has done him in dispensing with any more of that anxious searching which he found necessary in attaining it. 'Detailed criticism,' he says, 'of Dr. Newman's position, with its various assumptions and complex confusion of thought, is, of course, here impossible' (p. 669). Of course; impossible, and therefore let alone.

Marvellous is the power of a Fundamental View. There is said to have been a man who wrote English History, and could not be persuaded that the Heptarchy was over, or Queen Anne dead, I forget which; and who, when pressed with a succession of facts to the contrary, did but reply, as each came before him, 'O but, excuse me, *that* was an exception!' Dr. Fairbairn reminds me of that man.

N.B. – The paging, in quotations made from 'The Contemporary Review', follows the paging of that work, viz, pp. 663, 664, 665, 667, 668, 669, 673.

List of Letters by Correspondents

Abbreviations used in addition to those listed at the beginning of the Volume:

A.   Original Autograph.
Bodleian   Bodleian Library, Oxford.
C.   Copy, other than those made by Newman.
D.   Draft by Newman.
Georgetown   The University of Georgetown, Washington, D.C.
H.   Holograph copy by Newman.
Harrow   Dominican Convent, Harrow, Middlesex.
Keble   Keble College, Oxford.
Lond.   London Oratory.
Magd.   Magdalen College, Oxford.
Oriel   Oriel College, Oxford.
Oscott   Oscott College, Birmingham.
Pembroke   Pembroke College, Oxford.
Ph.   Photographic copy.
Pr.   Printed.
Pusey   Pusey House, Oxford.
S.J. Dublin   The Jesuit Fathers, 35 Lower Leeson Street, Dublin.
S.J. Lond.   The Jesuit Fathers, 114 Mount Street, London.
Stoke   The Dominican Convent, Stoke-on-Trent.
Stone   The Dominican Convent, Stone.
Trinity   Trinity College, Oxford.
Ushaw   Ushaw College, Durham.

The abbreviation which describes the source is always the first one after the date of each letter. This is followed immediately by the indication of its present location or owner. When there is no such indication, it means that the source letter is preserved at the Birmingham Oratory. It has not been thought necessary to reproduce the catalogue indications of the Archives at the Oratory, because each of Newman's letters there is separately indexed, and can be traced at once.

After the source and its location have been indicated, any additional holograph copies (with their dates) or drafts are listed, and then, enclosed within brackets, any reference to previous publication in standard works.

Lastly, when it is available, comes the address to which the letter was sent.

Correspondent	Year	Date	Source	Location, Owner, Address
Acland, William Dyke	1890	10 May	C	
Airy, Osmund	1885	5 Dec	A	Liverpool University Library
Allies, T. W.	1885	12 Jan	C	
		10 Oct	C	
		10 Nov	C	
	1886	26 Feb	C	
		24 Mar	C	
		2 April	C	
		14 June	C	
		16 June	C	
		20 June	C	
	1887	27 May	C	
Althaus, T. F.	1885	13 Jan	A	Dr V. H. H. Green (V. H. H. Green, *Oxford Common Room*, London 1957, p. 322) *Ad.* T. F. Althaus Esqr/Tring Lodge/Tring
Archer, William Henry	1885	10 Mar	A	Melbourne University
Armstrong, Richard Acland	1886	25 April	C	
			D	(two)
	1887	23 Mar	C	
Audley, C. F.	1885	26 Oct	C	
Bagot, R.	1888	10 Jan	A	Newman Preparatory School, Boston
Bagshawe, John B.	1890	14 May	C	
Baker, Frederick	1890	8 Mar	C	
		3 June	C	
			D	
		14 June	C	
Baker, Sir George Sherston	1886	17 Mar	C	
Barry, William	1885	4 Nov	A	Oscott
			D	
	1886	8 Mar	A	Oscott
		4 April	A	Oscott
		28 Oct	C	
Bathurst, Catherine Anne	1886	6 June	A	Harrow
		27 Dec	A	Harrow
	1887	9 June	A	Harrow
Beaumont College	1889	21 Feb	Pr	Privately printed by the English Jesuits
Bedford, Henry	1885	12 Oct	C	
	1887	6 June	C	
	1888	27 Jan	C	
Bellasis, Clara	1888	7 June	A	
Bellasis, Edward, Junior	1885	15 May	A	*Ad.* Edward Bellasis Esqr/College of Arms/London/Queen Victoria Street
	1886	24 July	A	*Ad.* Edward Bellasis Esqr/College of Arms/London E C
	1887	24 June	A	
		14 Nov	A	(Edward Bellasis, *Coram Cardinali*, third impression, London 1917, p. 85 *Ad.* Edward Bellasis Esqr L H/College of Arms/London E C
	1890	21 Feb	A	
Bellasis, Mrs Edward	1887	18 Jan	A	
Berington, Charles Michael	1887	7 July	A	Record Office, Worcester
Blachford, Lord	1885	26 Jan	C	
		23 April	A	
		19 May	A	St John's Seminary, Camarillo, California
		23 May	C	

Correspondent	Year	Date	Source	Location, Owner, Address
		27 July	C	
		2 Sept	C	
		8 Sept	C	
		14 Sept	C	
		17 Sept	C	
		28 Dec	C	
	1886	4 Feb	C	(*Ward* II, p. 509)
		6 Feb	C	(*Ward* II, pp. 509–10)
		9 Feb	C	(*Ward* II, pp. 510–11)
		16 Feb	C	
		17 Feb	C	
		11 Mar	C	
		12 Mar	C	
		1 Oct	C	
		5 Oct	C	
		23 Nov	C	
	1887	20 Jan	C	
		23 Feb	C	
		2 April	C	
		14 April	C	
		18 July	C	
		30 Sept	C	
		17 Dec	C	
	1888	11 Jan	C	
		25 April	C	
		6 Aug	A	Maggs Bros.
		10 Sept	C	
		13 Oct	C	
		31 Oct	C	
		9 Dec	C	
	1889	22 Mar	C	
		5 May	A	Mrs Passy, Ivybridge
		6 July	C	
		6 Sept	C	
		28 Sept	C	
Blachford, Lady	1889	5 Nov	C	
		24 Nov	C	
Blake, Robert J.	1886	21 Feb	A	
Bloxam, J. R.	1885	23 Feb	A	Magd.
		26 Feb	A	Magd.
		9 June	A	Magd.
		15 July	A	Magd.
		4 Oct	A	Magd.
		20 Dec	A	Magd.
	1886	14 May	A	Magd. (*Newman and Bloxam*, p. 226)
		15 June	A	Pusey
Bodley, John Edward Courtenay	1889	26 Dec	C D	
Borlase, Mrs William	1885	30 Mar	A	Pusey
		28 Aug	A	Pusey *Ad.* Mrs Borlase/Farnham Rectory/Bishop Stortford/Essex
Bosworth Smith, R.	1885	22 Dec	D	
Bowden, Catherine, Sister Mary Alban	1886	27 Dec	A	Stone
Bowden, Charles	1886	26 Mar	A	Lond.
		11 May	A	Lond.
		16 May	A	Lond. vol. 15 *Ad.* The Rev/Fr Charles Bowden/The Oratory/London S W
	1887	1 Mar	A	Lond.
Bowden, Emily	1887	23 Dec	A	
Bowden, Mrs J. W.	1886	28 Mar	A	Lond. *Ad.* Mrs Bowden/11 Cromwell Road/South Kensington/Cromwell Road/London S W

Correspondent	Year	Date	Source	Location, Owner, Address
		30 May	A	Lond. *Ad.* Mrs Bowden/11 Cromwell Road/South Kensington/London S W
Bowden, Henry Sebastian	1887	2 Mar	A	Lond. vol. 15 *Ad.* The Rev Fr Sebastian Bowden/The Oratory/Kensington/London S W
Bowden, The Misses	1885	25 Dec	A	
	1890	21 Feb	A	*Ad.* The Misses Bowden/32 Thurloe Sqre/London S. W.
Bowles, Emily	1885	5 Jan	A	
		5 Feb	A	
		24 Dec	A	(*Ward* II, p. 524)
	1886	28 Feb	A	
	1887	3 Nov	A	
	1888	4 May	A	
		1 Nov	A	*Ad.* To Emily Bowden/11 Cromwell Rd/South Kensington
	1890	21 Feb	A	
Boyd, Mr	1885	end of year	D	
Boyle, G. D.	1885	17 Oct	C	
		2 Nov	C	
	1886	6 Sept	C	
Bramston, John	1887	30 Aug	C	
		8 Nov	C	
	1888	27 June	C	
	1889	15 Nov	C	
Braye, Lord	1885	9 Jan	A	St Augustine's, Datchet *Ad.* The Lord Braye/Stanford Park/Rugby
		7 Oct	A	St Augustine's, Datchet *Ad.* the same
	1886	30 Aug	A	St Augustine's, Datchet *Ad.* The Lord Braye/Stanford Hall/Rugby
		3 Sept	A	St Augustine's, Datchet *Ad.* the same
		8 Sept	A	St Augustine's, Datchet *Ad.* The Lord Braye/Stamford Park/Rugby
		8 Oct	A	St Augustine's, Datchet *Ad.* The Lord Braye/Stanford Park/Nr Rugby
	1887	20 Mar	A	St Augustine's, Datchet *Ad.* The Lord Braye/Stanford Park Rugby
		23 Mar	A	St Augustine's, Datchet *Ad.* the same
		26 April	A	St Augustine's Datchet *Ad.* the same
		late April	D	
		27 April	A	St Augustine's, Datchet
			D	
Bredin, James Crawford	1886	10 May	A	Oscott
		21 May	A	Birmingham Diocesan Archives
		23 May	C	
Bridgett, Thomas Edward	1885	27 April	A	
Brownlow, William Robert	1887	3 Jan	C	
Bunting, Percy William	1885	9 Sept	D	
		5 Nov	A	Chicago University Library
			D	
		10 Dec	A	Chicago University Library
	1886	6 Mar	A	Chicago University Library
Burgon, John William	1887	4 Dec	A	
		5 Dec	A	
Burns and Oates, Messrs	1885	27 July	D	

Correspondent	Year	Date	Source	Location, Owner, Address
	1886	21 June	D	
		8 Nov	C	
			D	
		11 Nov	D	
		14 Nov	D	
		10 Dec	D	
	1887	26 Feb	D	
		28 Feb	D	
		2 Mar	C	
		4 Mar	D	
		11 July	D	
		27 Oct	C	
			D	
		17 Dec	C	
Carritt, F. K.	1888	3 May	C	
Casas, N. J.	1886	15 June	D	
Chambers, E. K.	1887	15 Dec	A	Bodleian *Ad.* The Rev/E K Chambers/St Mary's Rectory/Blandford/Dorset
Chandler, Clara	1886	1 Aug	A	*Ad.* Miss C. M. Chandler/Denham Lodge/Putney Hill/London S W
Christie, Albany James, S.J.	1886	12 April	A	S..J. Lond.
		15 June	A	S.J. Lond.
Church, R. W.	1885	4 Jan	C	
		12 April	Pr	*Ward* II, p. 524
		4 Nov and later	C, Pr	*Ward* II, p. 513
	1886	25 Mar	Pr	*Ward* II, p. 526
		16 April	C	
		11 May	C	
	1887	3 July	Pr	*Ward* II, p. 529
		7 Aug	A	Pusey
		1 Sept	A	Pusey
	1888	22 Jan	A	Pusey *Ad.* The Very Rev./The Dean of St Paul's/Hyeres/*France*
		15 May	D	
		28 June	C	
		16 Sept	A	Pusey
	1889	9 Jan	C	
		9 Dec	A	Pusey
			D	
	1890	28 May	C	
Clarke, Richard Frederick, S.J.	1887	12 June	A	
			D	
		28 June	D	
Clifford, William, Bishop of Clifton	1886	25 Jan	A	Clifton Diocesan Archives *Ad.* The Hon./The Rt Rev./The Bishop Clifford/Prior Park/Bath
		30 Mar	A	Clifton Diocesan Archives
Cole, Laetitia	1887	18 Jan	D	
Coleridge, Henry James, S.J.	1885	2 Jan	A	S.J. Lond.
	1887	20 Mar	A	*Ad.* The Rev Fr Coleridge/Catholic Church/Farm Street/Berkeley Square/London W
		13 Nov	C	
	1888	26 June	A	S.J. Lond.
Coleridge, Lord	1888	4 Aug	Pr	E. H. Coleridge, *Life and Correspondence of Lord Coleridge*, London 1904, p. 358.
	1890	26 May	C	
Colyer, John Edmeades	1886	29 April	D	
Cope, Sir William Henry	1885	4 Mar	C	

Correspondent	Year	Date	Source	Location, Owner, Address
		9 Mar	C	
Cormack, George	1886	11 Nov	A	*Ad.* The Rev. George Cormack/ St Peter's/Broad Street/Birmingham
Cornish, Mrs	1886	2 Feb	C	
Cox, George William	1885	4 Mar	A	Catholic University of America
Craven, Mrs Augustus	1885	12 Nov	Pr	H. J. Coleridge, *Life of Lady Georgiana Fullerton*, from the French of Mrs Augustus Craven, London 1888, p. x (Mme Augustus Craven, *Lady Georgiana Fullerton, sa vie et ses oeuvres*, Paris 1888, pp. VII–VIII)
	1888	17 April	D	(Mme Augustus Craven, op. cit., p. VIII; H. J. Coleridge, op. cit., p. xi)
Cuervo, R. J.	1885	8 April	A	Instituto Caro y Cuervo, Bogota, Colombia
Darnell, Nicholas	1886	12 Nov	A	The Misses Darnell
Daughter of Mrs L. J. Watt	1885	30 July	C	
Davis, Walter L.	1885	20 Oct	A	Mrs Davis *Ad.* Walter L. Davis Esqr/55 Elgin Crescent/Kensington Park/London W
Deane, Miss Emmeline	1885	26 Sept	C	
	1887	3 Mar	C	(*Ward* II, pp. 527–8)
Deane, Miss Louisa	1886	18 Feb	C	
	1887	15 July	C	
		12 Aug	C	
	1888	26 May	C	
Deane, Louisa Elizabeth	1885	27 Feb	C	
	1886	11 Jan	C	
De Lisle, Margaret	1885	26 Jan	Pr	H. N. Oxenham, *Memoir of Lieutenant Rudolph de Lisle, R. N.*, London 1886, p. 277
		27 Feb	A	St Mary's Abbey, Mill Hill
		27 Oct	A	St Mary's Abbey, Mill Hill *Ad.* Miss de Lisle/St Mary's Abbey/ Mill Hill/London N W
		16 Dec	A	St Mary's Abbey, Mill Hill *Ad.* Miss de Lisle/St Mary's Abbey/ Mill Hill/Hendon N W
Denbigh, Earl of	1888	23 Aug	C	
Denny, Alexander	1885	12 Jan	D	
		15 Jan	D	
		20 Jan	D	
		23 Jan	D	
		8 Feb	D	
Dermey, Emma	1889	Dec	D	
de Vere, Aubrey	1885	6 Feb	A	National Library of Ireland
		28 Sept	A	National Library of Ireland
	1886	29 April	A	National Library of Ireland
		2 Sept	A	Bodleian
	1887	10 July	A	National Library of Ireland
	1888	15 May	A	National Library of Ireland
Dickins, Owen	1886	28 May	D	
Dillon, Lawrence	1888	13 Sept	Pr	[Lawrence Dillon] *On General Gordon's Copy of the Dream of Gerontius*, 1892, pp. 15–16
		23 Sept	C	
Dinzey, R. Burton, Junior	1886	19 Dec	Ph	*Ad.* R. Burton Dinzey/St Bartholomew/W.I.
Domenichetti, Richard Hippisley	1885	30 May	A	Felix Markham

Correspondent	Year	Date	Source	Location, Owner, Address
Drane, Augusta Theodosia	1887	4 May	C	
		31 Dec	C	
	1888	5 May	C	
		13 July	A	Stone
	1889	5 May	A	Stone
		21 July	A	Stone
	1890	23 Mar	C	
		29 April	A	Stone
		19 July	A	Stone
Dubois, Gertrude d' Aurillac	1885	12 Mar	A	Stanbrook Abbey
Eardley-Wilmot, Sir John Eardley	1890	31 July	C	
Editor of the Cambrian	1887	24 Aug	C	(*Newman at Oxford*, p. 81; the *Sheffield Evening Star*)
Editor of the Pall Mall Gazette	1885	16 April	Pr	The *Pall Mall Gazette* (18 April 1885), p. 2
	1886	16 Jan	Ph	The *Pall Mall Budget* (14 Aug 1890), p. 1054
Edwards, George T.	1885	1 Jan	A	St John's Seminary, Camarillo, California
		24 Jan	A	St John's Seminary, Camarillo, California
		5 Mar	A	St John's Seminary, Camarillo, California
	1886	1 Jan	A	St John's Seminary, Camarillo, California
		25 Feb	A	St John's Seminary, Camarillo, California
	1887	22 Jan	A	St John's Seminary, Camarillo, California
		24 Feb	A	St John's Seminary, Camarillo, California (*Ward* II, pp. 526–7)
	1888	10 Jan	A	St John's Seminary, Camarillo, California
		24 Feb	A	St John's Seminary, Camarillo, California
	1890	29 Jan	A	St John's Seminary, Camarillo, California (*Ward* II, p. 536)
Emly, Lord	1886	7 April	A	
	1890	3 May	A	(H. Tristram, *Newman and his Friends*, London 1933, p. 171)
Engelbach, G. F.	1887	21 Jan	A	Newman Preparatory School, Boston
Eyre, Charles, Archbishop of Glasgow	1888	24 Sept	A	
Fitzgerald, Geraldine Penrose	1885	20 May	A	
		5 Dec	A	*Ad.* Miss G. Fitzgerald/19 Norfolk Square/London W
Fortey, Emily	1887	4 Aug	C	
Fullerton, Alexander	1885	12 Nov	A	Maryfield Convent, Roehampton
	1886	25 Feb	A	Maryfield Convent, Roehampton
		29 Dec	A	Maryfield Convent, Roehampton
	1888	20 Feb	A	Maryfield Convent, Roehampton
Furse, Charles Wellington	1887	11 Nov	A	St George's, Bristol *Ad.* The Rev Canon Furse/All Saints/Shrewsbury
General Life and Fire Office	1886	19 July	D	
Gibbons, James, Archbishop of Baltimore	1885	10 Oct	A	Catholic University of America
	1886	28 May	A	Baltimore Cathedral Archives
		July	A	Baltimore Cathedral Archives
		23 Sept	A	Baltimore Cathedral Archives

Correspondent	Year	Date	Source	Location, Owner, Address
Gibbs, John Lomax	1885	5 Dec	A	*Ad.* The Rev J L Gibbs/Rectory/ Clyst St George/Topsham/Devon *readdressed* Tyntefield/Bristol
Giberne, Miss M. R.	1885	19 Aug	A	
		8 Sept	A	
Gilbert and Rivington, Messrs	1885	19 Jan	D	
	1886	16 June	D	
		15 July	D	
Gladstone, William Ewart	1888	6 Nov	A	British Museum (*Moz.* II, p. 415)
	1889	27 Jan	A	British Museum
Glover, John	1886	20 Mar	D	
Gordon, William Philip	1886	31 Jan	A	Lond. Vol. 11
		26 Mar	A	Lond. Vol. 11
		15 June	A	Lond. Vol. 11
		30 Nov	A	Lond. Vol. 11
		27 Dec	A	Lond. Vol. 11
	1887	29 Jan	A	Lond. Vol. 11
		15 April	A	Lond. Vol. 11
		14 Oct	A	Lond. Vol. 11
Gore, Charles	1885	16 May	D	
	1888	14 Nov	C	(G. L. Prestige, *The Life of Charles Gore*, London 1935, p. 80)
Greaney, William	1890	4 May	A	Birmingham Diocesan Archives
Greenhill, W. A.	1887	1 Mar	A	Oriel (The *Academy*, Vol. 38, No. 9561 (30 Aug 1890), p. 174)
Grosart, A. B.	1889	26 Dec	C	
Hardman, John, Junior	1885	end of year	A	Sister Mary Teresa Hardman
	1886	16 Nov	A	Sister Mary Teresa Hardman *Ad.* John Hardman Esqr/Hunter's Lane/Handsworth/Birmingham
Harris, Henry	1887	23 May	C	
Head, H. H.	1885	13 June	A	Dinand Library, Holy Cross College, Worcester, Mass.
Hecker, Isaac Thomas	1888	22 Jan	D	
Hennin, Bernard	1885	24 Feb	C	
Herbert of Lea, Lady	1886	1 Feb	A	
Hewit, Augustine Francis	1889	28 Feb	A	Paulist Fathers Archives, New York (*Ward* II, p. 535)
	1890	15 Mar	A	Paulist Fathers Archives, New York
Higgins, John	1888	13 May	D	
Hope, C. H.	1887	26 Mar	D	
Hope, Josephine	1887	21 June	A	The late Mrs Sheed (*Ward* II, pp. 528–9; Maisie Ward, *The Wilfrid Wards and the Transition*, pp. 152–3)
		28 Sept	A	The late Mrs Sheed
Hopkins, Gerard Manley	1885	27 Feb	A	Campion Hall, Oxford
	1886	25 Feb	A	Campion Hall, Oxford (C. C. Abbott, *Further Letters of Gerard Manley Hopkins*, second edition, London 1956, p. 413) *Ad.* The Rev Fr Hopkins S J/University College/ Stephen's Green/Dublin
	1887	3 Mar	A	Campion Hall, Oxford (C. C. Abbott, op. cit., pp. 313–14; *Ward* II, p. 527)
	1888	22 Feb	A	Campion Hall, Oxford (C. C. Abbot, op. cit., p. 414) *Ad.* Revd Fr. G. M. Hopkins/University College/Stephens Green·/Dublin
Hubbard, John Gellibrand	1887	3 Jan	D	

Correspondent	Year	Date	Source	Location, Owner, Address
Hunter, Sylvester, S. J.	1886	6 Oct	A	Stonyhurst College
Hutton, Richard Holt	1886	1 Mar	C	
		15 Mar	C	
Ilsley, Edward, Bishop of	1888	19 Mar	A	Birmingham Diocesan Archives
of Birmingham				
		5 May	A	Oscott
	1890	15 Mar	A	Birmingham Diocesan Archives
		17 Mar	C	
James, Margaret Ellen	1885	30 May	C	
Jenkins, Robert	1885	25 Aug	C	
Charles				
	1888	26 Feb	C	
		7 June	A	
Jeremy, Walter David	1887	27 Nov	A	Yale University
Jordan, Dr Robert	1889	Dec	D	
Kavanagh, James	1885	26 Jan	D	
Blake				
Keating, W. H.	1885	13 Jan	C	
		13 July	A	
Keon, Mrs	1886	9 Aug	C	
Kerr, Henry Schomberg	1889	29 May	A	
		31 May	A	
Kerr, William Hobart,	1886	14 May	D	
S.J.				
Knight, William	1887	7 Jan	A	Pierpont Morgan Library (William Knight, *Principal Shairp and his Friends*, London 1888, p. 387)
		20 Oct	D	Pierpont Morgan Library
		28 Oct	A	Peirpont Morgan Library
		3 Nov	A	Pierpont Morgan Library
		16 Nov	A	Pierpont Morgan Library
		19 Nov	A	Pierpont Morgan Library
		1 Dec	A	Pierpont Morgan Library
	1890	26 May	A	Pierpont Morgan Library
Langford, Mrs William	1890	2 Aug	C	
La Serre, H.	1886	30 May	C	
Lee, Ambrose	1889	5 May	A	Mrs Bond *Ad.* Ambrose Lee Esqr/9 Elm Place/South Kensington
		8 July	A	Mrs Bond *Ad.* Ambrose Lee Esqr/ Church of the Holy Trinity/ Lambeth
Lee, Frederick George	1887	11 Mar	A	Mrs Bond *Ad.* The Rev Dr Lee/ All Saints Church/Lambeth/London
		17 Oct	A	Mrs Bond *Ad.* The Revd Dr Lee/ Allsaints Vicarage/Lambeth/London S E.
Lee, Mrs Frederick	1888	15 May	A	Mrs Bond
George				
		16 May	A	Mrs Bond
		2 June	A	Mrs Bond
Legg, John Wickham	1885	20 Oct	A	Winchester Cathedral Library *Ad.* J. Wickham Legg Esqr/47 Green Street/Park Lane/London
Leo XIII	1887	15 May	D	
		25 Nov	D	
	1888	25 Nov	D	(three)
Liddon, H. P.	1885	26 June	A	Keble *Ad.* The Rev/Canon Liddon/ Amen Passage/Pater Noster/St Paul's/London E C
		20 Nov	A	Keble *Ad.* The Rev Canon Liddon/ Ch Ch/Oxford
		23 Nov	A	Keble *Ad.* The Rev Canon Liddon/ Ch Ch/Oxford

Correspondent	Year	Date	Source	Location, Owner, Address
	1886	18 Sept	A	Keble
		22 Sept (I)	A	Keble *Ad.* The Very Revd. Canon Liddon/Culdees/Muthill/Perthshire N. B
		22 Sept (II)	A	*Ad.* the same
	1887	23 Feb	A	Keble *Ad.* The Rev Canon Liddon/ Ch Ch/Oxford
		18 April	A	Keble *Ad.* The Rev/Canon Liddon/ Amen Buildings/St Paul's/London E. C.
		27 May	A	Keble *Ad.* The Rev./Canon Liddon/ Ch Ch/Oxford
		3 July	A	Keble *Ad.* The Rev. Canon Liddon/Ch Ch/Oxford
	1888	22 Feb	A	Keble *Ad.* The Revd Canon Liddon D D/Christ Church/Oxford
		22 April	A	Keble *Ad.* Revd Canon Liddon/ 3 Amen Court/St Paul's/London E. C.
		14 Dec	A	Keble *Ad.* Revd Canon Liddon/ Amen Court/London E. C.
	1890	21 Feb	A	Keble
Lilly, W. S.	1885	7 Jan	A	Cashel Archdiocese Archives
	1886	15 May	Pr	The *Fortnightly Review* (Sept 1890), p. 436
	1887		Pr	The *Fortnightly Review* (Sept 1890), pp. 436–7
	1889	Sept	Pr	The *Fortnightly Review* (Sept 1890), p. 437
Livius, Thomas	1885	11 Mar	A	Oriel
		21 April	A D	Oriel
		30 April	A	Oriel
		7 May	A	Oriel
		12 May	A	Oriel
		15 May	A	Oriel
		10 June	A	Oriel
		21 June	A	Oriel
		5 July	A	Oriel
	1888	10 Mar	A	Oriel
		11 April	A	Oriel
Lockhart, William	1888	25 Mar	A	Rosminian Archives, Wonersh
Longman, Charles James	1885	8 Jan	D	
		10 Jan	D	
		15 Jan	D	
		20 Jan	D	
		24 Jan	D	
		27 Jan	D	
		31 Jan	D	
		3 Feb (I)	D	
		3 Feb (II)	D	
		11 Feb (I)	D	
		11 Feb (II)	D	
		13 Feb	D	
		14 Feb	D	
		21 Feb	D	
		25 Feb	D	
	1886	8 May	D	
		21 July	D	
		25 Aug	D	
	1887	2 July	D	
		18 Dec	C	
	1888	5 Sept	C	
Lorain, Charles	1887	24 Mar	C	
Loyola, Mother Mary	1887	4 Oct	A	

Correspondent	Year	Date	Source	Location, Owner, Address
MacColl, Malcolm	1887	27 April	C	(*Malcolm MacColl Memoirs and Correspondence*, edited by G. W. E. Russell, London 1914, p. 307)
		11 May	A	Scottish Record Office
	1889	29 Dec	C	
	1890	16 Jan	C	(op. cit., p. 308)
McCorry, Joseph	1886	8 Mar	D	
McGedy, Frank	1888	20 Nov	A	Frank McGeady Esqre/Secretary of the/Law Union Insurance Cy/ 126 Chancery Lane/London W C.
McLaughlin, John	1887	12 Aug	C	
MacVeagh, Jeremiah	1887	16 Mar	C	
			D	
Magee, Reginald	1885	28 Oct	C	
Manning, Cardinal	1887	4 July	C	
Marson, Charles Latimer	1886	3 June	A	(Maurice B. Reckitt, *For Christ and the People*, London 1963, p. 98)
Martin, Lady	1890	14 May	C	
Martineau, Thomas	1885	9 Nov	D	
		10 Nov	D	
Maxwell-Scott, Hon. Mrs	1885	16 Nov	A	Abbotsford
	1887	19 Feb	A	Abbotsford
		27 Feb	A	Abbotsford *Ad.* The Hon/Mrs Maxwell Scott/Abbotsford/Melrose/N B
		28 Feb	A	Abbotsford *Ad.* The Honble Mrs Maxwell-Scott / Abbotsford / Melrose/N.B.
		2 Mar	A	Abbotsford *Ad.* The Hon Mrs Maxwell Scott/Abbotsford/Melrose /N.B.
		8 April	A	Abbotsford *Ad.* The Hon./Mrs Maxwell Scott/Abbotsford/Melrose/N B
	1888	18 April	A	Abbotsford
Metcalfe, John Henry	1885	16 Dec	A	Lond. Vol. 10
Meynell, Wilfrid	1885	20 Sept	D	
		28 Oct	D	
Miles, Alfred Henry	1887	24 June	A	Newman Preparatory School, Boston
Mills, Richard	1885	14 Feb	D	
Mivart, St George Jackson	1885	10 Oct	C	
Monteith, Joseph	1885	18 Aug	A	Major J. B. Monteith
Moore, G. Washington	1887	23 July	A	*Ad.* G Washington Moore Esq/ 16 New Burlington Street/London W
Morris, Charles Smyth	1885	4 Jan	A	
Morton, Thomas William, S.J.	1886	24 Feb	C	
Mozley, Anne	1885	14 Jan	A	Oriel
		16 Jan	A	Oriel
		26 Jan	A	Oriel
		10 Feb	A	Oriel
		19 Feb	A	Oriel
		26 Feb	A	Oriel
		3 Mar	A	Oriel
		13 Mar	A	
		16 Mar	A	
		18 Mar	A	
			D	
		20 Mar	A	Oriel
		22 Mar	A	
		24 Mar	A	
		30 Mar	A	

Correspondent	Year	Date	Source	Location, Owner, Address
		7 April	A	
		28 April	A	Oriel
		29 April	A	Oriel
		3 May	A	
		15 May	A	
		21 May	A	
		27 May	A	
		7 Sept	A	
		14 Sept	A	
		26 Oct	A	Rev. C. P. Spender
		1 Dec	A	
		3 Dec	A	
	1886	8 Feb	A	
		21 Sept	A	
		28 Nov	A	(*Moz.* I, pp. 17–18)
		10 Dec	A	Bodleian
	1889	13 Aug	A	
	1890	25 April	A	J. H. Mozley
Mozley, Fanny	1887	14 April	A	
		27 June	A	
Mozley, Francis Woodgate	1886	11 Jan	A	Grace Mozley
	1888	15 May (I)	A	Grace Mozley
		15 May (II)	A	Grace Mozley
Mozley, Jane	1885	27 Feb	A	A. C. Wood, Birmingham *Ad.* Miss Mozley/6 Lansdowne Road/Bedford
Mozley, John Rickards	1886	3 April	C	
Mozley, Mrs John Rickards	1887	1 Mar	A	Bodleian
Muirhead, James Patrick	1887	11 Jan	D	
Murphy, Mary	1885	7 April	Ph	John Oldcastle, *Cardinal Newman,* fourth edition, London n. d., p. 65
Murray, John	1887	30 Nov	C	
		2 Dec	C	
Newdigate, Alfred	1886	1 Aug	A	Mrs Newdigate
			D	
		31 Aug	A	Mrs Newdigate
		21 Sept	A	Mrs Newdigate
		29 Sept	A	Mrs Newdigate
		4 Oct	A	Mrs Newdigate
		12 Oct	A	Mrs Newdigate
		4 Nov	A	Mrs Newdigate
	1887	4 Mar	A	Mrs Newdigate
		14 April	A	Mrs Newdigate
			D	
		26 April	A	Mrs Newdigate
		9 Dec	A	Mrs Newdigate
Norfolk, Duke of	1885	6 April	A	The Duke of Norfolk
	1886	14 April	A	The Duke of Norfolk
			D	
	1887	10 Jan	A	The Duke of Norfolk
		14 Jan	A	The Duke of Norfolk
		17 Jan	A	The Duke of Norfolk
		12 April	A	The Duke of Norfolk
Northcote, J. Spencer	1885	2 Nov	A	Stoke
		18 Feb	C	
	1886	1 June	A	Stoke
		2 June	A	Stoke (*Butler* II, pp. 276–7; the *Oscotian* (1886), p. 61)
			D	
Oakley, John	1888	11 April	D	
Oates, Wilfrid	1885	17 Jan	D	
		8 Feb	D	
		15 Feb	D	

Correspondent	Year	Date	Source	Location, Owner, Address
		10 April	D	
	1888	26 Sept	C	
O'Bryen, Henry	1886	30 June	A	Catholic Presbytery, Corby Glen Lincs.
O'Conor, J. F. X., S.J.	1885	31 July	A	Georgetown
O'Hagan, John	1885	27 Dec	A	S.J. Dublin
Osborne, R. B. Godolphin	1887	24 June	C	
		24 July	C	
Ogle, John William	1885	4 Mar	A	Wellcome Institute Library
	1887	12 Aug	A	Wellcome Institute Library
Palgrave, Francis Turner	1885	11 Dec	C	
	1887	18 Jan	C	
	1887	18 Jan	C	
	1888	16 Oct	C	(G. F. Palgrave, *Francis Turner Palgrave*, London 1899, p. 211)
Palmer, Roundell, Earl of Selborne	1887	18 Nov	A	Lambeth Palace Library
Panton, Miss	1885	end of year	D	
Parocchi, Cardinal	1889	2 Oct	A	Archives of Vicariato, Rome (Urban Young, *Life and Letters of the Venerable Father Dominic*, London 1926, pp. 261–2)
Patterson, John Laird	1888	6 Feb	D	
Percival, John	1885	18 May (I)	A	Trinity
			D	
		18 May (II)	A	Trinity (*Ward* II, p. 525; *Newman and Bloxam*, p. 246)
Perraud, Adolphe, Bishop of Autun	1887	3 Dec	A	Archives of the French Oratory
Phelps, Hubert Hunter	1890	23 Mar	C	
Plummer, Alfred	1885	27 Feb	A	Pusey (Frank Leslie Cross, *John Henry Newman*, London 1933, pp. 181–2) *Ad.* The Rev. Dr Plummer/University/Durham
	1886	26 April	A	Pusey *Ad.* The Rev/Dr Plummer/University College/Durham
		29 April	A	Pusey *Ad.* The Rev Dr Plummer/University College/Durham
	1887	23 Feb	A	Pusey *Ad.* The Very Rev/Dr Plummer/The Castle/Durham
	1888	1 July	A	Pusey (F. L. Cross, op. cit., p. 182) *Ad.* The Revd Dr Plummer/The University College/Durham
Plumptre, Edward Hayes	1886	30 May	C	
		17 Nov	C	
	1889	6 April	C	
	1890	29 Jan	C	
		April or May	C	
Pollen, John Hungerford	1885	6 May	C	(Anne Pollen, *John Hungerford Pollen*, London 1912, p. 343; *Ward* II, pp. 524–5)
	1887	27 Aug	C	
Pollen, Mrs John Hungerford	1888	1 Feb	C	
Rampolla, Cardinal	1887	2 Aug	D	
Reeve, A.	1886	8 Nov	C	
Renouf, Peter le Page	1886	27 Mar	A	Pembroke (*D R* (1955), p. 456) *Ad.* P. le Page Renouf Esqr/46 Roland Gardens/South Kensington/London S W
Rivington, Francis	1890	2 June	D	
Rivington, W. J.	1888	25 Nov	A	
Robarts, Charles Nathaniel	1886	22 June	D	

Correspondent	Year	Date	Source	Location, Owner, Address
Rosebery, Earl of	1890	24 June	C	
Ryan, P. J., Archbishop of Philadelphia	1886	17 Feb	A	Historical Society of Philadelphia
Ryder, Charles	1885	4 Mar	A	*Ad.* The Rev C. E. Ryder/Catholic Church/Smethwick
		20 Mar	A	*Ad.* The Rev Charles Ryder/ Catholic Church/Smethwick/Birmingham
		23 Mar	A	*Ad.* The Rev C. E. Ryder/Catholic Church/Smethwick/Birmingham
Ryder, Henry Ignatius Dudley	1889	8 Jan	A	
Scratton, Thomas	1885	5 Nov	A	S.J. Dublin *Ad.* Thos Scratton Esqr/84 Stephen's Green S/Dublin
Secretary of the Catholic Young Men's Society	1885	28 July	Pr	*Report of the General Conference* at Edinburgh 1885, p. 40
	1886	2 Aug	Pr	*Report of the General Conference* at Dumfries, 1886, p. 77
	1887	July	Pr	*Birmingham Daily Post*
	1890	31 July	C	
Sheridan, Philip	1885	7 Jan	D	
Simeon, Lady	1885	1 Jan	C	
		8 Feb	C	
		22 July	C	
		21 Dec	C	
		24 Dec	C	
	1886	29 April	C	
		4 May	C	
		5 July	C	
		7 July	C	
		18 Nov	C	
	1887	24 Feb	C	
		27 July	C	
	1890	20 July	C	
Sinker, Robert	1887	6 Oct	A	*Ad.* Professor Sinker/Trinity College/Cambridge [readdressed] 10 Causeway
Smyth, Miss Laura	1886	22 July	D	
Snead-Cox, J. G.	1885	9 Sept	D	
		17 Oct	D	(two)
		20 Oct	D	
	1887	27 April	Pr	W. P. Neville [unpublished] *Notes on Cardinal Newman's Later Years*, p. 12 (The *Athenaeum* (23 Aug 1890), p. 258)
Stafford, L. J.	1887	14 July	A	University College, Dublin
Stanton, Richard	1885	6 Dec	A	(*Trevor* II, p. 629)
		4 Oct	A	
Stonor, Edmund	1885	13 April	A	Rev. H. Keldany
	1886	26 Nov	D	
		4 Dec	A	
	1887	13 Dec	A	Rev. H. Keldany
	1889	end of Nov	D	
	1890	8 May	C	
Spurrier, Alfred Henry	1886	11 Dec	Pr	*Ward* II, p. 526
Stewart, Charles J.	1886	15 Mar	C	
Stewart, James	1885	25 Jan	A	M. A. Bryne, Exeter College, Oxford
	1886	12 May	C	
Stricland, Paul	1887	26 May	C	
Sullivan, Mrs Timothy	1886	30 Oct	A	Mrs Sullivan, Dublin
Superior of the Visitation Convent, Autun	1885	15 Dec	D	
Sykes, Mrs	1890	22 Mar	C	

Correspondent	Year	Date	Source	Location, Owner, Address
Taylor, Fanny Margaret	1885	28 Feb	A	Maryfield Convent, Roehampton *Ad.* Miss Taylor/The Convent/ Brentford/Middx
Taylor, Felix	1887	20 May	A	Manchester College, Oxford *Ad.* Professor Felix Taylor/Manchester New College/London W C
Teeling, George	1885	3 Feb	A	Fort Augustus Abbey
Tew, Edmund Lawrence Hemstead	1887	24 Sept	A	Pusey
Thynne, Lord Charles	1885	1 Nov	C	
		10 Dec	C	
	1886	21 Dec	C	
	1887	28 Feb	C	
	1890	10 Mar	C	
Todd, Jane	1887	8 Dec	A	
Trevelyan, Edwin	1885	24 Oct	A	
Tyndall, Emma	1886	28 Nov	A	Dinand Library, Holy Cross College, Worcester, Mass.
Ullathorne, Bishop	1885	23 Mar	A	
	1886	1 Sept	Pr	*Letters of Bishop Ullathorne*, London n.d. [1892] pp. 482–3 (*Butler* II, p. 278; H. Tristram, *Newman and his Friends*, London 1933, p. 142)
	1887	8 May	A	
		23 May	A	
		23 June	A	
		11 Aug	A	
	1888	18 May	A	
Unknown Correspondents	1885	6 April	A	
		12 April	C	
		16 Dec	A	Newman Preparatory School, Boston
		end of year	D	
		end of year	Pr	The *Weekly Register* (16 Aug 1890), p. 212
	1886	26 Mar	A	Lond.
		31 Aug	A	Philip Reidy, Worcester, Mass.
		7 Dec	A	Georgetown
	1887	20 May	A	Regis College, Weston, Mass.
		30 Aug	A	(*The Philosophical Notebook of John Henry Newman*, Louvain 1970, p. 197)
	1888	12 May	D	
		29 Oct	A	Thomas Donnellan
	1889	21 June	A	
Walford, John Thomas, S.J.	1889	17 Jan	A	Stonyhurst College
		11 July	A	
Ward, F. R.	1890	14 May	C	
Ward, Mrs Richard	1885	4 Jan	A	
Ward, Wilfrid	1885	16 Mar	A	The late Mrs Sheed
		21 Mar	A	The late Mrs Sheed
	1886	5 April	C	
		21 June	A	The late Mrs Sheed
		23 June	A	The late Mrs Sheed
		27 June	A	The late Mrs Sheed
	1887	18 April	D	
		17 June	A	The late Mrs Sheed
		4 July	A	The late Mrs Sheed
		11 July	A	The late Mrs Sheed
		28 Sept	A	The late Mrs Sheed (*Ward* II, p. 529; Maisie Ward, *The Wilfrid Wards and the Transition*, I, London 1934, p. 153)

Correspondent	Year	Date	Source	Location, Owner, Address
	1888	27 Mar	A	The late Mrs Sheed
	1889	7 Jan	A	The late Mrs Sheed
		25 May	A	The late Mrs Sheed
Warren, T. Herbert	1886	28 May	A	Magd. (*Newman and Bloxam* p. 226)
Watt, Mrs F. J.	1885	22 July	C	
	1886	7 June	C	
	1887	23 Feb	C	
Waugh, John	1885	24 Mar	C	
Wegg-Prosser, Francis Richard	1887	24 Feb	A	Wegg-Prosser Papers, Maryhill House, Belmont, Hereford
Wenham, J. G.	1886	23 June	A	St Edmund's College, Ware
Whitley, Mrs Lucy	1890	17 June	C	
Whitty, Robert, S.J.	1886	17 May	A	S.J. Lond.
		3 June	A	S.J. Lond.
Whyte, Alexander	1885	31 Dec	A	New College, The Mound, Edinburgh (G. F. Barbour, *Life of Alexander Whyte*, eighth edition London 1925, p. 248) *Ad.* The Rev. Dr Whyte/52 Melville Street/ Edinburgh
Wilberforce, Henry Edward	1885	18 Feb	A	Ushaw
Wilberforce, Wilfrid	1885	19 Feb	A	Pusey *Ad.* Wilfrid Wilberforce/ 21 Brunswick Gardens/Kensington /London W
		9 June	A	
	1886	2 April	C	
			D	
Wilson, Mrs	1885	5 Feb	C	
Wilson, Robert James	1890	19 May	C	
Wolseley, Mrs	1885	19 June	A	
Wood, Alexander	1885	10 Oct	D	
Wood, Charles Lindley, Viscount Halifax	1886	15 Jan	A	Hinckleton Papers
Wood, W.	1890	8 June	C	
Woodgate, Henrietta	1886	23 Jan	A	Pusey *Ad.* Miss Woodgate/The Chase/Worcester Road/Malvern
		4 Oct	A	Pusey *Ad.* Miss Woodgate/The Chase/Worcester Rd/Malvern
	1887	6 June	A	Pusey *Ad.* Miss Woodgate/St John's Lodge/Crawthorne/Berks
	1888	1 May	A	Pusey
Woodlock, Bartholomew Bishop of Ardagh	1886	25 Oct	C	
		19 Dec	A	Georgetown
	1887	28 Feb	A	Georgetown
	1890	23 Mar	A	Georgetown (not seen)
			C	
Woods, Henry George	1887	16 May	A	Trinity
	1888	9 May	A	Trinity
Wright, Edward Perceval	1886	12 April	A	Dr Donald F. Winslow, Philadelphia Divinity School
Wright, H. W.	1885	23 Jan	A	Ferryhill North Church, Aberdeen
Yates, W. J. Haydon	1890	15 May	C	

MEMORANDA, ETC

Date		Source	Subject
1887	25 Mar	C	On Secrecy in Voting
	11 Sept	A	Note to Memorandum of 4 December 1881
1889	Dec	C	St Philip's Grammar School

LETTERS TO NEWMAN

		From	Inserted before Newman's of
1890	7 June	W. Wood	8 June

Index of Persons and Places

The index to Volume XXI contains notices of almost all the persons who occur in that volume, and the indexes to subsequent volumes notices of those who occur in them for the first time. These are not repeated, and so, for persons and places already mentioned in those volumes, reference back is here made by a (XXI) or (XXII) etc. inserted after such names.

References are given in the case of persons mentioned for the first time in this volume, to *The Dictionary of National Biography* or *The Dictionary of American Biography*, and failing them, to Frederick Boase, *Modern English Biography*, or Joseph Gillow, *Bibliographical Dictionary* of the English Catholics; also occasionally to other printed works. Much of the information is derived from the correspondence and other material in the archives of the Birmingham Oratory, and from various private sources.

SUPPLEMENT

Letters Found Too Late for Inclusion in Volumes XI–XXX

TO FREDERICK CHARLES HUSENBETH

Temple. London. November 20/45

My dear Sir,

I have been waiting several days before writing, wishing to be the first to communicate to you the intelligence about which your letter inquired, viz the reception of Mr F. W. Faber; when I found that his reception had taken place at Northampton, and that you would know of it as soon as any one.

It cannot be doubted that books so well known as your own must have had, and have, an important influence on the minds of religious persons who are external to the Church; and what you say of them does not surprise me.[1] But one of the most remarkable peculiarities and evidences of Catholicism is the variety of methods by which persons are led to it. As some are led by argument, so others by imagination, others by remorse and unrest. As far as I have means of knowing, none of these means have been primary in the Oxford movement — which has been a sort of quiet growth, and a dawning of light, in the soul — aided of course by external means, but not strictly referrible to them. And at this moment I think I see various persons who are (humanly speaking) sure to join the Church ultimately, but 'the times and seasons' are as much beyond human calculation, as that great Event of which Scripture thus speaks, or as the course of the wind which blows as it listeth.[2] It seems impossible to hurry them any more than hurry the growth of plants or children — one can but help and forward them, and watch opportunities.

I hope I am saying nothing wrong in the way of doctrine or opinion, for I feel I have a great deal to learn

I am, my dear Sir, Very sincerely Yours,
John H Newman

TO WILLIAM SANCROFT HOLMES[3]

Littlemore. December 5. 1845

My dear Sir,

I have been moving about till now, or you should have heard from me before this.

[1] When inquiring on 7 Nov. whether F.W. Faber was likely to become a Catholic, Husenbeth wrote that he admired his *Life of St Wilfrid*, and had published polemical works against his uncle G.S. Faber, adding: 'I have had the happiness to be assured by some of the converted clergy that my books against Faber had, under God's blessing, much forwarded their determination'.

[2] *Acts*, 1:7; *John*, 3:8.

[3] William Sancroft Holmes (1815–49), elder son of the Rev. John Holmes, of Gawdy Hall, Harleston, Norfolk, and of his wife Anne, daughter of W. Whitear, Rector of Ore, Hastings, was at Harrow School and Emmanuel College, Cambridge, Scholar 1835, B.A. 1839, M.A. 1842. In 1840 he married Hester Elizabeth, daughter of Davies Gilbert, M.P., of Eastbourne. Holmes was a J.P. and D.L. for Norfolk.

You speak as if I had given the world no warning of what was likely to happen to me; whereas in various ways for four years past I have shown that I could not hold the Anglican theory of Christianity. It is now above a year since my intention of joining the Church of Rome has been spoken of confidently by friends and foes without any denial from me.

You are mistaken in saying I have been rebaptized. Rebaptization is a sacrilege. If my former baptism in infancy was good which I believe it to have been, the water poured on me the other day was a mere empty form, without more efficacy in it than in my washing my face of a morning. So it was expressed by the administrator, for he said 'Si *non* es baptizatus, ego te baptizo —' The Church of Rome has not that confidence in Anglican baptisms, to dispense with this precaution, on the *chance* of baptism having been incorrectly performed in particular instances — and I confess that the *present* modes of baptizing in the English Church are fearfully dangerous. I fear that vast multitudes of children at this time are not baptized, though their parents think that they are.

I do trust that a person so religious, as your letter shows you to be, so munificent in your offerings to the Church, so catholicly minded, will be led on as others have been, however unworthy, to the full truth and the whole counsel of God[1] as revealed by His Son and lodged in His Church. Then all this bitter feeling will have been the means of inestimable good, and in you, as in other others whom at present you are shocked at, will be fulfilled the words, 'They that sow in tears, shall reap in joy.'[2]

If at any time I can be of service to you in reference to this great object, (as I have, according to your kind statement, been already of use to you,) pray enable me to be so

I am, My dear Sir, Yours faithfully John H Newman

TO THE ABBÉ JAGER

[1846?]

M. l'Abbe,

It was a great gratification to me to find you had done the authors of the Lives of St Stephen and St Wilfrid the honor of translating their works into French.[3] They form part of a projected series of Lives of English Saints, of which I was to have been Editor. This accounts for my initials appearing at the end of the Advertisement of St Stephen. The author of the former of the two Lives is M. Dalgairns, and of the latter M. Faber, both members of the University of Oxford, and friends of my own, and recent converts to the Catholic Church. M. Faber, the author of St Wilfrid gained the honours of his University and is distinguished for his poetical compositions: M. Dalgairns the

---

[1] *Acts* 20:27.
[2] *Psalm* 126:5.
[3] *Life of St Stephen Harding* and *The Life of St Wilfrid* were published in 1844

author of St Stephen was my first companion at Littlemore, and after living with me for three years and a half, applied to F. Dominic the Passionist for admission into the Church, brought him to me, and then proceeded to your own country to study with the hope of admission into holy orders.

And now M. L'abbe, you will see that though I am not the writer of the works in question, I am too nearly concerned with them to make it modest in me to praise – Else I would say how high they, as well as their authors, stand in my estimation and how great a benefit may be expected to follow from their extended circulation.

TO GEORGE TALBOT[1]

Littlemore Febr 5. 1846

My dear Talbot,

I am going to try your patience, as you kindly let me; and, as I write in a hurry, I hope I shall not be unintelligible as well as troublesome.

1. St John and perhaps Penny propose to make their appearance at the *New* College on Tuesday or Wednesday. 2. The books are to arrive at the Old College on Wednesday — please to order two rooms, viz the boys' play room (the large square room with a brick floor) and the Refectory to be carefully swept out for the purpose of receiving them. They will be unpacked all in one day, viz Thursday, as the boxes are to go back forthwith for a second load, and the books will be deposited on the floor of the two rooms, *on* the paper in which they are packed. St John, Penny and Morris will superintend the operation. 3. I conclude from what Morris tells me that the workmen are out of the house, and the smell of the paint is the sole remaining impediment to entering it. Will you then order at once 2 bottles of chloride of lime, and let it be put in open vessels in the rooms? 4 Will you order fires in *five* rooms, viz the Infirmary as it used to be, in the two rooms (next each other) on the same floor as the Infirmary and on the other (the right hand) side of the gallery and in the two rooms in which the books are to be unpacked, to begin on next Tuesday. 5. If there are coals enough to last 10 days, well — if not, will you order in a load (5 ton?) of coals 6. Will you ascertain and send me word at once the *hour* of Dr Acquaroni's Mass? as our day's arrangements will depend upon the hour, and we should like to know before St John leaves us. If you wish privately to know we should *prefer* it to be not later than seven; but do not let us interfere with Dr A's convenience or wishes.

I do not expect to get off till a day or so before Ash Wednesday at earliest.

We are very much concerned to hear from Mr Spencer of Dr Wiseman's indisposition — You may think how anxious it has made us. Do let us know something about him

Yours most sincerely John H Newman

[1] This letter has already been printed, from the draft.

TO EDWARD HEALY THOMPSON

Maryvale, ⟨(Old Oscott)⟩ Birmingham April 8. 1846

My dear Sir,

Your intention, as communicated to me by Mr Badeley, has given me the greatest pleasure — pray let me be of any use to you, which is in my power, in facilitating the steps necessary for putting it into execution.[1] We have very little to offer you here besides an hearty welcome — but that you shall have, if you like to pay us a visit. We are only two miles from St Mary's Oscott — and you would find in Dr Wiseman one who would be kindly attentive to all your wishes.

I am, My dear Sir, Very truly Yours John H Newman

TO EDWARD HEALY THOMPSON

Maryvale, Perry Bar, Birmingham April 27. 1846

My dear Mr Thompson,

In case you should expect to hear from me before your promised visit, I write a line to say what pleasure it will give us, as the time draws near which you named. I wish I could give you a more easy direction for finding this place, than telling you to take a fly at the Birmingham station — but at present we are in a very unformed state, and not the least as regards communication for letters, parcels, and persons with Birmingham. It is strange that we should be near such large masses of population, yet so entirely in the wilderness.

I shall read with great interest the MS you speak of, whether you send it by post or bring it with you[2]

Yours very truly John H Newman

TO JOHN BERRY WALFORD

Maryvale. April 29. 1846

My dear Sir,

We feel very much the kindness which has led to your wishing to join us here, but I do not think it an intention which it would be right to let you put in practice suddenly, as there are many reasons which must interfere in any case with such an arrangement. I need not trouble you with some of those which press most upon me, one of which I mentioned to Mr Lloyd, though I

---

[1] See letter of 5 April 1846 to Edward Badeley.
[2] See below, letter of 29 May 1846 to Thompson.

regret to say I expressed myself to him so imperfectly that he has not conveyed to you my meaning. Certainly I never meant to say that Dr Griffiths was the only obstacle to a person in your case coming here.[1]

I would propose you should come here to see us, if you would like to do so — but I am sorry to say I cannot do so just now, for we have not all our rooms furnished, and are expecting at this moment three or four guests. Should you in a little while hence be disengaged, and would honor us with a visit, it would give us great pleasure to see you

With Mr St John's kind remembrances,

I am, My dear Sir, Yours faithfully John H Newman

TO JOHN BERRY WALFORD

St Mary's Vale. Perry Bar Birmingham. May 28/46

My dear Mr Walford,

I wonder whether it would suit you to pay us the visit you kindly promised, at this time. Next week we are in retreat — and Lloyd too is away, but after the 7th there will be no obstacle on our part. I shall be very sorry if there is any on yours.[2]

With St John's best remembrances

I am, Very faithfully Yours John H Newman

TO EDWARD HEALY THOMPSON

Maryvale May 29/46

My dear Mr Thompson,

I thank you very much for your Pamphlet,[3] and am glad you see your plans more clearly before you than you did.

Do you know I am obliged to put you off on Wednesday? we are in retreat here from *Wednesday next till Saturday*, Dr Wiseman conducting it. You do not say when you leave this neighbourhood. I wish you may be able to come another day.

You ought to have some way of introducing your Pamphlet to the Universities etc. It is a difficulty at present.

Ever Yrs very sincerely John H Newman

---

[1] Walford had just become a Catholic. Thomas Griffiths was the Vicar Apostolic of the London District.
[2] See diary for 9 June 1846.
[3] *Remarks on Certain Anglican Theories of Unity*, London 1846. cf. letter of 14 July 1846 to J. M. Capes.

TO JOHN PARSONS

July 24. 1846.

My dear Mr Parsons,

I will beg you to give directions for the transference of the balance of my account, which is £303, 15. 5 to my account with the Birmingham Banking Company, (Agent Mr Beaumont) Bennetts Hill, Birmingham. A small balance has to be added to it from my Fund Account. And two sums have to be deducted for which I have given cheques though they have not been presented — one is for £11. 0. 4? drawn in favor of Mr Allen of Littlemore, the other for £39. 10. 6 drawn in favor of Mr Walsh, and in Mr Copeland's hands. These two sums I shall be obliged by your retaining at present and paying to the respective cheques.

I cannot close an account which I have had with the Old Bank for so many years, without expressing my thanks for the friendly attention which I have ever received from you, My dear Mr Parsons, and the other gentlemen of the firm, especially those, (some of them no more) towards whom I have had other relations besides that which occasions my present letter. With every best wish for the welfare of yourself and Mr Thomson, and all who are dear to you both, and with very kind and constant recollections of you all[1]

I am &c. J H N.

John Parsons Esqr

TO MRS JOHN MOZLEY[2]

St. Mary's Vale, Perry Bar, August 16, '46

My Very Dear Jemima,

I have ever been very ready to give you a full account of myself and my doings, but you have behaved towards me in a way which has been a virtual rejection of my offers.

It is now going on for three years since you knew of my extreme want of confidence in the English Church; and nearly from that time, or soon after, I said to you something like this: 'I do not want to discuss religious points with you — I wish simply, letting you have your opinion and keeping my own, to put you in possession of what I feel, and what I am doing, and to write easily to you, as if (as far as might be) there were no differences between us.'[3] One time I recollect, in 1844, thinking you cold, I remonstrated about it to John, saying I really could not tell you more about myself, if you responded so little.

---

[1] The Old Bank had been founded early in the century by Thomson and the father of John Parsons. It was in the High Street, Oxford, in Newman's parish of St Mary's.

[2] This letter has already been printed in note to that of 31 Oct. 1865 to Mrs John Mozley.

[3] cf. letters of 31 Aug. and 22 Sept. 1843 to Mrs John Mozley, *Moz.* II, pp. 421 and 424.

You replied by saying it was a mere accident.[1] This I refer to as showing the footing on which I all along wished to stand towards you.

But now after this what have you done? First of all, John, in spite of the above remonstrance, in answer to my question about his publishing my book, wrote me a letter, not merely declining it, but with such unnecessary harshness that, laden as I was with anxiety and with the effort to that work, so struck down my spirits on receiving it, that I could have gone to bed from very despair and grief. I walked out, instead of working, sick at heart, with hands hanging down and feeble knees. Job's comforter, he grounded his refusal mainly on a rumour (!) that my book was to be severe on the English Church, to which in matter of fact I had been tender even to the prejudice of my argument. It was conscientious in him, doubtless, but it was quitting that neutral ground which I had hoped to preserve between us, and taking a side and putting me on the other. I send that letter back to you, and never wish to see it again.

Then, when my great trial came, my own relations, and they only, were those who could find the heart, or the want of reverence, to write censoriously to me. Others, agreeing with me or not, thought that something was due to my long suffering; it was otherwise with those on whom I had nearer claims. You were their organ; for I will not believe of so gentle and kind a heart that all you said was your own. I will not believe that it was you, though it was your hand, in answer to my own affectionate and confidential letters of many months, that wrote to me in so cruel a way — that wrote, for instance, so prematurely about my remaining at Littlemore, as if it were modest or seemly in you to advise in a matter of detail one from whom you differed so widely in the greatest matters, or as if the World, which had parted company with me, had any claim to know my mind at once on a point of expedience.[2]

Such letters as these completely swept away that footing which for a year or two past I had been wishing to preserve with you. I could not press you further to what, perhaps, on a feeling of conscience, you rejected. Next, as if to show in a marked way your feeling against that footing, you kept silence about yourself and those about you. You went to the Isle of Wight; for five weeks I knew nothing of your movements. Dear Johnnie was burnt; I heard it first from the people at Littlemore.[3] Then after Frank's birth you kept silence for above two months.[4] Again, at Christmas I mentioned my intention of having called on my aunt in passing through Derby; your answer contained nothing which sounded like an encouragement to do so.[5]

Now, had my letters been full of controversial matter, there might have been an excuse for this; had I called on you to become a Catholic, you might fairly have retorted on me your protestation. But when I wanted simply to go

---

[1] Letter of 20 Nov. 1844, *Moz.* II, pp. 442–3.
[2] See letters of 9 and 14 Oct. 1845 to Mrs John Mozley.
[3] See letter of 10 May 1846 to Mrs J. W. Bowden.
[4] Francis Woodgate Newman was born on 5 April 1846
[5] see letter of 11 Jan. 1846 to Elizabeth Newman, and diary for 3 Sept. 1846.

on with you without controversy, and you on your part volunteered so high a tone towards me, and then on the back of it kept silence about yourself — of course, you had a right to do so, you might feel it a duty to do what no one else did, but — you cannot, my dear Jemima, be surprised that I should feel I could not, as I had forewarned you in 1844, go on telling you in an easy and familiar manner what concerned myself, as I could have wished to have done.

And now, my dearest Jemima, before answering me, do me the kindness to read over my letters to you from August, 1844, to Christmas last. It will not satisfy me that you verily wish to make matters up with me. I want you to feel that you have not been so kind and considerate as I have been. Better feel pain now than by and by.

Ever yours affectionately, John H. Newman.

P. S.   Your letter came this morning.

TO FREDERICK CHARLES HUSENBETH

St Mary's vale. Aug 30/46

My dear Sir

I do not like to leave England without sending you my farewell. It is my earnest hope, though going to Rome, that I may return soon. I think my place is here, as well as my home. But all these things are beyond us. Pray think of me sometimes, and give me the benefit of your prayers. I leave this place for good on Tuesday and am to cross the water on Saturday

Yours, My dear Sir, Very faithfully

John H Newman

P. S.   I thank you much for your kind present. I shall not forget Mrs Jones.[1]

TO EDWARD HEALY THOMPSON

(Private)   Collegio di Propaganda. Febr 3. 1847
My dear Thompson,

In the midst of your present troublesome occupation, in carrying your work against Allies through the Press[2] (for I have not heard that it is *yet out* — we have only been very glad to hear of the *announcement*) I am going to call off

---

[1] This was a lady who had long corresponded with Husenbeth and had become a Catholic but was persecuted by her husband in consequence.
[2] *The Unity of the Episcopate Considered, in Reply to the Work of The Rev. T. W. Allies, entitled, 'The Church of England cleared from the Charge of Schism . . .', London 1847.

your mind to another subject. Archbishop Polding (of Sidney) who is here, is very eager to establish a Missionary College for the Colonies in England. Meanwhile various persons, separate from each other, have wished to set up a College in which married converts could be Professors. There is more ability in the married converts, as a body, than in any set of recent Catholics, and the Church must not lose it. Before I left England, I heard a rumour about the likelihood of offering minor orders to them, which would place them in very much the same ecclesiastical situation as that in which most members of the Anglican Church regard their clergy.[1] Well, the plan is to have a College after the pattern of the Missionary College in which I am stationed myself here; viz a College of which the discipline is worked by resident Jesuits, and lectures given by non-resident professors — One of them here is actually a married man. The place, Leeds; because it is a Jesuit mission and for other reasons. (If you can get at Mr Haigh, the recent convert, I wish you would in confidence inform him of the plan.) Caswall and Simpson, who are here, are its immediate projectors. They have asked me to write to you, and to [T.W.] Marshall at Tours. What might not be done with a College worked by Jesuits, and lectured by you, Marshall, Northcote (who is also written to) Capes, Seager, and Caswall: — a large Church with many altars and masses as on the Continent, a thing unknown in an English mission — Directly a plan is *digested*, we should apply to Propaganda, which will be sure to take it up — but we must get up a plan *first*. Are you likely to be able to take part in it as a Professor? I hope so.

Yours very sincerely John H Newman

P. S.   St John desires his kind remembrances.

TO MRS LOCKHART

Mary vale. Perry Bar. Birmingham. Jan 12. 1848

My dear Mrs Lockhart,

I thank you with all my heart for your kind congratulations on my return, and all you say besides about me, and my words in time past, and your deeply interesting account of yourself. Indeed have you cause to bless the good Providence who has done all things so well for you, and, while He has led you to a sure resting place, has not sent you for it to a distance from William [Lockhart]. Give him my love, and beg him sometimes to think of us at Mass, as we will not forget to do for him.[2]

It will interest you to know, but don't tell it yet, that there is every probability of all Faber's party joining us, and becoming our novices. I hope I am

---

[1] See letters of 5 Aug. 1846 to Mrs J. W. Bowden and 10 Oct. 1850 to J. Spencer Northcote; also cf. that of 28 Nov. 1845 to James Hope.
All the names mentioned below are those of married clergymen who had become Catholics.
[2] Mrs Lockhart was trying her vocation in the convent of the Rosminian Order of Charity at Loughborough in Leicestershire. Her son was at the Rosminian mission at Shepshed.

not like David numbering the people, but, if all turns out as it promises, we shall soon count up as many as thirty. Dear Father Frederick [Bowles] has stayed behind at Rome for a while — but I hope will join us at Easter. At present I am here by myself, but am expecting two postulants hourly,[1] and perhaps some of our Fathers will come before the end of the week.

I hope we shall have a good deal of time to ourselves for the first year, though I dare say we shall do some little things at once. In course of time we shall form into distinct bodies and settle in distinct localities.

I have brought a brief with me from Rome, but at this moment am the only Oratorian in England. On the Conversion of St Paul, or on the Purification, I shall formally admit all my brethren.

Ever Your affectionate friend John H Newman

P. S.   Will you accept the inclosed, which has been blessed by the Holy Father?

TO MRS JOHN MOZLEY

Maryvale Febr 10 [1848]

My dear Jemima

Thank you for your kind invitation, which I gladly accept.

I have, I suppose, 20 odd miles to come in on Monday, and can't start from St Wilfrid's near Alton Towers, till after 10 perhaps — but I don't know — So the chance is, I don't get to Derby till 2. This being the state of the case, I suppose I could dine with you at your usual hour.[2]

Ever Yrs affectly John H Newman

TO WILLIAM COBB, S.J.

Maryvale. *Perry Bar* July 24/48

My dear Father Provincial,

Many thanks for your kind letter. I hardly knew that our proposal had reached you. I thought of making it, and got no good opportunity, and Dr Wiseman, I find, has kindly done it for me.[3]

Very gladly as I would do any thing I could to show my reverence and sympathy for the Society, our offer would have been an advantage to ourselves

---

[1] John and William Gordon.
[2] See diary for 14 Feb. 1848.
[3] For the proposal to lend St Wilfrid's, Cotton, to the Jesuits, see first note to letter of 20 Sept. 1848 to J. D. Dalgairns.

as well as to you, had it suited you — and this was one of the difficulties of making it. We should have been glad to *lend* Cotton Hall without any rent — but then, we know well we should have had the place well taken care of. It is a difficulty at present having so large an Establishment in the *country* — for you know Oratorians affect a Town life — What we shall do with it ultimately, we do not know; but at the moment we thought that getting the place for a while into good hands, would have postponed our difficulty.

I wish you had said something about the Father General's health — which must be much tried just now.[1] Pray ask him to have the charity to remember us sometimes in his prayers — and asking the same of yourself, I am,

My dear F. Provincial Very sincerely Yours in Xt

John H Newman Congr. Orat. Sac.

TO MONSIGNOR G. B. PALMA

Ex S. Maria in Valle Aug. 11. 1848[2]

Illustrmo at Colmo Domino Dño J. B. Canonico Palma &c &c

Litteras Tuas, Domine Illustrissime et Charissime, ut Tu volebas, sic ego amplexus sum, quasi ex Oraculo Vaticano prodierint; quanquam non ad fidem aut mores pertinuerunt illæ, sed ad res nostras et nostram agendi rationem. Neque iis quæ tam lucide explicasti, coactum obsequium exhibui: sed quod auctoritate tuâ ad me venit, id judicio meo et annorum usu jam mihi comprobatum fuerat.

Quòd si ad Excellentiam Tuam responsum hactenus non miserim, id ne tribuas negligentiæ meæ neve animo minus in Te grato; sed in causâ erat dubitatio in quam incidi, utrùm, in media hac rerum externarum perturbatione, illa quæ scripsissem ad Te aliquando essent perventura. Accedebat, quòd non erat in litteris Tuis, neque quod Tu à me respondendum proponeres neque quod ego à Te clarius prolatum desiderarem.

Quod ad nos attinet, firmissimam profecto spem habemus, fore, ut Congregatio nostra, temporis progressu, et stabilem in se formam, et locum suum inter Catholicos nostros obtineat. Fausta certè, opitulante Deo, non desunt auguria; neque est quod timeamus nisi animus noster imbecillis et exiguæ vires.

Tu vero, Domine Excellentissime, et nobis amicissime, qui in ipsâ Catholicitatis arce preces et sacrificia quotidie offers, ne sis immemor nostri, et præsertim humilitatis meæ.

Tui observantissimus et obsequentissimus

Ioannes H. M. Newman Congr. Orat. Sac.

---

[1] J. P. Roothaan was the General of the Jesuits, who were suffering from the revolutions of 1848.

[2] This letter has already been printed from Newman's draft. See notes there.

Maryvale Perry Bar Oct 12. 1848[1]

My dear Madam

The Catholic doctrine concerning Faith and Reason is this — that Reason proves that Catholicism *ought to* be believed, and that in that form it comes before the Will, which accepts it or rejects it, as moved by grace or not. Reason does not prove that Catholicism is *true*, as it proves mathematical propositions are true; but it proves that there is a *case* for it so strong that we see we ought to accept it. There may be many difficulties, which we cannot answer, but still we see on the whole that the grounds are sufficient for conviction. This is not the same thing *as* conviction. If conviction were unavoidable, we might be said to be *forced* to believe, as we are forced to confess that two sides of a triangle are greater than the third; but, while there is enough evidence for conviction, whether we *will* be convinced or not, rests with ourselves. This is what the Priest means, when, on being asked 'If a man has not evidence enough to *subdue* his reason, what is to make him believe?', he answers, 'His will.' And this is just our trial; and one man rejects what another accepts. On the contrary, were we *forced* to believe, as we are forced to believe mathematical conclusions, there would be no trial of our affections, nothing morally right in believing, or wrong in not believing.

The simple question then with you is, How [Have] you *sufficient grounds* for being convinced that the Catholic Church is from God? If you have, it is nothing to the purpose that you find it difficult to believe. Of course you do; for belief is a supernatural act; you must pray to God for the *will* to believe, and the will has the power to command the mind. *You can believe what you will*; the only question is whether your reason tells you you *ought* to believe, and I think it does.

I think it does; for consider, by way of contrast, whether you have any *comparable* grounds in behalf of any other religion. I am not arguing that *therefore* Catholicism is true; but merely I wish to illustrate to you what is *meant* by conviction. You seem to me to have a feeling towards Catholicism *different in kind* from any you entertain towards other religions. And I do not think you can be happy or have an easy conscience till you confess this in *act*, by becoming a Catholic. You *cannot* be a latitudinarian; I will not argue the matter with you, till I have cause to suppose it possible.

Nor is it any thing to you what God will do with others; to his own master he standeth or falleth. No one is a real heretic who is not *wilfully* so. I am ready to enlarge on this subject, if you wish me.

As to yourself, you are in a very critical state; your Lord is making trial of you, as when He was on earth. He calls and goes forward. He does not stay. I do not forget you at Mass, and I trust and am sure you will be led on with

[1] This letter has already been printed from Newman's draft. See the notes there.

14*

whatever trial and distress to do this great and necessary work, to lay hold of salvation now for the first and perhaps for the last time offered you. God has led you forward wonderfully; He has been so gracious with you that, instead of your starting forward in the first instance to follow your own will, He gave you grace to submit yourself to another, to submit to the direction of the holiest man you could find. He is now rewarding you for your corresponding so faithfully to His grace; He is showing you, that, useful as that honored and loved superior has been to you, he cannot be more to you than he is in himself, he cannot be your teacher in *the* faith, unless he were inspired, because he has never learned it. You are being led on from self discipline to knowledge; he has done his part, and hands you on; unwillingly indeed, but still he has but his measure, as we all have our own. Use him for what he was given for. If his teaching *is* correct, he is like St Paul, for from man he has not been taught it; nor do I think that he, or any other Anglo-Catholic, would submit to put down his entire creed in writing, and lay it before the world.

If, as I have said, those who believe have incidental difficulties in reason, in spite of their believing, and their merit arises out of this, you see what view I take of all you urge about what Catholics believe of the Blessed Virgin; — accept all this as the specific trial of your faith, and be sure that, when you are a Catholic, that very doctrine, which is now your burden, will become your reward. I never can think it right, any more than you, to separate the dry letter of the decrees of the Church from the existing belief of Catholics. The existing belief is the true comment upon the decree. You must hold *substantially* what St Alfonso holds; his words are *not* mere figures of rhetoric, though of course the expression of doctrine always does take a colour from nation, language, speaker etc. When we say that our Lady has the care of the goats, it cannot indeed be literally true, if by goats is meant the finally reprobate; but he means that, to those who are *all but* reprobate, or rather who *feel themselves* all but reprobates ⟨or who feel themselves reprobates⟩, Christ gives a last chance in the intercession of his Mother. As to her being the sole hope of sinners, this, I conceive, *is* literally true, *that is*, in the sense in which such words are commonly used. Thus the sole cause of our salvation is God, is Christ, is a certain illness or other providence, is baptism, is faith, is the Blessed Virgin, *in that sense in which she IS a cause*. In like manner our Lady has a delegated omnipotence *in her own sphere*, i.e. of *intercession*, as when Solomon said to his mother, 'Ask on, my mother, for I will not say thee nay.'[1] On the other hand, Esther was promised any thing from Ahasuerus, up to the *half* of his kingdom; i.e. she had, what may be called, a semi-omnipotence.[2] I will write more on this subject if necessary.

May God guide you forward is, My dear Madam, the fervent prayer of

Yours very sincerely John H Newman

[1] I *Kings*, 2:20.
[2] *Esther*, 5:3.

P. S.   Oct. 13. I do not see that any thing urged in the letter you send me touches on the view, which I took in my last, of gifts external to the Church.

First, however, I will make this remark on the instances of supposed miracles themselves. 'I know of a case in which a person, *having been solemnly warned against receiving Holy Communion* etc' The account of this comes from me. It was a frightful occurrence, but *I did not give ANY warning* to the person, having no cause whatever to do so. He was a person I did not like, and his death itself so far justified my dislike of him; but there is nothing *in the facts* to suggest a connexion between his death and the communicating, as a *warning* might connect them. As far as the facts go, his coming might be an expiring effort of grace. I mention this to show how narratives are (unconsciously) altered in passing from mouth to mouth. Perhaps this applies to some of the others.

Next as to the argument: — If a quasi miracle or apparent miracle is the sanction of an ordinance, why not of an individual? 'It is wholly different,' the letter says, 'to suppose that God gives a reward, e.g. to all earnest prayer, that faith, as such, has its degree of reward, and to suppose that He would countenance what would be a *delusion.*' Yet it is not less a delusion to believe in a self appointed preacher, than to believe in schismatical ordinance; if then a sensible inward benefit or an outward quasi-miracle does not guarantee the preacher, why should it the ordinance? There was Mr Bulteel at Oxford who seceded from the Establishment, about the year 1830, being a dissenter he went into the room of a person, who (if I recollect rightly) had long been confined to her bed and bade her get up and walk; and she did. Here, if I may use the words of the letter, Providence seemed to 'countenance a delusion'. Mr B spoke *in order* to effect a cure; the administration of the Lord's Supper, in the case of the lady in the small pox, was not so pointed an act; it was not an appeal to God; but Mr B. called on Him to pronounce in his favor by his very act. It was a challenge; as when Elijah said, 'Let it be known this day etc.' And the cure was sudden and complete, both maladies being, as the letter confesses of the small pox beyond the reach of medicine.

In the Christian Observer for Nov. 1830 you will find an account of the sudden recovery of Miss Fancourt, which avails similarly in the present argument. If it be objected, that it was intended and considered by the parties to be an answer to faith, still it was done by an individual, of particular views in religion, and was taken, I believe, to sanction his particular 'delusion.' — 'Do you believe that Jesus could heal you at this very time? Yes — Between these questions he was evidently engaged in prayer. Then he added, Get up and walk. He then laid hold of my hand' etc. p. 710.

There is another view that might be taken of some of these occurrences. You tell me that Dr Pusey suggests that your doubts about the Anglican Church 'come from Satan.' He precedes then and justifies me in the use of strong language. Now evil spirits cannot, strictly speaking, work miracles, but still the consolations which attend the Anglican Communion, may in some cases, (i.e. when used against the Church) without detracting from the religiousness of the individuals feeling them, be temptations, and come from Satan, as theologians actually do consider.

But further it is not the case, as is insisted on [in] your letter, that Anglicans *do* refer the grace they gain to the administration of the Lord's Supper. A small section may do so, but it is not the belief of the great body of the laity, no nor of the clergy. They impute the divine mercy to *faith*. This is a fact which no one can deny. 'When devotion increases among *us*, what is sought for is more frequent communion, and, in thousands of cases, the sacrament of absolution.' Thousands of cases surprises me; but were it so, what is this to the millions of the Church of England all over the earth through 300 years. In Wesley's time, which was a more remarkable revival than the present, sermons were every thing, sacraments nothing.

Did ever any *one whole* parish any where adopt the high Anglocatholic view? If not, what does the following passage mean? 'Unless we have sacraments, *all* would be *one great* fable and blasphemy; I cannot imagine any thing more frightful than that Priests should be giving and receiving absolution, *people* receiving *it* etc etc' That is, if a few learned persons rise up in an *existing* system, and preach a doctrine disowned by the mass of their brethren, it is blasphemy to suppose that God will not make his words good. Who bade them believe it? Rather, the argument may be retorted: — 'If the Church of England *has* the Sacrament of the Holy Eucharist, I cannot imagine any thing more frightful than priests consecrating and people receiving *who do not believe*; in the careless disposal of Christ's own flesh, the crumbs under which It lies left on the plate, the pieces suffered to fall about and kicked aside, the blood drunk as a refreshment or as a treat after the Service, or poured back into the bottle etc'. I might go on of course. And certainly it is an argument, which has for some time weighed on me, in corroboration of others more direct, in proof that the Anglican Church has not the Apostolic Succession.

But even had Anglicans the succession, and the power of consecration, you rightly observe that the miracle would only prove the Real Presence, not that the Anglican Church was not in schism. I do not recollect the profaneness of the Donatists to which the letter alludes.

JHN

(After Nov 1. my direction is St Wilfrid's Cheadle Staffordshire)

TO DAVID LEWIS

[1849?]

My dear Lewis,

This passage with the words I have put in, seems to me quite orthodox — but I am plagued, because I can't get a good and clear authority for using the words 'He who hath seen Me, hath seen the Father,' of our Lord's *human* nature.[1] Can you?

Ever Yrs, J H N.

TO WILLIAM HENRY COOMBES

St Wilfrid's, Cheadle
Jan 10. 1849

Revd Sir,

I hope I shall not be taking a liberty in asking of you the following favor — should you be unable to grant it, I shall cheerfully acquiesce in your inability to do so.

Our Congregation is about to take on itself the Series of Saints' lives sometime since commenced by Mr Faber; and one of the early Lives we propose to publish is that of St Francis de Sales by Marsollier.[2]

The favor we ask of you is to be allowed to avail ourselves of your Translation of it, instead of making a new one of our own. Besides the convenience, it would be a pleasure and honor to us to have in this way your name connected with our publication. However, there may be many reasons, of which we can know nothing, to render such an arrangement impracticable — at all events it will never be any regret to us to have attempted it, and thus to show our respect for a venerable priest who has lived through times when the Catholic Church had not the share of popularity and the hopeful prospects which she enjoys at present.

I am, Rev Sir, begging your good prayers, Yours very truly in Xt

John H Newman Congr. Or. Pres.[3]

TO ALEXANDER FULLERTON

Oratory, Birmingham, July 1. 1849[4]

My dear Mr Fullerton,

I am going to ask a favor and may be taking a liberty, but you will please tell me without ceremony, if I am — and will kindly think no more about it.

---

[1] *John*, 14:9. At this period, when he was assistant editor of the *Tablet*, David Lewis frequently consulted Newman.

[2] William Henry Coombes (1767–1850), one of the old Douay priests, who escaped to England in 1793, was from 1810 in charge of the mission at Shepton Mallet, until he retired to Downside in 1849. He translated Marsollier's *The Life of St Francis of Sales*, two volumes, Shepton Mallet 1812.

The *Life* eventually published in 1854 was a translation from the Italian of Pier Giacinto Gallitia.

[3] On 28 Feb. 1849 Newman wrote to one of the seven priests of the name Gillow, a letter sold at Christie's on 1 July 1970, 'I could not at the time make out whether you were one of the good Priests of the same name, whom I had the pleasure of seeing at Ushaw or elsewhere . . .'.

[4] This letter has already been printed, but from an incomplete copy.

By accident I have seen a copy of some Poems which Lady Georgiana has allowed to be circulated — articled "The Old Highlander and others;" and they interested me so much that I am led to ask you whether it is possible any where or any how to obtain a copy for myself.

Excuse the trouble of this question and believe me, My dear Mr Fullerton,

Very sincerely Yours in Xt

John H Newman Congr. Orat.

TO ABBÉ MOULINET, CURÉ OF POULAINES

[November 1849?][1]

Pater Reverende, et, perinde ut omnes Galliarum dignissimi sacerdotes, tenerrimo affectu à me prosequende,

Probè sacerdotem egisti tuæ gentis tam generosæ, tam benevolentis erga extraneos, tam charitate fervidæ. Ego profecto à tuis, tum quando regionem tuam, Romam ab Angliâ profectus, percurrebam, tum omni quidem tempore ea fraternitatis signa accepi, non pro dignitate accipientis sed ex plenissimo dantium amore præstita quorum numquam, Deo opitulante, sum obliturus. Faxit Deus ut nobilissima Ecclesia Galliarum in dies abundet magis in operibus illis ex quibus jam celebritatem habet et laudem omnium in orbe terrarum!

Jam vero, quod ad id attinet de quo me interrogas, Pater, vereor ut tibi possim satisfacere. Verissimum dixisti, mihi Romæ commoranti à gravissimis quibusdam viris esse suggestum, ut ad Anglicam Sacrarum Scripturarum versionem cogitationes meas converterem; at illud verum est quoque, id quod doleo maxime, eidem mihi, tot nascentis Congregationis nostræ curis et negotiis districto, tempus quo in tantum munus incumbam, nec vacare neque, ut puto, esse vacaturum.

Tu autem aliquando, Pater optime, memor sis humilitatis nostræ sive in missis celebrandis sive cùm Beatissimam Virginem Mariam adeas et credas me esse tibi charitate Catholicâ devinctissimum

J.H Newman

TO A RECENT CONVERT

Oratory Birmingham June 25/50

My dear[2]

I have thought often of your letter and you, though I wrote you so few lines. Now too I shall write few lines also, still I trust you will not refuse from

---

[1] Moulinet was the Curé of Poulaines, Valençay, near Tours. He wrote in Latin on 21 Nov., probably in 1849, to inquire whether the English translation of the Bible, which Newman was asked to make, when in Rome after becoming a Catholic, had been published. See letters of 10–11 Jan. 1847 to J. D. Dalgairns, and 17 Jan. 1847 to Bishop Wiseman.
[2] The name has been cut out.

me what comes from the true interest I feel in you, and my anxiety to hear about you. The first months of a convert's life are often trying amid their sweetness—for, as I have heard them say, they have both joys and sorrows they never had before. For me, so old a person cannot be supposed to have either— but so much I bear witness to, the trouble arising from the strangeness of a new position, and from a want of ascertaining what my own position exactly was. At first I was not clear that it was my duty to be a priest—and this trial, while the lot of only a few, was made heavier to me by various circumstances. And then when it was clear I was to be, it was very difficult to bring stiff old branches into a new form—and every successive step which was necessary for the end was, not a physical, but a parallel *mental* pain, though my will and desire was with the path chosen for me. And it was a trial to me going abroad, though I wished to go—indeed there was nothing which was not a burden. In a word, for this is the sum total of the whole—I was called into the Catholic Church, not for enjoyment simply, but for work also. And so, whom God calls, He calls in some way or other for service, for His glory;—and in time He makes His will clear to every one.

May you ever have the light and the comfort of His Grace, and the Sweetness of His Presence, and the protection of His Saints—and let me some-times have the pleasure of knowing you have it.

Ever Yours very sincerely in Xt

John H Newman Congr. Orat.

TO J. SPENCER NORTHCOTE

Oratory Birmingham July 19. 1850

My dear Northcote

It was a great pleasure to me to hear the news of your return, and after-wards to see your writing.

What F. Costa said was simply this: — that the Bishop of the place had made it excommunication for any one to enter the small Church, above Amalphi with any portion of the Holy Cross upon him — because the blood of St Pantaleone which is placed in a *fixed* reliquary above the Altar, at once begins to melt.[1]

Further, that he, not knowing the prohibition, entered the Church with a relic of the true Cross on him – and the priest, or whoever went with him, cried out 'Some one here has a piece of the true Cross about him —' for the blood was melting.

When this was told to F. Rossi of the Chiesa Nuova at Rome, he said, 'Well, *we* have a portion of S. Pantaleon's blood, and it is liquid —' or 'is liquid on certain days,' I forget which

---

[1] For this and what follows see letters of 15 and 17 Sept. 1847 to Mrs John Mozley and Henry Wilberforce.

Have you inquired into the miracles attending the blood of St Nicholas of Bari?

Perhaps you saw at Naples the liquefaction of St John B's [Baptist] blood on August 29, and of St Patrizia's(?) on the 25th?

You must be glad to get back, in spite of the *great* attractions of Italy, though it must be sad for your wife, to find a sister gone. Yet her death was so happy, you must believe you have an advocate in heaven.[1]

Don't fear you will not get on in some way or other. I should be rejoiced to see you, if you came this way. But your place is Clifton. Any one like yourself, so long in Italy, will be invaluable to the new converts there

Ever Yours affly John H Newman Congr. Orat.

TO CHARLES WATERTON[2]

Oratory Birmingham August 4. 1850

Sir,

I have no sort of claim on your attention, beyond that of being the son of a great Saint, who seems set on doing a good turn to this unhappy country. St Philip Neri lived when it fell away from the faith; he ever took an interest in the remnant of Catholic martyrs and confessors which remained to it in his day; and now, when God seems to have purposes of mercy towards it, he at once comes to it by means of that institution which he has founded and which has spread almost throughout the Catholic world. Every order and congregation in the Church has its own work; and ours especially lies among the population of great towns, and still more directly with the educated or half educated or professedly educated portion of it.

Here in Birmingham our object will be to influence the tone of thought and opinion prevalent in the various circles of society, high and low, to recommend Catholicism, to expose Protestantism, and especially to take care of young men. We have been here about a year and a half; and have been sufficiently blessed to feel sanguine that St Philip will make use of us here, if once we get established. We are collecting subscriptions for a Church, as the accompanying paper explains; and, knowing your zeal for the Catholic faith, we are sure that you will not be offended at least at our *applying* to you for assistance, being sure also that, if you do not grant it, you will have the best reasons for declining, and that, if you do, St Philip will not forget it.

Praying that all blessings may be poured on you in this world and the next from the Giver of good

I am, Sir, Your faithful Servant
John H Newman Congr. Orat.

---

[1] Mrs Northcote's sister was Mary Columba Poole. See letter of 9 July 1849 to her.
[2] This letter has already been printed from the draft.

TO MR BETTERIS

[The Oratory Birmingham 13 August 1850]

I do not wish to distress Mrs Tombs, but I wish to secure my money. I do not see why the two should not be compatible; I mean, why she cannot be just to me, and I am not severe to her.[1]

TO J. SPENCER NORTHCOTE

The Oratory Bm August 29/50

My dear Northcote

I find in Baronius's Martyrology under August 25, 'Neapoli S. Patritiæ Virginis;' so I doubt not my memorandum in my former letter to you was right.[2]

F. St John and I were taken to her Church, and saw the liquid blood — but we had not come in time to see it hard.

F. Costa brought us (in the Gesù at Naples) a portion of the blood of Da Ponte, and told us it would melt, if we said, I think, a Hail Mary, and it did — but St John shall write to you a more exact account of it.[3]

We saw at the Gerolamini a portion of the blood of some former father of the Oratory, which is always liquid.

We did not see the liquefaction of the blood of St Januarius. John Bowden did, if you choose to write to him for his account of it, directing to the London Oratory (24 King Wm Str. West)

How is it this miracle of liquefaction is so local — and not confined to saints?

Ever Yours most sincerely in Xt

John H Newman Congr. Orat

August 30.

[1] See letter of 3 July 1849 to Betteris, and those of 17 Oct. 1851 and 31 March 1852 to J. R. Bloxam.
[2] See above, letter of 19 July to Northcote, and references there.
[3] It was St John who made this experiment. His account (preserved with Newman's letter) reads: 'I thought to myself, I will try quietly what saying a few Hail Maries will do — so I got up, and went into Father Newman's room and took the vessel away without his observing it, and when in my own room I knelt down and took the bottle in my hands and looked at it. The Blood seemed quite hard; then I put it down and said the Hail Maries and took it up and looked at it. At first I saw nothing, it was as hard as ice, but looking earnestly, I saw evidently the blood moving slowly and heavily as in the former case [St Patrizia]. I was a good deal astonished and said to myself as well as I remember — well that is most wonderful. Then, I took it back to Father Newman's room and showed it him: and made him look. I think he said he could not see the appearance I spoke of. No — on second thoughts I think we both saw it this second time, but when he asked, are you sure it was not so at first; I said, I looked hard, but saw nothing like it. This is as far as I remember the history of this too curious fact . . .'

TO GEORGE OLIVER

Oratory Birmingham. February 9. 1851

My dear Revd Sir,

I felt much flattered by your kind letter, and thank you for the Pamphlet of the Dean's.[1] It is, as you say, very superficial; and for the moment will do harm to some persons, but I do not think the effect will last. Such publications are commonly put out on the spur of the moment. A Bishop has a daughter who is an Ultra-puseyite, or an Archdeacon's son has turned Papist, and in consequence the father writes a charge or a sermon against St Alfonso or against the Confessional. The production and its effect are as feeble as the motive cause is accidental.

I will speak to the Editor of the Rambler on the subject of it, as you suggest.

Pray accept my best thanks for the kind terms in which you speak of me — and add to your kindness by giving me sometimes some of your good prayers and believe me,

My dear Dr Oliver, Very truly Yours in Xt

John H Newman Congr. Orat.

TO CHARLES RUSSELL

Oratory Birmingham August 31. 1851

My dear Dr Russell,

There is a report, which I do not wish talked about, that Dr Achilli is going to prosecute me for what I copied about him from the Dublin in one of the Lectures I am delivering (of which, by the bye, I had made a memorandum to beg your acceptance, when they are finished.)

Now it strikes me you may know your namesake, Dr Russell, the Dominican, who is just come from Rome — or can tell me where he is and how I can get at him — or whether there is any one else who can give me information about Achilli, or how to get evidence against him.[2] I am told no time is to be lost.

Very truly Yours in Xt   John H Newman Congr. Orat.

[1] Thomas Hill Lowe, Dean of Exeter from 1839 until his death in 1861, was the author of several anti-Catholic pamphlets. One of them, a sermon on auricular confession, published in 1852, was disapproved of by Bishop Phillpotts.

[2] This was Bartholomew Russell O.P. See letters of 7 Sept. 1851 to Archbishop Cullen and 17 Sept. 1851 to Richard Stanton.

24 King Wm Street Sept 10/51

My dear Mr Lambert,

It gave me the greatest pleasure to receive your letter here, and to find that you approved of the line of action which I have recommended in my Lecture to Catholics at this time.[1] Of course all you suggest about political activity was included in my idea, but would not have been fitting on the occasion which led to my remarks.

What you say of Salisbury is a striking instance in point — but it could not yet be done generally. What we want is *education*. Look at the House of Lords — not one of our Peers can say a word in our defence; they have not the power.

Father Edward [Caswall] has been ill and confined to his rooms. I left him better

Believe me, My dear Mr Lambert, Very truly Yours in Xt

John H Newman Congr. Orat.

TO WILLIAM DODSWORTH

Oy Bm Sept 22/51

My dear Dodsworth,

I was very sorry to miss you in London. I inquired about you to no purpose. Do you know that Father Gordon has just gone off to the continent for three months. He has been unwell the whole year — and four medical men agree that his lungs are quite good, but that he wants rest. After some months absence he came here little better — so we have sent him off for three months — and he has gone in good spirits at the thought of seeing Rome and Naples, and the various Catholic treasures contained there. Father Darnell has gone with him – I hope they will return by Christmas.[2]

What a wonderful time it is! no one can say what is coming — Every thing seems going well, but we must expect trials.

I almost trust, when you return from Torquay, you would find us in our new house, if you came this way. *When* in it, if we are so prospered, we shall be able to lodge you with the consideration we should wish to show distinguished persons.

I am sorry about Hallam, poor old man — for he must be old now.[3]

Ever Yours affectly in Xt   John H Newman Congr. Orat.

[1] This was the last lecture in *Prepos.* 'Duties of Catholics towards the Protestant View', delivered on 1 Sept. 1851.
[2] See letter of 22 Sept. 1851 to Mrs J. W. Bowden.
[3] Henry Hallam the historian, 1777–1859. His wife died in 1846 and of their eleven children only four grew up. Of these Arthur died in 1833, Ellen in 1837 and Henry in 1850, only one daughter Julia, surviving.

24*

TO JEAN JOSEPH GAUME

Oratory Birmingham Sept 26. 1851

Very Revd M. L'Abbe

Your name is so well known for your works of learning and of charity, that I felt quite flattered at your kindness in sending me a copy of your new volume.[1] I should have acknowledged it much sooner, had I not been very busy with a volume of Lectures which I have been publishing.

I am perfectly sure that whatever you do must tend, as it is meant and offered, to God's glory and the good of His Church. It is the one object you set before you in your labours, and it must have an abundant blessing.

I have been particularly struck with various portions of your volume, and am sure that Catholics cannot be too much warned of the evil effects of the spirit you so justly call Pagan. At the same time, I have a difficulty in the notion of substituting Christian authors for heathen, in education, as far as regards Latin and Greek. I mean, I do not see how Greek and Latin can be taught, except as media of ideas, without the classics. The classics seem to me to do so very much in *forming a correct taste*. On the other hand, great as the Christian writers are, I hardly know who among them write with the simplicity, taste, and grace of the classics, but perhaps St Athanasius, and St Basil (neither of whom would do for boys) Lactantius, Sulpicius, and one or two others. I have been accustomed to think that, as Palestine has been the seat and fountain of supernatural truth, so Attica was chosen by Providence as the home and centre of intellectual excellence.[2]

However, I shall study your Volume, and doubt not I shall get great instruction from it — and begging your good prayers, I beg you to believe me, My reverend M' Abbe, Your reverence's humble Servt in Xt

John H Newman Congr. Orat.

TO THOMAS RICHARDSON

The Oratory Alcester Street Birmingham Nov 1. 1851.

Dear Sir

Will you be so good as to write me word at once, directing to '24 King William Street West, London' what took place between Dr Achilli's friends and you on the publication of the Article in the Dublin or of the Pamphlet about him. It is said that you challenged them to prosecute, and they did nothing. Did any thing pass, and how much?[3]

---

[1] *Le ver rongeur des sociétés modernes ou le paganisme dans l'éducation*, Paris 1851. See letter of 16 Sept. 1851 to Archbishop Cullen and note there; also *Idea*, pp. 9, 260–1, 269, and 372.
[2] See also letter below of 26 March 1852 to Thompson.
[3] See letter of 8 Sept. 1851 to Edward Badeley, and notes there.

I thank you for your letter received this morning, and for the papers you promise me.[1]

Yours faithfully John H. Newman.

P. S.   Since writing the above your parcel has come. I thank you for it, but return it, as it contains no documents.[2]

TO PETER COOPER

Oratory Bm November 13/51

My dear Dr Cooper,

I feel exceedingly the kindness of your letter just received.[3] Of the great honor done me I shall say nothing, for I shall have an opportunity of acknowledging it when the Primate's letter comes, meanwhile the thoughtfulness, with which amid your many occupations you have lost no time to acquaint me at once with the result of a meeting so interesting to me, demands my warmest thanks.[4] Pray for me, my dear Dr Cooper, that your confidence in me may not be thrown away, but that I may be able in sufficient measure to acquit myself of the great responsibilities thrown upon me.

Achilli's proceedings are against *me*. Should I be cast, I shall have to go to prison. At present he occupies, I am sorry to say, a good deal of my time. I am from London on *furlough*.

Very sincerely Yours in Xt   John H Newman

TO ROBERT AUGUSTINE WHITE, O.P.

Oratory Birmingham January 9 1852

My dear Fr White,

I wish to ask your Reverence one question, which my lawyers are desirous of having answered.

Achilli in his book writes as follows: 'The Dominicans, *contrary to the*

---

[1] Richardson wrote on 31 Oct. from Derby: 'I am requested by His Eminence Cardinal Wiseman to send you the M.S. copy, and the Proofs of the Article on 'Dr Achilli,' which appeared in the Dublin Review . . . Should we possess any other documents that would be useful, they will be most cheerfully sent to you.'

[2] Richardson made a copy (now in the Westminster Archives) of his reply on 3 Nov.: 'About the time the Pamphlet, the Life of Dr Achilli and the Dublin Review were selling, several persons called upon me, when in London at my place in Fleet Street, and talked about bringing actions against me as publisher, and the writer — I do not know Dr Achilli by sight he might be one of them, my reply to all, we were quite ready for the Dr or his friends, not one of whom I knew and they would not give their names — I am sorry the papers I sent you cannot be made use of.' On the documents Newman needed, see letter of 26 Nov. 1851 to W. G. Ward

[3] Of 12 Nov. announcing Newman's appointment as President of the Catholic University of Ireland. See letter of 16 Nov. 1851 to Archbishop Cullen, and references there.

[4] Cooper wrote: 'This communication is to prepare you for the more formal and official one which is to follow by tomorrow's post, from the Primate who presided, and who knows of my writing.'

practice of all other monastic bodies, in their religious profession, *make but one single vow*, which is that of *obedience*. My profession, therefore, was *nothing more* than a promise *to be obedient* to the superior of the Order . . . Had I belonged to any *other* order, I must have vowed *three* things . . . The Dominicans require obedience *only*'.

Might I ask if this statement is correct?[1]

I am, My dear Father begging your good prayers
Very truly Yours in Xt   John H Newman of the Oratory.

P. S.   The trial comes on in February. We need the prayers of all. Some things we hope to prove by legal evidence — but failure on any one point is sufficient for a verdict of guilty.

TO ROBERT AUGUSTINE WHITE, O.P. [?]

Oratory Birmingham January 17. 1852
My dear Revd Father,

Your kind and satisfactory letter came today, and I am much obliged to you for it.

It is a great consolation to me to hear of your good prayers for me. I know the value of them, and feel very grateful. Good must come of it, if I am so supported.

Achilli has just shown the white feather, though it involves a very anxious crisis. He is attempting to hinder me bringing my witnesses into Court, by going off on some technical objection

Yours, My dear F,[2] Very truly in Xt
John H Newman of the Oratory

TO JOHN HARDMAN

Edgbaston. Febr 17/52
My dear Mr Hardman,

I inclose a letter just received from Father St John, who has gone to Paris to arrange matters about the women there. I am sorry to say that Vincenzo, the husband of one of them, is getting violent at the delay. Some one tells me too that Keosse, the Armenian Priest from Malta, now in London, is put out about something or other.

I had written to Mr Lewin several days ago, to communicate with you or Mr Canning about the London expences (of witnesses)[3]

---

[1] Dominicans have always taken a single vow of obedience, which includes essentially those of poverty and chastity.
[2] Newman wrote here and erased the word 'Russell'. cf. letter above of 31 Aug. 1851 to Charles Russell.
[3] See letters of 22 and 29 Feb. 1852 to Ambrose St John and J. D. Dalgairns.

As I am oscillating between this place and Alcester Street, you cannot catch me just now — but I will call on you if you have any thing to say

Yours very truly in Xt   John H Newman

TO AN UNKNOWN CORRESPONDENT

Oratory Febr 22/52

Dear Sir

I am sorry to have kept you in suspence as regards your flattering proposal, but I was unwilling to give my answer in a hurry.

I have now decided with every acknowledgment of your attention, not to avail myself of it. My reasons are various, but very intelligible. First, I have scarcely written for thirty years on any subjects but theological, and it would take me a great deal of time to write on any other. And, if I did, I ought to do it, first of all, for the new Institution in Ireland of which I am President. And that Institution will so completely occupy my thoughts shortly, and demand my presence so urgently, that I am unable to promise myself either leisure for writing, or a date for delivering, any lecture in Birmingham of any kind.

Under these circumstances I am sure you will kindly accept my decision in the negative, and will believe me,

with much respect, Your faithful Servt

John H Newman

TO EDWARD HEALY THOMPSON

Oy Bm March 26/52

My dear Thompson,

I am very glad you are to have a voice in Dolman's Committee of Literature.[1] There should be certain principles in the selection of Books for translation. They should be books which have a reputation in their own country — not newly published books, except for established authors — not party works — etc etc. I was very sorry to see the Abbé Gaume's new work on the List. It is the book of a *school* or party — it has been answered — and the decision is sub judice. This is not a work which will recommend the Library. As well might you publish a work on Doctrinal Developments, or an Apology for Malebranche or De Bonald. The precipitancy is the worst part of the matter.[2]

I suppose Gorres's works have occurred to you — and Balmez — Klee[3] — what is the worth of Nicolai? there is a curious appendix on Napoleon's argu-

---

[1] 'Library of Translations from Select Foreign Literature', published by Charles Dolman, 61 New Bond Street.
[2] Dolman published Gaume's book in 1852 under the title of *Paganism in Education*, translated by Robert Hill. See above letter of 26 Sept. 1851 to Gaume.
[3] Heinrich Klee (1800–40), succeeded Möhler as Professor at Munich. Klee was a theologian well versed in Scripture and the Fathers.

ment for Christianity.[1] There is an interesting Life of Pius vi by Baldassari, or some such name, which, I think, would bear translating. Is Arnaud's (or whatever his name is) Life of Pius vii translated?[2] But I know too little of foreign literature to talk about it.

Wishing you and Northcote a full measure of influence in the project I am My dear Thomson Very sincerely Yours in Xt

John H Newman of the Oratory

TO EDWARD HEALY THOMPSON

Oy Bm Easter Tuesday [13 April] /52

My dear Thompson,

You must be careful of Moehler's Unité. F. St John translated it on his becoming a Catholic, and the Cardinal [Wisemen] plucked it, as (though good in parts) being Josephine or Gallican, or something or other. Perhaps this could be set right — if so, a translation is almost ready for you.[3]

I know nothing of Alzog, but will inquire.[4]

I suppose Rio does not go into dogmatics — for, being a lay man, he almost recognized, I am told, at least at one time, or was inclined to do so, the Anglican Church.[5]

You should be prepared, tho' I know nothing about it, for German circuitousness and prosiness in Hurter and Voight.[6]

Is Ratisbonne's enough of a book?[7] You see all this comes to nothing at all, for it is critical; and I suppose you have only to do with the theological question.

Will you kindly give the inclosed to Northcote?

Yours very sincerely in Xt   John H Newman of the Oratory

TO THE PUBLISHER OF THE TELEGRAPH[8]

June 8. 1852

Dr Newman begs the Publisher of the Telegraph to be so good as to send it to him at 'Oratory, Edgbaston Birmingham' England instead of in Harcourt Street.

---

[1] Auguste Nicholas in *Études philosophiques sur le christianisme,* third edition, Brussels 1849, II, pp. 352–6. Newman adapted Napoleon's argument in *O.S.* pp. 43–5.

[2] Pietro Baldassari, *Histoire de l'enlèvement et de la captivité de Pie VI,* Paris 1839, translated from the Italian. A. F. Artaud de Montor, *Histoire du Pape Pie VII,* two volumes, Paris 1836.

[3] Johann Adam Möhler's *Die Einheit in der Kirche,* Tübingen 1825, has not been translated into English. Möhler modified its subjective emphasis in later works; it has been of service to the ecumenical movement.

[4] Johann Baptist Alzog (1808–78), author of *Lehrbuch der Kirchengeschichte,* 1841, English translation, Cincinnati 1874.

[5] Alexis François Rio (1797–1874) friend of Montalembert, wrote on Christian art.

[6] Friedrich von Hurter (1787–1865), author of *Leben Innocenz III,* four volumes, Hamburg 1834–42; Johannes Voigt (1786–1863), German medieval historian, who wrote on St Gregory VII.

[7] In 1842 Alfonse Marie Ratisbonne published accounts of his conversion.

[8] A Dublin newspaper, published from 7 and 8 Lower Abbey Street.

Edgbaston. Birmingham July 4. 1852

My dear Mr Lambert

Your letter has followed me to Dublin and then back again; else, you should have received my thanks for it before now. I doubt not every thing will turn out well — the worst is over, the suspence. The poet says 'Thrice is he armed, who has his quarrel just —'[1] and the same kind of armour is it to have the common sense of mankind on one's side. A Judge and Jury can no more overcome the common sense of mankind, than they can walk through a stone wall. People say they dare not do any thing to me — but even if they do, that will not improve their cause, the reverse.

I am sorry to find that I am exchanging the criminal information on the part of Achilli for 'an indictment' on your part. Why must I not speak what seems to me a *fact* about Gregorian music? am I not very impartial? you see, I express a *fear* of Beethoven and Mozart, and express no fear, but an acquiesce in Gregorian.[2]

With many thanks for your kindness, and hoping you will come to hear our Gregorian Vespers in our new House, I am,

My dear Mr Lambert, Very sincerely Yours in Xt

John H Newman of the Oratory

Oscott, Birmingham July 13. 1852

Dear Sir,

I hope you will excuse this brief note, written amid the Business of the Synod.

I beg to acknowledge your kind contribution to the expenses of my late Trial and thank you also for the interest it evidences in it.[3]

Begging your good prayers, I am, My dear Sir,

Truly Yours in Xt, John H. Newman

---

[1] *King Henry VI*, Part 2, III, ii, 233.

[2] Lambert had evidently complained of the passage in *Discourses on the Scope and Nature of University Education*, Dublin 1852, pp. 111–15; *Idea*, pp. 78–81.

[3] This letter is among the Weld family papers in the Dorset County Records Office. Joseph Weld wrote: 'Lulworth Castle Sunday
Revd Sir
Will you allow me to send you a small contribution for the expenses of the Achilli trial — begging your prayers for myself and family'

TO J. SPENCER NORTHCOTE

Edgbaston Bm Sept 2/52

My dear Northcote,

I recollect the Modern Pilgrim's Progress very well, and thought it very clever when I read it.[1] I do not recollect being annoyed at the passage you mention, which is very amusing. On looking at it now, I should fancy it was written, when the author was rather put out with me — but this may be a mistake. Do not suppose I shall feel any annoyance at your publishing it, as it is; though the passage does not express my view of the subject. The trouble is, the palisade was *never* continuous or strong – it was made open originally to admit stragglers from the other side, (the Catholic) of the common, who would not have had courage to climb it; and it was put together *by bad workmen*, who had different notions, *how* the line was to be drawn — and beginning at different *ends* of the line, no wonder they did not *meet*, and complete their job. This is *my* account of the matter, but there is no reason you should not publish another — which is quite fair and I should *wish* the Parable published. Thank you for mentioning the matter to me.[2]

I have not seen Allies's Parable, which must be clever.

I have written to Capes once or twice, and got no answer (my letters did *not* require any) which made me very anxious about his health. I am glad you are taking the Rambler off his hands.

As to my Fund, people are most kind and liberal – and I am pained, yet honored, by their contributions – *but do not fancy I am out of the wood.* You cannot fancy what the expences will be. Sometimes I despair of any contributions reaching them

Ever Yrs affly in Xt   John H Newman of the Oratory

TO AUSTIN MILLS

[24 December 1852][3]

"cantata" My Ite missa est will be quite as good as their Deo gratias. The House is in great excitement

Ever Yours affly J H N.

P.S. 4. Query   ought I to wash palls and corporals, as well as mundatories?[4]

I shall say tonight's Mass for the Congregation, so we shall be saying Mass together, as if I were in Birmingham.

---

[1] 'The Modern Pilgrim's Progress, or the History of Puseyism in a Dream', was Maria Spencer Ruscombe Poole's account of the steps leading to her conversion in 1845. Newman quoted from it in *Apo.* pp. 218–19. It was published in the *Rambler* (Feb. 1853), pp. 122–35.

[2] See the *Rambler*, loc. cit., p. 126, for the palisade between the Catholic and the Anglican road.

[3] This is the missing last sheet of Newman's letter already printed, and refers to the Midnight Mass he was to sing at Abbotsford.

[4] Cloths used at Mass.

Abbotsford, Melrose Jan 1. 1853[1]

My dear Lady Georgiana

How I wish I could speak instead of writing to you, in answer to your question! I am so afraid of going off on a wrong tack, and saying what is nihil ad rem.

I have a great difficulty in knowing what books to recommend to you, for I cannot tell *how* I got myself the general impression and idea of the early Church which rests upon my mind. Sometimes some little fact, got one does not know where, is a suggestion opening a whole scene or prospect.

I dare say you know or have heard of Bekker's 'Gallus.' It is translated from the German and published by Parker in the Strand. You would of course get it in Paris in the original – perhaps in French. It is much to your purpose. He has also published a 'Charicles', which is a story embodying Greek manners, as Gallus embodies Roman, but I have not seen it. It is translated also.

You know of course Bingham's Antiquities – which, bating its Protestantism, is as instructive and interesting as it is learned.

The volumes in the Oxford Library of the Fathers, containing St Cyprian's Epistles, and Tertullian's Apology with notes by Pusey, might be useful to you; but Pusey's *doctrinal* notes, I believe, are grossly unfair. I do not know whether in the same Series a volume has yet appeared of 'Acts of Martyrdoms' (from Ruinart, I suppose) — if so, you should get [it]. One or two of these were published among the 'Records' in the Tracts for the Times. You should consult some book about the Catacombs — Father Marchi's (e.g.) at Rome — of which Mr Northcote gave specimens in the Rambler. A very curious defence has lately been written in France (by the Benedictines of Solesme?) of the Traditions of St Mary Magdalene at Marseilles, if your scene is to be France. Perhaps it is in French, but I do not know. Some years ago Mr Lockhart (Mrs Hope's Father) wrote a novel called 'Valerius', which you ought to see — It is a tale of early Christianity — as accurate about, as the 39 articles are an accurate representation of the early Creed — but *clever*, and would suggest ideas to you — but I dare say you know it. Some sketches in it struck me as very good. Sismondi too has written a novel, called, I think, Julia Severa — of Roman times — I never saw it.

One prominent feature in those times is the attempt to re-animate Polytheism — of which Julian's history (though later) is the best instance. I have never read the Abbe Blèterie's 'Julian' — it is praised a good deal — It is a small duodecimo, and you would see at once if it is to your purpose. You should get some account of the Neo-platonists (Plotinus etc) whose history bears on the revival of Paganism.

---

[1] This letter has already been printed, but from an incorrect copy. See notes there.

I have a chapter in my own Essay on Development (under the head of 'The First Test,') on the primitive centuries, which may suggest something to you. You would read it through in half an hour.

Tillemont's works, which you would be able to consult in any great city, (his 'Emperors' and his 'Ecclesiastical Memoirs,') are the most *accurate* of any history. Gibbon calls his minute diligence 'almost genius'. He would give you every fact about martyrdoms etc.

Fleury's Ecclesiastical History, which also you would find every where, is *to my mind* the most graphic of histories. (Others do not agree with me.) It is a *mere narrative* of the *whole* course of the times diligently drawn out.

You should be on your guard against Fleury's Gallicanism and Tillemont's Jansenism.

The Protestant Neander (History of the first three centuries) will also be of use to you, though he is very fanciful and dreamy.[2] You would get it at Paris in French or German.

You will have to ask leave, out of England, to read many of these books.

Do not let me frighten you by the number I have mentioned — dipping into books, or skimming them, and consulting them, is not *reading*. Besides, I have put down works on *various* subjects. If I must mention *one* book to the exclusion of all others, it would be Fleury's History; — but when you come to *write*, you will not be able to get on without a knowledge of Antiquities — so I add Bekker and Bingham.

Your difficulty will be character. This is the point in which you excel, and on which your works have hitherto turned — and female character. Now I do not know *what* work would help you to understanding the Roman female character. I suppose it was absolutely different in kind from the Protestant or English. I suppose a genuine Roman woman had very little education. The known *historical* specimens, on the other hand, were often monsters. I doubt whether any of them, heathen or Christian, had that peculiar refinement of feeling and complexity of motive and passion, which you delight to draw.

I thank you extremely for the gift of your new work, which I have read with the greatest interest. It is most powerful, but I cannot reconcile myself to the distressing parts. I am not complaining of them, but merely mean they are too painful for *me*. However, they are necessary for the moral — which, though not forced upon people, is clear. I cannot help thinking, that readers will be obliged to *feel* its moral, though they do not observe, or do not acknowledge it. I wish you had made Lady Clara less of a *sketch*. Now, I am ashamed of saying all this — it sounds so very cold, which is the feeling of all others, with which a reader will not, and cannot rise, from your volumes.

[1] Augustus Neander, *The History of the Christian Religion and Church during the Three First Centuries*, two volumes, London 1831, translated by Henry John Rose.

[2] The copyist, whose text was used in Volume XV, silently corrected Newman's 'Neander' to 'Baur'.

With every kind and best wish for the New Year to you and Mr Fullerton, I am, My dear Lady Georgiana, Very sincerely Yours in Xt

John H Newman of the Oratory

TO FREDERICK CHARLES HUSENBETH

Abbotsford January 19 1853

My dear Dr Husenbeth

Your most kind letter came just now and I sincerely thank you for it. Your approbation is very valuable to me. I never wrote a volume which has caused me more anxiety, from the responsibility attaching to it, and the deficiences of which I am sensible in myself for fulfilling that responsibility.[1] It is a great relief to me and encouragement for any one like you to praise it. People one lives with are not the best judges of what one does. Again I thank you for your letter.

The argument in my case takes place in the Queen's Bench tomorrow, as you will see before this reaches you. Then you will know, what neither of us know yet — the termination of the matter; for lawyers are confident that, if I gain a new trial, the affair will be at an end — on the other hand, if I do not get a new trial, then I shall be had up for judgment next week, and then certainly the whole matter will be at an end, which will be a good thing. Anyhow, give me your good prayers and believe me, Most sincerely Yours in Xt

John H Newman

(Excuse this strange paper; I am out in covers)[2]

TO WILLIAM MONSELL

[3 February 1853][3]

will ever allow Catholic youth to mix with Protestants as students, let alone the question of professors. Where Professors, or where students, are of distinct religions among themselves, there will be no genius loci, or at least no healthy genius. Religion will be either altogether excluded as a latent element — or you will have a number of small sectarian clubs, each representing its own religious tenets, and brim full of the odium theologicum.

I am sorry to say all this — but the more I think of it, and without denying that some arrangement is possible, (though I do not at present see how,) the more does the *principle* of the three Colleges seem inadmissible and the ultimate consequences of their existence evil.

I hope the tooth ache is gone

Ever Yrs affly J H Newman

---

[1] Newman's letter refers to *Discourses on the Scope and Nature of University Education*, in Husenbeth's copy of which it was found.
[2] Having no envelope, Newman folded and sealed his sheet.
[3] This letter was printed from the draft. The last sheet of the autograph is here reproduced.

TO EDWARD HEALY THOMPSON

Febr 9 [1853] Edgbaston

My dear Thompson

Pray excuse my seeming inattention — but, in spite of my medical advisers' having long told me to get some rest, I am pulled about in every direction. I returned last night from Bath, where I left dear Father Joseph all but dying. Now I find letters on my Table showing me I cannot quite yet put the Achilli matter off my mind[1]

I assure you nothing would please and gratify me more than to find you were willing to assist us in Dublin. I hope we shall be doing something in the way of arrangements immediately after Easter.

Thank you for your letters — I was particularly interested in the account you so kindly gave me of your Father's death. At the time my Masses were much taken up — but I meant to say one for him the first vacant day I had. I cannot name a day before Monday the 28; but if all is well, I will say a black Mass for him then.

Excuse this hasty letter and believe me

Very sincerely Yrs in Xt   John H Newman

TO JEAN FÉLIX NOURRISSON

Edgbaston Bm April 9. 1853

M. le Docteur,

Your obliging letter, which came to me yesterday, is very acceptable.[2] I feel grateful for the commendation it bestows on my volume, and the sympathy it expresses for myself. It has been a great encouragement to me to think that any thing I have written may subserve the great cause of education in so intellectual a country as France.

I know nothing of the circumstances of French publication — but I cannot doubt that any work, coming before the French Catholic world, with the protection of so respected a name as yours must be, would be successful.

There is only one question which at the moment I cannot solve. M. Gondon, who has translated some other works of mine, may already be occupied on a translation of this — but I do not think it likely. However, I will inquire at once and let you know.

[1] See letters of 7 and 10 Feb. 1853 to Edward Bellasis.
[2] Nourrisson wrote on 7 April from Claremont, where he was acting as a temporary tutor to the son of Louis Phillippe, to ask permission to translate *Discourses on the Scope and Nature of University Education*. See next letter.
  Jean Felix Nourrisson (1825–99), was a religious philosopher and held French Professorships of Philosophy, ending with that at the Collège de France in 1874.

Meanwhile, I beg to subscribe myself, M. le Docteur with profound respect,

Your faithful obedient Servt John H Newman of the Oratory

To M. le Dr Nourrillon etc etc

TO JEAN FÉLIX NOURRISSON

Edgbaston. Birmingham April 29. 1853.

My dear Sir,

I heard yesterday from a friend in Paris to the following effect:

'M. [Gondon] has just received from a Curé in the South of France a translation of a great part of your Lectures on the University already done. He thought them well translated, as far as appeared.'[1]

Under these circumstances I do not see how I can with any propriety or due respect for you, avail myself of your most flattering offer. I assure you it is a disappointment to me, for it would have been a great point to have had a translation of my book coming from so high a quarter, which could not have failed to carry weight with it. But it would be most unfair to you, and a wanton disregard of your valuable time and labour, not to have told you what is going on about my Volume in Paris, and my own judgment upon it.[2]

Should any thing bring you this way, I hope you will give me the satisfaction of thanking you in person.

I am, My dear Sir, with much respect, Your faithful Servant

John H Newman of the Oratory.

To M. le Docteur Nourrillon etc etc.

TO SIR JAMES STEPHEN

Edgbaston. Birmingham July 13. 1853[3]

My dear Sir,

I have never forgotten the kind hospitality you showed me at Kensington in January 1836, and am glad of this opportunity of recalling it to your memory.

The report, which you so considerately inquire about, is strangely incorrect, as I shall give you the means of ascertaining. That it has had any sort of foundation must be attributed to the circumstance of my having ever enter-

---

[1] Newman's correspondent was J. D. Dalgairns.

[2] The first part of *The Idea of a University* was not published in a French translation until that of Edmond Robillard and Maurice Labelle, Paris 1968, in the 'Textes Newmaniens' series.

[3] This letter has already been printed from the draft. See notes there.

tained such pleasant recollections of your friendliness towards me at the date I have mentioned, that it pained me to find that you had felt it a duty to express in print a contrary feeling.

I cannot tell whether you have ever seen my little work, called Loss and Gain, to which you allude, and in defence of which I have never felt it necessary to say one single word; but from the Lecture, which I take the liberty of inclosing, you will see that, as to the statement of yours to which I did allude, I agreed with it in substance, while I complained of it. The passage, and the only passage in which I have ventured to speak of any of your works, is in p 75 of the Lecture. It was delivered and published three years ago,

Allow me to thank you for the very kind and flattering terms in which you speak of me in your letter to Mr H Wilberforce, which he has forwarded to me, and to assure you that I am, with sincere kindness and warmth of feeling,

My dear Sir, Very faithfully Yours John H Newman

Sir James Stephen &c &c.

TO DOMINIC AYLWARD, O.P.

Edgbaston Bm July 27/53

My dear Revd Father,

No such paper as you speak of was sent to me, because, I suppose, we are not regulars. And we took no part in the deliberations of Regulars at the Synod this time year.[1] Therefore I felt I could not avail myself of the leave, you so kindly offered me. I hope every thing will turn out to the satisfaction of all parties. Is it true, as I was told, that you kept your Postulants at Hinckley, though the novices are at Woodchester? What makes me speak on the subject, is the interest I take in a youth who is going to you, with the intention of trying his vocation, next month.[2] He is of a consumptive family, and I really am afraid from what his mother tells me, that the new house at Woodchester will not be dry enough for him. I hope it is not taking a liberty speaking about him to you, but he is the son of my oldest and dearest friend, now dead, and I have known him and loved him from an infant.

I am, My dear Revd Father, Very truly Yours in Xt

John H Newman of the Oratory

[1] The First Synod of Westminster held at Oscott in July 1852 devoted its Decree XXVII to Regulars, and strongly recommended that members of Religious Orders, who had been appointed as missionary priests, should only be removed in consultation with the local bishop. A letter from the Congregation of Propaganda in Rome approved of this, but it was considered an infringement of the rights of Regulars. Aylward was chosen to represent the cause of independence in Rome.

[2] See diary for 22 July and letter of 24 Aug. 1853 to Mrs J. W. Bowden. Aylward was the Provincial of the Dominicans, 1850–4, living at Hinckley. In the latter year he became the first Prior of Woodchester.

37*

Edgbaston Birmingham July 27. 1853[1]

My dear Lady Georgiana,

I read with much interest and pleasure the Princess Volkonski's letter, and felt how kind it was in you to mention my name to her in connexion with her pious undertaking. But really I have no right to any such recommendation to her notice; and have enough things to answer for, without interfering in matters about which I know so little as religious associations.

I have sometimes been tempted to wish that there were some means of bringing together ladies who may be said to have a half vocation — or rather a whole vocation for a half-religious rule — that is, some rule of life answering to that of the Oratory, which consists of priests living under a rule, yet not religious. The bond in religion is the vow of obedience — with us it is the duty of charity. In a religious house no regard (except accidentally) is paid to the feelings of each other — whereas in the world society gets on, and a family gets on, by a refined system of mutual concession. Society is like a carriage going on springs, where every collision or jar is anticipated. Such is necessarily the case in any voluntary community. It is necessarily the principle of the Oratory, even if St Philip had not prescribed it, directly vows are excluded.

So much I may have wished as regards communities for women – but then I greatly doubt if it would be practicable. After all Priests are under the vow of their sacred vocation — which, if it does not include a vow of obedience to the Congregation to which they belong, is practically a strong protection to them in various ways against both the temptation to quit it, and neglect of the social duties it involves. But besides this, I am exceedingly doubtful whether, (without the bond of relationship, old friendship, or the like,) women could live together at all without a vow. It is remarkable that the Filippine at Rome, though founded on the model of the Oratory, are under vow.

I shall be very grateful to you, if you let me take your offer, of conveying my respects to the Princess, and my gratitude for her letter, instead of my writing myself, — as I know you will do it so much better than I could do.

It pleases me very much to find you and Mr Fullerton are back again. I am told that Lord Arundel's new home is near Newbury, which must be very pleasant for him and Lady A. considering your neighbourhood.

I will not forget your message about your Son, of whose health some one was giving me a very good account. Remember me most kindly to Mr Fullerton, and believe me to be, begging your good prayers for us,

My dear Lady Georgiana, Very sincerely Yours in Xt

John H Newman of the Oratory

[1] This letter has already been printed from an incomplete copy.

TO DOMINIC AYLWARD, O.P.

Edgbaston Bm Augt 3/53

Dear very Revd Father

I am sorry I have left you without an answer with reference to your kind wish that I should be at Woodchester tomorrow.[1] It would have been a great pleasure to me, had I been able to manage it — which I am not.

I fear from what you say that the point about which you are so anxious has not been settled in London to your satisfaction. So many things are but matters of experiment in the ecclesiastical changes which are now in progress, that I cannot doubt nothing will ultimately be settled on, but what works well.

Praying that this may be the case

I am, My dear Very Revd Father Very truly Yours in Xt

John H Newman

TO J. B. PAGANI

Edgbaston. August 15./53

My dear Very Revd Father

I write a hasty answer to your kind invitation, as this day is a busy one.

It would give me much pleasure to accept it, but I consider it is on the subject of the late orders which have come to England from Rome about the Religious Bodies here.

I anticipate from what I hear that we shall be subjected to inconvenience as well as they — but, as we have received no copy of the orders in question, and have no claim to be called Regulars, I feel I should be intruding into a matter not ours, if we attended the meeting.

Begging your good prayers for us,

I am, My dear Very Revd Father, Very respectfully and sincerely Yours

in Xt   John H Newman of the Oratory

The Very Revd Father Pagani

TO ISAAC WILLIAMS

Edgbaston Birmingham Aug. 18. 1853

My dear Isaac Williams,

I hardly like to send you what I fear may here and there pain you — but I do not like Keble not to know how far I have used his leave of borrowing from the Lyra[2]

Ever Yours affectionately John H Newman

[1] For the opening of the new church there, on the feast of St Dominic.
[2] Newman sent a copy of his *Verses on Religious Subjects*, Dublin 1853, which included many of his poems in *Lyra Apostolica*.

TO EDWARD HEALY THOMPSON

Sept 9/53

My dear Thompson

I did not mean merely a *consulting* Northcote when I talked of him as a Prefect of Studies or the like.[1] I meant a person who really would zealously give himself to the work, as an occupation, managing various details of various kinds. E.g. we want a new lodging house — it has to be found, terms satisfactorily settled, furnished and who are to go into it? where shall we find a Dean and tutor? what are the youths up to? what are their lectures to be? etc etc. I give this but as an instance which first occurs, to illustrate ten thousand matters not admitting of anticipation

Every Yrs J H N

P. S.   I am sorry to say I am not at all more confident than before that the Committee will do the handsome thing, or so put matters into my hands that I can consent to go over.

TO EDWARD HEALY THOMPSON

[23 October 1853][2]

My dear Thompson

I heard last night that I am called over to Dublin on my own terms — but things are not yet quite clear.

I don't think there is a chance of the University starting till next September; but I shall hasten *prior* arrangements as soon as I can. That is, I wish people to know as soon as possible what to *expect*.

Ever Yrs most sincerely John H Newman

P. S.   Will you send this on to Mr Stewart. De Vere will know it already.

TO EDWARD HEALY THOMPSON

Edgbaston Oct 29 [1853]

My dear Thompson

I go to Ireland for *a day* at the end of next week, if all is well.

On my return comes our Synod — When that is over, I propose to come to Clifton for a day to see you and Northcote, if he is visible and chooses . . .[3] I shall do nothing openly till January, but can make every thing quite clear and sure to you at once.

Ever Yrs John H Newman

[1] See the letters of 1, 7 and 13 Sept. 1853 to Thompson.
[2] See diary for 22 Oct. and letter of 23 Oct. to J. I. Taylor.
[3] See letter of 2 Nov. to Northcote.

TO EDWARD HEALY THOMPSON

Edgbaston Nov 7/53

My dear Thompson

I propose to start hence on Friday Morning, so as to get to you by the express due 12.30 at Bristol. Dr Gillow is kind enough to take me in. We must think of all we have to say. I was in Dublin for a few hours the day before yesterday — but quite long enough for my purpose[1]

Ever Yours most sincerely in Xt   John H Newman of the Oratory

TO EDWARD HEALY THOMPSON

Dec 6/53

My dear Thompson

Thank you for your letters. I have been paying the penalty of my journeyings about in a most severe cold, which has kept me to my room or bed for a very good fortnight.

I should else have written to Stewart — but I have a most frightful accumulation of letters and other work. Will you kindly direct the inclosed to him?[2]

Very sincerely Yrs J H Newman

I don't know Stewart's Christian name. Will you direct the letter?

TO EDWARD HEALY THOMPSON

Edgbaston. Dec 24/53

My dear Thompson

I am sorry for the cause of your expatriation, and hope you will not be caught by any Russian Privateer in returning. Bating the chance of this accident, I doubt not it will do you and Mrs Thompson a great deal of good. But avoid both the cold and the heat of Italy, I don't know which is worse. But perhaps you know the South better than I — though I have only certain recollections about you connected with letters from Nurenburgh, Ratisbon, or some or other German cities.

As far as I am concerned, I am very sorry you are going, for I wanted to have settled about preliminary examinations etc etc. At this *moment* I am badly off. Poor Wilberforce has just lost a child and the rest are ill — and Ormsby [sic] has just lost his mother. So that my movements are impeded. I have been writing to the Archbishop to make me take the oaths and set me off.[3]

One special idea I have (of course all this is secret) is to try to get an

[1] See diary for 5 and 11 November
[2] Letter of 6 Dec. to James Stewart.
[3] Letter of 24 Dec. to Archbishop Cullen.

influence over the principal schools and colleges in Ireland — we *depend* on them, and unless they send us well trained youths, we can do nothing.

With the best and kindest wishes of the season to you and Mrs Thompson

Ever Yrs most sincerely in Xt   John H Newman of the Oratory

TO MICHAEL O'SULLIVAN[1]

Edgbaston. Dec 26. 1853

My dear Mr O'Sullivan,

I beg to thank the Committee of the Poor Schools for their suggestion contained in your letter of the 14th Inst. It certainly might surprise Catholics who did not know the circumstances of the case that our Fathers should not show their interest in the schools by placing their names on the subscription list; and I hereby beg to set right the omission by offering the sum of £5 for myself for the year 1854.

I am sure however the Committee will feel I ought not to ask others of our congregation for a subscription, considering the circumstances in which they stand. You know how low the sum is fixed for a patrimony; and, though our average income individually exceed that sum, yet it is not anything like that of a secular priest, and we have all the pecuniary claims of secular priests upon us. We are severally in much distress how to manage the parochial charities, which we cannot avoid, and, I suppose, not above two or three of the whole congregation find it easy or possible to make both ends meet. For myself, it is a simple fact, that, putting aside what I am soon to receive from Ireland, I have barely a patrimony, and have got on from year to year on chance incomings, on which I could not reckon.

You know we are set up after the pattern of the Chiesa Nuova at Rome, and have the privilege of (dispensing) missionary work. From love and devotion to the Bishop, and from a sense of the spiritual needs of the place, we have been missionaries from the time we have been a congregation and though, according to the sacred maxim, 'the workman is worthy of his meat', never, either at Maryvale or Alcester St have we received any remuneration whatever from the Diocese.

Had we that salary which a mission implies, we should be able to do much more than we do, in the way of charitable contribution. Rather, I suppose, we should give every penny, after the supply of our own wants, to our mission. This source of income we have not; nay, we should decline it, if offered. But this is the reason, if at any time we have seemed slow to contribute to necessary objects external to our mission; and I am sure the Committee will be glad to be in possession of a statement, which would else be impertinent, but which, as things are, will enable them to set us right with any Catholics, who, not knowing our circumstances might be disposed to wonder at us.

---

[1] This letter differs somewhat from the draft which has already been printed.

We have laid out no small sums on the fittings up of Alcester Street, which we have freely made over to our successor; and we have promised the Bishop the sum of £160 to enable him to take up our work. Moreover, we have just built here, with our own money, a chapel, which has altogether cost us £1500, at least. I know the munificence of the clergy and laity of this place will make them the last persons to fall into the error, which besets ordinary men of supposing that *those who give most* (I do not mean ourselves) *have most to give*. But this I can say of *ourselves*, that our gifts in Alcester Street and here to our missions have simply crippled us, and that, our expenses have for several years so far exceeded our income, that for the moment we are in embarassment and anxiety.

Do not think, my dear Mr O'Sullivan, anything I have said, spoken in a tone of complaint. We are abundantly repaid for any sacrifices we have made or are making, by the sympathy shown us, and the example set us, and the prayers given us, by the clergy and laity of Birmingham; and, if I have enlarged on the matters which have been the subject of this letter, this has been, not only in answer to your invitation, but in order to substantiate, if possible, a sort of claim for the continuance of those charitable thoughts and feelings on their part, which have been so long our consolation.

Accept for yourself and the Committee the best wishes of this sacred season, and believe me,

My dear Mr O'Sullivan, Very sincerely yours in Xt

John H. Newman of the Oratory

TO EDWARD HEALY THOMPSON

Edgbaston. Jany 24. 1854

My dear Thompson,

I don't see I have any chance of writing for your Library — and I do not like promising, if I could, what would stand in the way of writing something else.[1] I might find a call for some particular book when I get to Dublin, and wish to set about writing it — then I should say 'I can't, for I have made that miserable promise to Burns and Lambert —' and it would go on fidgetting me, if I promised it — and I should say to myself a hundred times, 'How could I be such a fool, to lay myself under an engagement.'

I have had a sad hitch, and am not yet in Dublin — but I have got over it — and now have no doubt, which has never been my state before, that all will go on well. There was a chance of my going to Rome — don't mention all this.[2]

Turn in your mind what you would recommend as the subjects of an

---

[1] Thompson, with J. M. Capes and J. S. Northcote was the editor of the 'Popular Library', published by Burns and Lambert. Newman contributed to it *Callista* in 1855.

[2] See Newman's letters of 1 and 2 Jan. 1854, and also those of 15 Jan. to J. I. Taylor and 23 Jan. 1854 to Cardinal Wiseman.

entrance examination (first, considering whether it is expedient) What do you think of Iliad book 1. Æneid, book 1 one book of Euclid, or Algebra up to Quadratics; and the Gospel of St Matthew – the examination in the classics being *grammatical* — and in the Gospel simply in its *matter*.[1]

As to Ward's anxiety, I hardly know distinctly *what* he recommends in *theology* — E.g. in the Treatise de Deo, would it content him if a University Student knew the *attributes* of God, or should he understand 'ἐπίνοιαι or notiones', 'eminenter et formaliter', 'scientia media' etc. If the latter, I don't see my way to agree with him — if the former, a catechism will do it. In the Treatise de Fide, should he know the Objectum formale Quod and Quo, 'prudentia' and 'motiva credibilitatis —'[2]

I am exceedingly concerned to hear your account of yourself, but I trust a sojourn on the continent will quite set you up.

Ever Yours most sincerely in Xt   John H Newman of the Oratory

TO EDWARD HEALY THOMPSON

Oratory Birmingham April 21. 1854

My dear Thompson

You give a good account of yourself, but, while I feel Mrs Thompson's kindness in using her hand in my behalf, I am sorry I should not be able to see more of your own.

About ten days ago the Briefs came from Rome — and the Bishops are to meet on May 18. As this has not yet appeared in the Papers, it must be considered secret. Whether we shall be able to begin in September, I cannot say — but I consider it certain now that all matters will soon be put into my hands.

This is the only news I have to tell you, but it is complete news. I propose going to Dublin tonight

I am much concerned at what you say about your brother

Yours very sincerely in Xt   John H Newman of the Oratory

TO EDWARD HEALY THOMPSON

Birmingham May 24/54

My dear Thompson

At last we are afloat; but I don't expect to begin in earnest till after Christmas. I have always said we should want 6 months before starting. I have

---

[1] Thompson replied on 28 Jan. urging for the Dublin University entrance requirements similar to those in other universities.
[2] W. G. Ward had spoken to Thompson of his anxiety as to how religion would be taught in the university. Thompson now sent him Newman's questions. Ward replied on 29 Jan. in a letter to Mrs Thompson: 'Will you please tell Thompson I am really too busy to be able to write to JHN' and asked that he should explain to Newman, 'I was not meaning to make any definite producible and aggressive statement, but only in conversation stating a general impression'.

nothing more to tell you, except that every thing but the appointment of the sub rector is committed to me

I am on my way to London and to the north to beat up for patrons etc. and am to be back by Whitsunday for the installation

Ever Yours John H Newman of the Oratory

TO EDWARD HEALY THOMPSON

16 Harcourt Street Dublin June 21. 1854

My dear Thompson,

I am so busy I must be pardoned, if I have not written to you more fully — but, alas, I have nothing to say on the point I wish to write to you on.

You will see (if I did not tell you) that I have named *Nov* 3 — whereas I spoke to you of after Christmas, for our commencement. The truth is, I felt we were sure to be later than *whatever* date was fixed. If we do any thing in November, our classes will be made up of externs and strangers — which is no real work.

In confidence, I am sorry to say we have hardly any names sent in yet — and *till they are*, of course we cannot fix the time of your coming. You may think how this annoys me — You shall know how things progress. If you can help us in getting names, pray do. I much desire to have *English* students.

Give me a good account of your health. *When* you come, you will have a good deal of work — so make the most of the leisure

Ever Yours very sincerely in Xt

John H Newman of the Oratory

TO EDWARD HEALY THOMPSON

16 Harcourt Street Dublin June 28. 1854

My dear Thompson

I was very glad to have your letter, and so fair an account of yourself. Let me hear from you when you are coming here. I go over to England next week to return here in August. I do not recollect Paley's paper, but will try to find it. As to Paley, I sounded him about helping us, but he was very luke-warm,[1] I can't answer you about the Greek — am glad you like the [Catholic University] Gazette – and hope I shall not make a floor of it some fine Thursday

Ever Yrs most sincerely in Xt   John H Newman of the Oratory

E H Thompson Esqr

[1] See letter of 19 July to Robert Ornsby.

TO J. B. PAGANI

The Oratory Hagley Road Birmingham July 5/54

My dear Fr Pagani

Will you kindly allow me to put down your name on our University Books? It will involve neither trouble nor expence on your part — while it will be our gain. We want your good prayers, for we have many difficulties.

Very sincerely Yours in Xt   John H Newman of the Oratory

The Very Revd Fr Pagani &c &c.

TO EDWARD HEALY THOMPSON

The Oratory, Hagley Road Bm July 28/54

My dear Thompson

The third anniversary of the act of committing the famous Achilli Libel.

I am glad to hear so good an account of you — I wish I could give you *any* account of ourselves — that is, we are simply in the same uncertainty about the students — nor shall we be able to form a conjecture till November. I say this, that you may just know how things are. You and Stewart shall be employed immediately there is work. I am sanguine there will be, very soon after we open — but at present (I mention it in confidence) our list of students is limited to *three*.

I was glad to hear your brother was going to take Stewart's place in Sheffield.[1] He ⟨(Stewart)⟩ has not written to me since he returned from Ireland.

Very sincerely Yours in Xt   John H Newman of the Oratory

TO EDWARD HEALY THOMPSON

Oratory Bm August 12/54

My dear Thompson

Thank you for your anxiety and hint about A. de Vere. I was writing to him on some matter within this week, and took occasion to ask him how he stood disposed towards us — he has not answered yet.[2] I am sorry to hear your news, but am not surprised.

As to yourself, I can't help fearing that a letter I wrote you some time ago did not reach. It must have been immediately on Whit-sunday, in the beginning of June, if not before — I said that *November* was mentioned merely for the

---

[1] James Stewart was tutor to the sons of R. J. Gainford, at Darnell Hall, Sheffield. Thompson's brother was John Costall Thompson, who had become a Catholic, author of *The Vision of Liberty and other Poems*, privately printed 1848, which won the approval of Gladstone and Sir Henry Taylor. See *DNB*, 1901–1911, on Francis Thompson.

[2] See letter of 21 Aug. 1854 to Aubrey de Vere.

sake of mentioning a time — but that I had no notion that we should do any thing serious till after Christmas — and that I should not want you or Stewart till after Christmas. Then at a later date I wrote again — saying that from the absence of any names being given in, I really could not say that we should be able to find pupils for our purpose even then.[1]

As soon as ever there are pupils, you and Stewart shall have them ⟨(as I said, I think, in my second letter)⟩ — and I am doing all I can to get them. It is *the one* point, to which my exertions have been directed — not for its own sake so much, because I think their coming is only a matter of time, but because it disarranges all anticipations and preparations — e.g. such as yours, viz our not knowing.

As to your going to November, I think it is certainly a good thing to put into position — but I shall be very sorry that you should not know even exactly how things lie. Stewart has not written to me since his visit to Dublin, and I don't know what he has done.[2]

I am very glad to hear you are so much better, and that you are able to turn to your books

Ever Yours most sincerely in Xt   John H Newman

TO J. B. PAGANI

The Oratory. Hagley Road Birmm August 18/54

My dear Father Pagani,

Do you think you could kindly name one of your Fathers to be one of our University Preachers? It would only require of him one Sermon in the course of the year, and he would have ample notice beforehand.

Begging your good prayers, and those of your holy community I am
My dear Father Pagani, Sincerely Yours in Xt

John H Newman of the Oratory

The Very Revd Dr Pagani

TO J. B. PAGANI

The Oratory Birmingham August 21. 1854

My dear Dr Pagani

I thank you very much for your kind compliance with my request — and I hope you will not think me incroaching if I take two instead of one, since you give me three to choose from. Therefore, if you please, I will say Father Furlong and Fr Lockhart. It is impossible at this time to say when our Sermons

---

[1] Letters of 24 May and 21 June above.
[2] Thompson replied on 13 Aug. that Stewart intended to move to Dublin at the end of the month, and that he himself would go there early in Oct.

will commence — but the only way to begin at all, is to take steps towards beginning as soon as possible — which is the cause of my application now.[1]

I am, My dear Dr Pagani, Very sincerely Yours in Xt

John H Newman of the Oratory

The Very Revd Dr Pagani

TO EDWARD HEALY THOMPSON

The Oratory. Hagley Road Bm August 27/54

My dear Thompson

Thank you for your letter. I rejoice to hear so good an account of you, and only regret that you should be kept in this uncertainty.[2] But of course it is as trying to others, though in other ways — and I suppose is inseparable from important commencements.

The stamp has been ready some time for the [Catholic University] Gazette — but we had not any great use for it.[3]

I fear Dr Smith's book is in some way or other objectionable — but I may be wronging him. I thank you for the hint, and about Schmitz, but I will inquire.[4]

Ever Yours affly in Xt   John H Newman of the Oratory

P. S.   How many livery servants does Oakeley bring with him?

TO T. W. ALLIES

The Oratory Birmingham August 30. 1854.

My dear Allies,

I am sorry you have had to write for our return — which I inclose. We have not collected it long, I believe. Last year we had not a mission here. As to the Alcester Street collection of last year, I fear to fall between the new missioner and the old, and it was not collected.[5]

I have long wished to write to you to know how your views stand just now about the Lectures. Have you got your subject? One most interesting one would be the philosophy of the bearing and effect of the revival of learning upon the European kingdoms, which would indirectly, without seeming to do so, hit at the Protestant accounts of the Reformation in 16th century. Another would be the Balance of power; its history, how far it was known in Greece,

---

[1] See diary for 28 Feb. 1857, and letter of 3 Dec. 1856 below to Pagani.
[2] Thompson wrote on 26 Aug. that he would remain in England until he was wanted in Dublin.
[3] Over weight printed papers, for which a stamp had been obtained, could be sent by the penny post
[4] See letter of 7 July 1854 to Robert Ornsby. Thompson recommended the two works mentioned.
[5] T. W. Allies was secretary of the Catholic Poor School Committee.

etc, etc. On its being a substitute for the Pope's mediation in the Medieval Era, and its proposed issue in a board for deciding all differences between State and State according to the views of the Peace Society. Colonization would be another, e.g. whether it tended to republics etc, etc. But I only run on in this way, to have a claim on you for some report of your own thoughts.[1]

It is with great satisfaction I learn that something is to be done towards reformatory schools. I wish in fact Schools could be systematized. You have an immense field before you. Will any invitation of subscriptions towards reformatory schools come out soon?

Ever yrs affly in Xt   John H. Newman

TO DENIS FLORENCE MCCARTHY

Mount Salus. Dalkey Oct 11. 1854

My dear Mr McCarthy

If I had not been laid up with a slight accident this month past, I should have called on you before this to have had a talk with you on our proceedings next month.

Do you think you could give a course of Lectures in November and December? If you like it better, you should lecture merely to the members of the University, without admitting others. This would allow of your Lectures being more familiar and conversational, and would be less formidable than lectures open to the world, which might begin after Christmas. Besides, it might be a *rehearsal* of your matter.[2]

Very truly Yours John H Newman of the Oratory

D. F. McCarthy Esqr

TO EDWARD HEALY THOMPSON

Mount Salus Dalkey October 21/54

My dear Thompson

Pray thank Aubrey de Vere most warmly for his kindness to me — my 'titles' are quite correct. Of course I will put down his name thankfully.[3]

---

[1] See letter of 3 Sept. 1854 to Allies.

[2] McCarthy, Professor of Poetry, gave his inaugural lecture on 7 Dec. 1854, and began public lectures in Jan. 1855.

[3] Thompson, who after all had come to Ireland, wrote on 19 Oct. from Kingston:

'In a letter we had from A de Vere this morning he says, "I see that several people are getting their names 'put on the books of the University', I need not say that anything of this sort I should regard as a great compliment to me:— so pray manage it for me."'

He also tells us he is dedicating to you a Volume of Poetry,' and asked if the dedication to Newman described him correctly. See last note to letter of 25 Jan. 1855 to de Vere.

I am getting on, and am better every day — but very slowly.

As soon as ever the meeting takes place in November, I will tell you whether I shall want you sooner than Christmas — but I am as ignorant how things will be as ever.

Ever Yours John H Newman of the Oratory

E Healy Thompson Esqr

TO EDWARD HEALY THOMPSON

6 Harcourt Street Nov 10/54

My dear Thompson

Your letter has given me the most lively sorrow.[1] It had been my intention, even before it came, to come down to you this morning — but I am now hampered with an engagement. I send down a messenger, thinking to prevent your coming here.

What I think is best, is, that you should not tell people the whole state of the case — Say, what is quite true, 1. that you are not wanted at present. 2. that you think Tunbridge Wells will do you more good than Dublin just now.

People here will believe that you came here, *in case* we should want you directly, and have taken advantage of the delay to go elsewhere.

When we actually *do* want you, I will write to you and ask how you are. If you are well enough to come, so much the better — if not, then you shall resign – which I shall be truly sorry for.

I don't think it will do to seem to resign now — It will look as if I had acted hastily in publishing your name[2]

Ever Yrs J H Newman

TO EDWARD HEALY THOMPSON

The Oratory, Hagley Road Bm — Dec 31/54

My dear Thompson,

I hear a somewhat better account of you, which is pleasant. We have gone on very well for a first term. I don't know how it could have been better. Troubles, however, are sure to come from an external quarter. Don't repeat it, but I was told the other day that Dr McHale refused to join the Bishops'

---

[1] Thompson wrote on 9 Nov. that the Irish climate was seriously harming his health, and that he must return to England at once. Unless there were a very great change in his health he could never live in Ireland.

[2] Among the appointments announced in Oct. was that of Thompson as Lecturer in English Literature.

dinner at the Irish College at Rome the other day — and before he went from Ireland, he made a general protest against my appointments.[1]

As to English Literature, I suppose we ought soon to set about it in earnest. I see the report of the Committee on Indian Education, which is very important, lays especial stress on English.

Will you direct, seal, and forward the inclosed to A. de Vere.

Did I tell you I went down to Kingstown on the Sunday, and found to my regret you had left the Friday before?

With best wishes to you and Mrs Thompson for the New Year, which is 'overcast, and heavily with clouds brings on the day'

Most sincerely Yours in Xt John H Newman of the Oratory

E H Thompson Esqr

TO HENRY THOMAS ELLACOMBE

The Oratory Birmingham Jany 1. 1855

My dear Ellacombe

I am very much touched by your kindness in writing to me in your present affliction, and I earnestly trust and pray that you may be strengthened to support it. It is as great a trial as can be — except so far as the circumstance, that the dear child you have lost had already been removed from you by her devotion, has prepared you for it.[2]

When you wrote to me about her, I believe I was in too great perplexities myself to dare to be the guide of others; nor had I any right to inspire doubts by means of a position which implied the absence of them. As to her, God's ways are wonderful — that she has been a sacrifice to her strong religious feelings I do not doubt — may God reward her, as He rewards all who follow Him with a perfect heart.

For you, my dear Ellacombe, let me wish the best blessings of the new year, and more and more of God's grace to know how to please Him and to secure His promises

Very sincerely Yours John H Newman of the Oratory

The Revd H T Ellacombe

---

[1] See Archbishop MacHale's letter of 6 Oct. placed before that of 8 Oct. 1854 to him.

[2] Ellacombe, Rector of Clyst St George, Devon, wrote to announce the death of his daughter, Jane, on 27 Dec. She was one of the first members of Pusey's Sisterhood at Regent's Park in 1845. In 1844 she had been drawn to the Catholic Church, when her father, as Newman now reminds him, wrote about her case. Newman sent her to Pusey. Jane Ellacombe died in her father's house, weakened by her austerities. See also letter of 22 Dec. 1856 to Emma Langston.

51*

Oratory Bm Jan. 7. /55.

My dear Allies

I don't think much of your 22 years, seeing that once a scholar always a scholar; and have no compunction, since I am taking up the Classics after 25 or thereabouts, *without* having ever been a scholar.[1]

However, if it is a real annoyance to you to turn out what is beneath your high idea, give us Latin. Greek, however, is just what I can't get except from converts. I don't know what Hymn I said — it was my bad writing. Homeric metre will be capital.

I recollect, I spoke of the Pseudo-Gregory's — I mean, the drama.[2]

It was a great pleasure to me to see you in Dublin, and I only had a compunction at leaving you so much to yourself.

Ever yours John H Newman of the Oratory

The Oratory. Bm Jany 8/55

My dear Thompson,

Thank you most warmly for your kind letters, and pray accept my best wishes for the best blessings, according to the good Will of God, on you and Mrs Thompson for the ensuing year. I return to Dublin in a few days.

My notion is that the English Chair will be an important one, and take a good deal of work. But it would be a great thing to get A. de Vere at work any how — and therefore I would not ask much of him at first, if he would take it.

It ought to begin soon — I don't think I could give him longer time than to Easter — i.e. so that he would begin his Lectures after Easter.

If he came and resided and made it his business, it would be worth £300 a year — but if he gave merely courses of Lectures, I suppose it would be something like £50 a course.

I do not think I should be satisfied with his delaying his answer a long time — This I say to *you*. In the Poetry affair, he delayed from November to March — and just about a week after Mr McCarthy had accepted it, or rather proposed for it and been accepted, he then offered.[3]

---

[1] Archbishop Cullen wrote from Rome on 20 Dec. 1854, asking for a commemoration in Dublin of the doctrine of the Immaculate Conception, just defined. Newman asked Allies to make a contribution in Greek. See letter of 30 Dec. to him.

[2] *Christus Patiens*. Its authenticity has recently been upheld. See *Grégoire de Nazianze, La Passion du Christ*, edited by André Tuilier, Paris 1969.

[3] Thompson wrote on 1 Jan. that he had forwarded a note Newman had sent him for Aubrey de Vere. Thompson commented, 'There are many vexatious people, and Aubrey de Vere is among them.'

Fr Dalgairns is very busy just now. I have some notion that this work may be too learned for you. That it will be most interesting, I know well.[1]

Ever Yrs most sincerely in Xt   John H Newman of the Oratory
E H Thompson Esqr

TO MESSRS HOPE

Bm April 10/55

(Copy)
Gentlemen,

I have just read in the Times of today the following Advertisement:

'Just published, price half a crown number 90 of Tracts for the Times, with introduction and notes by the Revd James Frew — &c. London, Hope & Co. &c 16 Great Marlborough Street.'

I beg to inform you that the copyright of this Tract is mine — and, though I believe it is out of print at this time, this simply arises from there being as I conceive no sale for it, not from any disinclination of mine to re-publish it.

I am not aware that any recent act of Parliament on the subject of copyright has interfered with my proprietorship. If I am right in so thinking, and right in interpreting your advertisement, you are exposed to a legal process on my part.

As I am going to London tomorrow, I shall have an opportunity of consulting a legal friend and, should you have any remarks to favor me with, you may address them to the Oratory, Brompton Road.[2]

I am &c.

TO LADY GEORGIANA FULLERTON

Birmingham. June 4. 1855
My dear Lady Georgiana,

If I seem intrusive, you must excuse it on the ground of the interest which has always accompanied the thought of you in my mind, since the day you let me call on you years ago, as you passed through Oxford. I have already been saying Mass for your intention, though a black Mass has been impossible. And so have others here.

It would be presumptious in me to speak to you and Mr Fullerton of submission. However, let me bear witness, not only as a matter of faith, which we all receive, but as a point, which the experience of life has ever been impressing on me, more and more deeply, from my early youth down to this day, that unusual inflictions, coming on religious persons, are proofs that they are objects, more than others, of the love of God. Those whom He singularly and

---

[1] Thompson hoped that Dalgairns would contribute to his 'Popular Library'. Dalgairns's work was presumably *The German Mystics of the Fourteenth Century*, London 1858.

[2] Messrs Hope withdrew their edition. See letter of 28 April 1855 to them. Pusey republished *Tract XC* in 1865. See letter of 14 Nov. 1865 to him.

53*

specially loves, He pursues with His blows, sometimes on one and the same wound, till perhaps they are tempted to cry out for mercy.

He loves you in proportion to the trials He sends you. I am telling you no news; but a testimony, external to oneself, stengthens one's own; and perhaps my testimony may be given with greater energy and fervency of conviction than another's.

We are in His hands — and cannot be in better.

With every respectful and earnest feeling of sympathy with Mr Fullerton, I am,

My dear Lady Georgiana, Most sincerely Yours in Xt

John H Newman of the Oratory[1]

TO LADY GEORGIANA FULLERTON

6 Harcourt Street   Dublin June 13. 1855

My dear Lady Georgiana,

I was very grateful to you for your letter, which I did not expect: This requires no answer.

I hope to say Mass for you and Mr Fullerton every Thursday between this and Michaelmas Day.

Would that I could use words of real comfort. Words are weak — but the Mass is strong

Most sincerely Yours in Xt   John H Newman of the Oratory

The Lady Georgiana Fullerton

TO J. B. PAGANI

6 Harcourt Street Dublin July 10. 1855[2]

My dear Father Pagani

I write a line to your Reverence by way of condolence with you and your Fathers on the loss of your distinguished and holy Founder. The news took me by surprise, and concerned me very deeply, because, though he was so specially connected with your Body, a man like him is the property of the whole Church, while he is allowed to be on earth.

I fear his anxieties here must have shortened his life. I said a black Mass for him yesterday morning, and I hope he will not forget me as soon as he is in heaven, though he is there, we may well believe, already

I am, My dear Fr Pagani Very sincerely Yours in Xt   John H Newman of the Oratory

The Very Revd Dr Pagani

---

[1] This letter and the next have already been printed, but from incomplete copies.
[2] Part of this letter will be found in its place, in Italian translation. See also letter of 27 Oct. 1882 to Charles Kegan Paul.

TO JOHN HUNGERFORD POLLEN

Friday Nov 2 [1855]

My dear Pollen

I have wanted to see you for days out of mind — and too lame to walk and too busy to write

Ever yrs J. H. N.

TO JOHN HENRY PARKER

6 Harcourt Street Dublin March 26. 1856

My dear Mr Parker,

I have to thank you for agreeing with Mr Rivington to let me have the copyright of my Essay on Ecclesiastical Miracles, as I learn from his letter just now received.

While I am writing, I will ask you whether you can give me information on the subject of Gallandi's Bibliotheca, which I purchased of you some years ago. The copy was deficient — and the portion deficient was written out. I have never had the copy bound, and have unluckily mislaid or lost the written portion.

I want you to be so good as to tell me, if you can, *what* the part deficient was and of *how many* pages. If it did not cost too much, I should get it printed by my printer here. If I did that, I must ask you to get it roughly copied. But the first question is *what* the deficiency was, and of how many pages. I think I bought it of you about 1843.[1]

I hope you will be able to give me a good account of yourself. I am here till the end of next week, April 3; when I go to 'the Oratory, Birmingham.'

Very truly Yours John H Newman

J H Parker Esqr

TO MRS EDWARD HEALY THOMPSON

6 Harcourt Street Dublin May 13. 1856

My dear Mrs Thompson,

I am much concerned to hear of Mr Thompson's continued indisposition. It must be an extreme trial to you and to him. I had not heard of him for some time, nor did I know where he was. To us he has been a great loss; and, now that it is over, I reproach myself for taking so little pains, while you and he were here, to cultivate his and your acquaintance. But I was very busy just

---

[1] Newman's edition of Andrea Gallandi's *Bibliotheca Veterum Patrum* was that in fourteen volumes, Venice 1765. The title page of each of the volumes was missing, and was now supplied.

then, and I looked forward to the future as enabling me to postpone the pleasure of the moment.

But one must never anticipate any thing, or put off any thing in this life — How long my Congregation will let me be here, I know not. It is now all but 5 years since I have had my thoughts given to the University, and my movements dependent on its proceedings. This cannot last for ever. We have been exceedingly prospered, and I shall have a plea for retiring when things have got into their places.

With my best remembrances to Mr Thompson, and begging your good prayers

I am, My dear Mrs Thompson, Sincerely Yours in Xt

John H Newman of the Oratory

Mrs Thompson

TO HENRI LOUIS CHARLES MARET

Hagley Road Birmingham. England May 20. 1856

My dear Very Revd Sir,

I acknowledge with much gratitude your kindness in intending to send me a copy of your work. I shall receive it with great satisfaction and interest, as sure to throw light upon a very important subject of theology.[1]

I have not written in any Review for these ten years past, and, except one article then, for nearly 15 years.[2] And I am sorry to say, the University of Ireland has no connexion whatever with the Dublin Review. Were it in my power to serve you in any way, I would gladly — but a work like yours requires no service from any one such as I am.

I beg you to receive the homage of my truest respect and to believe me to be,

M. le Docteur Your obedient Servant in J.C.

John H Newman of the Oratory

A Monsieur Monsieur le Docteur Maret Paris

TO MESSRS BURNS AND LAMBERT

Dublin July 18. 1856

Messrs Burns and Lambert,

I hereby certify that I have transferred to you the right of making a translation in the German language of a work, of which I am Author, entitled 'Callista'

John H Newman

---

[1] Maret sent the first volume of his *Philosophie et Religion, Dignité de la raison humaine et nécessité de la révélation divine*, Paris 1856.
[2] The one article was *Lyra Innocentium, D R* (June 1846), pp. 434–61.

TO MRS WOOTTEN

August 17. 1856

My dear Mrs Wootten,

I was so glad to hear you mention Mr Walsh.[1] I have always a lively remembrance of his kindness to us as [at] Littlemore. It is 32 years since I first knew him, though he may not recollect me quite so long — and there is no one for whom I have a greater respect.

Do you think he would accept from me a Volume of Sermons

Most sincerely Yours in Xt   John H Newman

TO THE DUCHESS OF NORFOLK

The Oratory Birmingham August 18. 1856

My dear Duchess of Norfolk,

I am sure you will forgive me for writing you this letter, whether you are able to comply with its request or not. And considering the manifold claims great people have to endure from the whole world, I shall not be at all surprised, if I find I am asking what is impossible.

Miss French, whom you may recollect in Alcester Street, as an Irish Convert, cast off by her friends, and helping this Oratory in many good works, had a fever or pleurisy last winter, which for a while made us despair of her life. She recovered, but now Dr Evans, her medical adviser, says he will not answer for her life, unless she goes to the south for the winter. She starts for Paris next Friday to remain there a month; thence she will go to Italy as her physician may then advise her.

We are trying to gain her some addition to her means, which are very limited. Mr Monsell and another friend have each promised something. Her family have been applied to. They have assisted her in the course of the year, and now declare they have not got it in their power to do more. Should you find it possible to do any thing, I should be very grateful.

How melancholy the news is of Lord Shrewsbury's death! It has almost taken people's breath away.[2]

With my best respects to the Duke, and kindest thoughts of all your circle, I am, My dear Duchess of Norfolk, Very sincerely Yours in Xt

John H Newman of the Oratory

[1] Henry Walsh, Oxford lawyer. Newman consulted him again in 1864 about the purchase of land in Oxford.

[2] See letters of 30 Aug. 1856 to Miss M. R. Giberne and 29 Nov. 1857 to the Duchess of Norfolk.

The Oratory Birmingham August 20. 1856
My dear Duchess of Norfolk

We are very much obliged by your kind and most munificent contribution towards an object in which we are so much interested. I see of course very little of Miss French — but it has touched me much, whenever I come here, to see her going on and on in her quiet and unregarded exertions — and it has proportionally distressed us to find her health failing.

However, when her need comes, God is good to her. You have made us all very glad. We are not likely to forget you, as many as have been allowed to know you, even without this.

Ask Lady Victoria[1] to say a Hail Mary for me, — she has said one before now — and believe me to be,

My dear Duchess of Norfolk Most sincerely Yours in Xt

John H Newman of the Oratory

The Duchess of Norfolk

Dublin, October 25, 1856.[2]
My dear Arnold,

Will you allow me to call you so? How strange it seems! What a world this is! I knew your father a little, and I really think I never had an unkind feeling

---

[1] Eldest daughter of the Duchess.

[2] This letter has already been printed in a shorter form. See note there. It is printed here from the copy in the article by his son William T. Arnold, 'Thomas Arnold the Younger', the *Century Magazine* (May 1903), p. 127. William Arnold introduced the letter by inserting the greater part of his father's first letter to Newman, in the summer of 1855, which began their correspondence. See letter of 27 July 1855 to Lord Dunraven. It was written from Hobart Town, and is preserved in a copy made by Thomas Arnold's daughter Julia:
'Revd and Dear Sir

I entreat you to forgive the freedom which I take in addressing you, though an utter stranger to you. The name I bear is doubtless familiar to you, and were it necessary that you should know any particulars about myself personally, there are several Oxford men to whom I could refer you. Ward and Faber I knew among others: the latter rather well.

My excuse for writing to you and seeking counsel from you, is that your writings have exercised the greatest influence over my mind. I will try to make this intelligible in as few words as possible. My Protestantism which was always of the liberal sort and disavowed the principle of authority, developed itself during my residence at Oxford into a state of absolute doubt and uncertainty about the very facts of Christianity. After leaving Oxford I went up to London, and there, to my deep shame be it spoken, finding a state of doubt intolerable, I plunged into the abyss of unbelief. You know the nature of the illusions which lead a man to this fearful state far better than I can tell you; — there is a page in your lectures on the University system where you describe the fancied illumination and enlargement of mind which a man experiences after abandoning himself to unbelief [*Idea*, pp. 132–3], which when I read, it seemed as if you had looked into my very heart, and given in clear outline feelings and thoughts which I had had in my mind, but never thoroughly mastered.

In this state of mind I emigrated to New Zealand, in the year 1847; whence I was invited down here by the late Governor, Sir William Denison, to fill the post of Inspector of Schools. This I still hold. I married here in 1850, and have two children. Up to last October I remained in the same way of thinking; unable to pray, without peace and without God in the world.

towards him. I saw him at Oriel on the Purification before (I think) his death and was glad to meet him. If I said ever a harsh thing against him, I am very sorry for it. In seeing you, I shall have a sort of pledge that he at the moment of his death made it all up with me. Excuse me — I came here last night, and it is so marvellous to have your letter this morning. . . .

I write in great haste, as I have much to do today. May all blessings come upon you. . . .

Yours most sincerely in Christ,

John H. Newman.

TO DENIS FLORENCE MCCARTHY

6 Harcourt Street Oct 26. 1856

My dear Mr McCarthy,

It is with great sorrow that I saw yesterday your letter to Mr Scratton. I will urge you no more, but will, with great regret and with feelings of great respect for you, accept your resignation of your Professorship.

In various ways I fell into grievous sin; — and philosophy proved to be no preservative against it. At last by God's mercy, a meditation into which I fell on my unhappy and degenerate state was made the means, — a text from St Peter suddenly suggesting itself to my memory — through the violent contrast which I found to exist between the teaching of the Apostle and the state of my own soul, of leading me to inquire again, to pray again, and to receive again, most unworthy as I was, the previous gift of faith in Christ.

This however is not all. You who have said that a man who has once comprehended and admitted the theological definition of God, cannot logically rest until he has admitted the whole system of Catholicism [*Mix.* pp. 260–1], will not wonder if after having admitted Christianity to be an assemblage of real indubitable historical facts, I gradually came to see that the foundation of the One-Catholic Church was one of those facts, and that She is the only safe and sufficient witness, across time and space, to the reality of those facts and to the mode of their occurrence. These convictions, the meditations of each day only tend to strengthen, and I ardently long for the hour for making my formal submission to the Catholic Church. It is here however that my perplexities begin; – and it is to you, who can understand and enter into all such, and to whose writings I feel most deeply indebted, that I venture to come for a resolution of them.

First — Could you advise me as to the *time* of making such submission? My dear wife, who is without any positive religious convictions (in great measure, alas! through my fault) has imbibed the strongest prejudices against Catholicism, and I see no prospect, humanly speaking, of her altering her mind. My mother and sisters — all in England — are sincerely Protestant, and I cannot doubt that my conversion will be a serious blow to them. And it is impossible for a son to owe more to a mother in the way of tender respect and consideration than I do to mine. I could with difficulty bring myself to take any important step, without her having at least full *knowledge* of it beforehand.

Secondly. Do you think that after having joined the Catholic Church, I might lawfully continue to take an active share in the administration of a system of primary education such as that established in this colony — one which, while not excluding religious teaching from the schools, professes to treat all religions alike, and to make no distinction between the various denominations into which the population is divided. It is quite possible that the Government would call upon me to resign — but if they should not I should be glad to be advised how to proceed.

Lastly. If I had to give up my situation and to think of returning to England, could I rationally look forward with anything like confidence to obtaining employment in some Catholic seminary or college at home.

I need hardly say that I would wish you to regard this letter as in some sort a confession, so if you are so very kind as to reply to it, what you write shall not come either to the sight or the knowledge of any third person

Believe me to remain in hope

Sincerely Yours T. Arnold.

59*

It grieves me to think that we should have thoughtlessly pained you by printing your name. It was taken from the list in the Calendar as a matter of course

Earnestly hoping you will in no long time recover your health,

I am, My dear Mr McCarthy Very sincerely Yours

John H Newman

D. F. Mc Carthy Esqr

TO MOUNSTUART ELPHINSTONE GRANT DUFF[1]

6 Harcourt Street Dublin Novr 11. 1856

My dear Sir,

You must not think me neglectful of your kindness in lending me Cohen's book. Mr Stephen brought it when I was packing up for this place — and I know I shall be so overwhelmed with work here, night as well as morning, that it would be useless bringing it with me.

I return to Birmingham for a little while in a fortnight, when I promise myself the pleasure of availing myself of the interesting matter you have furnished for me

I am, My dear Sir, Very truly Yours John H Newman of the Oratory

M E Grant Duff Esqr

TO J. B. PAGANI

The Oratory, Birmingham Decr 3. 1856

My dear Father Provincial,

I did not write at once on the subject of the preaching, because from what I heard I thought there was a chance of seeing you in Dublin. It is very kind in you to meet my wishes so promptly. Now I write.

The first Sunday in Lent is, I think, March 1st — and the second, March 8th. Do you think you could favour us, yourself or your Fathers, with University Sermons, one on each of those two days?

What I wish to have, as you may desire me to say, is a plain searching exhortation, suited to the season, which may do us all good.[2]

Thanking you very much for your kindness, I am,

My dear Fr Provincial, Sincerely Yours in Xt

John H Newman of the Oratory

The Very Revd The Fr Provincial of the
Order of Charity

---

[1] cf. note to diary for 31 Dec. 1856. James Fitzjames Stephen was a close friend of Grant Duff

[2] See above, letter of 21 Aug. 1854 to G. B. Pagani.

TO EDWARD HEALY THOMPSON

April 28/57 Oratory Bm

My dear Thompson

I ought to have returned your letters before. Thank you for the sight of them.[1] I write in great haste, as now starting for Dublin

Ever Yours John H Newman

TO FREDERICK CHARLES HUSENBETH

The Oratory, Birmingham October 17. 1857

My dear Dr Husenbeth,

Our Cardinal, acting under decree of the 2nd Provincial Synod of Westminster, and with the concurrence of the Bishops, has done me the singular honor of committing to me the charge of revising our version of the Holy Scriptures. I am sure that, in a matter of this kind, you above most men, can suggest to me some remarks and rules, which may guide me in the very responsible and arduous undertaking. May I make this claim upon your kindness? also, will you allow me, when my work is more advanced, to send you specimens, or portions of it, for the benefit of your criticism?[2]

Excuse this trouble, and believe me always,

My dear Dr Husenbeth, Yours affly in Xt

John H Newman of the Oratory

The Very Revd Dr Husenbeth

P.S. The copies of your Drama, which you were kind enough to give me, never got to me.[3]

TO LADY GEORGIANA FULLERTON

The Oratory, Birmingham October 28. 1857

My dear Lady Georgiana,

I ventured to send you that small book, not as thinking that there was any thing in it which would be of especial interest to you, but in order to bring me

---

[1] See letters of 6 and 12 April 1857 to Thompson.
[2] See letter of 17 Oct. 1857 to Ralph Platt.
[3] This refers to Husenbeth's *The Convert Martyr. A Drama in five acts, Arranged from 'Callista:' by permission of its Author*, London 1857. See letters of 18 Feb. and 31 March 1857 to Husenbeth. He explained on 21 Oct. that he meant Newman to apply to the publisher for the number of copies he wanted.

to your mind, for I am getting very old now, and need the prayers of all who will be so kind as to think of me. And therefore I cannot help taking pleasure in the good opinion of others, as in yours, though I know in my conscience I am so unworthy of it, because it serves to give me a hope that they will remember me in sacred times and places. Pray do not forget to do that, my dear Lady Georgiana, and be sure that I try to do the like charitable office for you and Mr Fullerton.

Ever Yours most sincerely in Xt
John H Newman of the Oratory[1]

The Lady Georgiana Fullerton

TO FREDERICK CHARLES HUSENBETH

The Oy Bm Oct 28/57

My dear Dr Husenbeth

I thank you for your valuable suggestions. Be sure I have no idea of making the Protestant Version a Standard. I had not heard of the paragraph in the Literary Gazette.[2]

Thank you for correcting my mistake about Burns and your Drama

Yours affly in Xt   John H Newman of the Oratory

The Very Revd Dr Husenbeth V G

TO AUBREY DE VERE

The Oratory Birmingham Nov 23. 1857

My dear de Vere,

The inclosed will show you we are progressing — when will you give us an article?[3]

I did not answer your kind letter and its inclosure some months ago, first from idleness, secondly on the excuse that I did not know where you were. Nor do I now

Ever Yrs most sincerely John H Newman

A de Vere Esqr

[1] This letter has already been printed, but from an incomplete copy.

[2] Husenbeth wrote on 21 Oct., 'There is a serious apprehension lest an endeavour should be made to assimilate our version to that of the establishment. This fear has been strengthened by a paragraph in some respectable papers, such as the *Literary Gazette*, stating broadly that this is even one main object of your commission. This fear is the more natural from the preference which you must have from long habit for what is called the "authorised version", — a preference which old Catholics do not usually entertain, and which I own I could not feel.'

[3] The first number of the *Atlantis* appeared in Jan. 1858. Newman enclosed a prospectus.

TO FRANK SCOTT HAYDON

The Oratory Birmingham April 14. 1858

Dear Sir,

Your letter opens so very large a subject, that I regret I shall not be able to answer it in any time which is at my disposal.[1] Nor do you ask me — but wish me to do what I am ashamed to say I have not the means of doing, recommend you some book which treats upon it. The truth is, like many Oxford men who have become Catholics, my convictions have been the slow growth of years, and the truths which I accept with all my heart have been brought home to me by personal reflection much more than by consulting divines or controversialists — so that I am a very unfit person to seek information of on the subject.

But your letter also raises the question whether a proof of infallibility be *possible* from the nature of the case. Here I ought to be able to give you my own answer to it, certainly — but how can I do so without knowing what you already hold and what you do not? — First, I should say that *the word of God must* be infallible; if then God *has* spoken, what He has said must be true, and His organ of communication must be infallible. This I suppose you would allow, and then your question becomes this —, not, can the Infallibility of the Church be demonstrated, but can there be a demonstration (such as may legitimately be demanded) 1. that God has spoken. 2. that God has spoken by the Church.

Now, as to the former of these two propositions, if an inquirer be an orthodox Protestant Christian, whether High Church or Low Church, he has no doubt at all about answering it in the affirmative. He will say that there is *sufficient* proof that the Bible is the word of God, and therefore true. But if I were to ask him 'do you think the proof *infallible?*' he would not perhaps know what to answer, he might say yes, or he might say no — but any how he would say that it was *sufficient* — and, if I could convince him that it would not be sufficient, *unless* it were infallible, he would have no hesitation in saying that in that case the proof *was* infallible; — so sure would he be of it.

Now I do not know whether you would allow yourself to be either of the High Church or Low Church school, but there are so many able men who belong to both, that I think the fact that they consider the Bible the true word of the Infallible God, sufficient to suggest to you, that, without taking into account as worth any thing any reasonings of mine, which, as you truly say, 'public criticism has rejected,'[2] it is worth while inquiring what public

---

[1] See the first two notes to letter of 24 April 1858 to Haydon, already printed from the draft. The second note refers to this present letter of 14 April as missing. It has since come to light in America.

[2] In his letter of 12 April Haydon wrote: 'I have read with much interest many of your published works on questions between the Church of England and of Rome — and have often found myself accepting without doubt the reasonings which, to my astonishment, public criticism subsequently rejected.'

criticism says to the High Church or Low Church philosophy, or whether that public criticism does not proceed from men who do in their own persons *profess* the philosophical basis either of the High Church or Low Church School. I know well that the argument as you put it 'An infallible Church must have an infallible proof' is very common with Protestants; I have used it myself before now;[1] but I think it should be held by those only who are *not* Protestants, but go much further. For surely it is to say with Hume that Revelation is incapable of demonstration, or that it is more likely than [that] testimony should be false than miracles true.

If you ask me my own answer to the question, I shall feel only this reluctance in giving it, that it involves a great deal of definition and discrimination which I could not get through on a sheet of paper. I should have to determine what is meant by an infallible proof etc etc. Therefore I will only say this, that I agree with High Church and Low Church Protestant so far, as to be unable to see any metaphysical or a priori difficulty in holding on *moral* evidence and with a *moral* conviction that 'God is *infallible*, His word is *true*, and there is an *existing organ*, instrument, or record of His word —,' — and that I think the onus probandi lies with those who do feel it.

I cannot hope to satisfy you with a few words – but even a few words, written in good will, and with a prayer to be able to write them sincerely and faithfully, may elicit a response of faithful and sincere inquiry in the heart of him who reads them.

Yours, my dear Sir, Very faithfully John H Newman

F. Scott Haydon Esqr

TO EDWARD HEALY THOMPSON

The Oratory, Bm April 14. 1858

My dear Thompson

I am very sorry you should have this additional trial upon you — and I wish I had it in my power to relieve it.

It is true that a school is in contemplation here — but on a very small scale. And since it is quite an experiment, we should attempt, in the only master with whom we should begin, in additional to Fr Darnell, to get a person well known as connected with the Protestant public schools — and with such a person (to tell you in confidence) I have corresponded some weeks ago, with a prospect of success.[2] I cannot predict how the school will go on, and I suppose it will be long before we want any one else besides an usher to be with the boys out of school hours and at night.

---

[1] *V.M.* I, pp. 86–9.
[2] This was Thomas Arnold. See letter of 15 Dec. 1858 to him; also that of 16 Jan. 1859 to Edward Bellasis, and note to letter of 14 March 1858 to T. W. Marshall.

I am always glad to hear of you and about you — and, as you speak of strict confidence, I think it best to burn your letter[1]

Ever Yours most sincerely in Xt   John H Newman of the Oratory

E. H. Thompson Esqr

P. S.   The only thing that would reconcile me to the thought of your going abroad, would be, if it had a chance of benefitting your health. Let me know how you decide.

TO FRANK SCOTT HAYDON

The Oratory, Birmingham April 24. 1858[2]

My dear Sir

Your letter certainly puts forward an objection to religious evidence as far-spreading as it is deep; nor am I the person to undervalue it, though I utterly disallow its force for the purpose to which you put it. Thus to feel towards it implies no inconsistency, as I hope will appear from the answer I shall make to it.

You ask, 'Must there not be an infallible evidence for the existence of an Infallible Church?' I would rather word the question thus, — 'Can I be certain that God is true, and that God has spoken?' And I prefer to throw it into this shape, because I then understand what I mean better, while I keep to the real point which is necessary in the argument for Catholicism.

1. You would question whether it is possible, from the nature of the case and antecedently, that we should have an infallible proof that God has spoken, or spoken this or that; you question whether there is not an antecedent impossibility of an infallible proof even in mathematics. I am disposed to agree with you here; but then, I make a distinction between the *judgment* of the mind as to the cogency of a conclusion, and the *state* of mind consequent upon that judgment. The 47th proposition of Euclid book 1st is certainly open to the objection, that the proof involves a grasp of previous propositions, which I cannot trust my memory to have accomplished. In my *judgment* then it is not absolutely demonstrated, 'without the taint of probability;' but *certainty* is not this judgment, it is a *state of mind*, and in spite of my *judgment* in disparagement of the *proof*, I suppose I am *certain*, without any sort of apprehension lest I should be mistaken, that the proposition in question is *true*. At the same time I consider it will be granted me, that the state of mind, which we call certainty depends ultimately on the will, which *could* so act upon the mind, as to lead it (morbidly) to use that microscopic objection as an occasion of *doubting* the truth of the proposition in question.

---

[1] This probably referred to a family lawsuit. See letter of 13 Feb. 1859 to Thompson.
[2] This letter has already been printed from a draft. See the notes there.

In like manner, when I say that the existing proof, of a certain person or body being the oracle of that God who can neither deceive nor be deceived, is sufficient for certainty, I mean no more than that certainty is the state of mind to which that proof *legitimately* leads, and will lead unless an act of will is interposed to hinder such a result. How often do we say, 'I cannot prove it, but I firmly believe it, I am sure of it;' that is, 'though I cannot draw out a proof which is clear of all logical objection, I feel I possess one which is sufficient in reason for my accepting a certain conclusion.'

Am I not certain that England is an island? am I not certain that I shall die? yet let me try, if I can, to make out a demonstration for either proposition.

I may surely then take it as a *law* of the human mind that 'proof, speculatively incomplete, is sufficient (not only for practical, but) for speculative belief; or again, that 'objection and doubt are not correlatives.' (connatural?)

Am I to go on to doubt of the truth of the laws of the human mind? If so, there are no laws of *reasoning* inclusively. Am I to go on, till I am sceptical of my own scepticism, and, though I condescend *practically* to follow what is probable or what is safest, to be allowed rationally to entertain *speculative* doubts whether I live or feel?

2. This, however, you will say is a mere reductio ad absurdum, and not a positive answer to your difficulty. I am aware of it; and I must leave it so, though for myself, I *have* an answer which satisfies my own mind. Many persons indeed will think it a greater assumption than any other which I could possibly make; but it is *my* first principle, and first principles *must* be assumptions, and if it be a first principle which approves itself to me, it may approve itself to another. I am very diffident about it, yet I cannot think it arises from an idiosyncrasy.

I assume then the being and presence of a Moral Governor of mankind, and I look at every thing which comes to me as coming from Him. The question simply is, What are the laws of thought, of belief, of conduct, under which my mind lies? Whatever they are, they are His imposing. I have only to ascertain them. He might have willed, that, as the Angels, I should need no middle terms at all; and now that He teaches me by means of inferences, I may see clearly that it is His will, that is, that it is a law of my nature, that they need not be infallible ones. I may have clear intimations, from a diligent scrutiny into the phenomena of human life and the course of the world, that He does not mean doubt to be the necessary consequence of logical imperfection. That is, it may be my duty to do in religion, what I continually do in matters of this world.

If it is not impertinent then to refer to myself personally, I will say, that this sense of God's presence is the only protection which I have had (though an abundantly sufficient one) to keep me from unlimited scepticism. I expressed it in the first book I wrote, 26 years ago. In my work on the Arians, after speaking of the apparent unreality of all phenomena, I went on to say, 'Though, on the mind's first mastering this general principle, it seems to itself at the moment to have cut the ties which bind it to the universe, and to be floated off upon the ocean of interminable scepticism, yet a true sense of its own weakness brings it back, the instinctive persuasion that it must *be intended to rely on* something, and therefore that the information given to it, though philosophically inaccurate, must be practically certain, a *sure confidence in* the *love of Him* who cannot deceive, and who has impressed the image and the thought of Himself and of His will upon our original nature.' — Where by 'practically certain', I mean, 'practically sufficient for speculative certainty.'

Eleven years afterwards, in a University Sermon, I said the same thing: — 'Should any one fear, lest thoughts such as these should tend to a dreary and hopeless scepticism, let him take into account the Being and Providence of God, the Merciful and True, and he will at once be relieved of his anxiety. All is dreary, till we believe, what our hearts tell us, that we are subjects of His governance; nothing is dreary, all inspires hope and trust, as soon as we understand that we are under His hand, and that whatever comes to us is from Him, as a method of discipline and guidance. What is it to us, whether the knowledge He gives us be greater or less, if it be He who gives it? What is it to us, whether it be exact or vague, if He bids us trust it? Why should we vex ourselves to find whether our deductions are philosophical, provided they are religious?' etc etc

I do not know what others will think of such a view of the matter; for myself I can only say, that in matter of fact, from this abiding conviction that God is over us, though I am as keenly sensitive as any one to objections, I have at no time had any tendency to religious doubt.

3. Now I will suppose a powerful sceptical philosophy to bring out forcibly the 'taint of probability' attaching to mathematical demonstrations. In such a case surely it would not be preposterous in any one who felt it embarrass him in the prosecution of that science to repel doubt by a strong act of the will, and to make an act of faith in the conclusions of Euclid or Newton and that on the broad principle that objection is not necessarily the parent of doubt.

And in like manner I think it possible to have such evidence that the Church is the oracle of the Almighty, as to make it a duty towards Him to accept her as such, under the conviction that He would not have invested her with evidence of such quality, though not demonstrative, unless He had meant thereby to signify to us the objective truth of a conclusion, to which proof at least points; and this, something in the way that I understand the signs and signals of my superior, whom I know well, though they are not drawn out into formal sentences.

Excuse this long letter, which nevertheless is short for its subject.

Yours, my dear Sir, most truly John H Newman

F. Scott Haydon Esqr

TO FRANK SCOTT HAYDON

The Oratory Birmingham May 28. 1858

My dear Sir,

I interpret the end of your letter of the 6th to mean that you do not wish to continue our correspondence — and I can easily understand, from my own case, how the engagements you speak of may interfere with your doing so.[1]

And I think too, that no issue would be obtained from it, were it continued, while the term 'infallibility' remains undefined. I attempted to say what I myself took it to mean in the argument for the truth of the Catholic Religion. I do not gather from your letters whether you agree or differ in my interpretation — nor have you given any other instead. In consequence, I do not feel able to follow the course of your last remarks.[2]

However, have you not at least departed from the à priori ground which I understood you originally to select?

I am sorry to have given you the impression, that I hold it to be lawful or not unlawful for a man to make himself believe any conclusion he pleases, irrespective of evidence.[3] Still I think he is often able (unlawfully) to do so; though of course, the clearer the evidence, the harder is his task. Properly, however, I should not call it 'belief' or 'faith,' but 'persuasion', or some other less honorable term, when it is an act in opposition to reason.

I am, My dear Sir, with every kind wish and prayer for you,

Yours very truly John H Newman

F. Scott Haydon Esqr

TO ROBERT MONTEITH

The Oratory Birmingham August 12. 1858

My dear Mr Monteith

I thank you very much indeed for your considerate present. I was not in possession of the book, and it seems very interesting and useful. I see by it that the new translation of the Romans [is] published, which I am very glad to know.[4] Should you hear of any new publications of the kind, I should be much

---

[1] Haydon's letter of 6 May (misread as 8 May in last note to his letter of 24 April) ended: 'I cannot say how sincerely I sympathise with the latter sentences of your letter, nor how cordially I join in the prayer that I may be enabled to enquire humbly and faithfully, still supported by hope if not by Faith.' See end of letter of 14 April to Haydon.

[2] Towards the end of his letter Haydon argued that 'human language is at best often equivocal', and hence that no Revelation could be 'known *certainly* to be divine'. These considerations nonetheless established the necessity of some learned body to interpret any book which very probably contained a divine message. In his first letter of 12 April he had claimed that infallibility was useless unless it was 'à priori evident'.

[3] This Haydon argued at the beginning of his letter of 6 May.

[4] Monteith's present was *The Gospel according to St. John, after the Authorized Version*, 'Newly compared with the original Greek and revised, by five clergymen', second edition, London 1857. On the back of it *The Epistle to the Romans* was advertised as 'Preparing for publication, by the same revisers'.

obliged to you, if you would give me information about them, if you have five minutes to spare. For myself, till I get the University off my hands, which will be very soon now, I shall not be able to do much.

I am, My dear Mr Monteith Most truly Yours

John H Newman of the Oratory

R. J. I. Monteith Esqr

TO J. B. MORRIS

The Oratory Bm Septr 18. 1858

My dear Morris

I am sorry I have so carelessly expressed myself as to make you think I did not want you to write on the drift as well as the date of the book of Job. In my mind the two subjects were connected together, but, when I see your way of treating them, I find they form two subjects, not one. All I should ask your leave to do would be to put the two in successive numbers of the Atlantis, and then we should have the advantage of two articles from you instead of one.[1]

My real *difficulty* in your paper, as it stands, is the introduction of theology proper and of controversy. I feel that I simply should not *be allowed* in the pages of the Atlantis to attack Protestants, and to teach our sacred doctrines, as that of the Immaculate Conception B. M. V. and I suppose rightly, for I should be using the work for a purpose for which it was never intended.

I know that our line of writing is uncommonly *dry*, but it must be so — for we are concerned with facts, and arguments from facts, and nothing else.

Don't suppose I do not feel how much there is in your article — a great deal more than you have thought worth while to bring out — but I can no more change the character of the Atlantis, than I can of Euclid.

Yours affectly in Xto   John H Newman of the Oratory

The Very Rd J B Morris

P. S.   I suppose you have heard that Charles Marriott is dead.[2]

TO JAMES STEWART

The Oratory, Bm Octr 18. 1858

My dear Stewart

If I have not taken up your idea of matriculation, it is because I did not consider you had reduced it enough to shape. Are the persons you speak of to

---

[1] See letter of 7 Sept. 1858 to Morris; also the end of that of 31 Jan. 1859 to W. K. Sullivan.

[2] See letter of 18 Sept. 1858 to J. R. Bloxam.

be residents or non-residents? You must, please, bring the proposition under our rules, and see how it stands there. At first blush I do not see that they may not be 'non-residents', supposing they mean to go on to a degree — not that there need be any pledge — but it would be unmeaning if there was a *system* of matriculation without the curriculum.

If you mean to make an *addition* to the Statutes, put the proposed addition into form.[1]

Excuse my bad writing, but my fingers are quite tired out with correspondence etc.

Your account of Fr Flanagan makes me anxious. I too thought him thin, when I first saw him. He has gained flesh lately, but perhaps he had lost a quantity before.

Ever Yrs affly John H Newman

J. Stewart Esq.

MEMORANDUM. LETTERS TO THE RAMBLER

March 1/59

Correspondence

Subjects for Letters.

1. France and Austria

2. illustration of Döllinger's expression. history as in theologians.

3. on the force of the propositions condemned by the Congregation of Index lately about there being a *proof* of the Being of a God, immortality of soul etc.[2] What is meant by word 'proof.' whether 'sufficient proof' is not parallel to 'sufficient grace.'

4. on the magisterial sayings of Dmowski 'nefarious to deny general ideas,' etc of Liberatori, that Bacon diris devovit the Syllogism. etc. and not bringing out in the vernacular answers to difficulties etc.[3]

5 a defence of the principle of nationalism from 'What *can* they know at Rome of the intimate wants of a country? of the Authors to be put on the index, of what is possible' etc. e.g. the condemning Gothic vestments.

6 subject of *scandal* and not speaking out, e.g. about the Index.

Communication.

1. a continuation of the Church of the Fathers, beginning with St Jerome;

---

[1] See letter of 22 Nov. 1858 to Stewart.

[2] Augustin Bonnetty's traditionalism was condemned by the Congregation of the Index in June 1855 and he had to subscribe theses including 'Ratiocinatio Dei existentiam, animae spiritualitatem, hominis libertatem cum certitudine probare potest . . .' *Denzinger-Schönmetzer* 2812

[3] Joseph Aloysius Dmowski, S. J. was the author of *Institutiones Philosophicae*, two volumes, first edition, Rome 1840, fourth 1844. Matteo Liberatore, S. J. inaugurated the revival of Thomism with his *Institutiones Logicae et Metaphysicae*, Naples 1840–2, frequently re-edited.

or rather first with ⟨running off into⟩ an apology for freedom beginning with Baronius, Rinaldus etc. Ciaconius.[1]

Set of Articles on

1. The *real* reason for belief is *divine*, not argument — vid John xiv. *compared* with this all argument may be called only probable.

2 whether notes of Church need be more than primâ facie or probabilities.

3 on *presumptions* as opposed to *facts*, i.e. to Mill's philosophy.

4. on probability issuing in moral certainty.

SKETCH OF LETTER 'THE PROSPECT OF WAR'[2]

1 Dreadful a conflict between *the* two Catholic powers — in other times of world *more* great Catholic powers. scandal. Kilkenny cats.

2. Yet I don't see why we should reserve our sympathy for Austria. And in saying that I shield myself behind the present Pope.

3. We cannot forget that 'Pio Nono' was a cry synonymous with the freedom of Italy. Popes do not commonly change.

4. The Austrians sent a veto on his election, but were too late — Various incidents of him in 1846,7. Words quoted in Napoleon pamphlet.

5 It is very well to be conservative, but the question is of *what*? conservatism is not good in itself. Else Christianity would never have come into the world. Did the Austrians remain to the end of time, they would be brutal. Their shootings — the police man at Verona.

4. [sic] Nor is the status quo desirable in Italy. Describe state of relaxation of priests and religious. ⟨King of Naples in the hands, not of the priests, but of the police.⟩ little hold over the people — King of Naples keeping bishopricks open like Russia [?] — no confirmations — no bishop at Pantellaria. no priests. Discontent, tyranny; no enlightenment without infidelity. Instance of bad priest in St Alfonso's life. qu. whether any thing of the state of Italy can be made out of the processes in the Library?[3]

5 Roman treatment of the present Pope — 'vile.'

6. the state of Italy a great scandal to the Protestants

7. Lombardy. The late Archbishop of Milan fraternizing with English Protestants against Catholic Italians.[4] Dislike of Austrian Rule by Priests. Manzoni — Great cruelty to Austria. Nuns — St Ambrose chasing away Austrians.

8. Dreadful the prospect of the devastation of Temples and shrines — but

---

[1] Rinaldus was the Oratorian continuator of Baronius. Ciaconius was author of *Vitae Summorum Pontificum et Cardinalium*, 1601.

[2] This letter, dated 2 April, was published in the *Rambler*, and is printed in Volume XIX, Appendix I, pp. 534–8.

[3] i.e. the Processes of Canonisation of Saints in the library at the Birmingham Oratory.

[4] This was the Austrian, Cardinal Gaetano Gaysruck, who became Archbishop of Milan in 1817 and died in 1846. He is said to have been a zealous pastor, but more like a soldier than a bishop, and opposed to the re-establishment of the religious orders.

will not the French *hinder* this. Did a red revolution break out at Rome, ⟨or at Palermo⟩ what would become of the priests and relics — The French are not as the first Revolution, not as Napoleon I. They would repair

9 Hence the English so opposed to the French. It is edifying. They opposed Russia in favor of Turkey because she would go into the principalities — but when France in favor of Italy opposes Austria who will hold Italy under its grasp, they are indignant. What is the real reason? They were ready enough to interfere 11 years ago. Why, you can't have your cake and eat it. They have squandered millions and wasted the most precious blood on the Turk, and a burned child dreads the fire. They cannot go to war twice. And like the dog in the manger they don't like France to do what they have no mind to.

10 And then moreover, they are not quite sure that Louis Napoleon will put down the Pope — the contrary — and what is the good of putting Italy to rights, if it will take away their power of talking against the Pontifical government?

THE PROSPECT OF WAR[1]

Sir,

I do not yield to any one in sensitiveness at the thought of the scandal which is involved in the prospect of war between three Catholic powers, which at the present moment indeed is doubtful; but, even if it comes, I think that there are worse scandals than such a war, and that, in spite of its inexpressible horrors and its attendant miseries of every kind, good may come out of it.

I did not think so of the Russian war; no good could come out of a contest, entered upon with such negative objects. It was a war of mere jealousy against Russia. and it was difficult to see what could come of it but loss of blood and treasure. At the same time viewing the Russian war in its best light and the war which seems coming in its worst, there is so much of analogy between the two, that it does seem wonderful that Englishmen, that Catholics, should consider the Russian war a sacred crusade, and the war before us, if it is to be, an ambitious, unprincipled invasion ⟨attack⟩.

⟨In those last words I seem taking the side of France — and I avow I do not think her success would be the greatest of evils⟩ Now first I am no defender of Louis Napoleon, for the simple reason that no one can defend a person too reserved to be trusted. I am no lover of the cloudy Napoleonic oracles contained in his speeches whether from the throne or in the Moniteur. It is not the way to gain our confidence

spargere voces

In vulgum ambiguas et quaerere conscius arma

Once he has spoken clearly – and certainly the sun came out to burn not to

---

[1] This is a draft of the letter to the *Rambler* (May 1859), reprinted in Volume XIX, Appendix I, pp. 534–8. See notes there.

gladden. He has told us, in a passage of one of his works, to which attention has been drawn of late ⟨Treaties of 15⟩

Nor do I forget the acts of French Rulers towards Italy now for 4 centuries nearly. But I have nothing to do with the Emperor of the French or with his motives tho' I think it is not mere jealousy; but first with ourselves, and secondly with the cause of religion. I think ⟨believe⟩ our reprobation of Louis Napoleon's conduct not a little inconsistent, and I suspect our fear for the cause of religion is not a little shortsighted.

I suppose we shall grant our inconsistency as regards Sardinia. What on earth had Sardinia to do in reason or fairness with the Russian war? What excuse had she for going to war? ⟨Perhaps in consideration of the antiquity of her House he is allowed to be a knight errant But if it attacked Russia why not Austria⟩ She had not the zeal of France for the Holy Places; she had not the fears of England for Indian possessions. I suppose then it was her philanthropic wishes to benefit the Turkish Empire: *honesta oratio*; and has she not a still greater right to cherish patriotic ideas about Italy? Have the Neapolitans, the Sicilians, no wrongs as well as Anatolia or Syria? I really should like some explanation why we were so mute, or rather loud in our admiration, when Count Cavour went to war with Russia, and so shocked, so indignant when he goes to war with Austria. We are now surprised and angry in 1859 that she goes to the expense of an army so disproportionate to her position in Europe; this anomaly did not strike us in 1855. Sardinia will reply, that well-appointed armies which may allowably defend the Turks from the danger of Russian domination, may without much qualm[?] rescue the Italians from the present ⟨existing⟩ pressure of Austrian usurpation.

This brings us to the case of France. I can fancy the Russian minister saying to the French some ⟨three⟩ years since, when the negotiations commenced for peace at Paris 'you think it is all fair to be jealous of us, yet you allow the encroachments of your neighbour. Austria is both your Turk and Russian in one; more than Russian because she is an actual intruder into a country not hers; as much as Turk, because she rules by force not by reason, and is the enemy of all reform and improvement. We at least should be better than the Turks in Turkey: we were putting an end to her slave trade on the Eastern coasts of the Euxine, when your armies interfered to restore it; we were putting down an enemy of the Christian name, and you have fought us under the united symbols of the Cross and the Crescent. You made us keep our hands off the Turks whom all your past Popes had denounced; and yet you don't make Austria keep her hands off the Italians, though the present Pope took the field against her.' France ⟨Louis Napoleon⟩ understands well the force of these arguments, for the improvement of Italy is an old hobby of his, and his minister introduces the subject to plenipotentiaries.

Inconsistencies are but on the surface of political action; why is it really that Englishmen are so averse to the present war. First, because war is no longer a novelty, they know, alas, what it is; the upper classes know the cost in blood, and the middle and lower classes know the cost in pocket. On the Russian war followed the Indian revolt. They have had enough of a good thing. A burned child fears the fire, and not irrationally. It is a pity they could not be wise without the experience. Secondly they are jealous of France now, as they were jealous of Russia, and they look to their interests and their possessions, not to the formal position of things or to logical necessity. And further still, in spite of their bad opinion of Louis Napoleon, they think he has religion enough to have no bad intentions to the Holy See, but in his own way to mean the Pope well, and, though they might be tempted to go to war themselves to annihilate him, they do not like France to go to war to remove the scandals which encompass his throne. And I think he would. I think the scandals greater than a war ⟨1 priests would be murdered 2 be king or don't⟩

Here we are brought to the second and chief point on which I beg leave to say a word. It seems then both true, and if true, honest to say, that the state of the Pontifical States is a more grave and dangerous scandal to religion than a war between three Catholic powers, serious as that is. And, in saying so I am saying it under shelter of the Pope's own conduct, when he acted for himself on first coming to the throne. There is nothing to show that he has changed his mind. Whatever leaks out proves the contrary. He and Cardinal Antonelli send Mr Bowyer etc. Speak out he cannot, from his position; his duties as the head of the Church hinder his political action as a temporal prince. M. Gueronnière says this   quote   [1] He went as far as he could ten years ago in the way of emancipating himself from the thraldom in which he is held. In the Byzantine age, in the middle age, the Pope was held in one kind of thraldom; now he is in another. First he was in thraldom from the sucessors of Constantine, tho' Constantine was his deliverer — then from the successors of Charlemagne, though Charlemagne was his restorer — Imperialism and feudalism were his old jailors. I do not know history ⟨and present fact⟩ enough to define his present captivity I cant give it a name — I don't know where it came from — but it must be a captivity when Pius, who can do so much in the ecclesiastical line, is so impotent in the civil. Somehow or other it is connected with Austria. Do not we recollect how she tried to prevent his election [and] was just too late? how he was said to be a reformer because [before] it and proved himself so after it? how he failed, not from change of purpose, but because his instruments broke in his hands? because the contemptible population of Rome, and the do-nothing nobles needed an education before they could be a people, before they could be statesmen and ministers? Would he not have laymen at this minute for the organs of his administration, had things continued in the course in which his own large mind put them?

When he came to the throne, his feelings were averse to Austria, they were

---

[1] Evidently the pamphlet of le Vicomte de la Gueronnière, *Napoléon III et l'Italie*, published in Feb. 1859 and inspired by the Emperor. It suggested that in return for the Presidency of a federal Italy the Pope should relinquish part of his temporal power.

warm and confiding towards England and France. He threw himself upon England; the history of that year 1847 sufficiently shows it; as to France, he expressed his desire to visit her shores, till the revolution overtook her. On the other hand his feeling about Austria is conveyed in his words quoted in the late famous pamphlet of Louis Napoleon   (quote)

TO SIR JOHN ACTON

[8 June 1859][1]

P.S.   I suspect Arnold would not write without pay; His name would be good. I declined his offer, as being too late.   J H N.

TO A. H. H. JESSE[2]

The chief authors of this re-action were the Jesuits — and it gave rise to two separate protesting movements — one on the part of Baius — the other and more famous on the part of the Jansenists, who professed to take the part of St Augustine, and to enunciate his doctrine. *They were* certainly a kind of Calvinists — but, after a long struggle, were ejected from the Church. Whether St Augustine really sanctioned some things they said, is a contested point; doubtless he said strong things which no Catholic would say now; but they never have been said by the Church at any time.

I hope I have answered your difficulty, as far as a few words can do so.

No apology was necessary for your letter — had there been, the name of Jesse, so well known in the literary world, would have been a sufficient introduction

I am, Dear Sir, Very truly Yours

John H Newman

A. H. H. Jesse Esqr

P.S.   Many great divines have taken St Augustine's view of predestination The Dominicans took a line very much like his. The Jesuits took the opposite side. Till lately no Saint was known to be with them — but now they can appeal to two — to St Francis de Sales, of whom a letter has been found on the subject, and St Alfonso Liguori.[3]

---

[1] On 7 June Thomas Arnold asked Newman: 'Would you admit a short paper from me upon Mill's book on Liberty into the next number of the Rambler?' Newman wrote what follows on Arnold's note and sent it to Acton. The paper appeared in the *Rambler* for Nov. 1859.

[2] This is perhaps a mistake for John Heneage Jesse, the historical writer. See *DNB*, X 804.

[3] The letter of St Francis de Sales is that of 26 Aug. 1618 to Lessius. Annecy edition XVIII p. 271.

TO GEORGE W. B. STAR

The Oratory Bm Octr 21. 1860

My dear Mr Star

I felt very much for you on the receipt of your letter, though I have not answered you at once.

But I said Mass for the soul of the dear wife, from whom it has been the wise and loving Will of God to separate you, as early as I could, viz the 26th of last month.

And, as you wished, I recommended her to the prayers of the faithful on the first Sunday, and posted up the notice at the usual place in our Church.

God, who has inflicted so deep a wound, will by his grace support you under it, and heal it for you.

I was very much pleased you wrote to me

Pray for me and believe me Most truly Yours in Xt

John H Newman of the Oratory

Mr Star

TO FREDERICK WILLIAM TRENOW, O.P.

Private   The Oratory Bm March 20/61

My dear Fr Trenow,

We shall be very glad of a brother, and thank you for recommending one.

This, however, I must say, an Oratorian House is a trying one, in this way. We have not a rule, strong enough to support and carry on every one. And again, our Superiors are bound to use little else but gentleness and persuasion in their treatment of their subjects. Then again there are no vows. It is plain then that a specific vocation is necessary for the Oratory, and one not often found in devout but uneducated minds.

In addition to this, since we are but few, and very much engaged in our several ways, most of us out of doors, lay brothers are necessarily left to themselves more than is desirable, and more than our Rule *admits of*.

I say these things to you by way of enabling you to judge whether your protegé is likely to suit us. If you think he is, we will gladly receive him as a probationer-brother

Our Fathers desire their kindest remembrances, and, not forgetting you in their prayers, hope for yours in turn

Ever Yours very truly in Xt

John H Newman of the Oratory

The Revd Fr Trenow O S D.

76*

TO FREDERICK WILLIAM TRENOW, O.P.

The Oratory Bm April 26/61

My dear Fr Trenow

I hope you will pardon my silence

We shall be glad to see Edward Child at Whitsuntide, as he proposes. He must write a line to give us notice

Yours very sincerely John H Newman

TO MRS TYNDALE

The Oratory Birmingham Sunday [end of 1862?]

Dear Madam

On inquiry I find that our usual way is to perform the funeral rites in the chamber where the body lies before its removal for burial. Therefore, if you will kindly tell us what time will be suitable to you, one of our Priests shall come to your house for the purpose

Yours faithfully John H Newman

Mrs Tyndale

TO LADY GEORGIANA FULLERTON[1]

The Oratory Birmingham June 3. 1863

My dear Lady Georgiana

I thank you very much for the second copy of the offerings. After asking for it, I was half sorry, fearing it might in some way prove a trouble to you. I hope this has not been the case.

I am very glad you are going to Rome for so long, greatly as I know you will be missed at home. You have taken such hard work upon yourself, that you must have rest. It is a happy thing when a remedy is also a reward, and soul and body enjoy a common benefit

With all kind thoughts of Mr Fullerton

I am   Most sincerely Yours in Xt

John H Newman

The Lady Georgiana Fullerton

---

[1] This letter has already been printed, but from an incomplete copy.

The Oratory Bm Nov 22/63

My dear Sir

I hope you will excuse my delay in answering your question on the plea, which I am obliged to urge, of the various letters I have to write.[1]

I do not know whither exactly to direct you to find a distinct answer to the objection you mention — but I know one person who has been in controversy upon it, and I dare say, if you wished to know, he could give you some information.[2]

If a person said to me 'Catholic countries are morally worse than Protestant,' I should first ask for his proofs. I should inquire whether he spoke of town or country — and should urge that the multitude in towns, commonly speaking, have little practical religion at all, and that in consequence it was hardly fair to call them Catholic or Protestant, as far as *obedience to a rule of conduct*, was concerned. On the other hand I think a Catholic population has a *sense* of religion and a *knowledge* of the great principles of religion, natural and revealed, which a Protestant population has not — I mean has a sense of the presence of God, of a future state, of the fact and the evil of sin, and a habit of religious observance — and deeply lodged convictions of the truth of the Christian doctrines of redemption and grace. And secondly, I think that in a Catholic city would be found an antagonist mass of good, of piety, conscientiousness, purity, and charity, which was not to be found in a Protestant city, without denying of course that there was a religious remnant in a Protestant city also.

Next, I don't think it would be fair for a Protestant to take his own standard of good and evil, and judge by it. For instance, lying and cheating on a small scale are more despicable sins than the almost recognized and legalized frauds which are found through all classes in a mercantile community, and they lie more on the surface and obtrude themselves upon the notice of the stranger. The latter are the sins of English towns — the former of Naples or Palermo — Cheating may be a rule of the trade in England (e.g. the placing false marks on goods, the adulterations of food etc) but an Englishman, taken at random knows nothing about them — he goes abroad and in his first walk in a Southern town he has his pocket picked of his handkerchief, or the wrong number of zwanzigers given him in change. To illustrate what I mean by an example on the other side. We should consider how foreigners are shocked at the disorders of Regent Street, the Haymarket, the Strand etc every evening

---

[1] Faduilhe, who was the curate at St Peter's church, Woolwich, wrote on 9 Nov. that he had spoken with an artillery officer, ready enough to accept the chief points of Catholic doctrine, but who objected as 'a notorious fact that immorality is more prevalent and more rampant in Catholic Countries (France, for instance,) than it is on these shores'. Faduilhe thought he had read of statistics which contradicted this.

[2] See letter of 4 Oct. 1862 to W. J. O'Neill Daunt.

and night — yet I don't suppose London is more immoral than a foreign city, in spite of this.

All this being considering [sic], viz that cities are not the best measures of the excellence of rival religions, that it is difficult to get at a true insight of what the state of a place is, especially if we have not resided in it, and thirdly that we are apt to bring a standard of right and wrong and prejudices of our own in forming our judgment, I think our best way of proceeding is, first to take countries which we are likely to know best and on which public opinion and testimony can be brought to bear, and secondly to have recourse to statistics, as giving ascertained facts, as you yourself say.

As an instance of the first method of proceeding I would appeal to the populations, in the length and breadth of each island, of Great Britain and Ireland — and should be quite willing that the question should be decided by a comparison of the two.

As to Statistics, which is the second method I have mentioned, I believe there are a number of works which are much to your purpose — e.g. Mr Laing's I believe, a Scotch Presbyterian, whose evidence is considered much in favour of Catholicism[1]

Excuse these insufficient remarks — I have not studied the subject. Two Lectures in my own Volume of 'Anglican Difficulties' etc are in a measure upon it.[2]

I am, My dear Sir, Yours very faithfully

John H Newman of the Oratory

P.S.   France is hardly an instance of a Catholic country. I have been told that a third is Catholic, a third indifferent, and a third atheistic. As a country it fell off from Catholicism at the Revolution. I ought to have thanked you in my first lines for the very kind words which you use of me[3]

TO PETER GALLWEY, S.J.

The Oratory Bm Febry 26/65[4]

My dear Fr Gallwey,

In answer to your question, whether there is an opening for a Catholic periodical, say a monthly magazine, or a want of one, I should first of all say, that, as to whether there is a *call* for one, you, as seeing so many people, have

---

[1] Samuel Laing (1780–1868), author of *A Tour in Sweden in 1838 : comprising Observations on the Moral, Political, and Economical State of the Swedish Nation*, London 1839; *Observations on the Social and Political State of the European People in 1848 and 1849*, London 1850, and similar works.

[2] *Diff.* I, 'The social state of Catholic countries no prejudice to the sanctity of the Church'; 'The religious state of Catholic countries no prejudice to the sanctity of the Church.'

[3] Fadhuilhe wrote that, although not personally known to Newman, he appealed to him 'on the principle of the Angelic doctor, that the higher order of Angels teach the lower ones.'

[4] This letter has already been printed from an incomplete copy.

much more means of answering the question, than others have. In such matters, supply *must* precede and create demand; and such supply as your Society can furnish, considering the number of your able and learned men in the English and Irish provinces, must, I conceive, create the demand, considering the discretion and tact which the Society of Jesus applies to the execution of all its undertakings.

Putting then aside this part of the subject, I would rather speak of the need of such a publication. Here I would say, that as secular power, rank, and wealth are great human means of promoting Catholicism, so especially, in this democratic age, is Intellect. Without dreaming of denying the influence of the three first named instruments of success, still I think the influence attendant on a reputation for ability and cultivation of mind is at present greater than any of these. The Catholic body in England is despised by Protestants from their (unjust) idea of our deficiency in education, and in the power, which education gives, of bringing out, and bringing to bear, that force of natural talents, which Catholics possess as well as others. They have an idea that few Catholics can think justly or express themselves satisfactorily. A first-rate journal then, of which the staple was science, art, literature, politics etc. would be worth more to the Catholic cause, than half a dozen noblemen, or even than a millionaire.

Next, I think that Protestants are accustomed to look upon Catholics, as an un-English body, who take no interest in national questions, nay, are unable to do so, and useless or hostile to the public, and the mere instruments of a foreign power. A magazine then, which, without effort or pretence, in a natural way, took part in all questions of the day, not hiding that it was Catholic to the back bone, but showing a real good-will towards the institutions of the country, so far forth as they did not oppose Catholic truths or interests, showing that it understood them, and could sympathise in them, and showing all this in the medium of good English, would create in the public mind a feeling of respect and deference for the opinion of the Catholic body, which at present does not exist.

As to the *direct* inculcation of Catholic truth, as such, in a periodical of this kind, I should dread its effect. I conceive the Magazine would be useless (for the purposes which alone I contemplate) if once it came to be generally comsidered as an 'Ultra-montane organ.' It seems to me that, what is to be aimed at, is to lay a Catholic *foundation* of thought — and no foundation is above ground. And next, to lay it with Protestant bricks; I mean, to use, as far as possible, Protestant parties and schools in doing the work, as St Paul at Athens appealed to the Altar of the Unknown God.

Then, as to the good which such a Magazine would do to Catholic readers, I should consider it to consist in its making them what it is itself; in creating in them that enlargement and refinement of mind, that innocent and religious sympathy in national objects, that faculty of easy intercourse with Protestants, and that power of aiding them in lawful temporal objects, which would ultimately be a means, more than any other human means, of bringing converts into the Church from all classes of the community.

I am, My dear Fr Gallwey, hoping you will excuse these imperfect remarks Sincerely Yours in Xt

John H Newman

The Very Revd
    Fr Gallwey S J.

TO JAMES PARKER

The Oratory Birmingham March 19. 1865

My dear Mr Parker,

I recollect you perfectly, though you were not so important a person in those days as you are now. It concerns me much to hear of your Father's indisposition; he is well to be out of England in weather such as this is.[1]

As to your question, certainly I know nothing at all about the publication of the Hymns which you speak of. The Hymns in themselves, I suppose, cannot be made copyright — but if my preface and initials are added, the case is altered.[2]

If it is worth your while to accept the Copyright from me, you are very welcome to it. If you do not, I will write to Messrs Macmillan myself on the subject.

Very truly Yours John H Newman

James Parker Esqr

TO JAMES PARKER

Rednall April 29/65

Dear Mr Parker

I have received no explanation either from Mr Combe or Mr Macmillan. Now I come to think some years ago Mr Combe never answered a letter I sent him, and I do not know why.[3]

---

[1] James, now aged thirty-one, was the only son of John Henry Parker, and had succeeded to his bookshop and publishing business in Oxford.

[2] Alexander Macmillan republished in 1865 in one volume *Hymni Ecclesiae e Breviario Parisiensi* and *Hymni Ecclesiae e Breviariis Romano, Sarisburiensi, Eboracensi et aliunde*, published at Oxford by J. H. Parker in 1838, the former with an English, the latter with a Latin preface, both of them signed J.H.N.

[3] On 21 March James Parker replied to Newman's letter of 19 March that Alexander Macmillan had written to him about the new edition of *Hymni Ecclesiae*, saying 'that it was brought to him ready printed by Mr Combe of Oxford, and that he was only to act as agent, and further that he thought naturally Mr Combe had full authority to print the book.' James Parker was glad to be able to say that he had had no hand in this republication about which Newman had not been consulted. 'A wrong is clearly committed against you.'

I think I ought to have some explanation about my Preface — and should be much obliged to you to obtain me one.

A sort of practice has got in, I forget whether I told you so before, of reprinting publications of mine without my leave; and I think it ought to be stopped.[1]

Very truly Yours John H Newman

James Parker Esqr

P.S.   Please direct to me 'Oratory, Birmingham.'

TO JAMES PAGET

The Oratory June 4. 1865

Dr Newman returns his thanks to Mr Paget for his letter, and proposes to call on him on Wednesday morning next between eleven and twelve.[2]

TO ANNA SWANWICK

The Oratory Birmingham August 6. 1865

Dear Madam

I am very much obliged to my brother for gaining for me from the Authoress the favour of a copy of her translation of the Trilogy of Æschylus.[3] Yet I do not wonder that he should be desirous to show how apt a pupil he has had in an arduous line of study.

The finer poetry is, the more indigenous it is in its character. Æschylus presents no exception to this remark; and it is surprising to me that you have been able with so much energy and spirit to encounter the difficulties of his style and to trasmute him into clear and literal English

I am, Dear Madam, Truly Yours John H Newman

Miss A. Swanwick

[1] Thomas Combe was the Superintendent of the University Press, and had a publishing arrangement with Macmillan. Combe explained on 3 May to Newman that he understood John Henry Parker, the original publisher, had given him permission to reprint *Hymni Ecclesiae*. There had been a misunderstanding, and Combe offered to hand over to James Parker any profit that might accrue.

Combe called at the Birmingham Oratory in Sept. when Newman was away. See letter of 16 Oct. 1865 to Mrs Thomas Combe.

[2] See diary for 7 June, also letter of 14 Aug. 1865 to Paget.

[3] See letter of 22 Aug. 1865 to Anna Swanwick and note there.

TO CHARLES JOHN PRATT FORSTER

The Oratory Bm Novr 18. 1865

I will gladly send you a copy of Loss and Gain — and I hope without much delay.[1]

It grieved me very much to hear of the loss with [sic] the Ryde Mission has had. It must be especially severe to the Woods.[2]

Say some good prayers for me, and believe me to be

Most sincerely Yours in Xt

John H Newman of the Oratory

C. Forster Esqr

TO FREDERICK WILLIAM TRENOW, O.P.

The Oratory Birmingham Febry 10. 1866

My dear Father Trenow

Fr Bittleston has just shown me your letter to him, which has gratified me exceedingly. Indeed it would be strange if I did not feel it a great satisfaction, to have gained the approbation of your Fathers. My Pamphlet, short though it be, has been a matter of much anxiety to me, and, if it is in any respect useful, I shall feel it to be our Lady's goodness, who makes it so[3]

Very sincerely Yours in Xt   John H Newman of the Oratory

The Revd Fr Trenow O.P.

P. S.   I have reserved for a P. S. (which often is not the least important part of a letter,) to thank you personally, which I do with all my heart, for your Masses for me, and, while I pray that I may get the full benefit of them, in spite of my own unworthiness, I pray too, that, by the infinite value of the Sacrifice, they may redound in equal fulness of blessing upon the offerer himself.

TO MRS F. R. WARD

The Oratory Birmingham March 8. 1866

My dear Mrs Ward

Being still anxious about Trinity, I wrote to my nephew now in residence at Oxford.[4] I inclose his answer, which you may like to see. On the whole I

[1] The copy is now at Prinknash Abbey. It is inscribed, 'Charles J. P. Forster, with the Author's kind regards March 20/66'

[2] The death of the priest, Henry Telford. See letter of 11. Nov. 1865 to Charlotte Wood.

[3] *A Letter to Pusey.*

[4] Francis Woodgate Mozley was a Scholar of New College, 1864–9, and Alfred Dean Mozley a Scholar of Jesus College, 1866–71. For Newman's anxiety see letters of 17 Dec. 1865, 5 Jan. and 25 Oct. 1866 to Mrs F. R. Ward.

consider it favorable. Every College has its bad set — the question is whether a College has a good set too.

My nephew has misread me. I spoke of a rowing set of men — and he has read 'boating' for 'given to rows.'

Very sincerely Yours in Xt   John H Newman of the Oratory

Mrs Ward

TO E. E. ESTCOURT

The Oratory Bm June 30/67

My dear Canon Estcourt

I have just received the printed Circular about the Bishop's Testimonial — and ask you to be so good as to correct a mistake, when any new copies are struck off. Instead of 'Dr Newman,' read, 'The Fathers of the Oratory.'[1]

To make up £20 a year is a difficulty for all of us, though we gladly encounter it — but for me to promise so much would be an absurdity, since I have not the means. And I am the more anxious the mistake should be corrected, as, in spite of all that I have said to the contrary, there is, I believe, a general idea that I am very wealthy. No greater proof of this can be given than what I have had to write about this week. An Irvingite clergyman, of whom I know nothing, wrote to me to ask me to pay his journey to Rome, to be present at the Canonizations. Surprised as I was, I thought at least he had some notion of becoming a Catholic — but he answered me 'No, not at all' — he only wished to be at Rome on a great occasion — and in his justification he sent me a letter a priest had sent him, to the effect that there were various wealthy people to whom he might go for money — out of whom, the priest said, he advised him to go to *me*.

I suppose you have altogether given up the idea of a Public Meeting. For myself, I think Priests would not have any business there. It is the business of the laity — they ought to *defend* their priests, and they can do it in better ways, I think, than by a Public Meeting[2]

Yours most sincerely John H Newman

TO RICHARD WESTBROOK LAMB

The Oratory, Birmingham. August 19, 1867.

Dear Sir,

I enclose for your inspection a copy of the prospectus of our school. It will answer many of your questions. We have between 50 and 60 boys, of all ages, from seven or eight to seventeen. They are lodged under one roof, in several

---

[1] See letter of 17 July 1867 to J. Spencer Northcote.
[2] After the 'Murphy Riots' in Birmingham. See letters of 19 and 29 June 1867 to Mrs John Mozley and Mrs F. J. Watt.

houses, in three or four dormitories, each superintended by a master. The school was originally set up in order to secure the comfort and proper care of little boys; they are under the charge of an old friend of ours, a lady who is the widow of one of the later physicians at Oxford.[1]The subjects of study are Latin, Greek, Mathematics, French and History.

I am, dear Sir, Very faithfully Yours,

John H Newman of the Oratory.

TO RICHARD WESTBROOK LAMB

The Oratory, Birmingham. Sept. 9, 1867.

Dear Sir,

In answer to your questions, I have the pleasure of telling you that there is no fagging whatever in our school, that corporal punishment is in the hands of two priests, members of our body, who superintend the school, and that it is rarely administered. If you are acquainted with Mr. Waldron of Ballybrack near Bray, his sons, three of whom are with us, would be able to tell you whether our system was severe or not. We could receive your son at once, if you determined on sending him.

I am, dear Sir, Yours faithfully,

John H. Newman of the Oratory.

TO CANON DONNET

The Oratory 11 December 1867

[A letter of introduction for R. H. Milward] an eminent lawyer of Birmingham, who is called on important business to Brussels.

TO RICHARD WESTBROOK LAMB

The Oratory, Birmingham. June 3, 1868.

My dear Mr. Lamb,

We received with the greatest concern the news of your over-whelming affliction; and I pray with all my heart that that Merciful Father, who has so visited you, will support you under His mighty, but gracious Hand. No one can know but you, what you have to bear. I have said Mass for your dear wife, and rejoice to have once seen her.

I am very sorry to hear of Joseph's continued indisposition. It is a sad loss of time, but he is so good and promising a boy that I trust he will soon recover it. Give him my love and believe me to be,

My dear Mr. Lamb, Sincerely yours in Xt,

John H Newman of the Oratory.

[1] Mrs Wootten

TO SIR JOHN TAYLOR COLERIDGE

The Oratory Bm Febr 7. 1869

My dear Sir John,

I received your Life of Keble from the Sollicitor General yesterday, and I have already read it, so far as it is right to call that reading which of course has been hasty.[1]

I do not see there is one word that could distress me, even in those passages (and I think there are some) in which, lest you should pain me, you have suppressed my name. And there are many on the other hand, in which you have spoken of me with a kindness and consideration, for which I am thankful to you.

I wish he had not thought, as he expresses it in the case of R Wilberforce, that a Catholic could not be goodnatured; ⟨pp 364–403⟩[2] but, though he might hold it in the abstract, or of persons at a distance, he would not think it of such persons as he actually saw. I suppose he meant that severity in speaking against Anglicanism, which is necessary in a Catholic, is often, or always, an outlet of illnatured and spiteful feelings.

I have taken the liberty to add several remarks on particular passages of the Life. May I take the additional liberty of congratulating you both on the great pleasure, mixed with whatever deep sadness, you must have felt in writing it, and on the successful accomplishing of an interesting and touching memorial of so dear a friend.

I am, My dear Sir John, with much respect,

Your faithful Servant John H Newman

Sir John T. Coleridge &c &c.

N.B.

p 215. Keble also wrote Numbers 52, 54, 57, 60. Four Saints' Day Sermons, which I believe were to have been parts of a course.[3]

[1] *A Memoir of the Rev. John Keble, M.A.* The Solicitor General was Sir John Duke Coleridge, later Lord Coleridge, son of the author.

[2] On p. 364, Keble's letter of 6 Oct. 1853 to Sir John Taylor Coleridge was quoted, about the possibility of Robert Wilberforce's conversion: 'But I really cannot imagine a person of his truthfulness, learning *and good temper*, putting up with the Roman system as a Convert.' On p. 403, Keble's letter of 6 Nov. 1854 to the same correspondent referred to Robert Wilberforce after his conversion. After speaking of the loss of an American friend, Professor Henry Reed in the sinking of the *Arctic*, Keble wrote: 'But the comfort in thinking of such as he (no doubt) was, is solid and growing, — not so the thought of poor dear R.W., whose departure touches *me* almost more nearly than any one's; except, perhaps that of Newman himself. I did not until very lately think that he would really go *there*. I thought he was too good tempered, besides his learning and truthfulness.'

[3] On p. 215 only *Tracts* 4, 13, 40 and 89 were attributed to Keble. In the third edition, 'With Corrections and Additions,' p. 224, Coleridge added a note: – 'To these I find now on the best authority ought to be added Numbers 52, 54, 57, 60, four Sermons on four Saints' Days. These on the same authority were to have been parts of a course.'

p 219. When, in 1841, I told Archbishop Howley (through another) that one of the *prospective* Tracts was a second part of 89 by Keble, it either did not move him at all, or moved him against acquiescing in the continuance of the Series. I give the impression on my mind, and my traditional memory, without any distinct remembrance, except that Keble's intention was certainly mentioned to him.[1]

p. 243. The Preface to Froude's Remains, consisting of 22 pages, is certainly Keble's, not mine, except the portion about 'Romanism' from p ix to p xv. I speak of the Preface to the First Series — The Preface to the Second Series is all Keble's, except a few formal lines at the end, which I think are mine.[2]

p 257. Lord Dudley's words are, 'I saw D. the other day in town. It is quite astonishing that with such an understanding and such acquirements, his manners should be so entirely odious and detestable. How you could live with him without hating him, I do not understand. Clever as he is, there must be some great defect in his mind, or he would try to make himself a little more sufferable.' p 58[3]   For Keble's sake, and from faith [?] in Keble, I had a rap at Lord Dudley for it in my review of Davison's works in the British Critic; but I confess that, in spite of my then and present admiration of Davison's abilities and writings, he was an awful man for young Masters to meet in Common Room, and in what I have said I may have done Lord Dudley something like the injustice which he has done to Davison.[4]

p 265. Yes — Mr Benson gave the name 'Tractarian' to us in his Sermon. I thought no one recollected this but myself. It pained me very much at the time, for the very reason that any title implied us to be a *party* — and I could not bear that we should be so thought — as I had a sort of contempt for parties, and party-leaders as being a sort of demagogue[s].[5]

[1] On p. 219 Coleridge regretted that *Tract* 89 'remains a fragment only.' No change was made in the third edition.

[2] On p. 243 Coleridge said of Hurrell Froude's *Remains*: 'for although Mr. Newman wrote the admirable preface, and was the ostensible publisher, Keble shared in the preparation, and insisted on partaking of the responsibility.' This was altered to: 'it was published in 1838 and 1839 in two Parts, and to each is prefixed a well-considered and able preface, written by Keble; with the exception however as to the second of a few formal lines at the close, but as to the first, of the portion from p. ix to p. xv. This last vindicates Froude from the imputation of Romanism, in the sense of favouring the Roman Catholic Church, or of being disloyal in any true sense to the Anglican, by citations from the "Remains" themselves. These excepted parts are, as I now learn, by Dr. Newman, who was the publisher of the work; Keble, however, shared largely in the preparation, and insisted on partaking of the responsibility.' cf. letters of 7 April 1876 and 19 June 1878 to W. J. Copeland, and notes there.

[3] Coleridge quoted a letter of Keble's about John Davison's *Remains*, which he was preparing for publication: 'I am just now, puzzling myself how, in the quietest and best way, to counteract the ill and false impression which the Bishop of Llandaff and poor Lord Dudley have been spreading abroad concerning his conversation.' Keble went on to call them 'the unworthy sentences'. Coleridge remarked 'I have not the means of ascertaining what "the unworthy sentences" were'. Newman quotes them from *Letters of the Earl of Dudley to the Bishop of Llandaff* Edward Copleston, London 1840. Coleridge altered his sentence in the third edition p. 268, to, 'It is not material now to ascertain what "the unworthy sentences" were'.

[4] The *British Critic* (April 1842), pp. 368–9; republished with alterations in *Ess.* II, pp. 377–8.

[5] The reference to Christopher Benson, Master of the Temple was not altered.

p. 284. I could say something on authority in corroboration of what is here said. I knew intimately Keble's extreme tenderness of conscience, and how, under the 'desolating anxiety' of those years, he would even, as I think he did, accuse *himself* (without any sort of foundation) of being in some way or other the cause of those events which caused him so much sorow.[1]

p 351. I suppose mention is somewhere made of Keble's memoir of Scott's Life in the British Critic — but it has not caught my eye.[2]

p. 480 I believe there is a slight inaccuracy in Mr H's [Hedgeland] statement. In *1843*, in respect to the letter in which I disclosed to Mr Keble my distinct belief that the Roman Communion was the Church of the Apostles (I have given some portion of my letter from my own notes in my Apologia p 335,) in order to prepare him I inclosed it in a cover, and upon the cover I wrote 'Read the inclosed, when you are by yourself,' or some words to that effect. This is what led him, as he told me he did in his reply to betake himself to the chalk pit. Mr H. places it in *1845*.[3]

p 517. To be quite accurate, the letter should run, 'This was in September 1865. But when, on the 11th etc' For the 12th was the day on which I went to Hursley.[4]

TO HENRI LOUIS CHARLES MARET, BISHOP OF SURA

The Oratory Bm Novr 6. 1869

Monseigneur

I beg to acknowledge the honour you have done me in giving me a copy of your most learned work on the General Council.[5]

---

[1] See Newman's Notice of 19 June 1878 about Keble's letters of 1843-5.

[2] In the third edition, p. 365, Coleridge referred to this article in the *British Critic* (Oct. 1838), reprinted in *Keble's Occasional Papers and Reviews*, Oxford 1877, on Lockhart's *Life of Sir Walter Scott*.

[3] This quotation from a letter of Mr Hedgeland to the *Guardian* was left unchanged, at p. 495.

[4] Coleridge left as it was written Newman's letter of 17 Sept. 1868.

[5] *Du concile général et de la paix religieuse, première partie la constitution de l'église et la périodicité des conciles généraux, memoire soumis au prochain concile oecuménique du Vatican,* two volumes, Paris 1869.

Maret had already written:

'Cabinet de l'Évêque de Sura. Paris, le 9 8bre 1869 Mon très révérend Père

Je trouve une occasion excellente pour vous envoyer l'ouvrage, en deux volumes, que je viens de publier, et qui vous avait été annoncé dès l'année dernière.

J'y traite de la constitution de l'Eglise et de la périodicité conciliaire, comme du moyen le plus puissant de l'accomplissement de la mission du Christianisme dans ce monde. Je ne dis rien de mon chef, dans une si grave matière, mais il me semble que, dans les circonstances si décisives où nous sommes, ces idées doivent être soumises à la sagesse du Concile. Je reste dans les doctrines de Boussuet, un peu modifiées et développées dans leurs conséquences.

Peut-être ce travail plaira en Angleterre, aux hommes modérés, parmi nos frères. Peut-être pourra-t-il contribuer au bien de quelques âmes! C'est le voeu que je forme, et la récompense que je demande à Dieu. Je combats des projets extrêmes qui me paraissent pleins de dangers, heureux, vénéré Docteur, si mon livre peut un moment fixer votre attention, et obtenir votre approbation!

J'ai l'honneur d'être, avec respect, mon révérend Père, votre bien humble et dévoué serviteur et frère en N. S.

† H.L.C. Evêque de Sura'

88*

I hope to gain much instruction from it, and am sure I shall — but it has a far higher destiny than that of profiting an individual such as I am.

It is an important contribution to our ecclesiastical literature and, in placing it in our Congregational Library, I look forward to its instructing and edifying Catholic students, after my time[1]

I am, Monseigneur, with profound respect, Your faithful Servt in Xt

John Henry Newman

Sa Grandeur Monseigneur Maret Evêque de Sura.

TO DENIS SHYNE LAWLOR

The Oratory Jany 31. 1870

My dear Sir

I feel the great kindness you have done me in sending me your Volume.[2] It is a beautiful and interesting work, and I thank you sincerely for it.

Also let me thank you for the friendly words which you use of me in your letter, and for the compliment you pay me in the quotations which you make from my writings in your Introduction.[3]

I am, My dear Sir, with true respect,

Most faithfully Yours John H Newman

D. Shyne Lawlor Esqr

TO JOHN HENRY PARKER

The Oratory August 6. 1870

Dear Mr Parker

I fear Mr Neville and I took a great liberty with you in sending or taking to you the Photographs — I forget the circumstances, it is so long ago – and I sincerely thank you for the kindness with which you, (or Mr George,) have taken them in charge, and been at the trouble of selling them. I fear we must have in some way acted unusually — but Mr Neville is on the continent and I cannot recollect what took place[4]

I am, My dear Mr Parker, Very truly Yours

John H Newman

[1] Maret was 'a known upholder of the old Gallican school', and the sending of his book, published in Sept. 1869, to every bishop of the Catholic world 'let loose a great wave of controversy'. Cuthbert Butler, *The Vatican Council*, London 1930, I, p. 120.

[2] *Pilgrimages in the Pyrenees and Landes*, London 1870.

[3] Announcing on 25 Jan. that he was sending his book, Lawlor spoke of his 'great admiration and profound respect' for Newman. In his Introduction, pp. XVII–XVIII, he quoted from *Diff*. II, p. 84, on the paramountcy of Christ, and on pp. XIX–XX from *Mir.*, pp. 74 and 106. Most of the book described shrines of our Lady, and miracles, including those at Lourdes.

[4] Parker wrote on 5 Aug., 'I had not heard of these photographs before now and am glad to get more of them.' Mr George was his book-keeper.

Aug. 6. 1870

Received from Mr George the sum of One Pound, Eighteen shillings for the sale of Photographs

John H Newman

TO FREDERICK WILLIAM TRENOW, O.P.

The Oratory August 31./70

My dear Fr Dominic[1]

Your letter is very kind, and I thank you for it. Fr Suffield's change can hardly be called a private grief of your Order — it is a public distress and scandal to all Catholics, from the confidence they have placed in him, and the love they have borne and bear him.[2]

He may say what he will, and increase the scandal inconsiderately by saying it, but I will never believe that for ten years he has been giving missions and retreats, and speaking of our Lord's incarnation, resurrection, and Presence in the Holy Eucharist, all the while without any belief in miracles.

No, what has brought out this sad event, without which it would not have occurred, is, the recent occurrences at Rome.[3] Indeed, though he tried to deny it, yet he confessed to me that those occurrences gave an edge to his convictions; and steel will not cut or damage, till an edge is given it.

I see no signs whatever of madness in him, an imputation easy to make, and impossible to repel. That a man's brother is mad, is an *antecedent* reason why *perhaps* he *will* go mad, but no proof that he has gone mad. If my lungs are in a healthy state, you can't prove me in a consumption, because my brother died in one. There is nothing that Fr S. says, that a hundred, a thousand, sane men have said and say [sic]. And, as to his Father being a Unitarian, it does not matter what he *is*, so much as what he has *ceased* to be. He has left the Church; and his Father being a Unitarian could not make him do that. The scandal is *less* than if he had become an Anglican.

That he has been in a state of excitement is undeniable — but it would tell against him still more, if he had taken the act in cool blood. The worst thing against him *now*, is that he *is* so *very cool*. Pray for us all and believe me

Sincerely Yours John H Newman

---

[1] This was the name he had taken as a Dominican.
[2] See letters of 17 July 1870 to Suffield, and 8 Aug. 1870 to Mrs William Froude; also those of 12, 13 and 14 Aug. 1870 to Henry Wilberforce.
[3] i.e. those at the first Vatican Council, which culminated in the definition of papal infallibility on 18 July.

TO PATRICK KENNEDY

The Oratory Decr 7. 1870

Dear Mr Kennedy

I thank you for your curious and amusing collection of Irish Tales.[1] I am very glad to have it

Yours truly John H Newman

TO WILLIAM JEROME WATMOUGH, O.S.B.

The Oratory Febry 20. 1871

My dear Fr[2]

Thank you for your very kind letter. I beg also to thank you very heartily for your pains in verifying me by St Thomas—and should feel great interest if, at your leisure, you let me see your papers.

As to Retreats, I am not qualified to speak — but as they occur only once in the year, they certainly seem to me good things. Whether they [are necessary] for those who live in cloister out of the world, as certain classes of nuns, I cannot tell; because I know nothing about nuns. But for those who mix much in the world, at first sight they promise much advantage.

Whether missions should be given often in one place, is quite another question. Were I a parochus in a large parish, and had long experience, I should be able to answer your question — but you think far too much of me to fancy I can do so, as I am.

As to the mode of giving it, the more one can realize oneself eternal things, the greater and more blessed is the effect of the words spoken. Experience at least tells us this. I have known, for that reason, sermons, which seemed the most empty of matter, produce a wonderful effect, through God's mercy. If a man feels that God sends him to speak to His sinful people, what can He desire to feel more? To realize that God is using us, is the best source of eloquence.

As far as I know, visiting is a loss of time.

It is kind in you to wish me to write on the Infallibility of the Pope — but tomorrow I am 70, and I don't expect to write another book

Very sincerely Yours John H Newman

---

[1] *The Fireside Stories of Ireland*, Dublin 1870.

[2] The name has been almost completely cut out, but a letter from Watmough to Newman shows his interest in the reception among Catholic reviewers of *A Grammar of Assent*, and the accord of that work with St Thomas Aquinas. 'I believe that from your various works passages could easily be produced proving that you agree perfectly with St Thomas . . .'

Watmough, an Ampleforth monk working in the poor parish of St Augustine, Great Howard Street, Liverpool, ended his undated letter (probably early in 1871): 'Sympathising with you in the great injustices that have of late been done to you by Protestant and Catholic Journals — Believe me to be Yours very sincerely'.

TO J. SPENCER NORTHCOTE

The Oratory March 26. 1872

My dear President

Fr St John is away. I have answered you as well as I can — but we don't quite see the bearing of many of the questions in a University[1]

Very sincerely Yours John H Newman

[1] Northcote enclosed a long list of printed questions, in connexion with the inquiry into the state of Catholic higher education. One questionnaire had already been sent out. See letter of 18 Feb. 1872 and subsequent ones, to Northcote.

The second set of questions were answered as follows:

'A. 1. What has been the average number (during the last five years) of boys or young men studying in your college, *below Theology*? ⟨The average, during each of the last five years, is 77 boys⟩

    2. How are these numbers made up in respect of nationality? Thus, how many are there whose parents reside in Great Britain, or Ireland, or the Colonies, or in Foreign countries? ⟨22 not of the United Kingdom in the five years⟩

    3. What proportion in numbers do lay-students bear to clerical students? ⟨There are no clerical students⟩

    4. What proportion is intended for professional, what for commercial pursuits?

B. 1. What is the number of forms or classes? and by what names are they called? ⟨Six forms, and, as a cross division, three classes⟩

    2. What is the work done by each of the four highest classes below Theology?

    N.B. Detailed information of the amount of work done in each subject in each year would be be very acceptable.

    3. What is the time and value assigned to the respective subjects of study in these classes?

    4. Have you any reason to believe that parents would desire a change in this course? and if so, what change?

    5. Is any room allowed for choice of other subjects? or are all the subjects of study compulsory on all members of each class? ⟨No.⟩

    6. In case of choice, is there any limit to that choice? And is an extra fee exacted for instruction in each subject chosen ⟨No⟩

C. 1. What means are taken to test the work done? Are periodical examinations held? ⟨yes.⟩ By whom? ⟨by some of the Fathers⟩ In what subjects? ⟨in all.⟩ Do these examinations extend to all the classes and all the boys of each class? ⟨yes⟩ or what exceptions are made?

    2. What weight have these Examinations in determining the position of each boy in his class? ⟨Some weight, but not decisive.⟩

D. 1. What is the number and arrangement of hours of study and recreation on regular school-days? What are the usual holidays and half-holidays? How many vacations in the year? and how long?

E. 1. What time is devoted to religious instruction?

    2. What is the nature and extent of religious instruction given?

    3. What time is devoted to religious exercises?

F. 1. What scholarships, exhibitions, prizes, or other rewards are established in the School? or in connection with it?

    2. By whom and on what principles are they severally awarded? and to proficiency in what subjects?

    3. How far do such rewards bear upon the regular work of the students?

G. 1. Is the School in connection with any University? ⟨no⟩

    2. What is the number of students, lay or clerical, who go through any University course?

    3. What is the number of students who go through any course of higher studies as distinguished from both School course and University course?

    4. What is the nature, extent and ordinary duration of such studies?

    5. How many matriculate? and for what purpose?

    6. How many take degrees? and for what purpose?

    7. What are the advantages, material or intellectual, arising from connection with an University?

    8. Have you any conscientious objection to connexion with the London or other Universities? ⟨yes⟩ If so, what? ⟨religious and moral⟩ Is it the subjects or books pro-

TO THE MARCHIONESS OF LOTHIAN

                                          The Oratory Febry 16. 1873
My dear Lady Lothian

I hope I may ask you to take the trouble of sending the inclosed cheque to the Treasurer of your excellent Society.[1]

I know how kind and complimentary your wish is that I should be the person selected to receive contributions to it in this Diocese, nor could I possibly refuse the request, coming from you. At the same time I could not promise to collect for its object, sacred as it is; for our local wants are so great, that we are crippled for want of money in our most necessary parochial duties. I sometimes think we shall have to shut up our poor school from our inability to meet its current expenses. Our offertory does not clear the current expense of our Church. We complain that all the money centers in London. I know how religiously it is spent there — but our people here have not any religiously to spend

I am, My dear Lady Lothian, Most truly Yours

                                          John H Newman

The Marchioness of Lothian

TO SIR GEORGE BOWYER

                                          The Oratory Febry 26. 1875
My dear Bowyer

I hope you will accept the copy I send by this post.[2] And, instead of your own which I keep, I ask your acceptance of the edition with my *Postscript* in answer to 'Vaticanism' when it is ready

                    Yours most sincerely John H Newman

posed, or the nature and extent of the course, or the character of the examinations? In what are they defective or otherwise?

9. Are you aware of any evil results having actually come from such connection, especially in respect to mental or metaphysical philosophy?

H. 1. Have you any suggestions which seem to you of an immediately practical character to make with a view to the encouragement, promotion, or general organization of the higher studies, subsequent to the complete school course existing in our Catholic Colleges?

2. Are you of opinion that there is any want with reference to preparation for Competitive Examinations, or in the matter of technical education which it is important to supply? If so, can you suggest the means?

3. Do you think it would be useful to establish some system of prizes to be contended for by all the Catholic Colleges *inter se*? and can you suggest any means whereby this could be done, without interfering with the internal independence of each college?

                    ⟨in the absence of Fr St John
                                          John H Newman'⟩

[1] This was for the work of a convent newly established in London, the Helpers of the Holy Souls, 23 Queen Anne Street.

[2] This was a copy of *A Letter to the Duke of Norfolk* in which Newman wrote 'To Sir George Bowyer Bart with the affectionate regards of the Author'

TO FRANCIS KERRIL AMHERST, BISHOP OF NORTHAMPTON

The Oratory June 2. 1875

My dear Lord

I am sure you will pardon my delay in answering your most kind letter. I have been so thoroughly overset by Fr St John's sudden death, when we thought that he was getting well.

That translation of Fessler, to which, as also to my own Pamphlet you so kindly refer, was the additional weight which overcame him. I did not know at the time, but he told me afterwards he had worked at it six hours a day, to bring it out as soon as possible after my Letter. He went through it again most conscientiously for the second edition. Even as it was, he had too much work, and great anxieties and sorrows.[1]

He used to the last the rosary you gave him on your return from the Holy Land to Rome in 1847 — as I do, and shall mine (please God) which you gave me at the same time

Begging your blessing on me in my very deep distress, I am,

Your Lordship's faithful Servant John H Newman

The Bishop of Northampton

TO B. M. PICKERING

The Oratory Aug 19. 1877

Dear Mr Pickering

Though my letter crossed yours, I take it for granted that you have taken the satisfaction I expressed at the look of my Volume to be virtually an answer to your question[2]

Very truly Yrs John H Newman

TO VERNON THOMAS GREEN

The Oratory Septr 22. 1878

Dear Mr Green

I think your letter very kind, and thank you for it. And I do not forget this is the anniversary of the opening of Littlemore Church in 1836.

Thank you too for the lines — which were quite new to me. Have they ever been in print, in Dean Swift's works or elsewhere?

When I left you the other day, I went straight to Mr Knowles's in Holywell — and told him, as I thought you would let me, to act under your directions. I suspect nothing can be done prominent enough to answer the purpose

---

[1] See letter of 9 May 1875 to Mrs Henry Wilberforce.
[2] This refers to *V.M.*

I had in view. Why I have been anxious about it, has been because, at the time it was put up, a friend shocked me by saying that it would be mistaken for an Annunciation. A Catholic would never so mistake it, for the Angel is always represented kneeling[1]

Yours very truly John H Newman

TO JOHN CUTHBERT HEDLEY

The Oratory Novr 2. 1878

My dear Lord

I shall feel much pleasure in your Lordship's call, as you propose on Tuesday next at two or three o'clock[2]

Begging your blessing I am Your faithful Servt

John H. Newman

The Rt Revd Bp Hedley

TO JOHN NORRIS

Rugby June 30. 1879

My dear John

James Michael must be at New Street station at 10.35 tomorrow morning in order to take charge of our luggage in a separate car, and leave us two at liberty.

I am not aware of any ceremony beyond that of some Father (Austin) giving me holy water at the Church door. But, if any thing more is necessary, you must come up at 10.35 and tell me. If I am strong enough, I shall attempt a few words after the Te Deum

Ever Yours affly John H Card. Newman

P.S.   We could not get a bed in London[3]

TO JOHN SHERLOCK

The Oratory Aug. 17. 1879

My dear Mr Sherlock

I am sure I gladly would do any thing I could to aid you in so good an undertaking, and I hope you will accept the inclosed check as a proof of my sincerity.[4]

---

[1] Newman, who had visited Littlemore on 10 Sept. 1878, wished an alteration made to his mother's monument there. Green, who was Vicar of Littlemore, sent on 20 Sept. the address of a firm that would do the work.

[2] See diary for 5 Nov.

[3] See diary for 1 July 1879.

[4] Sherlock, who was the priest at St Michael's, Moor Street, Birmingham, wrote on the autograph '£20:0:0 J S'.

But, to speak honestly, I have a great dislike of Bazaars, and cannot get myself to take part in them; so I cannot help you in that way.

But don't tell this, for I should be very much hurt to take a different line from the Bishop

Yours most sincerely John H Card. Newman

TO JOHN CUTHBERT HEDLEY

The Oratory April 13. 1880

My dear Lord

I thank your Lordship for what I must not call your sad tidings, when they are to tell me that a good and faithful servant of his Lord is taken to his reward, and having spent a long life in his work, transmits his high and sacred duties to other men.[1]

Your invitation of me to the funeral is very kind. I cannot avail myself of it for I am confined to my bedroom with a severe cold which has taken away my voice, and hinders me saying Mass. Of course I shall say Mass for the good Bishop as soon as I am able. And none of us will delay

Your Lordship's faithful Servt John H Card. Newman

The Right Revd Bp Hedley

TO JOHN CUTHBERT HEDLEY

The Oratory Oct 21. 1880

My dear Lord

I congratulate your good Fathers and yourself on the happy and successful opening of the monastery and College of St Benedict at Fort Augustus.

Also I beg to offer you my best thanks for the valuable memorial of it contained in the sermon which your Lordship has been so kind as to send me, and in the report of the proceedings which attended it[2]

Your faithful Servt in Xt   John H. Card. Newman

TO RICHARD WESTBROOK LAMB

The Oratory, Birmingham. Easter Day [17 April] 1881.

My dear Mr. Lamb,

I heard the mournful news just as I was vesting for Mass this morning, and I changed my intention and said Mass for your dear son and for you.[3]

---

[1] Thomas Joseph Brown, Bishop of Newport, died on 12 April. Bishop Hedley was his auxiliary, and succeeded him.

[2] The buildings of Fort Augustus Abbey were opened on 31 Aug. and the preacher was the Prior, Jerome Vaughan. cf. letter of 12 July 1880 to him.

[3] Richard Lamb's son Joseph, who had been at the Oratory School, died on 16 April 1881.

I know what a deep grief your loss will be to you, and of course I can say nothing which you have not said to yourself. But I can speak for myself and for all who knew him here, of the affection which we felt for him, and the great esteem and may I say respect, with which his uniform good conduct and religious bearing inspired us. We can even rejoice, amid our disappointment at the premature death of so good a youth, as you cannot yet, that he has been spared the trials of life and has been taken so soon so safely to his reward. What has been your object and aim since the day he was born, but that he should be trained and prepared for Heaven? and now Almighty God has given you what you have so anxiously desired.

May the blessings of this sacred season be a consolation and support to you in your distress.

Most truly yours John H. Card. Newman.

TO WILLIAM KENWORTHY-BROWNE

Bm. July 5. 1882

Dear Sir

We shall be glad to avail ourselves of your services in our School for a year from next September. The salary we offer is £80 with board and lodging.

We shall be very much pleased if it would suit you to come here at once. We would employ you in making a catalogue for our books, and you would see something of the boys before the vacation. We should wish to consider this catalogue a separate employment[1]

Very truly Yours John H Card Newman

W. K. Browne Esqr

TO ANTHONY TROLLOPE

Birmingham Oct 28, 1882

My dear Mr Trollope

I should not have ventured to trouble you with any so-called remedy for the attacks from which Lord Emly he said you suffered [sic], had not what he happened to say of your case been so parallel to that of a very dear friend of mine, now departed. I have seen enough of the caprice and subtle nature of asthma, hastily to suggest a relief.[2]

My friend, Mr Hugh Rose, whose name I dare say you recollect, could not sleep in Kings College, but was safe at his parsonage house of St Thomas' hospital over the water. But my friend *here* had no difficulty in sleeping in any

---

[1] Kenworthy-Browne went up to Exeter College, Oxford, in 1879, took his B. A. in 1881, and became a Catholic in 1882.

[2] This is Newman's reply to Trollope's letter of 27 Oct., printed in note to letter of 26 Nov. 1882 to Lord Emly.

town, here or abroad, nor any part of the country — but was simply debarred from going to a cottage on the slope of a well wooded hill, where he had bought land, and laid out a garden, after numberless trials, suffering on the 2nd or 3rd night most cruelly.[1]

I am sorry Lord Emly took from hence a specimen of the paper; it was at least seven years old, and was not to be depended upon.

It is very kind of you to express pleasure at hearing of my admiration of your novels. Many of them I read again and again. I have just been re reading one for the third time, (which I first read about 1865 when) I was at our Cottage [sic].

Excuse my mistakes in writing. It is old age.

Your faithful servant John H. Card. Newman.

TO M. J. MURPHY

The Oratory, Birmingham, July 20th, 1883.

Dear Professor Murphy,

I am much pained to hear of Dr. Kane's death. It recalls to my mind the friendly and familiar intercourse I had with him so many years ago. At that time Cardinal Cullen sanctioned the prospect of the establishment of a house of the Oratory at Dublin, and Dr. Kane was one of those who showed special interest in the undertaking. And now I hear of his death, I have the most pleasant and affectionate recollections of him. God rest his soul, or rather, may he pray for us.[2]

Your faithful servant, John H. Card. Newman.

P. S.   I am much touched to be told of his people's intended altar to our great Saint, in his parish church. May I offer £5 for that object?[3]

TO JOHN CUTHBERT HEDLEY, BISHOP OF NEWPORT

The Oratory Bm Sept 25. 1883

My dear Lord

I thank you for some favorable words you have used to the Bishop of Clifton regarding some notes of mine which I showed him on the Inspiration of Scripture.[4]

---

[1] This refers to Ambrose St John and Rednal. Hugh James Rose was Perpetual Curate of St Thomas's, Southwark.

[2] When Newman was in Dublin, Kane helped to serve the University Church, and wanted to join the proposed Oratory there.

[3] Kane was parish priest of Baltinglass, and it was decided that his memorial should be an altar dedicated to St Philip Neri in the church of the place.

[4] See first note to letter of 25 Sept. 1883 to Bishop Clifford, who wrote that Bishop Hedley would be only too happy to publish in *D R*.

I wish I felt myself at liberty to avail myself of your offer to admit it into the Dublin Review, but I am under some kind of engagement of long standing to use it in another way[1]

I am, My dear Lord Your Lordship's faithful Servt

John H Card. Newman

The Rt Rev The Bishop of Newport

TO W. J. O'NEILL DAUNT

a long time under the shadow of our [Ora]tory [an]d have attached himself to our members [before] the novici[ate]

Con[sider]ing what you
[answer]ing more at length than I can in the four pages of a letter

I am, My dear Sir, Very truly Yours

John H Newman

W. J. Daunt Esqr

TO THE MARCHIONESS OF LOTHIAN

[1860?]

I love him very much,[2] nor do I forget his dear brother whom I saw once at Ushaw, and who has been taken away. He made a great impression upon me. I mention his name every day in my Mass, ever since his loss. He is in heaven, I doubt not, and I hope he says a prayer for me there.[3]

TO WILLIAM MONSELL

[After 10 June 1863]

With many thanks

J H N

P. S.   I had some of the Catacomb Pictures which you gave me put in your room on purpose that you might see them. Do you recollect our talking of them in the Summer? They were very welcome.

J H N

[1] Newman's article was to appear in the *Nineteenth Century*.
[2] Lord Ralph Kerr.
[3] On Lord John Kerr, who died as a boy, see letters of 3 June 1854 to Ambrose St John and 26? January 1855 to Lady Lothian.

TO WILLIAM NEVILLE

[undated]

My dear W

Will you have the above *after* tomorrow put up.

I wished much to make the *bracketed* passages clearer — but can't find my MS which you have

J H N

TO WILLIAM NEVILLE

Tuesday

My dear William

I have thought a good deal about the place for the (97) shed — and I think it will be safest to put it where we meant to put the porch of the Church, viz across the back of Mrs Wootten's Houses Therefore I think it will be well, (if Edward does not object, — and I *have* now written to him) *if you give orders to that effect*

Ever Yrs affly J H N

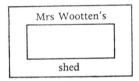

TO WILLIAM NEVILLE

Friday

My dear W

In the mahogony paper rack on the small table on which stands my writing desk

there ought to be a sheet of proof of my New Edition beginning with p. 169 and ending with p 192 — If you find it, please, send it per orphanum

Ever Yrs affly J H N

TO THE DUCHESS OF NORFOLK

which was a new thing with him. However, I comfort myself with thinking that it was drowsiness, and the laziness, which is akin to it, which was the cause of his re-

We owe much to the prayers of our friends, and they must not leave off.

After showing this letter to the Duke, I will ask you to burn it

Ever Yours most sincerely John H Newman

TO J.T. [?] WALFORD

My dear Walford

Have you not sent me a letter not mine?

Ever Yrs   John H Newman

TO AN UNKNOWN CORRESPONDENT

I did not till today ascertain your proper address, else I should have acknowledged your very welcome letter and your beautiful book sooner. But you will quite understand me when I desiderate one thing in it. You quote most touchingly ⟨affect[ing]ly⟩ the words of St Francis, St Ignatius, St Philip Neri and other saints, dead Saints. Are only dead Saints our consolation? Does not the heart cry out, 'half in dim fear, in anger half, My Mother is not here?'[1] You say at p 297 'If *our eyes were* opened, we should see Angels, and speak of blessed ones'; then, why are our eyes *not* opened. Why have we not faith, instead of sight, to fulfil in us ⟨our thoughts and hearts⟩ the wonderful text 'Ye are come etc' Hebr. xii[2]

May all the blessings of the coming joyful season come down upon you.

[1] 'Heard ye the quick appeal, half in dim fear
    In anger half, "My mother is not here".'
These were the last lines of the first verse of Keble's poem on our Lady, 'Mother out of Sight', referring to the neglect of her among Anglicans. It was written for *Lyra Apostolica*, 1846, but only published in Sir J. T. Coleridge's *A Memoir of the Rev. John Keble*, Oxford 1869, pp. 305–9, third edition pp. 316–20. Also in the appendix to *Lyra Innocentum*, 1903, p. 312.

[2] *Hebrews*, 12:22–4. 'But ye are come unto Mount Sion, and unto the city of the living God, the heavenly Jerusalem, and to an innumerable company of angels, to the general assembly of the firstborn, which are written in heaven, and to God the Judge of all, and to the spirits of the just men made perfect, and to Jesus the mediator of the new convenant ...'

List by Correspondents of Letters in the Supplement

Abbreviations used in addition to those listed at the beginning of the Volume:

A.	Original Autograph.
Bodleian	Bodleian Library, Oxford.
C.	Copy, other than those made by Newman.
D.	Draft by Newman.
H.	Holograph copy by Newman.
Lond.	London Oratory.
Oscott	Oscott College, Birmingham.
Pr.	Printed.
S.J. Lond.	The Jesuit Fathers, 114 Mount Street, London.

The abbreviation which describes the source is always the first one after the date of each letter. This is followed immediately by the indication of its present location or owner. When there is no such indication, it means that the source letter is preserved at the Birmingham Oratory. It has not been thought necessary to reproduce the catalogue indications of the Archives at the Oratory, because each of Newman's letters there is separately indexed, and can be traced at once.

After the source and its location have been indicated, any additional holograph copies (with their dates) or drafts are listed, and then, enclosed within brackets, any reference to previous publication in standard works.

Lastly, when it is available, comes the address to which the letter was sent.

Correspondent	Year	Date	Source	Location, Owner, Address
Acton, Sir John	1859	8 June	A	Acton Papers, Cambridge University Library
Allies, T. W.	1854	30 Aug	C	
	1855	7 Jan	C	
Amherst, Francis Kerril, Bishop of Northampton	1875	2 June	A	S.J. Lond.
Arnold, Thomas	1856	25 Oct	Pr	William T. Arnold, 'Thomas Arnold the Younger', *Century Magazine*, New York (May 1903), p. 127 (Mrs Humphry Ward, *A Writer's Recollections*, London 1918, p. 21)
Aylward, Dominic, O.P.	1853	27 July	A	Dominican Provincial Archives
		3 Aug	A	Dominican Provincial Archives
Betteris, Mr	1850	13 Aug	Pr	John Wilson's Catalogue 8
Bowyer, Sir George	1875	26 Feb	Ph	
Burns and Lambert, Messrs	1856	18 July	A	Dr Donald F. Winslow, Philadelphia Divinity School
Cobb, William, S. J.	1848	24 July	A	S.J. Lond.
Coleridge, Sir J. T.	1869	7 Feb	A	

Correspondent	Year	Date	Source	Location, Owner, Address
Coombes, William Henry	1849	10 Jan	A	Douai Abbey
Cooper, Peter	1851	13 Nov	A	St Mary's Tallaght
Daunt, W. J. O'Neill			A	Mills Memorial Library, McMaster University, Hamilton, Ontario
Dodsworth, William	1851	22 Sept	A	Nicholas Theis, Luxembourg
Donnet, Canon	1867	11 Dec	Pr	John Wilson, Catalogue 16
Editor of the Rambler	1859(I)		D	
	1859(II)		D(two)	
Ellacombe, Henry Thomas	1855	1 Jan	A	Bodleian
Estcourt, E. E.	1867	30 June	A	Oscott
Faduilhe, Alfred	1863	22 Nov	A	Douai Abbey
Forster, Charles John Pratt	1865	18 Nov	A	Prinknash Abbey
Fullerton, Alexander	1849	1 July	A	S.J. Lond.
Fullerton, Lady Georgiana	1853	1 Jan	A	S.J. Lond.
		27 July	A	S.J. Lond.
	1855	4 June	A	S.J. Lond.
		13 June	A	S.J. Lond.
	1857	28 Oct	A	S.J. Lond.
	1863	3 June	A	S.J. Lond.
Gallwey, Peter, S.J.	1865	26 Feb	A	Anthony D. Bischoff, S.J.
Gaume, Jean Joseph	1851	26 Sept	A	Archives of the Assumptionists, Rome Ad. Au R R Monsieur/M. L'Abbé Gaume etc etc./Rue Cassette 4/Paris/France
Grant-Duff, Mountstuart Elphinstone	1856	11 Nov	A	
Green, Vernon Thomas	1878	28 Sept	A	Anglican Church, Littlemore
Hardman, John	1852	17 Feb	A	Newman Preparatory School, Boston
Haydon, Frank Scott	1858	14 April	A	Gordon N. Ray, New York
		24 April	A	Gordon N. Ray, New York
			D	
		28 May	A	Gordon N. Ray, New York
Hedley, John Cuthbert	1878	2 Nov	A	Douai Abbey
	1880	13 April	A	Douai Abbey
		21 Oct	A	Douai Abbey
	1883	25 Sept	A	Douai Abbey
Holmes, William Sancroft	1845	5 Dec	A	John Sparrow, All Souls College, Oxford Ad. W. Sancroft Holmes Esqr/Gaudy Hall,/Harleston,/Norfolk
Hope, Messrs	1855	10 April	D	
Husenbeth, Frederick Charles	1845	20 Nov	A	Rose Memorial Library, Drew University, Madison, New Jersey
	1846	30 Aug	A	Dr Donald F. Winslow
	1853	19 Jan	A	The Friary, Woodford Green, Essex Ad. The Very Revd/Dr Husenbeth/Cossey/Norwich
	1857	17 Oct	A	Dr Donald F. Winslow
		28 Oct	A	Dr Donald F. Winslow
Jager, Abbé	1846		D	
Jesse, A. H. H.	1860		A	The Right Rev. Paul Verschuren, Suomessa, Finland
Kennedy, Patrick	1870	7 Dec	A	Stonyhurst College
Kenworthy-Browne, William	1882	5 July	A	Douai Abbey
Lamb, Richard Westbrook	1867	19 Aug	A	Richard Lamb
		9 Sept	A	Richard Lamb
	1868	3 June	A	Richard Lamb Ad. Richard Lamb, Esq/134, King's Road, Brighton
	1881	17 April	A	Richard Lamb Ad. Richard Lamb Esq./29 Great Cumberland Place,/London W.

Correspondent	Year	Date	Source	Location, Owner, Address
Lambert, John	1851	10 Sept	Ph	
	1852	4 July	Ph	
Lawlor, Denis Shyne	1870	31 Jan	A	O'Connell Museum, Derrynane *Ad.* D. Shine Lawlor Esqr/ Darrynane Abbey/Caherciveen/ *Ireland.*
Lewis, David	1849		A	Lond.
Lockhart, Mrs	1848	12 Jan	A	Rosminian Archives, Wonersh
Lothian, Marchioness of	1873	16 Feb	A	Society of Helpers, 1 Gloucester Avenue, London N.W. 1
	1860?		Pr	*Cecil Marchioness of Lothian,* edited by Cecil Kerr, London n.d. [about 1920] p. 147
McCarthy, Denis Florence	1854	11 Oct	A	*Ad.* D. F. McCarthy Esqr/29 Blessington Street/Dublin
	1856	26 Oct	A	*Ad.* D. F. McCarthy Esqr/29 Blessington Street/or Cavendish Row
Maret, Henri Louis Charles	1856	20 May	A	Archives of the White Fathers, Rome *Ad.* A Monsieur/Monsieur le Docteur Maret &c &c/Le Doyen/de la Faculté de Theologie/ Paris/France
	1869	6 Nov	A	Archives of the White Fathers Rome
Mills, Austin	1852	24 Dec	A	
Monsell, William	1853	3 Feb	A	last sheet (*Campaign,* p. XLIII)
			D	
	after 10 June 1863		A	
Monteith, Robert	1858	12 Aug	A	
Morris, J. B.	1858	18 Sept	A	Quarr Abbey
Moulinet, Abbé, Curé of Poulaines	1849	23 Nov	D	
Mozley, Mrs John	1846	11 Aug	Pr	The *British Weekly* (17 Sept 1936), p. 475
	1848	10 Feb	A	
Murphy, M. J.	1883	20 July	Pr	M. Comerford, *Collections Relating to the Dioceses of Kildare and Leighlin,* Dublin 1883, p. 331
Neville, William		[undated]	A	
		Tuesday	A	
		Friday	A	
Norfolk, Duchess of	1856	18 Aug	A	Duke of Norfolk
		20 Aug	A	Duke of Norfolk
		[undated]	A	Duke of Norfolk
Norris, John	1879	30 June	A	Douai Abbey
Northcote, J. Spencer	1850	19 July	A	Hawkesyard Priory
		29 Aug	A	Hawkesyard Priory
	1852	2 Sept	A	Hawkesyard Priory
	1872	26 Mar	A	Oscott
Nourrisson, Jean Félix	1853	9 April	A	Bibliothèque de l'Institut Catholique, Paris
			D	
		29 April	A	Bibliothèque de l'Institut Catholique
Oliver, George	1851	9 Feb	A	Iona College, New Rochelle, N.Y.
O'Sullivan, Michael	1853	26 Dec	A	Archbishop's House, Birmingham
			D	
Pagani, J. B.	1853	15 Aug	A	Rosminian Archives, Wonersh
	1854	5 July	A	Rosminian Archives
		18 Aug	A	Rosminian Archives
		21 Aug	A	Rosminian Archives
	1855	10 July	A	Rosminian Archives, Stresa (F. Paoli, *Life of Rosmini,* Turin 1880, p. 555; Claud Leetham, *Rosmini,*

Correspondent	Year	Date	Source	Location, Owner, Address
				London 1957, p. 481; *Vita di Antonio Rosmini, scritta da un sacerdote dell'Instituto di Carita, riveduta ed aggiornata da G. Rossi, Rovereto 1959, p. 560*
	1856	3 Dec	A	Rosminian Archives, Wonersh
Paget, James	1865	4 June	A	Andrew B. Myers, New York
Palma, Monsignor G. B.	1848	11 Aug	A	Segreteria delle Lettere Latine, 1848, Magg.–Nov. (Appendice), Archivio Segreto Vaticano
			D	
Parker, James	1865	19 Mar	A	Douai Abbey
		29 April	A	Douai Abbey
Parker, John Henry	1856	26 Mar	A	Douai Abbey
	1870	6 Aug	A	Douai Abbey
Parsons, John	1846	24 July	D	
Pickering, Basil Montagu	1877	19 Aug	A	*Ad.* B. M. Pickering Esqr/196 Piccadilly/London W
Pollen, John Hungerford	1855	2 Nov	C	
Publisher of the Telegraph	1852	8 June	A	Newman Preparatory School, Boston *Ad.* Publisher of the Telegraph/New [. . .] Office/7 and 8 Lower Abbey Street/Dublin
Richardson, Thomas	1851	1 Nov	C	Westminster Archives, Bagshawe Papers (at 4 June 1852)
Russell, Charles	1851	31 Aug	Ph	
Sherlock, John	1879	17 Aug	A	Meath Diocesan Archives
Star, George W. B.	1860	21 Oct	A	Mrs Slevin
Stephen, Sir James	1853	13 July	A	Dawson's of Pall Mall
			D	
Stewart, James	1858	18 Oct	C	
Swanwick, Anna	1865	6 Aug	A	
Talbot, George	1846	5 Feb	A	English College, Rome
Thompson, Edward Healy	1846	8 April	A	Catholic Record Society *Ad.* The Reverend/E. H. Thompson
		27 April	A	Catholic Record Society
		29 May	A	Catholic Record Society
	1847	3 Feb	A	Catholic Record Society *Ad.* The Revd E. Healy Thompson/Prior Park/Bath./*Inghilterra/* (to be forwarded immediately)
	1852	26 Mar	A	Catholic Record Society
		13 April	A	Catholic Record Society
	1853	9 Feb	A	Catholic Record Society
		9 Sept	A	Catholic Record Society
		23 Oct	A	Catholic Record Society
		29 Oct	A	Catholic Record Society
		7 Nov	A	Catholic Record Society
		6 Dec	A	Catholic Record Society
		24 Dec	A	Catholic Record Society
	1854	24 Jan	A	Catholic Record Society
		21 April	A	Catholic Record Society
		24 May	A	Catholic Record Society
		21 June	A	Catholic Record Society
		28 June	A	Catholic Record Society
		28 July	A	Catholic Record Society
		12 Aug	A	Catholic Record Society
		27 Aug	A	Catholic Record Society
		21 Oct	A	Catholic Record Society
		10 Nov	A	Catholic Record Society
		31 Dec	A	Catholic Record Society
	1855	8 Jan	A	Catholic Record Society
	1857	28 April	A	Catholic Record Society
	1858	14 April	A	Catholic Record Society

Correspondent	Year	Date	Source	Location, Owner, Address
Thompson, Mrs Edward Healey	1856	13 May	A	*Ad.* Mrs Thompson,/10 Portland Place/Torquay/Devon
Trenow, Frederick William, O. P.	1861	20 Mar	A	Hawkesyard Priory *Ad.* The Revd Fr Trenow O S D./Catholic Church /Stoke upon Trent
		26 April	A	Hawkesyard Priory *Ad.* The Revd Fr Trenow O. P./Catholic Church/ Stoke upon Trent
	1866	10 Feb	A	Hawkesyard Priory *Ad.* The Revd Fr Trenow O. P./The Priory/ Hinckley
	1870	31 Aug	A	Hawkesyard Priory *Ad.* The Revd/ Fr Trenow/The Convent/Stone/ Staffordshire
Trollope, Anthony	1882	28 Oct	C	Princeton University Library
Tyndale, Mrs	1862	end of year	A	Dinand Library, Holy Cross College, Worcester, Mass.
Unknown	1850	25 June	A	Princeton University Library
Correspondents	1852	22 Feb	A	
	[undated]		D	
Vere, Aubrey de	1857	23 Nov	A	St Joseph's Seminary, Dunwoodie
Walford, John Berry	1846	29 April	A	Dr P. A. Walford
		28 May	A	Dr P. A. Walford
Walford, J. T.	[undated]		A	John Tracy Ellis
Ward, Catherine	1848	12 Oct	A	Newman Preparatory School, Boston
			D	
Ward, Mrs F. R.	1866	8 Mar	A	S.J. Lond.
Waterton, Charles	1850	4 Aug	A	
			D	
Watmough, William Jerome, O.S.B.	1871	20 Feb	A	Douai Abbey
Weld, Joseph	1852	13 July	A	Dorset County Records Office
White, Robert Augustine, O. P.	1852	9 Jan	A	St Mary's Tallaght
		17 Jan	A	Conventual Archives, St Mary's Priory, Pope's Quay, Cork
Williams, Isaac	1853	18 Aug	A	Gloucestershire Records Office *Ad.* The Revd Isaac Williams/Stinchcombe/Dursley/Glocestershire
Wootten, Mrs	1856	17 Aug	A	

MEMORANDA, ETC

	Date	Source		Subject
1859	1 Mar		D	Letters to the Rambler

Note. The autographs of the following letters are in the Jesuit Archives, Farm Street, London.
23 Jan. 1850 to Francis Clough, S.J.
7 Jan 1859 to Thomas Harper, S.J.
25 July 1862 to George Lambert, S.J.
12 Sept 1862 to John Henry Wynne, S.J.

Index of Persons in the Supplement